The

ULTIMATE
PASTA

and

NOODLE
COOKBOOK

The
ULTIMATE
PASTA
and
NOODLE
COOKBOOK

SERENA COSMO

CIDER MILL PRESS

BOOK PUBLISHERS
KENNEBUNKPORT, MAINE

13-Digit ISBN: 9781604337334
10-Digit ISBN: 1604337338

This book may be ordered by mail from the publisher. Please include $5.99 for postage and handling. Please support your local bookseller first!

Books published by Cider Mill Press Book Publishers are available at special discounts for bulk purchases in the United States by corporations, institutions, and other organizations. For more information, please contact the publisher.

Cider Mill Press Book Publishers
"Where good books are ready for press"
PO Box 454
12 Spring Street
Kennebunkport, Maine 04046

Visit us on the Web!
www.cidermillpress.com

Cover design by Mallory Grigg

Interior design by Jaime Christopher

Typography:
Adobe Garamond, Brandon Grotesque, Lastra, Sackers English Script

Image Credits:
Front cover photo © StockFood / Firmston, Victoria
Illustrations on page 67-127 by Yi Bin Liang

Photos by Serena Cosmo appear on pages 156, 157, 166, 171, 172, 180, 184, 193, 206, 214, 221, 224, 229, 230, 233, 234, 239, 240, 267, 275, 276, 281, 284, 289, 304, 309, 324, 328, 335, 356, 365, 368, 371, 374, 377, 378, 383, 386, 418, 427, 428, 437442, 451, 458, 487, 490, 497, 498, 503, 506, 509, 510, 517, 530, 535, 541, 542, 547, 548, 553, 554, 561, 562, 567, 570, 579, 586, 595, 602, 609, 612, 615, 616, 627, 640, 647, 648, 655, 656, 661, 664, 671, 680, 683, 684, 693, 703, 704, 709, 718, 723, 724, 727, 728, 731, 732, 736, 745.

Supplemental photographs and illustrations are used under official license from Shutterstock.com

Printed in China

1 2 3 4 5 6 7 8 9 0

First Edition

To Erik, Alexia, & Kira,

for your love, laughter, and belief

CONTENTS

ACKNOWLEDGMENTS

Writing this book has required that I, a highly social, extroverted person, spend a considerable amount of time by myself fraternizing with more books and resources than I can count and stirring things up at the stove. While I was often the only person in the room for months on end as I slowly chipped away at writing and photographing this book, I certainly never felt alone.

My family, friends, editor, and the wonderful folks over at Cider Mill Press have made me feel supported throughout this long, arduous, and continuously compelling process.

In particular I want to extend a world of gratitude to the following people:

Cider Mill Press Book Publishers LLC: My heartfelt thanks go out to all of you wonderful folks. John Whalen, for giving me, an untested, unproven food writer, the opportunity to work with your publishing company to create a book about one of my greatest loves, pasta; Alex Lewis, for somehow finding me and my food blog, *Rustic Plate,* online and asking me to participate in this fantastic project; and Brittany Wason and Kelly Gauthier, for being there every step of the way with thoughtful guidance and prompt answers to any questions I had (and for forwarding me amazing food-related music you found online!). I can't imagine working with a better, sharper, nicer, more helpful group of people. You have made my foray into the world of writing books about as wonderful as I could ever have hoped for or imagined.

Pam Hoenig, my fearless editor: Your invaluable, thoughtful, and exacting editing has pushed me and I have become a better recipe writer in particular because of you. I so enjoy your spunk and respect your experience and perspective (it especially came in handy during those times when we negotiated 24-hour deadlines and 72 hours worth of work!).

Writing this book has also enabled me to develop a small army of "friends" who have guided me as I dove deeply into the world of pastas, noodles, and dumplings. I don't know how I would have completed this book without availing myself of their considerable counsel. While I have learned countless invaluable things on this journey from so many cookbook authors and food bloggers, I feel particularly indebted to the following culinary luminaries:

Oretta Zanini de Vita and Maureen B. Fant: Through the course of several years of researching every crevice of the vast culinary expanse that is Italy, Ms. Zanini de Vita has amassed a defining library of Italian pastas, many of which were a dying tradition, in her seminal book, the *Encyclopedia of Pasta.* What a fantastic legacy she leaves us. Because of her comprehensive research and passion, many of the ancient pastas she resuscitated in written form are currently being revived by chefs and home cooks eager to retain this invaluable culinary heritage. I have learned so much about my own people's food from her exhaustive efforts and have added pastas that had been previously unfamiliar to me to my own repertoire. Ms. Fant, Ms. Zanini de Vita's translator and dear friend, has helped me to not feel so alone in today's oftentimes clinical and precise approach to cooking ("add THIS much of THIS exact ingredient and cook it for precisely THIS amount of time"). In the book *Sauces & Shapes: Pasta the Italian Way:* she helps readers to understand that food is as mercurial as people. It is not static. Consequently, cooking entails tasting ingredients when necessary to assess how best to work with them. Her no-nonsense and humorous approach is invaluable because I believe it can aid in returning the art of cooking to the sensual, creative, and practical expression it has always been meant to be.

Marc Vetri: Because of Mr. Vetri's highly instructional and inspiring book, *Mastering Pasta*, I have reached a new defining paradigm in my own understanding of the role of flour in pasta (and bread, for that matter). Prior to reading his book, I had been under the impression that flour was just a bag of white powder used to make pastas, bread, cakes, and scones. But that would be like saying that all mushrooms are the same, without accounting for the innumerable variations of shapes, flavors, and textures that each brings to a dish. Mr. Vetri has helped me to understand the difference in the quality of flour and what it contributes to fresh pasta, as well as the importance of drying pasta, which significantly contributes to its texture when executed properly. Thanks to his tutelage, I now buy wheat berries and own a KitchenAid KGM Grain Mill attachment, which allows me and my family to enjoy the enhanced flavor and texture of pasta made with just-milled flour.

Leela Punyaratabandhu: I picked up her fantastic book *Simple Thai Food* in an effort to assuage my family's unrelenting appetite for Thai food. While the recipes in her book would certainly qualify as simple enough, Ms. Punyaratabandhu brings a whole other dimension to her recipes and book through her masterful instructions and her frank, helpful opinions about ingredients and cooking techniques. I believe you can learn how to cook just by making every single one of her recipes. Through her book I learned of her food blog *shesimmers.com* (She Simmers). I don't know why but the first time I saw her blog's name, I read it incorrectly as *She Shimmers*. That name, however wrong, has stuck with me ever since, probably because I find her so remarkably knowledgeable and likable that I wouldn't be at all surprised to learn that some sort of ethereal light emanates from her.

Andrea Quynhgiao Nguyen: Prior to writing this book, my entire experience of dumplings revolved around devouring as many as I could while retaining some semblance of dignity. After spending many happy hours reading and experimenting (not to mention eating the results!) with the recipes in her exacting book *Asian Dumplings: Mastering Gyoza, Spring Rolls, Samosas, and More*, I now feel like a competent dumpling maker. This fledgling feeling of proficiency would not have been possible without her book. Her passion for her culinary heritage is evident in every single word, as expressed by the level of detail in describing every single technique. I loved learning about the "belly" of the wrappers and how it plays a pivotal role in ensuring that dumplings have an even distribution of dough-to-filling throughout for maximum enjoyment. She has made so many of these minute yet essential details so clear to understand and execute.

A wide-armed thank you to my two precious *terroriste* daughters, Alexia and Kira. For six months they both (for the most part) patiently waited to get their mother back. I don't know what I would have done without their frequent visits as I holed myself up in some remote part of the house to sneak a few hours' worth of writing. Their hugs, kisses, and words of encouragement were priceless and kept me going when I was tired. *Vi voglio un sacco di bene, ragazze!*

Grazie, mamma e papa'. This book would also not have been possible without the *infarinatura* (training and knowledge) that I received from my parents, Claudia and Nicola, from the time I could first walk. While I do not possess a culinary degree nor have I studied for years under renowned culinary masters, I have nevertheless attended the "Claudia and Nicola Food University," where I viscerally lived the food experience since I could hold a spoon and feed myself. Since I can remember, we dissected every meal we have ever eaten together. "This could have used a little more sage," "That could have been cooked just a couple more minutes to crisp up the outside more," "These mussels aren't as tasty as last week's but the condiment is still good." To outsiders, we must have appeared to be psychopathically overcritical, but the truth is . . . no one in our family ever took offense. We were just having a conversation, one that happened to revolve around our most fervent desire to heighten everything we ate to its outmost potential. I would not have the relationship with food that I have today without both of them.

I would also like to express my gratitude to the readers of my blog and column, *Rustic Plate*. Your support, questions, and helpful comments mean more to me than you'll ever know.

Last but first in my heart, I send my undying love and gratitude to my husband, Erik. He alone is to be credited if I am a food writer today. Erik started encouraging me to write

about food more than ten years ago, and I wouldn't listen (surprise, surprise). I always associated food writing with some of the snootier magazines in circulation at the time, which seemed to take great pride in turning the simple act of cooking into a vehicle for snobbery and elitism ("Drizzle with *Acetaia Leonardi Reserva Oro* balsamic vinegar, or other 100-year-old balsamic vinegar. . ." Phewy!), and I couldn't relate to that. Without his gentle (and sometimes not so gentle!) prodding, I may have never embarked on this writing adventure. What can I say? He wore me down. I wasn't initially convinced, but it was the doing of it that got me hooked, because it wasn't until I began writing a local food column that I realized food writing was what I chose to make of it. Since then I have found the refreshing voices of other writers who take pride in celebrating food in a way that makes it feel more approachable.

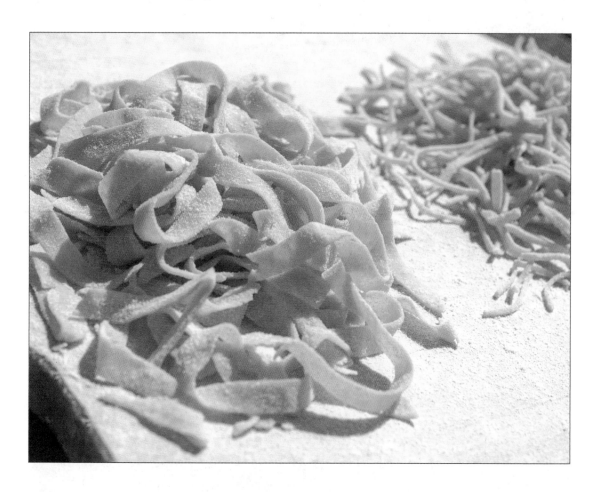

FOREWORD

My first vivid memory of food recalls a slice of lasagna. I ate it at a gathering organized around my family's departure from Italy to the United States. I was nine.

Though I had only just finished third grade, I understood the meal to be a momentous occasion. Soon my family and I would travel thousands of miles away from all the smiling faces seated around the large table my mother had reserved for us at a lovely nearby trattoria. Soon I would not be seeing all my aunts, uncles, and cousins at my grandparents' home every Sunday afternoon for dinner. Soon I would leave my friends, the city in which I was born, and the only life I ever knew. Mostly, I tried to focus on playing with my cousins and on trying to avoid being hugged by one sentimental family member or another. It was a strange day to say the least. Thank goodness for lunch.

When the first course arrived, the proprietor presented me with a perfectly square, piping hot slice of porcini lasagna. It was the most spectacular dish that I had ever tasted in my short life. (This is not an insignificant disclosure, since my mother is an excellent cook and makes delicious lasagna.) Who knows? Maybe it was the fresh air of the Piedmont mountains, in which this rustic trattoria was cozily nestled. Maybe it was because, for several hours leading up to lunch, I had been playing frenetically with my cousins and I was really hungry. Or maybe it was because it was, hands-down, a most spectacular, wondrous slice of lasagna.

I asked my mother if I could order another slice. And then another. And then another. I remember my mother looking at me quizzically. Accustomed to scolding me for fidgeting too much and for eating too little, she was clearly unfamiliar with the placid, raven-

ous child I had temporarily become. But she kept motioning to the proprietor to bring me another slice, and I kept eating them.

By the time the second slice arrived my cousins had already excused themselves from the table and were busy chasing each other around a nearby hill, but I didn't care. I had fallen in puppy love.

Funny, but I still think of that lasagna from time to time, the way a sports fan might reminisce about a particularly satisfying win. I believe that day's lasagna experience forever cemented my complete and unabashed adoration for pasta in particular and for food in general. I mean, it brings so much joy!

Granted, the foundation for this sort of ardor was already strong. Since I can remember, food has been the axis around which my family has revolved, and my parents' activities always seemed to be planned around growing, making, procuring, and eating it. My dad grew his own vegetables and tended to the fruit trees on our property. My mom, a no-nonsense cook with an affinity for rustic food, always seemed to be in the kitchen preparing something tasty.

Even family friendships connected us to food. Two of my parents' closest friends were farmers and I spent many happy weekends on their farm gathering eggs from their sassy chickens, biting into baby carrots I had just plucked from the ground, and helping to stomp grapes wearing galoshes twice my size. Once I even inadvertently started a tractor and had to be chased down by my panicked father because I didn't know how to turn it off. (He didn't find that particular adventure nearly as titillating as I did.) I still remember the shiny silver handgun my dad's friend Gianni used every year to kill a poor unsuspecting pig and all the work involved

in curing the meat and making a variety of sausages. I always felt sad for the poor fellow but somehow figured out a way to enjoy all the sausages in which he played the starring role.

One could argue that this sort of passion can be attributable to our Italian heritage (all Italians love food, right?), but I think that my family, while certainly not an anomaly among Italians, had an almost obsessive-compulsive quality to their preoccupation with food. Every ingredient had to be just right, and it was not at all unusual for my family to embark on a full-day excursion just to go pick up a special block of cheese or a particularly tasty case of olive oil from some small village renowned for the food item. And the thing is . . . all that care always translated well on the plate.

Moving to America only reinforced this obsession because my parents now had to work harder to procure the ingredients that their daily lives required. My mother continued to regale us daily with a wide variety of homemade pasta dishes, gnocchi (including my favorite, *gnocchi alla Romana;* see page 232 for my recipe), soups, roasts, and vegetables that made us feel as though we never left our beloved boot. But good bread and tasty everyday wine remained elusive in the rural part of Pennsylvania where my father's job had moved us.

Always the problem solver, my father, an engineer by profession and an artist by sensibility, embarked on a study of wine and bread-making that yielded unbelievably flavorful and full-bodied homemade wine and crusty loaves filled with coveted air pockets. He also developed a focaccia recipe so delicious that he could not attend a party without being asked to bring one or two.

Within a couple of years, walking through the doors of our home in Pennsylvania was like entering Italian sovereign territory. Our beloved dishes, in a sense, became our home.

This cultural imprint runs deep.

So deep, in fact, that I have become my own version of my food-obsessed parents. As my own family will attest, not always laudably, I am fairly persnickety about the quality of my ingredients and the techniques that go into preparing properly cooked food. It seems almost inevitable that I would use my journalism degree to write about it.

I started a food blog, *Rustic Plate,* in 2013 as a way to celebrate the deep and grounding flavors of simple rustic foods, many of them pasta dishes, that brought me and my family such comfort and nourishment. I found the experience of recording my cooking exploits so satisfying that it inspired me to pitch a local column, also called *Rustic Plate,* to my local newspaper. It is now published in several newspapers across the state.

When Cider Mill Press reached out and asked me to write this book, I couldn't have been more thrilled (and honored). Not just because, as a pasta lover, I get cranky if two days go by without eating a bowl of something containing my beloved food, but also because pasta philosophically falls in line with my belief that staples like pasta, noodles, rice, and potatoes are the invaluable foundation of a wholesome, satisfying, and earth-sustaining diet. In addition, once combined with sauces and condiments or added to stews, soups, and braises, they offer us an almost infinite array of flavors, textures, ingredients, and aromas.

Writing this book has been a fantastic journey. It has deepened my level of understanding and appreciation for pastas, noodles, and dumplings around the world. It has also unequivocally proven to me that there is always more to learn about these versatile and deliciously satisfying staples.

I have made many friends along the way. Not friends I meet for coffee, mind you, but cookbook authors who have guided me throughout the process of learning everything I could about the art of making pasta, noodles, and dumplings. I've perused the pages of their books so many times that they feel like old friends, and I mention them all by name and by their extraordinarily instructional books in the acknowledgment section. My greatest wish is to someday be able to shake their hands and to express my undying gratitude for their generosity of knowledge and spirit.

Another great wish of mine is that you, the reader, will find inspiration in the pages of this book. Inspiration that turns into a pasta, noodle, or dumpling dish so delicious that it makes your loved ones smile, perhaps even purr, as you all enjoy a wonderful meal together. Good food is such a satisfying unifier.

But enough talk, let's make some pasta together!

Serena

INTRODUCTION

Pasta and noodles were destined to attract universal attention and affection.

Versatile, wholesome, and inexpensive, they represent a tradition based equally in the home, in the culinary artisan's workshops and, in the last 300 years, factories. Pasta and noodles provide the proverbial blank canvases onto which we have been able to apply our preferences for ingredients, flavorings, and cooking techniques. Whether freshly homemade or mass produced, they remain an ideal platform for individual creativity in kitchens throughout the world.

Many countries on the Eurasian continent, from Germany and Turkey to Central Asia and the Middle East, possess a long and rich tradition of pasta. The true homelands of pasta, however, have been China and Italy, which evolved two separate but complementary culinary traditions based on a vast body of knowledge acquired through generations and developed through specific techniques and skills. Separately and at their own pace, each culture developed its own specifically designed culture of pasta products, which spread, initially throughout their respective countries, and then to the rest of the world.

China spearheaded the charge in understanding the properties of wheat dough. In their hands, it became the first malleable material from which they produced foods like breads and noodles. Dough enabled them to rely on foodstuffs that were more than simply the direct harvest of their natural environment— a momentous accomplishment. Because the Chinese never had access to the durum wheat used by the Italians to make what became their fabled dried pasta, they became masters of transforming the soft wheat that grew on their

fertile plains into a wide array of pasta and noodle products.

One thing is clear: The paths leading to the creation of the Chinese noodle and Italian pasta cultures were separate and distinct. Writer and food science expert Kantha Shelke, in her book *Pasta and Noodles: A Global History*, aptly compares the two traditions as "twins separated at birth and raised in entirely different worlds, developed unique interpretations with different personalities that characterize two archetypal cultures: one peninsular and insular and the other remote and separate."

Their histories, though, do share one unifying characteristic. In both cases, the fruits of their inventive processes captured the imagination, heart, and palate of patricians and commoners alike, a feat few foods have accomplished. As such, regardless of socioeconomic position, nationality, religion, or culture, their ability to bring the universal themes of care, love, and hospitality to their recipients remains forever unchanged.

Throughout the process of writing this book about pasta and noodles, people have often asked how all my newfound knowledge has affected my viewpoint on the subject. In no uncertain terms, learning about the evolution of pasta and noodles has given me an infinite amount of respect and appreciation for the seemingly bottomless ingenuity and creativity of our human race. As the American historian Charles Perry points out, the defined geometrical shape of pasta and noodles clearly bears the impression of the human intellect. Over time and through trial and error, men and women throughout the world figured out how to turn grains and other materials into flour and

those flours into pasta and noodles of infinite shapes, sizes, and flavors. While the endeavor was undoubtedly motivated initially by the universal need of placating hunger, it evolved into a highly developed expression of love and creativity. If it had not, we would still have only a handful of rudimentary pasta shapes and noodles instead of the hundreds, many of them delicate works of art, that surround us today.

This cookbook was conceived to provide readers with a comprehensive accounting of many of the pastas and noodles found throughout the world. This accounting is by no means exhaustive, as the sheer number of pasta and noodle variations would create a book too heavy to hold and too corpulent to stay together. Consequently we have amassed an array of the most common pasta products, both modern and ancient.

One final note: While we are on the topic of recipes, I feel strongly about mentioning that while my indefatigable editor Pam and I have taken the utmost care to ensure the recipes we present are clear, complete, and correct, I would like to add that recipes, at best, still represent a mere roadmap to creating a given dish. Prolific writer and cookbook author Maureen Fant, co-author of the terrific book *Sauces & Shapes:*

Pasta the Italian Way, explains this in a playful and amusing way: "Anyone who has ever consulted an Italian cookbook understands that no speaker of English would have the patience to cook from a book of truly Italian recipes, with their refusal to take positions. (Q: How long [to cook it]? A: How should I know? It's *your* stove! Q: How much salt? A: Taste the capers!)"

While we can estimate, through experience and an understanding of the cooking process, how much moisture is needed in a recipe or how long a given ingredient needs to cook before going on to the next step, real world factors can oftentimes affect our results in unexpected ways. Humidity can change how much liquid you need to add to your dough, a lazy oven can require you to bake a dish longer than specified, or very watery zucchini will take longer to soften and turn brown . . . these are the sorts of everyday, banal circumstances that can throw off the precise following of a recipe (usually only ever so slightly). Whenever possible, we include both a time and a visual cue in an effort to give you the information you need to successfully execute the recipe. In case your experience deviates from both, and unfortunately it is bound to happen sooner or later, use your instincts and common sense.

The HISTORY of NOODLES & PASTA

Poor Marco Polo. Relegated to an entertaining pool game for children, he has been stripped of the lore of having introduced pasta to the Italians. In fact, historical records show that pasta was being produced in Sicily a full century before Mr. Polo returned from his fabled expedition across Asia. (He made a considerable contribution to the Western world nonetheless. His writings about the Orient helped open up maritime routes to the spices of the Far East, which until then had been transported by land through the Middle East.)

Since the dismissal of Mr. Polo's alleged culinary contribution, scholars have been left with the arduous task of piecing together the twisted travails of this mythical food staple. It has not been easy. The origins of pasta are cryptic at best. Historical records suggest that, throughout time, different and distant cultures have engaged, separately, in the activity of making pasta and noodles.

Recent research reveals a similar dynamic in the development of agriculture. While it had been previously believed that the earliest farmers came from a homogenous population living in the Fertile Crescent, a region in the Middle East that includes modern-day Israel, Palestine, Iraq, Jordan, Syria, and parts of Iran and Turkey, new findings suggest that those populations were genetically distinct from one another and didn't intermingle for thousands of years while simultaneously growing crops and herding animals. Perhaps it is no happy accident that most ancient civilizations were built in fertile valleys bordering important rivers like the Euphrates, Tigris, and China's Yellow River (Huang He).

Incomplete historical records have also made it difficult to find a link between Italian pasta and Asian noodles, the ancestors of all pasta and noodles worldwide. Silvano Serventi and Francoise Sabban, in their engrossing and exhaustively researched book *Pasta: The Story of a Universal Food,* explain this void beautifully: "In fact, the turbulent and fascinating history of the middle land bounded by these two gastronomic territories has yet to be written. The vocabulary of a great many languages in Eastern Europe and in the Turkish, Arabic, and Persian spheres clearly indicates that pasta has traveled widely, leaving traces in some cases difficult to follow, hinting at complex events that, for now, remain enigmatic."

Forces, some whose lasting impact reach beyond our ability to effectively research them, have indeed played a role in bringing us our beloved pasta and noodles. But the research points us to separate histories, and thus requires that their stories be told separately.

THE HISTORY OF NOODLES

The story of Asian noodles begins in the ancient cradle of Chinese civilization known as the Central Plain. Situated in northern China in the lower reaches of the Yellow River, its fertile plains possessed the ideal soil for the cultivation of the indigenous grain millet. Recent archeological findings reveal that early inhabitants there eventually developed the milling technology necessary to turn millet into flour, as evidenced by a bowl of 4,000-year-old long, thin yellow noodles found at an archeological site on the Yellow River in 2012. Scientists discovered that the noodles were made from two varieties of ground millet, evidencing an already high level of food processing during the ancient Shang Dynasty. (It is worth noting that not all scientists agree with this analysis, claiming that millet does not possess the gluten content needed to be shaped into strands without the assistance of some other type of flour or starch. As it stands, the earliest undisputed record of noodles appears in a book written during the Han Dynasty, sometime between 25 BCE and 220 CE.)

For centuries the people of northern China continued to eat millet, mostly in the form of gruel, until wheat was introduced by Central Asian traders around 4,500 years ago. Initially this "new" grain was not widely used, and was often confused with barley, another non-native grain. Scientists speculate that people initially dismissed wheat because, unlike millet, it could not be eaten whole and required the removal of its hard outer layer. Given the primitive grindstones of the time, processing wheat was arduous and time consuming, causing people to continue gravitating toward millet.

This all changed around the 3rd century (201 BCE to 220 CE) during the Han Dynasty, when the building of the Silk Road forged a network of trade routes that linked Chinese regions and fostered commerce with the Western world. It was along those newly built roads that merchants carried more technologically advanced grindstones that made it significantly easier to mill and, consequently, consume wheat.

With easier access to wheat, it did not take long for the ingenious Chinese to understand the versatility and possibilities of wheat once it was combined with water, prompting the creation of a new category of food called *bing*. By the end of the Han Dynasty in the 3rd century, rare texts began using the word *bing* to

describe dishes made of kneaded wheat dough, including pasta products, leavened breads, and flatbreads. Over time, the use of the word *bing* came to represent so many food products that it required distinctions. The dictionary *Shiming* (thought to date from 200 CE), which described *bing* as the product of a well-blended mixture of flour and water, categorized it according to appearance into "barbarian *bing*" *(hubing)*, tortoise shell-shaped food (research has revealed this to be flatbreads); "steamed *bing*" *(zhengbing)*, little leavened breads; "broth *bing*" *(tangbing)*, noodles cooked in broth; "scorpion *bing*" *(xiebing)*, deep-fried dough in the shape of scorpions; "marrow *bing*" *(suibing)*, a baked mixture containing flour, water, marrow, and honey; "gold *bing*" *(jinbing)*, in the shape of gold ingots; and "lace *bing*" *(suobing)*, in the shape of lace.

Just a few decades later, the Chinese stopped using these compound words, dropping the term *bing* altogether and giving noodles names such as *bozhuang, qisou,* and *angan*, as well as naming them after objects, such as "dagger laces" and "dog tongues." As *bing's* popularity grew, in large part due to increasingly easier access to milled wheat flour, it slowly evolved from a predominantly imperial food to a widespread staple. According to chef and award-winning cookbook author Najmieh Khalili Batmangliji, "By the end of the Han dynasty, China already had developed the technique for swinging dough into individual strands. These were boiled and served with a range of seasonings, and although they were generally considered common food, they were so delicious that even the emperor ate them."

Over the course of the next 400 years, pasta products continued to become increasingly popular and spread throughout China, becoming a staple of the working class. A set of fifteen ancient *bing* recipes were printed in a 6th century book titled *Qimin Yaoshu*, or "Techniques Essential for the Subsistence of Common People." Of all the recipes, three were made from wheat flour, one from a combination of wheat

flour and millet, and two from starch, in addition to recipes for white bread, flatbreads, and cakes. (The inclusion of recipes for *bing* made from starches indicates an already established practice of gelatinizing this gluten-less substance in order to shape the dough into pasta products.)

It is during the Song Dynasty, in the 12th and 13th centuries, that wheat-based products start to be referred to as *mian*, leaving *bing* to exclusively signify flatbreads. As such, *bing* began to be sold in bakeries and pastry shops, while savory *mian* began to be sold in specialized noodle shops and to appear on the menus of specialty restaurants called "pasta shops," with names like *jisi mian*, or "minced chicken noodles," *sanxian mian*, or "three-freshness," and *shuihua mian*, or "pasta slipped into water."

A proliferation of *hundun* or "dumplings" also appear during this time period. While their existence had been previously documented in earlier periods, it is at this point that they explode in popularity and become available in a wide variety of shapes and fillings and start being sold in specialty shops and begin to appear on the restaurant menus in large urban areas. Being able to make thin dumpling wrappers becomes a prized culinary art form.

Rice noodles entered the *mian* lexicon as a result of a geopolitical development. A centuries-old sustained barbarian offense, which culminated in the 13th century, shifted the center of Chinese civilization to southern China, prompting many people from northern China to migrate to the south in search of opportunities. Once settled, these predominantly wheat noodle eaters found it difficult to acclimate to the local custom of eating rice. To adapt, northern cooks began to prepare noodles using rice flour, since wheat flour needed to be imported and was prohibitively expensive.

At the turn of the 15th century, the household encyclopedia titled *Jujia Biyong Shilei Quanji* differentiated noodles and dumplings. It distinguished between "moist pasta dishes" such as *mian*, in which flour was mixed with cold water and whose dough was then cooked in water or broth, and "dry pasta dishes" such as *jiao, mantou,* and *baozi,* in which flour was mixed with boiling water and the resulting dumplings then steamed.

Noodles and dumplings in China reached their evolutionary peak during the Ming Dynasty (1368–1644) and have remained relatively unchanged since that time, with the notable exception of the famed *yifu mian,* or "egg noodles," which were invented in the 18th century during the Qing Dynasty.

The ever increasing supplies of flour enabled imperial chefs, artisan noodle makers, and homemakers alike to discover the versa-

tility flour offered when combined with water and to create noodles of different widths and a variety of filled dumplings.

By the 17th century, the fruits of their labor and ingenuity began to look very similar to the noodles we consume today. Interestingly, despite their prevalence, few noodles were known on a national scale, as the Chinese tended to create regional specialties that stayed within their geographic areas, and the production of noodles was not industrialized until the 20th century, an unsurprising development considering that in 1913 only 50 industrial-scale mills existed throughout China.

THE HISTORY OF PASTA

If we were to follow the scent of pasta back through the centuries, the journey would not begin in Italy but most likely in Greece or the Middle East.

Etymology, or the history of words, intimate that pasta may have first appeared during ancient Greek civilization in the first millennium CE. Called *laganon,* it was a freshly prepared broad flat cake made from a mixture of wheat flour and water or the juice of crushed lettuce. Spiced and fried, it was consumed as an everyday food and was subsequently adopted by the Romans. Anna Del Conte, a prolific Italian-born food writer whose works cover the history of food, shares in her book *On Pasta* that it is very likely that a precursor to pasta could date back that far. "Not only pasta itself," she writes, "but also one of its many names, lasagna, since *laganon* led to the Latin *laganum*—mentioned by Horace in one of his Satires, and by Cicero, who loved to eat it. In Neapolitan dialect a rolling pin is still called a *laganatura.*" An archeological finding dating back to the 4th century BCE lends credence to this theory. The bas-relief, unearthed in an Etruscan tomb located 30 miles north of Rome, depicts a rolling pin and rolling board, very similar in appearance to

what we use today, used to prepare a spelt dish resembling lasagna.

It is also possible that Libyan Arabs brought a dried form of pasta to Italy during their conquest of Sicily in the late 7th century (601 CE–700 CE). It is most likely the origin of the dried pasta that began to be produced in great quantities in southern Italy around that time, since its ability to easily reconstitute into a hot and nutritious meal made it highly desirable. How the inhabitants consumed the pasta unfortunately is not known, though to this day many old Sicilian pasta recipes still include Arab-introduced ingredients like raisins, cinnamon, spinach, and eggplant.

The Romans, in their conquests, introduced pasta throughout Europe, though it was made from local soft wheat, and not the durum wheat for which Italian pasta is predominantly known (it had not yet become a staple in the area). The tradition of using soft wheat to make fresh pasta continues to this day, as evidenced by fettuccine and tagliatelle, traditional from central Italy to the Western Alps, and *spätzle* in Austria, Switzerland, and parts of Germany.

For several centuries, pasta's trail goes cold. Its absence from ancient texts may be attribut-

WHERE DOES THE WORD *MACARONI*, OR *MACCHERONI*, COME FROM?

The word *maccheroni* comes from the Sicilian term for "making dough forcefully." Until the automation of pasta making, making pasta from milled wheat (semolina) was a laborious and painstaking undertaking. Because the semolina flour used for the task was granular like sugar and not powdery like typical flour, it was both difficult to form into dough and often required a full day of kneading. The most tenable approach to kneading the dough for that long was to use men's feet. Throughout the south, beginning in the 16th century, barefoot men could be seen treading dough to make it malleable enough to roll out (a far cry from today's FDA regulations). The dough was then extruded through pierced dies by a large screw press powered by two men or one big horse.

This unique way of kneading dough, considered barbaric by the aristocratic class, continued at least until the beginning of the 20th century, when advancements in the mass production of pasta enabled the process to be executed mechanically.

able to pasta living in the shadow of the two more popular staples of the time, bread and gruel. As such, until the Renaissance, historical documents referencing pasta are rare. Here are a few of the more significant mentions that have been found:

◆ The first clear Western reference to dried noodles cooked by boiling appeared in the Jerusalem Talmud during the 5th century CE. Written in Aramaic, it describes a debate over whether noodles, referred to as *itriyah* (for more on this, see page 27), violated Jewish dietary laws. (It should be noted that by the 10th century, *itriyah* became associated exclusively with the durum wheat dried noodles one could buy at the market, as opposed to fresh homemade pasta made from soft flour.)

◆ An early 5th-century cookbook, attributed to Apicius, describes a dish called *lagana,* which contained layers of dough and a meat or seafood filling.

◆ In the 9th century, during the Muslim reign of Emir Abdurrahman II in Spain, the Arab minstrel Ziryab is known to have sung songs extolling the beauty of various shapes of pasta and the importance of eating them elegantly.

◆ The term *vermicelli* entered the pasta lexicon by appearing, for the first time, in the 11th-century cookbook *De Arte Coquinaria Per Vermicelli e Maccaroni Siciliani,* or "The Art of Cooking Sicilian Vermicelli and Macaroni," written by Martino Corno, the chef to the matriarch of Aquileia.

Otherwise, dried pasta lived in relative recorded silence. By the 12th century, references to pasta began to appear more regularly, as more and more people began to appreciate the attributes and convenience of dried pasta. The arduous and time-intensive process involved in making it and the need to import its flour from Sicily or Puglia, however, priced it out of reach for all but the wealthy. As a result, common laborers could only consume it on special occasions like weddings and religious holidays. (It is worth noting that the commercial pasta shops of the time hired night watchmen to protect their coveted goods.) Pasta was considered such a luxury, in fact, that in 1279 a Genoan soldier named Ponzio Baestone bequeathed in his last will and testament a *"bariscella peina de macarone,"* or a small basket of macaroni.

The German poet Walther von der Vogelweide mentioned pasta when he described the Sicilian's love of *maccheroni* combined with a sweet sauce, while the Arab geographer Muhammad al-Idrisi, commissioned to explore the island and write a book about his experiences, described the people of the Sicilian town of Trabia making a thread-like food made from the flour of hard wheat and exporting it all over the country. Called *itriyah*, the Arab word for string, the pasta eventually became known as *tria* and *trii*, which to this day remain terms for spaghetti in parts of Sicily and southern Italy.

The development of fresh and dried pasta as a culinary art took off, as with so many things, during the Renaissance, when it started to be produced by rudimentary factories. By the 15th century, the production by craftsmen of *fidei*, the word for pasta in local Italian dialect, became widespread from southern Italy all the way up the coast to Liguria, as evidenced by a surviving document of the Corporation of Pasta-Makers from 1571 found in Naples and a manuscript establishing "Rules for the Pasta-Masters' Art Corporation" in Savona, located near Genoa, in 1577.

Producing pasta in larger quantities lowered its price, making it more affordable to the masses, and historical references to pasta dishes such as ravioli, gnocchi, and vermicelli began to appear with increasing frequency across the

PASTA HIGH ON THE HOG

In Medieval and earlier times, the elites were the only class of people wealthy enough to have the great pleasure of eating fresh pasta. Served as a side dish and cooked well beyond today's "al dente" designation, pasta was either served as pockets of dough stuffed with cheeses and meats or layered with other foods in baked dishes resembling lasagna.

By the time of the Renaissance, it had gained such popularity that it was included in banquets, prepared in predictably opulent fashion. Perhaps one of the most memorable and illustrious examples of the gluttonous use of pasta involved the papal chef and cookbook author Bartolomeo Scappi. Considered a celebrity chef by today's standards, he regaled the Vatican with courses consisting of boiled chicken and ravioli filled with a mixture of pork belly, cow udders, roast pork, local cheeses, sugar, herbs, spices, and raisins, as well as dough enriched with goat's milk and egg yolks and seasoned with grated cheese, sugar, butter, cinnamon, and a cheese similar to mozzarella.

Perhaps not surprisingly, the 16th-century Italian author Giulio Cesare Croce added macaroni to his list of "fattening dishes."

Italian peninsula. By the 15th century, a book by Father Bartolomeo Secchi titled *De Honesta Voluptate et Valetudine,* or "On Honorable Pleasure and Health," mentions a long and hollow pasta called macaroni and a pasta similar to present-day soup noodles.

Although both dried and fresh pasta had become increasing popular among all classes, the introduction of a machine in Naples that extruded pasta from a die in the 17th century made pasta production more efficient and allowed production to be scaled up. The production of durum wheat also shifts to Naples around this time. Though Sicily historically had been the major supplier of the grain in medieval times, the soil around Naples turned out to be well-suited for growing durum wheat and its climate, replete with mild air from the sea and hot winds from the nearby mountains, ideal for drying pasta.

The abundance of significantly less expensive dried pasta turned it into an important food staple for the commoner. This was especially true in the city of Naples, which witnessed a remarkable growth of pasta shops, from 60 in 1,700 to 285 in 1785 (it is believed this boom was also attributable to economic conditions that caused the prices of meat and vegetables to skyrocket and to religious edicts that frequently restricted eating meat). Regardless of the reason for its increased popularity, Neapolitans began to be commonly called *"mangia-maccheroni"* or "macaroni-eaters." Commoners bought pasta from vendors called *maccaronaros,* who cooked it on the streets over charcoal-stoked fires, and ate it on the spot with bare hands, plain or sprinkled with grated sheep or goat's cheese.

But southern Italy wasn't alone in its appreciation for pasta. In 1740, the city of Venice issued Paolo Adami a license to open the first pasta factory, a rudimentary operation consisting of an iron press powered by several boys. Twenty years later, the Duke of Parma, Don Ferdinando of Bourbon, approved a ten-year monopoly for the production of dried pasta in the city of Parma.

It was also at this point in history that pasta began to officially travel outside of Italy as a food staple that kept well in a ship's stores for long voyages. Paul-Jacques Malouin, a French scientist inspired by the industrial production techniques he witnessed in Naples, brought a kneading machine and screw press to Paris in 1767 and introduced the city to the noodle-making trade of *"vermicilier."* Thomas Jefferson is also believed to have attempted to bring a "macaroni" machine to America in 1789, after serving as an ambassador to France. While his attempts to ship the machine were futile, he nevertheless brought cases of dried pasta back with him. Later, he invented his own pasta machine.

In 1862, the unification of Italy under King Vittorio Emanuele II, the ruler of Sardinia, created peace among the warring states. Now able to travel safely, Italians were exposed to the pasta-making techniques and recipes of other regions, causing an explosion in creativity and the proliferation of many additional shapes. Perhaps the main reason for pasta's dramatic spread in popularity was the invention of powerful kneading and extruding machines, which enabled factories to replace manpower with steam or hydraulic power. By 1878, the time-consuming process of separating semolina flour from the bran was mechanized with the development of the Marseillais purifier. Invented in Marseille, France, this machine had mechanical sifters. Four years later the first hydraulic press appears, followed by the first steam-powered mill two years later. Dried pasta became easier to produce than ever before.

These significant developments made dried pasta easier to produce than was ever possible with handmade fresh pasta and cheaper to purchase. New industrial developments made it possible to to create new and imaginative pasta shapes. By the end of the 19th century, pasta factories produced an assortment that ranged from 150 to 200 different shapes. The first patented pasta machine further revolutionized the pasta industry in 1933. Able to mix, knead, extrude, and dry pasta in one continuous process, it facilitated the vast production of pasta shapes and sizes that have carried on their legacy to this day.

INGREDIENTS

Making pasta is not rocket science. At the end of the day, it can be as simple as combining two ingredients, eggs and flour, or flour and water. My own anecdotal experience is a case in point. For 45 years, my mother has made pasta following my grandmother's recipe, which is essentially "one egg per person and as much flour as the egg can take." She doesn't worry about whether the eggs are medium, large, or extra large, and I don't believe it has ever occurred to her to purchase special flour for the task. She uses the trusty all-purpose flour she keeps on hand for making anything and everything and manages to make tender and delicious tagliatelle and ravioli every single time.

Should you decide to use the all-purpose flour in your food pantry and good quality eggs, I assure you that you will make pasta more delicious than anything you could purchase fresh from the market, even those from high-end grocers. Your pasta will be tender and absolutely satisfying and the journey can end right there for you.

If, on the other hand, you would like to delve deeper into understanding the finer subtleties of the ingredients that go into pasta making, I invite you to read on. Once you begin experimenting with different types of flour and ingredients, you will see and taste the different nuances in the pasta for yourself. It is a profoundly satisfying journey.

FLOUR: THE FOUNDATION OF PASTA AND NOODLES

A passion for making pasta translates into knowledge of flour. There's no way around it. Otherwise it is like wanting to fly a hot air balloon without understanding the role that air density plays in the process. In this book, we will closely examine the flours traditionally used in the preparation of pasta, noodles, and dumplings, the preponderance of which come from wheat berries and rice. (Pastas and noodles are also made from a variety of other grains and from non-grain based ingredients, and this book will cover the major players later in this chapter.)

Protein (and Gluten) in Flour
Before we embark on introducing the main types of flour available to us in our pasta, noodle, and

dumpling making exploits, it is important to understand the role that protein plays in flour and how it affects our dough. Once water is added to flour and the kneading process begins, two proteins, glutenin and gliadin, come into contact and form a bond that creates a continuous network of fine strands in the dough known as gluten. This network is what gives dough its structure and strength; the more of these two particular proteins that a flour contains, the stronger its gluten network will be once turned to dough. This network is what gives dough its structure and strength.

Author and food scientist Harold McGee in his seminal book *On Food and Cooking* shares that the Chinese call gluten "the muscle of

flour." It is an apt description because gluten is what gives dough its elasticity, which is the ability to stretch and bounce back, and its plasticity, which is the ability to take on a shape and keep it. The right amount of gluten results in a pasta dough that is easier to knead, to roll through the pasta machine, and to stretch without tearing when handled. This explains why bread flour contains higher amounts of protein and why pasta, which needs to be more malleable, requires less.

Wheat Flour

Wheat flour is the product of the annual grass we know as wheat, a grain so ancient that its primitive relatives were discovered in some of the world's oldest excavation sites, dating back more than 9,000 years ago, in eastern Iraq. For thousands of years the wheat plant cross-bred arbitrarily with other plants and grasses, evolving into several different wheat species. One of them, *Triticum aestivum,* proved particularly desirable because it contains glutenin, which produced a more elastic and malleable dough that was easier to shape into a variety of foods. We began to cultivate it more than 8,000 years ago and it

now accounts for 90% of the wheat grown around the world.

Within the *T. aestivum* genus, wheat is generally categorized by whether it is hard or soft, red or white, winter or spring. For the purposes of this book, we will focus on flours that tend to fall within the red (more flavorful, wheatier), soft (less gluten, more malleable dough), and winter (slightly less gluten than spring) categories, as they tend to produce better tasting pastas with a slightly chewy yet tender texture.

Accounting for most of the remaining 10% of world wheat production is *Triticum durum,* known as durum wheat. Similar to *T. aestivum,* it originated in the Middle East and spread to many parts of the Mediterranean Basin before Roman times. Deep amber in color and rich in protein, durum wheat is ground into semolina flour and used to make almost all of the commercial dry pasta typically sold in boxes or see-through plastic packaging. Durum wheat differentiates itself considerably among other grains because its flour contains the gluten protein gliadin, which is extensible rather than elastic, which means that its dough can be rolled easily into sheets and the resulting pasta dries without breaking and reliably holds intricate shapes.

Before we begin exploring the different flours used in pasta making, it is worth noting that flour is not a static product. If "a rose is a rose is a rose" in Gertrude Stein's world, then "flour is not flour is not flour" in ours. In other words, the bag of flour in your pantry is probably very different from your next door neighbor's. In fact, flour can be as unique as a proverbial snowflake and varies greatly depending on whether it comes from a nearby mill or is produced by a regional manufacturer or a nationally recognized one. That's because when flour is milled, its composition, and thus performance, depends on the wheat grain variety, growing season, the soil in which it is grown, protein content, milling technique, temperature of the grain at the time of milling, and storage. National brands are the exception. Blended specifically for consistency, they combine different hard and soft wheat varieties to guarantee certain protein level compositions in their flour. Because of this, they are often the flour of choice among professional bakers looking for predictable and reliable results in their baked goods.

The decision ultimately is yours. As I mentioned earlier, fresh pasta made with a national brand of flour and good quality eggs will be delicious. Its only shortcoming will be its flavor, which will be rather neutral and contain none of the aromatic notes of nuts, tobacco, and even grass that you would find in a freshly milled flour.

Unbleached All-Purpose Flour

Typically produced from a blend of hard, high-protein bread flours and soft, low-protein pastry flours, all-purpose flour contains a moderate level of protein that ranges from 9% to 12% in national flour brands but that can go as low as 7.5% protein in small regional brands. Blended and milled to be versatile, it is strong enough to make bread and soft enough to create tender, delicate scones, cakes, and biscuits. It also makes perfectly tender pasta, though combining it with other flours such as durum wheat or semolina, creates tastier and slightly firmer results. Avoid bleached flour whenever possible, as it is treated with chemicals like benzoyl peroxide and chlorine gas to speed up the flour's aging process. The unbleached version is aged naturally with oxygen, which slowly oxides the flour over time. The natural process is more time-intensive, which makes unbleached flour slightly more expensive than the bleached version. All-purpose flour is also available pre-sifted, a process that aerates the flour to make it lighter than standard all-purpose flour. However, since all flour has a tendency to settle and become more compact during storage, it is advisable to always sift flour when needed.

"00" Flour

Produced from soft wheat, finely ground, and almost talcum-like, "00" flour is fairly low in protein content. It is the flour of choice in most Italian homes and among Chinese noodle makers because it produces soft dough that is easy to roll and yields pastas and noodles that are smooth and silky. Tender egg pastas such tagliatelle, *garganelli,* and *corzetti* have most likely been prepared with "00" dough and eggs. Occasionally the categorization of "00" flour causes some confusion because despite always being finely milled into powdery form, it can be made from soft or hard varieties of wheat and consequently contains different percentages of protein by weight. Soft wheat is lower in protein and creates soft and tender pasta that readily absorbs and takes on the flavor of a tasty sauce. Hard wheat is higher in gluten content and creates a sturdy dough that is ideal for trapping air bubbles, like bread dough, but that makes it almost impossible to roll out into sheets for pasta. When purchasing it, you will find "00" flour designated for bread and pizza or for pasta, with protein contents ranging from 5% to 12%. Be sure to select the "00" flour designated for making pasta and not for bread. If this flour is not readily available in your area, it is only a click away on the internet.

Semolina Flour and Durum Flour

Both types of flour come from milling protein-rich durum wheat berries and have the highest protein content of any flour. Semolina comes from milling the innermost layer, called the endosperm, of the berry. It is characteristically golden yellow in color as a result of its high concentration of carotenoids (the same compounds responsible for the carrot's orange color) and coarse. It creates a strong pasta dough that holds any shape and that strengthens when heated. Experienced pasta makers often add small amounts of semolina flour to pasta dough made predominantly with "00" flour to add pleasant chewiness and a subtle nutty flavor and to increase the dough's stretchability during rolling. Semolina flour also makes an excellent alternative to cornmeal, and can be dusted on pasta and pasta-making surfaces to prevent sticking. Occasionally the word *semolina* causes some confusion because it is not always associated with wheat and is also used to describe the innermost layer of any grain, such as corn and rice.

Durum flour has a very fine texture that makes it look like yellow-hued all-purpose flour. A by-product of milling semolina flour, it creates a malleable pasta dough that is easily fed through pasta makers and that will curl or bend during cooking.

Again, if these flours are not readily available in your area, look for them online.

Whole Wheat Flour

Ground from hard red spring or winter wheat, this flour is ground from the entire wheat berry: the endosperm, germ, and bran. Brownish and lightly speckled, whole wheat adds a full-bodied and wheat-y flavor that, due to the tannin in the outer bran, at times can teeter on bitterness. Chock full of naturally occurring vitamins, minerals, and fiber, it is a viable option for health-oriented individuals who don't mind its strong flavor. For better results, it is advisable to add some all-purpose flour to make the resulting dough more pliable and

rollable and the pasta more tender. Whole wheat flour tends to absorb more moisture than white flour, so you'll need to adjust for that if you're making a substitution in a recipe. There is also white whole wheat flour, which is ground from hard white spring or winter wheat berries; it possesses the same nutritional profile as whole wheat flour but is milder in flavor and lighter in color.

Rice Flour

Ground from long- or medium-grain hulled white rice or whole grain brown rice, rice flour consists mostly of starch and contains only a small amount of protein. Flours ground from white and brown rice perform similarly in noodle recipes, though they differ slightly in flavor and coloring (noodles made from brown rice flour also take longer to cook). Commonly used in Asian countries to make a variety of noodles, dumplings, and pancakes, it is an excellent gluten-free substitute for wheat flour and therefore ideal for people who are gluten intolerant. Coarsely ground rice flour can also be used for dusting pasta and pasta-making surfaces to prevent sticking instead of cornmeal or semolina.

There is also sweet rice flour, which is ground from short-grain glutinous or "sticky" rice. It has the highest starch content among rice flours and becomes moist, firm, and sticky when cooked. Its pleasantly chewy texture makes it an ideal binder for Asian noodles, dumplings, buns, and pastries but it cannot be used as a substitute for regular rice flour.

Other Flours

One problem with using whole grain and alternative flours in pasta making is that there's a lot less consistency from brand to brand than with white flours, especially national brands. For instance, one brand of flour might be milled a little coarser than another. What that means is that measurement of flour can be difficult if a recipe doesn't specify an amount for alternative flours.

MILLING YOUR OWN FLOUR

Home milling may seem like a huge investment of time and effort to create something that we can access so effortlessly in a high-quality bag of wheat flour. Let's explore why some people decide to go the extra mile and grind their own berries to make flour for pasta.

First, home milling allows us to maximize the freshness and subtle sweetness of every batch of wheat berries that we grind into flour. This is especially important as it relates to making pasta. Consider that once a wheat berry is cracked, it begins to lose its flavor and aroma and that, within three days of milling, it has lost nearly half of its flavorful oils and 90% of its flavor compounds. Marc Vetri, restaurateur par excellence and author of the cookbook *Mastering Pasta*, likens milling the wheat berry to that of coffee beans. "For the best taste, you need to grind them fresh and use them right away. Otherwise, all the flavor and aroma just fade away." Because of this, only grind as much flour as you plan to use, as freshly ground whole grains contain oils that get rancid very quickly. Whole grain kernels, on the other hand, will keep indefinitely when stored in a cool, dry place.

Grinding your own flour also retains more nutrients because the milling process grinds the whole berry, which includes the endosperm, from which all-purpose flour is made, along with bran and germ for added fiber and nutrition.

Finally, you can feel confident that the powdery flour you are using to make pastas, noodles, dumplings, and even bread contains no fillers or additives. It is a pretty unique and satisfying experience. In addition to wheat berries, you can grind a wide variety of grains, dried beans, seeds, and nuts that include rice, buckwheat, rye, spelt, barley, garbanzos, oats, millet, kamut, quinoa, peas, mung beans, and lentils.

If the idea of grinding your own flour interests you, purchase wheat berries online or, preferably, from a local mill and then grind them using an inexpensive KitchenAid burr grinder attachment, a reasonably priced tabletop mill, or a manual grinder for a real hands-on experience.

Or, if milling your own isn't in the cards, seek out freshly milled flour from a local mill.

QUICK REFERENCE
1 cup of wheat berries produces a scant 1 ¾ cups flour
1 pound of wheat berries equals approximately 4 ½ cups flour

But even if you know the correct measurement, you're not home free. Whole grain flours can absorb a lot more water than white flours. If your chosen brand of flour isn't the same one the recipe writer was using, you still might end up with a dough that is too wet or too dry, even though your measurements are completely accurate. If you use a lot of whole grain and alternative flours, be ready to adjust the amount of water as needed.

Spelt Flour

Ground from *Triticum aestivum* subsp. *spelta,* spelt flour is subtly sweet. And while it is high in protein, those proteins are largely not the gluten-producing kinds (though it does contains some, so spelt is not gluten free). As a result, it is considered a weak gluten flour and a dough made with it will be very crumbly and will require that the pasta sheets to be rolled out thicker than normal. For best results, use it only in pasta dough recipes crafted specifically for spelt.

Farro Flour

Produced from milled emmer wheat *(Triticum turgidum dicoccum),* farro flour is high in protein and lightly tan in color. Emmer wheat was heavily cultivated in the Mediterranean Basin and Middle East until durum and hard wheat became more popular during Roman times. It is used most often in the northern Italian regions of Umbria and Tuscany to make artisanal pasta. While high in protein content, it produces weak gluten networks that, similar to spelt, make the dough very crumbly and require the pasta sheets to be rolled out thicker than normal.

Buckwheat Flour

Bold, nutty flavored, and gluten-free, this flour is ground from the grain-like seeds of the buckwheat *(Fagopyrum esculentum)* plant. Despite its name, buckwheat is not related to wheat, but rather is a member of the sorrel and rhubarb family. A hearty plant, it thrives in cold weather and grows in Siberia, in northern Japan, and in the alpine areas of Italy and France and is used to make Japanese soba noodles and Italian *pizzoccheri* pasta. Because this flour contains no gluten, its dough tends to dry out very quickly and crumble when rolled, while the resulting noodles are very fragile. For easier kneading and rolling and better overall results, use a combination of roughly 80 percent buckwheat flour and 20 percent wheat flour, as that little bit of wheat flour helps hold the dough together and gives it enough elasticity to roll out.

Rye Flour

Ground from the cereal grains of rye grass *(Secale cereale),* a member of the wheat family (Triticeae). Because it is difficult to separate the germ and bran from the endosperm of rye, rye flour usually retains a large quantity of nutrients, in contrast to refined wheat flour. Its flour produces gluten that is less elastic and is quite sticky on its own, so for easier kneading and rolling and better overall results, use roughly 30 to 50 percent rye flour and make up the difference with durum flour, which adds strength to the dough and mellows out rye's earthy and slightly spicy and sour flavor.

Chickpea Flour

Frequently packaged under its Indian names, gram or besan flour, or as garbanzo flour, this flour is ground from nutritious, fiber-rich chickpeas. The flour can be made with either roasted or unroasted chickpeas; when using it to make pasta or dumplings, use the unroasted kind. Because this flour contains no gluten, its dough tends to dry out very quickly and crumble when rolled, while the resulting noodles are very fragile. For best results, use a combination of roughly 25 percent chickpea flour and 75 percent wheat flour.

Storing Flour

I recommend refrigerating all flour if you have the space, but if not, always refrigerate whole wheat flour, as the rich oils in the germ of the wheat berry tend to get rancid. Always bring flour to room temperature before using it for pasta making.

EGGS: TENDER PASTA'S
NOT-SO-SECRET INGREDIENT

For the purposes of making pasta, or eating the best, most wholesome food possible for that matter, it is best to secure the best quality eggs available to you.

Eggs play a vital role in many fresh pasta recipes. Not only do they enrich the pasta from a nutritional standpoint, they also add an appealing pale yellow color and a subtle egg flavor to the dough. Eggs also contribute two additional elements that may perhaps be more important to a pasta maker. First, they provide more protein, which, when combined with the gluten in the dough, enhances the structure of the dough, making it elastic, soft, and easier to roll out thinly without tearing, resulting in a tender, smooth, and springy pasta. Secondly, the egg whites give additional heft and firmness to the dough while preventing the loss of starch as the pasta cooks.

It is important to use eggs that have a vibrantly orange yolk, as it is a sign of a healthy, happy, and well-fed chicken. Egg yolks get their color from carotenoids, the same compounds that give carrots their color, which are also responsible for strengthening the chicken's immune system. Because chickens only hatch eggs if they have sufficient levels of carotenoids, the yolks possess deep hues of dark gold and orange. Paler yolks are often a result of chickens feeding on barley or white cornmeal, foods that don't nourish them as completely as a carotenoid-enhancing diet based on yellow corn and marigold petals.

Using brown or white eggs is up to the discretion of the individual pasta maker, since they both share the same nutritional profiles and taste the same. Their color difference essentially rests, rather inanely, on whether the chicken breeds have white earlobes, which produces white eggs, or brown earlobes, which produces brown ones. Pasta connoisseur and author of the wonderful book *Making Artisan Pasta* Aliza Green makes a good argument for buying brown eggs. First, brown eggs come from larger breeds that eat more, take longer to produce their eggs, and produce eggs with thicker protective shells, which prevents internal moisture loss over time, thus helping them to maintain their freshness. Also, because brown eggs are considered a specialty product, she adds, their quality tends to be higher.

I wholeheartedly concur with Ms. Green but have to admit that I choose brown eggs, I suppose, because I am a romantic at heart. My hand is always drawn to their container because they are just prettier. They also take me back to my childhood and to the verdant rustic setting of a Piedmontese farm owned by dear family friends, where we never left a visit without at least a dozen of their fresh brown eggs carefully wrapped in old newspaper.

In my opinion, the quality and freshness of an egg and its temperature at time of use (it's always best to use eggs at room temperature because the flour has an easier time absorbing them) are more important than its particular size or weight. It pleases some people to get very scientific and measure each and every ingredient with a scale. And the truth is that they get excellent results and have a satisfying experience in the process. My father, an engineer through and through by training and profession, certainly falls in this category. He wouldn't dream of making his memorably crusty and delicious focaccia and pretzel-like *taralli* without weighing every last ingredient (including the small amount of fennel seeds that go in the *taralli*!). His baked results are always exceptional. While I applaud that level of precision and know firsthand how inherently satisfying it is from years of watching my father's satisfied face as he fastidiously weighed everything, I also believe there's room for a more relaxed, yet still effective approach. After all, men and women were eyeballing ingredients for centuries before standardized measuring cups and weights became commonplace.

Egg Grades

Because the quality of any food we create is the sum of all the ingredients that we use to create it, it behooves us to use the best quality eggs at our disposal.

Eggs in the United States are graded according to the thickness of their shell and the firmness of their egg whites. Agricultural advances have made it possible for large egg producers to assess the quality of each individual egg and to efficiently sort them by size, weight, and quality. With almost scientific precision, eggs are graded AA (top quality), A (good quality found in most supermarkets), and B (substandard eggs with thin shells and watery egg whites that don't reach consumers but are used commercially and industrially). They are also further categorized by size: medium, large (the most common size), and extra large. The past decade or so has also seen a rise in popularity of free-range and organic eggs. The product of smaller-scale enterprises, these chickens are fed organic feed and are caged with slightly more space at their disposal than standard chicken farms. While the jury is still out on whether this last category tastes betters, it nonetheless constitutes an additional, and perhaps politically oriented, option for pasta makers.

Freshness

Due to the industrialization of chicken farming, it has never taken less time for eggs to reach our supermarket shelves.

For the purposes of making pasta, it is best to secure the freshest eggs available, so check the expiration dates before buying them and buy them when they are well within that window.

In making pasta it is important to avoid cold, so use room temperature eggs. Also, do not work on a naturally cold surface such as marble or stainless steel. Wood is best; otherwise Corian or linoleum will work. If you do not make perfect pasta dough the first time don't be discouraged.

WATER

The water you use can influence dough quality depending on its mineral content and temperature.

Mineral-rich water from your tap is best for pasta dough. The only exception is if your water is particularly hard, or excessively high in minerals like magnesium and calcium. In that case, you may be better off using spring water, as too much of these minerals can produce a tighter gluten network in the dough and result in a firmer, and sometimes too firm, dough.

Always use tepid water, around 105°F (or two parts cold water to one part boiling water), as it makes it easier for the flour to absorb the liquid. Exceptions to this guideline exist and generally involve Asian noodles and dumpling wrappers that require boiling water to activate gluten.

SALT

Using a pinch or two of fine-grain iodized salt (table salt) or slightly coarser kosher salt both work nicely and contribute a hint of salty flavor to your pasta. I recommend not using fine or coarse sea salt, as their high mineral content can cause dough to develop a tighter gluten network and result in a firmer, and sometimes too firm, pasta.

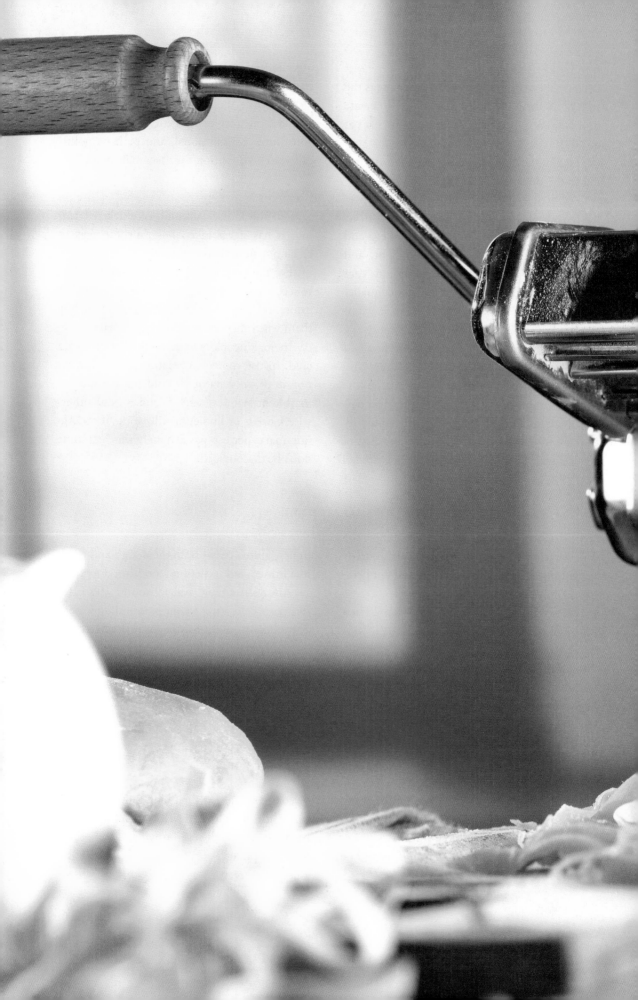

EQUIPMENT

At most, making basic pasta shapes like *tagliatelle* or lasagna sheets requires a work surface, measuring cups, a rolling pin, a knife, and your hands for mixing and kneading. But you don't even need a rolling pin if your goal is making pasta shapes like long and thick *pici* or, ear-shaped *orecchiette*. In other words, you can make pasta with the equipment you most likely have right now in your kitchen. This fact does not negate the usefulness of other tools that turn pasta making into an easier, faster, and even more consistent process. I will also add that, in my opinion, the tools listed under "Must Have" are indispensable. As luck would have it, they are also among the least expensive of all the pasta-making tools.

MUST HAVE

Baking Sheets

Pasta and dumpling makers can never have enough baking sheets. Thankfully, they stack and don't take up much space in the kitchen. The standard size, considered a half-sheet pan, is 13 x 18 inches, and three of them should suffice for most jobs. If you frequently make large batches of pasta and have the storage space, consider investing in a couple full-size sheet pans, which measure 18 x 26 inches.

Bench Scraper

Also known as a bench knife, a scraper is a flat, thin blade with a handle that is used to manipulate dough and to scrape up any leftover dough from the work surface. Look for one made from stainless steel with a wide handle that you can comfortably hold. They are also super handy for transporting delicate dumplings or pasta shapes from the cutting board to the cooking water.

Colander

Every kitchen needs a good stainless steel colander. It is indispensable for draining pasta, noodles, and just washed vegetables. Look for one with well-distributed holes for fast and thorough draining, and with a rounded base (not three feet) for extra stability in the sink or on counter tops. If you frequently cook more than a pound of pasta at a time, invest in a large-capacity colander. If you cook a lot of small pasta, you may also want to consider purchasing a large, fine-meshed sieve.

Flour Dredger

A cylindrical metal container with a slightly domed and perforated top, a dredger allows you to easily sprinkle a light coat of flour on pasta as you make it. (A flour sifter can be used in the same manner but is messier.)

Grater

Many recipes in this book call for grated cheeses, garlic, and ginger. When it comes to grating cheese, a classic and well-constructed box grater gives you four sides of various sized holes that allow you to grate cheese or other items from a coarse to a fine texture. Sturdy rotary cheese graters make grating cheese a breeze, but need to be strong enough to withstand the pressure that is applied to the handle as it is turned (metal models are usually best). Finer grating, like that typically required for garlic, ginger, lemon zest, lemongrass, or nutmeg, requires a Microplane grater, which essentially pulverizes each ingredient and makes it undetectable, except for the flavor, in your dishes.

Measuring Cups

While there are people out there who swear by their digital scales, millions of pounds of pasta have surely been made throughout time by women who have eyeballed their flour quantities. In comparison, measuring cups are much more accurate. The most effective way of using them involves filling them, scoop by spoon, until they are overflowing and then leveling them with a knife or other straight-edged tool. Scooping the flour right out of its container tends to pack the flour and ends up giving you more flour than the recipe actually calls for, with varying and not always stellar results.

Parchment Paper

I have come to believe that parchment paper is the most undervalued tool in the kitchen, and doubly so if you make your own pasta. Besides making it a cinch to clean up roasted chickens or cookie trays, it creates a fabulous nonstick surface for gnocchi and dumplings (always remember to dust them with a little flour). You can purchase it as pre-cut sheets or rolls, though I prefer the latter because it is customizable and eliminates unnecessary waste. If you live near a restaurant supply store, you can purchase it in big boxes, which is great because you can go through a LOT of parchment paper in the kitchen.

Pastry Cutter

Designed as a small rotating disc connected to a handle, a pastry cutter quickly and efficiently cuts sheets of dough into pasta ribbons with smooth borders or, when using a ridged pastry cutter, ruffled ones. Some models come with both smooth and ridged wheels. Look for models made from stainless steel with a wide, grip-friendly handle. You can also find cutters with five evenly spaced wheels that, depending on how far apart they are positioned, can make a variety of pasta ribbons. I even saw a stainless steel model that allows you to evenly adjust the space between the wheels, giving the pasta maker creative license to make ribbons of varied widths.

Pasta Fork

Also known as "spaghetti servers," these oversized, pronged forks help you toss and serve long-stranded pastas like spaghetti and linguine. With their nice, long handle, I also use them to easily retrieve a strand or piece of pasta when I am checking on its level of doneness toward the end of the cooking time.

Rubber Spatula

Helpful in getting every last tasty bit of sauce or mixed ingredients out of pots and bowls, they can also be used to gently mix gnocchi with their sauce without damaging or smushing them. All you have to do is slowly slide it along the side of the bowl, which helps to move the gnocchi into the sauce.

Glass or Stainless Steel Bowls

Mixing, resting, and holding pasta dough requires bowls. I recommend ones made of glass or stainless steel because they are "nonreactive," meaning they will not give your dough a metallic flavor (aluminum and copper are "reactive" and should not be used). Make sure to have several medium and large bowls on hand.

Small Paring Knife

Handy for cutting small ingredients you may need in your pasta preparations and for cutting rolls of dough into gnocchi or dumplings. Versions with thick, easy-to-hold handles help your hand not to cramp up during lengthy tasks.

Spider Strainer

A skimmer shaped like a wide, shallow wire-mesh basket with a long handle, it is used to remove and drain dumplings and filled pasta from boiling water and to skim foam from the surfaces of boiling broths. I find it more effective than a slotted spoon because it can retrieve more dumplings and filled pasta at one time, it's deep enough to prevent any of them from falling back into the water, and allows the water to drain super quickly.

VERY USEFUL TO HAVE

Bamboo Dumpling Spatula

Found in restaurant supply and housewares shops in most Chinatowns, this thin, inexpensive (around $3) spatula is used by professional dumpling makers to efficiently scoop and place filling onto wrappers without sticking.

Chinese Steamer

Widely available at Asian markets, specialized cookware shops, and online, Chinese steamers are the most effective way to steam dumplings. It is an ingeniously designed piece of equipment, comprised of a large bottom pan in

which to pour the water, a number of stackable perforated trays that hold the dumplings, and a domed lid that allows the steam to circulate as it contains it. You can find them made out of stainless steel or aluminum (more durable and more expensive) or bamboo (more aesthetically pleasing and less expensive but also less durable and prone to mildew). Asian dumpling expert Andrea Quynhgiao Nguyen recommends using a 12-inch-wide, stainless steel steamer or a 10-inch-wide bamboo steamer (which will be placed inside a skillet and therefore needs to be narrower).

Food Mill

A food mill is a good tool to own if you make your own tomato sauce from fresh or canned tomatoes. Blenders and food processors are not good for pureeing tomatoes because they macerate the seeds, which are bitter, and integrate them into the puree rather than separate them from the pulp as food mills do. Most food mills come with two or three interchangeable blades for fine to coarse purees of uniform consistency. Stainless steel models, though more expensive, are sturdier and will not rust. If using a food mill to rice potatoes (some people do it; I don't recommend it), make sure that they are very well boiled or baked to facilitate what might otherwise be a very frustrating process of having to continuously push bits of potatoes into the blades.

Gnocchi/Garganelli Board

Traditionally used to make and process butter, this tool is now used to make beautifully ridged homemade gnocchi and *garganelli,* a rolled pasta similar to penne. It consists of a ridged board, typically 8 x 4 inches, with a handle and typically comes with a mini rolling pin that is used to roll thin squares of rolled-out pasta to create *garganelli.* I find the pin is too thick and consequently makes humongous *garganelli;* I've taken to using the wider end of a chopstick for the job and am much happier with the considerably more petite results.

Mortar and Pestle

A tool comprised of a hefty bowl, typically marble or ceramic, and a thick, oblong pestle used to pound ingredients, such as herbs, garlic, spices, and nuts. It is considered the best tool for making pesto.

Pasta and Noodle Drying Rack

Many households have their own unique method for drying pasta: some hang it over the backs of chairs, over a kitchen broom suspended between two chairs, or on kitchen towels dusted with semolina flour. Those are perfectly effective options. If you are dying to own a pasta drying rack, look for a model that is easy to assemble and store, has a stable base that won't tip over under the weight of the hanging pasta, and that is tall enough to allow your pasta to hang adequately without half of it laying on the counter.

Pasta Cutters

Hand-held tools shaped like cookie cutters that are used to cut shapes from a sheet of rolled out dough. Available with smooth or fluted edges, they come in a variety of shapes and sizes.

Pierogi and Dumpling Makers

Designed to create perfectly sized pierogies and dumplings, these come in individual molds or in multiple, evenly spaced molds of varying numbers, all of which cut, seal, and separate them. They come in a variety of sizes. The molds sometimes come with a plastic tray designed to make indentations in the sheet of dough, which enables you to more easily center the mounds of filling.

Potato Ricer

Shaped like a huge garlic press, a potato ricer essentially presses cooked potatoes through holes of varying width to create fluffy, silky mashed potatoes without overprocessing them. This is important because boiled potatoes are packed with starch. When they are mashed or mixed in a food processor, their cells break apart and release the starch, which turns the potatoes into a pasty, gluey mess. Potato ricers manage to break potatoes down using the least amount of motion, resulting in a great texture. I have had mine for 25 years and can't imagine making gnocchi and mashed potatoes without it. (It is also great for removing excess water from spinach and getting the filling of deviled eggs and avocados slated for guacamole to a uniform degree of smoothness.)

Ravioli Molds

Designed to create evenly spaced and sized ravioli, these molds also cut, seal, and separate them. They come in a variety of sizes and shapes. While typical units make 12 ravioli at a time, you can also find ones that make 24, 36, and 48. Models sometimes come with a mini rolling pin the length of the mold's width or a plastic tray designed to make indentations in the sheet of dough, which enables you to more easily center the mounds of filling in each ravioli compartment.

Ridged Rolling Pins

Those who have the muscle power and patience to roll their dough into thin sheets can consider purchasing a handled rolling pin with ridges. Specifically spaced or designed to cut a variety of pasta shapes, they can make pappardelle, tagliatelle, fettuccine, spaghetti, and even ravioli.

Wooden Pastry Board

A pastry board is a square or rectangular piece of smooth wood used for kneading and rolling out dough or cutting out pasta shapes. Buy as large a pastry board as your kitchen counter can handle and you can easily store. The benefit of using a pastry board over a counter top is related to temperature; wood is always warmer than granite, formica, and cement and dough rolls out better in a warmer environment.

NICE TO HAVE

Chitarra Pasta Maker

Used to make sturdy, square-shaped *spaghetti alla chitarra* (also known as *maccheroni alla chitarra*; see page 159 for a recipe), this unusual tool is a rectangular pasta maker invented in the Abruzzo region of central Italy around the 1800s. Literally "guitar" in Italian, a *chitarra* looks like a double-sided harp set on a wooden frame slightly larger than a shoebox. Typically two-sided, it is strung with wires set ³⁄₁₆ inch (for tagliatelle) apart on one side and ⅛ inch (for *spaghetti alla chitarra*) apart on the reverse side. All one has to do is set a thick sheet of dough on the wires and run a rolling pin up and down the frame until the dough gets pushed through the wires to create the strands.

Corzetti Stamp

A hand-held wooden embossing tool used to make *corzetti* pasta (see page 175 for a recipe), small, thin pasta discs from northern Italy known for their beautifully engraved designs. Resembling a shorter version of an old-fashioned wooden peppermill that has been cut in half, the stamp consists of two pieces: the base, which has a ridged border to cut the pasta on one side and an embossed design on its other side, and the top, which functions as a press and has another embossed design on its flat side. Once the disc is cut, it is pressed between the two embossed designs, resulting in a beautifully decorated piece of pasta. The easiest way to find them is online and I've discovered a site, *artisanalpastatools.com,* that makes beautiful stamps, following the Italian tradition, right here in the United States.

Heavy-Duty Stand Mixer

Making pasta and dumplings requires a lot of mixing and kneading, which is where the

strength of a mixer really comes in handy. Some doughs, especially those made with large quantities of semolina or durum flour, are quite stiff and consequently difficult to work. A good-quality stand mixer can step in and take over, unlike hand-held mixers whose motors may burn out. The brand KitchenAid sells a variety of attachments that roll dough, cut pasta of different shapes and sizes, and even makes ravioli in no time.

Food Processor

In addition to mixing, chopping, and pureeing ingredients, food processors can also make pasta dough. When you press down on the machine's designated dough button, its fast-working blade quickly mixes eggs into flour and gives the resulting dough a good kneading at the same time, resulting in a soft and supple dough.

Manual Pasta Maker

People who love the feeling of handling pasta dough may consider purchasing a manual pasta makers. Sturdy, reliable, and inexpensive, these machines turn out, with the help of a manually operated crank, sheets of pasta for making lasagna, cannelloni, and filled pastas. The units attach to your counter top with an adjustable clamp to prevent them from moving and come with adjustable rolls (which typically range from ¼ to ¹⁄₁₆ inch) that make it easy to vary the thickness of the pasta sheets. They also usually come with built-in cutters for fettuccine and tagliolini (some models include spaghetti) and you can purchase separate attachments to make angel hair, linguine, and spaghetti. They are made either from chrome steel or stainless steel, the latter of which is sturdier and more durable. Electric motors can be purchased separately to motorize your manual pasta machine, if you like. Look for a machine of high quality to spare yourself the aggravation of mechanical malfunctions and broken parts. Make the best possible decision for yourself by researching all the machines that fall within your desired price point, checking Consumer Reports and assessing the ratings and reviews on reputable sites like Amazon.

The Advantages of a Manual Pasta Maker

◆ Considerably less expensive (typically around $50) than an electric pasta maker

◆ Gives you control, when rolling out dough, over the pasta sheet's thickness and width

◆ Rolls out flat pasta sheets of a consistent thickness

◆ Gives you an authentic experience of making your own pasta at home

The Disadvantages of a Manual Pasta Maker

◆ Continuously turning the crank over an extended period of time requires muscle power

◆ The rollers and mechanism can be time-consuming to clean

◆ Learning the process involved in rolling and cutting the dough requires a learning curve

Electric Pasta Machine

People who frequently make pasta may consider purchasing a partially or fully automated electric pasta machine, which mechanically pushes the dough through rollers or shaping dies for a nearly hands-free experience. Some models require you to make and to knead the dough beforehand, while other (more expensive) models simplify the process by enabling you to add flour and eggs or water in the designated opening for ingredients and letting it do all the mixing and kneading. Regardless of the model type and brand, it is important to note that electric pasta machines, unlike bread machines, require your full participation. Not only will you need to press a button to signal the machine to stop kneading and start cutting, but you will also need to cut pasta strings, ribbons, and tubes as they are extruded to their appropriate lengths. In other words, the machine may be electric, but it's not a passive process.

Similar to manual pasta machines, the electric versions are capable of making a limited number of pasta varieties straight out of the box (the number varies depending on the cutting dies that come with the brand or model) and you can purchase additional dies to expand the number of shapes you can make.

Finally, look for a machine of high quality to spare yourself the aggravation of mechanical malfunctions and broken parts. Make the best possible decision for yourself by researching all the machines that fall within your desired price point, checking Consumer Reports and assessing the ratings and reviews on reputable sites like Amazon.

The Advantages of an Electric Pasta Machine
◆ Potentially saves you substantial amounts of physical labor and time. Machines with powerful engines have the extrusion force (1,600 pounds of force is considered good for an electric machine) to turn out a pound of pasta in just 15 minutes

◆ After an initial learning curve, it enables you to make your own pasta easily and conveniently

◆ With the purchase of additional cutting dies, users can make a wide variety of pasta shapes, which kids especially love

◆ Nonstick coating on rollers makes them very easy to clean.

The Disadvantages of an Electric Pasta Machine
◆ Considerably pricier than manual pasta makers (noncommercial models typically range between $150 to $400)

◆ Only the pricier models knead the dough for you

◆ Dough sometimes can get stuck in the mechanism and the cutters are sometimes difficult to clean.

◆ Machines with plastic dies make pasta that is unpleasantly thick and well outside standard size

◆ Some models are very loud when operating.

Tortilla Press
Traditionally used to flatten corn or flour dough into tortillas, this handy device has been adopted in many Asian homes as a speedier way to form round dumpling wrappers of even thickness. Made from cast iron, cast aluminum, plastic, or wood, it is comprised of two flat discs, connected on one side, that can be pressed together using a lever. They can be found in Latino grocers and online.

Spätzle Maker
A simple tool designed to make the thick noodle-like dumplings called *spätzle*. It comes in three versions:

◆ One looks like a large-holed cheese grater, long enough to fit over a pasta pot, whose hopper attachment is first filled with dough and then slid back and forth over the holes to create the *spätzle*. I have never owned this version but read many comments online that suggest it makes a bit of a mess.

◆ One resembles, in form and function, a potato ricer. Though it has been reviewed as the easiest to use, I find that it tends to make fairly skinny *spätzle*. If you want to re-create this dumpling's rustic stoutness, this is not the tool for you.

◆ One resembles a ¾-inch shallow, flat colander, wide enough to fit over a pasta pot. Batter is poured in and pushed through the holes into the boiling water with a sturdy plastic scraper. I have owned this version and returned it. My experience was that the colander became super hot and was essentially cooking the batter-like dough before it could be pressed through the holes with the scraper (in the interest of full disclosure, I may have filled the pot too high with water).

After seeing a YouTube video of an ancient, charming Austrian woman making *spätzle* using just a knife and a narrow, handled wooden cutting board, I have adopted her age-old and efficient technique. For instructions, see page 257.

FRESH & DRIED
PASTA & NOODLES
and HOW *to* COOK THEM

Americans consume a paltry 26 pounds of pasta a year as compared to the average of 60 pounds that Italian men, women, and children consume. While considerably smaller, this consumption nevertheless is still a lot of pasta! And it leaves the American consumer with plenty of pasta decision-making to do when visiting the neighborhood grocer. Ultimately, you need to decide between the more expensive fresh pasta and the large assortment of dried pasta most supermarkets carry these days. And if dried pasta is what you are seeking, you will need to decide between nationally and internationally recognized, mass-produced brands and more expensive artisan pastas made by smaller, lesser known producers.

In the following paragraphs, I will make distinctions between the fresh and dried pastas and the roles they play in our dishes. In these days of "fresh is best," it would seem that fresh pasta would be the preferred, better choice over dried pasta, but that is not necessarily the case. In truth, we need both because, depending on the texture we seek or the sauce that we intend to pair that pasta with, they lend their invaluable characteristics to our culinary landscape. Unique in their own right, they are as equally indispensible as ying and yang or a full-bodied barolo and a light prosecco. Choosing between the two can feel like being forced to designate one of your children as your favorite. I firmly believe the world needs both.

Similarly to any other product on the market, you can find high-end forms of both pastas, as well as less pricy supermarket versions. The choice of fresh or dry predominantly comes down to personal preference.

FRESH PASTA & NOODLES

This is the pasta normally associated with the type that is made at home. It can also be purchased fresh. You have probably seen the long ribbons of fresh pappardelle, lasagna sheets, and thin strands of spaghetti in the refrigerated case of high-end supermarkets and gourmet stores. Often labeled "hand-made" or "house-made," they distinguish themselves from dried pasta with their smooth, velvety texture, tenderness, higher prices, and considerably shorter shelf life. The assumption is that these pastas are locally made with the freshest of ingredients, while dried pasta is shipped over long distances and has been sitting on shelves for unknown periods of time.

In actuality, there are widely fluctuating levels of quality between brands of fresh pasta. If you're lucky and live near a store that makes pasta daily from good-quality flour and eggs, consider yourself charmed. While these outstanding pasta-making operations do exist, they are far and few between. Most often, the "fresh" pasta sold in supermarkets is filled with preservatives and other ingredients (a good rule to follow is to walk away from fresh pasta that contains ingredients that are difficult to pronounce).

At its purest, fresh pasta is made from a simple dough of a soft wheat flour, usually all-purpose flour or "00" wheat flour, eggs, and occasionally a little water or olive oil. The dough is then kneaded like bread dough, pressed through rollers until it's as thin as desired, and, finally, cut into long noodles. Dough containing egg is especially important when making an assortment of filled pastas like tortellini and ravioli, as it produces a strong, malleable dough that withstands the slight tugging and handling required to form them. Finally, this type of pasta dough cannot be extruded to form a shape like penne or rigatoni, as you can do with the dough from which they make dried pasta, because the gluten networks in the dough are not strong enough to hold the shape. Because of this, fresh pasta doesn't expand very much when boiled.

Fresh pasta, which possesses varying levels of egg flavor, is at its best when paired with butter-, cream-, and cheese-based sauces when thin and with unctuous meat or hearty mushroom or vegetable sauces when thicker.

DRIED PASTA & NOODLES

An essential cupboard staple, dried pasta is versatile, convenient because of its long shelf life, and easy and quick to cook. It can be found in every supermarket, predominantly sold in cardboard boxes or see-through plastic packaging.

Made from finely ground semolina flour (called *semola di grano duro*), water, and sometimes salt, dried pasta is produced mechanically. Its combination of ingredients produces a hard, difficult-to-knead paste that is then pushed through molds and cut into the multitude of pasta shapes we know and love. It is then fully dried, which is what enables it to have an almost indefinitely long shelf life. The higher protein content of the semolina flour is what makes the dough better able to sustain the rigors of extrusion and the drying process while retaining the integrity of the pasta's texture. It is also what gives it its signature firm texture and is what makes the pasta almost double in size as it cooks as it reabsorbs all the moisture given up during the drying process and more.

Dried pasta, which possesses a rather neutral and subtle wheat-y flavor, is at its best when paired with savory or spicy oil- or tomato-based sauces that contain vegetables, meats, or fish.

Artisanal vs. Commercially Produced Dried Pasta

As with every other form of traditional food, enormous variations exist in the quality of the many brands out there, especially between mass-produced and artisanal varieties. While store shelves accommodate them all, it's important to understand what differentiates one from the other.

The good news is that all Italian dried pasta, as per a law passed in 1967, must be made from high-quality 100 percent durum semolina flour. This is good news because it ensures that, once cooked, the pasta will retain its shape and pleasantly chewy texture, and won't become a mushy, globby mess. The similarities end there, however, and in order to fully appreciate them, perhaps it would be helpful to understand how dried pasta is produced.

Once the dough has been mixed and kneaded, it is extruded through thick perforated discs called "dies." The perforations on the discs, which have notches and holes of different shapes and sizes, give pasta its curves, curls, and straight lines as the dough is pressed through them.

The material from which these dies are made is important, because it creates different results. Artisanal pasta is slowly extruded through bronze, rather than Teflon, dies. This is a significant distinction because bronze dies, which are very expensive to produce, create pasta with a microscopic roughness and almost white surface. This surface tends to be more porous and more closely mimics homemade pasta in its ability to hold onto sauces effectively. Pasta made with less expensive and longer-lasting Teflon dies, the industry standard, is extruded more quickly and comes out smooth, slick, and shiny, which, as you might guess, does not hold sauces as well.

Additionally, slower extrusion usually yields a superior pasta because it protects the gluten in the dough and preserves its texture. Mass production, on the other hand, tends to extrude the dough quickly and forcefully, generating unwanted heat that damages the texture and flavor of the pasta.

Some savvy mass producers have begun using bronze cut dies in their manufacturing process, and advertise it readily on their packaging. While a terrific and advantageous development for consumers, using bronze dies remains just one of the two factors that separates mass-produced pasta from artisanal.

The other factor is, incredibly, how the pasta is dried once shaped.

Up until the early 20th century, all Italian pasta was dried in the sun, often for up to a week to reach the optimal level of desiccation. Once the first pasta-drying machine was invented in 1919, the process predictably changed. Since then, the drying process has become automated for both artisanal and mass-produced pasta, but the method employed by each is very different.

The smaller artisanal pasta makers dry their pasta at much lower temperatures over a longer period of time. They may take at least 24 and up to more than 50 hours to dry their pasta. This slow drying takes place in very warm (but never high heat) environments, starting at a high humidity that is slowly reduced with the passage of drying time, enabling the pasta to dry without damaging the texture of the finished product.

Faster-moving, more cost-conscious mass producers often dry their pasta at high heat in a matter of hours. While this approach does remove the appropriate amount of moisture from the pasta, ensuring long shelf life, it also essentially "toasts" the pasta, which breaks down its gluten network, making it more brittle and affecting its texture once cooked.

COOKING PASTA

Great attention is given to the ingredients and techniques that go into making delicious homemade pasta. As crucial as both elements are to the ultimate flavor and texture of pasta and noodle dough, they are just part of the equation that enables us to plate a satisfyingly chewy finished dish. Cooking and seasoning pasta in a way that maximizes its flavor and texture are equally important.

The connection between both parts of the process is akin to preparing diamonds for the jewelry display case. First, you must select a high-quality rough diamond (the ingredients) and then "cut" it to its desired shape (the technique). But what if the gem cutter stopped there, without sanding and polishing it? The potentially gorgeous precious stone would have rough edges and a cloudy surface and would not be nearly as valuable on the market. Similarly, making delicious and well-crafted pasta only takes us halfway to realizing its full potential; cooking and serving it properly brings us the rest of the way, and takes only a handful of additional minutes at most.

PASTA PER PERSON

Before cooking the pasta, it is important to determine how much of it needs to be cooked. Generally, the per-person rule is 3 ounces (85 grams) for a starter portion and 4 ounces (115 grams) for a main course. This is clearly a guideline. I am sure I am not the only person to know outliers who seem either to survive on air or to eat their weight in pasta.

The amount of pasta per person also depends on the richness of its sauce or condiment. In other words, a plain, refreshing tomato sauce will not be as filling as a preparation that includes braised Swiss chard and calamari, and will require a larger amount of pasta for satiety. Most of the recipes in this book are on the heartier side and are therefore geared towards requiring a 3-ounce serving of pasta per person.

I am often asked whether there is any difference between cooking dried and fresh pasta and I always respond in the same way: "*Gli spaghetti amano la compagnia*," or "Spaghetti love company," which is how an Italian would explain that both require the same attention and care, though fresh pasta requires a little less of it since it cooks faster. At the end of the day, whether we are cooking fresh or dried pasta, we are striving for a precise characteristic: when we cut into a strand or tube of cooked pasta, it will have a uniform color on the inside except for a whisper of a tiny spot in the middle, regarded as the *anima*, or "soul" of the pasta, which retains a hint of white rawness. In order to achieve it, we need to drain the pasta when it is still a few minutes away from that perfect state of "tender but still pleasantly chewy," as it will continue to cook with its residual heat.

Below you will find helpful tips on cooking pasta to maximize its flavor and texture.

Use a Large Pot.
Cooking 1 pound of pasta requires 4 to 5 quarts of water, making a 6- or 8-quart pot filled about three quarters of the way ideal. That size allows each piece or strand of pasta ample water real estate to plump up as needed. If the space is not there, the pasta becomes mushy and sticky as its starch begins to release and to take over the little water that exists. If you need to cook 2 pounds of pasta, don't cook it in the same pot, but use two large pots instead. Otherwise, not only will the pasta not have enough space in the water to cook and plump up properly, but the water will take too long to return to a boil, affecting the cooking process. This general guideline applies even more to larger pasta shapes, as they are more prone to breaking or tearing when confined to a smaller boiling area. As a result, I again recommend using two big pots when boiling larger shapes like *paccheri* (huge pasta tubes) and *conchiglione* (oversized sea shells).

Salt the Pasta Water.
Always. In Italy, they describe perfect pasta water as being as salty as the Mediterranean Sea and not the Atlantic Ocean. That's because in order to taste good, pasta needs to be boiled in salted water (always add the salt once the water is boiling because doing it before that makes it take longer for the water to come to a boil). Most any salt will do, with the sole exception of iodized salt, which adds a subtle metallic

flavor to the water. In reality, the type of salt you use is less important than using the proper amount. The general rule is 1 tablespoon of salt per 4 cups of water. It sounds very specific and calculated but, in time, practice and experience will develop your ability to effectively "eye ball" the right amount. The important thing is that you add enough because salt, much like butter and bacon, makes everything taste better. For this very reason, salting the water is absolutely essential. Even though most of the salt will go down the drain the moment the pasta hits the colander, the pasta nevertheless will have absorbed a minute amount of it during cooking, and will transfer that additional seasoning to your finished dish. The bottom line is that even the tastiest and most savory of sauces will not be able to compensate for improperly salted pasta, and the final dish will suffer.

Do Not Add Oil to the Pasta Pot.

Save the oil for your salads instead. Its presence is occasionally credited with preventing the pasta from sticking together or the pasta water from boiling over, and if that's the case, I can sell you this little thing called the Brooklyn Bridge. In reality, the general consensus is that adding oil does more harm than good. It gives you a greasy pot to clean and, much worse, leaves a thin film of oil on the pasta that prevents the sauce from sticking to it. To prevent sticking, stir the pasta continuously for the first minute that it is added to boiling water. It is the easiest, most effective, and mess-proof way of preventing the pasta from sticking together as it begins to release its starch in the water. Once the first minute passes, you can transition to an occasional stir until the pasta is done. To prevent boiling over, be watchful as the pasta cooks. If you see the water begin to foam and rise up along the top of the pot, you can quickly tame it by slightly reducing the heat and giving the water a good stir.

Add Pasta to Furiously Boiling Water.

This is not a persnickety rule for hoity-toity foodies. Full on boiling water prevents the pasta from getting mushy and that first minute when the pasta hits the water is critical to its final texture because it controls the amount of starch that the pasta immediately releases. That is why you will sometimes read in recipes to immediately cover the pot after you've added the pasta, so it can start boiling again as quickly as possible. I personally don't use a lid because it wouldn't allow me to continuously stir the pasta for the first minute it hits the water (the most effective technique I've found to prevent the pasta from sticking together). If you decide to use a lid, just make sure to quickly give the pasta a good stir before adding the lid and to remove the lid as soon as the water starts boiling again, causing the water to boil over the pot in Mt. Vesuvius-like fashion. Another alternative is to prop your lid halfway open with a wooden spoon, which also prevents the water from overheating and spilling over. To be honest, I grew up with a slew of Italian women who never once covered their pots with a lid and I can't say I've ever tasted any quality deficiencies in their pasta dishes.

Use a Wooden Spoon or Fork to Stir the Pasta.

Many reasons exist to use them over their metal equivalents. Unlike metal utensils, wooden spoons don't have sharp angled edges that can bruise, crush, or tear pasta as you stir; they don't conduct heat, which means they won't accidentally burn you if left in or over a pot for too long (though they may occasionally warp on you); and they won't scratch nonstick surfaces. They also won't make clangy noises when you stir, which makes for a more Zen-like experience. Finally, while plastic utensils don't have as many disadvantages as metal ones, they are sensitive to heat, may melt at very high temperatures, and may also contain the toxic industrial chemical BPA. Bottom line: You can't go wrong using wooden utensils.

Set a Timer.

This may sound silly, but unless you have otherworldly powers of focus and concentration, set a timer for your pasta. I was once called un-Italian (the nerve!) for doing so, but I often get distracted by children, pets, and other dishes cooking on the stove and the timer prevents me from forgetting about the pasta and overcooking it. I usually set the timer two minutes shy of the cooking directions on the pasta packaging. After that, I babysit it so I can drain it the minute it's cooked but still firm.

Always Reserve at Least 1 Cup of Pasta Water Before Draining It.

The pasta cooking techniques described below may not require you to use all of it, but it is handy to keep on hand. You can always add a small amount in the event you find your finished dish to be a little too dry. As a bonus, the starch in the water will help the sauce cling to the pasta. Because of this I consider it the holy grail of the pasta cooking process.

Cook the Pasta Just Before Serving It.

Freshly cooked pasta is at its peak, both in terms of flavor and texture. If you must prepare it in advance, boil it in salted water 3 minutes short of its directed cooking time and immediately drain and rinse it with cold tap water to stop it from cooking further. Transfer it to a bowl, add ½ tablespoon of oil for every 12 ounces of pasta, and toss to evenly coat. Cover and set aside (or refrigerate for longer periods). When ready to use, add it to unsalted boiling water and boil it until heated through and tender but chewy, about 2 minutes. Drain and immediately combine with its sauce.

Don't Overcook It.

The time required to cook pasta varies depending on its quality, thickness, size, and shape and on whether it is fresh or dried (dried takes longer). Consequently, any time directives given in recipes are ballpark numbers at best, and ultimately leave the cook in charge of monitoring the cooking process. The best way to assess whether it is cooked enough is to begin tasting it toward the last few minutes of its cooking time. It is not unusual, especially when one is still developing an understanding of the natural rhythm of the process, to taste a piece of pasta two or three different times. As you taste it for doneness, you are looking for a tender but still pleasantly chewy texture, otherwise known as *al dente* (the seasoning technique I recommend using below actually requires you to drain the pasta when it is tender but still very firm, but that will be explained later in this section).

SEASONING PASTA

This book veers away slightly from the standard approach of combining fully cooked pasta with a sauce by adding an additional "seasoning" technique, which in Italy is called *pasta saltata in padella*. Before explaining the exact steps involved, it may be helpful to explain what the technique does and how it contributes to preserving the integrity of the pasta's texture.

At the end of the day, pasta is very porous by nature, the fresh variety especially so but even the dried version. Once it is added to boiling water, its unquenchable thirst begins, which is what makes it plump up as it cooks. This absorptive quality doesn't stop once the pasta is drained; in fact, pasta remains as parched as ever. The worst thing you could do to it at this point is to drain it well, dish it out into a bowl, and top it with sauce. Lacking any liquid to absorb, the pasta quickly becomes pasty and tough instead of tender and pleasantly chewy.

A way to avoid this degradation of the pasta's texture involves keeping the pasta well hydrated until it is plated. The process, as described below, takes about 3 to 4 minutes at most to execute and promotes two benefits. First, it melds the pasta and sauce together more effectively by incorporating some reserved pasta water, which contains starch. Second, it enables the pasta to absorb the flavoring of the sauce, resulting in an even tastier finished dish.

Seasoning Technique for Pasta to Be Served with a Cooked Sauce

This technique (to be used with ragùs and other sauces) involves immediately joining just drained pasta with a small amount of reserved pasta water and a small amount of oil or butter (depending on the nature of the sauce) and then cooking it the rest of the way in part or all of the sauce.

1. Cook the pasta in salted water according to package or recipe instructions and then drain it 2 minutes short of its directed cooking time. The pasta at this point will be soft but still very firm and would be considered slightly too firm to enjoy.

2. Right before draining the pasta, reserve 1 cup of pasta water. (Some will probably remain unused, but it's good to have just in case your pasta ends up being a little dry once combined with the sauce.)

3. Drain the pasta and return the pot to the burner. Immediately turn the heat to high, add a half tablespoon of oil (for oil-based sauces) or half tablespoon of butter (for butter-based sauces) and the amount of reserved pasta water specified in the recipe (if using recipes outside this book, the general rule is to use ¼ cup for every 12 ounces of pasta you are cooking). Because this process is time-sensitive and thus requires efficiency, it is helpful to have those things measured out and by the stove before draining the pasta.

4. Quickly add the just drained pasta to the pot and toss until most of the fat and pasta water gets absorbed (you may still see some areas on the bottom of the pot with a film of bubbling liquid). This usually takes about 30 seconds or

so, which goes to show you just how thirsty the pasta is.

5. Immediately add all or part of the sauce, depending on what the recipe directs. Continue cooking the pasta on high heat, tossing continuously, for 1 ½ to 2 minutes.

6. Transfer the pasta to warmed bowls, and top with additional sauce if appropriate.

Seasoning Technique for Pasta to Be Served with a Fresh Uncooked Sauce

Use this technique for pestos, raw tomato sauces, or when simply tossing freshly cooked pasta with cheese. It involves immediately joining fully cooked, just drained pasta to a slightly larger amount of reserved pasta water.

1. Cook the pasta in salted water according to package or recipe instructions and then drain it when it reaches the perfect firmness for eating, otherwise known as *al dente*.

2. Right before draining the pasta, reserve 1 cup of pasta water. (Some will probably remain unused, but it's good to have just in case your pasta ends up being a little dry once combined with the sauce.)

3. Drain the pasta and remove the pot from the stove. Return the pasta to the pot and immediately add at least ¼ cup of the pasta cooking water (more if specified by recipe) and the sauce. Because this process is time-sensitive, it is helpful to have the water measured out and by the stove before draining the pasta.

4. Toss well and add a little more pasta water if the pasta seems a little dry. An additional benefit to this technique is that the pasta is really hot when it gets combined with the condiment, enabling the sauce to better adhere to the pasta.

5. Transfer the pasta to warmed bowls.

Seasoning Technique for Pasta to Be Used in a Salad

This technique involves cooking the pasta until it is perfectly firm yet tender, or *al dente,* and then immediately stopping it from cooking to retain its chewy texture and coating it with oil to prevent it from sticking.

1. Cook the pasta in salted water according to package or recipe instructions and then drain it the moment it becomes firm and pleasantly chewy, or *al dente*.

2. Drain the pasta and immediately rinse it with cold tap water to stop the pasta from cooking further.

3. Drain well once again and transfer to a bowl.

4. Immediately add the pasta salad dressing and other ingredients, toss to evenly coat, and serve. Alternatively, if not using the pasta right away, add half tablespoon of olive oil per 12 ounces of pasta and toss to evenly coat (doing this prevents the pasta from sticking together and from drying out). Cover and set aside until ready to season with dressing.

COOKING ASIAN NOODLES

If you've entered an Asian supermarket or searched for Asian noodles online, you've probably been mesmerized by the large array of choices available to us today. While it is wonderful to have so many choices, it can often leave Western home cooks confused, particularly those new to this genre of noodles confused or baffled. Further complicating the situation, Asian noodles are made with a broader range of flours (and starches) than Western-style pasta and often require different cooking methods. It's enough to leave even the most adventurous cook a little flummoxed.

Because describing how to cook every single variety of Korean, Japanese, Thai, Vietnamese, and Chinese noodle would require a gargantuan book, I have opted to write about the noodles most widely called for in recipes and have categorized them based on whether they are made from wheat (which sometimes include eggs), rice and starch, or specialized flours. Japanese noodles are the only exception to this categorization; I have grouped them together because they all require a specialized cooking technique.

Finally, you will notice how some of the directives that follow include a rather large variation in cooking or soaking times. For instance, rice sticks have an indicated soaking time that ranges from 5 to 40 minutes! It is difficult to be more precise than that because the term *rice sticks* refers broadly to a variety of rice noodles that, while they all require soaking in water, are markedly different from each other and consequently not interchangeable.

But that's not all. Noodles sometimes contain starches or other flours that also affect their cooking time. Udon noodles are a good case in point. I have seen a wide variety of noodle recipes that require udon noodles to be boiled for anywhere from 30 seconds to 4 minutes when fresh and from 5 to 12 minutes when dry, which is a surprising range given that the shape and size of the noodles remain constant.

Ultimately, as with cooking regular pasta, noodles need tending if you want to cook them well. My advice is to identify brands of noodles that you like and to continue using them so that, in time, you can avoid needing to guess (and test) how long of a boil or soak each one requires.

On a personal note, I will add that while I include directions for preparing fresh, frozen, and dried noodles whenever applicable (not all versions are available in all noodles varieties), I highly recommend using fresh or frozen noodles whenever possible. They have by far a better texture (springier and less gummy) and, as an added bonus, require less time to cook. Follow package directions because some noodles require overnight defrosting while others need to be thrown in boiling water while still frozen. If you are lucky enough to find fresh noodles, treat them like you would egg pasta and refrigerate them until you are ready to cook. Unopened they will last a week in your refrigerator and, once opened, 2 to 3 days.

Wheat Noodles

This particular category of Asian noodles is the most similar to Italian pasta. Those made from wheat flour and water are extruded into different shapes and sizes and are available predominantly in dried form, though you can find them fresh or frozen in well-stocked Asian markets. Wheat and egg noodles are a huge category unto themselves and function as an umbrella term that includes thin, wide wonton noodles, lo mein, Hokkien noodles, Hong Kong-style chow mein, and *misua*. The difference among them, and thus the different names, is dictated mostly by their thickness and in what dishes each noodle is used.

These noodles, when yellow, either contain real eggs, yellow food coloring (always check the packaging), or an added alkali like lye water (it releases a yellow pigment as it interacts with the flour and water). The addition of alkali is especially prevalent in Western China, as it creates a firmer, chewier noodle, which is preferred there.

Because this particular category is so similar to Italian pasta, I am including a list of general guidelines, similar to those I shared with you regarding cooking Italian pasta, to ensure perfectly cooked noodles every time.

◆ Cook them in plenty of rapidly boiling water or broth in a pot that is ample enough to give them the room to expand properly. Boiling 1 pound of noodles requires 4 to 5 quarts of water or broth, making a 6- or 8-quart pot filled about three quarters of the way ideal.

◆ Don't add oil to the cooking water because it will interfere with the sauce's ability to stick to the noodles.

◆ It is important to remember that most noodles should be stirred immediately for at least 30 seconds upon being placed in the water and then occasionally as they cook. This prevents them from clumping together and also keeps them from sticking to the bottom of the pot.

◆ Once the noodles are done cooking, you can, depending on the recipe directions, either incorporate them with the other elements of the dish or shock them in ice water or run them under cold water to stop them from cooking further. If using right away, add them immediately to your soup, stew, etc. If not, transfer them to a bowl and toss them with just enough of a neutral oil (grapeseed or peanut oil works well) to keep from sticking and drying out. Cover and set aside or, if cooking them much later, refrigerate and bring back to room temperature before using.

◆ Once plated, the noodles should be eaten right away while fresh and piping hot for the best flavor.

Wheat Flour Noodles

The oldest form of noodle, Chinese wheat flour noodles are used mainly in soups and soup-like stews. Made exclusively from wheat flour and water, they vary in thickness, come round or flat in shape, are generally white or yellow-beige in color (which means they contain either food coloring or an alkali), and are most commonly found in dried form.

Method: Boil in plenty of boiling water until just tender, drain, rinse under warm water, drain again, and add to soups and stews. Cook fresh noodles for 2 to 4 minutes, dried noodles for 4 to 7 minutes (times vary depending on size and thickness).

Egg Noodles

Made from wheat flour, eggs, and water, egg noodles lend their firm and addictively chewy texture to stir-fries; the thicker variety is often used in soups. Found in various shapes and widths, they range in color from golden to a suspiciously bright yellow (always check the label for food coloring).

Method: Egg noodles are first boiled and then cooked in some sort of fat, along with other ingredients, or added to soups. Cook them in plenty of boiling water until tender but still firm, similarly to *al dente* pasta. Depending on shape and width, cook fresh noodles for 2 to 4 minutes, dried noodles for 4 to 9 minutes.

Rice Noodles

Rice Stick Noodles

Made from rice flour and water, rice stick noodles are used predominantly in soups and stir-fries. White, translucent, and typically flat or round, they can be found in a variety of shapes and sizes, ranging from vermicelli thinness to a width of more than ¼ inch. Their packaging will indicate whether the rice sticks are made in China, Thailand, or Vietnam, since all three countries use them.

Method: Soak in room temperature water anywhere from 20 to 40 minutes, depending on the size of the rice sticks. Drain and rinse with cold water, and drain again, which stops the cooking process and prevents the noodles from sticking together. (If you are preparing these noodles in advance and find that they are sticking together, just rinse under some additional cold water.) Once softened in water (you should be able to easily wrap a noodle around your finger without breaking it) and pleasantly chewy, they are ready to be cooked an additional 2 to 3 minutes in soups and 1 to 2 minutes in stir-fries (make sure you add them to their designated soup, stir-fry, or salad immediately upon draining them, as they tend to quickly get sticky). Because these noodles are cooked twice, it is important that you soak them until they are still quite chewy. You don't want to soak them until they are completely tender because they become mushy once cooked further. If using them in salads, soak them until completely tender and then combine them quickly with the dressing.

Sen Lek

Thin and flat, *sen lek* noodles are predominantly sold dried and their width can vary from slightly larger than ¹⁄₁₆ inch to just under ⅜ inch (the ideal width for pad Thai (see page 438) is around ⅛ inch).

Method: If ⅛ inch or thinner, soak in room temperature water until the noodles are pleasantly chewy, 20 to 30 minutes. If the noodles are much thicker than ⅛ inch, the soaking technique will not work and they will need to be cooked in plenty of boiling water like Italian pasta. Drain the noodles well and finish cooking them by adding them to soups for 2 to 3 minutes or stir-frying for no more than a minute or two.

The directions for soaking *sen lek* noodles come straight from the wisdom and experience of my absolute favorite Thai food cookbook author and food blogger, Leela Punyaratabandhu. On her fantastic blog called *She Simmers*, she counsels cooks not to soak the noodles in boiling or hot water, a directive that is often found on rice noodle packaging. When exposed to boiling water, rice noodles release tons of starch and clump up, she explains. Out of curiosity, I tested noodles soaked in both room temperature and boiling water. I found, unsurprisingly, that the noodles soaked in room temperature water were springy, soft but pleasantly firm after 25 minutes of soaking, while those soaked in boiling water were soft but had a slick and slimy surface due to the starch.

Rice Vermicelli

Neutral and virtually flavorless, rice vermicelli is made from rice flour and water and is typically used in soups, stir-fries, spring rolls, and salads. Sold in large cellophane-wrapped bundles, vermicelli is very thin, wiry, and translucent. Rice vermicelli can also be deep-fried into crispy arrangements that resemble styrofoam serpents and are then topped with stir-fries or used as a whimsical-looking garnish.

Method: Soak in room temperature water anywhere from 5 to 20 minutes, depending on its width and length. Once softened and pleasantly chewy, drain, rinse with cold water, and drain again. (If you prepare these noodles in advance and find that they are sticking together, just rinse under cold water and loosen them gently with your fingers. Ideally, you want to add them to their designated soup, stir-fry, spring rolls, or salad immediately upon draining them, as they do tend to quickly get sticky.) The noodles are now ready to be cooked an additional 1 to 2 minutes in soups and stir-fries.

Because these noodles are cooked twice, it is important that you soak them until they are still quite chewy. You don't want to soak them until they are completely tender because they become mushy once cooked further in soups and stir-fries. If using them in spring rolls or salads, soak them until completely tender and then combine them quickly with the dressing. If deep-frying them, do not presoak before adding them to oil heated to 375° F, at which point they will puff up. To test the temperature, add one noodle: It should sizzle and puff immediately. Cook them for 5 to 10 seconds on each side (they usually are sold bundled, which makes it easy to fry). Use a wire skimmer or slotted spoon to keep the noodles submerged in the oil. Blot fried noodles on paper towels. They can be rewarmed in a 250°F oven.

Starch Noodles

Chinese Cellophane Noodles
Made from mung bean starch, cellophane noodles are often used in stir-fries and salads or are deep-fried. They are also a popular noodle in soups because their slippery, gelatinous texture readily absorbs the tasty broth. These opaque noodles, shaped either like thin, round strands or flat ribbons resembling fettuccine, are sold dried and in bundles.

Method: Because they are typically sold dry, bean threads first need to be soaked in hot water for 15 minutes before they are cooked or added to soups. Place the noodles in a heat-proof bowl, pour hot water over them, and let them soften until just tender. If cooking them in a soup, it is not necessary to soak the noodles before adding them. If deep-frying them, do not presoak before adding them to oil heated to 375°F, at which point they will puff up. To test the temperature, add one noodle: It should sizzle and puff immediately. Cook them for 5 to 10 seconds on each side (they usually are sold bundled, which makes it easy to fry). Use a wire skimmer or slotted spoon to keep the noodles submerged in the oil. Blot fried noodles on paper towels. They can be rewarmed in a 250°F oven.

Korean Sweet Potato Vermicelli
Made from sweet potato starch, these noodles are longer and slightly thicker and tougher than Chinese cellophane noodles and are typically used in stir-fries. Thin and grayish in color, sweet potato vermicelli turns translucent once cooked and has a pleasantly slippery texture and mild, earthy flavor.

Method: Because its typically sold dry, sweet potato vermicelli first need to be soaked in hot water for 10 to 15 minutes before they are stir-fried. Place the noodles in a heatproof bowl, pour hot water over them, and let them soften until just tender. Once softened in water, they are almost entirely cooked and require only a fast stir-fry, often no more than a minute or two, to finish cooking them.

Japanese Noodles
The Japanese are known for cooking their dried noodles by tempering the water in which they cook. The process involves adding the noodles to boiling water, allowing the water to come back to a boil and then adding a cup of cold

water, and repeating the process three or four more times until the noodles are tender but with a slightly firm bite.

Buckwheat Soba Noodles

Made from buckwheat flour or a mix of buckwheat and wheat or yam flour, soba noodles lend their characteristic nutty flavor to soups, salads, and stews. Most commonly sold in dried form (though you can find them fresh and frozen in well-stocked Asian markets), they are flat, taupe-colored, and slightly flecked.

Method: Cook in plenty of boiling water, using the cup of cold water technique three to four times, until just tender. Drain, rinse under warm water while still in the colander, drain again, and use. Some say that merely rinsing them under warm water is not enough to remove the substantial amount of starch from the soba noodles. Instead, they suggest transferring the drained noodles to a bowl of tepid water and literally massaging them with your fingers to remove the starch before draining them again. I have tried both approaches and found the latter results in slightly crisper noodles, with no hint of mushy texture on the surface. I will also admit that sometimes I am rushed and just rinse them rather aggressively under warm water and find them to be very pleasing nonetheless. Cook dried noodles for 4 to 5 minutes; fresh noodles for 1 to 2 minutes.

Ramen

Made from wheat flour, eggs, and water, ramen are typically used in soups, stir-fries, and stews. Long, thin noodles and off-white in color, they are shaped either as straight rods or crinkled into a brick shape and are sold fresh, dried, and frozen. The instant variety, with which most people are familiar, comes with a flavor packet and has been deep-fried (to remove excess moisture for longer shelf life).

Method: Cook in plenty of boiling water, using the cup of cold water technique three to four times, until just tender. Drain, rinse under warm water while still in the colander, drain

again, and use. Once fully cooked, unite the noodles with its intended dish as quickly as you can, because the longer they are exposed to the open air, the stickier they become. If using frozen ramen noodles, defrost them in the refrigerator overnight and then let them reach room temperature before boiling. Cook dried noodles for 4 to 5 minutes, fresh and frozen (defrosted and at room temperature) noodles for 2 to 3 minutes, and for instant, follow the instructions.

Somen

Made from wheat flour and water, somen are typically used in soups and salads. Thin, round, white noodles resembling vermicelli, they are found dried and often packaged in band-tied bundles.

Method: Cook in plenty of boiling water, using the cup of cold water technique three to four times, until just tender. Drain, rinse under warm water while still in the colander, drain again, and use. Cook for 2 to 3 minutes.

Udon

Made from wheat flour, eggs, occasionally tapioca starch, and water, udon noodles are too soft to be used in stir-fries, though their slippery, chewy texture makes them ideal for soups, stews, and noodle bowls. Fat and white, they are generally thick and square when fresh and flat and round when dried. They are also sold frozen and are perhaps the best option if you can't find fresh ones and aren't crazy about the flavor and texture of the dried ones.

Method: Cook dried udon in plenty of boiling water, using the cup of cold water technique three to four times, until just tender. Drain, rinse under warm water while still in the colander, drain again, and use. Fresh and frozen udon noodles can be boiled as you would regular pasta. Don't defrost the udon noodles before boiling, as they will turn gummy. Cook fresh noodles for 1 to 3 minutes, dried noodles for 11 to 12 minutes.

ENCYCLOPEDIA
of PASTA,
ASIAN NOODLES,
& DUMPLINGS

Human ingenuity (and gluttony!) has made it possible to amass a wealth of varied pastas, noodles, and dumplings throughout the centuries. No other staples in history have as many variations in shapes, tastes, colors, textures, and subtleties. Food historian Oretta Zanini de Vita identified more than 1,300 pasta shapes alone. I'm not quite that ambitious, but you'll find more than 340 different kinds of pasta shapes, Asian noodles, and dumplings of all kinds in these pages, with descriptions and information on their origins and how they are served.

PASTA SHAPES

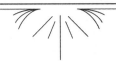

DECORATIVE SHAPES

1. Armoniche

Origin: Italy

Description: Literally "harmonicas," *armoniche* resemble the musical instrument, being shaped like wavy half ruffles curved around a cylinder. Made from durum wheat flour and water, they sometimes contain vegetable purees, like tomatoes or spinach, for added color.

Served: Their deep ridges make them ideal for chunky or coarsely textured meat- or vegetable-based sauces.

Also known as: *Radiatori* or "radiators" and *marziani* or "martians".

2. Assabesi

Origin: Italy

Description: A small grouping of minute pastas in different shapes, *assabesi* reflect Italy's enthusiasm for its military exploits in Africa in the late 19th century. *Assabesi*, which are shaped like small lemons with parallel ruffles near both ends, allude to the strategic purchase of the port of Assab on the Red Sea. Made from durum wheat flour and water.

Served: In broth.

Also known as: Other pastas in this category include small bow-shaped *bengasini*, tiny hat-shaped *tripolini*, and shell-shaped *abissini*.

3. Cappellacci dei Briganti

Origin: Central Italy (Molise and Lazio)

Description: Literally "brigands' hats," fingertip-sized *cappellacci dei briganti* resemble upturned brimmed hats. They are made from durum wheat flour, eggs, water, and salt.

Served: Typically served with lamb ragù and topped with grated Parmigiano.

4. Cencioni

Origin: Italy, with a number of variations specific to southern Italian regions of Basilicata, Puglia, Calabria, and Campania

Description: Literally "little rags," *cencioni* are large and petal-shaped, with a coarse texture on their concave side. Made from durum wheat flour and water.

Served: With a variety of hearty seafood-, meat- or vegetable-based sauces.

Also known as: A variation named *mischiglio*, found in the southern Italian region of Basilicata, is similarly shaped but made from durum wheat, barley, chickpea, and fava bean flour, and water and is served with tomato sauce and topped with crumbly *cacioricotta* cheese. This variety is also known as *pasta a mischiglio* and *misckiglio*. Another similarly shaped variation is named *strascinati*. Found in the southern Italian regions of Puglia, Calabria, Basilicata, and Campania, it is made from durum wheat flour and water, though alternative flours such as whole wheat, barley, toasted wheat flour, and semolina are occasionally substituted. This variety is also known as *cortecce, capunti, capuntini, cavati, cuppetiedde, mignuicchi, minchialeddi, minchjaleddi, pezzetelli, pizzidieddi, pizzarieddhi, rasckatieddi, stagghiotte, cantaroggni, chiancaredde, recchietedde,* and *minuich.*

5. Cencioni di Fave

Origin: Central Italy (Marche)

Description: Thick and rectangular or square in shape, *cencioni di fave* literally translates to "fava rags." Made from wheat flour, fava bean flour, and eggs.

Served: Typically served with sausage-based sauces, in bean soups, and with a tomato-based and meatless sauce known as *sugo finto,* or "fake sauce (see page 606)."

Also known as: *Cioncioni* and *concioni.*

6. Conchiglie

Origin: Throughout Italy, but with the one variation (*conchiglioni*) found predominantly in Campania

Description: Literally "seashells," seashell-shaped *conchiglie* are smooth or ridged and come in varying sizes. They are made from durum wheat flour and water.

Served: Smaller *conchiglie* are served in broth or soups and larger varieties are served with hearty meat-, seafood-, sausage-, or vegetable-based sauces.

Also known as: *Tofarelle, tofettine, abissini, arselle, cinesini, coccioline, cocciolette,* and *conchigliette.* The largest, called *conchiglioni* or "large shells," are found predominantly in Campania.

7. Corzetti

Origin: Northern Piedmont) and northeast Italy (Liguria)

Description: In existence since at least the 13th century, *corzetti* can be found in two shapes. The first, thin and coin-shaped, is made by pressing small pieces of flattened dough between two round, incised wooden molds. The second is thick and figure eight-shaped, and is made by pinching a chickpea-sized piece of dough. *Corzetti* are made predominantly from wheat flour, eggs, and water, though certain variations include oil, stale bread, or milk.

Served: With pesto or with mushroom-, walnut-, or cheese-based sauces

Also known as: *Croset, crosit, torsellini, crosetti, curzetti,* and *croxetti.*

8. Creste di Gallo

Origin: Italy

Description: Golden *creste di gallo,* literally "roosters' crests," are curved tubes of pasta with a Mohawk-like "hairstyle" made of ruffled pasta on their outer curve. Made from durum wheat flour and water, they are available in various sizes. A filled pasta by the same name is found in the central-eastern Italian region of Marche. It is made from durum wheat flour and eggs and is filled with a mixture of chicken, bread. and cinnamon.

Served: With a variety of meat- and vegetable-based sauces or, when small, in broth.

Also known as: *Griù.*

9. Dischi Volanti

Origin: Italy

Description: Literally "flying saucers," *dischi volanti* are medium-sized swirly discs. Particularly popular with children, they are made from durum wheat flour and water.

Served: With a variety of tomato- and meat-based sauces.

10. Farfalle

Origin: Italy

Description: Butterfly- or bow-shaped pasta with straight or ridged borders available in a variety of sizes. They are made from durum wheat flour and water when produced commercially and from flour and eggs when made by hand.

Served: Small shapes are typically served in broth, while larger ones are accompanied by a variety of meat-, cheese-, and vegetable-based sauces and topped with grated cheese.

Also known as: Literally "butterflies," *farfalle* are also known as *fiocchetti, stricchetti, sciancon, nocchette,* and *nocheredde.* Mass-produced versions are named according to their size. The small varieties are called *canestri, canestrini, lancette, galani, nastrini, nodini, stricchetti, stricchetti bolognesi,* and *tripolini,* while larger varieties are called *farfalle genovesi, farfalloni, francesine,* and *galani.*

11. Fisarmoniche

Origin: Italy

Description: Literally "accordions," *fisarmoniche* are shaped like large convex rectangles with parallel ridges that resemble the bellows of a real accordion. They recall a time when hunters would signal a successful hunt to their wives and fellow villagers by playing an accordion on their way home. Made from durum wheat flour and water.

Served: With a variety of sausage-, meat-, and vegetable-based sauces.

12. Foglie d'Olivo

Origin: Italy

Description: Shaped like elongated leaves, *foglie d'olivo* literally translates to "olive tree leaves." Made from durum wheat flour, pureed spinach, and water,

Served: With cream- or olive oil-based vegetable sauces.

13. Gigli

Origin: Italy

Description: Like the lily flower after which they are named, *gigli* are fluted in shape, with either smooth or wavy borders. Found in a variety of sizes, they are made from durum wheat flour and water.

Served: With meat- and vegetable-based sauces and in broth.

Also known as: *Riccioli, ballerina, cornetti, jolly,* and *campanelle.*

14. Gramigna

Origin: Northern (Emilia-Romagna and Friuli-Venezia Giulia) and central Italy (Marche)

Description: *Gramigna* comes in two distinct shapes and is made with varying ingredients, depending on how it is prepared. Handmade versions, made from durum wheat flour, type "00" flour, eggs, and at times spinach or saffron for color, look granular and elongated. Mass-produced versions, made only from durum wheat flour and eggs, vary in size from small to medium and look like skinny worms that curve in spiral-type fashion at one end.

Served: With tomato- and sausage-based sauces and topped with grated Parmigiano.

Also known as: *Crestine, margherite lisce, fagioletti, zitellini, tubettini lunghi, framignoni,* and *spaccatelle.*

15. Lanterne

Origin: Italy

Description: Deeply ridged and curved rectangles, *lanterne* literally means "oil lanterns." Made from durum wheat flour and water.

Served: With a variety of hearty meat-, tomato-, and vegetable-based sauces and topped with grated cheese.

16. Lorighittas

Origin: Sardinia

Description: Twirled thin strands of pasta shaped into narrow oval rings, *lorighittas* originate in the town of Oristano on Sardinia. Listed in the Italian national registry of traditional food products, their name derives from the Sardinian word *loriga,* which is the leather ring placed under the yoke of oxen. They are made traditionally from durum wheat flour, salt, and water,

though eggs are now often included.
Served: With a simple, spicy tomato sauce or with a chicken- or seafood-based sauces.

17. Nuvole
Origin: Italy
Description: Literally "clouds," *nuvole* are oblong, ribbed, and hollow in shape. They are made from durum wheat flour and water.
Served: With pesto or a variety of meat- or vegetable-based sauces.

18. Rocchetti
Origin: Central Italy (Umbria)
Description: Short, concave pasta, *rocchetti* are shaped either like elongated shells with many parallel ridges or like halved corrugated steel pipes. Made from durum wheat flour and water.
Served: With tomato- and meat-based sauces or baked with a variety of cheeses.

19. Ruote
Origin: Italy
Description: Literally "wheels," *ruote* are shaped like spoked wheels. Made from durum wheat flour and water, they are found in varying sizes.
Served: Larger sized "*route*" are served with a variety of tomato-, vegetable-, and meat-based sauces, while smaller sizes are served in broth.
Also known as: *Rotelle, rotelline,* and *rotine.* A variety with ridges is called *fiori or* "flowers."

20. Sagne Incannulate
Origin: Southern Italy (Puglia)
Description: *Sagne incannulate* are twirled ribbons of pasta pinched together at their ends to form an elongated teardrop. Made from durum wheat flour and water.
Served: With meat ragù.
Also known as: *Sagne 'ncannulate, lasagna arrotolate, sagne, lagane incannulate,* and *sagne torte.*

21. Sorprese
Origin: Italy
Description: Literally "surprises" in Italian, *sorprese* resemble smooth or ridged small baby clams with an indentation stretching from their border to the center. They are made from durum wheat semolina and eggs.
Served: In broth and legume soups.

22. Spighe
Origin: Italy
Description: A specialty pasta shape found throughout Italy, *spighe* are shaped like the outline of a pretty leaf. Made from durum wheat flour and water, they have a subtle golden color and are considered a favorite among children.
Served: Served with tomato-based sauces and in pasta salads.

23. Torchio
Origin: Italy
Description: Literally "torch," *torchio* are golden and torch-shaped. Made from durum wheat flour and water.
Served: With chunky meat- or tomato-based sauces.
Also known as: *Maccheroni al torchio* or "torch macaroni," trumpet pasta, and *campane* or "bells."

24. Csipetke

Origin: Hungary

Description: Shaped like flat, roughly torn pieces of dough, *csipetke* are made from wheat flour, eggs, and salt.

Served: In soups and stews. Most notably, they are frequently added to goulash.

25. Cuzzetielle

Origin: Southern Italy (Molise)

Description: *Cuzzetielle* are small rectangles of pasta with two side-by-side fingertip indentations that create a shallow curvature. Made from durum wheat flour and warm water.

Served: With meat ragù and topped with grated pecorino.

26. Filindeu

Origin: Sardinia

Description: Very thin, gauze-like pasta, *filindeu* literally means "the threads of God" and is possibly the most difficult and time-consuming of all pastas to make. Once made, the dough is pulled and folded with fingertips into 256 perfectly even strands, which are then stretched into needle-thin strings and placed diagonally across a circular frame in an intricate three-layer pattern. The resulting pasta weaves are dried in the sun and then broken into pieces. Made from durum wheat flour, water, and salt.

Served: In mutton broth and topped with sharp grated cheese.

Also known as: *Su filindeu.*

27. Fisckariedd'

Origin: Southern Italy (Basilicata)

Description: Flat, irregular, and oftentimes geometrically shaped, *fisckariedd'* are the odd-shaped leftover cuttings from ravioli-making and reflect a time when people wasted nothing, especially wheat and egg-enriched pasta dough. Made from durum wheat flour and eggs.

Served: In legume soups.

28. Ladittas

Origin: Sardinia

Description: Thick and slightly concave discs the size of walnuts, *ladittas* are made from durum wheat flour, lard, water, and salt.

Served: With a simple tomato sauce and topped with grated pecorino cheese or with *viscidu*, a local brined cheese made from goat or sheep's milk.

29. Maccheroni alla Pecorara

Origin: Southern Italy (Abruzzo)

Description: Thin or thick and irregularly shaped rings of pasta. Made from wheat flour, eggs, and water.

Served: With mutton ragù, a *carbonara*-style preparation made from pancetta, eggs, and grated cheese, or a vegetable-based sauce. They are always topped with grated pecorino cheese.

30. Maltagliati

Origin: Italy, but especially the northern regions of Lombardy, Veneto, Friuli, and Emilia-Romagna, the central region of Marche, and the southern region of Puglia

Description: Literally "badly cut," *maltagliati* are typically made from the dough left over from making tagliatelle and, as such, are irregularly or rhombus shaped. While typically made from wheat flour and either eggs or water, maltagliati's ingredients vary depending on geographical location: They contain the addition of Parmigiano in Lombardy, fine bran in the Marche, and they are made with buckwheat flour and butter in Friuli.

Served: In broth or with duck- or legume-based sauces.

Also known as: *Malmaritati, blecs, pizzocherini, straciamus, spruzzamusi, martaliai, preagge, bagnamusi, sguazzabarbuz, malintaia, strengozze, sagne "mpezze,* and *pizzelle.* A variant called *menuzze,* found in the central Italian region of Molise, are served in fish broth.

31. Mignaculis

Origin: Northern Italy (Friuli-Venezia Giulia)

Description: Thin, irregular strands of pasta that get their shape from being poured, as a watery batter, into a pot of boiling salted water. Made from wheat flour, salt, and water.

Served: In legume soups such as *fasui e mignaculis,* a thick and hearty soup featuring beans and potatoes.

32. Passatelli

Origin: Central (Umbria and Marche) and northern Italy (Emilia-Romagna)

Description: Coarse and worm-shaped flourless "pasta" made from Parmigiano, breadcrumbs, eggs, beef marrow, nutmeg, pepper, and, at times, vegetables, meats, or cold cuts like finely minced mortadella.

Served: Traditionally in broth, though now they are also served with clam-based sauces.

Also known as: *Lumachelle* or "little snails."

33. Pasta Strappata

Origin: Northern Italy (Friuli-Venezia Giulia), central Italy, and southern Italy

Description: Roughly torn pieces of dough, it's typically made from wheat flour and water, though variations exist; durum wheat flour is added in the south, Parimigiano or other grated cheeses and eggs are added in parts of the north, and spinach is added as a colorant in central Italy.

Served: With meat ragùs or a béchamel and prosciutto sauce.

Also known as: *Streppa e cacciatà, sciancui,*

schinkenfleckerln, strapponi, cannacce, carte da gioco, stracce, stracciatella, pasta straccia, pezzole, maccheroni all garfagnanina, cenciose, strappose, lacne stracciate, scinciata, frasquatuli, limbas 'e cane, and *pasta tappi tappi.*

34. Ricciolini

Origin: Northern Italy (Emilia-Romagna)

Description: Literally "little curls," *ricciolini* are lightly twisted rectangles. A staple of the area's Jewish cuisine, they are served traditionally on Yom Kippur. Made from durum wheat flour or finely milled type "00" wheat flour, eggs, and salt.

Served: In broth.

35. Streppa e cacciatà

Origin: Northwestern Italy (Liguria)

Description: Small, irregularly shaped pasta curls, *streppa e cacciatà* are made from wheat flour, water, salt, and small quantities of oil.

Served: In vegetable soups.

Also known as: *Streppa e caccia là* and *maccheroni strappati.*

36. Tatar Boraki

Origin: Armenia

Description: Rhombus-shaped pasta that translates roughly to "fresh pasta." Made with wheat flour, lukewarm water, eggs, egg yolks, salt, and occasionally sugar.

Served: With browned onions and a garlic yogurt sauce.

37. Testaroli

Origin: Northern Italy, specifically the valley of Lunigiana (along the border of the regions of Liguria and Tuscany)

Description: *Testaroli* date back to at least the Middle Ages and are considered to be among the earliest of pastas. Named after the traditional flat terra-cotta *testo* pan in which they are first cooked, which turns the dough into discs resembling crêpes, *testaroli* are then sliced into large triangular, rhombus, or rectangular shapes and scalded in boiling water. Made from durum wheat flour, salt, and water.

Served: Typically with pesto, though other sauces that include olive oil, pecorino, Parmigiano, and garlic are also used.

Also known as: *Testaroi, testaieu.*

38. Trahana
Origin: Greece, Cyprus, Turkey, Iran, Albania, Hungary, Egypt, Iraq

Description: Very small and hard pasta bits. Made predominantly from bread and semolina flours, it can vary quite a bit in ingredient composition. Different versions can contain goat or sheep's milk (sweet *trahana*), yogurt and milk (sour *trahana*), and vegetable pulp made from tomatoes, bell peppers, or onions (Lenten version). *Trahana* was prepared traditionally in the summer, when it was kneaded into a thick dough, air-dried in the sun, and then grated. Simpler contemporary techniques involve rolling out the dough, letting it dry, and then breaking it into very small pieces with a mallet.

Served: In soups or stews.

Also known as: *Kishk* in Egypt and *kushuk* in Iraq.

FLAT SHAPES

39. Abbotta Pezziende
Origin: Central Italy (Abbruzzo)

Description: Thin and rhombus-shaped *abbotta pezziende* means "feed the beggar" in Abbruzzese dialect. Made from durum wheat flour, water, and salt.

Served: It is served either with a simple tomato sauce and grated pecorino cheese or it is paired with pancetta and legumes, generally chickpeas or fresh fava beans.

Also known as: *Sagne a pezze.*

40. Blecs
Origin: Northern Italy (Friuli-Venezia Giulia)

Description: Thin and triangular pasta whose name means "patch" or "piece of cloth." Its name also reflects the area's proximity to Slovenia, where *bleck* means "piece of cloth." Made from buckwheat flour, wheat flour, eggs, occasionally butter, salt, and water.

Served: With butter and grated local cheeses or with sauces made from chicken, lamb, or rabbit.

Also known as: *Bleki, biechi,* and *maltagliati.*

41. Cresc'Tajat
Origin: Central Italy (Marche)

Description: Sturdy, flat, square- or rhombus- shaped pasta with straight or ridged edges. Made from wheat flour, corn flour, and warm water, though occasionally only corn flour, leftover polenta, and water are used.

Served: With tomato-, sausage-, or legume-based sauces.

Also known as: *Cresc'tajet, maltagliati, patacuc.*

42. Fregnacce
Origin: Central Italy (Lazio, Abruzzo, and Marche)

Description: Golden, wide, diagonally cut ribbons of pasta with smooth or ridged borders. The name means "pack of lies," "silliness," or "trifle" in dialect and reflects the ease involved in making this pasta shape. Handmade varieties are made with durum wheat flour and eggs, while mass-produced ones are made from durum wheat flour and water or eggs.

Served: With a variety of spicy meat- and vegetable-based sauces and topped with grated

pecorino cheese.
Also known as: *Paciocche, pantacce, frescacce.*

43. Lasagne Bastarde

Origin: Central Italy (Tuscany)

Description: Square- or rhombus-shaped pasta made from wheat flour, chestnut flour, salt, and water.

Served: With pesto or layered with ingredients such as cured fatback *(lardo)*, leeks, tomatoes, and cheeses and then gratinéed.

Also known as: Literally "bastard lasagna," *lasagne bastarde* are also known as *lasagna matte,* or "crazy lasagna," and *armelette.* A variation called *bastardui,* found in the northwestern region of Liguria, is made from wheat flour, water, and minced wild herbs and is shaped either like flat rhombuses or coarse gnocchi.

44. Mandilli de Sea

Origin: Northwestern Italy (Liguria)

Description: "Silk handkerchiefs" in Ligurian dialect, *mandilli de sea* are very thin and large pasta squares made from wheat flour, eggs, salt, and lukewarm water.

Served: With pesto, butter, and grated Parmigiano, or garlic-infused olive oil and grated Parmigiano.

Also known as: A variant called *fazzoletti* can also be rectangular in shape.

45. Paccozze

Origin: South-central Italy (Molise)

Description: Thin, very large, and rhombus-shaped, *paccozze* translate to "palm of the hand," which alludes to their considerable size. They are made from durum wheat flour, eggs, and salt and cooked in milk.

Served: With lamb ragù and topped with grated pecorino cheese.

Also known as: *Pizzelle,* a variation from the southern Italian region of Puglia, does not contain eggs.

46. Posutice

Origin: Istria, the peninsula on the Adriatic shared by Italy, Croatia, and Slovenia

Description: Rhombus or rectangular in shape, they are made from wheat flour and eggs.

Served: With a sauce made from olive oil and an anchovy-like small fish called *sardelle* or accompanied by dried cod *(baccalà)* and toasted breadcrumbs.

Also known as: *Pasutice.*

47. Ptresenelle

Origin: South-central Italy (Molise)

Description: This tiny, rhombus-shaped, green-hued pasta is named after parsley, which in Molisan dialect is *ptresine.* Made from durum wheat flour, eggs, parsley, and water.

Served: In chicken broth.

48. Quadrucci

Origin: Throughout Italy, with variations found in the south (Puglia, Molise, and Abruzzo) and in Hungary

Description: Literally "little squares," *quadrucci* are very thin squares of pasta that vary in size and ingredients according to their geographical location in Italy. While they are typically made from wheat flour and eggs, the dough can also be eggless or contain nutmeg, corn flour, or farro flour.

Served: In broth or legume-based soups.

Also known as: *Quadrellini, quadretti, quadrotti, quaternei, quadrelli pelosi* or "hairy squares," *patacchelle, squadruccetti, ciciarchiola, cicerchiole, tajurini,* and *lucciole* or "fireflies." A variation from Puglia, Molise, and Abruzzo is called *volarelle;* made from durum wheat flour and water, it is either deep-fried in olive oil or cooked in broth and served in soups featuring cardoons or beans. A much larger Hungarian version called *aproteszta* is 4 to 5 inches in width.

49. Sagne

Origin: Central (Molise, Lazio, Abruzzo, and Marche) and northern Italy (Friuli-Venezia Giulia)

Description: Thick, flat noodles whose length depends on where they are made. Made from wheat or farro flour, water, and occasionally eggs.

Served: With meat ragù, vegetable sauces, and in soups featuring *cicerchie*, a legume typical of central Italy.

Also known as: *Sagnarelle, sagnette, sagnettine, lis agnis, lasagnas, sagnotte, sagnozzi, lajanelle, makefante, sagne di casa, sagnatelle.*

50. Stracci

Origin: Northwestern (Liguria) and central Italy (Abruzzo, Molise, Lazio, and Marche)

Description: Literally "rags," thin and irregularly shaped *stracci* are made from wheat flour, eggs, and water, though whole wheat flour or fine bran is also occasionally used or included.

Served: With tomato-based sauce made with meats, sausages, or vegetables.

Also known as: *Stracce, sagne stracce.*

51. Stracci di Antrodoco

Origin: Central Italy (Lazio and Abruzzo)

Description: Large, crêpe-shaped pasta made from wheat flour, eggs, salt, and occasionally milk, the dough acquires a semi-liquid consistency that, once fried, creates "pasta crêpes."

Served: Typically filled with seasoned ground veal, *stracci di antrodoco* are covered with meat ragù and then baked.

52. Tacconi

Origin: Central (Umbria and Marche) and southern Italy (Abruzzo, Molise, Campania, and Sicily)

Description: Named after the large heels of sturdy clodhoppers, square- or rhombus-shaped *tacconi* of varying size are principally made from corn flour, type "00" wheat flour, and water, though durum wheat flour, whole wheat flour, or leftover polenta is occasionally added.

Served: Larger-sized *tacconi* are served with local sauces and topped with grated pecorino cheese, while smaller ones are served in broth or legume-based soups.

Also known as: *Tacconelle, taccozze de muline, taccozzelle, sagnarelle degli antichi, volarelle, taccù, cannarù, taccuna, taccuna de mulinu.*

53. Tacui

Origin: Northwestern Italy (Liguria)

Description: Sturdy, rhombus-shaped pasta made from chestnut flour, wheat flour, salt, and water. The inclusion of chestnut flour reflects a time when the rural poor could not afford to use what at the time was expensive wheat flour and resorted to using the bountiful supply of local chestnuts.

Served: With a pesto-like condiment containing basil, marjoram, and walnuts.

FOLDED OR ROLLED HOLLOW SHAPES

54. Busiata

Origin: Sicily and Sardinia

Description: Long, tightly spiraled ribbons of pasta that get their name from the rod, called *busa*, around which the pasta ribbons are wrapped. Made from semolina flour, water,

and occasionally olive oil.

Served: In mutton broth or with meat sauces made from lamb, veal, or boar and topped with grated pecorino cheese.

Also known as: *Maccarruna di casa, pirciati, filatu cu lu pirtusu,* and *busiati ribusiti.* A similarly shaped variation from Sicily named *busa* or *maccarones de busa* is made from durum wheat flour and water.

55. Cajubi

Origin: Southern Italy (Puglia)

Description: Long, narrow strips of pasta that get their shape by being loosely wrapped around a long, thin stick. Made from durum wheat flour, whole wheat flour, salt, water, and occasionally ground toasted wheat.

Served: In broth, topped with ricotta salata, or with vegetable-based sauces.

Also known as: *Cagghjubbi, cajubbi, ditalini, minchiareddhi, tubettini.*

56. Cavatelli

Origin: Southern Italy (Puglia and Campania) with a variation found in Hungary

Description: Shaped like bite-sized empty pea pod halves, *cavatelli* are made from durum wheat flour and water

Served: With a wide variety of meat- and vegetable-based sauces and topped with grated cheese.

Also known as: *Cazzarille, ciufele, cavatielle 'ncatenate, cecatelli, cantaroggni, cavatieddi, cavatielli, mignuicchi, strascenate, strascinati chiusi, tagghjunghele, cecatidde, cecatielle, cicatelli, raskatelli, capunti, capuntini, zinnezinne, cavateddri, rascatielli, rascatielli, rascatieddi, rasckatieddi, gnocculi, gnucchitti, cavatuneddi, cavasuneddi, lolli, gnocchetti, manatelle, orecchie di prete, strascinari,* and *truoccoli.* A variation named *pincinelle* is made with wheat flour, eggs, oil, and salt. A Hungarian variation, *csiga teszta,* is made from wheat flour or semolina flour and whole eggs.

57. Fileja

Origin: Southern Italy (Calabria, Campania, and Basicilata)

Description: Long, narrow ribbons of pasta that get their shape by being loosely wrapped around a long, thin stick. Made from durum wheat flour and water.

Served: With pork or lamb ragù, tomato sauce, or tossed with the spicy and spreadable Italian pork *salume* called *'nduja* and ricotta salata.

Also known as: *Filateddhi, filatelli, fusilli, maccaruni aru ferru, maccaruni 'i casa, scialatielli, sciliatelli, scilatelli, scivateddi, salatielli, strangugliapreviti, ricci di donna* or "woman's curls."

58. Garganelli

Origin: Central Italy (Emilia-Romagna, Umbria, and Marche)

Description: Named after the dialect word *garganel,* which means "chicken's gullet," *garganelli* are thin squares of ridged pasta rolled around a narrow stick. Its ingredients depend on how it is prepared. Handmade versions are made from wheat flour, eggs, and the occasional addition of Parmigiano and nutmeg, while mass-produced *garganelli* are made from durum wheat flour and eggs or water.

Served: Both varieties are served either in capon broth or with meat ragù.

Also known as: *Maccheroni al pettine* and *fischioni.*

59. Maccheroni con Lu Ceppe

Origin: Southern Italy (Abruzzo)

Description: This pasta is named named after *ceppe,* the smooth, thin stick used to make these sturdy, mid-sized tubes made from durum wheat flour, eggs, oil, and water.

Served: With meat ragù.

Also known as: *Torcinelli, ciufulitti.*

60. Minuich

Origin: Southern Italy (Puglia and Basilicata)

Description: Short, rectangular, twisted pasta that acquires its shape by being twirled around a knitting needle. Made from durum wheat flour or roughly ground semolina flour (called *semolone)* and water.

Served: With a variety of sauces that always

include abundant red pepper flakes as well as grated pecorino.

Also known as: *Capunti, ferricieddi, fusilli, minurich, ferriciedd', frizzuli, fusiedd', ciambodre, mignuicchi.*

61. Orecchiette

Origin: Southern Italy (Puglia)
Description: Literally "little ears," *orecchiette* are roughly shaped concave discs thought to resemble their Italian namesake. Made of durum wheat flour, type "0" wheat flour, and warm water.
Served: Traditionally with a condiment made from olive oil, garlic, and broccoli rabe, though they are also often combined with vegetable-, meat-, and mushroom-based sauces.
Also known as: *Orecchini, orecchie di prete, recchie, recchietedde, recchie de prevete, cicatelli, stacchiodde, tapparelle, hjubbi, strascnat, strascenate, pestazzule, stagghiotte, feneschecchie, chiancarelle, chaggrecchietelle, pizzarelle, pociacche,* and *pochiacce.* A Chinese variant called *māo ěr duŏ (see entry 140, p. 91)* literally means "cat's ears."

62. Pasta al Ceppo

Origin: Southern Italy (Abruzzo)
Description: Chewy, meaty pasta shaped like a cinnamon stick whose name means "pasta rolled by a stick." Made from durum wheat flour and water.
Served: With a variety of meat-, vegetable-, and sausage-based sauces.

63. Scorze di Mandorle
Origin: Southern Italy (Basilicata)
Description: Literally "almond shells," *scorze di mandorle* are small, round, roughly shaped discs that, once lightly curled with fingertips, resemble almond shell halves. Made from durum wheat flour, salt, and water.
Served: With lamb ragù or a tomato-based sauce containing garlic and red chile peppers

and topped with grated pecorino cheese.
Also known as: *Skorzel d'amell.*

64. Scorze di Nocella

Origin: Italy
Description: Literally "hazelnut shells," ash-colored or golden *scorze di nocella* resemble their namesake. While their ashen color is now achieved by toasting wheat, it used to come from using burnt grains, and reflects an economically depressed time when poor farm workers would rush to gather grains left over in the fields once landowners burned the remaining wheat stubbles after the harvesting season. Made from durum wheat flour, water, and occasionally either whole wheat flour or burnt or toasted wheat called "*grano arso.*"
Served: In broth or with ricotta or legumes.
Also known as: *Abissini, cappettine, scagghjuzze.*

65. Strangolapreti

Origin: Central, southern, and northern Italy (Friuli-Venezia Giuli)
Description: Loosely rolled and lightly twisted pasta rectangles, *strangolapreti* literally means "priest stranglers" or "priest chokers," alluding to what might happen if priests ate their parishioners' pasta dishes too quickly. They are made from water and a variety of flours, though bread, potatoes, fine bran, and cooked vegetables are used occasionally.
Also known as: *Strozzapreti, casarecce, gnocchi di prete, frigulelli, piccicasanti, strozzafrati, cecamariti, maccheroni alla molinara, strangulaprievete, stranguliaprjeviti, affogaparrini.*

66. Stringozzi

Origin: Northeastern (Emilia-Romagna) and central Italy (Lazio and Umbria)
Description: Long, sturdy, rectangular pasta ribbons made from farro flour, type "00" wheat flour, eggs, and water or from wheat flour, salt, and water.

Served: With sauces featuring ingredients such as local black truffles, lamb ragù, tomatoes, and porcini mushrooms.

Also known as: *Cariole, stringotti, umbricelli, strigliozzi.*

67. Sugeli

Origin: Northwestern Italy (Piedmont and Liguria, and the maritime Alps in particular)

Description: Shaped like small hats, *sugeli* are made from wheat flour, water, salt, and occasionally oil.

Served: With a sauce made from a fermented sour ricotta known as *brusso*.

Also known as: *Corpu de Diu* or "body of God."

CURVED OR SPIRALED TUBES

68. Cavatappi

Origin: Italy

Description: Literally "corkscrews" in Italian, *cavatappi* are smooth or ridged helix-shaped tubes made from semolina flour and water.

Served: With a variety of tomato-based sauces, as well as in salads, soups, and casseroles.

Also known as: *Cellentani, spirali, tortiglioni, fusilli rigati, serpentini, trivelle, stortelli, double elbows,* and *amori.*

69. Chifferi

Origin: Italy

Description: Smooth or ridged curved tubes made from durum wheat flour and water.

Served: With different condiments depending on their size.

Also known as: Smaller versions are served in broth or soups and are also known as *lumachine, lumachelle, lumachette, chifferini, chiocciole, genovesini, cirillini, gomitini, pipette, gobbini, gozzini,* and *stortini*, while larger varieties are served with sauces and are also known as *gomiti* or "elbows," *mezzi gomiti* or "half elbows," *chifferoni, gobboni* or "large hunchbacks," *stortoni* or "large bent ones," and *gozzettoni.*

70. Fusilli

Origin: Italy

Description: Fusilli come in a variety of shapes, lengths, and even colors, depending on how and where they are made. Handmade versions are shaped like narrow, twisted, rolled tubes of varying size and are made from durum wheat flour, occasionally type "00" wheat flour, and water or eggs. Mass-produced versions are shaped like solid or hollow spirals of varying size and are made of durum wheat flour and water.

Served: With many types of meat- and vegetable-based sauces and topped with grated cheese.

Also known as: *Macaron dell'alta lange, subioti, fusarioi, maccheroni bobbiesi, ciufolitti, sfusellati, zufoletti, gnocchi col ferro, feneschecchie, ferricieddi, fricelli, maccheroni a ferrittus, code di topo* or "tails of mice," *fusidde, fusille, maccarune a fierre, pizzarieddhi, firzuli, maccheroni chi fir, fischietti, fillil, fusiddri, filatelli, scilatielli, maccarones inferrettati, maccarones a ferrittus,* and *berriasa.* Mass-produced versions are also known as *fusilli ad alette, fusilloni, fusilli bucati* or "fusilli with a hole," *tricolor fusilli, fusilli lunghi* or "long fusilli," *gemelli* or "twins," *riccioli* or "curls," *spirali* or "spirals," and *tortiglioni.* Known as *spiralnudeln* in Germany.

71. Pipe Rigate

Origin: Northern and central Italy
Description: Literally "striped pipes," *pipe rigate* are hollow, curved pasta tubes that resemble snail shells. They are made with durum wheat flour and water.

Served: With hearty meat- or tomato-based sauces.

Also known as: *Pipette rigate* or "small ridged pipes" and *lumache* or "snails."

LONG TUBES

72. Bucatini

Origin: Italy
Description: Literally "small pierced ones," *bucatini* are mass-produced smooth, long-cut hollow tubes of varying widths and lengths made from durum wheat flour and water.

Served: With a variety of meat- or vegetable-based sauces. Occasionally they are also broken into bits and added to soups.

Also known as: *Boccolotti, candele, fidelini bucati, perciatelli, perciatellini, perciatelloni, candele* or "candles," *regine* or "queens," *ziti, zite, zitoni, zituane, mezzani, scaloppi, filatu cu la pirtusu, maccarruncinu, agoni bucati, bucatoni, spilloni bucati.* Known as *macaronade* in France.

73. Ferrazzuoli

Origin: Southern Italy (Calabria and Campania)
Description: Long-cut *ferrazzuoli* distinguish themselves by being so long that they need to be folded in half. Made from durum wheat flour and water.

Served: With a variety of meat- and vegetable-based sauces.

Also known as: *Cannucce* or "straws" when smaller in size.

74. Shtridhelat

Origin: Albanian communities in central Italy (Lazio, Abruzzo, and Molise) and southern Italy (Basilicata and Calabria)
Description: Long, thick, irregularly shaped tubes that have been pierced lengthwise with a long, thin utensil. Made from durum wheat flour, type "00" flour, and water.

Served: In legume soups or with a variety of meat- and vegetable-based sauces.

Also known as: *Maccar uni a cento, maccaruni a centinara, manare, maccheroni a fezze, manatelle, salatielli, scivateddi, sciliatelli, pasta alla molenara, jacculi.*

75. Ziti, Zite

Origin: Sicily
Description: Long, thick hollowed tubes whose name literally means "groom" or "bride." Traditionally prepared to help celebrate marriages, the Epiphany on January 6th, and other important holidays, they are now enjoyed year round. Made from durum wheat flour and water.

Served: With a variety of meat- and tomato-based sauces and topped with grated Parmigiano or pecorino cheese. They can also be broken into pieces and served in soups.

Also known as: *Maccheroni di zita, stivalette, pasta d'a festa.*

76. Ditalini

Origin: Italy

Description: Short, smooth, or ridged tubes of pasta found in varying small sizes. Made from durum wheat flour and water.

Served: In broth or legume- and vegetable-based soups.

Also known as: *Ditali* and *ditaletti* or "thimbles," *tubetti and tubettini* or "little tubes," *gnocchettini* or "little gnocchi," *gnocchetti di ziti, denti di cavallo* or "horse's teeth," *denti di vecchia* or "old woman's teeth," *magghietti, ganghi di vecchia* or "old woman's legs."

77. Fuži

Origin: Istria, the Adriatic peninsula shared by Italy, Slovenia, and Croatia

Description: *Fuži* resemble slightly flattened cylinders with pointy ends. Made from type "00" flour, eggs, and egg yolks.

Served: With hearty meat or mushroom sauces.

Also known as: An Italian variation, found in Friuli-Venezia Giulia, is called *fusi istriani* and occasionally contains pig's blood, which gives the pasta a darker color.

78. Gargati

Origin: Northern Italy (Veneto)

Description: Literally "gullets," *gargati* are short and ridged hollow tubes made from wheat flour and eggs.

Served: Traditionally with *consiero,* a ragù of mixed meats, or with *rovinassi,* a sauce made from chicken giblets or pigeon.

79. Maccheroni

Origin: Italy

Description: An umbrella term used throughout Italy to signify smooth or ridged and typically tubular pasta of varying shapes and sizes. When handmade, *maccheroni* are made with soft flour or durum wheat flour, eggs, and occasionally water; when mass produced, they are made with durum wheat flour and water.

Served: Extremely versatile, they are served with meat-, legume-, and vegetable-based sauces and topped with grated Parmigiano or pecorino cheese.

Also known as: *Macaroni, maccarrune 'e casa, maccarruni d'a zita, paste d'arbitriu, tufoli, cannerozzi, cannaroni, cannaruncielli.* Larger sizes are also known as *canneroni, cannerozzi, sigarette* or "cigarettes," *fascette* or *mezze fascette* or "wraps" and "half wraps," *schiaffetoni* and *schiaffoni* or "hard slap," *maniche* or "sleeves," *spolette, cannolicchi, diavolini* and *diavoletti* or "little devils," *stortini, svuotini, tubetti,* and *cannelli.* Small curved variations are called elbow macaroni in North America.

80. Mezze Maniche

Origin: Northern Italy (Emilia-Romagna)

Description: Literally "short sleeves," *mezze maniche* are short, stout cylinders with raised edges made predominantly from durum wheat flour and water, though farro flour is occasionally used

Served: In pasta salads and with meat-, cream-, and vegetable-based sauces.

Also known as: *Mezzemaniche* and *maniche di frate* or "friar's sleeves."

81. Paccheri

Origin: Southern Italy, region of Campania in particular

Description: Short, wide tubes of ridged or smooth pasta, their name derives from the Neapolitan word *paccaria,* or "slap," alluding to how the tubes slap a face when devoured too quickly. Made from durum wheat flour and water.

Served: With a variety of tomato-, seafood-meat-, and vegetable-based sauces.

Also known as: *Rigatoni, rigatoncini, tufoli rigati, moccolotti, maniche rigate* or "ridged sleeves," *maniche di frate* or "priest's sleeves," and *bombardoni* or "large explosions."

82. Penne
Origin: Italy

Description: Popular smooth or ridged tubes with straight or diagonal end cuts. *Penne* literally mean "quills," the hollow stems around which yarn is wound, though the name most probably refers to their similarity in shape to the old-fashioned pen called *pennino*. Made from durum wheat flour and water.

Served: They are served, depending on size, with a variety of meat-, tomato-, and vegetable-based sauces and in soups.

Also known as: *Mostaccioli, mostaccioli rigati, penne di ziti, penne di ziti rigati, ziti tagliati, ziti tagliati rigati, natalin, penne a candela* or "penne shaped like candles," *natalini* and *penne di Natale* or "Christmas penne," and *penne rigate* or "ridged penne." Smaller *penne* are also known as *pennette, penne di mezzane, pennette di mezzane rigate, pennette rigate, pennettine, penettine rigate, pennuzze,* *pennuzze rigate, pennine,* and *pennine rigate,* while very large *penne* are also called *zitoni, zitoni tagliati, penne di zitoni,* and *pennoni.*

83. Rigatoni
Origin: Southern Italy

Description: Large, thick, ridged tubular pasta. *Rigatoni* comes from the Italian word *rigato,* which aptly means "ridged." Made from durum wheat flour and water.

Served: With a variety of tomato-, meat-, and vegetable-based sauces.

Also known as: *Bombardoni, tortiglioni, cannerozzi rigati, tortiglioni, cannaroini, rigatoni romani, rigantonicini, trivelli, cappuccilli, calandreddi, scaffituni, maniche, tufoloni rigati.*

84. Trenne
Origin: Italy

Description: Short triangular tubes with pointed tips on both ends. Made from durum wheat flour and water.

Served: In baked dishes, in pasta salads, or either served with oil-based condiments and with meat- or vegetable-based sauces.

LONG RIBBONS

85. Battolli
Origin: Northwestern Italy (Liguria)

Description: Thick, flat noodles, *battoli* recall a time when many of the region's pastas were made with readily available chestnut flour. Made from wheat flour, chestnut flour, water, and occasionally eggs.

Served: Traditionally served with *pesto alla Genovese* or boiled potatoes and local white turnips called *naun* in Ligurian dialect.

86. Bavette
Origin: Northwestern Italy (Liguria)

Description: Long, flat, narrow ribbons of pasta of varying widths whose ingredients change depending on geographic location.

Served: Varieties made from durum wheat flour and water are typically served with seafood-based sauces and pesto or other herb-based sauces. Varieties made from durum wheat flour and eggs are typically served with meat- or cream-based sauces.

Also known as: The thinnest varieties are known as *linguine* and *linguettine* or "small tongues," *lingue di passero* or "sparrows'" tongues," and *bavettine.* Slightly wider ribbons are known as *trenette* and *trinette.* Even wider varieties are known as *tagliatelle, fettuccelle, fettucce romane, tagliarelli,* and *fresine.* Finally, the widest ribbons are known as *lasagnette, pappardelle,* and *lasagneddi.* A variety called *trenette avvantaggiate* or "pasta with advantages," is made with durum wheat flour, whole wheat flour, occasionally chestnut flour, and water, and alludes to how including whole wheat flour made it more affordable than the all-white flour counterparts. A variant called *fettuccine di assime* is made from matzo meal and eggs and is served in chicken, goose, or vegetable broth. A German variation called *bandnudeln* is made with wheat flour, eggs, and water.

87. Blutnudeln

Origin: Northern Italy (Trentino-Alto Adige)
Description: Thin, flat noodles made from rye flour, wheat flour, eggs, and pig's blood.
Served: With a browned butter and sage sauce and topped with a local cheese called *graukäse*.
Also known as: *Tagliatelle al sangue* or *pasta al sangue* or "blood tagliatelle or pasta."

88. Fettuce

Origin: Central and southern Italy
Description: Literally "ribbons" in Italian, *fettuce* are long, flat ribbons whose name varies depending on their width and thickness. Made from durum wheat flour and water.
Served: With a variety of meat- and cream-based sauces.
Also known as: *Fettucce rice, fettuccelle, fettuccine, fresine, lasagnette, nastrini, pappardelle, regfinelle, reginette, zagarelle,* and *filateddi*. In Eastern Europe they contain eggs and are called *szélesmetélt*.

89. Fieno di Canepina

Origin: Specific to the town of Canepina in the region of Lazio in central Italy
Description: Extremely thin, flat noodles made from wheat flour and eggs.
Served: With a variety of sauces containing meat or chicken giblets.
Also known as: *Maccaroni di canepina.*

90. Foglietti

Origin: Central Italy (Marche)
Description: Literally "small papers," *foglietti* are long, narrow, flat noodles. Now considered almost extinct, *foglietti* were enjoyed predominantly by the Italian Jewish community, who toasted the pasta before boiling it. Made from wheat flour and eggs.
Served: In broth or with sauces.

91. Lagane

Origin: Central (Lazio) and southern Italy (Puglia, Calabria, Campania, and Basilicata)
Description: Sturdy pasta ribbons of varying widths and lengths made from durum wheat flour, occasionally type "0" flour, water, and salt.
Served: In broth, legume soups, or with a condiment of onions and chickpeas.
Also known as: *Laganedde, laganelli, lane, lahane, laanedde, piatto del brigante, lane, lavane, lavanelle, laine, lacchene, tria.*

92. Maccheroncini di Campofilone

Origin: Central Italy (Marche)
Description: Extremely thin ribbons of pasta with an extraordinary aroma and texture, *maccheroncini di campofiline* are considered one of the best fresh egg pastas in Italy, even though it wasn't widely available in the country until the 1980s. Made from durum wheat flour and either egg yolks or whole eggs.
Served: With a variety of meat sauces.
Also known as: *Capellini di campofilone, maccarini.*

93. Maccheroni alla Chitarra
Origin: Southern (Puglia) and central Italy (Abruzzo, Molise, and Lazio)
Description: Sturdy, square-shaped spaghetti named after the tool used in making them, the *chitarra*, which consists of a wooden frame strung with parallel steel wires. Made from

durum wheat flour, eggs, and occasionally water.

Served: With mutton ragù, though they are often seasoned with variety of meat-, tomato-, and legume-based sauces.

Also known as: *Tonnarelli, crioli, caratelle, stringhetti.*

94. Mafalde

Origin: Italy

Description: Wide ribbons of pasta characterized by their long and fairly wide rectangular shape and curly edges. Made from durum wheat flour and water.

Served: With a variety of meat-, vegetable-, and mushroom-based sauces and topped with grated cheese.

Also known as: *Mafaldine, nastri* or "ribbons," *nastrini* or "little ribbons," *reginette* or "little queens," *reginette toscane* or "Tuscan little queens," *signorine* or "young misses," *sciabo, sciablo, tripolini, tagliatelle nervate, trine, trinette, ricciarelle, sfrese, sfresatine.*

95. Manate

Origin: Central (Abruzzo) and southern Italy (Basilicata)

Description: Long, thin, slightly irregularly shaped strands, this pasta shape dates back to the Middle Ages. The name, which means "by the handful," alludes to how the strands are made by rolling long ropes of dough around a hand. Made traditionally from durum wheat flour, salt, and water, though eggs and oil or lard are now often added,

Served: Traditionally with a ragù made of pork and lamb meat.

Also known as: *Manare, tratti, maccheroni alla molenara, manatelle.*

96. Pappardelle

Origin: Italy

Description: Wide strips of flat, sturdy pasta, their name is inspired by the verb *pappare*, which means "to eat with zeal" in Italian. Made principally from wheat flour and eggs, though mass-produced varieties are made from durum wheat flour and water.

Served: With meat ragù, typically game-based, and in baked dishes.

Also known as: *Paparele, paspadelle.*

97. Picagge

Origin: Northwestern Italy (Liguria)

Description: Thin, flat, wide pale, and golden or green ribbons, their name, taken from local dialect, refers to the ribbons dressmakers once used as decorative touches. Made from flour, eggs, oil, wine, salt, and occasionally chopped chard, borage, or marjoram as a green colorant.

Served: With pesto or with a sauce made from tomato, anchovies, and basil.

Also known as: *Piccagge, picaje.*

98. Pizzarelle

Origin: Central Italy (Lazio)

Description: Narrow, flat, sturdy ribbons of pasta made from corn flour, wheat flour, and warm water or eggs.

Served: With sauces featuring *baccala* (salted cod), snails, or mutton or the meat of castrated lambs.

99. Ramiccia

Origin: Central Italy (Lazio)

Description: Fine threads of pasta so thin that they are known to melt in the mouth. Made from wheat flour, eggs, and water

Served: With a sauce featuring either pork spareribs and liver sausage or finely diced meat.

100. Strettine

Origin: Northern Italy (Emilia-Romagna)

Description: Literally "little narrows," *strettine* are sturdy narrow, flat pasta ribbons made from wheat flour, stinging nettles or spinach, and eggs.

Served: With a tomato-less meat ragù and topped with grated Parmigiano.

101. Struncatura

Origin: Southern Italy (Calabria)

Description: Thick, flat, brownish rustic ribbons of pasta. Literally "sawdust," the name *struncatura* alludes to the former poverty of the region, as this pasta used to be made with the leftover sweepings of flour and bran from mill floors. Made from a variety of flours such as durum wheat, rye, and bran, and water.

Served: With a condiment made from olive oil, anchovies, garlic, and red pepper flakes and topped with toasted breadcrumbs.

102. Tagliatelle

Origin: Italy

Description: Long, flat, thin pasta strands whose name varies according to width, shape, and place of origin. Made from wheat flour, the occasional addition of durum wheat flour, eggs, and optional cooked spinach for color.

Served: With a variety of tomato- and meat-based sauces.

Also known as: Handmade varieties are also known as *tagliolini, tagliatelle smalzade, lesagnetes, bardele, maccheroni, tajulin sa'l sgagg, tajarille, tagghjarine, tagghjaridde, tagghiarini, taddarini, taglioli pelosi, pincinelle, tagliolini, tagliatini, taglierini, tagliarini, tagliolini pelosi, tajuli, tajurini, sciaquabaffi, curioli, bassotti,* and *fettuccine.*

Mass-produced varieties, most often sold shaped into nests, are also known as *nastri, fettucce romane, fettuccelle, fresine, tagliarelli,* and *capelvenere.* A variation named *fojade,* found in Lombardy, is made with flour, salt, eggs, and oil.

103. Tirache Trevigiane

Origin: Northern Italy (Veneto)

Description: Sturdy, thick, flat pasta ribbons, *tirache trevigiane* translates to "suspenders" in dialect. Made from wheat flour and water.

Served: They are most often used, broken into pieces, in the well-known pasta and bean dish called *pasta e fagioli.*

104. Toppe

Origin: Central Italy (Tuscany)

Description: Literally "patches," *toppe* are sturdy, flat, rather wide pasta ribbons made from durum wheat flour, type "00" wheat flour, and eggs.

Served: With a variety of tomato-based sauces or with a condiment made from olive oil, pepper, salt, and grated pecorino cheese.

105. Tria

Origin: Southern Italy (Puglia) and Sicily

Description: A pasta of Arab origin, *tria* are wide, thick ribbons made from durum wheat flour and eggs or water. Its name derives from *i·π≠riyah,* an Arabic word for pasta.

Served: They are served in a traditional pasta dish called *ciceri e tria,* which features chickpeas.

Also known as: *Ruvitti* and *tridde.*

106. Bigoli

Origin: Northern Italy (Friuli-Venezia Giuli and Veneto, particularly the city of Venice, and Istria, the Adriatic peninsula shared by Italy, Slovenia, and Croatia)

Description: Long, thick strands resembling oversized spaghetti. Once produced exclusively with buckwheat flour, they are now made from wheat flour, water, salt, and occasionally duck eggs.

Served: With meat- or vegetable-based sauces.

Also known as: *fusarioi*, though they are slightly thicker than *bigoli*.

107. Capelli d'Angelo

Origin: Italy

Description: Wire-thin, long-cut *capelli d'angelo* were considered the height of sophistication during the Renaissance because they were so difficult to make. They measure between 0.78 and 0.88 mm in diameter and are sold either fresh or dried, boxed in long single strands or, more typically, in nests to prevent breakage. Made from durum wheat semolina flour, and water or egg whites.

Served: In broth or soups or with thin, light sauces.

Also known as: Angel hair pasta, *barbine* or "little beards," and *cappellini* or "little hairs."

108. Bringoli

Origin: Central Italy (Umbria, Marche, and Tuscany)

Description: Long, very thick, and almost worm-shaped handmade noodles made from wheat flour, occasionally corn flour or durum wheat flour, and water

Served: With a variety of meat-, seafood-, and vegetable-based sauces.

Also known as: *Bringolo, brigonzolo, bringuili, biche, bringuli, ciriole*.

109. Cordeddi Cu Sucu

Origin: Southern Italy (Calabria)

Description: *Cordeddi cu sucu* are almost extinct thick, taupe-colored noodles characterized by their coiled appearance when uncooked. Made from rye flour, eggs, and milk.

Served: In tomato-less sauces that always include grated cheese and crushed red pepper flakes.

Also known as: *Cordelle calabresi*.

110. Cuzzi

Origin: Central Italy (Lazio)

Description: Coarse, thin, long *cuzzi* recall the days when peasants could not afford to eat pasta made exclusively from wheat flour. Made from corn flour, wheat flour, and warm water

Served: With a meat ragù or with oil-based condiments containing either walnuts and radicchio or mushrooms, tomatoes, and garlic.

Also known as: *Cellitti*.

111. Nouilles

Origin: Alsace, France

Description: Rich, short, almost paper-thin egg noodles, though in France the term also refers more generally to spaghetti or noodles. Made from wheat flour, eggs, warm water, salt, and vinegar, which tenderizes the dough.

Served: With a condiment of butter, poppy seeds, and chives, and topped with pan-fried crispy *nouilles* noodles.

112. Paglia e Fieno

Origin: Italy

Description: A combination of golden and green narrow strands of pasta whose name literally means "straw and hay." Made from durum wheat flour, eggs, water, and the addition of cooked spinach for the green variety.

Served: With ragùs and topped with grated Parmigiano.

113. Pici

Origin: Central Italy (Lazio)

Description: A very thick spaghetti whose name varies depending on geographical location. Made from finely milled type "00" wheat flour, warm water, and occasionally eggs

Served: Traditionally with a condiment of olive oil and grated pecorino cheese, though they are also often combined with a variety of vegetable-, tomato-, and meat-based sauces.

Also known as: *Pinci, lombrichelli, ombrichelli, lombrichi, umbrichelli, pisciarelli, ghighi, torcolacci, visciarelli, cechi, brigoli, bighi, culitonni, lilleri, filarelli, tortorelli, strigoli, stratte, schifulati.*

114. Schnalzernudeln

Origin: Northern Italy (Trentino-Alto Adige)

Description: An extremely thin spaghetti made using a pasta machine called *torchio*. Made from rye flour, ricotta, water, salt, and occasionally eggs, they are not boiled in water like most pasta but are instead browned in a generous amount of butter.

Served: Topped with grated cheese.

115. Spaghetti

Origin: Italy

Description: Arguably the most popular string-shaped pasta in the world, spaghetti is as synonymous with Italy as pizza. Coarse and irregularly shaped when handmade, spaghetti is now mostly extruded through dies, a process that makes the strands uniform in size and very smooth. Named after the diminutive form of *spago*, meaning "twine" or "thin string," they are made predominantly with durum wheat flour and water, though whole wheat flour or multi-grain flour are occasionally used.

Served: Very thin varieties are served in broth or with olive oil- or cream-based sauces, while thicker varieties are served with tomato-, vegetable-, or meat-based sauces or with an oil-based egg and pancetta condiment called *carbonara*.

Also known as: Thin varieties are also known as *spaghettini* or "small spaghetti," *capelli d'angelo* or "angel hair," *capellini* or "little hairs," *capelvenere* or "Venus' hair," *sopracapellini, fidelini, fedelini, mezzi vermicelli* or "half worms," *vermicelli* or *vermicellini* or "little worms." Thick varieties are also known as *spaghettoni* or "large spaghetti," *vermicelloni* or "fat worms," *vermicelloni gigantic* or "gigantic fat worms," and *filatelli.*

116. Stroncatelli

Origin: Italy, but particularly in central Italy (Marche) in Jewish communities

Description: Handmade long, thin strands made from durum wheat flour or type "00" wheat flour, salt, and eggs.

Served: In broth, sometimes with the addition of tiny meatballs.

Also known as: *Torcelli.*

117. Tajarin

Origin: Northwestern Italy (Piedmont)

Description: Considered the culinary jewel of Piedmont, *tajarin* are very thin, deep golden, delicate pasta strands made from wheat flour, eggs or just egg yolks, salt, and occasionally a small amount of oil or white wine.

Served: With rich meat ragùs or with condiments made from either oil and anchovies or butter and mushrooms.

Also known as: *Tajarin d'la nona* or "grandmother's *tajarin*," and *ceresolini*. A variation called *tajarin di meliga* is made with wheat flour, corn flour, and eggs.

118. Troccoli

Origin: Central (Lazio) and southern Italy (Abruzzo, Puglia, and Basilicata)

Description: Thick, irregular ribbons made with a special rolling pin with deep ridges called *u 'ntrucele*. Made from durum wheat flour or type "00" wheat flour, occasionally egg whites, and water.

Served: With meat ragù or a variety of seafood- and cheese-based sauces.

Also known as: *Torchioli, rentrocelo, ritrocilo, maccheroni al rintrocilo, truoccoli.*

119. Vipere Cieche

Origin: Central Italy (Lazio)

Description: Literally "blind vipers," *vipere cieche* are long, coarse handmade strands with rounded ends that are typically coiled, like sleeping vipers, once prepared and awaiting cooking. Made from wheat flour, water, and occasionally eggs.

Served: With a tomato and garlic sauce and topped with grated pecorino cheese.

SHORT STRANDS

120. Bricchetti

Origin: Northwestern Italy (Liguria)

Description: 1-inch-long spaghetti made from durum wheat and water. *Bricchetti* means *bastoncini* or "little sticks" in Genoese dialect.

Served: In fish broths or vegetable or legume soups.

121. Fideos

Origin: Spain, possibly of Greek or Persian origin

Description: Round 1-inch-long noodles made of durum wheat and water, they range in thickness from threads of angel hair (used in soups) to spaghetti-like cords (used in casseroles and paella).

Served: *Fideos* distinguish themselves by first being toasted in oil before being added directly to soups, casseroles, and occasionally paellas to cook.

Also known as: *Fideus* in Catalan.

122. Pizzoccheri

Origin: Northern Italy (Lombardy)

Description: Short, flat, thick ribbons made from buckwheat flour, type "00" wheat flour, water, and occasionally eggs and milk.

Served: With a condiment made of cheese, cooked potatoes, and Savoy cabbage or with butter and local cheeses such as *bitto* and *casera*.

Also known as: *Fugascion, pizzocher de tei.*

123. Sagne

Origin: Central (Abruzzo, Molise, Marche, and Lazio) and northeastern Italy (Friuli-Venezia Giulia)

Description: Thick, flat, mid-length ribbons made from wheat or farro flour, water, and occasionally eggs.

Served: With a variety of meat ragùs, vegetable sauces, and legume soups.

Also known as: *Sagnarelle, sagnettine, sagnette, sagnetelle, sagnotte, sagnozzi, sagne di casa, sagne 'mpezze, malefante, lis agnis, las agnas, lajanelle.*

124. Couscous

Origin: North Africa

Description: Tiny pasta granules found in many cuisines throughout the world, couscous is believed to have originated in North Africa when the Roman Empire ruled the area. Typically made from medium-grain semolina or barley flour and cold water.

Served: Mainly as a side to dishes containing vegetables, legumes, meat, or fish.

Also known as: *Cuscus, cuscuz.*

125. Frascarelli

Origin: Italy

Description: Tiny nuggets of pasta, served like polenta, whose ingredients vary depending on geographic location. Though typically made from semolina flour, eggs, and water, they also can include buckwheat flour in Trentino-Alto Adige, wheat flour and eggs in Tuscany, and wheat bran in the southern Puglia and Marche.

Served: In broth, in legume soups, or with oil-based condiments containing vegetables.

Also known as: *'nsaccaragatti, milchfrigelen, spruzzoli, fiscarielli, frascarielli, frascatielli, frascatelli, frascareji, frascatellene, picciasanti, infrascatiei, tritoli, bricioletti, 'ntrisi, 'ndromese, 'ndromisi, frascatole, frascatuli, piciocia, dromsat, 'ncucciatieddi.*

126. Fregola

Origin: Sardinia

Description: Coarse spheres twice the size of peppercorns, *fregola* is believed to have been brought to Sardinia by Ligurian immigrants from the Genoese colony of Tabarka in Tunisia. Made from durum wheat flour, wheat flour, salt, and water, *fregola* is dried and then toasted, a process that imparts a nutty flavor and maintains its considerable firmness during cooking.

Served: Most typically in a tomato-based sauce with clams or mussels, though it can also be added to soups or cooked gently in stock like risotto.

Also known as: *Fregula.*

127. Grumi di Grano Saraceno

Origin: Northern Italy (Trentino-Alto Adige)

Description: Small lumps of buckwheat pasta, *grumi di grano saraceno* aptly translates to "lumps of buckwheat grain." Traditionally from buckwheat flour, type "00" flour, and warm water or milk.

Served: In milk.

128. Millefanti

Origin: Southern Italy (Molise, Puglia, and Sicily)

Description: Short, thin strands or small lumps of pasta made from durum wheat flour, water, salt, and oil, or just durum wheat flour and water.

Served: In broth or bean-based stews, or with a variety of tomato-based sauces often containing legumes and vegetables.

Also known as: *Milafanti, malafanti, millafanti, melifanti, millefante, millinfranti, malefante, menafanti, menai, cettafanti, 'mbilembande, triddhi, tridde.*

129. Pasta Grattata

Origin: Italy

Description: Minute, irregularly shaped pasta obtained by either grating firm dough or by crumbling it by hand. Made from wheat flour, eggs, water, and occasionally parsley and grated pecorino cheese.

Served: In meat broths and legume soups.

Also known as: *Pasta grattada, pasta gratada,*

griebenes gerstl, gratadè, mignaculis, grattini, gratein, tridarini, mollichelle, 'nfranti, 'ntrisi, melempant, bilbanti, pasta rasa, pasta rattedda, grandinina, granite, triddi, farfel (in Jewish cuisine).

130. Pastine Minute

Origin: Italy

Description: Literally "tiny pastas," *pastine minute* is an umbrella term used to describe a variety of minute pasta that can be found, in a multitude of shapes and diminutive sizes. Made typically from durum wheat flour, eggs or water, and the occasional addition of semolina flour or salt.

Served: In broth, vegetable soups, stews, and salads.

Also known as: Generally named to reflect their shape, *pastine minute* are known as *quadretti* or "small paintings or notebooks," *quadrettini* or "very small paintings or notebooks," *quadrettini rigati* or "small ridged notebooks," *puntine* or "little points," *acini di pepe* and *pepperini* or "beads of peppers," *grandine* or "hail," *piombi* or "beads of lead," *funghetti* or "little mushrooms," *alfabeto* or "alphabet letters," *farfalline* or "little butterflies," *stelline* or "little stars," *conchigliette* or "tiny seashells," *margheritine* or "little daisies," *fiori di sambuco* or "elderflowers," *cuori* or "hearts," *fiochetti* or "little bows," *tempestine* or "little storms," *astri* or "aster flowers," *occhialini or* "small glasses," *occhi di trota* or "trout eyes," *occhi di passero* or "eyes of a sparrow," *ditaletti* and *ditalini* or "small thimbles," *coralli* and *coralline* or "small corals," *anelli* or "rings," *anellini* or "small rings," *grattini* or "small grated ones," *ruotine or* "little wheels," and *tubettini* and *tubetto minuto or* "minute tubes."

Seed-shaped varities are also known as *orzo* or "barley" (especially in Greece), *risoni* or "large rice," *punte d'ago* or "tip of a needle," *semi d'orzo* or "barley seeds," *semi d'avena* or "oat seeds," *semi di riso* or "rice seeds," *semi di melone* or "melon seeds," *semi di cicoria* or "chicory seeds," *semi di grano* or "wheat seeds," *pigne* and *pinolo* or "pine nuts," and *semi di mele* or "apple seeds." *Pastine minute* are also known as *farfel* in the Italian Jewish community and as *tarhonya* and *rivilchas* in Hungary.

ASIAN NOODLES

WHEAT NOODLES

131. Bakmi

Origin: China

Description: Introduced into Southeast Asia by the Chinese, *bakmi* are among the most popular hand-pulled noodles in Indonesian cuisine. Literally "meat noodles," they are made with wheat flour, water, and eggs and have a pale yellow color. While several variations of *bakmi* exist, their thickness generally falls between that of Japanese udon and Chinese-style egg noodles.

Served: In soups or stir-fries or seasoned with soy sauce and topped with sliced meats, usually pork, and accompanied by a bowl of broth. Dishes that use *bakmi* include *mie ayam, mee goring,* and *bami goreng.*

Also known as: *Bami, mi kuning,* and *mi telur.*

132. Biáng Biáng

Origin: Northwestern China, province of Shaanxi

Description: Touted as one of the "ten strange wonders of Shaanxi," *biáng biáng* noodles are popular because of their belt-like thickness and length. Initially considered rustic peasant food, these hand-pulled noodles have also gained popularity in restaurants because of the uniqueness and length of the noodle's Chinese characters, which are said to resemble the sound of its dough slapping on the counter as it is pulled. Made from wheat flour, water, salt, and occasionally an alkalizing ingredient.

Served: In hearty soups, topped with lots of red hot peppers.

Also known as: Belt noodles, ripped noodles, wide handmade noodles, *che mian, lapian, biangbiang, biángbiángmiàn,* and *yóupō chěmiàn.*

133. Chinese Egg Noodles

Origin: China

Description: Popular wheat-based noodles of varying shapes and thicknesses that derive their golden color from the inclusion of eggs and alkalized water, or—less desirably—yellow dye. The four most common types are: thin wonton noodles, wide wonton noodles, Hong Kong (or chow mein) noodles, and lo mein noodles.

Served: *Thin wonton noodles* are light, springy, and delicate and are best served in soups or simple dishes alongside ginger, scallions, and oyster sauce. *Wide wonton noodles* are, predictably, wider and thicker versions of their thin cousin. Due to their heartier size, they are often served in braised dishes that possess heavier flavors. *Chow mein noodles,* which literally mean "fried noodles," look like thin wonton noodles but come already parcooked in boiling water, which makes them ready for stir-frying without any further preparation. Chow mein noodles are also known as or Hong Kong noodles. *Lo mein noodles,* which literally mean "stirred noodles," are the thickest, densest, and least springy of the four noodles, which makes them ideal for stir-fry dishes with heavy or rich sauces.

Also known as: *Lao miàn, lo mi.*

134. Cumian

Origin: Northern China, province of Shanxi

Description: Literally "thick noodles," *cumian* are considered a staple and a popular street food in Shaanxi and Hong Kong. Made from wheat flour and water, they resemble a thicker version of Japanese udon noodles.

Served: They are the noodle of choice in the pan-fried pork and vegetables dish *dan dan*.

Also known as: *Cu mian.*

135. Dao Xiao Mian

Origin: Northern China, province of Shanxi

Description: *Dao xiao mian* are chewy noodles traditionally made with a special curved metal knife that creates the noodle's signature thicker-in-middle and thinner-on-the-sides shape. Made from high protein or bread flour and water, its dough is kneaded and then sliced directly over a pot of boiling water.

Served: In a variety of stir-fries and soups.

Also known as: Knife-shaved, knife-cut, or peel noodles, *daoxiao mian, dāo xiāo miàn, doe seuk mein.*

136. Ding Ding Chao Mian

Origin: Northwestern China, territory of Xinjiang

Description: *Ding ding chao mian* are very thick hand-pulled noodles that are then broken or sliced into approximately ¼-inch pieces, the approximate width of a chopstick. Made from wheat flour, water, and salt.

Served: In stir-fries.

Also known as: Fried crushed noodles.

137. Hui Mian

Origin: Central China, province of Henan

Description: Literally "braised noodles," these thick, chewy noodles are made from wheat flour, salt, and oil, hand-pulled into wide ribbons, and braised in rich broths.

Served: Braised in rich broths like mutton broth with coriander and dried kelp.

Also known as: Henan braised noodles, zhengzhou braised noodles.

138. Kesmé

Origin: Central Asia

Description: Primarily a homemade dish not often found in restaurants, *kesmé* is a traditional Central Asian noodle made by the Kazakhs. Made from flour, egg, water, salt, and milk, they are rustic flat, wide noodles of varying lengths.

Served: In soups (including one also called *kesmé*), mixed with rice in pilaf, or made into desserts.

Also known as: *Kespe, erişte*

139. Lamian

Origin: Central China

Description: One of the better known Chinese hand-pulled noodles, dense and springy *lamian* are popular in the Chinese-Muslim communities in central China, as well as throughout Asia and the Western world. Expert noodle makers pull noodles to order, thick or thin. Their length and thickness, which vary, are determined by the number of times the dough is folded onto itself to create the strands. Made from wheat flour, salt, and water often alkalized with *kansui* (lye) or *penghui*, a powder made by burning mugwort or a local tumbleweed called bitter fleabane into ash.

Served: In beef or mutton broth, soups, and stir-fries.

Also known as: *La mian, lā miàn, eghmen, lagʹmon, kalli, laai mein, ba mee, dau dau.* A thicker spiced version called *läghmän* is the national dish of Kyrgyzstan.

A BRIEF HISTORY OF INSTANT RAMEN NOODLES

Inspired by the food shortage lines he had witnessed after World War II in Japan, Japanese businessman Momofuku Ando, the founder of Nissin Foods, set out to invent an instant ramen that would help feed the masses.

In 1957, he began experimenting in a makeshift laboratory in his backyard to make a perfect instant ramen noodle that would reconstitute with boiling water. After months of trial and error, he discovered the magic formula when his noodles, made from wheat flour, palm oil, and salt, underwent the process of being kneaded, steamed, and then flash-fried.

He quickly developed a flavoring that he believed would appeal to taste buds in the West by taking cues from the popularity of chicken soup and, in 1958, he began marketing "Chikin Ramen" (Chicken Ramen). It quickly became a staple in Japan and then China.

Ever the entrepreneur, Mr. Ando realized in 1971 that people in the U.S. were breaking up their ramen noodles and eating them in a cup. This inspired him to create Cup Noodles, a ramen product that made it possible to package, prepare, and serve noodles all in one container. A revolutionary product, it enabled busy people to eat noodles anywhere and many versions of this iconic dish can be found today on supermarket shelves everywhere.

140. Mao Er Duo
Origin: China
Description: Literally "cat ears," *mao er duo* are hand-formed noodles that resemble Italian *orecchiette,* or "little ears," in shape. Depending on the region, they are made either from wheat flour, water, and salt or buckwheat flour, water, and salt, though both versions are shaped by rolling small pieces of dough over onto themselves into a tight curl.
Served: In stir-fries, typically with pork, cabbage, soy sauce, and black vinegar.
Also known as: Cat's ear noodles, *māo ěr duǒ du«í, maau yi do, mashi.*

141. Misua
Origin: Southeastern China (province of Fujian) as well as Taiwan and Singapore.
Description: Literally "thread noodles," *misua* are very thin, white, and salty noodles made from wheat flour, salt, and water. *Misua* are known for their suppleness and absorptive quality. They come in two shapes, flat and circular, and two colors, white and light brown, the last of which is achieved by steaming the noodles at high heat until they caramelize.
Served: With pork hocks in stews, soups, or stir-fries or topped with raw oysters or braised pig's intestines.
Also known as: Wheat vermicelli and longevity noodles, as well as *miswa, xian mian, mian xian, miàn xiàn, mi sua, misua,* and *gōng miàn* in China and *mee sua* in Thailand.

142. Naengmyeon

Origin: Korea

Description: Long, thin hand-made noodles that date back to the Joseon Dynasty in the late 14th century. Made from buckwheat flour, wheat flour, sweet potato starch, and water.

Served: Seasoned with a spicy dressing made primarily from red chili paste or with a tangy iced broth accompanied by julienned vegetables, pickled radishes, and hard-boiled eggs or slices of beef.

Also known as: *Raengmyeon*, *naeng-myeon*, *naengmyun*, and *naeng-myun*.

143. Pan Mee

Origin: Malaysia

Description: Literally "flat flour noodle," these egg noodles are popular among the Hakka, a Chinese people from the Hakka-speaking provincial areas of Guangdong, Fujian, Jiangxi, Guangxi, Sichuan, Hunan, Zhejiang, Hainan, and Guizhou. Made from wheat flour, eggs, water, and salt, the dough is hand-kneaded and then either torn into 2-inch-long pieces of dough or shaped into ribbons. *Pan mee* dough is sometimes colored using natural ingredients such as spinach (green), pumpkin (yellow), sweet potato (purple), and orange bell pepper (orange).

Served: Typically for breakfast, with a thick black soy sauce-based condiment, in curry or chili-based broths, and in soups that contain dried anchovies, minced pork, mushrooms, and leafy vegetables.

Also known as: *Mee hoon kuih, mee hoon kueh.*

144. Ramen Noodles

Origin: Japan

Description: A broad category of fresh and packaged noodles, ramen are predominantly associated with the pre-cooked manufactured Japanese noodles that are most often sold as dried noodle blocks with an accompanying seasoning packet. They are also available in single-serving cups and in vacuum-sealed packaging. Created by Taiwanese-Japanese inventor Momofuku Ando in 1958, ramen noodles have been hailed by the Japanese as their best 20th-century invention. Made from wheat flour, palm oil, and salt, the noodles are kneaded, steamed, and then either flash-fried (most common) or air-dried. Variations in salt content and flour exist, depending on regional preferences.

Served: In a variety of broths and as a side dish to eggs and vegetables.

Also known as: Instant noodles.

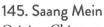

145. Saang Mein

Origin: China, region of Hong Kong in particular

Description: Quick-cooking thin noodles made from wheat and tapioca flours, salt, and water. *Saang mein* also contain a small amount of potassium carbonate, which is a chemical leavening compound that tenderizes the dough and gives the noodles their smooth and slippery texture.

Served: Hot either by themselves or mixed with cooked leafy green vegetables and seasoned with sesame oil and occasionally accompanied by hard-boiled eggs or meat.

Also known as: *shēng miàn.*

146. Shrimp Roe Noodles

Origin: Southern China, region of Hong Kong and province of Guangdong

Description: Thin, wiry noodles made from wheat flour, tapioca flour, salt, monosodium glutamate (MSG), and salty shrimp roe, which gives them their defining tiny black spots.

Also known as: Shrimp noodles.

147. Sōmen

Origin: Japan

Description: Very thin and white Japanese noodles made from wheat flour, occasionally eggs, salt, and water.

Served: Typically served chilled in hot weather,

accompanied by a dipping sauce.
Also known as: *Nyumen* when served in hot soups.

150. Udon
Origin: Japan
Description: Popular thick, chewy noodles, they are made from wheat flour, salt, and water.

Served: Hot in a variety of ways, though three popular options find them in mildly flavored broths topped with either thinly sliced scallions or tempura, with deep-fried tofu pockets called *aburaage*, or with half-moon-shaped fish cakes called *kamaboko*. They are also served cold, on their own, occasionally topped with the shredded seaweed *nori*, or in a cold soup made of unpasteurized soy sauce and *sudachi* citrus juice and topped with grated daikon.

Also known as: *Hiyamugi*, a slightly more slender variant, is typically white, though it can also be taupe or pink. *Sanuki udon*, a variant popular on the Japanese island of Shikoku, is characterized by its square shape and flat edges and is served in broth.

148. Sutamyeon
Origin: Korea
Description: Thick, flat, chewy noodles made from wheat flour, salt, and water, they are kneaded by hand to look like a thicker version of udon noodles.
Served: A key ingredient in the popular Korean black bean noodle dish known as *jjajangmyeon*.

149. Tasalsan Guril
Origin: Mongolia
Description: Wide, flat noodles made from wheat flour and water, they distinguish themselves from other noodles by first being pan-fried as pasta sheets, then hand cut into long ribbons.
Served: With any dish that requires fresh noodles, though they are frequently found in *tsuivan*, the traditional Mongolian meat and vegetable stew, and in hearty meat soups such as the popular *guriltai shul*.

RICE NOODLES

151. Bánh Canh
Origin: Vietnam
Description: Literally "soup cake," *bánh canh* are jumbo-sized noodles cut from thick sheets of uncooked dough. Made from rice flour, tapioca starch, and water, their color fluctuates from white to almost transparent depending on the ratio of starch to flour.
Served: In a variety of soups, the most common being *bánh canh cua,* a rich crab-based soup with quail eggs, and *bánh canh bánh canh chả cá,* a fish cake soup.

152. Idiyappam
Origin: India
Description: Thin, white, wiry noodles that have been in existence since the 1st century AD, *idiyappam* are a culinary specialty in the southern Indian states of Tamil Nadu, Kerala, and Karnataka, as well as in Sri Lanka and Malaysia. Made from rice or finger millet flour, water, sometimes ghee, and salt.
Served: For breakfast or as a main course for dinner in sweetened coconut milk or with spicy curries.
Also known as: *Semige, semé da addae, shavige, nooputt, noolputtu, putu mayam, putumayam,* and string hoppers.

153. Rice Vermicelli
Origin: Throughout China, Vietnam, Indonesia, Singapore, Malaysia, Philippines and Cambodia
Description: White, thin, and almost wiry rice noodles. Made primarily from rice flour and water, though tapioca starch or cornstarch are occasionally added to improve the noodles' transparency and increase its chewy texture.
Served: In soups, spring rolls, cold salads, and stir-fries.

Also known as: Rice noodles, rice sticks, dried rice noodles, and rice fettuccine. Slight variations of this noodle exist and are known as *mai sin, lai fun, bee sua, bee hoon, ho fun, chow fun, kwai tiu, kway teow, gǔo tiáo, shā hé fěn, hé fěn, lài fěn, mí fěn, mai fun, mai sin, hor fun, migàn, mǐ xiàn, laai fun* in China; *sevai* in Tamil; *pancit* and *pansit* in the Philippines; *bihun* in Malaysia; *bifun* in Japan; *sen mee* (very very thin and delicate noodles), *sen yai* (wide, flat noodles),

sen lek (used in *Pad Thai*), and *sen chan* (noodles from Chantaburi province, reputed as being the origin place of these noodles), *guay teow, khanohm jeen,* and *khanom chin* in Thailand; *bán pho* or *bánh phở* (fresh rice sticks), *bánh phở kho* (dried rice sticks), and *bun* in Vietnam; and *sevai, shyavige,* and *santhakai* in southern India. A thicker variety, called *guilin mǐfěn,* comes from the southern Chinese city of Guilin, where it is a breakfast staple.

EGG NOODLES

154. Ba Mee
Origin: Thailand
Description: Literally "egg noodles," *ba mee* are most commonly long, thin, and round in shape and are known for their canary yellow color, which they get from either eggs or food coloring. Made from wheat flour and eggs.
Served: In soups and as an accompaniment to roasted pork and duck dishes.
Also known as: *Ba mee haeng.*

155. Jook-sing
Origin: China
Description: Considered one of the rarer noodles in existence today, *jook-sing* literally means "bamboo rice noodles" since the dough, once kneaded, is manually pressed with huge bamboo logs. They are found predominantly in Macau and in parts of Hong Kong and Guangzhou, located in the southeastern province of Guangdong. Made from high-gluten wheat flour, water, duck eggs, and an alkaline solution.
Served: Most commonly in a soup with wonton dumplings or tossed in light soy sauce and topped with *char siu* pork slices.
Also known as: Bamboo pole noodles, bamboo rod noodles, bamboo noodles.

156. Kalguksu
Origin: Korea
Description: Literally "knife noodles," *kalguksu* are handmade egg noodles that are cut into strands with a knife. Made from wheat flour and eggs, though ground bean powder is occasionally added for texture.
Served: Considered a seasonal food consumed most often in summer, they are served traditionally added to seafood- or vegetable-based soups like *yachae kalguksu.*

157. Yi mein
Origin: Southern China, province of Guangdong
Description: Flat, narrow egg noodles, *yi mein* are known for their golden yellow color and pleasantly chewy, slightly spongy texture, which comes from using soda water, instead of regular water, along with wheat flour and eggs.
Served: In stir-fries, soups, and salads.

158. Youmian
Origin: Southern China, region of Hong Kong and province of Guangdong
Description: Literally "thin noodles," *youmian* are widely used in southern China, especially in the cuisines of Hong Kong and the southeastern province of Guangdong. Made from

wheat flour, eggs, and soda water, the last of which gives the noodles the unusually spongy, slightly chewy texture for which they are known.

Served: By themselves or in soups, broths, salads, stir-fries, and braises.

Also known as: *You mian*, *e-fu* noodles, *yee-fu* noodles, *yi* noodles, *yifu* noodles.

STARCH AND MISCELLANEOUS NOODLES

159. Cellophane Noodles

Origin: China

Description: Called crystal noodles and glass noodles because they become translucent once cooked, these thin, wiry noodles are typically sold bunched in dried form and then reconstituted in water before using. They are generally round, are available in a variety of thicknesses, and are very brittle when dry but become strong and firm once cooked. Made from a single or a mixture of starches such as mung bean, yam, potato, sweet potato, cassava, canna, or batata and water.

Served: In stir-fries, soups, hot pots, spring rolls, curries, salads, as a filling in dumplings, and even to simulate shark fins in vegetarian soups.

Also known as: Chinese vermicelli, mung bean vermicelli, bean threads, bean thread noodles, and cellophane noodles around the world; as *harumsame* in Japan (and made from potato starch or mung bean flour); *fěnsī*, *dōngfěn*, *suān là fěn*, and *saifun* in China; *soun* and *suun* in Indonesia; *sotanghon* in the Philippines; *phing* and *fing* in Tibet; *wun sen* or *woon sen* in Thailand; long rice in Hawaii; and *lialia* in Samoa. In Korea, they are called *gamjanongma guksu* when made with potato starch, *dangmyeon* when made from sweet potato starch, and *gamja guksu* when made with potato starch, rice flour, and glutinous rice flour. Wide, flat cellophane noodle sheets are called mung bean sheets.

160. Cheonsachae

Origin: Korea

Description: Slightly transparent, chewy noodles made from the jelly-like extract that remains after steaming the seaweed *kombu*.

Served: Bland in taste, they are generally served in a light salad or used as a garnish over sliced raw fish.

161. Dotori Guksu

Origin: Korea

Description: They come in two varieties: starch-based vermicelli and flour-based soba. The starch-based noodles, made from acorn starch and a combination of potato, rice, or arrowroot starch, wheat flour, salt and water, resemble very thin brown plastic threads when dry and have a very elastic, chewy texture once cooked. The flour-based noodles are as thick as spaghetti and made from acorn flour and a combination of grain-based flours such as buckwheat and corn, salt, and water. They differentiate themselves from standard buckwheat soba noodles by being more brittle, slightly saltier, and coarser in cut.

Served: As *dotori naengmyeon* (starch-based), they are served chilled with a dipping sauce, and as *donguri-men* (flour-based), they are served in stir-fries or chilled with a dipping sauce.

Also known as: Acorn noodles, *dotori naengmyeon*, *donguri-men*.

162. Lao Shu Fěn

Origin: China

Description: Literally "rat noodles," these are short, plump, and chewy noodles with tapered ends that make them resemble rats' tails. Made from wheat starch, tapioca starch, rice flour, salt, and boiling water, they fluctuate in color from white to almost transparent, depending on the ratio of starch to flour. White varieties contain more flour and the more transparent varieties contain more or all starch and tend to be more slippery once cooked.

Served: In stir-fries and soups, boiled and flavored with condiments, or cooked dry in a clay pot, such as in the dish *Clay-pot lao shu fen*.

Also known as: Rat noodles, silver needle noodles

163. Shirataki

Origin: Japan

Description: Thick, semi-translucent, and slightly rubbery in texture, *shirataki* are made from water and the fiber-rich starch of the konjac yam, also known as "devil's tongue." Because the noodles consist mainly of fiber and water, they are vegan, gluten free, and have near-zero calories. Packaged in water, they tend to have a fishy aroma that can easily be eliminated by rinsing them well under cold running water and drying them prior to cooking.

Served: In soups, stews, and stir-fries as a substitute for grain-based noodles.

164. Soba

Origin: North Japan

Description: Soba are firm, dark taupe, square-shaped noodles made from buckwheat flour and water. When made from buckwheat flour, wheat flour, and water, they are known as *nagano soba* or *ni-hachi soba*.

Served: Chilled, accompanied by a dipping sauce typically made of dashi, soy sauce, and wasabi, or in hot broth, often topped with vegetable or shrimp tempura.

Also known as: A variant called *okinawa soba* is made exclusively with wheat flour.

165. Tokoroten

Origin: Japan via China

Description: Believed to have been introduced to Japan from China over a thousand years ago during the Nara period, *tokoroten* are firm, square, and translucent. Made from the congealed jelly of *ogonori* and *tengusa* seaweed, the "dough" is then pressed through a traditional gadget called a *tentsuki*, which squeezes the jelly into noodles.

Served: They are served savory, with condiment variations that include vinegar, soy sauce, nori, hot pepper, mirin, and/or sesame seeds, or sweet, mixed a condiment of molten dark sugar.

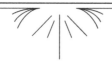

DUMPLINGS

FILLED DUMPLINGS

166. Ada

Origin: South India

Description: Large half-moon-shaped dumplings traditionally prepared for the Hindu festival *Onam*. Made of rice flour, water, coconut oil, and salt, they are filled, wrapped in banana leaves, and then steamed or boiled. Their filling can be savory but is typically sweet, and contains either jackfruit or a mixture of freshly grated coconut, jaggery, bananas, and spices.

Served: By itself as a snack or as breakfast accompanied by a cup of tea.

167. Agnolini Mantovani

Origin: Northern Italy (Lombardy)

Description: Presumed to have been created during the Renaissance for the princely House of Gonzaga in Mantua, they are slightly larger than their similarly shaped cousin the *tortellino*. Made with both "00" and durum wheat flours, eggs, and water or milk, they are filled with minced beef, the pork sausage *salamella*, Parmigiano, pancetta, spices, and herbs.

Served: In the broth, topped with Parmigiano.

168. Agnoli di Mostardele

Origin: Northwestern Italy (Piedmont)

Description: Considered a winter specialty, these triangular pasta pockets are made from wheat flour, bran, buckwheat flour, walnut oil, and eggs. They are traditionally filled with leeks and *mostardele*, a rustic salami made from wine, spices, and the nasty bits (or offal) of pigs.

Served: Typically served on top of a savory leek sauce, garnished with a little foaming butter and crispy julienned leeks.

169. Agnollotti Toscani

Origin: Central Italy (Lazio and Tuscany)

Description: Rectangular, inch-long pasta pockets made from wheat flour and eggs, they typically contain one of two classic fillings: ricotta and spinach or veal, brain, and chard.

Served: With a hearty meat sauce and Parmigiano.

Also known as: *tordelli, ravioli, tortelli*.

170. Agnolotti

Origin: Northwestern Italy (Piedmont)

Description: Rectangular, square or half-moon-shaped inch-long pasta pockets made with wheat flour and eggs, they are traditionally filled with a mixture of braised meats like pork, veal, and occasionally donkey, vegetables like cabbage or spinach, and aromatics. Three other fillings feature artichokes, ricotta and spinach, and fontina cheese, the latter of which are called *fagottini della bella rosina*.

Served: Seasoned with the juices of roasted meats or a browned butter and sage sauce and topped with Parmigiano.

Also known as: *Agnelotti, langaroli, agnulot, langheroli;* the miniature version is called *agnolotti del plin.*

171. Bánh bôt lo

Origin: Vietnam

Description: Small, half-moon-shaped, and almost transparent dumplings whose name translates loosely to "clear flour cake." Believed to have originated in the 19th century during the Nguyễn Dynasty, *bánh bánh bột lọ* are made with tapioca starch and water and filled with shrimp and pork belly.

Served: As an appetizer or snack topped with fried shallots and accompanied by a sweet chili fish sauce.

172. Bánh It

Origin: Central Vietnam

Description: Round and white sticky rice dumplings, *banh it* acquire a tea-like flavor due to the banana leaves on which they are steamed. Made from glutinous rice flour and water, they are filled with a mixture of ground pork, mushrooms, shrimp, onions, fish sauce, and spices.

Served: Warm accompanied by a dipping sauce.

173. Bansh

Origin: Mongolia

Description: A dumpling similar to its cousins *buuz* and *khuush-uur.* While the ingredients for the dough and filling are the same for all three, they differ in size, shape, and cooking method. *Bansh,* which look like a rose about to bloom, are the smallest of the three and are most often boiled. Made from wheat flour and water, they are filled principally with seasoned mutton or beef, though they may also contain a varied combination of onions, caraway seeds, garlic, sprouted fennel seeds, seasonal herbs, mashed potato, cabbage, and rice.

Served: In a savory broth, in milk tea, or with butter, condiments, and a few raw vegetables for decoration.

174. Baozi

Origin: China

Description: A generic name used to describe a bready steamed dumpling similar to the Chinese *jiaozi,* Mongolian *buuz,* Japanese *gyoza,* Korean *mandu,* and Nepalese *momo. Baozi* have a variety of fillings and come in two main sizes: "big bun" *dàbāo* and "small bun" *xiǎobāo.*

Served: With a dipping sauce.

Also known as: *Dàbāo, bao, bau, humbow, nunu, bakpao, bausak, pow, pau, paozu, pao.*

175. Barbagiuai

Origin: Northeastern Italy (Liguria)

Description: This popular appetizer is named after the legendary bearded (*barba*) Uncle Giovanni (*Giuà* in dialect) who invented these fried pasta pockets. Made from wheat flour, extra virgin olive oil, white wine, and water, they are filled with pureed winter squash, eggs, marjoram, and *cagliata,* a sharp regional cheese. Chard or spinach is sometimes used instead of squash.

Served: Predominantly as an appetizer.

Also known as: *Barbajuan, barbagiuan.*

176. Ba-Wan

Origin: Taiwan

Description: Large, tennis ball-sized steamed dumplings whose name translates to "meatball." Made either from tapioca pearls, water, and oil, or rice flour and corn or sweet potato starches, they are typically filled with a mixture of pork, shiitake mushrooms, bamboo shoots, and spices, though the ingredients often vary according to region.

Served: With a crisscross incision on top and topped with fresh cilantro leaves and a sweet and savory sauce made from oyster sauce, sugar, plum powder, and ketchup.

177. Bertù

Origin: Northern Italy (Lombardy)

Description: These half-moon-shaped filled dumplings date back to the mid-15th century, when they were made annually to thank the Virgin Mary for protecting local soldiers against the Turks in the victorious Battle of Lepanto. Made of whole wheat flour, salt, and eggs, they are shaped into 3-inch discs and filled with a mixture of the fresh pork sausage *cotechino*, Parmigiano, eggs, and nutmeg.

Served: As a starter pasta dish, typically with a butter sauce and pancetta.

Also known as: *Gai*, "donkey" in dialect, to reflect their similarity in shape to donkey ears.

178. Boraki

Origin: Armenia

Description: Popular dumpling shaped like small cylinders with an open top. Made from flour, egg, and water, they are filled with cooked minced beef, onions, oil, broth, salt, and pepper. Once assembled, *boraki* are first steamed in broth and then pan-fried.

Served: With yogurt and chopped garlic.

179. Buuz

Origin: Mongolia

Description: Shaped like the filled bindle of a runaway child, these steamed dumplings are eaten throughout the year, but especially during the Mongolian New Year celebrations. *Buuz* originates from the word *bāozi*, which means "steamed dumpling" in Mandarin. Made from flour and water, they are filled principally with seasoned mutton or beef, though they may also contain varying combinations of ingredients such onions, caraway seeds, garlic, sprouted fennel seeds, seasonal herbs, mashed potato, cabbage, and rice. *Buuz* are in some ways similar to its cousins, *khuushuur* and *bansh*.

While the ingredients for their dough and filling are the same, they differ in size, shape, and cooking method.

Served: Alongside fried bread and salad.

180. Cadunsei

Origin: Northern Italy (Lombardy)

Description: These half-moon-shaped dumplings are a culinary staple throughout the region's many summer festivals. They sometimes have an indentation in the middle that makes them look like a small boat, closely resembling the pasta shape Bertù (see number 177). *Cadunsei* have changed over the years due to Lombardy's increasing prosperity. While the dough used to be made with just wheat flour and water, today it also includes eggs. The filling, which originally contained chicken innards, aromatics, and ground peach kernels, now contains meats, salami, and crumbled amaretto cookies.

Served: As a starter, typically with a browned butter sauce.

Also known as: *Cahunhei* and *Casoncelli*.

181. Caicc

Origin: Northern Italy (Lombardy)

Description: Half-moon-shaped dumplings from the small town of Breno. Possibly Italy's largest dumplings, *caicc* measure 4 to 5 inches in length. Their name is Italian dialect for *cuneo*, which means "wedge." Made from wheat flour, a handful of buckwheat flour, eggs, and water, they are filled with meats, salami, mortadella, chard, raisins, crumbled amaretto cookies, breadcrumbs, aromatics, and spices.

Served: As a starter pasta dish, typically with a browned butter and sage sauce.

182. Calcioni

Origin: Central Italy (Marche)

Description: Large, half-moon-shaped dumplings considered a specialty of the small town of Treia. Made from wheat, water, and eggs, their filling contains sheep's milk ricotta, prosciutto, cheese, and varied aromatics that always include fresh marjoram. *Calcioni* are either pan-fried or boiled.

Served: With a rich meat sauce.

Also known as: *Calcione col sugo, carciù, cacui,* and *ravioli.* There is also a fried sweet pastry from the same area called *calcione dolce.*

183. Calhù

Origin: Northern Italy (Lombardy)

Description: Very small dumplings named after the baggy trousers that men wore as part of their traditional garb in Lombardy. Made from wheat flour, water, and eggs, their filling includes potatoes, salami, aromatics, and spices.

Served: With a browned butter and sage sauce and topped with freshly grated Parmigiano.

184. Calzoncelli

Origin: Southern Italy (Puglia)

Description: Shaped like half-moons or discs, these dumplings were served principally on feast days. The name *calzoncelli*, which it shares with a better known and more common sweet pastry from the same region, means "small trousers" in Italian. Made from durum wheat flour, water, and sometimes eggs, they are filled with eggs and either ricotta or meat.

Served: As a main course topped with a meat sauce or simply fried.

Also known as: *Agnolotti baresi, calzoncieddi, calzoncini, cazune.*

185. Calzonicchi

Origin: Central Italy (Lazio, specifically, the Italian Jewish community in Rome)

Description: Considered an integral part of the Jewish New Year (Rosh Hashanah) menu among the Roman Jewish community, these inch-long triangular dumplings translate in Italian to "little trouser legs." Made from wheat flour and eggs, their filling consists of calf's brains, onions, and spices.

Served: As a starter in broth or with a meat sauce.

Also known as: *Tortellini di cervello.*

186. Cannelloni

Origin: Italy

Description: One of the oldest pasta shapes in Italian culinary history, cannelloni began appearing in dictionaries in the mid-19th century. Cannelloni, which literally means "big tubes," are large rectangles of fresh pasta wrapped around a filling to form a roll. Homemade versions are made from wheat flour, eggs, and sometimes olive oil, while commercially produced versions contain only durum wheat flour and water. Found throughout Italy, cannelloni allow different regions of Italy to express their culinary preferences through the filling, which can feature meat, fish, cheese, and/or greens.

Served: Typically baked covered in béchamel sauce and served as a main course.

Also known as: *Cannaciotti, canneroncini, canneroni, manfriguli, manfrigoli, cannarune, cannarunciedde, cannaroni, cannoli, crusetti,* and, in the United States, manicotti.

187. Cappellacci di Zucca

Origin: Central Italy (Emilia-Romagna, the city of Ferrara in particular)

Description: Considered the signature dish of Ferrara, these dumplings date back to the Renaissance, when they were prepared for the princely Este family that ruled the area. Made from wheat flour and eggs, its filling is made exclusively from *barucca,* a locally grown sweet squash, Parmigiano, sugar, nutmeg, and, at times *mostarda,* an Italian candied fruit condiment with a piquant mustard syrup

Served: With a rich meat sauce or a browned butter and sage sauce and topped with freshly grated Parmigiano.

Also known as: *Caplaz* in local dialect, to reflect

the dumplings' resemblance to the straw hats worn by local peasants.

188. Cappelletti

Origin: Central Italy, (Emilia-Romagna)

Description: Literally meaning "little hats," these bite-size dumplings resemble nurses' caps. Made from "00" wheat flour and eggs, they have two different types of filling. The first contains a variety of meats and spices, while the second uses soft regional cheeses like ricotta, *cacao raviggiolo, stracchino,* and/or *cassatella,* as well as nutmeg, lemon zest, and sometimes seasonal greens.

Served: Traditionally in capon broth, though other meat broths can be used.

Also known as: *Caplet.*

189. Cappieddi 'I Prieviti

Origin: Southeastern Italy (Calabria)

Description: From the region of Calabria, located on the easternmost tip of the Italian boot, this filled dumpling is shaped like a three-cornered hat and its name literally means "priest's hat" in dialect. Made from durum wheat flour, salt, eggs, and sometimes water, they are filled with eggs, soppressata, *provola* cheese, and spices. Although quite rare today, they still appear on tables on holidays and special occasions.

Also known as: *Cappelli del prete* and *tricorni.*

190. Casonsei

Origin: Northern Italy (Lombardy)

Description: In existence since the 14th century, these half-moon-shaped dumplings have changed quite a bit over time and continue to do so. Made from wheat flour, eggs, salt, and sometimes olive oil, *casonesi* vary in size from place to place. While at various points in history they have been filled with either pears, cheese, and spices or amaretto cookies and candied fruit, you now find them, depending on the city, filled with a varied combination of ingredients that can include meats, vegetables cooked in lard, potatoes, sausage, garlicky salami, and/or cheeses.

Served: With butter, local grated cheese and, depending on the area, poppy seeds.

Also known as: *Casoncelli, casonzieri ciaorncie.*

191. Cepelinai

Origin: Lithuania

Description: The national dish of Lithuania, *cepelinai* are large, croquette-shaped boiled dumplings. Made from a fairly precise ratio of grated raw and riced cooked potatoes, along with eggs and seasonings, they are traditionally filled with ground meat, scallions, and spices, though cheese and mushrooms are sometimes included.

Served: With a sour cream-based sauce or with sour cream and the condiment *spirgučiai,* which is made with fried onions and pork belly.

Also known as: *Didžkukuliai.*

192. Chao Shou

Origin: Southwestern China (Sichuan)

Description: The name of these thin-skinned boiled dumplings literally means "folded arms," alluding to how their skins are wrapped, with one corner crossed over the other and then pinched together. Made from wheat flour and water, they are filled with pork, scallions, ginger, wine, eggs, oil, and spices.

Served: In bowls with a garlicky and hot soy sauce-based condiment and topped with chopped scallions.

Also known as: *Hong you chao shou, hong you yuntun.*

193. Che Troi Nuoc

Origin: East and Southeast Asia

Description: Soft, chewy, and round, these are savory-sweet dumplings made from glutinous rice flour and boiling water, and filled with mung bean paste, shallots, and salt.

Served: In a warm, thick, sweetened broth

made with fresh ginger, brown and white sugar, and water, and topped with a coconut sauce and toasted sesame seeds.

194. Chiburekki

Origin: Eastern Europe
Description: These deep-fried large, half-moon-shaped dumplings are the national dish of the Crimean Tatars and a popular snack and street food throughout Central Asia, Russia, Ukraine, Turkey, Uzbekistan, and Romania. Made from wheat flour, water, oil, and salt, they are filled with minced meat, cilantro, parsley, scallions, and spices.
Served: Alone or with sour cream or sprinkled with ground sumac.
Also known as: *Chebureki*. A baked *chiburekki* variation also exists and is called *töbörek*.

195. Chiu-Chao Fun Gow

Origin: China and Taiwan
Description: Delicate steamed dim sum dumplings. Made from tapioca and wheat starches, boiling water, vegetable oil or lard, and salt, they are primarily filled with a mix of pork and dried shrimp, along with chopped roasted peanuts, jicama, cilantro, and shiitake mushrooms.
Served: With soy sauce and chile garlic sauce for dipping.
Also known as: *Chaozhou fun guo, chao zhou fen guo, fun quor, fun gor, fen guo, gok zai, chiu chow dumplings, teochew dumpling, hung gue, fun kor.*

196. Chuchvara

Origin: Uzbekistan and Tajikistan
Description: *Chuchvara* are very small boiled dumplings that resemble nurses' hats. Made from wheat flour, eggs, water, and salt, they are filled with a mixture of seasoned meats that, in observance of Islamic dietary rules, do not include pork.
Served: In a clear soup or on their own, accompanied either by vinegar, a sauce made of chopped greens, tomatoes, and sour cream, or

suzma, a fermented Turkic dairy product similar to strained yogurt.
Also known as: *Dushpara, tushpara, tushbera, tushbera, dushbara.*

197. Cjalsons

Origin: Northeastern Italy (Friuli-Venezia Giulia)
Description: Believed to have ancient Arab origins. Made from wheat flour, eggs, and sometimes boiled potatoes, these boiled crescent-shaped dumplings have as many name variations as they do fillings. The only unifying ingredient in every *cjalson* is cheese, as local fertile hills provide farm animals with ample grazing.
Served: With a traditional sauce made of melted butter, smoked ricotta, and aged local cheeses.
Also known as: *Agnolotti, cialcions, cjarsons, cialzons, ciargnei.*

198. Coronette

Origin: Southern Italy (Campania)
Description: Possibly the only Italian dumpling to have two different shapes and sizes—small half-moons and considerably larger triangles. Literally "little wreaths," these wavy-edged ravioli are made from wheat flour and eggs, and filled with ricotta and parsley.
Served: With traditional condiments from the area.

199. Culingionis

Origin: Sardinia
Description: These dumplings are formed in various shapes, though the most diffused resemble leaning figs topped with a fishbone-like pattern. Made of durum wheat flour type "00," lard, salt, and water, they are filled with a variety of ingredients, depending on where they are made on the island. Popular combinations include local fresh pecorino, chard, and saffron; mixed meats that always contain lamb; potatoes and pecorino; eggplant, chard, and walnuts; and

mint-scented ricotta.

Served: With a hearty meat or tomato and basil sauce, depending on the filling.

Also known as: *Culurzones, kulurjones, culurjones, angiolottus, culurzones, spighitti.*

200. Da Lian Huo Shao

Origin: China

Description: Pan-fried pancake-like dumplings the size of a large chocolate bar that are popular in Beijing, *da lian huo shao* can be traced to the time of Emperor Guangxu, during the Qing Dynasty in the late 1700s. Made from wheat flour, water, and sesame oil, they are most often filled with pork and fennel, pork and cabbage, lamb and scallions, or with a variety of vegetable combinations.

Served: Traditionally served with a small bowl of vinegar for dipping, along with a bowl of sweet and sour soup made of chicken blood and tofu.

201. Daizi Jiao

Origin: China

Description: Popular steamed dim sum dumplings. Made from wheat and tapioca starch, salt, oil, and boiling water, they are filled principally with fresh and dried scallops, ginger, Chinese chives, carrots, Shaoxing rice wine or dry sherry, soy sauce, and spices.

Served: With a dipping sauce.

202. Dan Jiao

Origin: China

Description: Traditionally eaten during Chinese New Year celebrations, these golden egg dumplings from Beijing resemble miniature omelets. Made from eggs, cornstarch, and salt, they are typically filled with pork, scallions, wine, sesame oil, and seasonings.

Served: With a dipping sauce, in broth, or in hot pots.

203. Dushbara

Origin: Azerbaijan

Description: Diminutive dumplings that resemble Italian tortellini. It is said that every Azerbaijani woman needs to know how to make them small enough to be able to fit 10 on a soup spoon. Made of wheat flour, egg, water, and salt, they are filled with minced lamb or beef, onion, and spices.

Served: In broth and topped with mint and a mixture of crushed garlic and vinegar.

Also known as: *Dushbere, dushpara,* düşbere.

204. Fara

Origin: Northern India (Uttar Pradesh and Bihar)

Description: These large, half-moon-shaped dumplings are a popular snack and breakfast item. Made with fine semolina, cumin, salt, water, and either rice or whole wheat flour, they are filled with spiced ground lentils.

Served: Alone or with green chutney.

Also known as: *Faraa, peetha, pitha, goojha, gujha, gooja, goitha.*

205. Fattisù

Origin: Northern Italy (Emiglia-Romagna)

Description: *Fattisù* are shaped like old-fashioned candies with twisted wrappings on both ends. Their name comes from *"fare su,"* which refers to the twisting action of closing the pasta dough. Made from wheat flour, eggs, and water, they are filled with Savoy cabbage, sausage, and local cheeses.

Served: With melted butter and grated local cheeses.

206. Fioroni

Origin: Southwestern Italy (Campania)

Description: These 4-inch-long dumplings presumably get their name from their close resemblance to a variety of fig

named *fiorone*. Made of wheat flour, lard, eggs, and salt, they are filled with Neapolitan salami, young and aged pecorino cheese, and eggs.
Served: Unlike most filled pastas, which require boiling, *fioroni* are drizzled with oil and baked. Some areas of Campania make smaller versions that are fried and served as an appetizer.

207. Gattafin
Origin: Northwestern Italy (Liguria)
Description: *Gattafin* are large, triangular dumplings. Their name derives from *gattafura*, a term that in the 14th century referred both to the pasta *raviolo* and to cake. Made of wheat flour, olive oil, water, and salt, they are filled with chard, eggs, cheese, and marjoram. its filling resembles another traditional dish from Liguria, the savory Easter pie *torta pasqualina*.
Served: Deep-fried in Ligurian olive oil and served piping hot.
Also known as: *Gattafuin*.

208. Gow Choy Gao
Origin: Southern China, province of Guangdong
Description: Dim sum dumplings known for the green hue that peeks through their translucent wrappers. The color is due to the dumpling's generous inclusion of *jiu cai*, or Chinese chives. Made from wheat and tapioca starches, peanut oil, salt, and boiling water, they are filled predominantly with shrimp and the garlicky chives.
Served: Steamed, accompanied by a dipping sauce. They are sometimes shaped into hockey puck-sized packets and fried.
Also known as: *Jiu cai xia bao, jiucai jiao, gao choi ha gao, gao choi gau*.

209. Guangdong Chunjuan
Origin: Southern China, province of Guangdong
Description: Cantonese spring rolls resembling gold bars and traditionally savored during the Chinese Spring Festival.

Guangdong chunjuan are known for their thin skins and delicate meat and vegetable fillings. Made from wheat flour, salt, water, and eggs, they are typically filled with pork, shrimp, scallions, vegetables, oyster sauce, and spices.
Served: With dipping sauce.

210. Guan Tang Bao
Origin: East-central China, province of Jiangsu
Description: These steamed round soup dumplings have the same circumference as a large coffee mug with a very thick, almost leathery wrapper. Made from wheat flour and boiling water, they are filled with pork, spices, and congealed broth.
Served: With a straw inserted into a dime-sized opening on top to allow one to drink the hot soup within.

211. Guōtiē
Origin: China
Description: More popularly known by Americans as pot stickers, these pan-fried dumplings are the crusty, thicker-skinned cousins of the boiled *shui jiao* dumpling (see entry). Made from wheat flour and water, they are filled with a variety of ingredients that range from pork and shrimp to bok choy, leeks, cabbage, ginger, and chives. In Muslim provinces they contain lamb.
Served: With a dipping sauce.
Also known as: *Wor tip, guo tie*.

212. Graviuole Molisane
Origin: Southern Italy (Molise)
Description: Square-shaped dumplings made from durum wheat flour, eggs, and salt, they are filled with ricotta, savory cheeses, vegetables, spices, and, occasionally, pork. In yesteryear, wild greens were used.
Served: As a first course with a rich and savory lamb ragù.
Also known as: *Ravioli alla montanara*.

213. Gujia

Origin: Northern India

Description: *Gujia* are crescent-shaped dessert dumplings with a rope-textured seal on the rounded side. Made of wheat and semolina flours and water, they are filled with a sweet mixture of roasted and grated dried fruits, coconut, a little semolina flour for crunch, and *khoya*, a ricotta cheese-like dairy product widely used in the cuisines of India, Nepal, Bangladesh, and Pakistan.

Also known as: *Guihia, purukiya.*

214. Gyoza

Origin: Japan

Description: The Japanese version of Chinese pan-fried *jiaozi* dumplings, *gyoza* differentiate themselves by having a much thinner skin and a crispy bottom. Made from wheat flour and water, they are traditionally filled with ground pork, chives, scallions, cabbage, ginger, garlic, soy sauce, and sesame oil, though a wide variety of other ingredients are used today. *Gyoza* are typically pan-fried (*yaki gyoza),* although they can also be boiled (*sui gyoza*) or deep-fried (*age gyoza*).

Served: Typically with a dipping sauce made of vinegar, soy sauce, and sometimes chile oil for breakfast and for lunch and dinner as an appetizer, side dish, or main course.

Also known as: *Guo tie,* pot stickers.

215. Har Gow

Origin: Southern China, province of Guangdong

Description: These translucently pinkish white, crescent-shaped steamed dumplings are a dim sum classic. Made from wheat flour and tapioca starch, oil or lard, salt, and boiling water, they are filled with shrimp, minced pork fat, bamboo shoots, scallions, Shaoxing rice wine, salt, and sugar.

Served: With a dipping sauce.

Also known as: *Xia jiao,* crystal shrimp dumplings. Vegetarian *har gow* are known as *chai kuih.*

216. Idrijski Žlikrofi

Origin: Western Slovenia, the town of Idrija in particular

Description: The town of Idrija and the surrounding areas have been famous since the mid-19th century for this small, pudgy, boat-shaped dumpling. Made from wheat flour, egg, and water or milk, they are filled with cooked potatoes, minced lard or smoked bacon, onion, seasoning, and herbs.

Served: On their own or as a side dish to meat, topped with pork rinds and various sauces, the most common being a mutton or rabbit and vegetable sauce called *bakalca.*

217. Knedle

Origin: Croatia

Description: Popular in Central and East European cuisines, *knedle* are boiled round dumplings the size of tennis balls. Made from mashed potatoes, eggs, butter, and flour, they are filled with pitted plums and, less frequently, also pitted apricots.

Served: As a dessert, main dish, or side dish, rolled in sugar and cinnamon or breadcrumbs seasoned with butter.

Also known as: *Knödel,* plum dumplings, *gombotzen, zwetschkenknodel, zwetschgenknodel, szilvasgomboc, knedle od sljiva, knedle sa sljivama, slivovi cmoki, slivkove knedle, svestkove knedliky, knedle ze sliwkami, gombotii cu prune.*

218. Ma Tuan

Origin: China

Description: Bronze-colored sweet fried dumplings that date back to the Tang Dynasty. Round and sesame-seed crusted, *ma tuan* are a staple on dim sum tables and at Chinese bakeries throughout the world. They are known for their hollow interior, which is caused by the expansion of the dough as it cooks. Made from glutinous rice flour, lard, sugar, and water, they are typically filled with sweetened black bean, red bean, or lotus nut paste.

Served: As a dessert or snack.

Also known as: *Zhimaqiu (*which translates to "sesame balls"), *matuan, maqiu, ma yuan, jeen doy, jin deui, jian dui, zhen dai.*

219. Jiaozi

Origin: Nepal

Description: Believed to have originated from Nepal, these steamed dumplings are now enjoyed throughout East Asia, particularly during the Chinese New Year festivities but also year-round in the northern Chinese provinces. *Jiaozi* translates to "tender ears" in Chinese, alluding to when they were used to treat frostbitten ears. Made from wheat flour and water, they are most commonly filled with pork, though they can also contain a wide variety of other ingredients such as lamb, vegetables, mushrooms, and even SPAM®.

Served: As an appetizer, side dish, or main course with a dipping sauce or vinegar with red pepper flakes.

Also known as: Similar to Chinese *baozi,* Mongolian *buuz,* Japanese *gyoza,* Korean *mandu,* and Nepalese *momo.* Also known as *shuijiao,* while pan-fried *jiaozi* are known as *jian jiao* or *gwou tei.*

220. Jiu Cai Bau

Origin: China

Description: Crispy pan-fried dumplings whose name literally means "chive box" because garlicky green Chinese chives can be seen peeking through their translucent skin. Shaped like turnovers with a rope-textured border, they range in size from an empanada to a calzone. Made with wheat flour and water, they are filled with mung bean threads, dried shrimp, ground pork, eggs, chives, salt, white pepper, and sesame oil.

Served: With vinegar or chili sauce.

Also known as: *Jiu cai he zi.*

221. Jiucai Jiao

Origin: China

Description: Pan-fried dumplings shaped like domes made with wheat and tapioca starches, salt, oil, and boiling water, they are filled principally with Chinese chives along with fresh and fried shrimp, soy sauce, Shaoxing rice wine, sugar, oyster sauce, and sesame oil.

Served: With a dipping sauce.

222. Kachori

Origin: India, Pakistan, and other parts of South Asia

Description: Shaped like lightly flattened golf balls, these fried dumplings are a popular snack. Made with wheat flour, oil, salt, and water, they are filled with heavily spiced yellow moong beans or horse beans.

Served: With a green or tamarind chutney.

Also known as: *Kachauri, kachodi, katchuri.*

223. Kalduny

Origin: Lithuania, Belarus, Poland

Description: Named after a Belarusian noble family, these pudgy, half-moon-shaped dumplings are made with wheat flour, eggs, water, and salt, and stuffed with a savory or sweet filling. Savory fillings include smoked ham and mushrooms or farmer's cheese and potatoes and, once cooked, are topped, respectively, with butter or thick sour cream. Sweet fillings consist of fresh or dried fruits that, once cooked, are topped with fruit syrups or sprinkled with cinnamon. Similar to the Russian *pelmeni* and Ukrainian *vareniki.*

Served: As a main course or dessert, depending on the filling.

Also known as: *Kolduny.*

224 Karanji

Origin: West-central India, state of Maharashtra

Description: These half-moon-shaped sweet fried dumplings are a culinary staple during Diwali, the annual Hindu festival of lights. Made of wheat and semolina flours, clarified butter, milk, and salt, they are filled with a mixture of unsweetened dried coconut, white sesame seeds, almonds, cashews, golden raisins, poppy seeds, and spices.

Served: Warm or at room temperature as a snack.

225. Kartoffelkloesse

Origin: Germany

Description: Large, round dumplings found in Germany, Austria, and the Czech Republic. Made from potatoes, wheat flour, cornstarch or potato starch, eggs, nutmeg, and salt, they are filled with a cube of sourdough bread.

Served: As a side with cabbage and any roast with gravy, though the most popular pairing is with sauerbraten.

226. Khinkali

Origin: Georgia

Description: Shaped like a filled bindle, these rich, soupy dumplings possess a substantial knot of dough at the top that is too thick and tough to eat and which is therefore discarded. Made from wheat flour, eggs, and water, they are filled with a variety of ingredients that include beef, pork, mushrooms, mashed potatoes, cottage cheese, a local fresh cow's milk cheese called *imeretian* and, in Muslim-majority areas, lamb. The traditional *khinkali* recipe, known as *khevsuruli* or *mtiuluri*, consists of pork, lamb or beef, onions, chili pepper, cumin, and salt, while an updated version, called *kalakuri*, also includes parsley or cilantro and crushed garlic.

Served: Plain or with black pepper.

227. Khuushuur

Origin: Mongolia

Description: A large handheld dumpling made from wheat flour and water, they are traditionally filled with minced mutton or beef, garlic, onion, and spices, though less common ver-sions containing potatoes, carrots, or cabbage also exist. *Khuushuur* are similar in some ways to their cousins, *buuz* and *bansh*. While the ingredients for their dough and filling are the same, they differ in size, shape, and cooking method. *Khuushuur*, the largest, are half-moon-shaped, and fried.

Served: With a carrot salad or lettuce and gherkins on the side, along with, unbelievably, ketchup or Maggi seasoning sauce.

228. Krafi

Origin: Northeastern Italy (Friuli-Venezia)

Description: Small and half-moon shaped, *krafi* are made from wheat flour, eggs, and oil, and filled with cheese, eggs, and sometimes a pinch of sugar.

Served: Seasoned with the pan juices of roasted meats and topped with freshly grated Parmigiano.

Also known as: *Crafi de Albona*.

229. Kreplach

Origin: Eastern Europe

Description: Dating back to Medieval times, these triangle-shaped dumplings made from wheat flour, eggs, and water, are filled with a varying combination of ingredients that can include chicken, beef, herbs, onion-spiced potatoes, and lightly sweetened dairy, the last of which is often enjoyed during the holiday of Purim.

Served: Deep-fried or in a rich chicken broth topped with sweet onion, dill, and black pepper.

230. Kroppkakor

Origin: Sweden

Description: Large round dumplings; they are particularly popular in northern Sweden. Made from potatoes and wheat flour, they are traditionally filled with pork and, less commonly, eel, herring, and smoked goose breast. *Kroppkakor* look very much like *pitepalt*, another Swedish dumpling, but are made from different ingredients: *krop-*

pkakor from boiled potatoes and wheat flour and *pitepalt* from raw potatoes and mostly barley flour.

Served: With butter, lingonberry preserves, crunchy bacon, and a glass of cold milk.

Also known as: *Kroppkaka.*

231. Labinksi Krafi

Origin: Eastern Croatia

Description: Traditional half-moon-shaped dumplings from the town of Labin. Made from wheat "00" flour, eggs, oil, and salt, they are filled with a semi-sweet mixture of at least two cheese varieties (from cow and sheep's milk), raisins, lemon zest, rum, and spices.

Served: The semi-sweet filling enables them to be served either as a starter, accompanied by a beef and chicken sauce, or as a dessert, topped with a sauce made from cherries and wine.

232. Laianelle

Origin: South-central Italy (Molise)

Description: These triangle-shaped dumplings are named after the rolling pin with which they are made. Made from durum wheat flour, eggs, and salt, they are filled with sheep's milk ricotta, nutmeg, and pepper.

Served: With a hearty lamb ragù and a generous topping of pecorino cheese.

Also known as: *Laganelle.*

233. Lemper Ayam

Origin: Indonesia

Description: A popular snack, these dumplings are cooked in and presented wrapped in banana leaves. Made from steamed sticky rice, they are filled with chicken, shallots, nuts, spices, coconut milk, and lime leaves.

Served: Warm or at room temperature alone or as a side dish.

234. Lo Mai Gai

Origin: Southern China

Description: Wrapped in lotus leaves, these popular dumplings resemble filled rectangular parcels. Made from white glutinous rice, they are filled with chicken, mushrooms, Chinese sausage, scallions, and sometimes dried shrimp or salted egg. There is a version, called *zongzi*, that is shaped like a pyramid and wrapped in bamboo leaves.

235. Luobo Si Su Bing

Origin: East-central China

Description: A Shanghai specialty, they are either round dumplings topped with a spiral pattern or oblong dumplings with a linear pattern; both are topped with toasted sesame seeds. Made from wheat flour, sugar, salt, lard or vegetable shortening, and warm water, they are filled with daikon radish, ham, scallions, oil, and spices.

236. Mandili 'Nversoi

Origin: Northern Italy (Piedmont)

Description: Literally "reversed handkerchiefs" in dialect, these dumplings resemble small, filled silk handkerchiefs that have been folded to create the shape of a triangle or rectangle. Made from durum wheat flour, water, and salt, they are filled with sausage, sweetbreads, chard, and cheese.

Served: With browned butter and sage or meat sauce.

237. Mandu

Origin: Korea

Description: Dumplings similar to Mongolian *buuz* and Turkish *mantı*. Made from wheat flour and water or wheat flour, glutinous rice flour, and boiling water, they are most often filled with a combination of ingredients that can include meat, tofu, vegetables, garlic, mushrooms, scallions, Chinese chives, toasted sesame oil, garlic, and ginger. A number of variants exist on the *mandu* theme, the most common being boiled *mulmandu*; pan-fried *gun mandu;* steamed *jjinmandu*; ball-shaped, wrapperless *gullin mandu;* pork and vegetable-stuffed *wang mandu;* rectangularly shaped and vegetable-filled *pyeonsu*; fish fillet-wrapped *eomandu;* pheasant, meat, beef, and tofu-stuffed *saengchi mandu;* pomegranate-shaped *seognyu mandu*; vegetable-stuffed *somandu*; and sea cucumber-shaped *gyuasang.*

238. Manti

Origin: Central Asia

Description: Popular in most Turkic cuisines, as well as throughout Central Asia and in Chinese Islamic cuisine, these slightly oval-shaped dumplings have a textured seam that resembles a fishbone on top. Made from wheat flour, eggs, oil, salt, sugar, and water, they are traditionally filled with a spiced meat mixture, usually lamb or ground beef, and sometimes pumpkin or squash are included. Typically boiled or steamed, *manti* vary significantly in size and shape depending on where they are made.

Served: With a variety of toppings that include butter, yogurt, sour cream, chile oil, spices, onion sauce, or a spicy tomato sauce.

Also known as: *Mantu, manty, klepe, kayseri mantisi, mantu kaddab, kaskoni.*

239. Mataz

Origin: Russia

Description: Popular among the Adyghe people of Russia, these half-moon-shaped dumplings have wavy, rounded edges. Made from wheat flour and water, they are traditionally filled with spiced lamb or ground beef, greens, onions, and spices. Mushrooms, potatoes, or cheese sometimes substitute for the meat.

Served: As a snack.

240. Maultasche

Origin: Germany, region of Swabia

Description: Large, rectangular dumplings, *maultasche* began appearing in German cookbooks in 1794 and have since earned the distinction of a "regional specialty." Made with wheat flour, salt, eggs, oil, and water, they are filled with spinach, onions, butter, stale bread, ground pork or beef, ham, or *schinkenwurst* (similar to bologna), eggs, breadcrumbs, spices, and parsley.

Served: Dressed in butter and onions, served in broth, or sliced up and pan-fried, along with onions and eggs.

241. Mezzelune

Origin: Northern Italy (Alto Adige/South Tyrol)

Description: Literally "half-moon," these dumplings are made from wheat and rye flours, eggs, olive oil, and water, and filled with ricotta, spinach, onion, garlic, Parmigiano, and nutmeg. There are also variations with potato, meat, beet, or sauerkraut fillings.

Served: As a starter with a brown butter and chive topping.

Also known as: Similar types of filled pasta can be found in other regions or areas of Italy: *casoncelli* in Lombardy, *cjarsons* in Friuli, and *casunziei* in the Dolomites. Also known as *schlutzkrapfen.*

242. Modak

Origin: West-central India, state of Maharashtra

Description: These sweet fried or steamed dumplings shaped like garlic heads have rounded pleats that come to a point. They are a traditional offering during the Hindu festival of Ganesh Chaturthi. Made from rice flour, ghee, and salt, they are filled with coconut and jaggery.

Served: Topped with a touch of melted ghee.

Also known as: *Kozhakkatta, modhaka, kadubu, modakam, modhakam, kozhakkattai, kudumu.*

243. Momo

Origin: Nepal and Tibet

Description: Though originating in Tibet and Nepal, these large, hearty dumplings are now considered a staple in Bhutan and the Darjeeling district of India. Shaped like a purse with a braided opening on top or as a round parcel, momo's dough is made from wheat flour and water. Traditionally filled with seasoned ground beef or yak meat, they now can also include pork, chicken, tofu, paneer or chhurpi cheese, cabbage, and/or potato.

Served: Steamed or fried with a fiery red chile-garlic-ginger-cilantro sauce called *sepen* and a bowl of broth.

Also known as: Similar to Chinese *baozi* and *jiaozi*, Mongolian *buuz*, Japanese *gyoza*, and Korean *mandu*. Also known as *momo-cha*.

244. Offelle

Origin: Northeastern Italy (Friuli-Venezia Giulia)

Description: Savory square dumplings that share the same name as a popular sweet treat traditionally served during Italy's Carnival celebration, especially in Friuli-Venezia Giulia. The word offa refers to Roman spelt cakes that were traditionally offered to the gods and has now come to mean "a portion of food reserved for the gods." Made of wheat flour, potatoes, eggs, and yeast, they are filled with meat, sausage, and spinach.

Served: As a starter, topped with melted butter and grated local cheese.

245. Onde Onde

Origin: Malaysia

Description: Small green, sweet, round dumplings coated with shredded coconut, *onde onde* get their celadon green color from fresh or frozen pandan, the aromatic leaves of a perennial grass. Made from glutinous rice flour and water infused with pureed pandan and vanilla extract, they are filled with palm sugar balls that melt once boiled. For best results, *onde onde* are served the same day they are prepared.

Served: As a snack or dessert.

Also known as: *Ondeh-ondeh, klepon.*

246. Pannicelli

Origin: Central Italy (Tuscany)

Description: Square dumplings whose name, which means "swaddling blanket," reflects their considerable 3-inch size. Made from wheat flour and eggs, they are filled with ricotta, local cheese, spinach or chard, and spices.

Served: With tomato sauce or gratinéed in the oven with butter and Parmigiano.

247. Pansotti

Origin: Northwestern Italy (Liguria)

Description: These dumplings can be found in the shape of a square, triangle, or half-moon. Made from wheat flour, water, and white wine, they are filled with ricotta, a mix of local wild herbs and greens, and Parmigiano.

Served: With a savory sauce made from pine nuts and walnuts.

Also known as: *Pansooti*, which in dialect means "potbellied," an allusion to what might happen by consuming too many.

248. Pelmeni

Origin: Russia

Description: Dumplings resembling small, pudgy flying saucers. While similar to Ukranian *vareniky* and Polish pierogi, *pelmeni* are known for their thin pasta shells and generous filling. Made of wheat flour, eggs, water, and salt, they are filled with a mixture of ground meats (pork, beef, lamb, mutton, or sometimes just fish), pureed onion, spices, and aromatics. *Pelmeni,* unlike *vareniky* and pierogi, are never sweet.

Served: In broth or boiled and served topped with butter or sour cream and chopped herbs.

249. Pierogi

Origin: Eastern Europe
Description: These half-moon-shaped dumplings with a pleated border were initially considered peasant food when they first appeared, most likely in Poland. Today they are the national dish of Poland, Ukraine, and Slovakia, as well as a culinary staple throughout Eastern Europe. Made from wheat flour, eggs, oil, water, and salt, they can be either savory or sweet. Savory fillings include combinations of mashed potatoes, meat, fried onions, farmer's cheese, cabbage, spinach, sauerkraut, and/or mushrooms. Dessert pierogi are filled with sweetened farmer's cheese, jam, pitted prunes, and/or fresh fruit.
Served: First boiled and then pan-fried, they are served topped with melted butter (for savory or sweet) or sour cream and fried onions (for savory).
Also known as: *Varenyky, bryndzové pirohy, colţunaşi, derelye.*

250. Pi.Fasaac

Origin: Northern Italy (Lombardy)
Description: These unusual dumplings have all but disappeared except as an offering during summer festivals. The name *pi.fasaac*, which means "swaddled newborn" in dialect, accurately depicts its shape. Made from wheat flour, water, oil, salt, and eggs, they are filled with local cheeses, breadcrumbs, aromatics, and spices.
Served: With browned butter and sage sauce.
Also known as: *Pipihahas, ravioli col manubrio* (ravioli with handlebars).

251. Pitepalt

Origin: Sweden
Description: Large, round dumplings named after the Swedish city Pitea, from which, it's believed, they originated. Made from grated raw potatoes mixed mainly with barley flour and small quantities of wheat flour, they are traditionally filled with bacon or minced meat. Many variations exist. The two most well known are filling-less *flatpalt* and *blodplat*, which contains the blood of cows, pigs, or reindeer.
Served: With melted butter, lingonberry preserves, crunchy bacon, and a glass of cold milk on the side.
Also known as: *Pitepalt* look very similar in shape to *kroppkakor*, another Swedish dumpling, but are made from different ingredients: *pitepalt* from raw potatoes and mostly barley flour and *kroppkakor* from boiled potatoes and wheat flour. Also known as *palt*.

252. Purulzoni

Origin: Sardinia
Description: Round or square dumplings fmade from durum wheat flour, salt, and lukewarm water, they are filled with sweetened fresh pecorino cheese from the northeast Gallura region of Sardinia.
Served: With a simple tomato and basil sauce.

253. Pyzy Ziemniaczane

Origin: Poland
Description: Large and round, *pyzy ziemniaczane* are the only Polish dumpling in the category of *kluski* (see entry) that have a filling. Made with boiled and finely grated potatoes, flour, eggs, and salt, they are filled with a wide variety of savory ingredients that include ground meats, vegetables, and aromatics. When made with a sweet filling, they are called *knedle*.

254. Qingtuán

Origin: East-central China, provinces of Jiangsu and Zhejiang, and the municipality of Shanghai
Description: These steamed green rice dumplings date back 2,000 years ago to the Zhou Dynasty. *Qīngtuán*, which contain a sweetened bean paste, are traditionally consumed in Shanghai to commemorate Tomb Sweeping Day every April. Their intense green hue used

to come exclusively from mixing the juice of the fragrant medicinal Chinese herb mugwort with glutinous rice flour; today it is also created by using any chlorophyll-rich juice. Their filling consists of sweetened bean or sesame paste.

Served: As a snack or dessert.

Also known as: *Qing tuan.*

255. Raviole Alagnesi

Origin: Northern Italy (Piedmont)

Description: These walnut-sized dumplings reflect the historical Germanic influence on northern Italian cooking. Made from corn flour, small quantities of wheat flour, stale bread, butter, and water, they are filled with sausage, salami, and local cheeses.

Served: Boiled in meat broth or milk and then served with melted butter and Parmigiano.

256. Ravioli

Origin: Northern Italy (Lombardy)

Description: World-renowned square dumplings with long historical roots. While mentions of a preparation similar to ravioli date as far back as the 12th century, they officially appeared in the Italian courts of Milan and Mantova in the 16th century. Over time, ravioli dispersed regionally and eventually into plebeian kitchens throughout Italy, where they were consumed on special holidays. Made from wheat flour, eggs, and sometimes water and salt, ravioli are shaped in rounds, half-moons, triangles, or rectangles and have an inexhaustible number of fillings that can contain meats, fish, ricotta, squash, spinach, and much more as their principal ingredient.

Served: Topped with local sauces and condiments.

Also known as: *Raviolini* and formerly known as *raffiolo, rafiolo, ravaiolo, raviuolo,* and *ravviolo.*

257. Ravioli alla Genovese

Origin: Northwestern Italy (Liguria)

Description: Rectangular dumplings made from wheat flour, eggs, and water, they are filled with a mixture that contains brains, sows' udders, pieces from the spinal cord of calves, vegetables, and spices. Other filling variations from Liguria include either squash or a mixture of greens, ricotta, pine nuts, and raisins.

Served: Traditionally served with a long-simmered and aromatic meat and mushroom sauce called *il tocco di carne* (the touch of meat).

258. Ravioli alla Napoletana

Origin: Southwestern Italy (Campania)

Description: Half-moon-shaped dumplings made from wheat flour, eggs, and water that are filled with mozzarella, ricotta, prosciutto, and spices.

Served: Traditionally served with the *ragù alla napoletana,* a rich and savory meat and tomato-based sauce.

259. Ravioli alle Cime di Rapa (Ravioli with Turnip Greens)

Origin: Southern Italy (Puglia)

Description: Large, half-moon-shaped dumplings that celebrate turnip greens, which are the horticultural pride of the extensive plateaus found in Puglia. Made from wheat flour, salt, eggs, and water, they are filled with, predictably, turnip greens that have been sautéed in local olive oil with garlic.

Served: With *ciccioli* (pork cracklings) and red chilis.

260. Ravioli Amari

Origin: Sicily

Description: Literally "bitter ravioli," these square dumplings are not bitter at all. The term *"amari,"* is used to distinguish them from the island's popular rich

pastry known as *ravioli*. Made from durum wheat flour, salt, and water, they are filled with ricotta and marjoram or sometimes mint.
Served: With a rich pork ragù.
Also known as: *Raviolia*.

261. Ravioli Della Pusteria (Ravioli of Puster Valley)

Origin: Northern Italy (Trentino-Alto Adige)

Description: These half-moon-shaped dumplings reflect, in their ingredients, the area's proximity to Austria and Switzerland and the seasonal availability of ingredients. Made from rye and wheat flours, eggs, oil, and water, they are filled with sauerkraut in the winter, nettles and poppy seeds in the spring, and spinach, ricotta, and potatoes in the summer.
Served: With melted butter and grated cheese.
Also known as: *Schlutzer*.

262. Ravioli di San Leo

Origin: Eastern Italy (Marche)
Description: Half-moon-shaped dumplings from the town of San Leo. Made from wheat flour, eggs, and water, they are typically filled with mixed wild greens, ricotta, Parmigiano, lemon zest, and spices, although their actual filling depends on what is available at any given time in the fields.
Served: With a hearty meat ragù and topped with grated local cheese.

263. Ravioli di Seirass e Maiale (Ravioli with Seirass Ricotta and Pork)

Origin: Northern Italy (Piedmont)
Description: Half-moon-shaped and sometimes green dumplings made from wheat flour, egg yolks, and, at times, spinach, they are filled with stewed pork and *"seirass"*, a fragrant local ricotta made from the individual or collective milk of cows, sheep, and goats.
Served: With a prized local butter that has been browned with sage, and topped with grated Parmigiano.

264. Ravioli Dolci di Ricotta (Sweet Ricotta Ravioli)

Origin: Southern Italy (Abruzzo)
Description: Half-moon-shaped dumplings that, despite their sweetness, are traditionally served as a first course at important functions. Made from wheat flour and eggs, they are filled with sheep's milk ricotta, sugar, lemon zest, and cinnamon.
Served: As a first course topped with melted butter and Parmigiano.
Also known as: *Ravioli materni* (maternal ravioli) and *u cazini* (dialect for "the calzone").

265. Raviore

Origin: Northwestern Italy (Liguria)
Description: Rectangular dumplings with twisted ends that resemble a life-size wrapped piece of candy, *raviore* are the gastronomic pride of Liguria. Made from wheat flour and water, they are filled with wild herbs and greens such as lemon verbena, wild spinach, costmary, mint, and nettles.
Served: With cream and chopped walnuts or with a traditional topping that includes butter, local pecorino cheese, and some of the dumpling's cooking water.

266. Rotolo Ripieno (Stuffed Roll)

Origin: Italy
Description: A relative newcomer to Italy's historical resume of pastas, *rotolo ripieno* has become popular throughout the boot, in no small part due to its ease of preparation. This filled pasta roll consists of a sheet of pasta spread with a savory filling that is then rolled up, wrapped in cheesecloth, boiled, and, once cooled, sliced into medallions. Made from wheat flour, eggs, and water (sometimes the eggs are omitted), they are filled with varying mixtures of ingredients that can include meats, cheeses, and fish. The filling is usually

bound with ricotta.

Served: Gratinéed with butter, béchamel, ragù, or tomato sauce.

Also known as: *Rotolo imbottito* (stuffed pasta), *pasta al sacco* (bagged pasta), *strudel*.

267. Rufioi della Valle dei Mòcheni

Origin: Northern Italy (Trentino-Alto Adige)

Description: This large, square-shaped filled pasta is named after the Mòcheni, an ethnic German minority that fled feudal wars to seek refuge in Trentino-Alto Adige. Made from wheat flour, eggs, water, and salt, they are filled with Savoy cabbage, leeks, grana Trentino cheese (a local cheese similar to Parmigiano), and cinnamon.

Served: As a starter with foaming butter and freshly grated grana Trentino.

268. Saku Sai Mu

Origin: Thailand

Description: A popular street food, *saku sai mu* are translucent round dumplings with a bumpy exterior. Made from tapioca pearls, salt, and boiling water, they are filled with pork or chicken, shallots, fish sauce, sugar, roasted peanuts, cilantro, and garlic.

Served: Bundled in lettuce and topped with cilantro, mint, and a piece of chile.

269. Samosas

Origin: India

Description: Golden dumplings shaped like slightly deflated pyramids, samosas are popular street food and a culinary staple in India, the Arabian peninsula, and Africa. Made from wheat flour, butter, water, and salt, they are typically fried, though baked versions also exist. Many *samosa* recipes are vegetarian and contain ingredients such as potatoes, onions, carrots, green peas, lentils, macaroni, and noodles, while meat-containing *samosas* are filled with minced lamb, beef, or chicken, vegetables, and spices.

Served: With a variety of chutneys.

Also known as: *Samoosa*.

270. Scarfiuni

Origin: Southern Italy (Puglia)

Description: Half-moon–shaped dumplings made from durum wheat flour, water, eggs, and salt, they are filled with ricotta and pecorino cheese.

Served: As a starter with a hearty meat ragù and pecorino.

Also known as: *Ravioloni*.

271. Scarpinocc

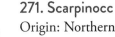

Origin: Northern Italy (Lombardy)

Description: "Shoe" in dialect, these bean-shaped dumplings resemble the traditional footwear worn by the citizens of the small town of Parre. Made from flour, milk, eggs, and butter, they are filled with cheese, breadcrumbs, garlic, and spices.

Served: As a starter with melted butter and grated local cheeses.

Also known as: *Betoi, orecchie*.

272. Schiaffettoni

Origin: Southern Italy (Campania, Molise, Puglia, Basilicata, Calabria)

Description: These dumplings used to resemble a stuffed and flattened roll with tightly sealed ends. Today's *schiaffettoni*, which literally mean "hard slaps," have become large, mass-produced rigatoni that can either be stuffed, like *cannelloni*, or used unstuffed empty in baked dishes. Made principally from durum wheat flour and eggs, though regular flour, water, and a small amount of olive oil can also be included, they are filled with meats and sausages.

Served: As a starter with a hearty meat ragù and red chile peppers.

Also known as: *Schiaffuni, schiaffune, sckaffune, scaffettune. Schiaffettoni*, when dried, are also known as *paccheri*.

273. Schultzkrapfen

Origin: Northern Italy (Trentino-Alto Adige)

Description: Half-moon-shaped dumplings from Trentino-Alto Adige that reflect the area's cultural ties and geographical proximity to Austria. Made from rye and wheat flours, eggs, oil, and water, they are filled with spinach, ricotta, potatoes, and, depending on the season, chives, nettles, poppy seeds, or sauerkraut.

Served: With melted butter and topped with local cheese, in particular a strongly flavored gray Austrian cheese named *graukäse*.

Also known as: *ravioli atesini, ravioli della pusteria, roffioi,* and *rofioi*.

274. Shanghai Wontons

Origin: East-central China, municipality of Shanghai

Description: Boiled dumplings that resemble tortellini but have a much sturdier skin to hold their substantial filling. Made from wheat flour and water, they are traditionally filled with pork, a delicate wild green known as shepherd's purse (or bok choy), sesame oil, soy sauce, and other seasonings.

Served: With a dipping sauce for breakfast, lunch and dinner.

275. Siu Mai

Origin: Inner Mongolia

Description: A popular dim sum offering, these golden, short, and cylindrically shaped dumplings are encased in frilly, paper-thin wrappers that leave the filling slightly exposed on top. Fillings vary with the region and ingredient availability. Traditional Cantonese *shumai* from the southeastern Chinese province of Guangdong contain ground pork, shrimp, pork fat, Chinese black mushrooms, scallions, ginger, Shaoxing rice wine, soy sauce, sesame oil, broth, and sometimes bamboo shoots or water chestnuts.

Served: Alone, or sometimes topped with crab roe or a whole shrimp, with a dipping sauce.

Also known as: *Shaomai, shao mai, shui mai, shu mai, sui mai, shui mei, siew mai, siomai, xiu mai, khanom chip.* A much smaller version of *siu mai*—called *fei cui shao mai*—also exists.

276. Shishbarak

Origin: Persia

Description: Believed to have originated in pre-Islamic Persia, these square dumplings resemble ravioli and are popular in Iraq, Lebanon, Syria, Jordan, and Palestine. Made from wheat flour, water, and salt, they are filled with ground beef, onions, herbs, and spices.

Served: In individual bowls with rice vermicelli and topped with a yogurt sauce.

Also known as: *Shish barak* and *tatarbari*.

277. Shuijiao

Origin: China

Description: Purse-shaped, juicy dumplings with a braid-like top that are essentially boiled *jiaozi (see jiaozi* entry). Traditionally consumed during Chinese New Year festivities, they are now a year-round food, especially in northern China. Made from wheat flour and water, they are typically filled with ground pork, Napa cabbage, ginger, scallions or Chinese chives, Shaoxing rice wine, oil, and spices, though ingredients often vary according to preference or ingredient availability.

Served: In broth or accompanied by a dipping sauce.

Also known as: *Shui jiao.*

278. Siomay

Origin: Indonesia

Description: Cylindrical dumplings encased in hollowed-out bitter gourds or large pieces of tofu. They are traditionally filled with a fish paste made principally of wahoo, although tuna, mackerel, and shrimp are also used.

Served: Considered a light meal or snack, they are cut into bite-size pieces and served topped with peanut sauce, sweet soy sauce, chili sauce, and/or a squeeze of kaffir lime juice. Other accompaniments include steamed cabbage and potatoes, and hard-boiled eggs.

Also known as: *Somay.*

279. Slicofi

Origin: Northeastern Italy (Friuli-Venezia Giulia)

Description: Rectangular dumplings made from flour, oil, and water, they are filled with potatoes, breadcrumbs, cheese, herbs, and sometimes ham.

Served: As a starter topped with buttered breadcrumbs.

Also known as: *Gnocchi di Idria, gnocchi di pasta ripieni di patate, slikrofi, zlikofi.*

280. Sui Kow

Origin: China

Description: Large half-moon-shaped dumplings with pleated edges, *sui kow* loosely translates to "water dog" or "water chestnut," possibly alluding to how they are often boiled and served in broth. Made from wheat flour, water, and salt, they are traditionally filled with whole shrimp, minced pork, chopped vegetables, water chestnuts, herbs, and spices.

Served: In broth with wonton noodles or steamed rice, though they can also be served alone in broth, deep-fried, pan-fried, or steamed as pot stickers.

281. Tang Yuan

Origin: China

Description: One of two sticky rice dumplings traditionally eaten during the Lantern Festival, held on the last day of the Chinese New Year festivities. (The other is *yuan xiao.* Unlike *yuan xiao*, which are made by continuing to dip the filling in water and then rolling it in glutinous rice flour until—in snowball fashion—

the dumpling skin is formed, *tang yuan*'s rice skin is kneaded by hand.) *Tang yuan* come in a variety of shapes, sizes, and colors, though traditionally they are round, slightly smaller than golf balls, and white. Made from glutinous rice flour and water, they become soft and chewy once boiled. Most often they are sweet and filled with sesame paste, ground peanuts, or red bean paste, though savory versions containing pork and green onions also exist.

Served: On their own or, more commonly, in a sweet bean, sesame, or ginger broth.

Also known as: *Tangtuan, tangyuan.*

282. Tordei

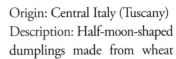

Origin: Central Italy (Tuscany)

Description: Half-moon-shaped dumplings made from wheat flour, eggs, salt, and water, they are filled with chicken giblets, mortadella, and aromatics.

Served: As a starter with local sauces.

283. Tordelli

Origin: Central Italy (Tuscany)

Description: These dumplings were historically made without meat in observance of religious fast days. Today, *tordelli* can be found with meat fillings (usually veal, sausage, or brains), chard, and grated cheese, though there are still vegetarian versions, the three primary ones being ricotta and grated cheese, just ricotta, and milk-soaked bread. Made from wheat flour, eggs, salt, a little milk, and extra virgin olive oil, they are half-moon-shaped and have ridged edges.

Served: As a starter with a hearty meat ragù. Or, on meatless days, with melted butter and grated cheese.

284. Tortelli

Origin: Northern (Lombardy) and central Italy (Emiglia-Romagna, Tuscany)

Description: These dumplings are now widespread throughout Italy. The word *tortelli*, which derives from *torta* or cake, started appearing in historic writings in the 14th century. *Tortelli* come in a variety of sizes and shapes, including square, half-moon, and twisted into roundish hat-like parcels. The filling varies as well, depending on the region, season, and preference.

285. Tortelli Bastardi

Origin: Northwestern Italy (Liguria)

Description: Literally "bastard *tortelli*," tortelli bastardi are half-moon-shaped dumplings whose inclusion of chestnut flour (along with wheat flour, eggs, milk, and salt) in the dough reflects the ample supply of chestnuts in the region's forests. They are filled with ricotta and grated cheese.

Served: As a starter with different local condiments.

286. Tortelli Cremaschi

Origin: Northern Italy (Lombardy)

Description: Triangular dumplings that originated from, and are named after, the city of Crema. Made from wheat flour, eggs, and water, they are filled with a mixture of crushed amaretto cookies, raisins, candied citron, a hard, spicy cookie named *mustazzitt*, mint, Parmigiano, and spices.

Served: As a starter with melted butter.

287. Tortelli del Melo

Origin: Central Italy (Tuscany)

Description: Square dumplings made from wheat flour, eggs, and water, they are filled with chard, local ricotta and other cheeses, breadcrumbs, and spices.

Served: As a starter, traditionally with a hearty meat ragù or a mushroom sauce.

Also known as: *Ravioli del melo*.

288. Tortelli del Montefeltro

Origin: Eastern Italy (Marche)

Description: Round dumplings named after the court of Montefeltro, which, in medieval times, was regarded as a beacon of culture and gastronomy. Made from wheat flour and eggs, they are filled with ricotta and other local fresh cheeses, lemon zest, and honey.

Served: As a starter with melted butter, sage, Parmigiano, and a local minty-tasting herb called *mentuccia*.

289. Tortelli del Mugello

Origin: Central Italy (Tuscany)

Description: Triangular dumplings made from wheat flour and eggs, they are filled with chestnuts, grated cheese, spices, and olive oil.

Served: As a starter with melted butter and topped with local cheese.

290. Tortelli di Patate

Origin: Central Italy (Tuscany)

Description: Large, square, potato-filled dumplings from Tuscany, which is known for its distinctive and delicately flavored tubers. Made from wheat flour, eggs, and salt, they are filled predominantly with cooked local potatoes as well as local cheeses and spices.

Served: As a starter with a hearty meat ragù.

291. Tortelli di Zucca

Origin: Northern Italy (Lombardy)

Description: Rectangular or half-moon-shaped dumplings from Lombardy, known for the delicately sweet pumpkins that grow in the fertile, foggy fields around Mantua. Made from wheat flour, eggs, and salt, they are filled predominantly with cooked pumpkin as well as local cheeses and spices.

Served: As a starter with a hearty meat ragù.

Also known as: *Tortei, blisgon*.

292. Tortelli Maremmani

Origin: Central Italy (Tuscany)

Description: Square dumplings from the Maremma Grossetana area of Tuscany. Made from wheat flour and eggs, they are filled with spinach or nettles, ricotta and local cheeses, and spices.

Served: As a starter with a hearty meat ragù.

293. Tortelli Romagnoli

Origin: Northern Italy (Emilia-Romagna)

Description: Triangular dumplings made from wheat flour and eggs, they are traditionally filled with local greens, ricotta, and nutmeg, though a variation with potatoes and ricotta also exists.

Served: As a starter with various sauces and sometimes with the wild spinach that grows abundantly in the pine forests around the city of Ravenna.

Also known as: *Cappelletti romagnoli.*

294. Tortelli Sguazzarotti

Origin: Northern Italy (Lombardy)

Description: Large, triangular dumplings made from wheat flour, eggs, and water, they are filled with just two ingredients: *borlotti*, or cranberry beans, and *salsa saorina*, a unique condiment made with walnuts, sugar, apples, squash, orange rind, and a dark, sweet, thick paste called *vincotto*. The name derives from the verb *sguazzare*, which means "to flounder," alluding to how the *tortelli* swim in the *salsa saorina.*

Served: Hot or cold, topped with *salsa saorina.*

Also known as: *Turtei sguassarot.*

295. Tortellini

Origin: Northern Italy (Emilia-Romagna)

Description: Ring-shaped dumplings that, along with *tagliatelle* and *lasagna*, make up the defining triumvirate of the cuisine of Bologna, the capital of the region of Emilia-

Romagna. Tortellini's defining characteristics are its diminutive size and the thinness of its pasta dough. Made from "00" wheat flour and eggs, they are traditionally filled with prosciutto, mortadella, a mixture of veal, beef, and pork, beef marrow, Parmigiano, and spices, though ingredients sometimes vary.

Served: As a starter in beef or chicken broth and topped with Parmigiano.

Also known as: *Presuner, cappelletti.*

296. Tortello sulla Lastra

Origin: Northern (Emilia Romagna) and central Italy (Tuscany)

Description: Literally *"tortello* on the slab," these rectangular dumplings are found in the mountainous terrain that connects the regions of Tuscany and Emilia Romagna. Made from wheat flour and the water in which the filling's pumpkin has cooked, they are filled with a mixture of pumpkin, potatoes, *lardo*, seasonings, and cheeses like *cacao raviggiolo* or pecorino.

Served: Plain and piping hot straight from a sandstone griddle, where they are cooked much like pancakes.

297. Turle

Origin: Northwestern Italy (Liguria and the Maritime Alps)

Description: Half-moon-shaped dumplings made with wheat flour, water, and sometimes eggs, they are filled with cooked potatoes and fresh mint.

Served: As a starter with butter, garlic or leeks, and hazelnuts, or with cream and walnuts. Both reflect the tradition of the region's *cucina bianca*, or "white cuisine," which distinguishes itself by the white color of many of its dishes.

298. Turtei della Valle Tanaro

Origin: Northern Italy

Description: Large, square dumplings from northern Italy, particularly in the upper Valle Tanaro area in the

Ligurian Alps. Made from flour, fresh local cream, and salt, they are filled with cooked potatoes and wild herbs such as nettle tips.
Served: Either deep-fried or cooked on a griddle.

299. Turtej Cu La Cua
Origin: Northern Italy (Emilia-Romagna)

Description: Unusually shaped, these dumplings look like teardrops with a braid on top and an elongated tail at one end. In fact, part of its name, *cu la cua*, means "with a tail." Traditionally made on the feast of St. John the Baptist to celebrate the successful completion of the green walnut harvest and the distillation of *nocino*, or walnut liqueur. Made from wheat flour and eggs, they are filled with either ricotta and greens or ricotta and mascarpone cheese.
Served: As a starter with a hearty meat ragù or with melted butter and Parmigiano.
Also known as: *Tortelli piacentini*.

300. Turtres Ladine
Origin: Northern Italy (Veneto and Trentino-Alto Adige)

Description: Large, round fried dumplings from the valleys straddling the regions of Veneto and Trentino-Alto Adige. *Turtres Ladine* derive their name from an ethnic group, the Ladins, who cultivate the area's mountainous terrain. Made from rye and wheat flours, eggs, water, butter, and salt, they are filled with onion, sauerkraut, juniper berries, and cumin.
Also known as: *Turtres de craut*.

301. Uszka
Origin: Poland

Description: Literally "little ears," *uszka* are dumplings that look like nurses' caps and are part of the traditional Polish and Ukrainian Christmas Eve menu. Made from wheat flour, eggs, water, and salt, they are filled predominantly with mushrooms as well as onion, garlic, breadcrumbs, and parsley.
Served: In clear broth or *barszcz* (Poland's version of *borscht)*, or as a side dish, drizzled with butter and sprinkled with chopped parsley.

302. Vareniky
Origin: Ukraine

Description: Similar in size and shape to Polish pierogi, *vareniky* are popular half-moon-shaped dumplings made with wheat flour, sour cream, butter, and eggs, and filled with potatoes and cheese.
Served: First boiled and then typically pan-fried with onions, *vareniky* are served, along with some of the cooked onions, topped with sour cream or *zazharka*, a condiment made of bacon, onions, and butter.
Also known as: *Varenyki*.

303. WonTon
Origin: China

Description: A dumpling found through China that varies in size and shape and is served in dozens of different ways. Made from flour, eggs, water, and salt, they are typically filled with ground pork and shrimp, though there are plenty of variations on this.
Served: In soups, or fried, or poached and accompanied by a dipping sauce. The smallest wontons, called *xiao huntun*, literally meaning "small wonton," are customarily served in a soup with condiments such as pickles, ginger, sesame oil, and cilantro.
Also known as: Yuntun tang, hong you yuntun, hunt un, pangsit, wantan, wanton, wuntun.

304. Xia Mia Chang
Origin: China

Description: A favorite dim sum offering, *xia mia chang* are translucent, roll-shaped steamed dumplings. Made with rice flour, cornstarch, tapioca starch, oil, salt, and water, they are filled with whole shrimp, oyster sauce, and sesame oil.

Served: Topped with thinly sliced scallions and accompanied by a dipping sauce.

Also known as: *Xia chang. Niu rou chang* and *ji si chang* are similar to *xia mi chang* but contain, respectively, minced beef and orange, and chicken and vegetables instead of shrimp.

305. Xian Shui Jiao

Origin: China

Description: Crispy-chewy deep-fried dumplings shaped and similar in size to eggs, *xian shui jiao* are a dim sum staple. Made from glutinous rice flour, wheat starch or potato flour, lard, sugar, and water, they are typically filled with a variety of ingredients that can include pork, mushrooms, sausage, vegetables, aromatics, coconut, and/or sweet bean paste. *Chashao xian shui jiao* and *shu cai xian shui jiao* are similar to *xian shui jiao* but their fillings contain, respectively, pork and mushrooms, and shrimp and vegetables.

Also known as: *Haam sui gok* in Cantonese.

306. Xiaolongbao

Origin: Southern China, region of Jiangnan

Description: These small soup-filled dim sum dumplings are named after *xiaolong*, the bamboo baskets in which they are traditionally steamed. Made from bread and wheat flours, oil, and boiling water, they are filled traditionally with pork, ginger, and seasonings, though variations exist that also include crab, roe, seafood, other meats, and vegetables. *Xiaolongbao* always contain cubes of congealed broth that, once heated, create the coveted "soup" experience.

Served: Steamed, often topped with crab roe.

Also known as: *Xiao long bao, xiaolong bao, xiao long bao, xiaolong mantou, sioh-lon meu-doe, xiaolong*-style *mantous.*

307. Yao Gok

Origin: Southeastern China, province of Guangdong

Description: Little, crunchy, purse-shaped dumplings made from wheat flour, eggs, oil, and sugar, they are filled with a mixture of coconut, ground peanuts and sesame seed, and sugar.

Served: Typically served as a sweet snack, though some savory versions of this dumpling also exist.

308. Yuan Xiao

Origin: China

Description: One of two sticky rice dumplings traditionally eaten during the Lantern Festival, held on the last day of the Chinese New Year festivities. (The other is *tang yuan*. Unlike *tang yuan*, in which the rice dough is kneaded by hand, *yuan xiao* are made by continuing dip the filling in water and then rolling it in glutinous rice flour until, in snowball fashion, the dumpling skin is formed.) *Yuan xiao* come in a variety of shapes, sizes, and colors, though traditionally they are round, slightly smaller than golf balls, and white. Made from glutinous rice flour and water, they become soft and chewy once boiled. Most often they are sweet and filled with red bean paste, walnuts, sesame paste, jujube paste, dried fruit, and rose petals, though savory versions containing meat and vegetables can also be found.

Served: On their own or, more commonly, in a sweet or savory broth.

Also known as: *Yuanxiao.*

309. Zembi D'Arzillo

Origin: Northwestern Italy (Liguria)

Description: These square dumplings derive their name from the Arab word *zembil*, which was a woven basket made of palm leaves used to transport fish, and *arzillo*, which describes the fragrance of just-caught fish and algae washed ashore. Made from wheat flour and water, they are filled with leftover cooked fish, ricotta, greens, eggs, and varied herbs that always include borage.

Served: As a starter with a tomato-based mushroom or seafood sauce.

Also known as: *Zembi darziglio*.

310. Zha Jiao
Origin: China

Description: Literally "fried dumpling" in Chinese, *zha jiao* are similar to fried wontons with the exception of their shape. While wontons have a considerable amount of crunchy wrapper, *zha jiao* have a meatier filling and are teardrop shaped with a braidlike closure on top. Made from wheat flour and water, they are filled with a variety of ingredients ranging from meat and seafood to vegetables.

Also known as: *Zha yuntun* are similar to *zha jiao*, except that their dough is made with wheat flour, salt, water, and eggs.

311. Zheng Jiao
Origin: China
Description: Literally "steamed

dumpling" in Chinese, *zehen jiao* are steamed *jiaozi* (see entry) that are crescent-shaped and have an elaborately pleated closure. Made from wheat flour and water, they are filled with a combination of ingredients that can include pork, beef, shrimp, cabbage, assorted vegetables, chives, and other spices and aromatics.

Served: With a dipping sauce.

Also known as: *Zhengjiao*.

312. Zongzi
Origin: China

Description: Triangular or cone-shaped rice dumplings traditionally eaten during the Duanwu Festival, though today they are consumed throughout the year. Made from glutinous rice, soy sauce, and salt, they are filled and then boiled or steamed, encased in bamboo leaves (traditionally) or lotus, maize, banana, canna, shell ginger, or pandan leaves. *Zongzi* have many regional variations and their fillings vary accordingly. They can include red bean paste, taro root, salted duck eggs, pork belly, shredded pork or chicken, peanuts, Chinese sausage, pork fat, and shiitake mushrooms.

Served: Alone or accompanied by a dipping sauce.

Also known as: *Zong, bakcang, bacang, zang, machang, pya htote, nom chang, bachang*.

DUMPLINGS WITHOUT FILLING

313. Banku
Origin: West Africa, Ghana in particular

Description: *Banku* are large, uneven tennis ball-sized dumplings. Made from fermented white corn dough, grated cassava root, and water, the dough turns into a thick, whitish, pastelike porridge that, once cooked, is shaped into spheres.

Served: In stews and soups.

314. Canederli
Origin: South-central Europe

Description: Literally "bread dumplings," these large dumplings are found in south-central Europe and in the northern Italian regions of Lombardy, Trentino-Alto Adige, and Friuli-Venezia Giulia. Made from stale bread, occasionally wheat flour, milk, eggs, prosciutto or speck, parsley, and Parmigiano, the dough is shaped, dredged in wheat flour, and boiled in broth or water.

Served: As a side dish topped with breadcrumbs toasted in butter or in broth.

Also known as: *Knodel, gnocchi di pane, canedeli, gnocchetti chiavennaschi.* A variation from Trentino-Alto Adige, *canederli di fegato,* replaces the prosciutto or speck with chicken liver and is served in broth.

315. Cassulli

Origin: Italy, the island of San Pietro

Description: Small concave dumplings from Carloforte, a fishing and resort town on San Pietro, located off the coast of Sardinia. *Cassulli* resemble Ligurian *corzetti* (see entry), likely the result of Ligurian immigrants who came to the island in the 18th century. When Barbary kings banned local fishing off the Ligurian coast, Charles Emmanuel III intervened by welcoming the displaced fishermen to the Isola di San Pietro. As a result, Ligurian dialect is still spoken there today. Made from wheat and durum wheat flours, water, and eggs

Served: With a tuna and tomato-based sauce.

316. Capunsei

Origin: Northern Italy (Lombardy)

Description: A specialty of the city of Cereta, these dumplings first became popular in the 15th century when the princely House of Gonzaga ruled the area. Made with breadcrumbs, grated cheese, eggs, butter, and nutmeg, they are shaped like elongated ovals with tapered ends and are cooked in beef broth.

Served: Topped with browned butter and sage sauce and grated cheese.

317. Ciciones

Origin: Sardinia

Description: Chewy and chickpea-sized, these boiled dumplings get their remarkable golden color from saffron, whose use is pervasive in Sardinian cuisine. Made from durum wheat flour, saffron, and water.

Served: With hearty meat sauces, topped with pecorino.

Also known as: *Pizzottis, ciuccionis, cravao, macarones coidos, cigiones, zizzones.*

318. Donderet

Origin: Northern Italy (Piedmont)

Description: Irregular-shaped dumplings made with wheat flour, milk, eggs, salt, and often boiled potatoes.

Served: With butter and grated local cheese. Traditionally, the butter used is the rich and distinctive *burro di malga,* which is made from the raw whole milk of local cows that graze on mountain pastures.

Also known as: *Dandarini, strangolapreti piemontesi.*

319. Dunderi

Origin: Southwestern Italy, along the Amalfi Coast

Description: Plump, bite-size rectangular dumplings made from wheat flour, ricotta, egg yolks, Parmigiano, nutmeg, and salt. They also occasionally include the zest from the celebrated lemons for which the area is so well known.

Served: With melted butter or tomato sauce.

320. Gnoc de Schelt

Origin: Northern Italy (Lombardy)

Description: These small dumplings made from wheat flour, chestnut flour, buckwheat flour, eggs, milk, and salt are practically extinct now. The inclusion of a variety of flours reflects a time when the inhabitants of struggling rural economies needed to use any and all local ingredients at their disposal for survival.

Served: With a simple tomato sauce.

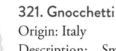

321. Gnocchetti

Origin: Italy

Description: Smaller versions of *gnocchi* (see entry), these diminutive, typically spherical dumplings can be found throughout Italy with innumerable variations in the ingredients and shapes. Made from water, salt, and soft wheat flour or durum wheat flour or a mixture of the two, they can also include cornmeal, buckwheat and/or chestnut flours, or breadcrumbs. A richer *gnocchetti* variety containing eggs and at times either boiled potatoes or ricotta also exists. Mass-produced varieties, which look like smooth or ridged elongated concave shells, are made from durum wheat flour and water.

Served: With a variety of meat, cheese, and vegetable sauces and in legume or vegetable soups. Mass-produced *gnocchetti* are also served in plain broth.

Also known as: *Torsellini, gnocchetti de gris, sbirici, zlicnjaki, pestarici, gnuchet, maccheroni matti, gnocchi al latte, battollo, topini, suricitti, gnocchetti alla dispreta, falchetti, frascarelli, gnucchitti pilusi, gnocchi 'ncotti, cianfrachiglie, suricidde,* and *gnucchetti*. A variety called *gnochi mes'ci d'castagne* is made with chestnut flour.

322. Gnocchetti di Tricarico

Origin: Southern Italy (Basilicata)

Description: Cylindrical, bite-size dumplings found in the region of Basilicata, particularly in the little town of Tricarico. Made from durum wheat flour and water.

Served: With traditional local sauces that often include vegetables and cheeses.

Also known as: *Cantarogn*, which sometimes also contain eggs.

323. Gnocchi di Patate

Origin: Italy

Description: Popular throughout Italy and in many parts of the world, potato *gnocchi* are soft, pillowy, bite-size oval dumplings that often carry a ridged pattern. Considered the ancestor of almost all Italian pasta, *gnocchi* were originally made from flour or stale bread and water, but as society became more economically comfortable, eggs and potatoes were added to the dough. Made from cooked potatoes, wheat flour or durum wheat flour, eggs, and salt, they are shaped into slightly concave mounds to facilitate the cooking process. Mass-produced varieties are made only from durum wheat flour and water.

Served: With a variety of meat and cheese sauces, topped with grated Parmigiano, or in legume soups.

324. Gnocchi di Semolino

Origin: Italy

Description: Rich and almost custardy dumplings found in the central region of Lazio, as well as Sardinia, Trentino, Umbria, and Friuli-Venezia Giulia. Made from semolina flour, eggs, milk, butter, Parmigiano, and salt, the dough is cooked on the stove before being spread out on a flat surface and cut into thick medallions, cookie-cutter style.

Served: Most often served topped with grated Parmigiano and melted butter and browned in the oven, though sometimes they are topped with meat ragù and grated pecorino.

Also known as: *Gnocchi alla romana, pillas.*

325. Gnocchi di Zucca

Origin: Northern Italy (Valle d"Aosta, Veneto, Friuli-Venezia Giulia)

Description: Literally "pumpkin gnocchi," *gnocchi di zucca* are irregularly shaped, orange-hued dumplings. Made from wheat flour, pumpkin, eggs, salt, and sometimes Parmigiano, they can also contain lemon zest, nutmeg, and a few drops of Marsala wine.

Served: With browned butter and sage sauce, topped with grated Parmigiano, or covered in fontina cheese and broiled.

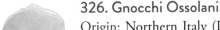

326. Gnocchi Ossolani

Origin: Northern Italy (Lombardy and Piedmont)

Description: Nutritionally rich spiced dumplings, *gnocchi ossolani* are particularly prevalent in Val d'Ossola. Made from wheat flour, chestnut flour, pumpkin, potatoes, eggs, salt, and spices, they are shaped into slightly concave, ridged mounds.

Served: With browned butter and sage sauce and topped with grated Parmigiano.

327. Gnoche de Ciadin

Origin: Northern Italy (Veneto)

Description: Literally "basin gnocchi," these irregularly shaped, bite-sized dumplings get their name from the wooden bowl, *ciadin*, in which they are traditionally prepared. *Gnoche de ciadin* are made from wheat flour, eggs, and milk.

Served: Most often with melted butter and grated local cheese.

328. Gnudi

Origin: Central Italy (Tuscany)

Description: An old term that literally means "nude," *gnudi* refer to ravioli (see entry) without pasta pockets, or "nude fillings." The preparation originated in Tuscany but they are now prepared throughout Italy. Made from wheat flour, chard or other similar greens, ricotta, grated cheese, sometimes eggs, and spices.

Served: With meat sauces or browned butter and sage sauce, topped with Parmigiano.

Also known as: *Malfatti, ravioli gnudi, strangolapreti, strozzapreti.*

329. Halusky

Origin: Central and Eastern Europe

Description: Thick, soft, oval-shaped dumplings made from wheat flour, water, and the occasional addition either of grated potatoes or eggs, *halusky* resemble plumper, smoother German *spätzle* (see entry).

Served: With a variety of presentations that can include cabbage, hard-boiled eggs, and stews. When served with the condiment *bryndza*, made from sheep's milk cheese and fried bacon bits, the combination becomes the Slovak national dish, *bryndzové halušky.*

Also known as: *Galuska, haluska, nokedli, galusca, virtinukai.*

330. Kenkey

Origin: West Africa, Ghana in particular

Description: Large, irregularly shaped dumplings, *kenkey* are considered a staple. They are made from a fermented white corn dough that is more akin to a thick, paste-like porridge that, once cooked halfway, is wrapped in banana leaves and steamed.

Served: In stews and soups or as a side to meat dishes.

331. Kluski Leniwe

Origin: Poland

Description: Diamond-shaped dumplings called "lazy dumplings" because of the ease of their preparation. Made from the fresh Polish cheese *twarog*, flour, eggs, salt, and sugar.

Served: First boiled and then pan-fried in butter, they are served topped with toasted buttered breadcrumbs, sugar, and cinnamon. Served as a main course.

332. Kluski Slaskie

Origin: Poland, region of Silesia in particular

Description: Small, plump, dome-shaped dumplings made from mashed potatoes, potato flour, eggs, and salt, they have a distinctive dimple in the middle.

Served: As a main course with roasts or topped with a variety of sauces or bacon cracklings.

Also known as: *Gumiklyjzy,* Silesian dumplings. A variation called *kluski czarned* (also known as *kluski żelazne, kluski żelazne, kluski szare,* black dumplings, iron dumplings, and gray dumplings) contains grated potatoes, which give them a darker appearance.

333. Kluski Lane

Origin: Poland

Description: Stringlike dumplings known as "poured noodles," *kluski lane* are very similar in appearance to German *spätzle* (see entry). Made from a thin batter of eggs, milk or melted butter, flour, and salt, they are formed by pouring thin streams of batter into boiling water or directly into soup.

Served: In broth, sometimes with vegetables.

334. Kluski Kladzione

Origin: Poland

Description: Irregularly shaped noodles known as "laid dumplings." Made from eggs, milk, flour, salt, and sometimes whipped egg whites or soda water, they are formed by dropping, or "laying," dough into boiling salted water with the help of a spoon or knife.

Served: In soups, by themselves drizzled with melted butter and accompanied with sautéed onions or bacon, and as a side to meat dishes.

335. Knodel

Origin: Central and Eastern Europe

Description: Round, mandarin orange-sized boiled dumplings, found particularly in Germany and Austria, *knodel* derive their name from the Latin word *nodus,* or "knot." Made from potatoes, flour, eggs, and salt.

Served: As a side to roast duck, with a variety of roasted meats and gravy, in soups, and sometimes as a dessert.

Also known as: *Cnigle, klöße, klösse, knedlík, knedlička, canederli alla Tiralese.*

336. Kopytka

Origin: Poland

Description: Literally "little hooves," *kopytka* are hoof-shaped potato dumplings popular in Polish, Belarusian, and Lithuanian cuisines. Made from grated potatoes, flour, eggs, and salt, they are typically first boiled and then pan-fried, although in Belarusian and Lithuanian cooking they are first baked and then boiled or stewed.

Served: With a variety of toppings such as sautéed onions and bacon, mushroom sauce, and cheese.

Also known as: *Kapytki.*

337. Malloreddus

Origin: Sardinia

Description: Shaped like plump shells with a ridged surface, *malloreddus* are saffron-hued dumplings made from durum wheat flour (this kind of wheat has grown on the island since Roman times), saffron, water, and salt. Two variations exist. The first, *maccarronis de orgiu,* contains barley flour, and the second, *chiusone,* is more closed in shape.

Served: With hearty sauces containing meat or sausage or with tomato sauce, topped with grated pecorino cheese.

Also known as: *Macarones caidos, macarones cravaos.*

338. Pantruca

Origin: Chile

Description: Flat, irregularly shaped dumplings made from flour, water, salt, and oil.

Served: In vegetable soups or broth topped with chopped parsley.

Also known as: *Pancutra, pancucha.*

339. Paternoster

Origin: Central Italy (Abruzzo and Lazio)

Description: Literally "Our Father," these bite-sized dumplings are partic-

ularly found in the town of Leonessa, which is located in northern Lazio. Named after a prayer, *paternoster* reflect a time when housewives recited prayers as a way of measuring the pasta's cooking time. Made from flour and water, they are shaped into dumplings that are then rolled over the tines of a fork or a special comb created for this very purpose to give them ridges.
Served: With a ricotta-based sauce.

340. Pidiyum Kozhiyum

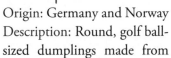

Origin: Southern India, state of Kerala
Description: A culinary staple of the St. Thomas Christians (they are also known as Syrian Christians) of Kerala, these white, round dumplings date back to the 4th century. Made from roasted rice flour, grated coconut, shallots, garlic, and spices, they are boiled in a thick, whitish sauce made from coconut milk and rice flour.
Served: With beef dishes and chicken curries.
Also known as: *Pidi.*

341. Raspeball

Origin: Germany and Norway
Description: Round, golf ball-sized dumplings made from cooked and raw potatoes and barley and wheat flours.
Served: With boiled meats, smoked sausage, steamed rutabaga, crispy bacon bits, and melted butter.
Also known as: *Klubb, kumle, komle, kompe, baller, potetball.* When fresh or salted minced fish is added to the potato dough, *raspeballs* become *fiskeball.*

342. Shlishkes

Origin: Hungary
Description: Small, pudgy, oval-shaped dumplings popular in Hungarian and Ashkenazic cooking. Made from potatoes, flour, eggs, and salt.
Served: Rolled in breadcrumbs that have been toasted in butter or with onions fried in *schmaltz,* or rendered chicken fat.
Also known as: *Shlishkas, krumplinudli, nudli, kopytka.*

343 Spätzle

Origin: Germany
Description: Literally "small sparrows," *spätzle* are small, soft, irregularly shaped boiled dumplings that can be found in the cooking of Germany (particularly in the south), Austria, Switzerland, Hungary, and Alsace in France. Prior to being mass-produced, spätzle were made either by hand or with a spoon and its shape was thought to resemble the bird after which they are named. Made from semolina flour, eggs, salt, and sometimes water. Two sweet variations using fruit also exist, *apfelspätzle* (apple *spätzle*) and *kirschspätzle* (cherry *spätzle*).
Served: In soups, with roasted meats and gravy, with lentils and sausages, or with fried onions and cheese.
Also known as: *Spätzli, chnöpfli, knöpfle, nokedli, csipetke, galuska.*

344. Topfenknodel

Origin: Czech Republic
Description: Originally from the western region of Bohemia, these large, round dumplings are now also popular in Austrian and German cuisines. Made from the thick, tangy curd cheese quark (also known as *topfen),* butter, bread, eggs, sour cream, semolina flour, salt, lemon, and vanilla sugar.
Served: With sour cream or rolled in sweetened breadcrumbs.
Also known as: *Turos gomboc, syrove knedliky, kluskiin.*

FRESH PASTA
& NOODLES

*I*conic Italian film director and screenwriter Federico Fellini was right: Life is a combination of magic and pasta. Mix flour with water, add an egg and a dash of imagination. Wave a wooden spoon, and poof! Before your eyes appears an almost infinite array of shapes such as whimsical *farfalle* or "butterflies," cute *orecchiette* or "little ears," thick, stringlike udon noodles, and stubby, hearty *ding ding chao mian* or "stir-fried noodle cubes." Like magic, you have tender or chewy comfort in a bowl.

THREE-EGG BASIC PASTA DOUGH

YIELD: A LITTLE OVER 1 POUND; ABOUT 6 SERVINGS / ACTIVE TIME: 1 HOUR / TOTAL TIME: 1 ½ HOURS

This recipe is your standard, go-to recipe when you want to simplify the pasta making process and still get delicious results. Suitable for hand- or machine-rolling, it forms a malleable and nicely golden-hued dough that is a pleasure to knead by hand since it resembles PlayDoh in texture and produces tender pasta. For best results, all the ingredients—even the flours—need to be at room temperature. Keep in mind that the thickness suggestions for each pasta shape are just suggestions. If you prefer any pasta shape slightly thicker or thinner, you are the master of your own dining destiny.

Suitable for fettuccine, *pappardelle, tagliatelle, maltagliati, quadretti, farfalle, fazzoletti, cappellacci dei briganti, ravioli, ravioloni, caramelle, pansoti, tortellini, tortelloni, agnolotti, anolini,* and *cappellacci di zucca* (butternut-squash stuffed pasta).

INGREDIENTS:

2 ¾ cups all-purpose flour

3 large eggs

1 egg yolk

1 Mixing and kneading the dough by hand: On a flat work surface form the flour into a mountain-like mound. Create a well in the center, then add the eggs, egg yolk, and 2 tablespoons water. Using a fork or your fingertips, gradually start pulling the flour into the pool of egg, beginning with the flour at the inner rim of the well. Continue to gradually add flour until the dough starts holding together in a single floury mass, adding more water—1 tablespoon at a time—if the mixture is too dry to stick together. Once the dough feels firm and dry, and can form a craggy looking ball, it's time to start kneading.

Begin by working the remaining flour on the work surface into the ball of dough. Using the heel of your hand, push the ball of dough away from you in a downward motion. Turn the dough 45 degrees each time you repeat this motion, as doing so incorporates the flour more evenly. As you continue to knead, you'll notice the dough getting less and less floury. Eventually it will have a smooth, elastic texture. If the dough still feels wet, tacky, or sticky, dust it with flour and continue kneading. If it feels too dry and is not completely sticking together, wet your hands with water and continue kneading. Wet your hands as many times as you need in order to help the flour shape into a ball.

Knead for 8 to 10 minutes. It seems like a long time, but it accomplishes two things.

1. It creates a dough that is smooth and springy.

2. It eliminates any air bubbles and bits of unincorporated flour in the dough.

The dough has been sufficiently kneaded when it is very smooth and gently pulls back into place when stretched.

Mixing and kneading the dough with a mixer: Put the flour in a large bowl. Create a well in the center. Using a hand-held or stand mixer fitted with the dough (spiral) attachment, set the speed to 1 or 2 and slowly add half of the eggs and 1 tablespoon water while mixing. Mix until the wet ingredients have been fully incorporated into the flour, then add the remaining eggs and another tablespoon water and continue to mix on low speed until fully incorporated. Soon the dough will begin coming together in a single floury mass. Add water—1 tablespoon at a time—if the mixture is too dry to stick together. Add flour—1 teaspoon at a time—if the mixture is too wet and sticky. Once the dough feels firm and dry, and can be formed into a coarse looking and slightly tacky ball, it's time to start kneading.

Turn the speed on the mixer to medium-high, typically notch 4, and mix for 8 to 10 minutes. The dough has been sufficiently kneaded when it is very smooth and gently pulls back into place when stretched.

2 Resting the dough: Wrap the ball of dough tightly in clear food wrap and let rest for 1 hour—2 hours is even better if you have the time. If using within a few hours, leave it out on the kitchen counter, otherwise refrigerate it (it will keep for up to 3 days). If you do refrigerate it, however, the dough may experience some discoloration (but it won't affect the flavor at all).

3 Rolling the dough: Cut the dough into four even pieces. Set one piece on a smooth work surface and wrap up the rest in clear food wrap to prevent drying. Shape the dough into a ball, place it on the surface, and, with the palm of your hand, push down on it so that it looks like a thick pita. Using a rolling pin, roll the dough to ½ inch thick. Try as much as possible to keep the thickness and width of the dough "patty" even, as it will help

the dough fit through the pasta machine more easily.

Set the pasta machine for the flat roller (no teeth) on the widest setting (typically notch 1). Now feed the dough into the rollers. As a rather rough, thick sheet of pasta comes out the other end, make sure to support it with your hand or fingers. Fold the sheet of dough over itself twice, as you would a letter, and then turn the folded dough on its side and feed it back into the machine again. Repeat this folding and feeding it back into the machine three more times. This process is called "laminating" and it makes the dough more sturdy and manageable to handle.

Set the machine to the second-widest setting (typically notch 2) and feed the dough into the rollers. Again, support the pasta as it comes out the other side. Again fold it as you would a letter and feed it into the rollers on its short side; repeat this three more times.

Set the machine to the third-widest setting (typically notch 3) and feed the dough into the rollers. Again, support the pasta as it comes out the other side. Again fold it as you would a letter and feed it into the rollers on its short side; repeat this three more times.

Set the machine to the second-smallest setting (typically notch 4). Feed the pasta into the rollers. Again, support the pasta as it comes out the other side. At this point, there is no need to laminate the pasta.

Stop rolling at this point if making sheets of pasta ⅛ inch/2mm thick for pansoti, agnolotti, maltagliati, farfalle, and cappellacci dei briganti. If you like your fettuccine, pappardelle, and tagliatelle a little thicker, then this is the setting for you.

Set the machine to the smallest setting (typically notch 5). Cut the pasta sheet in half and feed it into the rollers. Again, support the pasta as it comes out the other side.

This last setting makes pasta sheets so thin (about 1/16 inch/1.5 mm thick) that you can see light through them. It is ideal for filled pastas like ravioli, ravioloni, tortellini, tortelloni, ano-

lini, cappellacci di zucca, and *caramelle,* whose fillings can easily be overshadowed by too much surrounding dough, as well as *fazzoletti* and *quadretti.* If you like your *fettuccine, pappardelle,* and *tagliatelle* very thin, then this is the setting for you.

The just rolled pasta will be very delicate, so be gentle handling it. If the pasta sheet is too long to easily handle, carefully cut it in half. Lightly dust each sheet with flour and lay it on a surface lined with wax or parchment paper. Repeat all the above steps with the remaining pieces of dough.

4 Drying the sheets of dough: Pasta dough needs to be allowed to dry for approximately 15 minutes after it has been rolled out and before it is cut into strands or other shapes. This drying time makes the dough less sticky and easier to handle. Keep in mind that when the pasta is very thick or wide it will need to be turned over to ensure thorough and even drying (not necessary for thin noodles). Pasta sheets are now ready to be shaped or cut according to recipe requirements.

The notable exception to this rule is if you are making stuffed pasta. In this case, not letting the dough dry is best because the slight stickiness helps the pasta adhere better and creates a better seal.

5 Drying the cut pasta before cooking: Once fresh pasta has been cut (see the individual recipes), toss it with semolina flour and then place it on a lightly floured surface (again, with semolina flour) and allowed it to dry for at least 15 minutes before cooking. This drying period is important because it allows the pasta to dry enough to become firmer and less sticky, which prevents the pasta from sticking together as it cooks (shaped pasta also holds its shape better when allowed to dry slightly before cooking). More specific drying times are indicated in individual pasta recipes. Just note that the drying process can be fickle. Depending on temperature, humidity levels, and the size of the noodles or pasta, the process may take a longer or shorter period of time than stated in the recipes. It is probably best to avoid making pasta on very humid days. If you can't avoid it, turn on the air conditioning or even a movable fan to help the air circulate more effectively.

EGG PASTA DOUGH *with* DURUM FLOUR

YIELD: ¾ POUND PASTA; 4 SERVINGS / ACTIVE TIME: 1 HOUR / TOTAL TIME: 1 ½ HOURS

Restaurants often include durum flour in their pasta because it makes the resulting pasta sturdier, less likely to stick, and more difficult to overcook. They also add olive oil to make the dough stretchier and easier to handle. I recommend using this recipe when you are making pasta that will not be used right away or when you are making large portions for a crowd (this recipe can be doubled and tripled). It is also ideal for people who love a substantial chew in their pasta and is well suited for both spaghetti and linguine, since they are at their best when they still have a pleasant bite to them.

This particular combination of flours initially creates a dough that is tough to knead (it feels like a new, unworked block of clay). It softens substantially after two hours of resting and is very easy to roll into sheets. Once cooked, it remains very firm and springy. For best results, all the ingredients—even the flour—need to be at room temperature,

This dough is suitable for linguine, spaghetti, and *spaghetti alla chittara.*

Note: Spaghetti and linguine require their own designated attachments on a pasta maker and need to be purchased separately. Follow the manufacturer's directions to prepare them once you've rolled the dough to its specified thickness.

INGREDIENTS:

- 1 cup + 3 tablespoons finely milled type "00" wheat flour OR 1 ⅓ cups + 1 tablespoon all-purpose flour

- 7 tablespoons durum flour

- 1 ½ teaspoons salt

- 8 large egg yolks

- 2 tablespoons extra virgin olive oil

1 Mixing and kneading the dough by hand: On a flat work surface combine the flours and salt and form it into a mountain-like mound. Create a well in the center, then add the egg yolks, olive oil, and 2 tablespoons water. Using a fork or your fingertips, gradually start pulling the flour into the pool of egg, beginning with the flour at the inner rim of the well. Continue to gradually add flour until the dough starts holding together in a single floury mass, adding more water—1 tablespoon at a time—if the mixture is too dry to stick together. Once the dough feels firm and dry, and can form a craggy looking ball, it's time to start kneading.

Begin by working the remaining flour on the work surface into the ball of dough. Using the heel of your hand, push the ball of dough away from you in a downward motion. Turn the dough 45 degrees each time you repeat this motion, as doing so incorporates the flour more evenly. As you continue to knead, you'll notice the dough getting less and less floury. Eventually it will have a smooth, elastic texture. If the dough still feels wet, tacky, or sticky, dust it with flour and continue kneading. If it feels too dry and is not completely sticking together, wet your hands with water and continue kneading. Wet your hands as many times as you need in order to help the flour shape into a ball.

Knead for 8 to 10 minutes. It seems like a long time, but it accomplishes two things.

1. It creates a dough that is smooth and springy.

2. It eliminates any air bubbles and bits of unincorporated flour in the dough.

The dough has been sufficiently kneaded when it is very smooth and gently pulls back into place when stretched.

Mixing and kneading the dough with a mixer: Put the flours and salt in a large bowl and stir well with a spoon. Create a well in the center. Using a hand-held or stand mixer fitted with the dough (spiral) attachment, set the speed to 1 or 2 and slowly add half of the egg yolks, 1 tablespoon of oil, and 1 tablespoon water while mixing. Mix until the wet ingredients have been fully incorporated into the flour, then add the remaining egg yolks and oil and another tablespoon water and continue to mix on low speed until fully incorporated. Soon the dough will begin coming together in a single floury mass. Add water—1 tablespoon at a time—if the mixture is too dry to stick together. Add flour—1 teaspoon at a time—if the mixture is too wet and sticky. Once the dough feels firm and dry, and can be formed into a coarse looking and slightly tacky ball, it's time to start kneading.

Turn the speed on the mixer to medium-high, typically notch 4, and mix for 8 to 10 minutes. The dough has been sufficiently kneaded when it is very smooth and gently pulls back into place when stretched.

2 Resting the dough: Wrap the ball of dough tightly in clear food wrap and let rest for 1 hour—2 hours is even better if you have the time. If using within a few hours, leave it out on the kitchen counter, otherwise refrigerate it (it will keep for up to 3 days). If you do refrigerate it, however, the dough may experi-ence some discoloration (but it won't affect the flavor at all).

3 Rolling the dough: Cut the dough into four even pieces. Set one piece on a smooth work surface and wrap up the rest in clear food wrap to prevent drying. Shape the dough into a ball, place it on the surface, and, with the palm of your hand, push down on it so that it looks like a thick pita. Using a rolling pin, roll the dough to ½ inch thick. Try as much as possible to keep the thickness and width of the dough "patty" even, as it will help the dough fit through the pasta machine more easily.

Set the pasta machine for the flat roller (no teeth) on the widest setting (typically notch 1). Now feed the dough into the rollers. As a rather rough, thick sheet of pasta comes out the other end, make sure to support it with your hand or fingers. Fold the sheet of dough over itself twice, as you would a letter, and then turn the folded dough on its side and feed it back into the machine again. Repeat this folding and feeding it back into the machine three more times. This process is called "laminating" and it makes the dough more sturdy and manageable to handle.

Set the machine to the second-widest setting (typically notch 2) and feed the dough into the rollers. Again, support the pasta as it comes out the other side. Again fold it as you would a letter and feed it into the rollers on its short side; repeat this three more times.

Set the machine to the third-widest setting (typically notch 3) and feed the dough into the rollers. Again, support the pasta as it comes out the other side. Again fold it as you would a letter and feed it into the rollers on its short side; repeat this three more times.

Stop rolling at this point if making pasta shapes ⅛ inch/3 mm thick like spaghetti alla chitarra and spaghetti.

Set the machine to the second-smallest setting (typically notch 4). Feed the pasta into the rollers. Again, support the pasta as it comes out the other side. At this point, there is no need to laminate the pasta.

Stop rolling at this point if making sheets of pasta ⅛ inch/2mm thick for linguine.

The just rolled pasta will be very delicate, so be gentle handling it. If the pasta sheet is too long to easily handle, carefully cut it in half. Lightly dust each sheet with flour and lay it on a surface lined with wax or parchment paper. Repeatall the above steps with the remaining pieces of dough.

4 Drying the sheets of dough: Pasta dough needs to be allowed to dry for approximately 15 minutes after it has been rolled out and before it is cut into strands or other shapes. This drying time makes the dough less sticky and easier to handle. Keep in mind that when the pasta is very thick or wide it will need to be turned over to ensure thorough and even drying (not necessary for thin noodles). Pasta sheets are now ready to be shaped or cut according to recipe requirements.

The notable exception to this rule is if you are making stuffed pasta. In this case, not letting the dough dry is best because the slight stickiness helps the pasta adhere better and creates a better seal.

5 Drying the cut pasta before cooking: Once fresh pasta has been cut (see the individual recipes), toss it with semolina flour and then place it on a lightly floured surface (again, with semolina flour) and allow it to dry for at least 15 minutes before cooking. This drying period is important because it allows the pasta to dry enough to become firmer and less sticky, which prevents the pasta from sticking together as it cooks (shaped pasta also holds its shape better when allowed to dry slightly before cooking). More specific drying times are indicated in individual pasta recipes. Just note that the drying process can be fickle. Depending on temperature, humidity levels, and the size of the noodles or pasta, the process may take a longer or shorter period of time than stated in the recipes. It is probably best to avoid making pasta on very humid days. If you can't avoid it, turn on the air conditioning or even a movable fan to help the air circulate more effectively.

ALL YOLK PASTA DOUGH

YIELD: ¾ POUND; 4 SERVINGS / ACTIVE TIME: 1 HOUR / TOTAL TIME: 1½ HOURS

INGREDIENTS:

- 1½ cups all-purpose flour
- ⅓ cup + 2 tablespoons finely milled "00" flour
- 8 large egg yolks
- 3 tablespoons tepid water, more if needed

Dough made exclusively with egg yolks has a beautiful rich and golden color and makes smooth and very tender pasta. Just as importantly, it is easier to roll out without tearing. Because of this, it is an excellent dough for making thin, fragile pasta strands or miniature filled pasta. Once cooked, it is very tender and yielding, and readily absorbs pasta sauces. For best results, all the ingredients—even the flours—need to be at room temperature. Finally, because this dough is made exclusively from egg yolks, it will discolor rather quickly. As such, I recommend making this variation when you are planning on using it right away because it does tend to develop an unattractive light green tint to it, even when refrigerated and perfectly safe to eat.

Suitable for lasagna, *sagne chine, cannelloni, tajarin, rotoli,* angel hair, and *tagliolini.*

Note: Unlike the other pasta shapes in this recipe, which can be made with standard pasta makers or by hand, angel hair requires its own designated attachment on a pasta maker and needs to be purchased separately. It is the only way to create the strand's round shape. For best results, roll the dough through the thinnest setting on your pasta maker and then run it through the angel hair cutter like you would with fettuccine and *tagliatelle.* You can, of course, dust the pasta sheets, roll them up, and then slice them into paper-thin slivers, but they will not be round.

1 Mixing and kneading the dough by hand: On a flat work surface combine the flours and form it into a mountain-like mound. Create a well in the center, then add the egg yolks and water. Using a fork or your fingertips, gradually start pulling the flour into the pool of egg, beginning with the flour at the inner rim of the well. Continue to gradually add flour until the dough starts holding together in a single floury mass, adding more water—1 tablespoon at a time—if the mixture is too dry to stick together. Once the dough feels firm and dry, and can form a craggy looking ball, it's time to start kneading.

Begin by working the remaining flour on the work surface into the ball of dough. Using the heel of your hand, push the ball of dough away from you in a downward motion. Turn the dough 45 degrees each time you repeat this motion, as doing so incorporates the flour more evenly. As you continue to knead, you'll notice the dough getting less and less floury. Eventually it will have a smooth, elastic texture. If the dough still feels wet, tacky, or sticky, dust it with flour and continue kneading. If it feels too dry and is not completely sticking together, wet your hands with water and continue kneading. Wet your hands as many times as you need in order to help the flour shape into a ball.

Knead for 8 to 10 minutes. It seems like a long time, but it accomplishes two things.

1. It creates a dough that is smooth and springy.

2. It eliminates any air bubbles and bits of unincorporated flour in the dough.

The dough has been sufficiently kneaded when it is very smooth and gently pulls back into place when stretched.

Mixing and kneading the dough with a mixer: Put the flours in a large bowl and stir well with a spoon. Create a well in the center. Using a hand-held or stand mixer fitted with the dough (spiral) attachment, set the speed to 1 or 2 and slowly add half of the egg yolks and 1 tablespoon of the water while mixing. Mix until the wet ingredients have been fully incorporated into the flour, then add the remaining egg yolks and another tablespoon water and continue to mix on low speed until fully incorporated. Soon the dough will begin coming together in a single floury mass. Add water—1 tablespoon at a time—if the mixture is too dry to stick together. Add flour—1 teaspoon at a time—if the mixture is too wet and sticky. Once the dough feels firm and dry, and can be formed into a coarse looking and slightly tacky ball, it's time to start kneading.

Turn the speed on the mixer to medium-high, typically notch 4, and mix for 8 to 10 minutes. The dough has been sufficiently kneaded when it is very smooth and gently pulls back into place when stretched.

2 Resting the dough: Wrap the ball of dough tightly in clear food wrap and let rest for 1 hour—2 hours is even better if you have the time. If using within a few hours, leave it out on the kitchen counter, otherwise refrigerate it (it will keep for up to 3 days). If you do refrigerate it, however, the dough may experience some discoloration (but it won't affect the flavor at all).

3 Rolling the dough: Cut the dough into four even pieces. Set one piece on a smooth work surface and wrap up the rest in clear food wrap to prevent drying. Shape the dough into a ball, place it on the surface, and, with the palm of your hand, push down on it so that it looks like a thick pita. Using a rolling pin, roll the dough to ½ inch thick. Try as much as possible to keep the thickness and width of the dough "patty" even, as it will help the dough fit through the pasta machine more easily.

Set the pasta machine for the flat roller (no teeth) on the widest setting (typically notch 1). Now feed the dough into the rollers. As a rather rough, thick sheet of pasta comes out the other end, make sure to support it with your hand or fingers. Fold the sheet of dough over itself twice, as you would a letter, and then turn the folded dough on its side and feed it back into the machine again. Repeat this folding and feeding it back into the machine three more times. This process is called "laminating" and it makes the dough more sturdy and manageable to handle.

Set the machine to the second-widest setting (typically notch 2) and feed the dough into the rollers. Again, support the pasta as it comes out the other side. Again fold it as you would a letter and feed it into the rollers on its short side; repeat this three more times.

Set the machine to the third-widest setting (typically notch 3) and feed the dough into the rollers. Again, support the pasta as it comes out the other side. Again fold it as you would a letter and feed it into the rollers on its short side; repeat this three more times.

Set the machine to the second-smallest setting (typically notch 4). Feed the pasta into the rollers. Again, support the pasta as it comes out the other side. At this point, there is no need to laminate the pasta.

Set the machine to the smallest setting

(typically notch 5). Cut the pasta sheet in half and feed it into the rollers. Again, support the pasta as it comes out the other side.

This last setting makes pasta sheets so thin (about 1/16 inch/1.5 mm thick) that you can see light through them. It is ideal for lasagna, sagne chine, cannelloni, tajarin, rotoli, angel hair, and tagliolini.

The just rolled pasta will be very delicate, so be gentle handling it. If the pasta sheet is too long to easily handle, carefully cut it in half. Lightly dust each sheet with flour and lay it on a surface lined with wax or parchment paper. Repeat all the above steps with the remaining pieces of dough.

4 Drying the sheets of dough: Pasta dough needs to be allowed to dry for approximately 15 minutes after it has been rolled out and before it is cut into strands or other shapes. This drying time makes the dough less sticky and easier to handle. Keep in mind that when the pasta is very thick or wide it will need to be turned over to ensure thorough and even drying (not necessary for thin noodles). Pasta sheets are now ready to be shaped or cut according to recipe requirements.

The notable exception to this rule is if you are making stuffed pasta. In this case, not letting the dough dry is best because the slight stickiness helps the pasta adhere better and creates a better seal.

5 Drying the cut pasta before cooking: Once fresh pasta has been cut (see the individual recipes), toss it with semolina flour and then place it on a lightly floured surface (again, with semolina flour) and allow it to dry for at least 15 minutes before cooking. This drying period is important because it allows the pasta to dry enough to become firmer and less sticky, which prevents the pasta from sticking together as it cooks (shaped pasta also holds its shape better when allowed to dry slightly before cooking). More specific drying times are indicated in individual pasta recipes. Just note that the drying process can be fickle. Depending on temperature, humidity levels, and the size of the noodles or pasta, the process may take a longer or shorter period of time than stated in the recipes. It is probably best to avoid making pasta on very humid days. If you can't avoid it, turn on the air conditioning or even a movable fan to help the air circulate more effectively.

WHOLE WHEAT PASTA DOUGH

YIELD: 1 ¾ POUNDS; 8 TO 10 SERVINGS / ACTIVE TIME: 1 HOUR / TOTAL TIME: 1 ½ HOURS

Perfect for chewy pappardelle or linguine. Whole wheat pasta pairs well with thick, creamy sauces.

INGREDIENTS:

- 4 cups + 2 tablespoons finely ground whole wheat flour
- 1 ½ teaspoons salt
- 4 large egg yolks
- 1 tablespoon extra virgin olive oil

1 Mixing and kneading the dough by hand: On a flat work surface combine the flour and salt and form it into a mountain-like mound. Create a well in the center, then add the egg yolks, olive oil, and 2 tablespoons water.

Using a fork or your fingertips, gradually start pulling the flour into the pool of egg, beginning with the flour at the inner rim of the well. Continue to gradually add flour until the dough starts holding together in a single floury mass, adding more water—1 tablespoon at a time—if the mixture is too dry to stick together. Once the dough feels firm and dry, and can form a craggy looking ball, it's time to start kneading.

Begin by working the remaining flour on the work surface into the ball of dough. Using the heel of your hand, push the ball of dough away from you in a downward motion. Turn the dough 45 degrees each time you repeat this motion, as doing so incorporates the flour more evenly. As you continue to knead, you'll notice the dough getting less and less floury. Eventually it will have a smooth, elastic texture. If the dough still feels wet, tacky, or sticky, dust it with flour and continue kneading. If it feels too dry and is not completely sticking together, wet your hands with water and continue kneading. Wet your hands as many times as you need in order to help the flour shape into a ball.

Knead for 8 to 10 minutes. It seems like a long time, but it accomplishes two things.

1. It creates a dough that is smooth and springy.

2. It eliminates any air bubbles and bits of unincorporated flour in the dough.

The dough has been sufficiently kneaded when it is very smooth and gently pulls back into place when stretched.

Mixing and kneading the dough with a mixer: Put the flour and salt in a large bowl and stir well with a spoon. Create a well in the center. Using a hand-held or stand mixer fitted with the dough (spiral) attachment, set the speed to 1 or 2 and slowly add half of the egg yolks and 1 tablespoon water while mixing. Mix until the wet ingredients have been fully incorporated into the flour, then add the remaining eggs and oil and another tablespoon water and continue to mix on low speed until fully incorporated. Soon the dough will begin coming together in a single floury mass. Add water—1 tablespoon at a time—if the mixture is too dry to stick together. Add flour—1 teaspoon at a time—if the mixture is too wet and sticky. Once the dough feels firm and dry, and can be formed into a coarse looking and slightly tacky ball, it's time to start kneading.

Turn the speed on the mixer to medium-high, typically notch 4, and mix for 8 to 10 minutes. The dough has been sufficiently kneaded when it is very smooth and gently pulls back into place when stretched.

2 Resting the dough: Wrap the ball of dough tightly in clear food wrap and let rest for 1 hour—2 hours is even better if you have the time. If using within a few hours, leave it out on the kitchen counter, otherwise refrigerate it (it will keep for up to 3 days). If you do refrigerate it, however, the dough may experience some discoloration (but it won't affect the flavor at all).

3 Rolling the dough: Cut the dough into four even pieces. Set one piece on a smooth work surface and wrap up the rest in clear food wrap to prevent drying. Shape the dough into a ball, place it on the surface, and, with the palm of your hand, push down on it so that it looks like a thick pita. Using a rolling pin, roll the dough to ½ inch thick. Try as much as possible to keep the thickness and width of the dough "patty" even, as it will help the dough fit through the pasta machine more easily.

Set the pasta machine for the flat roller (no teeth) on the widest setting (typically notch 1). Now feed the dough into the rollers. As a rather rough, thick sheet of pasta comes out the other end, make sure to support it with your hand or fingers. Fold the sheet of dough over itself twice, as you would a letter, and then turn the folded dough on its side and feed it back into the machine again. Repeat this folding and feeding it back into the machine three more times. This process is called "laminating" and it makes the dough more sturdy and manageable to handle.

Set the machine to the second-widest setting (typically notch 2) and feed the dough into the rollers. Again, support the pasta as it comes out the other side. Again fold it as you would a letter and feed it into the rollers on its short side; repeat this three more times.

Set the machine to the third-widest setting (typically notch 3) and feed the dough into the rollers. Again, support the pasta as it comes out the other side. Again fold it as you would a letter and feed it into the rollers on its short side; repeat this three more times.

Stop rolling at this point if making pasta shapes ⅛ inch/3 mm thick like spaghetti alla chitarra and spaghetti.

Set the machine to the second-smallest setting (typically notch 4). Feed the pasta into the rollers. Again, support the pasta as it comes out the other side. At this point, there is no need to laminate the pasta.

Stop rolling at this point if making sheets of pasta ⅛ inch/2mm thick for maltagliati, farfalle, and cappellacci dei briganti. If you like your fettuccine, pappardelle, and tagliatelle a little thicker, then this is the setting for you.

Set the machine to the smallest setting (typically notch 5). Cut the pasta sheet in half and feed it into the rollers. Again, support the pasta as it comes out the other side.

This last setting makes pasta sheets so thin (about ⅟₁₆ inch/1.5 mm thick) that you can see light through them. It is ideal for fazzoletti and quadretti. If you like your fettuccine, pappardelle, and tagliatelle very thin, then this is the setting for you.

The just rolled pasta will be very delicate, so be gentle handling it. If the pasta sheet is too long to easily handle, carefully cut it in half. Lightly dust each sheet with flour and lay it on a surface lined with wax or parchment paper. Repeat all the above steps with the remaining pieces of dough.

4 Drying the sheets of dough: Pasta dough needs to be allowed to dry for approximately 15 minutes after it has been rolled out

and before it is cut into strands or other shapes. This drying time makes the dough less sticky and easier to handle. Keep in mind that when the pasta is very thick or wide it will need to be turned over to ensure thorough and even drying (not necessary for thin noodles). Pasta sheets are now ready to be shaped or cut according to recipe requirements.

The notable exception to this rule is if you are making stuffed pasta. In this case, not letting the dough dry is best because the slight stickiness helps the pasta adhere better and creates a better seal.

5 Drying the cut pasta before cooking: Once fresh pasta has been cut (see the individual recipes), toss it with semolina flour and then place it on a lightly floured surface

(again, with semolina flour) and allow it to dry for at least 15 minutes before cooking. This drying period is important because it allows the pasta to dry enough to become firmer and less sticky, which prevents the pasta from sticking together as it cooks (shaped pasta also holds its shape better when allowed to dry slightly before cooking). More specific drying times are indicated in individual pasta recipes. Just note that the drying process can be fickle. Depending on temperature, humidity levels, and the size of the noodles or pasta, the process may take a longer or shorter period of time than stated in the recipes. It is probably best to avoid making pasta on very humid days. If you can't avoid it, turn on the air conditioning or even a movable fan to help the air circulate more effectively.

CHESTNUT PASTA DOUGH

YIELD: 1 POUND; 6 SERVINGS / ACTIVE TIME: 1 HOUR / TOTAL TIME: 1 ½ HOURS

This mixture of flours creates a pasta whose nutty, earthy chestnut flavor shines through and can easily be shaped into *tagliatelle* or simple flat shapes like *maltagliati*.

INGREDIENTS:

- 1 ¼ cups chestnut flour
- ¾ cup finely milled type "00" wheat flour **OR** 1 cup all-purpose flour
- ⅔ cup semolina flour
- ½ teaspoon salt
- 4 large eggs
- 2 egg yolks
- 1 tablespoon extra virgin olive oil

1 Mixing and kneading the dough by hand: On a flat work surface combine the flours and salt and form it into a mountain-like mound. Create a well in the center, then add the eggs, egg yolks, olive oil, and 2 tablespoons water. Using a fork or your fingertips, gradually start pulling the flour into the pool of egg, beginning with the flour at the inner rim of the well. Continue to gradually add flour until the dough starts holding together in a single floury mass, adding more water — 1 tablespoon at a time — if the mixture is too dry to stick together. Once the dough feels firm and dry, and can form a craggy looking ball, it's time to start kneading.

Begin by working the remaining flour on the work surface into the ball of dough. Using the heel of your hand, push the ball of dough away from you in a downward motion. Turn the dough 45 degrees each time you repeat this motion, as doing so incorporates the flour more evenly. As you continue to knead, you'll notice the dough getting less and less floury. Eventually it will have a smooth, elastic texture. If the dough still feels wet, tacky, or sticky, dust it with flour and continue kneading. If it feels too dry and is not completely sticking together, wet your hands with water and continue kneading. Wet your hands as many times as you need in order to help the flour shape into a ball.

Knead for 8 to 10 minutes. It seems like a long time, but it accomplishes two things.

1. It creates a dough that is smooth and springy.

2. It eliminates any air bubbles and bits of unincorporated flour in the dough.

The dough has been sufficiently kneaded when it is very smooth and gently pulls back into place when stretched.

Mixing and kneading the dough with a mixer: Put the flours and salt in a large bowl and stir well with a spoon. Create a well in the center. Using a hand-held or stand mixer fitted with the dough (spiral) attachment, set the speed to 1 or 2 and slowly add half of the eggs and oil and 1 tablespoon water while mixing. Mix until the wet ingredients have been fully incorporated into the flour, then add the remaining eggs and another tablespoon water and continue to mix on low speed until fully incorporated.

Soon the dough will begin coming together in a single floury mass. Add water—1 tablespoon at a time—if the mixture is too dry to stick together. Add flour—1 teaspoon at a time—if the mixture is too wet and sticky. Once the dough feels firm and dry, and can be formed into a coarse looking and slightly tacky ball, it's time to start kneading.

Turn the speed on the mixer to medium-high, typically notch 4, and mix for 8 to 10 minutes. The dough has been sufficiently kneaded when it is very smooth and gently pulls back into place when stretched.

2 Resting the dough: Wrap the ball of dough tightly in clear food wrap and let rest for 1 hour—2 hours is even better if you have the time. If using within a few hours, leave it out on the kitchen counter, otherwise refrigerate it (it will keep for up to 3 days). If you do refrigerate it, however, the dough may experience some discoloration (but it won't affect the flavor at all).

3 Rolling the dough: Cut the dough into four even pieces. Set one piece on a smooth work surface and wrap up the rest in clear food wrap to prevent drying. Shape the dough into a ball, place it on the surface, and, with the palm of your hand, push down on it so that it looks like a thick pita. Using a rolling pin, roll the dough to ½ inch thick. Try as much as possible to keep the thickness and width of the dough "patty" even, as it will help the dough fit through the pasta machine more easily.

Set the pasta machine for the flat roller (no teeth) on the widest setting (typically notch 1). Now feed the dough into the rollers. As a rather rough, thick sheet of pasta comes out the other end, make sure to support it with your hand or fingers. Fold the sheet of dough over itself twice, as you would a letter, and then turn the folded dough on its side and feed it back into the machine again. Repeat this folding and feeding it back into the machine three more times. This process is called "laminating" and it

makes the dough more sturdy and manageable to handle.

Set the machine to the second-widest setting (typically notch 2) and feed the dough into the rollers. Again, support the pasta as it comes out the other side. Again fold it as you would a letter and feed it into the rollers on its short side; repeat this three more times.

Set the machine to the third-widest setting (typically notch 3) and feed the dough into the rollers. Again, support the pasta as it comes out the other side. Again fold it as you would a letter and feed it into the rollers on its short side; repeat this three more times.

Stop rolling at this point if making pasta shapes ⅛ inch/3 mm thick like pappardelle, spaghetti alla chitarra, corzetti, spaghetti, and pierogi.

Set the machine to the second-smallest setting (typically notch 4). Feed the pasta into the rollers. Again, support the pasta as it comes out the other side. At this point, there is no need to laminate the pasta.

Stop rolling at this point if making sheets of pasta ⅛ inch/2mm thick for lasagna, tortelloni, pansotti, agnolotti, anolini, maltagliati, cannelloni, tagliatelle, strozzapreti, cappellacci dei briganti, fettuccine, linguine, and garganelli.

Set the machine to the smallest setting (typically notch 5). Cut the pasta sheet in half and feed it into the rollers. Again, support the pasta as it comes out the other side.

This last setting makes pasta sheets so thin (about ⅟₁₆ inch/1.5 mm thick) that you can see light through them. It is ideal for filled pastas like ravioli, fazzoletti, culurgiones, and cappellacci, whose fillings can easily be overshadowed by too much surrounding dough.

The just rolled pasta will be very delicate, so be gentle handling it. If the pasta sheet is too long to easily handle, carefully cut it in half. Lightly dust each sheet with flour and lay it on a surface lined with wax or parchment paper. Repeat all the above steps with the remaining pieces of dough.

4 Drying the sheets of dough: Pasta dough needs to be allowed to dry for approximately 15 minutes after it has been rolled out and before it is cut into strands or other shapes. This drying time makes the dough less sticky and easier to handle. Keep in mind that when the pasta is very thick or wide it will need to be turned over to ensure thorough and even drying (not necessary for thin noodles). Pasta sheets are now ready to be shaped or cut according to recipe requirements.

The notable exception to this rule is if you are making stuffed pasta. In this case, not letting the dough dry is best because the slight stickiness helps the pasta adhere better and creates a better seal.

5 Drying the cut pasta before cooking: Once fresh pasta has been cut (see the individual recipes), toss it with semolina flour and then place it on a lightly floured surface (again, with semolina flour) and allow it to dry for at least 15 minutes before cooking. This drying period is important because it allows the pasta to dry enough to become firmer and less sticky, which prevents the pasta from sticking together as it cooks (shaped pasta also holds its shape better when allowed to dry slightly before cooking). More specific drying times are indicated in individual pasta recipes. Just note that the drying process can be fickle. Depending on temperature, humidity levels, and the size of the noodles or pasta, the process may take a longer or shorter period of time than stated in the recipes. It is probably best to avoid making pasta on very humid days. If you can't avoid it, turn on the air conditioning or even a movable fan to help the air circulate more effectively.

SPICED PASTA DOUGH

YIELD: ¾ POUND; 4 SERVINGS / ACTIVE TIME: 1 HOUR / TOTAL TIME: 1 ½ HOURS

Often decadently colored by spices, this egg pasta dough lends a hint of spicy or peppery flavor to every dish it touches. Perfect for flat, simple shapes of pasta or long strands.

1 Mixing and kneading the dough by hand: On a flat work surface combine the flours, spice, and salt and form it into a mountain-like mound. Create a well in the center, then add the egg yolks, olive oil, and 2 tablespoons water. Using a fork or your fingertips, gradually start pulling the flour into the pool of egg, beginning with the flour at the inner rim of the well. Continue to gradually add flour until the dough starts holding together in a single floury mass, adding more water — 1 tablespoon at a time — if the mixture is too dry to stick together. Once the dough feels firm and dry, and can form a craggy looking ball, it's time to start kneading.

Begin by working the remaining flour on the work surface into the ball of dough. Using the heel of your hand, push the ball of dough away from you in a downward motion. Turn the dough 45 degrees each time you repeat this motion, as doing so incorporates the flour more evenly. As you continue to knead, you'll notice the dough getting less and less floury. Eventually it will have a smooth, elastic texture. If the dough still feels wet, tacky, or sticky, dust it with flour and continue kneading. If it feels too dry and is not completely sticking together, wet your hands with water and continue kneading. Wet your hands as many times as you need in order to help the flour shape into a ball.

Knead for 8 to 10 minutes. It seems like a long time, but it accomplishes two things.

1. It creates a dough that is smooth and springy.

2. It eliminates any air bubbles and bits of unincorporated flour in the dough.

The dough has been sufficiently kneaded when it is very smooth and gently pulls back into place when stretched.

Mixing and kneading the dough with a mixer: Put the flours, spice, and salt in a large bowl and stir well with a spoon. Create a well in the center. Using a hand-held or stand mixer fitted with the dough (spiral) attachment, set the speed to 1 or 2 and slowly add half of the egg yolks and oil and 1 tablespoon water while mixing. Mix until the wet ingredients have been fully incorporated into the flour, then add the remaining egg yolks and oil and another tablespoon water and continue to mix on low speed until fully

INGREDIENTS:

- 1 ¼ cups durum flour

- ⅓ cup + 2 tablespoons finely milled type "00" wheat flour OR ½ cup all-purpose flour

- 1 ¾ tablespoons freshly ground black pepper, five-peppercorn medley, smoked paprika, ground cinnamon, or ground cumin (you can use all of one spice or a mix, as you prefer)

- 1 ½ teaspoons salt

- 9 large egg yolks

- 2 tablespoons extra virgin olive oil

incorporated. Soon the dough will begin coming together in a single floury mass. Add water—1 tablespoon at a time—if the mixture is too dry to stick together. Add flour—1 teaspoon at a time—if the mixture is too wet and sticky. Once the dough feels firm and dry, and can be formed into a coarse looking and slightly tacky ball, it's time to start kneading.

Turn the speed on the mixer to medium-high, typically notch 4, and mix for 8 to 10 minutes. The dough has been sufficiently kneaded when it is very smooth and gently pulls back into place when stretched.

2 Resting the dough: Wrap the ball of dough tightly in clear food wrap and let rest for 1 hour—2 hours is even better if you have the time. If using within a few hours, leave it out on the kitchen counter, otherwise refrigerate it (it will keep for up to 3 days). If you do refrigerate it, however, the dough may experience some discoloration (but it won't affect the flavor at all).

3 Rolling the dough: Cut the dough into four even pieces. Set one piece on a smooth work surface and wrap up the rest in clear food wrap to prevent drying. Shape the dough into a ball, place it on the surface, and, with the palm of your hand, push down on it so that it looks like a thick pita. Using a rolling pin, roll the dough to ½ inch thick. Try as much as possible to keep the thickness and width of the dough "patty" even, as it will help the dough fit through the pasta machine more easily.

Set the pasta machine for the flat roller (no teeth) on the widest setting (typically notch 1). Now feed the dough into the rollers. As a rather rough, thick sheet of pasta comes out the other end, make sure to support it with your hand or fingers. Fold the sheet of dough over itself twice, as you would a letter, and then turn the folded dough on its side and feed it back into the machine again. Repeat this folding and feeding it back into the machine three more times. This process is called "laminating" and it makes the dough more sturdy and manageable to handle.

Set the machine to the second-widest setting (typically notch 2) and feed the dough into the rollers. Again, support the pasta as it comes out the other side. Again fold it as you would a letter and feed it into the rollers on its short side; repeat this three more times.

Set the machine to the third-widest setting (typically notch 3) and feed the dough into the rollers. Again, support the pasta as it comes out the other side. Again fold it as you would a letter and feed it into the rollers on its short side; repeat this three more times.

Stop rolling at this point if making pasta shapes ⅛ inch/3 mm thick like spaghetti alla chitarra and spaghetti.

Set the machine to the second-smallest setting (typically notch 4). Feed the pasta into the rollers. Again, support the pasta as it comes out the other side. At this point, there is no need to laminate the pasta.

Stop rolling at this point if making sheets of pasta ⅛ inch/2mm thick for maltagliati, farfalle, and cappellacci dei briganti. If you like your fettuccine, pappardelle, and tagliatelle a little thicker, then this is the setting for you.

Set the machine to the smallest setting (typically notch 5). Cut the pasta sheet in half and feed it into the rollers. Again, support the pasta as it comes out the other side.

This last setting makes pasta sheets so thin (about 1/16 inch/1.5 mm thick) that you can see light through them. It is ideal for fazzoletti and quadretti. If you like your fettuccine, pappardelle, and tagliatelle very thin, then this is the setting for you.

The just rolled pasta will be very delicate, so be gentle handling it. If the pasta sheet is too long to easily handle, carefully cut it in half. Lightly dust each sheet with flour and lay it on a surface lined with wax or parchment paper. Repeat all the above steps with the remaining pieces of dough.

4 Drying the sheets of dough: Pasta dough needs to be allowed to dry for approximately 15 minutes after it has been rolled out and before it is cut into strands or other shapes. This drying time makes the dough less sticky and easier to handle. Keep in mind that when the pasta is very thick or wide it will need to be turned over to ensure thorough and even drying (not necessary for thin noodles). Pasta sheets are now ready to be shaped or cut according to recipe requirements.

The notable exception to this rule is if you are making stuffed pasta. In this case, not letting the dough dry is best because the slight stickiness helps the pasta adhere better and creates a better seal.

5 Drying the cut pasta before cooking: Once fresh pasta has been cut (see the individual recipes), toss it with semolina flour and then place it on a lightly floured surface (again, with semolina flour) and allow it to dry for at least 15 minutes before cooking. This drying period is important because it allows the pasta to dry enough to become firmer and less sticky, which prevents the pasta from sticking together as it cooks (shaped pasta also holds its shape better when allowed to dry slightly before cooking). More specific drying times are indicated in individual pasta recipes. Just note that the drying process can be fickle. Depending on temperature, humidity levels, and the size of the noodles or pasta, the process may take a longer or shorter period of time than stated in the recipes. It is probably best to avoid making pasta on very humid days. If you can't avoid it, turn on the air conditioning or even a movable fan to help the air circulate more effectively.

CITRUS PASTA DOUGH

YIELD: ¾ POUND; 4 SERVINGS / ACTIVE TIME: 1 HOUR / TOTAL TIME 1 ½ HOURS

Rich in the flavor of either lemon or orange, this flour combination works well with simple, flat shapes, long pasta strands, and seafood-oriented stuffed pasta.

INGREDIENTS:

- 1 ¼ cups finely milled type "00" wheat flour OR 1 ½ cups all-purpose flour
- ½ cup durum flour
- 1 ½ teaspoons salt
- 9 large egg yolks
- 2 tablespoons extra virgin olive oil

  Grated zest of 1 lemon or lime or ½ orange

1 Mixing and kneading the dough by hand: On a flat work surface combine the flour(s) and salt and form it into a mountain-like mound. Create a well in the center, then add the egg yolks, olive oil, citrus zest, and 2 tablespoons water. Using a fork or your fingertips, gradually start pulling the flour into the pool of egg, beginning with the flour at the inner rim of the well. Continue to gradually add flour until the dough starts holding together in a single floury mass, adding more water—1 tablespoon at a time—if the mixture is too dry to stick together. Once the dough feels firm and dry, and can form a craggy looking ball, it's time to start kneading.

Begin by working the remaining flour on the work surface into the ball of dough. Using the heel of your hand, push the ball of dough away from you in a downward motion. Turn the dough 45 degrees each time you repeat this motion, as doing so incorporates the flour more evenly. As you continue to knead, you'll notice the dough getting less and less floury. Eventually it will have a smooth, elastic texture. If the dough still feels wet, tacky, or sticky, dust it with flour and continue kneading. If it feels too dry and is not completely sticking together, wet your hands with water and continue kneading. Wet your hands as many times as you need in order to help the flour shape into a ball.

Knead for 8 to 10 minutes. It seems like a long time, but it accomplishes two things.

1. It creates a dough that is smooth and springy.

2. It eliminates any air bubbles and bits of unincorporated flour in the dough.

The dough has been sufficiently kneaded when it is very smooth and gently pulls back into place when stretched.

Mixing and kneading the dough with a mixer: Put the flours and salt in a large bowl and stir well with a spoon. Create a well in the center. Using a hand-held or stand mixer fitted with the dough (spiral) attachment, set the speed to 1 or 2 and slowly add half of the egg yolks and oil, the zest, and 1 tablespoon water while mixing. Mix until the wet ingredients have been fully incorporated into the flour, then add the remaining egg yolks and oil and another tablespoon water and continue to mix on low speed until fully incorporated. Soon the dough will begin coming together in a single floury mass. Add water—1 tablespoon at a time—if the mixture is too dry to stick together. Add flour—1 teaspoon at a time—if the mixture is too wet and sticky. Once the dough feels firm and dry, and can be formed into a coarse looking and slightly tacky ball, it's time to start kneading.

Turn the speed on the mixer to medium-high, typically notch 4, and mix for 8 to 10 minutes. The dough has been sufficiently kneaded when it is very smooth and gently pulls back into place when stretched.

2 Resting the dough: Wrap the ball of dough tightly in clear food wrap and let rest for 1 hour—2 hours is even better if you have the time. If using within a few hours, leave it out on the kitchen counter, otherwise refrigerate it (it will keep for up to 3 days). If you do refrigerate it, however, the dough may experience some discoloration (but it won't affect the flavor at all).

3 Rolling the dough: Cut the dough into four even pieces. Set one piece on a smooth work surface and wrap up the rest in clear food wrap to prevent drying. Shape the dough into a ball, place it on the surface, and, with the palm of your hand, push down on it so that it looks like a thick pita. Using a rolling pin, roll the dough to ½ inch thick. Try as much as possible to keep the thickness and width of the dough "patty" even, as it will help the dough fit through the pasta machine more easily.

Set the pasta machine for the flat roller (no teeth) on the widest setting (typically notch 1). Now feed the dough into the rollers. As a rather rough, thick sheet of pasta comes out the other end, make sure to support it with your hand or fingers. Fold the sheet of dough over itself twice, as you would a letter, and then turn the folded dough on its side and feed it back into the machine again. Repeat this folding and feeding it back into the machine three more times. This process is called "laminating" and it

makes the dough more sturdy and manageable to handle.

Set the machine to the second-widest setting (typically notch 2) and feed the dough into the rollers. Again, support the pasta as it comes out the other side. Again fold it as you would a letter and feed it into the rollers on its short side; repeat this three more times.

Set the machine to the third-widest setting (typically notch 3) and feed the dough into the rollers. Again, support the pasta as it comes out the other side. Again fold it as you would a letter and feed it into the rollers on its short side; repeat this three more times.

Set the machine to the second-smallest setting (typically notch 4). Feed the pasta into the rollers. Again, support the pasta as it comes out the other side. At this point, there is no need to laminate the pasta.

Stop rolling at this point if making sheets of pasta ⅛ inch/2mm thick for maltagliati, farfalle, and cappellacci dei briganti. If you like your fettuccine, pappardelle, and tagliatelle a little thicker, then this is the setting for you.

Set the machine to the smallest setting (typically notch 5). Cut the pasta sheet in half and feed it into the rollers. Again, support the pasta as it comes out the other side.

This last setting makes pasta sheets so thin (about 1/16 inch/1.5 mm thick) that you can see light through them. It is ideal for fazzoletti and quadretti. If you like your fettuccine, pappardelle, and tagliatelle very thin, then this is the setting for you.

The just rolled pasta will be very delicate, so be gentle handling it. If the pasta sheet is too long to easily handle, carefully cut it in half. Lightly dust each sheet with flour and lay it on a surface lined with wax or parchment paper. Repeat all the above steps with the remaining pieces of dough.

4 Drying the sheets of dough: Pasta dough needs to be allowed to dry for approximately 15 minutes after it has been rolled out and before it is cut into strands or other shapes.

This drying time makes the dough less sticky and easier to handle. Keep in mind that when the pasta is very thick or wide it will need to be turned over to ensure thorough and even drying (not necessary for thin noodles). Pasta sheets are now ready to be shaped or cut according to recipe requirements.

The notable exception to this rule is if you are making stuffed pasta. In this case, not letting the dough dry is best because the slight stickiness helps the pasta adhere better and creates a better seal.

5 Drying the cut pasta before cooking: Once fresh pasta has been cut (see the individual recipes), toss it with semolina flour and then place it on a lightly floured surface (again, with semolina flour) and allow it to dry for at least 15 minutes before cooking. This drying period is important because it allows the pasta to dry enough to become firmer and less sticky, which prevents the pasta from sticking together as it cooks (shaped pasta also holds its shape better when allowed to dry slightly before cooking). More specific drying times are indicated in individual pasta recipes. Just note that the drying process can be fickle. Depending on temperature, humidity levels, and the size of the noodles or pasta, the process may take a longer or shorter period of time than stated in the recipes. It is probably best to avoid making pasta on very humid days. If you can't avoid it, turn on the air conditioning or even a movable fan to help the air circulate more effectively.

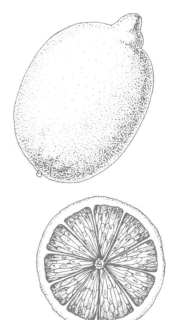

HERBED FRESH PASTA DOUGH

YIELD: 1 POUND / ACTIVE TIME: 1 HOUR / TOTAL TIME: 1 ¼ HOURS

For not a whole lot of extra effort or time, you can add vibrant color to your homemade pasta as well as a subtle hint of flavor that complements the sauce with which it will be paired. Colored and flavored dough is suitable for a variety of shapes such as linguine, *pappardelle, tagliatelle,* ravioli, tortellini, lasagna, *maltagliati, cannelloni, ravioloni, agnolotti,* and *cappellacci dei briganti.*

INGREDIENTS:

- ¼ cup packed fresh herb leaves like basil, cilantro, chive, parsley, or mint OR 1 ¼ tablespoons finely minced fresh thyme or rosemary
- 1 ¼ cups finely milled type "00" wheat flour OR 1 ½ cups all-purpose flour
- ½ cup durum flour
- 1 ½ teaspoons salt
- 9 large egg yolks
- 2 tablespoons extra virgin olive oil

1 Preparing the herbs: For herbs measured as whole leaves, bring a small saucepan of water to a boil. Add the herb leaves and blanch until they turn a brighter shade of green, about 10 seconds (this is done to fix the color of the herbs). Using a slotted spoon or strainer, transfer the leaves to a bowl of ice water to stop the cooking. Drain well and transfer, along with 3 tablespoons of the blanching water (let it cool first), to a mini food processor and process into a very smooth puree, with no flecks of herbs present. Skip this step if you are using the minced herbs.

2 Mixing and kneading the dough by hand: On a flat work surface combine the flours, salt, and minced herbs if using, then form the mixture into a mountain-like mound. Create a well in the center, then add the egg yolks, olive oil, herb puree if using, and 2 tablespoons water (use the blanching water if adding herb puree). Using a fork or your fingertips, gradually start pulling the flour into the pool of egg, beginning with the flour at the inner rim of the well. Continue to gradually add flour until the dough starts holding together in a single floury mass, adding more water—1 tablespoon at a time—if the mixture is too dry to stick together. Once the dough feels firm and dry, and can form a craggy looking ball, it's time to start kneading.

Begin by working the remaining flour on the work surface into the ball of dough. Using the heel of your hand, push the ball of dough away from you in a downward motion. Turn the dough 45 degrees each time you repeat this motion, as doing so incorporates the flour more evenly. As you continue to knead, you'll notice the dough getting less and less floury. Eventually it will have a smooth, elastic texture. If the dough still feels wet, tacky, or sticky, dust it with flour and continue kneading. If it feels too dry and is not completely sticking together, wet your hands with water and continue kneading. Wet your hands as many times as you need in order to help the flour shape into a ball.

Knead for 8 to 10 minutes. It seems like a long time, but it accomplishes two things.

1. It creates a dough that is smooth and springy.

2. It eliminates any air bubbles and bits of unincorporated flour in the dough.

The dough has been sufficiently kneaded when it is very smooth and gently pulls back into place when stretched.

Mixing and kneading the dough with a mixer: Put the flours, salt, and minced herbs if using, in a large bowl. Create a well in the center. Using a hand-held or stand mixer fitted with the dough (spiral) attachment, set the speed to 1 or 2 and slowly add half of the egg yolks, oil, and herb puree if using, and 1 tablespoon water while mixing. Mix until the wet ingredients have been fully incorporated into the flour, then add the remaining egg yolks, oil, and herb puree and another tablespoon water and continue to mix on low speed until fully incorporated Soon the dough will begin coming together in a single floury mass. Add water—1 tablespoon at a time—if the mixture is too dry to stick together. Add flour—1 teaspoon at a time—if the mixture is too wet and sticky. Once the dough feels firm and dry, and can be formed into a coarse looking and slightly tacky ball, it's time to start kneading.

Turn the speed on the mixer to medium-high, typically notch 4, and mix for 8 to 10 minutes. The dough has been sufficiently kneaded when it is very smooth and gently pulls back into place when stretched.

3 Resting the dough: Wrap the ball of dough tightly in clear food wrap and let rest for 1 hour—2 hours is even better if you have the time. If using within a few hours, leave it out on the kitchen counter, otherwise refrigerate it (it will keep for up to 3 days). If you do refrigerate it, however, the dough may experience some discoloration (but it won't affect the flavor at all).

4 Rolling the dough: Cut the dough into four even pieces. Set one piece on a smooth work surface and wrap up the rest in clear food wrap to prevent drying. Shape the dough into a ball, place it on the surface, and, with the palm of your hand, push down on it so that it looks like a thick pita. Using a rolling pin, roll the dough to ½ inch thick. Try as much as possible to keep the thickness and width of the dough "patty" even, as it will help the dough fit through the pasta machine more easily.

Set the pasta machine for the flat roller (no teeth) on the widest setting (typically notch 1). Now feed the dough into the rollers. As a rather rough, thick sheet of pasta comes out the other end, make sure to support it with your hand or fingers. Fold the sheet of dough over itself twice, as you would a letter, and then turn the folded dough on its side and feed it back into the machine again. Repeat this folding and feeding it back into the machine three more times. This process is called "laminating" and it makes the dough more sturdy and manageable to handle.

Set the machine to the second-widest setting (typically notch 2) and feed the dough into the rollers. Again, support the pasta as it comes out the other side. Again fold it as you would a letter and feed it into the rollers on its short side; repeat this three more times.

Stop rolling at this point if you are making thicker (about ¼ inch/6 mm) pasta shapes like pici.

Set the machine to the third-widest setting (typically notch 3) and feed the dough into the rollers. Again, support the pasta as it comes out the other side. Again fold it as you would a letter and feed it into the rollers on its short side; repeat this three more times.

Stop rolling at this point if making pasta shapes ⅛ inch/3 mm thick like pappardelle, spaghetti alla chitarra, corzetti, spaghetti, and pierogi.

Set the machine to the second-smallest setting (typically notch 4). Feed the pasta into the rollers. Again, support the pasta as it comes out the other side. At this point, there is no need to laminate the pasta.

Stop rolling at this point if making sheets of pasta ⅛ inch/2mm thick for lasagna, tortelloni, pansotti, agnolotti, anolini, maltagliati, cannelloni, tagliatelle, strozzapreti, cappellacci dei briganti, fettuccine, linguine, and garganelli.

Set the machine to the smallest setting (typically notch 5). Cut the pasta sheet in half and feed it into the rollers. Again, support the pasta as it comes out the other side.

This last setting makes pasta sheets so thin (about 1/16 inch/1.5 mm thick) that you can see light through them. It is ideal for filled pastas like ravioli, fazzoletti, culurgiones, and cappellacci, whose fillings can easily be overshadowed by too much surrounding dough.

The just rolled pasta will be very delicate, so be gentle handling it. If the pasta sheet is too long to easily handle, carefully cut it in half. Lightly dust each sheet with flour and lay it on a surface lined with wax or parchment paper. Repeat all the above steps with the remaining pieces of dough.

5 Drying the sheets of dough: Pasta dough needs to be allowed to dry for approximately 15 minutes after it has been rolled out and before it is cut into strands or other shapes. This drying time makes the dough less sticky and easier to handle. Keep in mind that when the pasta is very thick or wide it will need to be turned over to ensure thorough and even drying

(not necessary for thin noodles). Pasta sheets are now ready to be shaped or cut according to recipe requirements.

The notable exception to this rule is if you are making stuffed pasta. In this case, not letting the dough dry is best because the slight stickiness helps the pasta adhere better and creates a better seal.

6 Drying the cut pasta before cooking: Once fresh pasta has been cut (see the individual recipes), toss it with semolina flour and then place it on a lightly floured surface (again, with semolina flour) and allow it to dry for at least 15 minutes before cooking. This drying period is important because it allows the pasta to dry enough to become firmer and less sticky, which prevents the pasta from sticking together as it cooks (shaped pasta also holds its shape better when allowed to dry slightly before cooking). More specific drying times are indicated in individual pasta recipes. Just note that the drying process can be fickle. Depending on temperature, humidity levels, and the size of the noodles or pasta, the process may take a longer or shorter period of time than stated in the recipes. It is probably best to avoid making pasta on very humid days. If you can't avoid it, turn on the air conditioning or even a movable fan to help the air circulate more effectively.

SAFFRON PASTA DOUGH

Prepare the dough using 3 tablespoons water, 1 teaspoon (½ gram) saffron threads, 1 cup + 3 tablespoons finely milled type "00" wheat flour (or 1 ⅓ cups + 1 tablespoon all-purpose flour), 7 tablespoons durum flour, 1 ½ teaspoons salt, 8 large egg yolks, and 2 tablespoons extra virgin olive oil. Heat the water for 20 seconds in a microwave oven until very hot and steaming. Add the saffron threads, cover, and steep for 15 minutes. Pour the saffron water through a fine-meshed strainer, gently pressing down on the saffron threads to squeeze out any remaining color and flavor into the water. Discard the saffron threads and add the water as directed above instead of the blanching water.

RIBBON PASTA

YIELD: 6 SERVINGS / ACTIVE TIME: 1 HOUR / TOTAL TIME: 3 HOURS

Making your own pasta ribbons is akin to making your own pie crust, and adds a notch on the wooden spoon that identifies you as a cook. Best of all, ribbon pasta is the least time-consuming homemade pasta to make (35 minutes for pros and under an hour for novices) and doesn't even require special equipment if you are willing to expend plenty of elbow grease to roll out the dough into a thin sheet. I heard one food blogger say that he doesn't even own a rolling pin but uses an unopened wine bottle for the job!

Pappardelle are velvety wide and very thin egg ribbons, typically paired with sauces made from more exotic feathered and furry game such as duck and boar. In existence for more than 400 years, they get their name from the Italian verb *pappare,* which means to eat with gusto. Their narrower counterparts, in diminishing order of width, are *tagliatelle,* fettuccine, linguine, and *tagliolini.* I have included instructions on how to make fettuccine and *tagliolini* with a manual pasta maker, for those of you who own one, as they are the shape cutters included with the basic machine.

It is important to note that the thickness of all of these pasta ribbons is up to the discretion of the pasta maker (you have to love the control!). While Italians generally prefer thin, delicate ribbons, you will also find born-and-bred Italians who prefer a heftier bite to their noodles. As such, I will leave the desired thickness up to each individual pasta maker, though I recommend a thickness of either $\frac{1}{8}$ or $\frac{1}{16}$ inch, as it creates pasta sheets that are still sturdy enough to handle rolling without tearing.

Recommended sauces and pasta dishes: The general rule-of-thumb on pairing pasta ribbons with sauces is that the thicker the ribbons are, the heavier the sauce they can accommodate. Use your own preferences and discretion as your guide, since you are the one who ultimately has to enjoy your dining experience.

Pappardelle: Duck Ragù (page 600), Rabbit Ragù (page 603), Wild Boar Ragù (page 622), Mutton Ragù (page 643), Pappardelle with Wild Boar Sausage (page 526)

Tagliatelle: Chicken Liver, Guanciale, and Porcini Mushroom Sauce (page 598), Bolognese Sauce (page 629), Lamb Ragù (page 641)

Fettuccine: Creamy Leek Sauce (page 504), Meat Ragu with Bechamel Sauce (page 636), Asparagus and Ricotta Sauce (page 499), Fettuccine Alfredo (page 470)

Tagliolini: Fresh Mushroom Sauce (page 551), Caper and Lemon Sauce (page 481), Smoked Salmon and Asparagus Sauce (page 580)

INGREDIENTS:

1 recipe Three-Egg Basic Pasta Dough (page 131)

   Semolina flour for dusting

   Salt

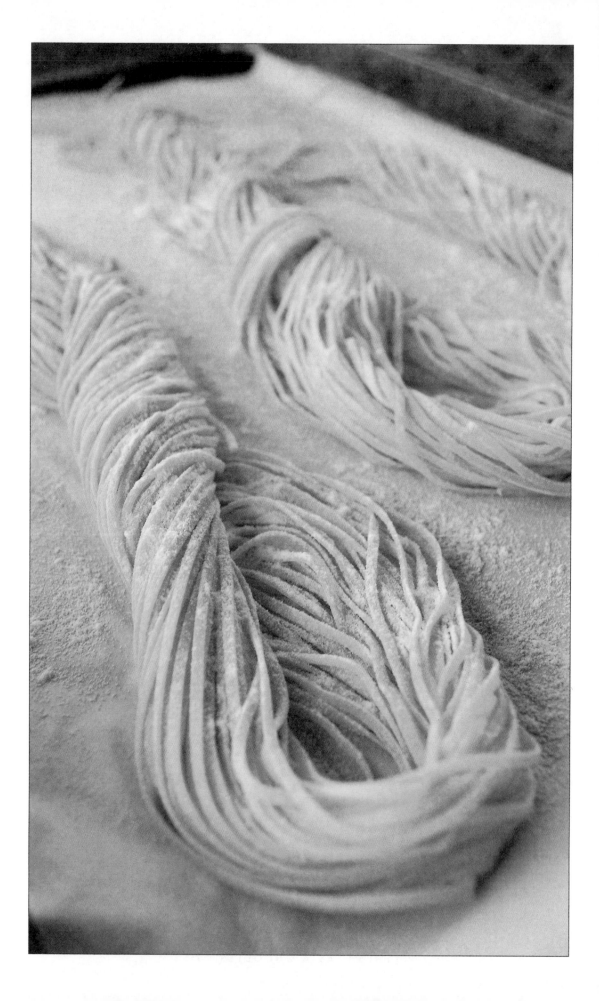

1 Prepare the dough as directed on pages 131–133, rolling the dough to the second thinnest setting (generally notch 4) or thinnest setting (generally notch 5 or 6) to form pasta sheets that are, respectively, ⅛ or ¹⁄₁₆ inch thick. Lay the pasta sheets on lightly floured parchment paper-lined baking sheets. Let the sheets air-dry for 15 minutes, turning them over halfway through (doing this will make them easier to cut).

2 Lightly flour the surface of a pasta sheet and gently roll it up, starting from a short end, to create a pasta roll. Use a very sharp knife to gently slice the roll across to your preferred width. You may find other sources that recommend widths that vary from the ones below, which is not surprising given the variations of measurements I've found in books and online. Again, select an approximate width that suits your fancy.

Pappardelle: 1- to 1 ½-inch-wide strips
Tagliatelle: ¾-inch-wide strips
Fettuccine: ½- to ¼-inch-wide strips

3 Lightly dust the cut roll with flour, then begin to gently unfold the strips, one by one, as you shake off any excess flour. Arrange them either straight and spread out or lay them down by shaping them in a coil (referred to as a bird's nest). Repeat with all the pasta sheets. Let air-dry for 30 minutes and then cook. Alternatively, cover them with a kitchen towel and refrigerate for up to 3 hours.

4 To cook the pasta ribbons, bring a large pot of water to a boil. Once it's boiling, add salt (1 tablespoon for every 4 cups water) and stir. Add the pasta and stir for the first minute to prevent any sticking and to disentangle the strands of pasta. *Tagliolini* will not require additional cooking so drain them as soon as they hit the water and you stir to disentangle them. Cook the remaining pasta ribbons until tender but still chewy, anywhere from 1 to 3 minutes. Drain and add them to the sauce of your choice.

SPAGHETTI ALLA CHITARRA

YIELD: 5 TO 6 SERVINGS / ACTIVE TIME: 1 HOUR / TOTAL TIME: 1 ½ HOURS

A specialty of the Italian region of Abruzzo, *spaghetti alla chitarra* or "guitar spaghetti" are long, thick, square noodles named after the rectangular stringed wooden tool that has shaped them since the early 1800s. The device is slightly larger than a shoebox and contains a number of evenly spaced strings designed to cut, with the applied pressure of a rolling pin, a pasta sheet into strands. When pasta strands occasionally remained attached to the "instrument," a simple strum across the strings would promptly dislodge them. Should you not own an Abruzzese *chitarra* (sadly most of us don't), you can improvise by rolling out well-floured thick pasta sheets and cutting them into ⅛-inch-wide noodles. Unlike other fresh egg pastas, which are usually delicate and rather silky, *spaghetti alla chitarra* is quite hearty in texture and requires a rich, punchy sauce and plenty of piquant pecorino cheese as accompaniments.

Suggested sauces and pasta dishes: Pici Pasta with Pecorino Cheese and Pepper (page 480), Chicken Liver, Guanciale, and Porcini Mushroom Sauce (page 598), Simple Roasted Tomato and Garlic Sauce (page 568), Puttanesca Sauce (page 494)

INGREDIENTS:

1   recipe Egg Pasta Dough with Durum Flour (page 134)

1   Prepare the dough as directed on pages 134–136, rolling the dough to the second thinnest setting (generally notch 4) for pasta sheets that are about ⅛ inch thick.

2   Cutting the noodles with a *chitarra:* Cut the sheets into lengths the size of your *chitarra.* Gather the trimmed dough together in a ball and run it through the pasta machine to create more sheets. Lay the pasta sheets on lightly floured parchment paper-lined baking sheets. Working with one pasta sheet at a time, lightly dust it with flour, then place it over the *chitarra.* Using a floured rolling pin, roll it back and forth over the sheet until the *chitarra* strings cut it into strands. Lightly dust the strands with flour and arrange them straight and spread out on lightly floured parchment paper-lined baking sheets. Repeat with the remaining pasta sheets.

Cutting the noodles by hand: Lightly flour the surface of a pasta sheet and gently roll it up, starting from a short end, to create a pasta roll. Using a very sharp knife, gently slice the roll into ⅛-inch-wide ribbons. Lightly dust the cut roll with flour, then gently begin to unfold the strips, one by one, as you shake off any excess flour. Transfer them to lightly floured parchment paper-covered baking sheets and arrange them straight and spread out. Repeat with the remaining pasta sheets.

3 However you cut the noodles, let them air-dry for 30 minutes, then cook. Alternatively, cover with a kitchen towel and refrigerate for up to 3 hours. Or freeze on the baking sheets, transfer to freezer bags, and store in the freezer for 3 to 4 weeks. Do not thaw them prior to cooking (they will become mushy), and add an extra minute or two to their cooking time.

4 To cook, bring a large pot of water to a boil. Once it's boiling, add salt (1 tablespoon for every 4 cups water) and stir. Add the pasta and stir for the first minute to prevent any sticking and to disentangle the strands of pasta. Cook until the pasta is tender but still chewy, 2 to 3 minutes. Drain and serve with the sauce of your choice.

PIZZOCCHERI

YIELD: 1 POUND; 6 SERVINGS / ACTIVE TIME: 1 HOUR / TOTAL TIME: ABOUT 1 ¾ HOURS

Pizzoccheri is a thick, purplish gray and hearty pasta from northwestern Italy's Valtellina area, though the residents of the canton of Graubünden in Switzerland may dispute this claim. Tasty, chewy, and hearty, it is ideal during cold winter months, particularly when combined with its traditional Valtellina condiment comprised of butter, fontina cheese, Parmigiano, potatoes, and cabbage. *Pizzoccheri* distinguish themselves from other substantial pastas by their inclusion of buckwheat flour, which gives them dark flecks and a subtle nutty, almost "hoppy" flavor (buckwheat is in fact used to make some gluten-free beers). For best results when working with buckwheat flour, I recommend using ingredients that are all at room temperature and warming up the water until it is almost too hot to comfortably touch (the warmth helps the buckwheat flour come together as dough).

Suggested sauces and pasta dishes: Pizzoccheri della Valtellina (page 477), Fonduta (page 472), Walnut, Black Garlic, and Mascarpone Sauce (page 476), Gorgonzola Cream Sauce with Pan-Toasted Spiced Walnuts (page 474)

INGREDIENTS:

- 1 cup buckwheat flour
- 1 cup all-purpose flour
- ½ teaspoon salt, plus more for the pasta water
- ¼ cup very warm but not boiling water, more as needed
- 2 large eggs

Semolina flour for dusting

1 Prepare the dough as directed on pages 134–135, resting it for 40 minutes. Cut the dough into quarters. Cover three pieces with clear food wrap to prevent them from drying.

2 Rolling the dough using a pasta machine: Lightly flour the piece of dough and, using a rolling pin, roll it into a band about 4 inches wide and 8 inches long. Run the band three times through the widest setting of the pasta machine. The dough will now be 12 to 15 inches long and 4 to 5 inches wide. Repeat this process with the remaining pieces of dough.

Rolling the dough by hand: Using a lightly floured rolling pin, roll the piece of dough into an approximately 10-inch square that is 3/16 inch thick, flouring it as little as possible but as much as necessary to keep the dough from sticking to the counter. Repeat this process with the remaining pieces of dough.

3 Regardless of the method in which the pasta has been rolled, hang the dough across a wooden drying rack (a broom handle set up between two chairs works nicely) and air-dry for 30 minutes, turning the sheets over twice during that time.

4 To make the *pizzoccheri,* lightly flour the surface of a dough sheet and gently roll it up, starting from a short end, to create a pasta roll. Using a very sharp knife, gently slice the roll across

into ⅓-inch-wide ribbons, taking care not to compress the roll too much as you slice through it. Repeat with the remaining pasta sheets. Lightly dust the pasta coils with flour, then unroll them and set on lightly floured parchment paper-lined baking sheets. Air-dry them for 30 minutes, then cook. Alternatively, cover with a kitchen cloth and refrigerate for up to 12 hours.

5 To cook the *pizzoccheri,* bring a large pot of water to a boil. Once it's boiling, add salt (1 tablespoon for every 4 cups water) and stir. Add the pasta and stir for the first minute to prevent any sticking and to disentangle the strands. Cook until the pasta is tender but still chewy, 4 to 5 minutes. Drain and add to the sauce of your choice.

LORIGHITTAS

YIELD: 6 SERVINGS / ACTIVE TIME: 2 ½ HOURS / TOTAL TIME: 3 ½ HOURS , PLUS A DAY OR MORE TO AIR-FRY

Sardinian *lorighittas,* twisted double strands of pasta shaped like large rings, are possibly the most beautiful of the Italian pastas. The name derives from *lorigi,* Sardinian dialect for "ring." They are only made in Morgongiori, a tiny village located in the center of the island. Originally they were prepared to celebrate All Saints' Day and were served with a thick tomato sauce and chicken, though they are now combined with a variety of sauces. Their twisted strands capture tasty sauce like no other.

Suggested sauces and pasta dishes: Sausage Ragù (page 617), Pasta with Mussels, Parsley, and Garlic (page 518), Scallop and Vidalia Onion Sauce (page 584), Spicy Tuna Sauce with Tomatoes (page 522)

INGREDIENTS:

- 2 ¾ cups semolina flour, plus more for dusting

- 1 teaspoon salt, plus more for the pasta water

- 1 cup + 1 tablespoon water

Change to Spicy Tuna Sauce with Tomatoes (page 522)

1 Put the flour and salt in a large bowl, mix well with a fork, and add the water. Mix with the fork until all the water has been absorbed, then start working the dough, still in the bowl, with your hands. In a few minutes the crumbly mixture will begin to come together into a grainy dough.

2 Transfer the dough, along with any bits of dough stuck to the side and bottom of the bowl and loose flour, to a work surface. Begin kneading the dough. Using the heel of your hand, push the ball of dough away from you in a downward motion. Turn the dough 45 degrees each time you repeat this motion, as doing so incorporates the flour more evenly. As you continue to knead, you'll notice the dough absorbing any remaining bits of loose flour. Eventually the dough's graininess will disappear, giving way to a smooth texture. Continue to knead the dough until it becomes smooth and firm, about 10 minutes. Cover the dough tightly in clear food wrap to keep it from drying out and let rest for 1 hour—2 hours is even better. If using within a few hours, leave out on the kitchen counter. Otherwise, put it in the refrigerator, where it will keep for up to 3 days.

3 Between the palms of your hands or on a lightly floured work surface, roll the dough into a 2-inch-thick salami and cut it across into 18 to 20 rounds of even thickness (the easiest way to do this is to cut the roll in half and continue cutting each piece in half until you have 18 to 20 pieces). Cover all the dough pieces but one to keep them from drying out.

4 Between the palms of your hands or on the work surface, roll the piece of dough into a long string, no thicker than

⅙ inch. Wrap the pasta string around the four fingers of one hand twice to form two pasta loops, then break the string off and pinch the two loose string ends together tightly to join them. You now have two pasta loops. (Should you find the resulting pasta loop too large, you can wrap the string of dough around three fingers instead of four.) Using the thumb and index finger of one hand, begin twirling the two pasta strings around each other to form a two-strand braid. Set them on lightly floured parchment paper-covered baking sheets so they are not touching. Repeat until all the dough is used. Should you find the dough becoming too dry as you try to shape the *lorighittas,* moisten your hands as you work the dough. Let them air-dry, flipping them over halfway through, for at least 1 day, then cook (these are best enjoyed as soon as they finish air-drying).

5 To cook the *lorighittas,* bring a large pot of water to a boil. Once it's boiling, add salt (1 tablespoon for every 4 cups water) and stir. Add the *lorighittas* and stir for the first minute to prevent any sticking. The cooking time varies a bit, depending on the *lorighittas'* thickness and how dry the pasta is prior to cooking (if they have been dried for 2 to 3 days, they can take as long as 25 minutes to cook). The *lorighittas* are done when they are soft but still pleasantly chewy. Drain and serve with the sauce of your choice.

RYE MAFALDE

YIELD: 1¼ POUNDS; 6 TO 8 SERVINGS / ACTIVE TIME: 45 MINUTES / TOTAL TIME: 1½ HOURS, PLUS 1 HOUR TO AIR-DRY

Found throughout Italy, *mafalde* are wide ribbons of pasta with ruffles on both of their long sides, which are fantastic at grabbing and holding onto sauce. You can make them using Three-Egg Basic Pasta Dough (page 131) but I love this version, with rye flour and caraway added. Perfect comfort food for the cold winter months.

Suggested sauces: Sauerkraut and Mascarpone Sauce with Crispy Corned Beef Strips (page 630), Fonduta (page 472), Aromatic Walnut Sauce (page 543), Gorgonzola Cream Sauce with Pan-Toasted Spiced Walnuts (page 474)

INGREDIENTS:

- 1 ¾ cups durum wheat flour, plus more for dusting
- 1 cup + 2 tablespoons dark rye flour
- 1 ½ teaspoons ground caraway seeds
- ½ teaspoon salt, plus more for the pasta water
- 3 large eggs
- 3 tablespoons warm water, more if needed
- Semolina flour for dusting

1 Prepare the dough as directed on pages 131–133, adding the caraway with the flours and salt and rolling the dough to the second thinnest setting (generally notch 4) for pasta sheets that are about ⅛ inch thick. Lay the pasta sheets on lightly floured parchment paper-lined baking sheets and air-dry for 15 minutes

2 Working with one pasta sheet at a time, lay it on a lightly floured work surface and trim the ends to create a rectangle. Using a ridged pastry cutter, cut the sheet across into 1-inch-wide strips. Lightly dust the ribbons with flour and set on parchment paper-lined baking sheet so they aren't touching. Repeat with the remaining pasta sheets. Allow them to air-dry for 1 hour, turning them over once halfway through, and then cook. Alternatively, you can place them, once air-dried, in a bowl, cover with a kitchen towel, and refrigerate for up to 3 days. Or freeze on the baking sheets, transfer to freezer bags, and store in the freezer for 3 to 4 weeks. Do not thaw them prior to cooking (they will become mushy), and add an extra minute or two to their cooking time.

3 To cook *mafalde,* bring a large pot of water to a boil. Once it's boiling, add salt (1 tablespoon for every 4 cups water) and stir. Add the pasta and stir for the first minute to prevent any sticking. Cook until the pasta is tender but still chewy, 3 to 4 minutes. Drain and serve with the sauce of your choice.

TAJARIN

YIELD: 4 SERVINGS / ACTIVE TIME: 2 ½ HOURS / TOTAL TIME: 3 ½ HOURS

Rich and golden, *tajarin* are very thin flat noodles from the northern Italian region of Piedmont. Made exclusively from flour and egg yolks, they are frequently paired with the decadently delicious juices of roasted meats like veal, pork, and chicken. Consider saving those juices next time you make a roast and trying them with *tajarin*. A cup is all you will need for this recipe.

Suggested sauces: Fresh Mushroom Sauce (page 551), Bolognese Sauce (page 629), Browned Butter and Sage Sauce (page 466)

INGREDIENTS:

1 recipe All-Yolk Pasta Dough (page 137)

Salt

1 Prepare the dough as directed on pages 137–139, rolling the dough to the thinnest setting (generally notch 5) for pasta sheets that are about ¹⁄₁₆ inch thick. Cut into 8-inch-long sheets. Lay the pasta sheets on lightly floured parchment paper-lined baking sheets. Air-dry for 15 minutes.

2 Working with one pasta sheet at a time, lightly dust it with flour, then gently roll it up, starting from a short end, to create a pasta roll. Using a very sharp knife, gently slice the roll across into ¹⁄₁₂-inch-wide strips. Lightly dust the cut roll with flour, then gently begin unfolding the strips, one by one, as you shake off any excess flour. Arrange them either straight and spread out or curl them in a coil that is referred to as a bird's nest. Repeat with all the pasta sheets. Allow them to air-dry for 30 minutes and then cook. Alternatively, you can place them, once air-dried, on a baking sheet, cover with a kitchen towel, and refrigerate for up to 3 days. I do not recommend freezing them because they are so delicate and susceptible to breaking.

3 To cook the *tajarin,* bring a large pot of water to a boil. Once it's boiling, add salt (1 tablespoon for every 4 cups water) and stir. Add the pasta and stir for the first minute to prevent any sticking and to disentangle the strands of pasta, particularly if you've nested them. Cook until the pasta is tender but still chewy, typically for no more than 2 minutes. Drain and serve with the sauce of your choice.

UMBRICELLI

YIELD: 6 SERVINGS / ACTIVE TIME: 1 HOUR / TOTAL TIME: 3 ¼ HOURS

Reminiscent of long earthworms, these chewy eggless noodles are most commonly found in the northern Italian region of Umbria. Their sturdy shape notwithstanding, *umbricelli* need to be cooked on the same day they are prepared, as their tender and simple dough tends to dry out and become brittle in a hurry.

Suggested sauces: Chicken Liver, Guanciale, and Porcini Mushroom Sauce (page 589), Creamy Mushroom Sauce (page 551), Mutton Ragù (page 643), Rabbit Ragù (page 603), Bucatini all'Amatriciana (page 492)

INGREDIENTS:

3 cups all-purpose flour

1 ½ teaspoons salt, plus more for the pasta water

1 cup tepid water

Semolina flour for dusting

1 Prepare the dough as directed on pages 131–133, rolling the dough to a thickness of ¼ inch (generally notch 2). Lay the pasta sheets on lightly floured parchment paper-lined baking sheets. Let the sheets air-dry for 15 minutes, turning them over halfway through (doing this will make them easier to cut).

2 Working with one pasta sheet at a time, place it on a lightly floured work surface. Using a sharp knife, cut across a short end of the sheet to make ½-inch-wide ribbons. Working with one ribbon at a time, roll it against the work surface with the palms of your hands, applying light pressure, until it is a rope 9 to 10 inches long, with tapered ends. Repeat with the remaining ribbons and remaining pasta sheets. Dust generously with flour, set on lightly floured parchment paper-lined baking sheets so they are not touching, and cover with clear food wrap to prevent them from drying. *Umbricelli* become dry and brittle fairly quickly and need to be cooked on the same day they are made, and preferably within 3 to 4 hours.

3 To cook the *umbricelli,* bring a large pot of water to a boil. Once it's boiling, add salt (1 tablespoon for every 4 cups water) and stir. Add the pasta and stir for the first minute to prevent any sticking. Cook until the pasta is tender but still chewy, about 4 minutes. Drain and add to the sauce of your choice.

PICI

YIELD: 4 SERVINGS / ACTIVE TIME: 1¼ HOURS / TOTAL TIME: 3¼ HOURS

Hefty hand-rolled pasta strings slightly thinner than a pencil, *pici* (or *pinci* as they are known in the Montepulciano area) originate in the province of Siena in Tuscany. No shrinking violet on the plate, they require a sauce savory and substantial enough to stand up to their corpulent size. Ready-made *pici* can often be found in gourmet stores and online, but they really are at their best when they are handmade and fresh. A very forgiving pasta shape, *pici* are expected not to be perfect and often vary in thickness within each noodle. They make up for their rustic imperfections by offering a wonderful, chewy bite. According to Oretta Zanini de Vita's *Encyclopedia of Pasta*, *pici* are sometimes made by adding semolina or farro flours, which makes the pasta a little rougher and easier to roll out by hand.

Suggested sauces sauces and pasta dishes: Bucatini all'Amatriciana (page 491), Pici with Crispy Anchovy Breadcrumbs (page 512), Pici Pasta with Pecorino Cheese and Pepper (page 480), Duck Ragù (page 600), "Fake" Sauce (page 606)

INGREDIENTS:

- 2 cups + 2 tablespoons finely milled type "00" wheat flour OR 2 ½ cups + 5 tablespoons all-purpose flour

- ½ teaspoon salt, plus more for the pasta water

- ⅔ cup warm water

- Semolina flour for dusting

1 Prepare the dough as directed on pages 131–133, rolling the dough to ¼ inch thick (generally notch 2). Lightly dust the sheets with flour and place on parchment paper-lined baking sheets. Let them air-dry for 15 minutes, which will allow them to dry just enough to make it easier to cut them.

2 Working with one pasta sheet at a time, place it on a lightly floured work surface and, using a pastry cutter, cut across its width into ⅓-inch-wide ribbons. To shape, join the two ends of each ribbon to double the strand and then, using the palms of your hands, roll the strand until it becomes a thick (about ⅙ inch) rope that is 9 to 10 inches long with tapered ends. Repeat with all the ribbons and pasta sheets. Lightly dust the *pici* with flour and set them on parchment paper-covered baking sheets so they aren't touching. Let air-dry for 30 minutes, then cook. Alternatively, you can place them, once air-dried and freshly dusted with flour, in a bowl, cover with a kitchen towel, and refrigerate for up to 3 days. Or freeze on the baking sheets, transfer to freezer bags, and store in the freezer for up to 2 months. Do not thaw them prior to cooking (they will become mushy), and add an extra minute or two to their cooking time.

3 To cook the *pici,* bring a large pot of water to a boil. Once it's boiling, add salt (1 tablespoon for every 4 cups water) and stir. Add the *pici* and stir for the first minute to prevent any sticking. Cook until they are tender but still chewy, 3 to 4 minutes. Drain and serve with your sauce of choice.

FARFALLE

YIELD: YIELD: ¾ POUND; 4 SERVINGS / **ACTIVE TIME:** 45 MINUTES / **TOTAL TIME:** 3 HOURS

These pretty butterfly-shaped creations (*farfalle* means butterfly in Italian) are exceptionally versatile, though they especially shine when combined with tomato- or cream-based sauces.

Suggested sauces: Classic Tomato Sauce (page 566), Fresh Tomato Sauce (page 565), Simple Roasted Tomato and Garlic Sauce (page 568), Creamy Leek Sauce (page 504), Walnut, Black Garlic, and Mascarpone Sauce (page 476), Rose Sauce (page 488)

INGREDIENTS:

1 recipe Egg Pasta Dough with Durum Flour (page 134–136)

Semolina flour for dusting

Salt

1 Prepare the dough as directed on pages 134–136, rolling the dough to the second thinnest setting (generally notch 4) for pasta sheets that are about ⅛ inch thick. Lay the pasta sheets on lightly floured parchment paper-lined baking sheets and cover loosely with clear food wrap. Work quickly to keep the pasta sheets from drying out, which makes it harder for the pasta to stick together.

2 Working with one pasta sheet at a time, place it on a lightly floured work surface and trim both ends to create a rectangle. Using a pastry cutter, cut the pasta sheet lengthwise into 1- to 1 ¼-inch-wide ribbons. Carefully separate the ribbons from each other, then, using a ridged pastry cutter, cut the ribbons into 2-inch pieces. To form the butterfly shape, place the index finger of your nondominant hand on the center of the piece of pasta. Then place the thumb and index finger of your dominant hand on the sides of the rectangle—right in the middle—and pinch the dough together to create a butterfly shape. Firmly pinch the center again to help it hold its shape. Leave the ruffled ends of the *farfalle* untouched. Repeat with all the pasta sheets. Set the *farfalle* on lightly floured parchment paper-covered baking sheets so they are not touching. Allow them to air-dry for at least 30 minutes and up to 3 hours, and then cook. Alternatively, you can place them, once air-dried, in a bowl, cover with a kitchen towel, and refrigerate for up to 3 days. Or freeze on the baking sheets, transfer to freezer bags, and store in the freezer for up to 2 months. Do not thaw them prior to cooking (they will become mushy), and add an extra minute or two to their cooking time.

3 To cook the *farfalle,* bring a large pot of water to a boil. Once it's boiling, add salt (1 tablespoon for every 4 cups water) and stir. Add the *farfalle* and stir for the first minute to prevent any sticking. Cook until the pasta is tender but still chewy, 2 to 3 minutes. Drain and serve with the sauce of your choice.

ORECCHIETTE

YIELD: 1 POUND; 6 SERVINGS / ACTIVE TIME: 1 ½ HOURS / TOTAL TIME: 4 TO 5 HOURS

True to their name ("little ears"), *orecchiette* are ear-shaped morsels that hail from the southern Italian region of Puglia. At their most perfect, *orecchiette* are approximately ¾ inch wide and slightly domed. Dragging each *orecchiette* across a flat work surface as it's formed causes the center to be thinner than the outer edges; when cooked, you end up with an enjoyable contrast in textures—the center thin and soft, the outer edges slightly thicker, with a pleasant chew. Homemade *orecchiette* tend to be much more tender than those that are commercially produced.

Suggested sauces and pasta dishes: Pasta with Broccoli Rabe (page 501), Pasta with Arugula and Potatoes (page 493), Sweetbreads, Tomato, and Caper Sauce (page 638), Wild Boar Ragù (page 622), Sausage Ragù (page 617)

INGREDIENTS:

- 2 cups semolina flour, plus more for dusting
- 1 teaspoon salt, plus more for the pasta water
- ¾ cup water, or more as needed

1 Combine the flour and salt in a large bowl. Add the water a little at a time while mixing with a fork. Continue mixing the dough until it starts holding together in a single floury mass. If it's still too dry to stick together, add more water, 1 teaspoon at a time, until it does. Work the dough with your hands until it feels firm and dry, and can be formed into a craggy looking ball

2 Transfer the dough to a lightly floured work surface and knead it for 10 minutes. Because it is made with semolina flour, the dough can be quite stiff and hard. (You can also mix and knead this in a stand mixer; don't try it with a hand-held mixer—the dough is too stiff and could burn the motor out.) Using the heel of your hand, push the ball of dough away from you in a downward motion. Turn the dough 45 degrees each time you repeat this motion, as doing so incorporates the flour more evenly. As you continue to knead, you'll notice the dough getting less and less floury. Eventually it will have a smooth, elastic texture. If the dough still feels wet, tacky, or sticky, dust it with flour and continue kneading. If it feels too dry and is not completely sticking together, wet your hands with water and continue kneading. Wet your hands as many times as you need in order to help the flour shape into a ball. After 10 minutes of kneading, the dough will only be slightly softer (most of the softening is going to occur when the dough rests, which is when the gluten network within the dough will relax). Shape into a ball, cover tightly with clear food wrap, and let rest in the refrigerator for at least 2 to 3 hours or, in refrigerator, for up to 2 days.

3 Cut the dough into four equal sections. Take one dough section and shape it in an oval with your hands and cover the remaining sections with clear food wrap to prevent drying Place it on a lightly floured work surface and, with the palms of your hands, roll it against the surface until it becomes a long ½-inch-thick rope. Using a sharp paring knife, cut the rope into ¼-inch discs, lightly dusting them so they don't stick together. Some pieces may get slightly smushed when cut; if they do, reshape them as needed.

4 To form the *orecchiette,* place a disc on the work surface. Stick your thumb in flour, place it on top of the disc, and, applying a little pressure, drag your thumb, and the accompanying dough, across to create an ear-like shape. Flour your thumb before making each *orecchiette* for best results. Lightly dust the *orecchiette* with flour and set them on lightly floured parchment paper-covered baking sheets so they are not touching. Allow them to air-dry for 1 hour, turning them over once halfway through, and then cook. Alternatively, you can place them, once air-dried, in a bowl, cover with a kitchen towel, and refrigerate for up to 3 days. Or freeze on the baking sheets, transfer to freezer bags, and store in the freezer for up to 2 months. Do not thaw them prior to cooking (they will become mushy), and add an extra minute or two to their cooking time.

5 To cook the *orecchiette,* bring a large pot of water to a boil. Once it's boiling, add salt (1 tablespoon for every 4 cups water) and stir. Add the *orecchiette* and stir for the first minute to prevent any sticking. Cook until they are tender but still chewy, 3 to 4 minutes. Drain and serve with the sauce of your choice.

CORZETTI

YIELD: 6 SERVINGS / ACTIVE TIME: 1 HOUR / TOTAL TIME: ABOUT 2 HOURS

These small, embossed discs of pasta from Liguria aren't stamped just to look beautiful. It serves a tasty functional purpose, which is to hold onto more of the sauce with which the pasta is paired. Look for the stamps online, which are crafted from wood and available with all sorts of lovely designs etched into them.

Suggested Sauces: Truffled Mushroom and Pine Nut Sauce (page 555), Basil Pesto (483), Aromatic Walnut Sauce (page 543), Signora Sofia's Spiced Pork Sauce (page 620), Lamb Ragù (page 641), Browned Butter and Sage Sauce and its variation (page 466), Rabbit Ragù (page 603).

INGREDIENTS:

- 2 cups finely milled type "00" wheat OR 2 cups + 5 tablespoons all-purpose flour
- 1 ½ teaspoons salt, plus more for cooking the pasta
- 1 large egg
- 1 tablespoon extra virgin olive oil
- ½ cup water, more if needed

  Semolina flour for dusting

1 Prepare the dough as directed on pages 131-133, rolling the dough to the thinnest setting (generally notch 5) for pasta sheets that are about ¹⁄₁₆ inch thick. Place on a lightly floured parchment paper-lined baking sheet, separating them with more lightly floured parchment sheets. Make sure to work quickly to keep the pasta sheets from drying out and becoming brittle.

2 Working with one pasta sheet at a time, place it on a lightly floured work surface. Using the *corzetti* stamp, which has a hollowed-out side that acts like a cookie cutter, cut the dough into discs. Place a disc of pasta on top of the stamped section of the *corzetti* stamp and, using the part of the stamp with the handle, gently press down to indent the round with the design. If you find the pasta sticking to the stamp, lightly flour the discs before pressing. Repeat with all the pasta sheets. Gather the scraps together into a ball, put it through the pasta machine to create additional pasta sheets, and cut those as well.

3 Set the *corzetti* on another parchment paper-lined baking sheet so they don't touch. Air-dry for an hour. Cook or cover and refrigerate for up to 24 hours. Or freeze on the baking sheets, transfer to freezer bags, and store in the freezer for 3 to 4 weeks. Do not thaw them prior to cooking (they will become mushy), and add an extra minute or two to their cooking time.

4 To cook the *corzetti*, bring a large pot of water to a boil. Once it's boiling, add salt (1 tablespoon for every 4 cups water) and stir. Add the *corzetti* and stir for the first minute to prevent any sticking. Cook until the pasta is tender but still chewy, 2 to 3 minutes. Drain and serve with the sauce of your choice.

RICOTTA CAVATELLI

YIELD: 6 SERVINGS / ACTIVE TIME: 1 HOUR / TOTAL TIME: 1½ HOURS

These ridged and elongated pasta curls get their name from the Italian word *cavato*, or "indented." So many size and name variations exist on the *cavatelli* theme that it's probably best to consider "cavatelli" an umbrella term, one used to describe plump dumplings that are traditionally shaped over a ridged surface or using a *cavatelli* maker. Chewy and extremely versatile, they can be paired with a variety of meat and vegetable sauces.

Suggested sauces and pasta dishes: Simple Roasted Tomato and Garlic Sauce (page 568), Chicken Liver, Guanciale, and Porcini Mushroom Sauce (page 598), Wild Boar Ragù (page 622), Fresh Fresh Mushroom Sauce (page 551), Signora Sofia's Spiced Pork Sauce (page 620), Pasta with Broccoli Rabe (page 501)

INGREDIENTS:

- 3½ cups all-purpose flour
- 1 teaspoon salt, plus more for the pasta water
- 1 15-ounce container (a little less than 2 cups) whole-milk ricotta cheese
- 2 large eggs

Semolina flour for dusting

1 Put the flour, salt, ricotta, and eggs in a large bowl and, using your hands, knead until the dough is fully combined and mostly smooth, about 10 minutes. Alternatively, you can add all the ingredients to a bowl and, using a hand-held or stand mixer fitted with the dough hook, mix until the dough is fully combined and mostly smooth, about 10 minutes.

2 Wrap the ball of dough tightly in clear food wrap and let rest for 1 hour. If using within 2 to 3 hours, leave out on the kitchen counter; otherwise refrigerate it for up to 3 days and bring back to room temperature before using.

3 Cut the dough into four pieces. Place one on a lightly floured work surface and wrap up the rest in clear food wrap to prevent drying. Divide the piece of dough into four pieces. Again, cover the three remaining pieces. Shape the dough into a long rope about the diameter of your index finger by rolling it on the surface with the palms of your hands. Repeat until you've formed long ropes from all of the dough. Keep them covered until you are ready to work with them.

4 Shaping *cavatelli* by hand: With a sharp paring knife, cut each rope into ¾-inch pieces. Place a small piece of pasta on a lightly floured surface. Shape the pasta by placing the side of your thumb on each piece of pasta and rolling it along the work surface (about an inch or so) while flicking your thumb up ever so slightly in the process. The flick creates a shallow indentation that helps the *cavatelli* to cook more evenly. Repeat with the remaining dough.

Shaping *cavatelli* using a *cavatelli* maker: Clamp a *cavatelli* maker to the edge of the counter. Cover the ropes of pasta generously with flour (it will help the dough not stick to the machine) and cover the ones you're not using as you work. Slowly feed one end of the dough rope into the *cavatelli* maker and turn the crank. It will soon grab the dough. Practice doing this at different speeds to achieve perfect results, as you may find turning it too fast will clog the machine with dough. The dough will come out, cut and shaped, on the other side. Rework any misshapen pieces back into a dough rope and try again.

5 Lightly dust the *cavatelli* with flour and set them on lightly floured parchment paper-covered baking sheets so they are not touching. Allow them to air-dry for 45 min-utes, turning them over once halfway through, and then cook. Alternatively, you can place them, once air-dried, in a bowl, cover with a kitchen towel, and refrigerate for up to 3 days. Or freeze on the baking sheets, transfer to freezer bags, and store in the freezer for 3 to 4 weeks. Do not thaw them prior to cooking (they will become mushy), and add an extra minute or two to their cooking time.

6 To cook the *cavatelli,* bring a large pot of water to a boil. Once it's boiling, add salt (1 tablespoon for every 4 cups water) and stir. Add the *cavatelli* and stir for the first minute to prevent any sticking. Cook until they float to the surface and are tender but still chewy, 4 to 5 minutes. Drain and serve with the sauce of your choice.

MALLOREDDUS

YIELD: 6 SERVINGS / ACTIVE TIME: 1 HOUR / TOTAL TIME: 1 ½ HOURS

A dumpling-like pasta from the island of Sardinia, *malloreddus* are shaped like ridged and elongated seashells. A lovely shade of gold, they contain saffron, which is cultivated on the island, and barley flour, which gives them a slightly sweet and nutty flavor. There is a mass-produced dried version (look for it online) that's also sold as *gnocchetti Sardi* or "little Sardinian gnocchi," but they aren't nearly as plump or, to my taste, satisfying in texture as homemade. *Malloreddus* are prepared most easily using a mechanical *cavatelli* machine, but they can also be shaped using a gnocchi board or the tines of a fork. In days gone by in Sardinia, they were formed by dragging bits of dough across a wicker basket called a *ciurili*.

Suggested sauces: Sausage Ragù (page 617), Lamb Ragù (page 641), Chicken Liver, Guanciale, and Porcini Mushroom Sauce (page 598), Wild Boar Ragù (page 622), Simple Roasted Tomato and Garlic Sauce (page 568), Classic Tomato Sauce (page 566), Fresh Tomato Sauce (page 565)

INGREDIENTS:

- **3 tablespoons water**
- **½ teaspoon (1 large pinch) saffron threads**
- **1 ¾ cups durum wheat flour**
- **1 cup + 2 tablespoons barley flour**
- **3 large eggs**
- **½ teaspoon salt, plus more for the pasta water**
- **Semolina flour for dusting**

1 Heat the water for 20 seconds in a microwave oven until very hot and steaming. Add the saffron threads, cover, and steep for 15 minutes. Pour the saffron water through a fine-meshed strainer, gently pressing down on the saffron threads to squeeze out any remaining color and flavor into the water. Set aside.

2 Make and knead the dough as directed on pages 131–133, adding the saffron water with the eggs. Wrap the ball of dough tightly in clear food wrap and let rest for 1 hour—2 hours is even better if you have the time. If using within a few hours, leave it out on the kitchen counter, otherwise refrigerate it (it will keep for up to 3 days). If you do refrigerate it, however, the dough may experience some discoloration (but it won't affect the flavor at all).

3 Cut the dough into four pieces. Wrap up the rest to prevent drying. Divide the piece of dough into four pieces. Again, cover the three remaining pieces. Place the smaller piece of dough on a lightly floured work surface. Shape the dough into a long rope about ¼ inch in diameter by rolling it on the surface with the palms of your hands. Repeat with the remaining dough and cover until you are ready to work shape the *malloreddus*.

4 Shaping *malloreddus* by hand with a gnocchi board: Using a sharp paring knife, cut the rope into ½-inch pieces, lightly dusting them with flour so they won't stick together. Place a piece

of dough on the gnocchi board. Dab a thumb lightly in flour, place it on the dough piece, and, using a little pressure, drag your thumb, and the accompanying dough, across to create a curled shape. Flour your thumb before making each *malloreddus* for best results.

Shaping *malloreddus* using fork tines: Using a sharp paring knife, cut the rope into ½-inch pieces, lightly dusting them with flour so they won't stick together. Place a piece of dough on the rounded side of a fork, right on the tines. Dab your thumb lightly in flour, place it on the dough piece, and, using a little pressure, drag your thumb, and the accompanying dough, across the length of the tines to create a curled shape. Flour your thumb before making each *malloreddus* for best results.

Shaping *malloreddus* with a *cavatelli* maker: Clamp a *cavatelli* maker to the edge of the counter. Dust the ropes of pasta generously with flour (it will help the dough not stick to the machine) and cover the ones you're not using as you work. Slowly feed one end of a dough rope into the *cavatelli* maker and turn the crank. It will soon grab the dough. Practice doing this at different speeds to achieve per-fect results, as you may find turning it too fast will clog the machine with dough. The dough will come out, cut and shaped, on the other side. Rework any misshapen pieces back into a dough rope and try again.

5 Lightly dust the *malloreddus* with flour and set on parchment paper-lined baking sheets so they are not touching. Allow them to air-dry for 45 minutes, turning them over once halfway, and then cook. Alternatively, you can place them, once air-dried, in a bowl, cover with a kitchen towel, and refrigerate for up to 3 days. Or freeze them on the baking sheets, transfer to freezer bags, and store in the freezer for up to 2 months. Do not thaw them prior to cooking (they will become mushy), and add an extra minute or two to their cooking time.

6 To cook the *malloreddus,* bring a large pot of water to a boil. Once it's boiling, add salt (1 tablespoon for every 4 cups water) and stir for the first minute to prevent any sticking. Cook until they are tender but still chewy, 6 to 7 minutes. Drain and serve with the sauce of your choice.

NODI

YIELD: 6 SERVINGS / ACTIVE TIME: 1 ½ HOURS / TOTAL TIME: 2 ½ HOURS

This is my own adaptation of a novel pasta I discovered on *Briciole* (or "crumbs" in Italian), a food-centric blog written by Simona Carini, a self-described peripatetic food storyteller. Inspired by the shape of the gondola, it's created by making a knot *(nodo)* in a thin rope of dough.

Suggested sauces: Sausage Ragù (page 617), Simple Roasted Tomato and Garlic Sauce (page 568), Sweetbreads, Tomato, and Caper Sauce (page 638), Bolognese Sauce (page 629)

INGREDIENTS:

- 1 ¾ cups + 1 tablespoon semolina flour, plus more for dusting

- 1 teaspoon salt, plus more for the pasta water

- ½ teaspoon finely ground fennel seed

- ⅔ cup warm water

1 Put the flour, salt, and ground fennel in a large bowl and add the water. Begin mixing with a fork until the mixture starts to roughly stick together and look coarse. Gather it together with your hands and transfer it to a lightly floured work surface.

2 Using the heel of your hand, push the ball of dough away from you in a downward motion. Turn the dough 45 degrees each time you repeat this motion, as doing so incorporates the flour more evenly. As you continue to knead, you'll notice the dough getting less and less floury. Eventually it will have a smooth, elastic texture. If it feels wet, tacky, or sticky, dust with flour and continue kneading. If it feels too dry and is not completely sticking together, wet your hands with water and continue kneading. Wet your hands as many times as you need in order to help the flour shape into a ball. Knead for 10 minutes.

3 Cover the dough tightly with clear food wrap to keep it from drying out and let rest for 1 hour—2 hours is even better. If using within a few hours, leave out on the kitchen counter. Otherwise, put it in the refrigerator, where it will keep for up to 3 days.

4 Between the palms of your hands or on a lightly floured work surface, roll the dough into a 2-inch-thick salami and cut it across into 18 rounds of even thickness (the easiest way to do this is to cut the roll in half and continue cutting each piece in half until you have 18 pieces). Cover all the dough pieces but one to keep them from drying out.

5 With the palms of your hands, roll the piece of dough left out into a long rope ⅛ inch thick. Now make the knots. Starting on one end of the rope, tie a simple knot, gently pull on both ends to slightly tighten the knot, then cut the knot off, leaving a tail on each side of about ⅜ inch long. Keep making

and cutting off knots in this manner until you use up all of the rope. Repeat with the remaining pieces of dough. Set the finished knots on lightly floured parchment paper-lined baking sheets so they are not touching. Allow them to air-dry for 2 hours, turning them over once halfway through, and then cook. Alternatively, you can place them, once air-dried, in a bowl, cover with a kitchen towel, and refrigerate for up to 3 days. Or freeze on the baking sheets, transfer to freezer bags, and store in the freezer for up to 2 months. Do not thaw them prior to cooking (they will become mushy), and add an extra minute or two to their cooking time.

6 To cook the knots, bring a large pot of water to a boil. Once it's boiling, add salt (1 tablespoon for every 4 cups water) and stir. Add the knots and stir for the first minute to prevent any sticking. The cooking time will vary, depending on their size and how dry they are, so let cook for 2 to 3 minutes, then start testing for doneness. You want the knots to be soft but still very firm. Drain and serve with the sauce of your choice.

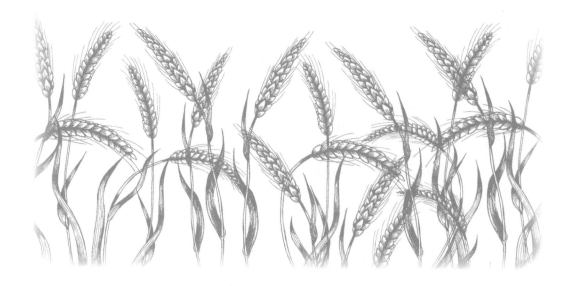

MALTAGLIATI

YIELDS: 6 SERVINGS / ACTIVE TIME: 1 HOUR / TOTAL TIME: 1 ½ HOURS, PLUS 2 HOURS TO DRY

Maltagliati translates to "badly cut" in Italian; they are similar to *fazzoletti* (page 184) in that they are both pieces of thinly rolled pasta dough. But while *fazzoletti* are cut into squares or rectangles, traditionally *maltagliati* were made from all the irregularly shaped trimmings leftover from cutting out the dough for pastas like ravioli, *anolini*, and *agnolotti*. Those pastas are generally made from pasta rolled out so thin, it's almost transparent; I prefer to prepare *maltagliati* from scratch so I can make them slightly thicker, for a bit more chew.

Suggested sauce and pasta dishes: Puttanesca Sauce (page 494), Fresh Mushroom Sauce (page 551), Duck Ragù (page 600), Truffled Mushroom and Pine Nut Sauce (page 555, Maltagliati with Creamy Lemon Sauce (page 469))

INGREDIENTS:

1 recipe Three-Egg Basic Pasta Dough (page 131)

Semolina flour for dusting

Salt

1 Prepare the dough as directed on pages 131–133, rolling the dough to the second thinnest setting (generally notch 4) for pasta sheets that are about ⅛ inch thick. Lay the pasta sheets on lightly floured parchment paper-lined baking sheets. Let the sheets air-dry for 15 minutes, turning them over halfway (doing this will make them easier to cut).

2 Lay a pasta sheet on a lightly floured work surface directly in front of you. Lightly flour the sheet, then fold it into thirds lengthwise, like you would a letter. Using a pastry cutter, cut the folded-up pasta into rough diamond and triangular shapes. No precision is required, so have fun with it. Gently toss the *maltagliati* with flour and transfer to lightly floured parchment paper-covered baking sheets. Repeat with all the pasta sheets. Allow them to air-dry for 2 hours, turning them over once halfway, and then cook. Alternatively, you can place them, once air-dried, in a bowl, cover with a kitchen towel, and refrigerate for up to 3 days. Or freeze them on the baking sheets, transfer to freezer bags, and store in the freezer for up to 2 months. Do not thaw them prior to cooking (they will become mushy), and add an extra minute or two to their cooking time.

3 To cook *maltagliati,* bring a large pot of water to a boil. Once it's boiling, add salt (1 tablespoon for every 4 cups water) and stir. Add the *maltagliati* and stir for the first minute to prevent any sticking. Cook until the pasta is tender but still chewy, about 2 minutes. Drain, add to the sauce of your choice, and serve.

FAZZOLETTI

YIELD: 6 SERVINGS / ACTIVE TIME: 1 HOUR / TOTAL TIME: 2 HOURS

Square or rectangular in shape, like the thin handkerchiefs they are named for, *fazzoletti* are easy to make. You don't have to be all that precise in how you cut them; they'll still taste delicious! I personally like cutting them into squares because I think they look better plated.

Suggested sauces: Puttanesca Sauce (page 494), Mutton Ragù (page 643), Chicken Liver, Guanciale, and Porcini Mushroom Sauce (page 598), Asparagus and Ricotta Sauce (page 499)

INGREDIENTS:

1   recipe Three-Egg Basic Pasta Dough (page 131)

Semolina flour for dusting

Salt

1   Prepare the dough as directed on pages 131–133, rolling the dough to the thinnest setting (generally notch 5) for pasta sheets that are about ¹⁄₁₆ inch thick. Lay the pasta sheets on lightly floured parchment paper-lined baking sheets and let them air-dry for 15 minutes.

2   Using a pastry cutter, cut each pasta sheet into as many 2 ½-inch squares or 1 ½ x 2 ½-inch rectangles as possible. Set them on lightly floured parchment paper-covered baking sheets so they are not touching. Gather the any scraps together into a ball, put it through the pasta machine to create additional pasta sheets, and cut those as well. Allow them to air-dry for 1 hour, turning them over once halfway, and then cook. Alternatively, you can place them, once air-dried, in a bowl, cover with a kitchen towel, and refrigerate for up to 3 days, or transfer them to freezer bags and freeze for up to 2 months. Do not thaw them prior to cooking (they will become mushy), and add an extra minute or two to their cooking time.

3   To cook the *fazzoletti*, bring a large pot of water to a boil. Once it's boiling, add salt (1 tablespoon for every 4 cups water) and stir. Add the *fazzoletti* and stir for the first minute to prevent any sticking. Cook until they are tender but still chewy, about 1 minute. Drain and serve with the sauce of your choice.

TROFIE

YIELD: 5 TO 6 SERVINGS / ACTIVE TIME: 40 MINUTES / TOTAL TIME: 50 MINUTES, PLUS 2 HOURS TO AIR-DRY

From the northwestern region of Liguria, *trofie* are very thin, short, chewy pasta spirals with pointed ends. Its name most likely derives from the verb *strofinare*, which means "to rub," reflecting how the small strips of dough are rubbed along a work surface to form their curled-up shape. Legend has it that Ligurian women would make them as they sat together by the sea waiting for their husbands to return from fishing excursions. Made only from flour, water, and a little salt, *trofie* are fairly neutral in flavor and are consequently at their best when paired with strongly flavored sauces like pesto, meat ragùs, and condiments made from varying combinations of vegetables and seafood.

Suggested sauces: Basil Pesto (page 483), Smoked Salmon and Asparagus Sauce (page 580), Hazelnut and Basil Sauce (page 485), Truffled Mushroom and Pine Nut Sauce (page 555), Sweetbread, Tomato, and Caper Sauce (page 638),

INGREDIENTS:

2 ¾ cups all-purpose flour

1 teaspoon salt, plus more for the pasta water

1 cup water

Semolina flour for dusting

1 Put the flour and salt in a large bowl, mix well with a fork, and add the water. Mix with the fork until all the water has been absorbed, then start working the dough, still in the bowl, with your hands. In a few minutes the crumbly mixture will begin to come together into a grainy dough.

2 Transfer the dough, along with any bits of dough stuck to the side and bottom of the bowl and loose flour, to a lightly floured work surface. Begin kneading the dough. Using the heel of your hand, push the ball of dough away from you in a downward motion. Turn the dough 45 degrees each time you repeat this motion, as doing so incorporates flour more evenly. As you continue to knead, you'll notice the dough absorbing any remaining bits of loose flour. Eventually the dough's graininess will disappear, giving way to a smooth texture. Continue to knead the dough until it becomes smooth and firm, about 10 minutes. Cover the dough with clear food wrap to keep it from drying out and let rest at room temperature for 1 hour—2 hours is even better.

3 Between the palms of your hands or on a lightly floured work surface, roll the dough into a 2-inch-thick salami and cut it across into eight pieces (the easiest way to do this is to cut the roll in half and continue cutting each piece in half until you have eight pieces). Cover all the dough pieces but one to keep them from drying out.

4 Shape the piece of dough into a ball, then roll it against the work surface with the palms of your hands until it's a long ½-inch-thick rope. Cut it into ½-inch pieces. Lightly dust the pieces with flour.

5 Working with one piece at a time, place it at the top of the palm of your nondominant hand. Place the tips of the fingers of your dominant hand on top of the dough (the fingers of both hands should be pointing in the same direction). Press down on the dough with your fingertips and roll the dough all the way down to the palm of your other hand. This action will cause the piece of dough to turn into a narrow spiral with tapered ends. Repeat with the remaining pieces of dough. Dust the spirals with flour and set them on lightly floured parchment paper-covered baking sheets so they are not touching. Allow them to air-dry for 2 hours, turning them over once halfway through, and then cook. Alternatively, you can place them, once air-dried, in a bowl, cover with a kitchen towel, and refrigerate for up to 3 days. Or freeze them on the baking sheets, transfer to freezer bags, and store in the freezer for up to 2 months. Do not thaw them prior to cooking (they will become mushy), and add an extra minute or two to their cooking time.

6 To cook *trofie,* bring a large pot of water to a boil. Once it's boiling, add salt (1 tablespoon for every 4 cups water) and stir. Add the pasta and stir for the first minute to prevent any sticking. Cook until the pasta is tender but still chewy, 3 to 4 minutes. Drain and serve with the sauce of your choice.

CAPPELLACCI DEI BRIGANTI

YIELD: 6 SERVINGS / ACTIVE TIME: 1 ½ HOURS / TOTAL TIME: 3 ½ HOURS

Shaped like old-fashioned pointy hats, *cappellacci dei briganti* (brigands' hats) pay homage to the 19th-century guerrilla fighters known as brigands, who wore these head garments as they rebelled against domestic and foreign occupiers during the Risorgimento, or the unification of Italy. Uniquely shaped, they are actually quite easy to make; all you need are pasta rounds, an index finger, and two fingertips from your other hand.

Suggested sauces: Sweetbread, Tomato, and Caper Sauce (page 638), Roasted Red Pepper, Creamy Corn, and Herb Sauce (page 558), Fresh Mushroom Sauce (page 551), Sausage Ragù (page 617)

INGREDIENTS:

1 recipe Three-Egg Basic Pasta Dough (page 131)

Semolina flour for dusting

Salt

1 Prepare the dough as directed on pages 131–133, rolling the dough to the thinnest setting (generally notch 5) for pasta sheets that are about ¹⁄₁₆ inch thick. Lay the pasta sheets on lightly floured parchment paper-lined baking sheets and cover loosely with clear food wrap. Work quickly to keep the pasta sheets from drying out, which makes it harder for the pasta to stick together.

2 Working with one pasta sheet at a time, use a 2-inch round stamp or pastry cutter to cut out as many discs as possible, covering them loosely with clear food wrap. Repeat with all the pasta sheets. Gather the scraps together into a ball, put it through the pasta machine to create additional pasta sheets, and cut those as well.

3 To shape the *cappellacci,* wrap a disc around your index finger, starting about ½ inch down from the fingertip, making sure one side of the disc overlaps the other side. Apply pressure to seal the two sides at the overlap and then gently fold up the rounded piece of dough at the bottom of the wrapped disc to create a "brim." The pasta should now resemble the hat after which it was named.

4 Transfer the "hats" to lightly floured parchment paper-covered baking sheets, arranging them so they are not touching. Allow them to air-dry for 30 minutes, then cook. Alternatively, after they have air-dried, transfer to a bowl, cover with a kitchen towel, and refrigerate for up to 2 days, or Or, freeze them on the baking sheets, transfer to freezer bags, and store in the freezer for 3 to 4 weeks. Do not thaw them prior to cooking (they will become mushy), and add an extra minute or two to their cooking time.

5 To cook the *cappellacci,* bring a large pot of water to a boil. Once it's boiling, add salt (1 tablespoon for every 4 cups water) and stir. Add the pasta and carefully stir for the first minute to prevent any sticking. Cook until the pasta is tender but still chewy, 2 to 3 minutes. Drain and serve with the sauce of your choice.

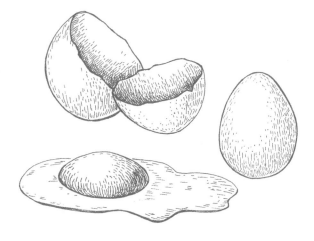

QUADRETTI

YIELD: ¾ POUND PASTA; 6 SERVINGS / ACTIVE TIME: 45 MINUTES / TOTAL TIME: 3 HOURS, PLUS 2 DAYS TO AIR-DRY

Quadretti, which means "little squares" in Italian, belong to the minute or "tiny" pasta family and are always cooked in broth. Though they are not similar in size, *quadretti* are like *maltagliati* (page 183) in that, traditionally, they were made from the trimmings left over from making other pastas and dumplings. This particular shape is very small and delicate and therefore lends itself well to clear broths and consommés that can be enhanced with vegetables cut in julienne strips.

Suggested broths: Capon or Chicken Stock (page 749), Mixed Meat Stock (page 750)

INGREDIENTS:

1   recipe Three-Egg Basic Pasta Dough (page 131)

Semolina flour for dusting

1 Prepare the dough as directed on pages 131–133, rolling the dough to the thinnest setting (generally notch 5) for pasta sheets that are about ⅟16 inch thick. Cut the sheets into 24-inch-long rectangles. Lay the pasta sheets on lightly floured parchment paper-lined baking sheets. Let the sheets air-dry for 15 minutes, turning them over halfway through (doing this will make them easier to cut).

2 Fold each pasta sheet in half lengthwise, so that it becomes 12 inches long. Then fold it in half again lengthwise so it's 6 inches long. Fold it one more time so that you have a roll of pasta 3 inches across. Cut across the roll with a sharp knife to make nested strips ⅛ inch wide. Now cut across those strips in ⅛-inch increments to create tiny pasta squares. Lightly dust them with flour and gently separate them. Transfer to parchment paper-lined baking sheets, spreading them out in a single layer. Repeat with the remaining pasta sheets. Air-dry for 2 days. At that point, you can store them in an airtight container at room temperature or in the freezer for up to 2 months. Do not thaw them prior to cooking (they will become mushy), and add an extra minute or two to their cooking time.

3 To cook *quadretti,* add them to a finished soup and simmer until tender but still chewy, 3 to 4 minutes. Keep in mind that pasta—even tiny pasta—can absorb a lot of liquid. If you want to cook it right in the soup, make sure you have enough liquid so that the pasta doesn't end up absorbing most of it and/or be careful how much pasta you add, or cook the pasta separately in water, then add it to individual soup bowls before ladling in the soup.

GARGANELLI

YIELD: YIELD: 1 ½ POUNDS; 6 SERVINGS / ACTIVE TIME: 1 ½ HOURS / TOTAL TIME: 3 ½ HOURS

Garganelli, yet another of Bologna's many gastronomic contributions, are made by rolling pasta squares into tubes. The dough needs to be pliable and velvety soft in order to be rolled properly, which is done around a thin stick or, better yet, a chopstick. When rolling out the dough square to form the *garganelli* tube shape, you have the option of doing so on a smooth surface or on a ridged wooden gnocchi board. I prefer to use the board because it creates ridges on the surface of the pasta that aid in capturing more savory sauce when they are served.

Suggested sauces and pasta dishes: Kira's Garganelli Pasta with Cream, Ham, and Peas (page 533), Hearty Meat Sauce with Bracciole and Spare Ribs (page 624), Roman-Style Tripe Sauce (page 634), Roasted Red Pepper, Creamy Corn, and Herb Sauce (page 558)

INGREDIENTS:

- 2 ¼ cups semolina flour, plus more for dusting
- 1 ½ teaspoons salt, plus more for the pasta water
- 3 large eggs
- 2 tablespoons extra virgin olive oil
- 2 tablespoons water

1 Prepare the dough as directed on pages 131–133, rolling the dough to the second-thinnest setting (generally notch 4) for pasta sheets that are about ⅛ inch thick. Lay the pasta sheets on lightly floured parchment paper-lined baking sheets, covering them loosely with clear food wrap. Work quickly to keep the pasta sheets from drying out, which makes it harder for the pasta to stick together.

2 Working with one pasta sheet at a time, lightly dust it with flour. Using a pastry cutter, cut it into 1 ½-inch-wide strips. Cut the strips into 1 ½-inch squares. Repeat with the remaining pasta sheets. Cover them loosely with clear food wrap. Gather any scraps together into a ball, put it through the pasta machine to create additional pasta sheets, and cut those as well.

3 To make each *garganello,* place one square of pasta dough on a lightly floured work surface (or gnocchi board if you have one) with one of the corners pointing toward you. Using a chopstick, gently roll the square of pasta around the chopstick, starting from the corner closest to you and rolling away from you to the corner furthest from you until a tube forms. Applying downward pressure as you do this will give the pasta square a ridged texture, if you're doing it on a gnocchi board.

4 Once completely rolled, press down slightly as you roll one final time to seal the ends together, then carefully slide the pasta tube off the chopstick and lightly dust with flour. Set them on lightly floured parchment paper-covered baking sheets so they are not touching. Allow them to air-dry for 1 hour, turning them over once halfway, and then cook. Alternatively, you can place them, once air-dried, in a bowl, cover with a kitchen towel, and refrigerate for up to 3 days, or transfer them to freezer bags and freeze for up to 2 months.

Do not thaw them prior to cooking (they will become mushy), and add an extra minute or two to their cooking time.

5 To cook the *garganelli*, bring a large pot of water to a boil. Once it's boiling, add salt (1 tablespoon for every 4 cups water) and stir. Add the *garganelli* and stir for the first minute to prevent any sticking. Cook until they are tender but still chewy, 2 to 3 minutes. Drain and serve with your sauce of choice.

TESTAROLI

YIELD: 6 SERVINGS / ACTIVE TIME: 1½ HOURS / TOTAL TIME: 1½ HOURS

Testaroli, also known as crépe pasta, is a flat, rhombus-shaped pasta that that is a specialty of Lunigiana, an area that straddles the regions of Liguria and Tuscany. Considered one of the earliest recorded pastas, *testaroli* are a direct descendant of the porridges that were cooked over hot rocks during the Neolithic Age. Its name derives from *testo,* a special pan made of two terra-cotta or cast iron halves in which they are cooked. A most unusual type of pasta by Italian standards, they resemble thin, soft pancakes and are first cooked with dry heat inside the *testo* and then boiled. Since I don't own a *testo,* I've adapted my *testaroli*-making by using a helpful tutorial I found on the wonderfully informative website Serious Eats.

Suggested sauces: Aromatic Walnut Sauce (page 543), Basil Pesto (page 483)

INGREDIENTS:

- 1½ cups durum flour

- 1 cup + 2 tablespoons semolina flour, plus more for dusting

- 2 teaspoons salt, plus more the pasta water

- 2⅔ cups water

- 2 tablespoons extra virgin olive oil, more if needed

1 Stir the flours and salt together in a large bowl. Add the water in a thin, steady stream, whisking continuously. Once it's added, you should have a very thin batter, like crêpe or thin pancake batter. You can make the batter up to 2 hours in advance, cover, and leave at room temperature, or refrigerate for up to 2 days (bring back to room temperature before proceeding).

2 Put the olive oil a small bowl and set it near the stove, along with a heat-proof kitchen brush. Heat a 6-inch nonstick skillet over medium-low heat until a drop of water bounces off the surface, then brush it lightly with the oil. Pour a little less than ¼ cup of the batter into the center of the hot skillet at the same time you tilt the skillet in all directions. (Doing both simultaneously is very important because it helps to spread the batter evenly in the skillet and also creates a perfect circle.) The batter should cover the entire bottom of the skillet in a light coating. Let it cook for 30 seconds or so, until it is lightly browned on the bottom. Gently lift an edge with a spatula to assess the color.

3 Shake and jerk the pan by its handle to dislodge the crêpe, then turn it over with your fingers, a spatula, or toothpick. Cook the crêpe on the other side for another 15 to 20 seconds. When finished, the pancake should be thin, browned, and crispy on the surface while still moist on the inside.

4 Transfer the pancake to a wire rack to cool. Avoid stacking them or overlapping them too much, as they can get soggy. Cook or cool completely, put in a plastic bag, and refrigerate for up to 2 days or freeze for several weeks (thaw before proceeding). Using a pizza or pastry cutter, slice the cooled *testaroli* into rhombus shapes.

5 To cook the *testaroli*, bring a large pot of water to a boil. Once it's boiling, add salt (1 tablespoon for every 4 cups water) and stir. Take the pot off the heat and add the *testaroli*, stirring well. Using a strainer, remove them from the water after 3 minutes and serve with the sauce of your choice.

SOUR TRAHANA

YIELD: 2 CUPS; 8 SERVINGS / ACTIVE TIME: 1 HOUR / TOTAL TIME: 4 TO 5 HOURS

Found throughout Greece, Turkey, Albania, Bulgaria, and Egypt, *trahana* is a crumb-like fermented wheat product that is either treated like rice or pasta and added to stews and soups or consumed like porridge. According to Diane Kochilas, the author of *The Food and Wine of Greece*, it was considered a food staple for the working poor. "Until a generation ago, sour *trahana* was the shepherd's and farmer's breakfast. It was made at the end of every summer all over Greece in preparation for the winter months," she explains. *Trahana* can be made from flours as varied as wheat, cracked wheat, bulgur, semolina, and chickpea and can contain pureed vegetables. In Greece, *trahana* is considered sweet when made with wheat or semolina flour and sheep or goat's milk and sour when yogurt and lemon juice are added to the milk and bulgur flour. Making it in the traditional manner is a rather elaborate and time-intensive process that starts with a thick, porridge-like dough that is fermented for days and then spread out on netting to air-dry in the hot summer sun. Once dried, it is broken or grated into bits that resemble panko breadcrumbs, and can be stored in airtight jars for months. I include a recipe for basic sour *trahana* and a sweet *trahana* version made with pureed vegetables. You can also buy *trahana* ready made online or in a specialty or Middle Eastern food store.

Suggested pasta dishes: Trahana with Green Beans and Tomatoes (page 549), Trahana with Chicken, Red Pepper, and Thyme (page 596)

INGREDIENTS:

- 1 ½ cups coarse bulgur
- 1 cup whole goat's milk or cow's milk
- ½ cup whole-milk Greek yogurt
- ¾ tablespoon fresh lemon juice
- Salt and freshly ground black pepper
- Extra virgin olive oil

1 Put the bulgur, milk, yogurt, lemon juice, and salt and pepper to taste in a medium saucepan over medium heat and bring to a gentle simmer, stirring occasionally to prevent the bulgur from sticking to the bottom of the pan. Continue cooking and occasionally stirring until the mixture becomes very dense and almost solid, 15 to 20 minutes. Remove from the heat.

2 Preheat the oven to 250°F degrees (yes, 250°F) and line a baking sheet with parchment paper. Using a rubber spatula that has been lightly greased with olive oil (to prevent sticking), spread the bulgur mixture over the parchment, filling the entire baking sheet in an even ¼-inch-thick layer.

3 Place the sheet in the oven and bake until the bulgur mixture is completely dry and brittle, 3 to 4 hours (it should color only slightly). If the edges start to brown, remove that portion and

return the pan to the oven until all of the *trahana* is completely dry.

4 Remove from the oven. When cool enough to handle, break the sheet of dough into granules. Once fully cooled, transfer to airtight jars. Store in a cool, dry place for 3 to 4 months.

5 Because of the amount of liquid *trahana* absorbs when it cooks, to keep it from absorbing too much of the broth of a soup, I find it best to cook it first in water, then drain and rinse under cold running to remove any sticky surface starch. Then I add it to each serving of soup. If you place it in the bowl, then ladle the hot soup on top, the soup will warm it up almost instantly. To cook *trahana*, bring a large pot of water to a boil. Once it's boiling, add salt (1 tablespoon for every 4 cups water) and stir. Add the *trahana*, reduce the heat to low, and simmer until they are tender but still chewy, about 20 minutes, then drain.

SWEET TRAHANA

YIELD: 3 CUPS; 6 SERVINGS / ACTIVE TIME: 1 ½ HOURS / TOTAL TIME: 5 HOURS

Possibly the world's oldest "fast food," *trahana* is believed to have originated from the gruel that Greek and Roman foot soldiers ate daily as they conquered the world. Apicius, the 1st-century Roman cookbook author, describes a *trahana*-like gruel called *tractae* that was used to enrich foods. This particular version, typical of the Greek island of Chios, is considered "sweet," though it does not contain sugar, because it gets its moisture from yogurt and the puree of vegetables and not from the addition of milk and lemon juice, otherwise known as "sour milk."

1 Bring a medium pot of water to a boil. Blanch the tomatoes in the boiling water for 1 minute. Use tongs to remove them to a cutting board and let cool until you can handle, then remove their skins. Cut them into quarters, remove the seeds, and chop.

2 Heat a large skillet over medium-low heat for 2 to 3 minutes, raise the heat to medium, add the tomatoes, the pepper, the onion, savory, and salt and pepper to taste, and stir. Bring to a boil, reduce the heat to low, cover, and cook for 40 minutes, stirring occasionally. Remove from the heat and let cool. It will look like watery, chunky tomato sauce.

3 Once cool, transfer the mixture to a food processor or blender and process to a smooth puree. Strain through a food mill or fine-meshed strainer directly into a large bowl. It will look like thick vegetable puree. Add the semolina flour and a generous pinch of salt and mix thoroughly. Cover with clear food wrap and let rest at room temperature for 1 hour, to allow the semolina to absorb the vegetable liquid.

4 Line two rimmed baking sheets with parchment paper. Add the yogurt to the semolina mixture and stir well. Add the bread flour and mix with a wooden spoon until a dough forms.

5 Preheat the oven to 200°F.

6 Transfer the dough to a lightly floured work surface. Dust the dough with flour and begin kneading. Using the heel of your hand, push the dough away from you in a downward motion. Turn the dough 45 degrees each time you repeat this motion, as doing so incorporates the flour more evenly. Knead for 8 to 10 minutes. As you continue to knead, you'll notice the dough getting less and less floury. Eventually it will have a smooth, elastic texture.

INGREDIENTS:

3   very ripe plum tomatoes

1   red bell pepper, seeded and cut into fine dice

1   large onion, diced

¾   tablespoon dried thyme or savory

     Salt and freshly ground black pepper

2   cups semolina flour, plus more for dusting

½   cup whole milk Greek yogurt

1 ¾   cups + ½ tablespoon bread flour

7 Divide the dough into three pieces, patting each one into a ¼-inch-thick round resembling a fat pita bread. Place the rounds on the prepared baking sheets and place on the center rack. Lower the oven temperature to 175°F and bake for 1 hour. Flip the rounds, return to the oven, and bake for another hour. Remove from the oven. At this point, the rounds should be quite firm but not rock hard. Let cool.

8 Once cool, break each round in half and then grate all the pieces, using the large holes on a box grater, resulting in large crumbs. Spread the crumbs on the baking sheets and bake again at 175°F, until they are rock hard, which will take about 1 ½ hours. Remove from the oven and let cool. Once completely cool, cook or store in an airtight container at room temperature for up to 6 months.

9 Because of the amount of liquid *trahana* absorbs when it cooks, to keep it from absorbing too much of the broth of a soup, I find it best to cook it first in water, then drain and rinse under cold running to remove any sticky surface starch. Then I add it to each serving of soup. If you place it in the bowl, then ladle the hot soup on top, the soup will warm it up almost instantly. To cook *trahana*, bring a large pot of water to a boil. Once it's boiling, add salt (1 tablespoon for every 4 cups water) and stir. Add the *trahana*, reduce the heat to low, and simmer until they are tender but still chewy, about 20 minutes, then drain.

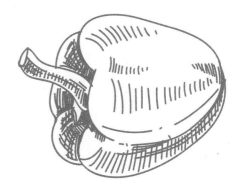

ARMENIAN EGG NOODLES
with ONIONS *and* GARLIC YOGURT

YIELD: 5 TO 6 SERVINGS / ACTIVE TIME: 1¼ HOURS / TOTAL TIME: 1½ HOURS

A cornerstone of Armenian cooking, *tatar boraki* is a rhombus-shaped egg noodle typically served with browned onions and garlic-spiked yogurt. Tasty comfort food, they are frequently prepared at large family gatherings.

INGREDIENTS:

1   cup warm water

1   large egg + 1 large egg yolk, at room temperature, beaten

1   tablespoon sugar

    Salt

2 ½ cups all-purpose flour, or more as needed

3   tablespoons unsalted butter

3   tablespoons extra virgin olive oil

2   large yellow onions, minced

1   cup plain Greek yogurt

3   garlic cloves, minced

    Freshly ground white pepper

2 bay leaves

1   Put the water, eggs, sugar, and 1 teaspoon salt in a large bowl and whisk well. Start adding the flour, ½ cup at a time, and work it in, first with a spoon and then with your hands, on a work surface. Continue adding small amounts of flour until the dough is smooth and no longer sticky, about 10 minutes. Cover the dough with clear food wrap and let it rest at room temperature for 1 hour.

2   While the dough rests, heat a large skillet over medium heat for 2 to 3 minutes, then add the butter and olive oil. When the oil begins to swirl and the butter starts to bubble, add the onions. Cook, stirring occasionally, until they are golden, about 10 minutes. Remove from the heat.

3   While the onions cook, stir the yogurt, garlic, and salt and pepper to taste together in a small bowl. Set aside.

4   Roll and cut the noodles. Divide the dough into three equal portions for easy rolling. (Keep the dough you're not working with covered so it doesn't dry out.) Place one portion on a lightly floured work surface and roll it out with a lightly floured rolling pin to a circle approximately 15 inches in diameter. Dust lightly with flour when needed to make rolling easier. Using a sharp knife or fluted pastry cutter, cut the pasta into rhombuses. Arrange the noodles in a single layer on a lightly floured parchment paper-lined baking sheet. As you continue making *tatar boraki,* keep adding layers of parchment paper lightly dusted with flour to stack them vertically. Repeat with the remaining dough.

5   Bring a large pot of water to a boil. When it's boiling add salt (1 tablespoon for every 4 cups water) and the bay leaves and stir. Add the noodles (you may need to do this in batches) and stir for the first minute to prevent any sticking. Cook until they float to the surface, 4 to 6 minutes. Using a strainer, transfer the *tatar boraki* to a warmed serving bowl.

6 When half the noodles are cooked, top with half of the sautéed onions and half of the garlic yogurt. Top that with the remaining cooked *tatar boraki,* then finish with a final layer of onions and then the garlic yogurt. Gently toss to combine and serve piping hot.

BAY LEAVES

Use dried bay leaves in this recipe, and all future dishes that you prepare. Dried bay leaves contribute a subtle herbal taste to dishes that rounds out the flavor of the meal. In contrast, fresh bay leaves are overpowering in taste and are not recommended for cooking unless they are removed before the dish is served.

CHINESE EGG NOODLES

YIELD: ABOUT 1 POUND; 6 SERVINGS / ACTIVE TIME: 45 MINUTES / TOTAL TIME: 1 HOUR

This springy, chewy noodle is especially versatile and can be used in lo mein and chow mein dishes as well as soups. It is very forgiving and is an especially excellent option for the novice noodle-maker. The technique for slicing the noodles makes you the master of your own destiny, allowing you to cut the dough into thin strands or thick, meaty ribbons. Unlike Italian egg pasta dough, which only needs to be kneaded, this Chinese egg noodle recipe requires that its dough be "beaten" with a rolling pin. This technique gives noodles a superior "elastic band"-like bounce referred to as *sans kansui*, and recalls the dying art of making *jook-sing* noodles, which requires men to pummel the dough with giant bamboo poles.

INGREDIENTS:

2 cups all-purpose flour, plus more for dusting

1 teaspoon salt

2 large eggs, lightly beaten

3 to 4 tablespoon water, more if needed

1 Mix the flour and salt together in a large bowl. Add the eggs and mix until a floury dough forms. Add 3 tablespoons of the water and continue to mix until you almost can't see any remaining traces of flour. If you find, even after adding the water, that your dough is still very floury, add more water, 1 tablespoon at a time, and continue mixing it with your hand until the dough starts coming together more easily. Start kneading the dough in the bowl with your dominant hand (it is okay to have some loose flour at the beginning of this process). Continue kneading in the bowl until a smooth ball forms; this may take about 10 minutes of kneading. Wrap the dough tightly in clear food wrap and let rest at room temperature for 40 to 50 minutes to allow the gluten in the dough to relax.

2 Unwrap the dough and place it on a lightly floured work surface. Using a rolling pin, begin "beating" the dough, turning it over after every 10 whacks or so. Continue doing this for 6 minutes. Then shape the dough into a ball, cover with clear food wrap, and let rest at room temperature for another 30 minutes.

3 Return the dough to the work surface (no need to flour again). Cut it in half and wrap one half in clear food wrap to prevent drying. Roll the other half into a large, thin sheet about twice the length and breadth of the length of your rolling pin (you should be able to almost see your hand through it). Lightly flour both sides of the sheet of dough and then fold the sheet of dough twice over itself to create a three-layered fold (like a letter).

Using a very sharp knife, slice across the roll into evenly spaced strands. (You can make them as thin or thick as you'd like or your recipe directs.) As you cut the dough, be sure to hold the knife perpendicular to the surface and lightly push the newly cut strip away from the roll with the knife to completely separate it. Continue until you have cut the entire roll, then lightly dust the slivered pasta with flour to prevent any sticking. Transfer the noodles to a parchment paper-lined baking sheet, shaking off any excess flour if necessary. You can leave them nested or unspool them according to your preference, as either way they will unravel and straighten once boiled. Repeat with the remaining dough. Cook or cover and refrigerate for up to day. Or freeze on the baking sheets, transfer to freezer bags, and freeze for 3 to 4 weeks. Do not thaw them prior to cooking (they will become mushy), and add an extra minute or two to their cooking time.

To cook, bring a large pot of water to a boil and add the noodles. Stir for the first minute to separate the strands and prevent any sticking. Cook until they are tender but still chewy; the time will depend on the thickness of the noodle. It is best to start taste-testing them after a couple of minutes. Drain and use as directed in the particular recipe.

UDON NOODLES

YIELD: 6 SERVINGS / ACTIVE TIME: 1 HOUR / TOTAL TIME: 3 HOURS

Thick, chewy, soft, slippery, and almost irresistibly gummy, Japanese udon noodles are at their best when made fresh. The packaged dried versions are thinner and shorter and their texture does not hold up to hearty flavorings. Thankfully Asian supermarkets sell them both fresh and frozen—or make them yourself!

INGREDIENTS:

- ¼ cup + 2 tablespoons warm water
- 1 teaspoon fine sea salt
- 2 ¼ cups cake flour or finely milled type "00" wheat flour
- Potato starch or cornstarch for dusting

1 Stir the water and salt together in a small bowl until the salt dissolves.

2 Mixing and the kneading the dough by hand: Put the flour in a large bowl and make a well in the center. Add the salted water in a stream while stirring the flour with a spoon. Once all the water has been added, begin working the dough with your hands to incorporate all the floury clumps into one mass. If the dough is too dry to come together, add plain water, 1 teaspoon at a time, and continue to mix until the dough sticks together in a firm mass.

Transfer the dough to a very lightly floured work surface. Knead the dough with the palm of your dominant hand, turning it 45 degrees with each pressing, until the dough becomes uniformly smooth and it slowly springs back when pressed by a finger, about 10 minutes.

Mixing and kneading the dough in a stand mixer: Put the flour in the bowl of a stand mixer fitted with the paddle attachment. Turn the mixer on low speed and add the salted water in a steady stream. Once the water has been added, stop the mixer and check the dough. If still floury and clumpy, turn the mixer on medium speed and add plain water, 1 teaspoon at a time, until the dough sticks together in a firm mass. Swap the paddle attachment for the dough hook and knead on medium speed until all of the dough gathers around the hook, about 10 minutes. The dough should be soft and silky.

3 Cover the dough tightly with clear food wrap and let rest for 1 to 2 hours to relax the gluten.

4 Cut the dough into two pieces. Set one on a lightly floured work surface and wrap the other in clear food wrap to prevent drying.

5 Pat the piece of dough into a rectangular shape and, using a lightly floured rolling pin, roll the dough into a rectangle that is ⅛ inch thick. Lightly dust the dough with flour, then fold it twice over itself to create a three-layered fold (like a letter).

6 Using a very sharp knife, slice across the roll into ⅛-inch-wide strands. As you cut the dough, be sure to hold the knife perpendicular to the surface and lightly push the newly cut strip away from the roll with the knife to completely separate it. Continue until you have cut the entire roll, then lightly dust the slivered pasta with flour to prevent any sticking. Transfer the noodles to a parchment paper–lined baking sheet, shaking off any excess flour if necessary. Repeat with the remaining dough. Udon noodles quickly turn brittle and break when handled, so cook as soon as you finish making them.

7 To cook, bring a large pot of water to a boil. When it's boiling, add salt (1 tablespoon for every 4 cups water) and stir. Add the noodles and stir for the first minute to separate the strands and prevent any sticking. Cook until they are tender but still chewy, 3 to 4 minutes. It is best to start taste-testing them after a couple of minutes. Drain and use as directed in the particular recipe.

TAIWANESE HAND-PULLED NOODLES

YIELD: 5 TO 6 SERVINGS / ACTIVE TIME: 3 HOURS / TOTAL TIME: 3 ½ HOURS

For centuries the Taiwanese have been hand-pulling smooth, springy, chewy noodles by twisting, stretching, and folding dough in just the right way. It's almost a mystical experience to witness. And the delicious results of that labor are added to soups and stir-fries for maximum enjoyment.

Traditionally, hand-pulled noodles were made including the ashes of a grass native to China. Its addition was important since the ashes contained an alkaline agent that encouraged the dough to absorb more water and to create more gluten networks, which in turn enabled the dough to be pulled sooner and longer. Most of today's noodle pullers now use an additive made mostly from potassium carbonate. This recipe uses an even more common ingredient, baking soda, to good effect.

I hesitated to include this fantastic recipe in the book because making hand-pulled noodles involves kneading techniques that are quite challenging to fully and clearly describe in words. For this reason, I encourage readers to go to YouTube and search "hand-pulled noodles" to avail themselves of the very helpful videos cooks have posted there. Should your first attempts not turn out as you would like, please do not be disheartened. Professional noodle pullers typically train for at least a year with a noodle master before they are allowed to make noodles for customers.

INGREDIENTS:

- 1 ⅓ cups bread flour
- 1 tablespoon + 2 teaspoons all-purpose flour
- ½ teaspoon salt
- ¼ teaspoon baking soda
- ½ cup warm water
- Cake flour for dusting
- ½ tablespoon peanut or grapeseed oil (optional)

1 Mix both flours, the salt, and baking soda together in the bowl of a stand mixer fitted with the paddle attachment. Turn the mixer on medium speed and add the water in a slow stream; mix until the dough is very smooth, which will take about 15 minutes. Remove the dough from the bowl, wrap in clear food wrap, and let rest for 1 hour at room temperature.

2 Return the dough to the bowl of the mixer and swap the paddle attachment for the dough hook. On speed 3, knead the dough until it is smooth and has no give to it, like Play-Doh; this will take about 15 minutes.

3 Transfer the dough to a lightly floured work surface (use cake flour). Shape it into a thick sausage and then start rolling it back and forth on the surface with the palms of your hands until it becomes a ¾- to 1-inch-diameter rope 2 to 2 ½ feet long.

4 Lightly dust the work surface again with cake flour. Holding the long rope by both ends, snap the center of the rope against the floured surface. Then bring the ends together, as if you

are holding the joined ends of a noose, and twist both ropes of dough to create a two-roped braid. Reshape the braid back into a sausage and roll it back and forth on the surface with the palms of your hands until it becomes a rope 2 to 2 ½ feet long.

5 Repeat Step 4 until the dough is soft, pliable, and does not spring back when you push a finger into it. This may take 10 to 15 minutes, depending on the ambient temperature, humidity, and even altitude.

6 To pull the noodles, reshape the braid back into a sausage and roll it back and forth on the surface with the palms of your hands until it becomes a rope 2 to 2 ½ feet long a final time. Take hold of each end with your hands and stretch the rope as long as you can, opening your arms as wide as you can. Bring both ends together to create a loop of dough. Fold that loop in half to create four strands of dough. Once again, holding both ends of the dough, stretch your arms as wide open as you can. Bring the ends of the end together and fold in half to create eight strands. Continue this process until you have achieved the desired thickness in the noodle.

7 When you are done, gently tear off the thick meeting point of ends of the noodles (where you've been holding them with your hands). Dredge the noodles in cake flour and shake off the excess.

8 To cook, bring a large pot of water to a boil. Add the noodles and stir for the first minute to separate the strands and prevent any sticking. Cook until they are tender but still chewy, 1 to 3 minutes, depending on their thickness. Start testing them after a minute. Drain. Use immediately as directed in your recipe or toss with ½ tablespoon oil to prevent sticking, cool, and store in an airtight container in the refrigerator for up to 2 days. To reheat them, put them in boiling water for 45 to 60 seconds, using chopsticks to gently separate them.

CAT'S EAR NOODLES

YIELD: ABOUT 1 POUND; 5 TO 6 SERVINGS / **ACTIVE TIME:** 20 MINUTES / **TOTAL TIME:** ABOUT 3 HOURS

Small pillows of dough shaped like cat ears, *mao er duo* are the Chinese equivalent of *orecchiette*. Like their Italian counterpart, making them involves the tricky technique of curling pieces of dough using a thumb. Once mastered, the process produces a chewy noodle that adds satisfying heft to soups and stir-fries.

INGREDIENTS:

½ cup + 2 tablespoons warm water, more if needed

1 teaspoon salt

2 ¾ cups cake flour or finely milled type "00" wheat flour

Potato starch or cornstarch for dusting

1 Stir the water and salt together in a small bowl until the salt dissolves.

2 Mixing and kneading the dough by hand: Put the flour in a large bowl and make a well in the center. Add the salted water in a stream while stirring the flour with a spoon. Once all the water has been added, begin working the dough with your hands to incorporate all the floury clumps into one mass. If the dough is too dry to come together, add plain water, 1 teaspoon at a time, and continue to mix until the dough sticks together in a firm mass.

Transfer the dough to a very lightly floured work surface. Knead the dough with the palm of your dominant hand, turning it 45 degrees with each pressing, until the dough becomes uniformly smooth and it slowly springs back when pressed by a finger, about 10 minutes.

Mixing and kneading the dough in a stand mixer: Put the flour in the bowl of a stand mixer fitted with the paddle attachment. Turn the mixer on low speed and add the salted water in a steady stream. Once the water has been added, stop the mixer and check the dough. If still floury and clumpy, turn the mixer on medium speed and add plain water, 1 teaspoon at a time, until the dough sticks together in a firm mass. Swap the paddle attachment for the dough hook and knead on medium speed until all of the dough gathers around the hook, about 10 minutes. The dough should be soft and silky.

3 Cover the dough tightly with clear food wrap and let rest for 1 to 2 hours to relax the gluten.

4 Cut the dough into two pieces. Set one on a work surface lightly dusted with potato starch and wrap the other in clear food wrap to prevent drying.

5 Pat the piece of dough into a rectangular shape and, using a rolling pin lightly dusted with potato starch, roll the dough into a rectangle that is ¼ inch thick. Dust lightly with potato

starch and cut across into ½-inch-wide strips, then cut each strip into ½-inch squares. Dust the squares with potato starch to prevent any sticking. Repeat with the remaining dough.

6 To shape the *mao er duo,* place a dough square on a lightly floured work surface. Using your thumb, push on the square in a down and forward motion so that the square curls up slightly into a bit of a cone shape. Repeat with the remaining squares.

7 Lightly dust the *mao er duo* with potato starch and transfer to a parchment paper-lined baking sheets. For best results, they should be cooked within 30 minutes of preparation.

8 To cook the *mao er duo,* bring a large pot of water to a boil. Once it's boiling, add salt (1 tablespoon for every 4 cups water) and stir. Add the *mao er duo* and stir for the first minute to prevent any sticking. Cook until they are tender but still chewy, about 6 minutes. Drain and use as directed in your recipe.

DING DING CHAO MIAN NOODLES

YIELD: 1 ⅓ POUNDS; 4 TO 5 SERVINGS / ACTIVE TIME: 1 HOUR / TOTAL TIME: 1 ½ TO 3 HOURS

This short "noodle," which is as thick as the wide end of a chopstick, shares the same name as a popular Chinese lamb, tomato, and pepper stir-fry dish from Xinjiang. Literally "stir-fried noodle cubes," chewy *ding ding chao mian* are also known as *soman* and *din din soman* in Central Asia.

INGREDIENTS:

- ¾ cup hot but not boiling water
- ⅛ teaspoon salt
- 2 ⅓ cups all-purpose flour, plus more for dusting
- Grapeseed oil for brushing work surface and tossing with noodles if needed

1 Put the water and salt in a small bowl and stir until the salt dissolves.

2 Mixing and kneading the dough by hand: Put the flour in a large bowl and make a well in the center. Add the salted water slowly while stirring the flour with a wooden spoon. Once all the water has been added, begin working the dough with your hands (the mixture will have cooled enough in the mixing process to be able to do so) to incorporate all the floury clumps into one mass. If the dough is too dry to come together, add more hot water, 1 teaspoon at a time.

Transfer the dough to a very lightly floured work surface. Knead the dough with the palm of your hand, turning it 45 degrees with each pressing, until the dough becomes uniformly smooth and it slowly springs back when pressed by a finger; this will take about 15 minutes. Return the dough to the bowl.

Mixing and kneading the dough with a stand mixer: Fit the mixer with the paddle attachment. Put the flour in the bowl. With the mixer running on medium speed, add the salted water and mix until all the flour has been incorporated into the dough and a ball forms. Remove the paddle attachment and, using a spatula, remove any dough stuck to it. Now attach the dough hook and knead on low speed until all of the dough has gathered around the hook, about 10 minutes. The dough will be soft and silky. Scrape the dough off the hook and return to the bowl.

3 Cover the bowl tightly with clear food wrap and let rest at room temperature for anywhere from 30 minutes to 2 hours (the longer the better, depending on how much time you have). Once rested, the dough can be used right away or refrigerated for up to 24 hours and used once it has been brought back to room temperature.

4 Once the dough has rested, prepare a large work surface by brushing it with a thin layer of oil. Place the dough on top and, using your hands, press it into a ⅓-inch-thick rectangular sheet. Brush the top of the dough with oil as well, then cover loosely with clear food wrap. Let rest for 20 minutes.

5 Bring a large pot of water to a boil.

6 Slice the sheet of dough widthwise into 12 strips. Separate them slightly as you cut them to prevent them from sticking together.

7 Working with one strip at a time, gently but firmly pull the strip with both hands until it becomes ¼ inch thick, then return it to the work surface. Repeat this process with the remaining 11 strips. Once finished, brush the strips lightly with oil to prevent sticking.

8 Line all the strips next to one another and, using a sharp knife or pastry cutter, cut them across into ⅓-inch pieces. Brush them again lightly with oil to prevent sticking (should they stick anyway, they will separate in the boiling water when you cook them). Cook them as soon as you cut them.

9 To cook the noodles, bring a large pot of water to a boil. When the water is boiling, add salt (1 tablespoon for every 4 cups water) and stir. Add the noodles and stir for the first minute to prevent any sticking. Once the noodles float to the top, continue to cook until they are cooked but still firm and very chewy, 2 to 3 minutes (timing depends on the thickness of the noodles). Drain and rinse well under cold water to remove the surface starch and to stop them from cooking. Drain again and use as directed in the desired recipe. If not using right away, transfer the noodles to a bowl and drizzle with a little grapeseed oil. Toss well, cover, and set aside or refrigerate for up to 24 hours.

GNOCCHI, SPÄTZLE, & OTHER DUMPLINGS

*N*onna, *zeidy, halmoni, nai nai, oba-chan, oma, mor mor,* or *babcia.* No matter how you say it, in every culture around the world, no food is more synonymous with grandmother than dumpling. Whether made from potatoes and served with a sauce, or rice flour and served in a soup, dumplings deliver portions of comfort, goodness, and love. Pull up a chair, sweetie, and eat. Everything will be just fine.

POTATO GNOCCHI

YIELD: 8 SERVINGS / ACTIVE TIME: 1 ½ HOURS / TOTAL TIME: 2 ¼ HOURS

Nubby, ridged, and slightly creviced, potato gnocchi (gnocchi di patate) are arguably the most well known of all Italian dumplings. Extremely versatile because of their neutral flavor, these tender, pillowy mounds can be combined with a variety of sauces for maximum enjoyment.

Much ado has been made over how best to prepare them so they are as tender as possible. As it turns out, the potato variety is not nearly as important as using the minimum amount of flour to bind the dough. After much experimentation, and some helpful guidance from the good folks at *Cook's Illustrated*, I've discovered that baking—not boiling—the potatoes creates the best results, because this dry-heat method of cooking them doesn't add more moisture to the already water-filled vegetable. Regardless of the method I use, I also include instructions on how to boil the potatoes, for those of you who, like my beloved mother, feel more comfortable following the traditional way of cooking them.

Suggested sauces: Signora Sofia's Spiced Pork Sauce (page 620), Lamb Ragù (page 641), Rabbit Ragù (page 603), Fonduta (pages 472), Gorgonzola Cream Sauce with Pan-Toasted Spiced Walnuts (page 474), Pesto (page 483)

INGREDIENTS:

- 3 pounds (about 6) potatoes (Yukon Gold are best but russets will do)
- 2 large eggs
- 2 ½ cups all-purpose flour, plus extra for dusting
- 1 tablespoon salt
- ¼ cup freshly grated Parmigiano-Reggiano cheese, plus more for dusting

1 Bring a large pot of water to a boil and add the potatoes. Cook them until you can easily insert a knife through the thickest part of a potato, 35 to 40 minutes. Alternatively, you can also bake the potatoes. Prick them several times with a fork and bake them, covered in aluminum foil, on a baking sheet at 425°F for 45 minutes or so.

2 When the potatoes are cool enough to handle, peel off their skin if boiled or scoop the flesh out of their skin if baked. Pass them through a potato ricer while still warm. Alternatively, you can place them in a wide, shallow bowl and press them with a potato masher until smooth. Create a mound on your work surface (do not use a food processor or blender, as it works the potatoes too thoroughly, which will then affect the texture of the gnocchi). Create a small crater in the middle of the mound. Add the eggs, 1 ½ cups of the flour ,and the salt, then start working it into a dough with your hands. Knead the dough as you add the remaining 1 cup flour, pressing down and away from you with the heel of your hand. Then fold the dough, turn it 45 degrees, and

repeat the process. As soon as it forms into a nonsticky ball of dough, stop adding flour. The secret to making tender gnocchi is to add just enough flour so that the dough sticks together and not a flicker more. Form the dough into a mound.

3 Lightly flour the work surface and rip off a handful of dough. Shape it into a thick sausage, then, using the palms of your hands, roll it into a long ¾-inch-thick rope. Cut it across into ½-inch pieces.

4 After you finish cutting each rope, give the gnocchi ridges. (The ridges are not just a decorative element, though they do make them look pretty. They actually serve two purposes: They create a little crevice in the back of the gnocchi, which helps them cook more evenly, and they allow more of the sauce to stick to the gnocchi, enhancing everyone's eating experience.) To create the ridges, gently roll each piece on a gnocchi board or on the back of the tines of a fork. This may take a little practice. At times you may find the dough sticking to the board or fork. When this happens, which is not at all uncommon, sprinkle the board with or dip the fork into flour before you press the *gnoccho* against it.

5 When finished, put the gnocchi on a parchment paper-lined baking sheet so they don't touch and lightly dust with flour. Once you run out of room, cover them with another sheet of parchment and begin stacking them vertically. Repeat with the remaining dough. Cook or cover and refrigerate for up to a day. Or freeze on the baking sheet, transfer to freezer bags, and store in the freezer for up to 3 months.

6 In preparation of boiling the gnocchi, place the Parmigiano in the bottom of a large heat-proof bowl.

7 Bring a large pot of water to a boil. Once it's boiling, add salt salt (1 tablespoon for every 4 cups water) and stir. Cook the gnocchi in batches of 20 to 25. They will immediately plummet to the bottom of the pot. Do not touch them. Within a minute or two, they will start to float up to the top. Cook them for another minute or so. Remove them with a strainer, gently shaking them over the pot to remove any excess moisture, then transfer them to the bowl with the Parmigiano. Add a ladleful of whatever sauce you are using and a dusting of Parmigiano, and toss gently (I slowly run a rubber spatula along the side of the bowl, which works really well in combining them without smushing the gnocchi). Continue in this manner until all the gnocchi are cooked.

8 Divide the sauced gnocchi among warmed bowls. Serve piping hot topped with a little additional sauce, if desired, and a final dusting of Parmigiano.

POTATO GNOCCHI *with* TOMATO SAUCE *and* MOZZARELLA

YIELD: 8 TO 10 SERVINGS / ACTIVE TIME: 30 MINUTES / TOTAL TIME: 2 ½ HOURS

A classic summer dish from the sunny Italian region of Campania, and the coastal town of Sorrento in particular, *gnocchi alla Sorrentino* is a wonderful combination of sweet tomato sauce, molten mozzarella, and piquant pecorino cheese. If you can find *mozzarella di bufala*, mozzarella made from the milk of the Italian water buffalo, it will lend its distinctive subtly tart tanginess and raise the dish to even greater heights.

1 Preheat the oven to 425°F. Grease either a 9 x 13-inch baking dish or individual gratin dishes with butter.

2 Put a few tablespoon of the hot tomato sauce in a bowl large enough to hold all the gnocchi.

3 Bring a large pot of water to a boil. Once it's boiling, add salt (1 tablespoon for every 4 cups) and stir. Cook the gnocchi in batches of 20 to 25. They will immediately plummet to the bottom of the pot. Do not touch them. Within a minute or two, they will start to float up to the top. Cook them for another minute or so. Remove them with a strainer, gently shaking them over the pot to remove any excess moisture. Transfer them to the bowl, add another few tablespoons of sauce, a handful of mozzarella cubes, and a sprinkling of the Parmigiano and pecorino, and toss gently with a rubber spatula until well combined. (I slowly run a rubber spatula along the side of the bowl, which works really well in combining them without smushing the gnocchi). Continue in this manner, using up all the pecorino cheese, half of the Parmigiano, and enough of the sauce so that all of gnocchi are thoroughly and abundantly coated.

4 Pour the gnocchi into the prepared dish or carefully spoon into individual gratin dishes and top with the remaining ½ cup of grated Parmigiano. Place on the center rack and bake until the mozzarella has melted and the gnocchi are hot, 10 to 15 minutes. Remove from the oven and let cool for a few minutes, then garnish with the basil and serve.

INGREDIENTS:

Butter for greasing the baking dish

2½ to 3 cups Classic Tomato Sauce (page 566), warmed

Salt

1 recipe Potato Gnocchi (page 219) prepared through Step 5 or 3 pounds store-bought potato gnocchi

1 pound mozzarella cheese, preferably di bufala, cut into small cubes

1 ½ cups freshly grated Parmigiano-Reggiano cheese, divided

1 cup freshly grated pecorino Sardo

Thinly sliced fresh basil leaves for garnish

POTATO GNOCCHI
with TRUFFLED CHEESE SAUCE

YIELD: 6 SERVINGS / ACTIVE TIME: 15 MINUTES / TOTAL TIME: 25 MINUTES (GNOCCHI NOT INCLUDED)

Known as *gnocchi alla bava* (literally "drool gnocchi" in Italian), this is a traditional dish from the alpine region of Aosta Valley (Valle d'Aosta), an area celebrated for its rich dairy products. Potato gnocchi's pleasant chewiness is a perfect accompaniment to the creamy cheese sauce. But should you not have time to make gnocchi, or even go get them at the store, please feel free to use just about any dry pasta shape under the sun with this sauce.

1 Heat the cream in a medium saucepan over low heat until it is almost bubbling. Add the cheeses, truffle oil, and pepper to taste and cook, stirring occasionally and gently, until the cheeses melt.

2 Put a few tablespoon of the hot cheese sauce in a warmed bowl large enough to hold all the gnocchi.

3 Bring a large pot of water to a boil. Once it's boiling, add salt (1 tablespoon for every 4 cups) and stir. Cook the gnocchi in batches of 20 to 25. They will immediately plummet to the bottom of the pot. Do not touch them. Within a minute or two, they will start to float up to the top. Cook them for another minute or so. Remove them with a strainer, gently shaking them over the pot to remove any excess moisture. Transfer them to the bowl, add another few tablespoons of sauce, and toss gently with a rubber spatula until well combined (I slowly run a rubber spatula along the side of the bowl, which works really well in combining them without smushing the gnocchi). Add more gnocchi and sauce to the bowl in this manner until they are all cooked.

4 Ladle the gnocchi into warmed bowls and serve piping hot, topped with a few cracks of white pepper and a sprinkling of parsley.

INGREDIENTS:

- 2 cups heavy cream
- 1 ½ cups freshly grated Parmigiano-Reggiano cheese
- ¼ pound Fontina cheese (preferably from Valle d'Aosta), grated
- 1 ½ teaspoons truffle oil
  Freshly ground white pepper
- ½ recipe Potato Gnocchi (page 219) prepared through Step 5 or 1 pound store-bought potato gnocchi
  Chopped fresh parsley for garnish

ARUGULA GNOCCHI *with* HERBED CHEESE

YIELD: 6 SERVINGS / ACTIVE TIME: 1 ½ HOURS / TOTAL TIME: 1 ¾ HOURS

Essentially gnocchi with a smooth, unridged surface, these are known as *chicche* in Italy. They are the kind of dumpling a doting Italian grandmother or great-aunt might make for the apple of her eye. This particular version stretches the term *rustic* a tad by incorporating peppery arugula and creamy Boursin cheese into its dough.

Suggested sauces: Fonduta (page 472), Gorgonzola Cream Sauce with Pan-Toasted Spiced Walnuts (page 474), Truffled Mushroom and Pine Nut Sauce (page 555), Smoked Salmon and Asparagus Sauce (page 580)

INGREDIENTS:

- ½ pound arugula, trimmed of thick stems
- 1 ½ pounds (about 3) Yukon Gold or russet potatoes
- 1 large egg
- 2 tablespoons extra virgin olive oil
- 1 ⅔ cups all-purpose flour, plus more for dusting
- ¼ cup freshly grated Parmigiano-Reggiano cheese
- 3 tablespoons Boursin cheese
- 2 teaspoons salt

    Freshly ground white pepper

1 Wash the arugula but don't pat it dry. Place a 10-inch skillet on the stove and turn the heat to medium-high. Add the arugula, with the water still clinging to it, by the handful. Mix well with tongs until the leaves have softened but are still bright green. Drain in a colander. When cool enough to handle, squeeze any remaining water out of the arugula and mince it. Set aside.

2 Bring a large pot of water to a boil, then add the potatoes. Cook until you can insert a knife through the thickest part of a potato with no resistance, 35 to 40 minutes, then drain. You can also bake the potatoes. Prick them several times with a fork and bake at 425°F for 45 minutes or so.

3 As the potatoes cook, put the arugula, egg, and olive oil in a mini food processor and pulse until smooth.

4 When the potatoes have cooled enough to handle, peel off their skins or scoop the flesh out of their skins. Pass them through a potato ricer directly into a large bowl. Alternatively, you can place them in a wide, shallow bowl and press them with a potato masher until smooth. Add the arugula mixture, flour, cheeses, salt, and pepper to taste and mix with your hands until the dough comes together.

5 Transfer the dough to a lightly floured work surface and knead for 5 minutes. Using the heel of your hand, push the ball of dough away from you in a downward motion. Turn the dough 45 degrees each time you repeat this motion, as doing so incorporates flour more evenly. As you continue to knead, the dough will become soft and smooth. Form the dough into a 2 ½-inch-thick salami. Cut it across into 8 equal pieces (the easiest

way is to first cut the roll in half and continue cutting each piece in half until you have 8 pieces). Cover all the dough pieces but one with clear food wrap to prevent them from drying.

6 On a lightly floured work surface, with the palms of your hands, roll out the small piece of dough into a long ½-inch-thick rope. Cut it across into ¾-inch pieces. Repeat with the remaining dough. Put the *chicche* on parchment paper-lined baking sheets so they don't touch and sprinkle lightly with flour. Cook or cover and refrigerate for up to a day. Or freeze them on the baking sheets, transfer to freezer bags, and store in the freezer for 3 to 4 weeks. Do not thaw them prior to cooking (they will become mushy), and add an extra minute or two to their cooking time.

7 Bring a large pot of water to a boil. Once it's boiling, add salt (1 tablespoon for every 4 cups water) and stir. Adjust the heat so that the water is boiling gently and not furiously. Add the gnocchi in batches of 20 to 25. They will immediately plummet to the bottom of the pot. Do not touch them. Within a minute or two, they will start to float up to the top. Cook them for another minute or so. Remove them with a strainer, gently shaking them over the pot to remove any excess moisture, then transfer them to a warmed serving bowl. When they are all cooked, add the sauce of choice and gently toss with a rubber spatula to combine (I slowly run a rubber spatula along the side of the bowl, which works really well in combining them without smushing the gnocchi). Ladle into warmed bowls and serve piping hot topped with a light dusting of white pepper.

BACCALÀ GNOCCHETTI
with RADICCHIO CREAM SAUCE

YIELD: 8 SERVINGS / ACTIVE TIME: 1 ½ HOURS / TOTAL TIME: 2 HOURS, PLUS 3 DAYS FOR SOAKING THE BACCALÀ

Adding *baccalà* (dried salted cod) to the potato mixture yields a chewier texture and a milder flavor. You'll have to plan ahead, though, as the salt cod requires three days of soaking to soften and lose enough of its salt to become tasty. I especially love this sauce with it because the peppery notes of the radicchio balance out the whisper of sweetness the salt cod brings to the *gnocchetti*. There are four varieties of radicchio, but the one most commonly found in the United States is Chioggia. It resembles a small, dark crimson cabbage and is available at most well-stocked supermarkets throughout the year. Of all the radicchio, it has the strongest flavor. If you prefer a little less boldness, consider using the Treviso variety. It looks like a larger, awkwardly shaped crimson Belgian endive, and lends mellower astringency to the sauce.

1 Three days before you intend to make the *gnocchetti,* place the *baccalà* in a large bowl with a wide bottom and completely submerge in water. Cover and refrigerate. Change the water twice a day, morning and evening. This step removes excess salt from the salt-cured cod and makes it edible. When ready to cook, drain the *baccalà,* remove any remaining skin or bones, dry with paper towels, and mince. Set aside.

2 Bring a large saucepan of water to a boil and add the potatoes. Cook them until you can easily insert a knife through the thickest part, 30 to 40 minutes. Drain and, when cool enough to handle, remove their skins. While still very warm, pass the potatoes through a potato ricer into a large bowl. Alternatively, you can place them in a wide, shallow bowl and press them down with a potato masher until smooth. Dump the potatoes out onto a work surface and spread it out to help cool it and allow as much of the steam to dissipate as possible.

3 Once cool enough to handle, around 5 to 8 minutes, evenly sprinkle the potatoes with the cheese, lemon zest, ⅓ cup of the *baccalà,* the flour, beaten egg, and salt and pepper to taste on top. Using a bench scraper, begin mixing the added ingredients into the still warm potatoes. Mix until the dough begins sticking together. Continue working the dough for another minute or two until it has an even consistency and the ingredients are thoroughly mixed in. You may find you need to add a little more flour, a tablespoon at a time, to create a nonsticky ball of dough.

INGREDIENTS:

GNOCCHETTI:

5 ounces baccalà

1 ⅓ pounds (about 2) Yukon Gold or russet potatoes

⅓ cup freshly grated manchego cheese

Grated zest of 1 lemon

¾ cup all-purpose flour, or more as needed

1 large egg, beaten

Salt and freshly ground white pepper

SAUCE:

3 tablespoons unsalted butter

1 large head radicchio, cored and shredded

Salt and freshly ground white pepper

1 ½ cups heavy cream

Juice of ½ lemon

3 tablespoons warm water

½ c up loosely packed fresh parsley leaves, chopped

4 Shape the dough into a square block and lightly flour the work surface. Using a knife or bench scraper, cut off a slice 1 inch in thickness. With the palms of your hands, roll the dough into a long ½-inch-thick rope, then cut it across into ½-inch pieces. Put them on a parchment paper-lined baking sheet so they don't touch and lightly sprinkle with flour. Repeat with the remaining dough.

5 Cook or cover and refrigerate for up to a day. Or freeze them on the baking sheet, transfer to freezer bags, and store in the freezer for 3 to 4 weeks.

6 Make the sauce. Heat a large skillet over medium heat for 2 to 3 minutes, then add the butter. When it melts and stops foaming, add the radicchio, a couple pinches of salt, and white pepper to taste and stir. Cook, stirring a few times, until the radicchio wilts, about 5 minutes. Add the warm water and cook until the radicchio softens, another 4 to 5 minutes. Using a slotted spoon, transfer the radicchio to a bowl and cover to keep warm. Add the cream to the skillet and bring to a gentle boil. Reduce the heat to low and cook until the sauce is thick and reduced, about 15 minutes.

7 While the sauce simmers, bring a large pot of water to a boil. When it's boiling, add salt (1 tablespoon for every 4 cups water) and stir. Adjust the heat so that the water is boiling gently and not furiously. Add the *gnocchetti* in batches of 20 to 25. They will immediately plummet to the bottom of the pot. Do not touch them. Within a minute or two, they will start to float up to the top. Cook them for another minute or so. Remove them with a strainer, gently shaking them over the pot to remove any excess moisture, then transfer them to a large warmed bowl, tenting it loosely with aluminum foil to keep them warm.

8 Pour enough of the reserved *gnocchetti* cooking water to cover the bottom, by ¼ inch, of a skillet large and deep enough to hold the finished dish. Turn the heat to medium and once the water starts to simmer, add the remaining *baccalà* and cook for 2 minutes. Add the lemon juice, radicchio, cream, and parsley and continue cooking, gently stirring, until it begins to gently bubble. Add the *gnocchetti* and gently toss with a rubber spatula to combine (I slowly run a rubber spatula along the side of the bowl, which works really well in combining them without smushing the *gnocchetti*). Bring the mixture back to a gentle boil, then ladle into warmed serving bowls. Serve piping hot, topped with a light dusting of white pepper.

CHEESY CHOCOLATE GNOCCHI

YIELD: 8 SERVINGS / ACTIVE TIME: 45 MINUTES / TOTAL TIME: 2 HOURS

While these brown-hued potato gnocchi (*gnocchi al cacao*) contain cocoa and a tiny amount of sugar, they nevertheless remain savory dumplings. I have found they taste best with a rich, creamy sauce, to better accentuate their subtly smoky, woodsy flavor. When combined with any of the sauces suggested below, they become a rather rich and filling dish that can be served as a main course or, in smaller portions, as a starter.

Suggested sauces: Walnut, Black Garlic, and Mascarpone Sauce (page 476), Aromatic Walnut Sauce (page 543), Creamy Mushroom Sauce (page 551)

INGREDIENTS:

- 1 ½ pounds (about 3) Yukon Gold potatoes
- 1 ¾ cups all-purpose flour, or more as needed
- 2 tablespoons unsweetened cocoa powder
- 2 teaspoons sugar
- ½ teaspoon ground cinnamon
- 5 ounces room temperature Brie cheese, rind cut off
- 2 large eggs, lightly beaten
- 1 tablespoon salt, plus more for cooking the gnocchi
- Freshly ground white pepper

1 Bring a large pot of water to a boil and add the potatoes. Cook until you can easily insert a knife through the thickest part, 35 to 40 minutes. Alternatively, you can bake them. Prick them several times with a fork and bake at 400°F for 45 minutes or so. When the potatoes are cool enough to handle, peel off their skins.

2 While still very warm, pass the potatoes through a potato ricer directly over a large bowl. Alternatively, put them in a wide, shallow bowl and press with a potato masher until smooth. Add the flour, cocoa, sugar, cinnamon, Brie, eggs, 1 tablespoon salt, and white pepper to taste. Mix well with your hands until you have a cohesive dough. Continue kneading in the bowl until the dough is smooth, about 5 minutes. (To test the dough, bring a small saucepan of water to a boil. Drop in a small ball of dough and wait until it floats to the surface, which should take about a minute and no longer than two If the ball falls apart or has a really soft and mushy texture, knead more flour, 1 tablespoon at a time, into the dough.)

3 Shape the dough into an approximately 1 ½-inch-thick sausage, then cut it across into ten even pieces. Place a piece on a lightly floured work surface. Using the palms of your hands, roll the piece back and forth until it becomes a long ½-inch-thick rope. Cut the rope across into ⅓-inch pieces. Repeat with the remaining dough. Transfer the gnocchi to a lightly floured parchment paper-lined baking sheet so they are not touching. Cook or cover and refrigerate up to 2 days. Or freeze on the baking sheet, transfer to a freezer bag, and store in the freezer for 3 to 4 weeks. Do not thaw them prior to cooking, and add an extra minute or two to their cooking time.

4 Bring a large pot of water to a boil. Once it's boiling, add salt (1 tablespoon for every 4 cups water) and stir. Add the gnocchi in batches and cook until they float to the top, 2 to 3 minutes. Taste test one to make sure they're fully cooked. Using a strainer, remove from the water, gently shaking them over the pot to remove excess surface moisture. Transfer to a warmed serving bowl and tent loosely with aluminum foil while you cook the remainder.

5 Once they are all cooked, add the desired sauce and gently toss with a rubber spatula to combine, then serve.

ROMAN-STYLE SEMOLINA GNOCCHI

YIELD: 4 SERVINGS / ACTIVE TIME: 45 MINUTES / TOTAL TIME: 1¼ HOURS

Gnocchi alla Romana's very name discloses its origins, the city of Rome and surrounding Lazio region. Made from a polenta-like semolina mixture that is cooled, stamped into rounds, and baked topped with dots of butter and Parmigiano, these savory dumplings possess a subtle sweetness. Possibly as tasty as the dumplings themselves are the scraps that remain from cutting the sheet of dough into rounds. You can bake them along with the rounds, or you can dip them into lightly beaten egg, dredge in breadcrumbs, fry in a little oil, and enjoy as a crispy gift to the cook!

INGREDIENTS:

5 ½ cups whole milk

9 tablespoons unsalted butter, divided, plus more for buttering the baking dish

Salt

2 cups semolina flour

1 ½ cups freshly grated Parmigiano-Reggiano cheese, divided

3 large egg yolks, at room temperature

1 teaspoon freshly grated nutmeg

⅓ cup Gorgonzola cheese, crumbled

1 Bring the milk, 1 tablespoon of the butter, and a pinch of salt to a gentle boil in a large saucepan over medium heat. Add the semolina in a thin stream, stirring continuously with a wide whisk to keep lumps from forming. Bring back to a gentle boil. Reduce the heat to low and simmer, stirring occasionally, until the mixture becomes very thick, 18 to 20 minutes.

2 Remove from the heat and whisk in 4 tablespoons of the butter and ¾ cup of the Parmigiano. Wait 5 minutes and then add the egg yolks, one at a time, whisking well after each addition. Taste for seasoning and add salt if needed.

3 Wipe down a large wooden cutting board with a wet sponge. Spread the hot semolina mixture on the board and, using a wide, flat spoon, spread it over the board so that it's about ¾ inch thick. Let it cool for 1 hour.

4 Preheat the oven to 425°F. Butter a large shallow baking dish.

5 Using a 2-inch round cutter, cut as many rounds as you can from the cooled semolina. To make cutting the semolina easier, dip the cutter in a small bowl of cold water between cuts. Start by placing the misshapen leftover cuttings, in an even layer, in the bottom of the baking dish. Cover with slightly overlapping semolina rounds. Sprinkle with the nutmeg and remaining ¾ cup Parmigiano. Cut the remaining 4 tablespoons butter into bits and distribute on top. Place on the center rack and bake until the top is golden brown, about 20 minutes. Let cool for 10 minutes, then serve.

BAKED SPINACH *and* RICOTTA GNOCCHI
with SAGE BUTTER

YIELD: 4 SERVINGS / ACTIVE TIME: 45 MINUTES / TOTAL TIME: ABOUT 1 HOUR

This recipe was inspired by the interestingly named Italian Swiss chard-stuffed dumpling from the northern region of Trentino-Alto Adige called *strangolapreti,* or "priest chokers" (allegedly named so as to recount how gluttonous priests of yesteryear would apparently eat them so zealously that they risked choking on them).

After several attempts at making these gnocchi in the traditional way, by boiling, I was unhappy with the resulting watery lumps and decided to bake them. This yielded a moist but dry and pleasantly meaty texture.

INGREDIENTS:

- 2 ½ cups whole milk ricotta
- 2 10-ounce containers baby spinach leaves
- 4 garlic cloves, unpeeled
- Handful fresh basil leaves, gently torn into pieces
- ½ cup all-purpose flour
- 1 teaspoon freshly grated nutmeg
- ¾ cup freshly grated Parmigiano-Reggiano cheese, plus more for serving
- 4 large egg yolks
- Salt and freshly ground white pepper
- 8 tablespoons (1 stick) unsalted butter
- 5 to 6 fresh sage leaves

1 Spoon the ricotta into a fine-meshed strainer lined with cheesecloth that has been set over a large bowl. Let it drain for 30 minutes. Then, gather the cheesecloth in a bundle and squeeze it, tourniquet style, to squeeze any remaining water from the ricotta. Set aside. Rinse the spinach; don't bother to pat dry.

2 Bring a small saucepan of water to a boil and add the garlic cloves. Cook for 4 minutes, then drain (this mellows out their flavor just a bit). Let cool and remove the skins.

3 Place a large skillet over medium-high heat. Add the spinach (with the water still clinging to it) by the handful. Mix well with tongs until the leaves have softened but are still bright green. Drain in a colander. Once cool enough to handle, squeeze any remaining water out with your hands and mince.

4 Preheat the oven to 350°F. For the easiest possible clean-up, line two large baking sheets with aluminum foil, including the raised sides, and then with parchment paper trimmed to fit the pan bottoms.

5 Place the torn basil leaves and boiled garlic halves in a mini food processor and pulse until the mixture resembles pesto without the oil. Scrape down the side of the processor with a rubber spatula as needed so everything gets chopped finely. Transfer it to a large bowl along with the drained ricotta, spinach, flour, nutmeg, Parmigiano, egg yolks, and salt and pepper to taste and mix very well. Roll the dough into balls that are slightly smaller than golf balls. Put them on the prepared baking sheet spaced about 1 ½ inches apart.

6 Place 2 tablespoons of the butter in a small microwave-friendly dish and heat for 30 seconds, until melted. Brush the gnocchi with the melted butter. Place in the oven and bake until lightly golden brown on top, 15 to 20 minutes.

7 As the gnocchi bake, melt the remaining 6 tablespoons butter in a large heavy skillet over medium-low heat. Add the sage leaves and cook until the edges curl and the butter turns an amber color, about 6 minutes.

8 Place the gnocchi on a platter, pour the sage butter over them, sprinkle with Parmigiano, and serve piping hot.

BUTTERNUT SQUASH GNOCCHI

YIELD: **4 SERVINGS** / **ACTIVE TIME:** 45 MINUTES / **TOTAL TIME:** 1½ HOURS

Irregularly shaped gnocchi di zucca from Lombardy are one of the easiest and speediest of dumplings to make, as the dough is dropped by the teaspoonful into the boiling water. Speed and ease aside, what will have you making these tasty morsels over and over again is the nuanced flavor of lemon zest and nutmeg in every bite. It has become such a family favorite that my daughter accuses me of not loving her if I don't make them at least three times every fall.

INGREDIENTS:

- 1 **3-pound butternut squash**
- 1 **tablespoon olive oil**
- 3 **large eggs**
- 1 **tablespoon salt, plus more for cooking the gnocchi**
- 1 **tablespoon sugar**
- 2 **teaspoons freshly grated nutmeg**
- **Grated zest of 1 lemon**
- **2 tablespoons Marsala wine (optional)**
- 2 **cups all-purpose flour**
- 6 **tablespoons (¾ stick) unsalted butter**
- 8 **fresh sage leaves**
- **Freshly ground black pepper**
- **Freshly grated Parmigiano-Reggiano cheese for serving**

1 Preheat the oven to 400°F. Slice off the top and bottom off the squash. Rest it on its widest end and, using a heavy kitchen knife, slice down vertically. If it's difficult to do (it is for me), use a rubber mallet to tap gently on the pointy side of the blade. Work as slowly as you need to and wedge the knife all the way to the base of the squash. When you have the two separated squash halves, use a spoon to scrape out the seeds and fibrous insides. Prick the flesh with a fork. Brush all the cut surfaces lightly with the olive oil (I use my hands to do this) and place, cut side down, on a parchment paper-lined baking sheet. Place on the center rack of the oven, lower the temperature to 375°F, and roast until you can easily pierce the squash with a fork, 40 to 45 minutes. Remove from the oven and let cool, then scoop the soft flesh off the skins with a large metal spoon.

2 While still very warm, pass the squash through a potato ricer directly over a large bowl. Alternatively, you can place it in a wide, shallow bowl and press it with a potato masher until smooth. Measure out 3 cups of the squash flesh and place it in a large bowl. Add the eggs, salt, sugar, nutmeg, lemon zest, and Marsala if using. Using a stand mixer fitted with a whisk attachment, mix until well combined. Replace the whisk attachment with the dough hook and slowly begin adding the flour. Mix thoroughly until well blended and the dough starts to pull away from the side of the bowl. If the flour you added has not made that happen, continue to add flour, 1 tablespoon at a time, until it does. (Alternatively, you can mix it by hand.)

3 Bring a large pot of water to a boil. Once it's boiling, add salt (1 tablespoon for every 4 cups water) and stir. Then, using two teaspoons, make little dumplings from the dough. Do this by scooping up a teaspoon of dough with one teaspoon and using the other teaspoon to scrape it off into the boiling water. That's really

it! Work in batches. Don't add more than 15 to 20 gnocchi to the pot at a time. Once each batch has cooked about 2 minutes, you'll see the gnocchi floating on the surface of the water. That's how you know they are done cooking. Scoop them up with a strainer or large slotted spoon and give them a quick jiggle over the pot of water to drain excess water. Transfer to a warmed serving bowl and loosely tent with aluminum foil to keep warm as you cook the remainder.

4 When you've added your last batch of gnocchi to the boiling water, heat a small saucepan over medium heat for 2 to 3 minutes, then add the butter. When it's melted, add the sage and cook for several minutes, until the butter starts to lightly brown. Pour the sage butter over all the gnocchi and mix gently. Serve piping hot topped with a couple cracks of pepper and a dusting of Parmigiano (or serve the grated cheese in a bowl at the table).

RICOTTA GNOCCHETTI

YIELD: 6 SERVINGS / ACTIVE TIME: 40 MINUTES / TOTAL TIME: 50 MINUTES

Airy and light, these diminutive gnocchi almost scream for a savory powerhouse of a sauce to highlight their pillowy deliciousness. Thanks to Food & Wine Test Kitchen whiz Justin Chapple, I learned a simple trick that takes a lot of the time and hassle out of making them. It involves tying kitchen string to both handles of a large stockpot and then using it to "cut" the *gnocchetti* dough as it is being squeezed from a pastry bag. The secret to successfully using this unique technique is to work quickly, as your hands will be close to boiling water. I've tried this method and, quite honestly, found that filling the pastry bag with dough was more burdensome a task than having my hands close to the water. I admit to feeling rather invincible when cutting all those gnocchi in what felt like a flash.

Suggested sauce and pasta dishes: Aromatic Walnut Sauce (page 543), Wild Boar Ragù (page 622), Truffled Mushroom and Pine Nut Sauce (page 555), Basil Pesto (page 483), Pasta with Broccoli Rabe (page 501)

INGREDIENTS:

Salt

1 15-ounce container (a little less than 2 cups) whole-milk ricotta

2 large eggs, lightly beaten

1½ cups freshly grated Parmigiano-Reggiano cheese, plus more for serving

1 teaspoon freshly grated nutmeg

Leaves from 1 small sprig fresh thyme, minced

Freshly ground white pepper

1¼ cups all-purpose flour

1 Tie a piece of kitchen string around both handles of a large stockpot filled with water. You want the string to run taut across the top of the pot, above the water. Bring the water to a boil. When it's boiling, add salt (1 tablespoon for every 4 cups water) and stir.

2 While the water comes to a boil, combine the ricotta, eggs, Parmigiano, nutmeg, thyme, a couple pinches of salt, and pepper to taste in a large bowl. Add the flour and, using your hands, mix until just combined. At this point, the dough should feel wet and slightly sticky. Don't add more flour and don't overwork the dough, as both will make the *gnocchetti* tough.

3 Working in batches, spoon enough dough to halfway fill a pastry bag with an open tip. Holding it over the boiling water, lightly squeeze the bag to release a half inch or so of dough, then rub it across the kitchen string to "cut" it off. Continue like this until the pastry bag is empty. Cook the *gnocchetti* until they float to the surface of the water, about 3 minutes. Using a strainer, transfer them to a warmed serving bowl. Tent loosely with aluminum foil to keep warm. Repeat until all the dough is used up. Serve with your sauce of choice. The cook gnocchetti can be refrigerated, covered, for up to 2 days.

CHICKPEA GNOCCHETTI

YIELD: **4 SERVINGS** / ACTIVE TIME: **1 ½ HOURS** / TOTAL TIME: **1 ½ HOURS**

This is my adaptation of a fantastic recipe in one of my favorite pasta cookbooks, *Pasta By Hand,* by Jenn Louis. I am a sucker for chickpeas, and as soon as I saw her Chickpea Gnocchetti, I just had to try it and was pleased with the *gnocchetti's* subtle flavor of chickpeas. I will warn you that the dough is very tacky during kneading; don't be tempted to add more flour. I added it the first time I made them and ended up with hard gnocchi. Instead, generously flour your work surface and you will end up with a very malleable dough that you can roll without sticking. Even so, these rustic *gnocchetti* are dense and very chewy, very different in texture—but wonderful in their own right—than pillowy potato gnocchi.

Suggested sauces and pasta dishes: Fava Bean, Pancetta, and Pecorino Condiment (page 608), Pasta with Arugula and Potatoes (page 493), Roasted Red Pepper, Corn, and Herb Sauce (page 558), Signora Sofia's Spiced Pork Sauce (page 620)

INGREDIENTS:

- 1 **14-ounce can chickpeas or 1 ⅓ cups cooked chickpeas**
- 2 **large eggs**
- 1 **tablespoon water**
- 1 ½ **cups all-purpose flour**
- 1 ½ **teaspoons salt, plus more for cooking the gnocchetti**

  Semolina flour for dusting

- ½ **cup freshly grated Parmigiano-Reggiano cheese, plus more for serving**

1 Drain and rinse the chickpeas well in a colander under cold running water. Using your thumb and index finger, remove the outer skin from each chickpea (this is optional but it creates a smoother dough).

2 Put the chickpeas, eggs, and water in a food processor and process into a smooth puree. Transfer the puree to a medium bowl and add the flour and salt. Knead by hand in the bowl until a soft, tacky dough forms, 7 to 8 minutes. (This dough has no stretch whatsoever. If you poke it with a finger, the indentation should remain.)

3 Lightly flour the work surface. Tear off a handful of the dough and cover the rest with clear food wrap to keep it from drying out. Shape the dough into a long rope about ½ inch in diameter by rolling it on the surface with the palms of your hands. Using a sharp paring knife, cut it into ⅓-inch pieces. Dust the pieces lightly with flour.

4 Making the *gnocchetti* with a gnocchi board: Place a piece of dough on the gnocchi board. Dab a thumb lightly in flour, place it on the dough piece, and, using a little pressure, drag your thumb, and the accompanying dough, across the board to create a curled shape. Flour your thumb before making each *gnocchetto* for best results.

Making the *gnocchetti* with fork tines: Place a piece of dough on the rounded side of a fork, right on the tines. Dab your thumb lightly in flour, place it on the dough piece, and, using a little pressure, drag your thumb, and the accompanying dough, across the length of the tines to create a curled shape. Flour your thumb before making each *gnocchetto* for best results.

5 However you form them, lightly dust the *gnocchetti* with flour and place on a parchment paper-lined baking sheet so they are not touching. Cook or cover and refrigerate for up to a day. Or freeze on the baking sheets, transfer to freezer bags, and store in the freezer for 3 to 4 weeks. Do not thaw them prior to cooking, and add an extra minute or two to their cooking time.

6 To cook the *gnocchetti*, bring a large pot of water to a boil. While it comes to a boil, put the Parmigiano in a large heatproof bowl. Once the water is boiling, add salt (1 tablespoon for every 4 cups water) and stir. You will need to cook the *gnocchetti* in batches. Add them three handfuls at a time and stir for the first minute to prevent any sticking. Cook until they float to the top, 3 to 4 minutes. Using a strainer, transfer them to the bowl, add a ladleful of the chosen sauce, toss gently to coat, and cover the bowl with aluminum foil to keep warm. Keep cooking and saucing the *gnocchetti* in this way until they are all cooked, then serve with a final sprinkling for Parmigiano (or pass the grated cheese at the table).

CHICKPEAS

Chickpeas' nutty flavor will complement each of the suggested sauces for this dish in a distinct and delectable style. This legume, also known as the garbanzo bean, will add a boost of protein and fiber to this recipe. In addition, the health benefit of eating chickpeas encompasses lowering cholesterol, regulating digestion, and more.

CANEDERLI *with* SPECK *and* TOASTED CARAWAY BREADCRUMBS

YIELD: 5 TO 6 SERVINGS / ACTIVE TIME: 10 MINUTES / TOTAL TIME: 20 MINUTES

Plump, meaty, walnut-sized bread dumplings, *canederli* come to us from the Austrian-influenced northern Italian region of Trentino-Alto Adige, also known as Südtirol. Traditionally, *canederli* contain speck, a delectable pork product akin to prosciutto that is native to the area. Cured and smoked, it has a much lighter flavor than the heavily smoked hams found north of the Alps, but is more robust than the more delicate and mildly sweeter prosciuttos produced in more southern areas of Italy, like prosciutto di Parma or prosciutto di San Daniele.

Canederli are frequently served in a rich broth or as an accompaniment to roasted or braised meats. My favorite way to enjoy these substantial morsels is to treat them like gnocchi, though their size makes it more practical to serve them on a bed of sauce as opposed to mixing them with it. I generally present them as a first course with browned butter sauce, though they go quite nicely with a rich mushroom sauce or, as mentioned above, with broth.

Suggested sauces or broth: Browned Butter and Sage Sauce (page 466), Creamy Mushroom Sauce (page 551), Fonduta (page 472), Gorgonzola Cream Sauce with Pan-Toasted Spiced Walnuts (page 474), Capon or Chicken Broth (page 749)

INGREDIENTS:

- 5 ½ tablespoons unsalted butter, divided
- 1 medium yellow onion, minced
- Salt
- 1 ½ tablespoons extra virgin olive oil
- ¾ cup dry breadcrumbs
- Freshly ground black pepper
- Handful fresh parsley leaves, minced
- 3 large eggs
- 1 cup whole milk
- ½ pound day-old crusty bread, crusts removed and cut into small cubes
- ¼ pound sliced speck or prosciutto, minced
- ½ cup thinly sliced fresh chives
- ¾ cup all-purpose flour, or more if needed
- 1 ½ teaspoons caraway seeds

1 Heat a large skillet over medium-low heat for 2 to 3 minutes. Add 1½ tablespoons of the butter and increase the heat to medium. Once it's melted and stops foaming, add the onion and a couple pinches of salt and stir. When the onion mixture starts to sizzle, adjust the heat to low, cover, and cook, stirring occasionally, until very soft, about 20 minutes. Remove from the heat.

2 Heat the largest skillet you have over medium heat for 2 to 3 minutes. (The width of the skillet is important because it allows more of the breadcrumbs to have direct contact with the heat.) Add the olive oil and turn the heat up to medium-high. Once the oil begins to swirl on the surface but is not yet smoking, add the breadcrumbs and ¼ teaspoon each of salt and pepper. Cook, stirring frequently, until the crumbs are a deep golden color, 3 to 4 minutes. Transfer to a bowl and toss with half of the parsley. Set aside.

3 Whisk the eggs and milk together in a large bowl. Add the onion, bread, speck, chives, ¾ teaspoon salt, and a couple of good cracks of pepper and, using your hands, mix until the bread cubes break down and a runny mixture develops. Add the flour and continue working the mixture with your hands until it starts to come together as a dough. If it doesn't stick together, add more flour, 1 tablespoon at a time, and continue to mix with your hands until it does. Once finished, the dough will be slightly sticky to the touch. Keep a small bowl of water nearby so you can moisten your hands as you shape the *canederli* (it will prevent the dough from sticking to your hands). Pinch off enough of the dough to form a ball the size of a walnut, then roll it on a floured work surface. Put on a parchment paper-lined baking sheet so they don't touch. Cook or cover and refrigerate for up to 2 days.

4 Bring a large pot of water to a boil. Once it's boiling, add salt (1 tablespoon for every 4 cups water) and stir. Add all the *canederli*, dropping them as close to the water as possible to prevent water splashes that could burn your hand. Turn the heat down to medium and cook until they are cooked through (test one), about 15 minutes. You want the water to be just below the boiling point as you cook them. Using a strainer, transfer them to a warm platter.

5 Heat a large skillet over medium-low heat for 2 to 3 minutes. Add the remaining 4 tablespoons butter and increase the heat to medium-high. Once it's melted and stops foaming, add the *canederli*. Cook, carefully turning them over every minute or so, until golden, about 5 minutes.

6 Divide the *canederli* among warmed plates and serve piping hot sprinkled with the toasted breadcrumbs, the remaining parsley, and caraway seeds.

CARAWAY SEED

In this recipe, caraway seeds add a distinct peppery and earthy element. Though they can be sharp and bitter, these seeds also possess a slight citrusy flavor. Paired best with savory meals, these seeds will enhance this buttery recipe.

SPINACH MALFATTI

YIELD: 4 SERVINGS / ACTIVE TIME: 40 MINUTES / TOTAL TIME: 50 MINUTES

Large, misshapen dumplings made from flour, spinach, and either eggs or fresh ricotta cheese, *malfatti* taste a whole lot better than they look. Even their name, which means "badly formed" in Italian, contributes to this moist and chewy dumpling's inevitable sense of inferiority. Regardless, once matched with a bright tomato sauce or a rich savory browned butter sauce, *malfatti* prove adroitly satisfying and filling with their earthy spinach flavor and warming aroma of nutmeg.

Suggested sauces: Browned Butter and Sage Sauce or its variation (page 466), Classic Tomato Sauce (page 566), Fresh Tomato Sauce (page 565)

INGREDIENTS:

- 2 pounds fresh spinach
- 4 large eggs, lightly beaten
- 1 ¼ cups all-purpose flour
- 1 teaspoon freshly grated nutmeg
- Salt and freshly ground white pepper

1 Trim the heavy stems from the spinach and swish it around in a large bowl of cold water. Drain; shake the leaves but don't worry about water that remains clinging. Put a large skillet on the stove and turn the heat to medium-high. Add the spinach and cook until the leaves have wilted but are still bright green. Transfer to a colander. When cool enough to handle, squeeze any remaining water out of the spinach, then mince, transfer to a medium bowl, add the eggs, and mix well with a whisk. Add the flour, nutmeg, and a few pinches of salt and white pepper and, using a wooden spoon, mix until the dough looks like thick muffin batter.

2 Bring a large pot of water to a boil. Once it's boiling, add salt (1 tablespoon for every 4 cups water) and stir. Move the bowl of batter next to the stove. You'll need two teaspoons. Dip one teaspoon into the dough to draw out a rounded dollop. Using the second teaspoon, scrape the dough off the first teaspoon into the boiling water. Work quickly to cook about 15 *malfatti* (no more) at a time. Cook until they float to the surface, 2 to 3 minutes. Using a strainer, remove them from the water, gently shake over the pot to remove excess water, and transfer to a large warmed bowl. Tent loosely with aluminum foil to keep warm while you cook the remainder. Toss with the sauce of your choice and serve.

PIZZICOTTI

YIELD: 6 SERVINGS / ACTIVE TIME: 1 HOUR / TOTAL TIME: 3 ½ HOURS

Small rustic dumpling from Tuscany, *pizzicotti* translate to "pinches," most likely because they are formed by pinching off pieces of yeasted dough, then added to boiling water to cook. Why the addition of yeast to a pasta dough? Because these noodles were a happy by-product of making something else, in this case, bread.

Suggested sauces or pasta dishes: Arrabbiata (page 489), Bucatini all'Amatriciana (page 491), Signora Sofia's Spiced Pork Sauce (page 620), Lamb Ragù (page 641), Rabbit Ragù (page 603), Roman-Style Tripe Sauce (page 634)

INGREDIENTS:

- **4** cups all-purpose flour
- **2 ½** teaspoons active dry yeast
- **2** teaspoons salt, plus more more to cook the pizzicotti
- **1 ¼** cups warm water

  Semolina flour for dusting

1 Combine the flour, yeast, and salt in a large bowl. Add the water, a little at a time, while mixing with a fork. Continue mixing the dough until it starts holding together in a single floury mass. If it's still too dry to stick together, add more water, 1 teaspoon at a time, until it does. Work the dough with your hands until it feels firm and dry, and can be formed into a craggy looking ball.

2 Transfer the dough to a lightly floured work surface. Using the heel of your hand, push the ball of dough away from you in a downward motion. Turn the dough 45 degrees each time you repeat this motion, as doing so incorporates the flour more evenly. As you continue to knead, you'll notice the dough getting less and less floury. Eventually it will have a smooth, elastic texture. If the dough still feels wet, tacky, or sticky, dust it with flour and continue kneading. If it feels too dry and is not completely sticking together, wet your hands with water and continue kneading. Wet your hands as many times as you need in order to help the dough shape into a ball. The dough has been sufficiently kneaded when it is very smooth and gently pulls back into place when stretched; this will take 8 to 10 minutes.

3 Put the dough in a large bowl and cover tightly with clear food wrap. Let it rise in a warm place (I put it in my cold oven with the light turned on, covered with my "dough" blanket, a small, heavy blanket I use exclusively in the kitchen to keep doughs warm and happy) until the dough doubles in volume, about an hour. Remove the dough from the bowl and, using both hands, knead it in the air just enough to remove any trapped air inside. Put it on a parchment paper-lined baking sheet, cover with a kitchen towel, and let rise for another hour in a warm place.

Once again, remove the dough from the bowl and, using both hands, knead it in the air just enough to remove any trapped air inside.

4 Bring a large pot of water to a boil. Once it's boiling, add salt (1 tablespoon for every 4 cups water) and stir. Also, have your sauce ready and put the Parmigiano in a large heatproof bowl.

5 To make the *pizzicotti,* pinch off peanut-size pieces of dough (it's fine if they are irregularly shaped). When you have done that, drop them in the boiling water. (You may want to do this in several batches.) Cook until they float to the surface, 2 to 3 minutes. Remove with a strainer, giving them a gentle shake to remove any water from their surface, and transfer to the bowl and toss with the sauce of your choice.

WHITE PEPPER

White pepper is typically used instead of the common black pepper for aesthetic purposes in certain dishes, or for its distinct earthy flavor in some meals. Because the previous recipes only call for a small amount of white pepper, you can substitute it for black pepper. Though both types of peppercorn originate from the same plant, white peppercorn is left to ripen longer, then soaked and fermented. Eventually, the black shell is peeled off, revealing the milky white center.

PISAREI

YIELD: 6 SERVINGS / ACTIVE TIME: 1 HOUR / TOTAL TIME: 1 ½ HOURS

These bean-shaped little dumplings (whose name translates into "baby penises"—go figure!) come from the Italian region of Emilia-Romagna and are always served in soup, particularly Pisarei Pasta and Cranberry Bean Soup (page 398), from Piacenza.

INGREDIENTS:

2 cups dry breadcrumbs

3 ½ cups all-purpose flour

2 teaspoons salt, plus extra for the cooking water

1 cup + 2 tablespoons just boiled water, more if needed

1 Put the breadcrumbs in a food processor and pulse until very finely ground. Transfer them to a large bowl and add the flour and salt. Mix well. Add the water a little, mixing with a spoon. Once cool enough to handle, start kneading the dough with your hands until it stops feeling granular and starts feeling silky, 5 to 6 minutes. Cover with clear food wrap and let it rest at room temperature for 30 minutes to an hour.

2 Tear off a chunk of dough. Keep the rest of the dough covered to prevent drying. Using the palms of your hands, roll the dough back and forth on an unfloured work surface until it becomes a long rope about ¾ inch in diameter. Cut the rope across into ¼-inch pieces. Shape the pasta by placing the side of your thumb on each piece of pasta and rolling it along the work surface (about an inch or so) while flicking your thumb up ever so slightly in the process. The flick creates a shallow indentation that helps the *pisarei* to cook more evenly. Repeat with the remaining dough. Set them on lightly floured parchment paper-covered baking sheets so they are not touching. Cook or cover and refrigerate for up to a day. Or freeze on the baking sheets, transfer to freezer bags, and store in the freezer for 3 to 4 weeks. Do not thaw them prior to cooking (they will become mushy), and add an extra minute or two to their cooking time.

3 To cook the *pisarei,* you can add them to simmering soup that's ready to be served and cook until tender but still chewy, about 5 minutes. Keep in mind that the pisarei—even tiny pasta—can absorb a lot of liquid. If you want to cook it right in the soup, make sure you have enough liquid so that pasta doesn't end up absorbing most of it and/or be careful how much of it you add or cook the pisarei separately in water, then add it to individual soup bowls before ladling in the soup.

PASSATELLI

YIELD: 8 SERVINGS / ACTIVE TIME: 20 MINUTES / TOTAL TIME: 2 ½ HOURS

Resembling golden, stubby caterpillars, *passatelli* originated in the Italian regions of Umbria, Emiglia-Romagna, and the Marche. Their name, which means "to be passed through," alludes to how they are made, the dough pushed through the large holes of a potato ricer. Not technically a pasta (nor a gnocchi), they are treated like pasta, served in meat or seafood broths or sauced. But no two ways about it, you will need a potato ricer or a spätzle maker to make them. The directions are for cooking them in water, but you can cook them directly in the broth if you intend to serve them that way; for this amount of *passatelli,* use 3 quarts of broth to ensure there is enough left for serving after the *passatelli* cook (they absorb a decent amount of liquid).

Recommended sauces: Braised Swiss Chard and Squid Sauce (page 589), Sausage Ragù (page 617), Fresh Mushroom Sauce (page 551), Sweetbreads, Tomato, and Caper Sauce (page 638).

INGREDIENTS:

- 1 ¼ cups extra-fine breadcrumbs
- 1 ¼ cups freshly grated Parmigiano-Reggiano cheese
- 2 tablespoons unsalted butter, melted
- Handful fresh parsley leaves, minced
- 3 large eggs
- 1 teaspoon freshly grated nutmeg (if serving with a meat broth or sauce) or grated zest of 1 lemon (if serving with a seafood broth or sauce)
- 1 teaspoon salt, plus more for the cooking water
- ½ teaspoon freshly ground white pepper

1 Put the breadcrumbs, Parmigiano, butter, parsley, eggs, nutmeg or lemon zest, salt, and pepper in a large bowl and mix well with your hands to create a thoroughly homogenous, firm but slightly sticky dough. If it feels too wet, add more breadcrumbs, 1 tablespoon at a time, being careful not to make the mixture too dry and crumbly, as it won't stick together. Cover with clear food wrap and let rest at room temperature for 15 minutes.

2 Bring a small saucepan of water to a boil. Once it's boiling, test the texture of the dough by forming a small ball and dropping it in. If it falls apart, add another egg to the dough and mix thoroughly. If it stays together, proceed.

3 Spoon enough dough to fill half the potato ricer or spätzle maker chamber, then press to squeeze the dough through. As they come out the other side, cut the strands into 1 ½-inch lengths directly onto a parchment paper-lined baking sheet. Gently separate them so they don't touch. Repeat with the remaining dough. Air-dry for 1 ½ hours, then cook (these are best enjoyed as soon as they finish air-drying).

4 To cook the *passatelli,* bring a large pot of water to a boil. Once it's boiling, add salt (1 tablespoon for every 4 cups water) and stir. Turn the heat down so it's gently (not vigorously) boiling. Pick up the parchment paper on both ends and tip it so that the *passatelli* slide directly from the paper into the water. Cook until they float to the surface, about 4 minutes. Let them cook for a minute longer. Remove using a strainer, gently shaking them over the pot to remove any excess water. Add to the sauce of your choice.

MENIETTI

YIELD: 6 SERVINGS / ACTIVE TIME: 1 HOUR / TOTAL TIME: 1 HOUR, PLUS AN HOUR TO AIR-DRY

Tapered, almost worm-like dumplings from the Italian region of Liguria, *menietti* are traditionally served in vegetable soups. Humble and rustic in appearance, they offer a most satisfying chew and are very filling.

INGREDIENTS:

- 1 ¾ cups all-purpose flour
- 1 teaspoon salt, plus more for the cooking water
- ⅓ cup whole milk, room temperature
- 2 tablespoons extra virgin olive oil
- Semolina flour for dusting

1 Combine the flour and salt in a large bowl. Add the milk and olive oil and, using a fork or your hands, mix well to form a coarse, floury dough. Transfer to a lightly floured work surface and begin to knead the dough. Using the heel of your hand, push the dough away from you in a downward motion. Turn the dough 45 degrees each time you repeat this motion, as doing so incorporates the flour more evenly. As you continue to knead, you'll notice the dough getting less and less floury. Eventually it will have a smooth, elastic texture. If the dough still feels wet, tacky, or sticky, dust it with flour and continue kneading. If it feels too dry and is not completely sticking together, wet your hands with water and continue kneading. Wet your hands as many times as you need in order to help the dough shape into a ball. Knead for 8 to 10 minutes.

2 Working with a teaspoon of the dough at a time, roll it between the palms of your hands until it becomes a narrow, 1 ¾-inch-long, almost worm-like roll with tapered ends. Repeat until all the dough is shaped. Set them on lightly floured parchment paper-covered baking sheets so they are not touching. Allow them to air-dry for 1 hour, turning them over once halfway through, then cook. Alternatively, you can place them, once air-dried, in a bowl, cover with a kitchen towel, and refrigerate for up to 3 days. Or freeze them on the baking sheets, transfer to freezer bags, and store in the freezer for up to 2 months. Do not thaw them prior to cooking (they will become mushy), and add an extra minute or two to their cooking time.

3 Because of the amount of liquid they absorb when they cooks, to keep the *menietti* from absorbing too much of the broth of a soup, I find it best to cook them first in water, then drain and rinse under cold running to remove any sticky surface starch. Then I add them to each serving of soup. If you place them in the bowl, then ladle the hot soup on top, the soup will warm them up almost instantly. To cook *menietti*, bring a large pot of water to a boil. Once it's boiling, add salt (1 tablespoon for every 4 cups water) and stir. Add the *menietti* and stir for the first minute to prevent any sticking. Cook until they are tender but still chewy, 7 to 8 minutes, then drain.

SORCETTI

YIELD: 6 SERVINGS / ACTIVE TIME: 1 HOUR / TOTAL TIME: 1½ HOURS

These rustic potato dumplings from the eastern Italian region of the Marche differ from gnocchi in that the potatoes aren't riced after they're cooked but rather mashed, which yields a pleasantly grainy texture. *Sorcetti* pair well with hearty sauces. Instead of spinach, feel free to substitute Swiss chard, dandelion greens, or mustard greens.

Suggested sauces: Signora Sofia's Spiced Pork Sauce (page 620), Lamb Ragù (page 641), Rabbit Ragù (page 603), Mutton Ragù (page 643), Walnut, Black Garlic, and Mascarpone Sauce (page 476)

INGREDIENTS:

- **2 10-ounce containers baby spinach leaves**

- **1¼ pounds (about 3) russet or other baking potatoes**

- **2 large eggs**

- **1 teaspoon salt, plus more for the cooking water**

- **Freshly ground black pepper**

- **⅔ cup all-purpose flour, or more as needed**

- **Semolina flour for dusting**

1. Rinse the spinach and drain; leave the water clinging to the leaves. Place a large skillet on the stove and turn the heat to medium. Add the spinach by the handful and mix well, using tongs, until the leaves slightly wilt but are still bright green. Drain in a colander. When cool enough to handle, squeeze out any remaining water with your hands and mince. Transfer to a paper towel-lined bowl to absorb any excess moisture.

2. Put the potatoes, unpeeled, in a medium saucepan. Cover them with cold water, bring to a gentle boil over medium-high heat, and cook until you can easily pierce the center of each with a knife, about 25 minutes. Drain in a colander. When cool enough to handle, remove and discard the skins and chop them into large pieces. Transfer to a wide, shallow bowl and mash with a potato masher until smooth. Add the spinach, eggs, salt, and pepper to taste and mix well with a spoon until well combined. Add the all-purpose flour and mix, using your hands, until well combined and the dough sticks together as a mass, adding more flour if necessary. It will feel very sticky and soft to the touch.

3. Transfer the dough and any loose scrapings to a lightly floured work surface and knead. Using the heel of your hand, push the ball of dough away from you in a downward motion. Turn the dough 45 degrees each time you repeat this motion, as doing so incorporates the flour more evenly. As you continue to knead, you'll notice the dough getting less and less floury. Eventually it will have a smooth, elastic texture.

4. Between the palms of your hands or on a lightly floured work surface, roll the dough into a 2-inch-thick salami and cut it across into 18 rounds of even thickness (the easiest way to

do this is to cut the roll in half and continue cutting each piece in half until you have 18 pieces). Cover all the dough pieces but one to keep them from drying out.

5 Between the palms of your hands or on the work surface, roll the remaining piece of dough into a long ½-inch-thick rope, dusting with just enough flour, if any is needed, to keep it from sticking. Cut the rope into ¾-inch pieces. Lightly dust the pieces with flour and place on parchment paper-lined baking sheets so they are not touching. Repeat with the remaining dough. Cook or cover and refrigerate for up to 2 days. Or freeze on the baking sheets, transfer to freezer bags, and store in the freezer for 3 to 4 weeks. Do not thaw them prior to cooking (they will become mushy), and add an extra minute or two to their cooking time.

6 To cook the *sorcetti,* bring a large pot of water to a boil. Once it's boiling, add salt (1 tablespoon for every 4 cups water), stir, and lower the heat to medium-high to maintain a gentle boil. Add the sorcetti and stir for the first minute to prevent any sticking. Cook until they float to the surface and are tender but still chewy, 2 to 3 minutes. Drain and serve with the sauce of your choice.

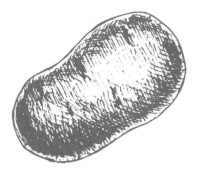

FRASCARELLI

YIELD: 4 SERVINGS / ACTIVE TIME: 2 ½ HOURS / TOTAL TIME: 4 ½ HOURS

Frascarelli are unusual dumpling-like nuggets found throughout central and southern Italy. Traditionally served mounded on a plate and smothered in sauce, they are reminiscent of polenta. I discovered them while perusing Francine Segan's *Pasta Modern* cookbook. She described them as the "world's easiest pasta," which struck me as a very attractive feature in homemade pasta. After making these rustic and pleasantly chewy pasta morsels, I concluded that their considerable ease of preparation is slightly offset by the rather time-consuming multi-step process entailed in making them. *Frascarelli* are made by drizzling beaten eggs, a few drops at a time, into a baking pan filled with flour. These egg drizzles are then covered up with flour and then the whole pan of flour is poured through a sieve to reveal a multitude of freshly formed *frascarelli*. The process then begins all over again. Thankfully, I entered an almost zen-like state of egg dripping and flour sifting meditation as I prepared them and found myself marvelously relaxed (the glass of wine helped) once my egg mixture was finished. But I also wasn't in a hurry and suggest you may not want to be in one either.

Suggested sauces: Classic Canned Tomato Sauce (page 566), Fresh Tomato Sauce (page 565), Simple Roasted Tomato and Garlic Sauce (page 568), Creamy Mushroom Sauce (page 551), Meat Ragù with Bechamel Sauce (page 636)

INGREDIENTS:

- **2 cups semolina flour, plus more for dusting**
- **2 cups all-purpose flour**
- **¼ cup water**
- **2 large eggs**
- **Grated zest of 1 lemon**
- **Salt**

1 Place both flours in a large, deep baking dish and mix well to combine.

2 Beat the eggs, water, lemon zest, and a couple pinches of salt together in a medium bowl. Set the bowl right next to the baking dish.

3 Using a basting brush, dip the brush into the egg mixture, then let it drip into the flour. Keep repeating this until there are drippings over the entire surface of the flour (but be careful—don't glop it on). Lightly sprinkle more flour over the egg-streaked areas.

4 Using the fingertips and thumb of your dominant hand, gently work the egg mixture into the flour until little pasta nuggets form. With your hands, gently transfer the pasta nuggets from the flour to a colander, then shake off any excess flour. Transfer the *frascarelli* to a clean cotton dishcloth.

5 Repeat steps 3 and 4 until the egg mixture is all used up, adding more flour to the baking dish if needed. Air-dry for 2 hours, then cook (these are best enjoyed as soon as they finish air-drying).

6 To cook the *frascarelli*, bring a large pot of water to a boil. Once it's boiling, add salt (1 tablespoon for every 4 cups water) and stir. Add the *frascarelli* and stir for the first minute to prevent any sticking. Cook until they are tender but still chewy, 9 to 10 minutes. Drain and serve with the sauce of your choice.

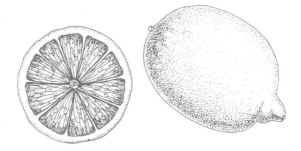

FRASCARELLI *with* SWISS CHARD *and* PARMIGIANO

YIELD: 6 SERVINGS / ACTIVE TIME: 1 ½ HOURS / TOTAL TIME: 3 ½ HOURS

Frascarelli, little nuggets of egg pasta from the Italian region of Umbria, are often treated like polenta because of their porridge-like appearance. In this recipe, they are topped with a savory mixture of Swiss chard and golden beets, whose subtle sweetness lightens up this delicious and nourishing dish. *Frascarelli,* as delicious as they are, are time consuming to make and best saved for a lazy weekend day. Should you have a lovely bunch of Swiss chard to dispense with, I suggest using ziti or penne to make a weeknight version of this dish.

Other recommended pasta shapes: penne, ziti

INGREDIENTS:

Salt

1 bunch (about 1 pound) Swiss chard, stems trimmed

1 recipe Frascarelli (page 254)

4 tablespoons (½ stick) unsalted butter

1 teaspoon freshly grated nutmeg

Freshly ground black pepper

⅓ cup freshly grated Parmigiano-Reggiano cheese

1 Bring a large pot of water to a boil. Once it's boiling, add salt (1 tablespoon for every 4 cups water) and stir. Add the Swiss chard and, once the water comes back to a boil, blanch for 2 minutes. Using a strainer or tongs, transfer to a colander and rinse under cold water. Reduce the heat of the water to a gentle boil (if it's boiling too furiously, it risks breaking up the *frascarelli* as they cook). Add half of the *frascarelli* and cook, gently stirring once or twice to prevent any sticking, for 10 minutes. Using a strainer or a large slotted spoon, transfer them to a large warmed bowl and tent with aluminum foil to keep warm. Repeat with the remaining *frascarelli.*

2 As the *frascarelli* cook, flatten out each chard leaf on a cutting board and make incisions with a knife on both sides of each stem. Discard the stems. Pile all the flattened and stem-less leaves on top of each other and slice them across into 2-inch-wide ribbons.

3 Put a large skillet over medium-high heat and add the butter. Once it stops foaming and little brown bits develop on the bottom of the skillet, add the *frascarelli.* Gently toss to coat with the butter. Add the Swiss chard and nutmeg and fold gently into the pasta to evenly coat it with butter. Let cook until everything is heated through, another minute or two.

4 Divide among six warmed bowls. Serve piping hot topped with a good crack of pepper and sprinkled with the Parmigiano (or pass it at the table).

SPÄTZLE

YIELD: 6 SERVINGS / ACTIVE TIME: 1 HOUR/ TOTAL TIME: 1 ½ HOURS

Literally "little sparrows" in German, *spätzle* can be found throughout Germany and Austria and in the mountainous regions of northern Italy. They are very simple—but satisfying—dumplings made from flour, eggs, milk, and salt (though you can find versions that include such additions as herbs or beets). If you're going to make *spätzle*, consider buying a *spätzle* maker, but it's not necessary and my directions assume you don't have one. In addition to the sauces listed below, *spätzle* are fantastic served as a side dish with any kind of braised or roasted meat dish, tossed with the juices or gravy.

Suggested sauces: Browned Butter and Sage Sauce and its variations (page 466), Rabbit Ragù (page 603), Wild Boar Ragù (page 622)

INGREDIENTS:

- ¼ cup packed fresh basil, chive, parsley or thyme leaves (optional; if you add the herbs, decrease the milk to 1 cup)
- 2 ½ cups all-purpose flour
- 1 tablespoon salt, plus more for the cooking water
- 2 large eggs
- 1 ¼ cups milk, more if needed

  Extra virgin olive oil for tossing

1 If adding the herbs, bring a small saucepan of water to a boil. Add the herbs and blanch until they turn a brighter shade of green, about 10 seconds. Using a slotted spoon, transfer the leaves to a bowl of ice water to stop the cooking. Drain well and transfer, along with 2 tablespoons of cooled blanching water, to a mini food processor and puree until very smooth, with no flecks of herbs present. Set aside.

2 Stir the flour, salt, eggs, milk, and herb puree if using together until just combined. Continue to stir until the mixture becomes somewhat shiny, 7 to 8 minutes. Cover the bowl with clear food wrap and let rest at room temperature for 1 hour. At this point, the dough should be more like pancake batter, so if it seems too thick, add room temperature milk (microwave it for a few seconds if necessary), 1 teaspoon at a time, until the consistency becomes thinner.

3 Bring a large pot of water to a boil. Once it's boiling, add salt (1 tablespoon for every 4 cups water) and stir. Reduce the heat so the water is gently boiling. Line a baking sheet with parchment paper.

4 To make and cook the *spätzle*, place the bowl of batter near the stove. Get a narrow heatproof cutting board with a handle (it needs to be narrow enough that it can be partially dipped in the pot of boiling water). Dip the board in the water, then pull it out and spoon a cup of the batter onto it. Quickly dip the board back in the water for a second to wet the dough and then, using

your knife, flatten the dough so that it's about ¼ inch thick and covers a good part of the cutting board. Begin cutting small slices, about ⅛ inch thick and 1 ½ to 2 inches long, of the dough directly into the boiling water. Stir the pot from time to time with a long wooden spoon to dislodge any *spätzle* stuck to the bottom. Cook until they float to the surface, about 1 minute. Quickly remove them with a strainer and transfer to the prepared baking sheet. Drizzle with the oil so that they don't stick together and tent loosely with aluminum foil to keep them warm. Repeat with the remaining dough, then serve the *spätzle* with the sauce of your choice.

CHARD SPÄTZLE

YIELD: 4 SERVINGS / ACTIVE TIME: 1½ HOURS / TOTAL TIME: 2½ HOURS

Making your own soft and chewy *spätzle* dumplings requires a little more time than opting for boxed pasta, but of all the homemade pastas, it is one of the quickest to make. Feel free to substitute spinach, mustard greens, collards, or kale for the chard, though the mustard greens, collards, and kale are heartier leaves and will need to cook longer, anywhere from 10 to 20 minutes depending on their size and thickness, in order to wilt.

Suggested sauces: Fonduta (page 472), Gorgonzola Cream (page 474), Aromatic Walnut Sauce (page 543)

INGREDIENTS:

- Salt
- 2 pounds Swiss chard or spinach
- 4 extra large eggs
- 1 teaspoon freshly grated nutmeg
- 2 cups all-purpose flour, or more if needed
- ¼ cup water
- Extra virgin olive oil for drizzling

1 Trim away the stems from the chard or spinach. Bring a large pot of water to a boil. Once it's boiling, add salt (1 tablespoon for every 4 cups water) and stir. Add the greens and cook until wilted, about 3 minutes. Using a strainer, transfer the greens to a colander set in a large bowl (reserve the cooking water to cook the spätzle). Rinse the greens under cold water. Drain well and, using your hands, squeeze them to remove as much liquid as possible. Transfer to a kitchen towel and pat dry.

2 Put the greens, eggs, 1 ½ tablespoons salt, and nutmeg in a food processor and pulse until the greens are mostly shredded. Add the flour and water and process until the mixture is smooth, about 3 minutes, occasionally stopping to scrape the mixture down from the sides. Transfer the batter to a medium bowl. Cover with plastic wrap and let rest for 1 hour at room temperature. At this point, the dough should be more like pancake batter, so if it seems too thick, add room temperature milk (microwave it for a few seconds if necessary), 1 teaspoon at a time, until the consistency becomes thinner.

3 Bring the pot of water you used to cook the greens in back to a boil. Reduce the heat so the water is gently boiling. Line a baking sheet with parchment paper. You will be working in batches.

4 To make and cook the *spätzle,* place the bowl of batter near the stove. Get a narrow heatproof cutting board with a handle (it needs to be narrow enough that it can be partially dipped in the pot of boiling water). Dip the board in the water, then pull it out and spoon a cup of the batter onto it. Quickly dip the board back in the water for a second to wet the dough and then, using

your knife, flatten the dough so that it's about ¼ inch thick and covers a good part of the cutting board. Begin cutting small slices, about ⅛ inch thick and 1 ½ to 2 inches long, of the dough directly into the boiling water. Stir the pot from time to time with a long wooden spoon to dislodge any *spätzle* stuck to the bottom of the pot. Cook until they float to the surface, about 1 minute. Quickly remove them with a strainer and transfer to the prepared baking sheet. Drizzle with the oil so that they don't stick together and tent loosely with aluminum foil to keep them warm. Repeat with the remaining dough, then serve with the sauce of your choice.

POLISH POTATO DUMPLINGS
with BACON *and* ONIONS

YIELD: 4 TO 6 SERVINGS / ACTIVE TIME: 40 MINUTES / TOTAL TIME: 1 HOUR

These filled dumplings, known as *pyzy*, are traditional to Polish and Ukrainian cooking. They use potatoes in both the wrapper and the stuffing, which can also include ground meat. This is a quicker, unfilled version. Adding the potato flour and potato starch left behind from the grated potatoes will help keep the dumplings together.

INGREDIENTS:

- 2 ½ pounds russet potatoes, peeled, divided
- Salt
- 2 large eggs, beaten
- 1 cup all-purpose flour, or more as needed
- 1 tablespoon potato flour
- 2 tablespoons olive oil
- 6 ounces thick-sliced bacon, cubed
- 1 large yellow onion, sliced into thin slivers

1 Bring a large pot of water to a boil. Cut half the potatoes into chunks (leave the other half whole and uncooked). When the water is boiling, add salt (1 tablespoon for every 4 cups water) and stir. Add the potato chunks and cook until you can easily pierce through the chunks with a fork. Drain and return them to the pot, leaving the pot over the still warm but turned-off burner to dry out for a few minutes. Pass them through a potato ricer directly into a large bowl. Alternatively, you can place them in a wide, shallow bowl and press them down with a potato masher until smooth.

2 While the potatoes are cooking, grate the raw potatoes by hand or in a food processor using a very fine grater. Place the grated potatoes in a kitchen towel or in several layers of cheese-cloth and twist and squeeze the cloth over a bowl to remove as much water as possible from them. Put them in the bowl with the riced potatoes. Carefully pour out the water from the other bowl, saving the potato starch that has settled at the bottom. Transfer the starch to the bowl of potatoes. Add the eggs, 2 teaspoons salt, and both flours and mix thoroughly; it should hold its shape when squeezed together in your hand. If it's sticky, add more all-purpose flour, 1 tablespoon at a time, until it has the proper consistency. With slightly floured hands, roll spoonsful of the dough into balls slightly larger than golf balls. Cook or cover and refrigerate for up to 24 hours.

3 Make the topping. Heat a large skillet over medium heat for 2 to 3 minutes. Add the olive oil and heat for a minute or two, then add the bacon and onion. Cook until the onion is golden and the bacon crispy, stirring occasionally, about 12 minutes. Keep warm.

4 Bring a large pot of water to a boil. When it's boiling, add salt (1 tablespoon for every 4 cups water) and stir. Carefully

drop in the dumplings a few at a time (the closer to the surface of the water you drop them, the less likely they are to splash water and burn you). Cook until the dumplings float to the surface, 4 to 5 minutes. Taste test one for doneness. You should not taste the flavor of raw flour if properly cooked. Using a strainer or large slotted spoon, transfer the dumplings from the water to a colander to drain. Continue to cook the remaining dumplings.

5 Transfer the cooked dumplings to a warmed serving platter, spoon over the topping, and serve piping hot.

MATZO BALLS

YIELD: 24 MATZO BALLS; 6 TO 8 SERVINGS, WITH SOUP / ACTIVE TIME: 45 MINUTES / TOTAL TIME: 1½ HOURS

Matzo balls are soup dumplings that are part of the Ashkenazic cooking tradition. They can be airy or dense and chewy, depending on how they are made. This particular recipe falls somewhere in between; whipping the egg whites separately from the yolks adds a degree of lightness. Traditionally made matzoh balls are particularly scrumptious because they contain schmaltz, or rendered chicken fat. Using butter, as some recipes counsel, does not produce the same results because schmaltz, unlike butter or oil, contributes a subtle and savory fried chicken flavor to everything it touches. That is probably why, since discovering matzo balls many years ago, I have not been able to fully enjoy chicken soup with noodles.

INGREDIENTS:

- 4 large eggs, separated
- 1 small yellow onion, grated
- ¼ cup Chicken Schmaltz (page 748)
- ¼ cup chicken broth, or more if needed, at room temperature
- Handful fresh parsley leaves, minced
- 1 teaspoon salt
- ¼ teaspoon freshly ground white pepper (optional)
- 1½ cups matzo meal, or more if needed

1 Mix the egg yolks, onion, chicken fat, broth, parsley, salt, and pepper together thoroughly in a large bowl. Add the matzo and mix well with a wooden spoon.

2 Put the egg whites in a medium bowl and whisk vigorously until they begin to thicken and turn glossy. (You can use a hand-held mixer, but be careful not to overheat them, otherwise the matzo balls will be too airy.) Add the whites to the matzo mixture, a little at a time, and fold until mostly incorporated, with a few streaks of white remaining. (If the mixture seems too runny, add more matzo meal, 1 tablespoon at a time, until it turns into a loose paste. If the mixture seems too thick, add more broth, 1 tablespoon at a time, until it turns into a loose paste.) Cover with clear food wrap and refrigerate for 45 minutes to chill the paste until it is stiff enough to roll it into balls.

3 Fill a small bowl with water and place it next to your work surface. You will use it to moisten your hands before touching the matzo ball mix, to keep it from sticking. With moistened hands, grab a golf ball-sized piece of mixture and roll it into a ball. Place the matzo balls on a plate. Repeat until the matzo mixture is gone. Cook or cover with clear food wrap and refrigerate for up to a day.

4 To cook matzo balls, add them to boiling broth or soup, one at a time. The balls will begin to float within 5 minutes. When they do, reduce the heat to low, cover, and simmer for 20 minutes. Serve with the broth or soup.

KOREAN RICE CAKES

YIELD: 4 SERVINGS / ACTIVE TIME: 45 MINUTES / TOTAL TIME: 1¼ HOURS

Tteok are chewy steamed rice cakes shaped like narrow cylinders that can be prepared in countless ways. They figure into celebratory dishes served during Korean New Year festivities as well as simpler preparations for weeknight family dinners. You can find them shaped like small, 2-inch-long cylinders or in oval slices, which have been cut on the diagonal from the cylinders. You can treat the *tteok* slices as you would gnocchi or other unfilled dumplings, serving them with sauces or in soups or stir-fries.

INGREDIENTS:

- **2** cups rice flour
- **½** teaspoon salt, plus extra for the cooking water
- **¾** cup boiling water if using a microwave, 1 cup if using a steamer

  Cabbage leaves (optional)

- **1** teaspoon toasted sesame oil, plus more for rubbing on hands to shape the rice dough

1. Mixing and heating the dough using a microwave: Put the flour, salt, and boiling water in a medium microwave-friendly bowl and mix until it looks like a thick, white paste. Cover the bowl with clear food wrap, leaving a small gap to let the steam release, and microwave for 2 minutes. Mix the dough with a wooden spoon. Cover again and microwave for 2 minutes.

   Mixing and heating the dough with a steamer: Put the flour, salt, and boiling water in a medium bowl and mix until it looks like a thick, white paste. Bring 3 cups water to a boil in a large pot. Line a steamer with cabbage leaves or parchment paper cut to the size and shape of your steamer with lots of small incisions made in it to allow steam to circulate. Set the rice dough in the steamer so it's at least ½ inch away from the sides of the steamer. Place the steamer in the pot over the boiling water (it should not touch it), cover, and steam over high heat until the dough is shiny and slightly translucent, about 25 minutes.

2. Brush your work surface with the sesame oil. Put the hot dough on the surface and, using a pestle, smooth meat mallet, or the end of a rounded rolling pin, pound the dough until it is smooth and elastic, about 5 minutes.

3. With the palms of your hands, roll the dough into a 3-inch-diameter sausage and cut into eight equal pieces (the easiest way is to first cut the roll in half and then continue cutting each piece in half until you have eight pieces). Roll each piece into a cylinder that is approximately ¾ inch wide and 4 inches long.

4. Rub your palms with a little sesame oil and gently rub the rice cakes to coat them with a thin sheen of oil (this prevents any sticking). Cut each rice cake in half and roll each piece into a 10-inch-long cylinder. Let the cylinders sit out, uncovered, at

room temperature for 3 to 4 hours, until significantly hardened. Then slice, on the diagonal, into ¼- to ⅙-inch-thick slices or however thick your recipe directs. Use immediately or refrigerate them in a single layer (not touching) on baking sheets for up to a day or freeze, transfer to freezer bags, and store in the freezer up to 3 months. Do not thaw them prior to cooking (they will become mushy), and add an extra minute or two to their cooking time.

5 To cook, bring a large pot of water to a boil. Once it's boiling, add salt (1 tablespoon for every 4 cups water) and stir. Add the rice cakes, stirring for the first minute to prevent any sticking. Cook until they are tender but still chewy, 3 to 4 minutes. Drain and use as directed in your particular recipe.

KOREAN RICE CAKES *with* UYGHUR-STYLE LAMB *and* THREE-PEPPER SAUCE

YIELD: 6 SERVINGS / ACTIVE TIME: 15 MINUTES / TOTAL TIME: 45 MINUTES , PLUS 2 HOURS MARINATING

The Uyghurs, a Turkic ethnic group that now lives primarily in the Xinjiang Uyghur Autonomous Region of China, are known for toasting their spices to further coax out their flavor. An added benefit to this technique is that it highlights cumin's earthy quality while simultaneously diminishing its bitter notes. What I find particularly satisfying about this tasty one-pot dish featuring spiced lamb morsels and stir-fried peppers are the Korean *tteok*. Chewy steamed rice cakes, *tteok* come in two varieties: 2-inch-long narrow cylinders called *tteokbokki* or *tteokggochi,* and thin slivers cut on the diagonal from *tteok* cylinders called *tteokguk tteok*. This recipe uses the cut slivers, which you can either easily make from scratch or find, typically in 2-pound bags, in the freezer section of well-stocked Asian markets.

1 Put the lamb in a large bowl.

2 Heat a small skillet over medium heat for 2 to 3 minutes. Add the coriander and cumin and toast, stirring, until they become fragrant, 2 to 3 minutes. Pour the spices over the lamb and add the garlic, Aleppo pepper, black pepper, and fish sauce and mix well. Cover and marinate in the refrigerator for 2 to 3 hours. Take out of the refrigerator at least 45 minutes prior to cooking as it needs to be at room temperature.

3 Bring a large pot of water to a boil. Once it's boiling, add salt (1 tablespoon for every 4 cups water) and stir. Add the rice cakes and cook according to the recipe or package instructions.

4 While the rice cakes cook, heat a wok or large skillet over medium heat for 2 to 3 minutes. Once very hot (you can test by adding a drop of water; if it bounces off the surface, it's ready), add the oil and turn the heat up to medium-high. Add the lamb and cook until nicely browned on all sides, about 5 minutes. Add all the peppers, the scallions, and a pinch of salt and stir-fry for 4 minutes. Add the bok choy stems and a pinch of salt and stir-fry for 2 minutes. Add the bok choy leaves and stir-fry for another minute.

5 Drain the rice cakes, add to the skillet, and toss to combine.

6 Divide among six warmed plates, garnish with cilantro, and serve piping hot with lime wedges.

INGREDIENTS:

- 2 pounds lamb shoulder, trimmed of fat and cut into 2-inch cubes
- 1 tablespoon ground coriander
- 2 teaspoons ground cumin
- 3 garlic cloves, grated or minced
- 1 tablespoon Aleppo chile flakes or red pepper flakes
- 2 teaspoons freshly ground black pepper
- 1½ tablespoons fish sauce, plus more for serving
- Salt
- 4 cups Korean rice cake slivers, homemade (page 264; use the whole recipe) or store-bought
- 1 tablespoon safflower oil
- 1 large red bell pepper, seeded and cut into ¾-inch dice
- 1 large yellow bell pepper, seeded and cut into ¾-inch dice
- 4 poblano peppers, seeded and cut into ¾-inch dice
- 1 bunch (5 or 6) scallions, trimmed and cut into ½-inch pieces on the diagonal
- 4 baby bok choy, stems and leaves divided, cut into bite-size pieces
- Handful chopped fresh cilantro for garnish
- Lime wedges for serving

KOREAN RICE CAKES
with SHIITAKE MUSHROOMS *and* PORK

YIELD: 4 SERVINGS / ACTIVE TIME: 25 MINUTES / TOTAL TIME: 45 MINUTES

INGREDIENTS:

- 1 **cup dry white wine**
- 4 **tablespoons toasted sesame oil, divided**
- 1 **pound Chinese pork sausage, removed from casings and crumbled**
  Salt
- 1 **bunch (5 or 6) scallions, trimmed and thinly sliced**
- 10 **medium shiitake mushrooms, stems discarded and caps minced**
- 1 **tablespoon gochujang**
- ½ **red onion, thinly sliced**
- 1 **tablespoon miso**
- 1 **tablespoon tomato paste**
- 1 **pound Korean rice cakes, 1 recipe homemade (page 264) or store-bought**
- 2 **handfuls fresh basil leaves**
  Thinly sliced fresh basil and toasted sesame seeds for garnish

Shaped like narrow cylinders, Korean *tteok* are steamed, chewy rice cakes that come in two varieties: 2-inch-long narrow cylinders called *tteokbokki* or *tteokggochi,* and thin slivers cut on the diagonal from *tteok* cylinders called *tteokguk tteok.* This recipe uses the long cylindrical *tteokbokki,* which you can either easily make from scratch or find, typically in 2-pound bags, in the freezer section of well-stocked Asian markets. The rich, spicy notes in the sauce come from *gochujang,* Korea's national condiment, made from red chiles, glutinous rice, fermented soybeans, and salt.

This recipe calls for Asian pork sausage. Known commonly by the Cantonese generic name of *lap cheong,* Asian pork sausages come in many varieties. They can be fresh, smoked, made from pork or from liver and some have been dried to the point of being rock hard. Their two unifying characteristics are their marked sweetness and their almost-paste like texture. For this recipe, I suggest heading to your local Asian market and looking for fresh Chinese sausage. Considerably less shriveled and softer, the links will feel heavy and greasy and may contain little chunks of pearly fat. Their high level of sugar makes them brown quickly, so be sure not to step away from the stove when cooking them.

1 Bring the wine to a boil in a small saucepan and continue to boil until reduced almost by half (this will concentrate its flavor, including acidity and sweetness).

2 Heat a large skillet over medium-low heat for 2 to 3 minutes. Raise the heat to medium and add 2 tablespoons of the sesame oil. When the surface of the oil begins to swirl, add the crumbled sausage and a couple pinches of salt. Stir well and cook until the fat in the sausage begins to render, about 8 minutes. Add the scallions, mushrooms, and a couple pinches of salt and stir.

3 Put the *gochujang,* onion, miso, reduced wine, tomato paste, and a couple pinches of salt in a food processor or blender and pulse until smooth. Add the basil leaves and pulse until you can just barely see green flecks. Add the pureed mixture to the skillet, stir, and raise the heat to medium-high. Once the mixture begins to gently boil, reduce the heat to low and cook until the sauce becomes fairly thick, 8 to 10 minutes.

4 While the sauce is cooking, bring a large pot of water to a boil. Once it's boiling, add salt (1 tablespoon for every 4 cups water) and stir. Add the rice cakes and stir for the first minute to prevent any sticking. Cook according to the package or recipe instructions until they are tender but still chewy. Drain and place, not touching, on a kitchen towel.

5 Heat another large skillet over low heat for 2 to 3 minutes. Add the remaining 2 tablespoons sesame oil and turn the heat to medium-high. When the oil begins to swirl on the surface, add the rice cakes and cook, stirring occasionally, until they turn a caramel color on all sides and are heated through, 3 to 4 minutes. Add them to the skillet with the sauce and toss to coat them with it.

6 Divide the sauce and rice cakes among four warmed bowls and serve piping hot garnished with the thinly sliced basil and sesame seeds.

GOCHUJANG

This Korean condiment is made from red chili, soybeans, wheat, and salt. Gochujang will add a savory, spicy and sweet taste to this dish. The spice level varies by brand, so be sure to taste test the condiment before you add it to this dish.

RAVIOLI, POTSTICKERS, & OTHER FILLED PASTAS & DUMPLINGS

Marie von Ebner-Eschenbach once said, "What delights us in visible beauty is the invisible." She was talking, of course, about filled pastas and dumplings. Strip away the glitz and look beyond the dazzlingly shaped tender exteriors to the real treasures buried within. Whether filled with a mixture of savory meats, poultry, seafood, vegetables, or fruits, served up in a soup or steamed or pan-fried, and offered with a sauce, they provide whimsical sustenance with every bite.

RAVIOLI *with* SAUSAGE *and* BROCCOLI RABE

YIELD: 4 TO 6 SERVINGS / ACTIVE TIME: 2 HOURS / TOTAL TIME: 3 HOURS

Ravioli are one of the oldest types of pasta, and related forms of this dish are believed to date back to early Roman times, though they don't actually begin appearing in historical manuscripts until the 12th century. Filled with varying mixtures of meats, vegetables, and/or cheeses, they can be shaped like squares, discs, or triangles and are typically 1¾ inches wide. You can make *raviolini* using this recipe by placing ½ teaspoon of filling spaced 1 inch apart on the pasta sheets and then cutting them into 1-inch squares. Similarly, you can make *ravioloni* by placing 2 tablespoons of filling spaced 4 to 6 inches apart on the pasta sheets and cutting them into 4- to 6-inch squares. I include instructions for making ravioli by hand and with a ravioli maker tray mold.

Suggested sauces: Browned Butter and Sage Sauce (page 466)

---

1 Discard any discolored leaves from the broccoli rabe. Detach the florets from the tops of the stems, rinse under cold water, and set aside. Trim off and discard the last 2 inches of the stems. Using a sharp paring knife, cut off the leaves and place in a bowl. Peel the skin from the thicker stalks and cut them crosswise into thin slivers. Add the leaves and stems to a bowl of cold water, swish around to remove dirt, and then transfer to a colander. Rinse under cold water.

2 Bring a medium saucepan of water to a boil. Once it's boiling, add salt (1 tablespoon for every 4 cups water) and stir. Add the peeled stems and cook for 2 minutes, then add the leaves and cook for 4 minutes. Add the florets and cook for 2 minutes. (Note: If the stalks are still crisp, they will remain bitter.) Reserve ¼ cup of the cooking water and drain the greens. Once cool enough to handle, mince.

3 Heat a large skillet over medium heat for 2 to 3 minutes. Add the olive oil and let it heat for a couple of minutes. Add the sausage, breaking it into small pieces with a potato masher or wooden spoon as it cooks. Add the broccoli rabe, garlic, red pepper flakes, and salt and black pepper to taste, and stir. Add the reserved broccoli rabe cooking water and simmer until the sausage is cooked through and there is no liquid left in the pan, 5 to 6 minutes. Transfer to a medium bowl and let cool, draining off excess liquid—if any—that may accumulate. Once cooled, add the cheeses and mix well. Set aside. The filling can be prepared a day ahead; cover, refrigerate, and bring back to room temperature before proceeding.

INGREDIENTS:

FILLING:

½ pound broccoli rabe

Salt

2 tablespoons extra virgin olive oil

½ pound sweet Italian sausage, casings removed

2 garlic cloves, thinly sliced

¼ teaspoon red pepper flakes

Freshly ground black pepper

½ cup freshly grated Parmigiano-Reggiano cheese

½ cup freshly grated pecorino Sardo (preferable) or pecorino Romano

DOUGH:

Three-Egg Basic Pasta Dough (page 131-133)

Semolina flour for dusting

Salt

4 Prepare the dough as directed on pages 131–133, rolling the dough to the thinnest setting (generally notch 5) for pasta sheets that are about 1/16 inch thick. The pasta sheets will be very long on this setting. Cut them into 12½-inch-long lengths. Lay the cut pasta sheets on lightly floured parchment paper-lined baking sheets and cover loosely with clear food wrap. Work quickly to keep the pasta sheets from drying out, which makes it harder for the pasta to stick together.

5 Forming the ravioli by hand: Place a sheet of dough on a lightly floured work surface and fold it in half lengthwise. Lightly tap on the folded edge to create a guideline. Unfold the dough so that it's laying flat, the fold line now delineating two pasta strips that are still connected. Place balls of filling about the size of hazelnuts in the center of one pasta strip, spacing the mounds, from the top to the bottom of the strip, about 1¾ inches apart. Should the dough have become a little dry during this process, lightly moisten the pasta border with a fingertip dipped in water (it's helpful to have a small bowl of water nearby for this purpose). Cover the filling with the other half of the sheet of dough. Using your fingertips, gently but firmly press down the dough around each filling mound. As you do this, try to push out any air from around the filling (this keeps the ravioli from coming apart in the water when boiling due to vapor pressure). Press one more time to ensure you have a tight seal. Using a ridged pastry cutter, slice between the mounds to create squares approximately 1¾ inches in size.

Forming the ravioli with a ravioli maker tray mold: Lightly dust the metal ravioli mold with flour, then place a sheet of dough on top. Gently press the plastic mold over the pasta sheet to create depressions (should you press too hard and tear the dough, simply ball it back up and roll it through the machine again). Place approximately 2 teaspoons of filling in each depression. Remove any filling that falls on the surrounding dough. Gently tap the metal mold on the table a few times to help remove any air bubbles that may be trapped underneath the filling. Should the dough have become a little dry during this process, lightly moisten the pasta border with a fingertip dipped in water. Lay another sheet of dough over the mold. As you do this, gently press down with the palm of your hand to push out any air within the ravioli. Run a rolling pin over the surface of the ravioli mold until the ridges of the ravioli beneath become visible. Carefully flip the mold over and gently remove it. If some of the ravioli get stuck to the mold, gently tap one edge of the mold against the table. Gently pull the ravioli apart. Should they still be slightly attached to each other, use a ridged pastry cutter to cut them apart.

6 No matter how you form them, set the ravioli on lightly floured parchment paper-covered baking sheets so they are not touching. Allow them to air-dry for 2 hours, turning them over once halfway through, and then cook. Alternatively, you can place them, once air-dried, in a bowl, cover with a kitchen towel, and refrigerate for up to 3 days. Or freeze on the baking sheets, transfer to freezer bags, and store in the freezer for 3 to 4 weeks. Do not thaw them prior to cooking (they will become mushy), and add an extra minute or two to their cooking time.

7 To cook the ravioli, bring a large pot of water to a boil. Once it's boiling, add salt (1 tablespoon for every 4 cups water) and stir. Carefully drop the ravioi into the boiling water and stir for the first minute to prevent any sticking. Cook until they are tender but still chewy, about 3 minutes. Drain and serve with the sauce of your choice.

PLANTAIN RAVIOLI *with* CHIPOTLE *and* CHORIZO SAUCE

YIELD: 4 SERVINGS (22 DUMPLINGS) / **ACTIVE TIME:** 1 HOUR / **TOTAL TIME:** 1½ HOURS

This tasty and spicy ravioli dish uses an unexpected ingredient—plantains. Also known as "cooking bananas," plantains are starchier, mealier, and slightly larger versions of regular bananas and can be added to a variety of different kinds of dishes, depending on their level of ripeness. This recipe requires them to be semi-ripe, which means they need to be light to dark yellow, with some dark streaks in the peel and browning on both tips. Though plantains at this stage of ripeness are lightly sweet, this dish remains firmly in the savory world and is helped considerably to this end by the addition of two delicious ingredients. The first is fresh chorizo sausage. Also known as Mexican chorizo, fresh chorizo is made from ground pork, chiles, and spices and can be found in the fresh sausage section of most well-stocked supermarkets. Substitute spicy Italian sausage if you cannot find it (without fennel seed, if possible; and if you can't get it without, spend a few minutes plucking out as many of the seeds as possible once the meat is removed from the casings). The second ingredient is fresh queso, a soft, mild white cheese made from cow's milk or a combination of cow and goat's milk. It is treated like feta cheese and crumbled over everything. Finally, you can choose to make your own richer and more pliable wrappers with the basic egg dough recipe on pages 131–133, though using store-bought wonton wrappers ensures that you can prepare this appetizing dish even faster.

---

1 Prepare the sauce. Heat a large skillet over medium-low heat for 2 to 3 minutes. Add the chorizo, turn the heat up to medium, and, using a potato masher or wooden spoon, press down on the sausage to break it up into crumbles. Cook until the sausage has browned, 5 to 10 minutes, stirring occasionally. Transfer the sausage to a small bowl, leaving the fat behind in the skillet, and set aside.

2 Add the garlic, shallots, and a pinch of salt to the fat in the skillet and cook until the shallots turn translucent, stirring a few times, about 5 minutes. Add the lime juice and stir well, scraping up any browned bits from the bottom of the pan. Add the cooked chorizo back to the skillet along with the chipotles, broth, and pepper to taste, and stir. Raise the heat to medium-high and bring the mixture to a boil. Remove ½ cup of the liquid and add the cornstarch, whisking well to integrate. Add the corn-

INGREDIENTS:

SAUCE:

- 1 pound fresh chorizo, casings removed
- 4 garlic cloves, minced
- 2 small shallots, minced
- Salt
- Juice of 2 limes
- 2 canned chipotles in adobo sauce, minced
- 3 cups chicken broth
- Freshly ground black pepper
- 2 tablespoons cornstarch

RAVIOLI:

- 2 light to dark yellow semi-ripe plantains
- 4 cups chicken broth
- 4 cups water
- 1 chicken bouillon cube
- 1 cinnamon stick
- 6 whole cloves
- ½ nutmeg, freshly grated
- Salt
- 8 ounces queso fresco cheese, plus more for serving
- 1 10-ounce package round wonton wrappers (square are okay)
- Chopped fresh cilantro for garnish

starch slurry to the skillet and lower the heat to medium, stirring constantly. The sauce will begin to thicken. Taste for seasoning, adding more salt and pepper if needed. Take the skillet off the heat and cover. You will need to rewarm it once the ravioli are finished.

3 Rinse and scrub the plantains well. Cut off the ends and slice each plantain in half, widthwise. Make a small lengthwise nick in each plantain peel (makes it easier to remove the peel once cooked). Add them to a medium pot, along with the broth, water, cinnamon stick, cloves, nutmeg, and a few pinches of salt, and stir. Bring the mixture to a boil, add the bouillon cube, stir until it dissolves, then reduce the heat to medium-low. Simmer until the plantain peels start to open up and separate slightly from the flesh, 20 to 25 minutes. Remove from the liquid and, when cool enough to handle, remove the peels. Put the plantains in a food processor or blender and process into a thick, sticky paste. Transfer to a bowl and add the crumbled queso fresco and a pinch of salt. Mix well (the mixture is very thick and I find it easier to mix it with my hand). The mixture will look thick, coarse, and tacky. Taste for salt.

4 Assemble the ravioli. Keep a damp paper towel over each open package of wonton wrappers (this prevents them from drying out). Fill a small bowl with water. Line a baking sheet with parchment paper.

5 Place a wonton wrapper in front of you. Place 1 tablespoon of filling in the center of the wrapper. Wet the edges of the wrapper with a moistened finger and place another wonton wrapper on top. Press the edges together to ensure a tight seal, making sure to remove excess air from inside the ravioli as you seal it. Put the ravioli on the prepared baking sheet. Repeat until you have used up all the filling. Arrange the ravioli on the sheet so they don't touch. When you run out of room, cover the layer of ravioli with another sheet of parchment and continue to arrange the ravioli in this way. Cook or freeze them on the baking sheets, transfer to freezer bags, and store in the freezer for up to 1 month. Do not thaw them prior to cooking (they will become mushy), and add an extra minute or two to their cooking time.

6 Bring a large pot of water to a boil (at this time, also bring the sauce back to a simmer over medium heat). Once the pasta water is boiling, add salt (1 tablespoon for every 4 cups water) and stir. Gently drop all the ravioli into the water and stir for the first minute to prevent any sticking. Once they float to the surface, cook for another 2 minutes. Using a strainer, transfer them to a surface lined with parchment paper to air-dry for a minute.

7 Ladle enough sauce to cover the central part of four warmed bowls. Arrange cooked ravioli on top of the sauce. Top with a small dollop of sauce, crumbled queso fresco, and cilantro and serve piping hot.

TORTELLINI *with* PORK, CHICKEN, *and* PARMESAN FILLING

YIELD: 6 SERVINGS / ACTIVE TIME: 2 HOURS / TOTAL TIME: 3 HOURS

The culinary pride of Emilia-Romagna, tortellini are so delicious that the cities of Bologna and Modena continue to lay claim to being their birthplace. Affectionately nicknamed *ombelico*, or "belly button," they can be made with either round or square pieces of pasta. Extremely versatile, they are generally filled with meat or cheese and are served in broth or with rich sauces. If you want to serve them in broth, cook them directly in the broth.

Suggested sauces and broths: Browned Butter and Sage Sauce (page 466), or served in Capon or Chicken Stock (page 749) or or Mixed Meat Stock (page 750)

1 Heat a large skillet over medium-low heat for 2 to 3 minutes, then add the butter. While it heats, pat the pork and chicken with paper towels to absorb any surface moisture, then sprinkle them with salt and pepper. Once the butter has melted and stopped foaming, add the pork and chicken to the skillet. Raise the heat to medium-high and brown one side for 2 minutes, until golden brown. Flip the pieces over and cook the other side for 2 minutes. Add the sage and rosemary and stir for a couple of minutes. Adjust the heat to low, cover, and cook until the meat is cooked all the way through, about 12 minutes. Remove from the heat, discard the herbs, and let cool.

2 Put the pork and chicken in a food processor along with the prosciutto and process until ground. Transfer the mixture to a bowl, add the Parmesan, egg, nutmeg, lemon zest, the oily condiment leftover from cooking the meats (including the crispy bits stuck to bottom of the skillet), and salt and pepper to taste, and mix until thoroughly combined. Taste for seasoning and add more salt and pepper if needed. The filling can be prepared a day ahead; cover, refrigerate, and bring back to room temperature before proceeding.

3 Prepare the dough as directed on pages 131–133, rolling the dough to the thinnest setting (generally notch 5) for pasta sheets that are about 1/16 inch thick. Lightly dust the sheets with flour and transfer them to lightly floured parchment paper-lined baking sheets. Cover loosely with clear food wrap. Work quickly to keep the pasta sheets from drying out, which makes it harder for the pasta to stick together.

INGREDIENTS:

FILLING:

- 3 tablespoons unsalted butter
- ¾ pound pork tenderloin, cut across into 1 ½-inch-thick medallions
- ¾ pound boneless, skinless chicken breast, cut in small pieces
- Salt and freshly ground white pepper
- 3 fresh sage leaves
- 1 small sprig fresh rosemary
- 4 ounces prosciutto, cut into pieces
- 1 cup freshly grated Parmigiano-Reggiano cheese
- 1 large egg, lightly beaten
- 1 teaspoon freshly grated nutmeg
- Grated zest of ½ lemon

DOUGH:

- 1 recipe Three-Egg Basic Pasta Dough (page 131)
- Semolina flour for dusting
- Salt

4 Working with one pasta sheet at a time, place it on a lightly floured flat work surface and, using a round stamp or pastry cutter, cut as many 1 ¼-inch rounds or squares out of it as possible. Transfer the rounds or squares to lightly floured parchment paper-lined baking baking sheets and cover with clear food wrap. Repeat with all the pasta sheets. Gather the scraps together into a ball, put it through the pasta machine to create additional pasta sheets, and cut those as well.

5 Place ½ teaspoon filling in the center of each round or square. Should the dough have become a little dry during this process, lightly moisten the pasta border with a fingertip dipped in water (it's helpful to have a small bowl of water nearby for this purpose). Fold the dough over to form a half-moon or a triangle. Now draw the two corners together; if using a pasta round, this will form a nurse's cap; for a square, it will have a kerchief shape. Press down around the joined sides to create a tight seal. As you do this, try to push out any air from around the filling (this prevents the tortellini from coming apart in the water when boiling due to vapor pressure). Press one more time to ensure you have a tight seal. Lightly dust with flour, and set on a parchment paper-covered baking sheet so that they are not touching. Repeat with the remaining dough and filling. Allow them to air-dry for 2 hours and then cook. Alternatively, you can place them, once air-dried, in a bowl, cover with a kitchen towel, and refrigerate for up to 3 days. Or freeze them on the baking sheets, transfer to freezer bags, and store in the freezer for up to 2 months. Do not thaw them prior to cooking (they will become mushy), and add an extra minute or two to their cooking time.

6 To cook the tortellini, bring a large pot of water to a boil. Once it's boiling, add salt (1 tablespoon for every 4 cups water) and stir. Carefully add the tortellini and stir for the first minute to prevent any sticking. Cook until they are tender but still chewy, 2 to 3 minutes. Remove the tortellini with a strainer and serve with the sauce of your choice.

TORTELLONI *with* PORCINI *and* GOAT CHEESE FILLING

YIELD: 6 SERVINGS / ACTIVE TIME: 2 HOURS / TOTAL TIME: 2 ½ HOURS

Tortellini's much larger cousins, *tortelloni* are puffy, kerchief-shaped filled pockets of pasta from the regions of Tuscany and Emilia-Romagna. While typically filled with ricotta and leafy greens, *tortelloni* can also contain other mixtures, like pumpkin and crushed amaretto cookies. This particular filling is my own creation and combines three of my favorite ingredients: porcini, subtly sweet leeks, and tangy goat cheese.

Suggested sauce: Browned Butter and Sage Sauce (page 466)

INGREDIENTS:

FILLING:

1 ounce dried porcini mushrooms

1 large leek

1 tablespoon extra virgin olive oil

1 tablespoon unsalted butter

Salt

1 10.5-ounce log goat cheese, at room temperature

Freshly ground white pepper

DOUGH:

1 recipe Three-Egg Basic Pasta Dough (page 131)

Semolina flour for dusting

Salt

1 Put the porcini in a small bowl with enough warm water to cover them and let soak until softened, about 15 minutes. Lightly run your fingers across all the pieces to dislodge any dirt or debris. Gather them in your hand and gently squeeze over the bowl to remove excess water, then chop. Strain the soaking liquid through a small paper towel-lined strainer; set aside.

2 Trim away the root end and dark green leaves of the leek, keeping only the white and light green parts. With a sharp knife, cut the leek in half lengthwise and remove the two outer layers. Cut the halves vertically into thin slivers. Place them in a large bowl of water and swish around to remove any dirt. Drain well, then transfer to a kitchen towel. Set aside.

3 Heat a large skillet over medium-low heat for 2 to 3 minutes, then add the olive oil and butter. When the butter has melted and stopped foaming, add the leek and a few good pinches of salt, and stir. Raise the heat to medium. When the leek starts to sizzle, adjust the heat to low, cover, and cook, stirring occasionally until very soft, about 15 minutes. Add the mushrooms and a pinch of salt and stir. Raise the heat to medium and cook, stirring occasionally, until the mushrooms soften, about 5 minutes. Transfer the mixture to a medium bowl and let fully cool, then add the goat cheese and white pepper to taste and mix to thoroughly combine. The filling can be prepared a day ahead; cover, refrigerate, and bring back to room temperature before proceeding.

4 Prepare the dough as directed on pages 131–133, rolling the dough to the thinnest setting (generally notch 5) for pasta sheets that are about 1/16 inch thick. Lightly dust the sheets with flour and place on parchment paper-lined baking sheets. Cover

loosely with clear food wrap. Work quickly to keep the pasta sheets from drying out, which makes it harder for the pasta to stick together.

5 Working with one pasta sheet at a time, place it on a lightly floured flat work surface and, using a round stamp or pastry cutter, cut as many 3-inch rounds or squares as possible, covering them with clear food wrap. Repeat with all the pasta sheets. Gather the scraps together into a ball, put it through the pasta machine to create additional pasta sheets, and cut those as well.

6 Place an generous teaspoon of filling in the center of each pasta round or square. Should the dough have become a little dry during this process, lightly moisten the pasta border with a fingertip dipped in water (it's helpful to have a small bowl of water nearby for this purpose). Fold the dough over to form a half-moon or a triangle. Now draw the two corners together; if using a pasta round, this will form a nurse's cap; for a square, it will have a kerchief shape. Press down around the joined sides to create a tight seal. As you do this, try

to push out any air from around the filling (this prevents the *tortelloni* from coming apart in the water when boiling due to vapor pressure). Press one more time to ensure you have a tight seal. Lightly dust with flour, and set on parchment paper-covered baking sheets so that they are not touching. Repeat with the remaining dough and filling. Allow them to air-dry for 2 hours and then cook. Alternatively, you can place them, once air-dried, in a bowl, cover with a kitchen towel, and refrigerate for up to 3 days. Or freeze them on the baking sheets, transfer to freezer bags, and store in the freezer for up to 2 months. Do not thaw them prior to cooking (they will become mushy), and add an extra minute or two to their cooking time.

7 To cook the *tortelloni,* bring a large pot of water to a boil. Once it's boiling, add salt (1 tablespoon for every 4 cups water) and stir. Carefully drop the *tortelloni,* a few at a time, into the boiling water. Stir for the first minute to prevent any sticking. Cook until they are tender but still chewy, about 3 minutes. Drain and serve with the sauce of your choice.

AGNOLOTTI *with* CABBAGE *and* MEAT FILLING

YIELD: 80 TO 90 AGNOLOTTI; 4 TO 6 SERVINGS / ACTIVE TIME: 1 ½ HOURS / TOTAL TIME: 3 ½ HOURS

Hailing from the northern Italian region of Piedmont, *agnolotti* are small filled pastas known for being easier to make than their more demanding cousins, tortellini and ravioli. This particular version is meat based, though you can also find them filled with spinach and ricotta. If you use leftover roast to make this scrumptious filling, be sure to save some of the roast's cooking juices and stir 3 to 4 tablespoons of it into the filling for additional flavor.

Suggested sauces: Browned Butter and Sage Sauce or its variation (page 466)

1 Trim away the root end and dark green leaves of the leek, keeping only the white and light green parts. With a sharp knife, cut the leek in half lengthwise and remove the two outer layers. Cut the halves vertically into thin slivers. Place them in a large bowl of water and swish them around to remove any dirt. Drain well, then transfer to a kitchen towel. Set aside.

2 Grind the meat in a food processor to a fine paste. Transfer to a medium bowl, add the Parmigiano, egg, nutmeg, white pepper, and few pinches of salt, and mix until well blended.

3 Heat a large skillet over medium-low heat for 2 to 3 minutes, then add the butter. When it's melted, add the leek and cabbage and a few good pinches of salt, and stir. Raise the heat to medium. When the vegetables start to sizzle, adjust the heat to low, cover, and cook, stirring occasionally, until all the vegetables are very soft and wilted, about 15 minutes. (If using meat leftover from a roast, add any reserved meat juices at this point. Raise the heat to medium and cook for 5 minutes, stirring a few times, until some of the juice evaporates.) Remove from the heat and let the mixture fully cool. Once cooled, add to the meat mixture. Mix thoroughly and set aside. The filling can be prepared a day ahead; cover and refrigerate, and bring back to room temperature before proceeding.

4 Prepare the dough as directed on pages 131–133, rolling the dough to the second-thinnest setting (generally notch 4) for pasta sheets that are about ⅛ inch thick. Cut the pasta sheets into approximately 12-inch-long pieces. Lay the cut pasta sheets on lightly floured parchment paper-lined baking sheets and cover

INGREDIENTS:

FILLING:

1 small leek

½ pound each sliced roast beef and roast pork OR 1 pound of either meat

¼ cup freshly grated Parmigiano-Reggiano cheese

1 large egg

1 teaspoon freshly grated nutmeg

½ teaspoon freshly ground white pepper

Salt

2 tablespoons unsalted butter

½ medium head Savoy cabbage, cored and finely shredded

DOUGH:

½ recipe Three-Egg Basic Pasta Dough (page 131)

Semolina flour for dusting

Salt

them loosely with clear food wrap. Make sure to work quickly to keep the pasta sheets from drying out, which makes it harder for the pasta to stick together.

5 Place a 5½- to 6-inch-wide (depending on pasta maker) sheet of dough on a lightly floured work surface and fold it in half lengthwise. Lightly tap on the fold to create a guideline in the pasta sheet. Unfold the dough so that it's laying flat, with the fold line now delineating two still-connected pasta strips that each measure 2 ¾ to 3 inches in width.

6 Working from top to bottom, place 1 tablespoon of filling 1 ½ inches apart in the center of one pasta strip. Should the dough have become a little dry during this process, lightly moisten the pasta border with a fingertip dipped in water (it's helpful to have a small bowl of water nearby for this purpose). Cover the filling with the other half of the sheet of dough. Using your fingertips, gently but firmly press down the dough around each filling mound. As you do this, try to push out any air from around the filling (this keeps the *agnolotti* from coming apart in the water when boiling due to vapor pressure). Press one more time to ensure you have a tight seal.

7 Using a ridged pastry cutter, cut the dough between the filling in equal increments to create 8 *agnolotti*. Transfer them to lightly floured parchment paper-covered baking sheets, arranging them so they are not touching. Repeat until you've used up all the dough and filling. Allow them to air-dry for 2 hours, turning them over once halfway, and then cook. Alternatively, you can place them, once air-dried, in a bowl, cover with a kitchen towel, and refrigerate for up to 3 days or transfer them to freezer bags and freeze for up to 2 months. Do not thaw them prior to cooking (they will become mushy), and add an extra minute or two to their cooking time.

8 To cook the *agnolotti*, bring a large pot of water to a boil. Once it's boiling, add salt (1 tablespoon for every 4 cups water) and stir. Carefully drop the *agnolotti* into the boiling water and stir for the first minute to prevent any sticking. Cook until they are tender but still chewy, 4 to 5 minutes. Remove the *agnolotti* with a strainer, gently shaking them over the pot to remove excess moisture. Serve with the sauce of your choice.

ANOLINI *with* CHEESY BREADCRUMB *and* PARSLEY FILLING IN BROTH

YIELD: 8 SERVINGS / ACTIVE TIME: 2 ½ HOURS / TOTAL TIME: 3 ½ HOURS

Hailing from the Italian city of Parma, famed for bringing us Parmigiano-Reggiano, *anolini* are filled pasta discs traditionally served in a rich and savory broth during the Christmas holidays and other special occasions. The success of this delicate dish lies in the quality of its ingredients and the care taken in their preparation. In other words, please make this with homemade broth. While *anolini* are typically meat-filled, I have taken to filling them with a tasty breadcrumb and *Parmigiano* mixture that feels quite "meaty" in texture and whose savory flavor is quite satisfying despite being remarkably light.

1 Mix the breadcrumbs, chicken broth, and a couple pinches of salt together in a large bowl. Let stand for 5 minutes to give the breadcrumbs a chance to absorb the broth. Add the Parmigiano, nutmeg, egg, parsley, a pinch of salt, and white pepper to taste and mix until well combined. Try pressing the mixture together in a ball. If it holds, the filling is done. If it's too moist, add more breadcrumbs, 1 teaspoon at a time, until the mixture can form into a ball. If it's too dry, add more broth, 1 teaspoon at a time, until the mixture can form into a ball. Set aside. The filling can be prepared a day ahead; cover, refrigerate, and bring back to room temperature before proceeding.

2 Prepare the dough as directed on pages 131–133, rolling the dough to the second-thinnest setting (generally notch 5) for pasta sheets that are about ¹⁄₁₆ inch thick. Cut the pasta sheets into approximately 12-inch-long pieces. Lay the cut pasta sheets on lightly floured parchment paper-lined baking sheets and cover loosely with clear food wrap. Work quickly to keep the pasta sheets from drying out, which makes it harder for the pasta to stick together.

3 Place a 5 ½- to 6-inch-wide (depending on the pasta maker) sheet of dough on a lightly floured work surface and fold it in half lengthwise. Lightly tap on the fold to create a guideline in the pasta sheet. Unfold the dough so that it's laying flat, with the fold line now delineating two still-connected pasta strips that each measure 2 ¾ to 3 inches in width.

4 Place balls of filling about the size of hazelnuts in the center of one pasta strip, spacing the mounds, from the top to the

INGREDIENTS:

FILLING:

1 ¼ cups dry breadcrumbs

½ cup warm chicken broth

Salt

1 ¼ cups freshly grated Parmigiano-Reggiano cheese

½ teaspoon freshly grated nutmeg

1 large egg, lightly beaten

Handful fresh parsley leaves, minced

Freshly ground white pepper

DOUGH:

½ recipe Three-Egg Basic Pasta Dough (page 131)

Semolina flour for dusting

Salt

TO SERVE:

10 cups Capon or Chicken Stock (page 749)

Freshly grated Parmigiano-Reggiano cheese

bottom of the strip about 2 inches apart. Should the dough have become a little dry during this process, lightly moisten the pasta border with a fingertip dipped in water (it's helpful to have a small bowl of water nearby for this purpose). Cover the filling with the other half of the sheet of dough. Using your fingertips, gently but firmly press down the dough around each filling mound. As you do this, try to push out any air from around the filling (this keeps the *anolini* from coming apart in the water when boiling due to vapor pressure). Press one more time to ensure you have a tight seal.

5 Use a 2-inch round stamp or pastry cutter, centering it over each mound of filling, to cut out each *anolino*. Transfer them to lightly floured parchment paper-covered baking sheets, arranging them so they are not touching. Allow them to air-dry for 2 hours, turning them over once halfway, and then cook. Alternatively, you can place them, once air-dried, in a bowl, cover with a kitchen towel, and refrigerate for up to 3 days, or transfer them to freezer bags and freeze for up to 2 months. Do not thaw them prior to cooking (they will become mushy), and add an extra minute or two to their cooking time.

6 To cook the *anolini,* bring the broth to a boil in a large pot, then turn the heat down just a bit so it's not at a raging boil (which could tear the *anolini* apart). Carefully drop all the *anolini* into the broth and stir for the first minute to prevent any sticking. Cook until they are tender but still chewy, 2 to 3 minutes. Using a strainer or large slotted spoon, transfer the *anolini* to large shallow soup bowls, ladle hot broth over them, and serve sprinkled with Parmigiano (or offer the grated cheese at the table).

BUTTERNUT SQUASH-STUFFED CAPPELLACCI

YIELD: 4 SERVINGS / ACTIVE TIME: 2 HOURS / TOTAL TIME: 3 HOURS

This is the signature dish of Ferrara, the quaint cobblestoned city in the northern Italian region of Emilia-Romagna. *Cappellacci di zucca* are typically served with a butter-based sauce but occasionally you see them joining forces with a light meat sauce, and the result is quite delicious.

Suggested sauces: Browned Butter and Sage Sauce and its variation (page 466), Signora Sofia's Spiced Pork Sauce (page 620), Rabbit Ragù (page 603)

INGREDIENTS:

FILLING:

- 1 ½ pounds butternut squash
- 1 tablespoon extra virgin olive oil
- ¾ cup freshly grated Parmigiano-Reggiano cheese
- 2 large egg yolks
- 1 ½ tablespoons dry breadcrumbs
- 1 teaspoon freshly grated nutmeg
- Salt and freshly ground white pepper

DOUGH:

- ½ recipe Three-Egg Basic Pasta Dough (page 131)
- Semolina flour for dusting
- Salt

1 Preheat the oven to 400°F. Slice the top and bottom off the squash. Rest it on its widest end and, using a heavy kitchen knife, slice down vertically. If it's difficult to do (it is for me), use a rubber mallet to tap gently on the pointy side of the blade. Work as slowly as you need to and wedge the knife all the way to the base of the squash. When you have the two separated squash halves, use a spoon to scrape out the seeds and fibrous insides. Prick the flesh with a fork. Brush all the cut surfaces lightly with the olive oil (I use my hands to do this) and place, cut side down, on a parchment paper-lined baking sheet. Place on the center rack of the oven and roast until you can easily pierce the squash with a fork, 40 to 45 minutes. Remove from the oven and let cool, then scoop the soft flesh off the skins with a large metal spoon. Run the squash flesh through a potato ricer directly over a medium bowl. Alternatively, you can place in a food processor or blender and process until smooth. Add the Parmigiano, egg yolks, breadcrumbs, nutmeg, and salt and pepper to taste and mix until thoroughly combined. Try pressing the mixture together in a ball. If it holds, the filling is done. If it's too moist, add more breadcrumbs, 1 teaspoon at a time, until you can form it into a ball. If it's too dry, add olive oil, 1 teaspoon at a time, until it will hold together. The filling can be prepared a day ahead; cover, refrigerate, and bring back to room temperature before proceeding.

2 Prepare the dough following the directions on pages 131–133, rolling the dough to the thinnest setting (generally notch 5) for pasta sheets that are about 1⁄16 inch thick. Transfer them to lightly floured parchment paper-covered baking sheets, covering them loosely with clear food wrap. Work quickly to keep the pasta sheets from drying out, which makes it harder for the pasta to stick together.

3 Working with one sheet at a time, place it on a lightly floured work surface in front of you. Using a pastry cutter, cut each sheet into as many 3-inch squares as possible. Place the finished squares on a lightly floured parchment paper-lined baking sheet so they don't touch and cover them lightly with clear food wrap. Repeat with all the pasta sheets. Gather the scraps together into a ball, put it through the pasta machine to create additional pasta sheets, and cut those as well.

4 To make the *cappellacci,* place a square of dough on a lightly floured work surface in front of you. Place 1 tablespoon of filling in the center. Should the dough have become a little dry during this process, lightly moisten it with a fingertip dipped in water (it's helpful to have a small bowl of water nearby for this purpose). Fold one of the corners over the filling to create a triangle, tightly sealing both sides. As you do this, try to push out any air from around the filling (this prevents the *cappellacci* from coming apart in the water when boiling due to vapor pressure). Bring the two longest corners of the triangle together to form a kerchief shape. Press tightly to seal. Dust with flour

and transfer them to lightly floured parchment paper-covered baking sheets, arranging them so they are not touching. Repeat with the remaining squares and filling. Allow them to air-dry for 2 hours, turning them over once halfway, and then cook. Alternatively, you can place them, once air-dried, in a bowl, cover with a kitchen towel, and refrigerate for up to 3 days or transfer them to freezer bags and freeze for up to 2 months. Do not thaw them prior to cooking (they will become mushy), and add an extra minute or two to their cooking time.

5 To cook the *cappellacci,* bring a large pot of water to a boil. Once it's boiling, add salt (1 tablespoon for every 4 cups water) and stir. Carefully drop them into the boiling water and stir for the first minute to prevent any sticking. Cook until they are tender but still chewy, 5 to 6 minutes. Using a strainer or large slotted spoon, remove the *cappellacci,* gently shaking them over the pot to remove excess moisture. Serve with the sauce of your choice.

CAPPELLETTI *with* PORK *and* PROSCIUTTO FILLING IN BROTH

YIELD: 6 SERVINGS / ACTIVE TIME: 2 ½ HOURS / TOTAL TIME: 3 ½ HOURS

Cappelletti, or "little hats" in Italian, are plump, meat-filled morsels traditionally served in a rich capon broth. In many parts of Italy, they are a beloved part of the Christmas menu, though they are also often seen on Sunday dinner tables and for special occasions.

1 Heat a large skillet over medium-low heat for 2 to 3 minutes, then add the butter. While it heats, pat the pork and chicken with paper towels to absorb any surface moisture, then sprinkle them with salt and pepper. Once the butter has melted and stopped foaming, add the pork and chicken to the skillet. Raise the heat to medium-high and brown one side for 2 minutes, until golden brown. Flip the pieces over and cook the other side for 2 minutes. Add the sage and rosemary and stir for a couple of minutes. Adjust the heat to low, cover, and cook until the meat is cooked all the way through, about 12 minutes. Remove from the heat, discard the herbs, and let cool.

2 Put the pork and chicken in a food processor along with the prosciutto and process until ground. Transfer the mixture to a bowl, add the cheeses, egg, nutmeg, lemon zest, the oily condiment leftover from cooking the meats (including the crispy bits stuck to bottom of the skillet), and salt and white pepper to taste, and mix until thoroughly combined. Taste for seasoning and add more salt and pepper if needed. The filling can be prepared a day ahead; cover, refrigerate, and bring back to room temperature before proceeding.

3 Prepare the dough following the directions on pages 131–133, rolling the dough to the thinnest setting (generally notch 5) for pasta sheets that are about ¹⁄₁₆ inch thick. Transfer them to lightly floured parchment paper-covered baking sheets, covering them loosely with clear food wrap. Work quickly to keep the pasta sheets from drying out, which makes it harder for the pasta to stick together.

4 Working with one sheet at a time, place on a lightly floured work surface in front of you. Using a pastry cutter, cut each sheet into as many 2-inch squares as possible, covering them loosely with clear food wrap. Repeat this with all the pasta sheets. Gather the scraps together into a ball, put it through the

INGREDIENTS:

FILLING:

3 tablespoons unsalted butter

¾ pound pork tenderloin, sliced in medallions

¾ pound boneless skinless chicken breast, cut into pieces

Salt and freshly ground white pepper

3 fresh sage leaves

1 small sprig fresh rosemary

4 ounces sliced prosciutto

4 ounces camembert cheese, rind removed

1 cup freshly grated Parmigiano-Reggiano cheese

1 large egg, lightly beaten

1 teaspoon freshly grated nutmeg

Grated zest of ½ lemon

DOUGH:

1 cup + 3 tablespoons finely milled type "00" wheat flour OR 1 ⅓ cups + 1 tablespoon all-purpose flour

½ teaspoon salt

2 large eggs, room temperature

1 large egg yolk

Semolina flour for dusting

FOR SERVING:

8 cups Capon or Chicken Stock (page 749) or Mixed Meat Stock (page 750)

pasta machine to create additional pasta sheets, and cut those as well.

5 To make the *cappelletti,* place a square of dough on a lightly floured working surface. Place 1 ½ teaspoons of filling in the center. Should the dough have become a little dry during this process, lightly moisten the pasta border with a fingertip dipped in water (it's helpful to have a small bowl of water nearby for this purpose). Cover with another square of dough and fold one of the corners over the filling to create a triangle, tightly sealing both sides. As you do this, try to push out any air from around the filling (this prevents the *cappelletti* from coming apart in the water when boiling due to vapor pressure). Bring the two longest corners of the triangle together to form a kerchief shape. Press tightly to seal. Toss with flour, then set on a well-floured parchment paper–covered baking sheet so they are not touching, and cover with a kitchen towel. Repeat with the remaining dough and filling. Allow them to air-dry for 2 hours, turning them over once halfway, then cook. Alternatively, you can place them, once air-dried, in a bowl, cover with a kitchen towel, and refrigerate for up to 3 days. Or freeze them on the baking sheets, transfer to freezer bags, and store in the freezer for up to 2 months. Do not thaw them prior to cooking (they will become mushy), and add an extra minute or two to their cooking time.

6 To cook the *cappelletti,* bring the broth to a boil in a large pot, then turn the heat down just a bit so it's not at a raging boil (which could tear the *cappelletti* apart). Carefully drop all the *cappelletti* into the broth and stir for the first minute to prevent any sticking. Cook until they are tender but still chewy, 3 to 4 minutes. Using a strainer or large slotted spoon, transfer the *cappelletti* to large shallow soup bowls, ladle hot broth over them, and serve.

CARAMELLE *with* ROASTED BUTTERNUT SQUASH, PARMESAN, *and* GORGONZOLA FILLING

YIELD: 6 SERVINGS / ACTIVE TIME: 2 HOURS / TOTAL TIME: 3 HOURS

Aptly named "candies" in Italian, *caramelle* are pudgy filled pastas that do indeed look like pieces of wrapped candy with twists on both ends. I've filled this version with butternut squash and gorgonzola cheese, but you can use a mixture of spinach and ricotta, mushrooms and goat cheese, or roasted eggplant and chervil cheese to name three. The filling options are endless, which means you can enjoy these savory treats in a variety of ways.

Suggested sauces: Creamy Leek Sauce (page 504), Browned Butter and Sage Sauce (page 466), Aromatic Walnut Sauce (page 543)

1 Preheat the oven to 400°F. Slice the top and bottom off the squash. Rest it on its widest end and, using a heavy kitchen knife, slice down vertically. If it's difficult to do (it is for me), use a rubber mallet to tap gently on the pointy side of the blade. Work as slowly as you need to and wedge the knife all the way to the base of the squash. When you have the two separated squash halves, use a spoon to scrape out the seeds and fibrous insides. Prick the flesh with a fork. Brush all the cut surfaces lightly with olive oil (I use my hands to do this) and place, cut side down, on a parchment paper-lined baking sheet. Place on the center rack of the oven, lower the temperature to 375°F, and roast until you can easily pierce the squash with a fork, 40 to 45 minutes. Remove from the oven and let cool, then scoop the soft flesh off the skins with a large metal spoon. Run squash flesh through a potato ricer directly over a medium bowl. Alternatively, you can place in a food processor or blender and process until smooth. Add the breadcrumbs, cheeses, egg yolks, nutmeg, and rosemary and mix well. The filling can be prepared a day ahead; cover, refrigerate, and bring back to room temperature before proceeding.

2 Prepare the dough as directed on pages 131–133 rolling the dough to the thinnest setting (generally notch 5) for pasta sheets that are about 1/16 inch thick. Cut the pasta sheets into approximately 12-inch-long pieces. Lay the cut pasta sheets on lightly floured parchment paper-lined baking sheets and cover loosely with clear food wrap. Work quickly to keep the pasta sheets from drying out, which makes it harder for the pasta to stick together.

INGREDIENTS:

FILLING:

- 1 ½ pounds butternut squash

  Olive oil for brushing

- ¼ cup soft breadcrumbs

- ½ cup freshly grated Parmigiano-Reggiano cheese

- ¼ cup crumbled gorgonzola cheese

- 2 large egg yolks

- 1 teaspoon freshly grated nutmeg

- 10 fresh rosemary leaves, minced

DOUGH:

- 1 recipe Three-Egg Basic Pasta Dough (page 131)

  Semolina flour for dusting

  Salt

3 Working with one sheet at a time, place it on a lightly floured work surface in front of you. Using a ridged pastry cutter, cut each sheet into as many 2 ½-inch squares as possible. Set the squares on lightly floured parchment paper-lined baking sheets, making sure they don't touch and cover them loosely with clear food wrap Repeat with the remaining pasta sheets. Gather any scraps together into a ball, put it through the pasta machine to create additional pasta sheets, and cut those as well.

4 To make the *caramelle,* lay out 12 to 14 pasta squares at a time and place 2 teaspoons of filling in the center of each. Should the dough have become a little dry during this process, lightly moisten it with a fingertip dipped in water (it's helpful to have a small bowl of water nearby for this purpose). Fold one edge of the square over the filling, to create a rectangle, aligning it with the other edge. Press down around the joined sides to create a tight seal. As you do this, try to push out any air from around the filling (this keeps the *caramelle* from coming apart in the water when boiling due to vapor pressure). Press one more time to ensure you have a tight seal. Twist the ends of the rectangle in opposite directions and pinch the end joints to create a tight seal. Repeat until you have used up all the pasta squares and filling. Set them on lightly floured parchment paper-covered baking sheets so they are not touching. Allow them to air-dry for 2 hours, turning them over once halfway, and then cook. Alternatively, you can place them, once air-dried, in a bowl, cover with a kitchen towel, and refrigerate for up to 3 days. Or freeze on the baking sheets, transfer to freezer bags, and store in the freezer for up to 2 months. Do not thaw them prior to cooking (they will become mushy), and add an extra minute or two to their cooking time.

5 To cook the *caramelle,* bring a large pot of water to a boil. Once it's boiling, add salt (1 tablespoon for every 4 cups water) and stir. Carefully drop the *caramelle* into the boiling water and stir for the first minute to prevent any sticking. Cook until they are tender but still chewy, 3 to 4 minutes. Using a strainer or large slotted spoon, remove the *caramelle,* gently shaking them over the pot to remove excess surface moisture. Serve with the sauce of your choice.

CJALSÒNS *with* SMOKED RICOTTA *and* BUTTER

YIELD: 6 SERVINGS / ACTIVE TIME: ABOUT 1 HOUR / TOTAL TIME: ABOUT 1 ½ HOURS

From the Carnia area of the Italian region of Friuli, *cjalsòns* are filled pastas that combine the sweetness of raisins and chocolate with the earthy flavor of cooked spinach. This mixing of sweet and savory flavors, a fairly typical combination in certain parts of Italy, may seem like an exotic main dish to some. As a Piedmontese, I grew up unaccustomed to such pairings, which is why I found this recipe, from Micol Negrin's excellent cookbook *Rustico,* so intriguing. This is my adaptation of that recipe.

1 Put the raisins in a small bowl, cover with warm water, and soak for 20 minutes. Drain and transfer to a paper-towel lined plate to absorb any surface water.

2 Rinse the kale and parsley. Lightly shake them but don't pat them dry. Put a large skillet on the stove and turn the heat to medium-high. Add the kale and parsley and stir with tongs until the leaves soften but are still bright green, 4 to 5 minutes. Transfer to a colander. When cool enough to handle, squeeze out any remaining water with your hands. Mince.

3 Put the breadcrumbs, minced greens, raisins, eggs, chocolate, chile powder, sugar, lemon zest, cinnamon, nutmeg, and salt to taste in a large bowl and mix well. The filling can be prepared a day ahead; cover, refrigerate, and bring back to room temperature before proceeding.

4 Prepare the dough following the directions on pages 131–133, rolling the dough to the thinnest setting (generally notch 5) for pasta sheets that are about 1/16 inch thick. Lay the cut pasta sheets on lightly floured parchment paper-lined baking sheets and cover loosely with clear food wrap. Work quickly to keep the pasta sheets from drying out, which makes it harder for the pasta to stick together.

5 Working with one sheet at a time, place on a lightly floured work surface in front of you. Using a 2-inch round stamp or pastry cutter, cut as many rounds as possible. Repeat this with all the pasta sheets. Set them on lightly floured parchment paper-covered baking sheets so they don't touch and cover loosely with clear food wrap. Gather the scraps together into a ball, put it through the pasta machine to create additional pasta sheets, and cut those as well.

INGREDIENTS:

FILLING:

- 2 tablespoons golden raisins
- 2 pounds baby kale leaves
- 2 handfuls fresh parsley leaves
- 2 cups soft breadcrumbs
- 3 large eggs
- 1 ½ ounces bittersweet chocolate, grated or chopped
- ½ teaspoon ground ancho chile powder or red pepper flakes
- 2 teaspoons sugar

  Grated zest of 1 lemon
- ½ teaspoon ground cinnamon
- ½ teaspoon freshly grated nutmeg

  Salt

DOUGH:

- 2 ¾ cups all-purpose flour
- 1 teaspoon salt
- 3 large eggs
- 3 tablespoons whole milk, more if needed

  Semolina for dusting

  Salt

SAUCE:

- 6 tablespoons (¾ stick) unsalted butter
- ¾ cup grated smoked ricotta cheese, or crumbled ricotta salata plus 3 drops of liquid smoke, or regular ricotta cheese
- ¼ cup milk (only needed if using regular ricotta)
- 1 teaspoon sugar

6 Place 2 teaspoons of filling in the center of each round. Should the dough have become a little dry during this process, lightly moisten the pasta border with a fingertip dipped in water (it's helpful to have a small bowl of water nearby for this purpose). Gently pull one side of the round outward and then over the filling so that it joins the side touching the work surface. As you do this, try to push out any air from around the filling (this prevents the *cjalsòns* from coming apart in the water while boiling due to vapor pressure). Press one more time to ensure it is tightly sealed. Repeat with the remaining rounds and filling. Set them on lightly floured parchment paper-covered baking sheets so they are not touching. Cook or cover and refrigerate for up to 3 to 4 hours.

7 To cook the *cjalsòns*, bring a large pot of water to a boil. Once it's boiling, add salt (1 tablespoon for every 4 cups water) and stir. Drop them into the boiling water and stir for the first minute to prevent any sticking. Cook until they are tender but still chewy, 3 to 4 min-

utes. Transfer them with a strainer to a warmed serving bowl.

8 If using smoked ricotta or ricotta salata: As the *cjalsòns* cook, heat a small saucepan over medium-low heat for 2 to 3 minutes, then add the butter. When it has melted, remove from the heat, cover, and keep hot. When the *cjalsòns* are cooked, pour the hot butter over them and gently toss to combine. Top sprinkled with the ricotta or ricotta salata and sugar and serve piping hot.

If using regular ricotta: As the *cjalsòns* cook, heat a small saucepan over medium-low heat for 2 to 3 minutes, then add the butter. When it has melted, remove from the heat, cover, and keep hot. Put the ricotta, milk, and sugar in a microwave-friendly bowl or measuring cup and microwave for 1 minute to warm up. Stir to combine well. When the *cjalsòns* are cooked, pour the hot butter over them and gently toss to combine. Ladle the ricotta sauce on warmed plates and top with the buttered *cjalsòns*. Serve piping hot.

CULURGIONES

YIELD: 6 SERVINGS / ACTIVE TIME: 2 HOURS / TOTAL TIME: 3 ¼ HOURS

This recipe is an adaptation from one of my two favorite books on pasta, *Mastering Pasta* by Marc Vetri (the other is *Pasta By Hand* by Jenn Louis). Coming from northern Italy as I do, I am sad to say that I had never heard of *culurgiones,* unique filled dumplings from the island of Sardinia, before picking up the book. Resembling teardrops with a zipper-like seal, they take some time to master, but you can always roll the pasta dough and create simple half-moon shapes (or use pre-made round Asian wrappers). Hardcore pasta makers knowledgeable in the art of making *culurgiones* may not approve of the inclusion of an egg and oil in this recipe. They may argue that resting a simple dough comprised of flour, water, and salt for at least 2 hours is enough to yield a tender dough. Should you want to give it a try (the dough will be slightly more difficult to roll and shape), try using 1 ½ cups semolina flour, 1 teaspoon salt, and ½ cup warm water, being sure to let the dough rest for 2 hours. I personally found Mr. Vetri's version very malleable and am quite happy to continue using it.

Suggested sauces: Sweetbread, Corn, and Jalapeño Sauce (page 676), Browned Butter and Sage Sauce (page 466), Fresh Mushroom Sauce (page 551)

---

1 Heat a large skillet over medium-low heat for 2 to 3 minutes. Add the butter and turn the heat up to medium. Once the butter has melted and stops foaming, add the onions and a couple pinches of salt and stir. Cook, stirring occasionally, until deep golden brown and soft, about 20 minutes.

2 While the onions cook, bring a medium saucepan of water to a boil, then add the potatoes. Cook until you can easily insert a knife through the center of a cube, 15 to 20 minutes. Drain, place in a wide, shallow bowl, and press them with a potato masher until smooth. Add the cooked onions, cheese, cilantro, and salt and pepper to taste. Mix until well combined. Let cool to room temperature before using. The filling can be prepared a day ahead; cover and refrigerate, and bring back to room temperature before proceeding.

3 Prepare the dough as directed on pages 131–133, rolling the dough to the thinnest setting (generally notch 5) for pasta sheets that are about 1/16 inch thick. Lightly dust the sheets with flour and place on parchment paper-lined baking sheets.

INGREDIENTS:

FILLING:

- 3 tablespoons unsalted butter

- 3 medium white or yellow onions, minced

- Salt

- 1 ½ pounds russet potatoes, peeled and cut into 1-inch cubes

- 1 cup freshly grated Parmigiano-Reggiano cheese

- 2 handfuls fresh cilantro leaves, minced

- Freshly ground black pepper

DOUGH:

- 2 ¼ cups semolina flour

- 1 ½ teaspoons salt

- ¾ cup water, or more as needed

- 1 large egg

- 1 tablespoon extra virgin olive oil

Make sure to work quickly to keep the pasta sheets from drying out and becoming brittle.

4 Working with one pasta sheet at a time, place it on a lightly floured work surface and cut out as many rounds with a 3-inch biscuit or cookie cutter as possible. Repeat with all the pasta sheets. Gather the scraps together into a ball, put it through the pasta machine to create additional pasta sheets, and cut those as well.

5 To fill the *culurgiones,* place a round in the palm of your slightly cupped hand and hold it so that it takes the shape of a taco. Place 1 tablespoon of the filling in the center. Pinch one end of the "taco" to begin and then, very similarly to braiding hair, start by pinching a small section of one side of the pasta over the other side. Now, like braiding, reverse the order and pinch the other side of the pasta. Repeat this pattern until you work your way to the

other end of the "taco," then pinch and twist the dough into a point (which creates the teardrop look). Repeat with the remaining dough and filling. Put the filled *culurgiones* on lightly floured parchment paper-lined baking sheets so they don't touch. Cook or cover and refrigerate for several days. Or freeze on the baking sheets, transfer to freezer bags, and store in the freezer for 3 to 4 weeks. Do not thaw them prior to cooking (they will become mushy), and add an extra minute or two to their cooking time.

6 To cook the *culurgiones,* bring a large pot of water to a boil. Once it's boiling, add salt (1 tablespoon for every 4 cups water) and stir. Carefully add the *culurgiones,* stirring for the first minute to prevent any sticking. Cook until they are tender but still chewy, 3 to 4 minutes. Remove them with a strainer and serve with the sauce of your choice.

BACCALÀ PYRAMIDS *with* GREEN OLIVES

YIELD: 6 SERVINGS / ACTIVE TIME: 45 MINUTES / TOTAL TIME: ABOUT 1 HOUR, PLUS 2 TO 3 DAYS TO SOAK THE BACCALÀ

Meant to be served as a tapas-like appetizer, these moist dumplings derive their delicate flavor from *baccalà,* salted and dried cod. Very popular in Italy, it was traditionally served on Christmas Eve and on Fridays, in observance of religious edicts. Today it is consumed throughout the year seasoned with tomato sauce, braised onions, or myriad other toppings. Making this dish does require planning. Because *baccalà* is heavily salted, it needs to be soaked in water or milk (considered more effective at extracting salt from the *baccalà*) for no less than 48 to 72 hours and its liquid, which becomes very salty after 12 hours of soaking, must be changed at least twice a day. While it sounds like a lot of work, in reality it only takes a few minutes a day to prep it, and what it gives back, in terms of flavor and a satisfyingly chewy texture, is tenfold. Finally, to maximize this dish's flavor, use brined cured olives from a good-quality supermarket or gourmet grocer, as olives from a can lack the flavor and texture to properly contribute their fruity and pungent characteristics to the dumplings. I recommend using arbequina green olives if you can find them, though manzanilla olives, which are much larger, are a good substitute.

1 Three days ahead, place the *baccalà* in large bowl with a wide bottom and completely submerge it in water or milk. Cover and refrigerate. Change the liquid twice a day, morning and evening.

2 When ready to cook, drain the *baccalà,* remove any remaining skin, dry with paper towels, and chop into small pieces. Transfer to a medium saucepan and add the potatoes, water, 1 cup milk, and a few good cracks of pepper. Bring to a gentle boil, then cook over medium-low heat, stirring occasionally, for 45 to 50 minutes. In that time, the *baccalà* and potatoes will break up and the sauce will become thick. Taste for seasoning and add salt or pepper as needed.

3 As the *baccalà* and potatoes cook, prepare the sauce. Heat a wide skillet over medium heat for 2 to 3 minutes. Add 2 tablespoons of the olive oil and turn the heat up to medium-high. Heat for a couple of minutes, then add the tomatoes, olives, and salt and pepper to taste. Cook for a couple of minutes, until the tomatoes begin to burst. Add the tomato sauce and bring to a boil. Reduce the temperature to low and simmer for 5 minutes. Remove from the heat, cover, and set aside.

INGREDIENTS:

- 1 pound baccalà (dried and salted cod)
- 1 cup milk (more if you are using milk to soak the baccalà)
- 1 ½ pounds (about 3) Yukon Gold potatoes, peeled and cubed
- 1 cup water
- Freshly ground black pepper
- Salt
- 4 tablespoons extra virgin olive oil, divided
- 1 pint yellow grape tomatoes
- ¼ pound pitted green olives
- 1 ¼ cups plain tomato sauce of your choice
- 1 recipe Spiced Pasta Dough (page 146), made with a five-peppercorn spice blend, OR 1 12-ounce package (42 to 48) 3-inch square wrappers
- Handful fresh parsley leaves, chopped

PEPPER RELISH:

- 4 jalapeño peppers, seeded and roughly chopped
- ½ red bell pepper, seeded and cut into several pieces
- ½ large red onion, roughly chopped
- 1 tablespoon nonpareil capers, rinsed and drained
- 3 tablespoons extra virgin olive oil

4 Prepare the dough as directed on pages 146–148, rolling the dough to the thinnest setting (generally notch 5) for pasta sheets that are about 1/16 inch thick. The sheets will be very long on this setting. Cover loosely with clear food wrap to prevent them from drying. Make sure to work quickly to keep the pasta sheets from drying out, which makes it harder for the pasta to stick together. Cut them into approximately 6-inch squares and then cut each 6-inch square into four 3-inch squares. Repeat with the remaining dough.

5 Place 1 tablespoon of filling in the center of each square. Should the dough have become a little dry during this process, lightly moisten the pasta border with a fingertip dipped in water (it's helpful to have a small bowl of water nearby for this purpose). Join all four corners together over the filling to form a pyramid. As you do this, try to push out any air from around the filling (this prevents the pyramids from coming apart in the water when boiling due to vapor pressure). Repeat with the remaining dough and filling. Put the dumplings on lightly floured parchment paper-covered baking sheets so they don't touch. Let them air-dry for 2 hours, turning them over after an hour. Cook or transfer to a bowl, cover with a kitchen towel, and refrigerate for up to a day. Or freeze them on the baking sheets, transfer to freezer bags, and store in the freezer up to a month. Do not thaw them prior to cooking (they will become mushy), and add an extra minute or two to their cooking time.

6 Bring a large pot of water to a boil. Once it's boiling, add salt (1 tablespoon for every 4 cups) and stir. Carefully add the pyramids and stir for the first minute to prevent any sticking. Cook until they are tender but still chewy, about 3 minutes.

7 While the pyramids cook, reheat the tomato sauce over medium-high heat. Also, make the pepper relish. Put the peppers, onion, and capers in a mini food processor and process into a thick paste. Transfer to a small bowl, then, whisking continuously, slowly add the olive oil in a stream until everything is very well mixed. Use or cover and refrigerate for up to 4 days.

8 When the pasta has cooked, carefully scoop the dumplings out with a strainer and add them to the piping hot tomato sauce in the skillet. Cook for 1 to 2 minutes, then remove from the heat and drizzle the remaining 2 tablespoons oil over the top.

9 Divide the pyramids evenly among six warmed bowls, spoon over the sauce, sprinkle with parsley, and serve.

HERB *and* CHEESE-FILLED PANSOTI
with AROMATIC WALNUT SAUCE

YIELD: 6 SERVINGS / ACTIVE TIME: 45 MINUTES / TOTAL TIME: 1 ½ HOURS

Kerchief-shaped filled pasta, *pansoti* (or *pansotti*) come from the Italian region of Liguria. In Ligurian dialect their name means *pansa*, or "big belly," alluding to their hefty size. It is almost impossible to make authentic *pansoti*, which require a mixture of wild herbs indigenous to the fertile hills of Liguria, as well as *prescinsêua*, a fresh local cheese that's kind of a cross between ricotta and sour cream. This is a tasty approximation, served with the traditional walnut sauce.

1 Pinch or cut the leaves away from the stems. Keep the sturdier greens like beet greens, kale, and spinach separate from tender herbs and greens like mâche, parsley, and watercress. Wash them separately, swishing them in a large bowl of cold water. Drain well.

2 Bring a large pot of water to a boil. Once it's boiling, add salt (1 tablespoon for every 4 cups water) and stir. Add the sturdier greens and scallions, stir, and cook for 4 minutes. Now add the herbs and more tender greens and cook for 30 seconds. Drain in a colander and rinse with cold water to stop the cooking process. Squeeze the greens and herbs to remove excess water. Mince everything together.

3 Transfer the greens and herbs to a large bowl, add the eggs, cheeses, breadcrumbs, olive oil, nutmeg, and salt and white pepper to taste, and mix well. The filling can be prepared a day ahead; cover, refrigerate, and bring back to room temperature before proceeding.

4 Prepare the dough as directed on pages 131–133, rolling the dough to the second-thinnest setting (generally notch 4) for pasta sheets that are about ⅛ inch thick. Transfer them to lightly floured parchment paper-covered baking sheets and cover loosely with clear food wrap. Work quickly to keep the pasta sheets from drying out, which makes it harder for the pasta to stick together.

5 Working with one sheet at a time, place on a lightly floured work surface in front of you. Using a pastry cutter, cut each sheet into as many 3-inch squares as possible, covering them loosely with clear food wrap as they are

INGREDIENTS:

FILLING:

- 2 pounds mixed greens and fresh herbs (make sure to include at least 3 to 4 different kinds): endive, arugula, spinach, radicchio, beet greens, kale, spinach, mâche, parsley, watercress, chervil, and/or the feathery leaves from fennel bulb
- Salt
- 1 bunch (5 or 6) scallions, trimmed and thinly sliced
- 3 large eggs, lightly beaten
- ¾ cup freshly grated Parmigiano-Reggiano cheese, divided
- ½ cup whole-milk ricotta cheese
- ¼ cup freshly grated pecorino Romano
- ¼ cup soft breadcrumbs
- 2 teaspoons extra virgin olive oil
- 1 teaspoon freshly grated nutmeg
- Salt and freshly ground white pepper

DOUGH:

- 1 recipe Three-Egg Basic Pasta Dough (page 131)
- Semolina flour for dusting
- Salt

FOR SERVING:

- ¼ cup freshly grated Parmigiano-Reggiano cheese
- 1 recipe Aromatic Walnut Sauce (page 543)

done to prevent them from drying. Repeat with all the pasta sheets. Gather all the dough scraps together into a ball, put it through the pasta machine to create additional pasta sheets, and cut those as well.

6 Place a teaspoon of filling in the center of each square. Should the dough have become a little dry during this process, lightly moisten the pasta border with a fingertip dipped in water (it's helpful to have a small bowl of water nearby for this purpose). Fold the dough over to form a triangle. Draw the two corners together; it will have a kerchief shape. Press down around the joined sides to create a tight seal. As you do this, try to push out any air from around the filling (this prevents the *pansoti* from coming apart in the water when boiling due to vapor pressure). Press one more time to ensure you have a tight seal. Lightly dust with flour and set on a parchment paper–covered baking sheet so they aren't touching. Repeat with the remaining dough and filling. Allow them to air-dry for 2 hours, turning them over once halfway through, and then cook. Alternatively, you can place them, once air-dried, in a bowl, cover with a kitchen towel, and refrigerate for up to 3 days. Or freeze on the baking sheets, transfer to freezer bags, and store in the freezer for up to 2 months. Do not thaw them prior to cooking (they will become mushy), and add an extra minute or two to their cooking time.

7 To cook the *pansoti*, bring a large pot of water to a boil. Once it's boiling, add salt (1 tablespoon for every 4 cups water) and stir. Reduce the heat to medium. Add the *pansoti* in batches and stir for the first minute to prevent any sticking. Cook until they float to the surface, 3 to 4 minutes. Remove them using a strainer, gently shaking them over the pot to remove excess moisture. Transfer to a warmed serving bowl and tent with aluminum foil to keep warm as you cook the remainder.

8 When all the *pansoti* are cooked, add the Parmigiano and walnut sauce to the bowl and toss gently until the *pansoti* are well coated with both. Serve piping hot.

PIEROGIS *with* POTATO, ONION, *and* FARMER'S CHEESE FILLING

YIELD: 4 SERVINGS / ACTIVE TIME: 2 HOURS / TOTAL TIME: 3 HOURS

These dumplings, known as *pierogi* in Poland and *varenyky* in the Ukraine, are endlessly versatile and seriously comforting. In addition to potatoes, onions, and cheese, they can be filled with mushrooms, sauerkraut, meat, even fruit. I've included directions for making the dumplings with a pierogi form and by hand, if you don't own one.

1 Prepare the dough. With a stand mixer, use the paddle attachment and put the cream cheese, egg, and salt in the bowl. Mix on medium speed until smooth. Add the water and mix until smooth. Swap the paddle for the dough hook. With the mixer running, slowly add the flour and continue to mix until you have a dough that pulls away from the side of the bowl. If mixing by hand, put the cream cheese, egg, and salt in a large bowl. Use a large whisk, first pressing down on the cream cheese to break it up and then whisking the mixture until it's smooth. Add the water and mix again until it's smooth. Add the flour and, using your dominant hand, mix until the dough comes together in a well-blended mass.

2 Transfer the dough to a lightly floured work surface and knead. Using the heel of your hand, push the ball of dough away from you in a downward motion. Turn the dough 45 degrees each time you repeat this motion, which will help to distribute the flour evenly through the dough. As you continue to knead, you'll notice the dough getting less and less floury. Eventually it will have a smooth, elastic texture. If it feels wet, tacky, or sticky, dust it with flour and continue kneading. If the dough feels too dry and is not completely sticking together, wet your hands with water and continue kneading. Wet your hands as many times as you need to get the proper texture. Total kneading time will be 8 to 10 minutes.

3 Wrap the dough tightly in plastic wrap and let rest for 1 hour at room temperature. (At this point, you can also refrigerate it up to 3 days. Be warned, however, that the dough may discolor; this won't affect the flavor in any way.)

4 Prepare the filling. Bring a large pot of water to a boil and add the unpeeled potatoes. Cook them until you can easily insert a knife through the thickest part, 30 to 40 minutes. Drain

INGREDIENTS:

DOUGH:

- 5 ounces cream cheese
- 1 large egg, at room temperature
- 1 teaspoon salt
- 2 tablespoons warm water
- 1 ¼ cups all-purpose flour, plus more if needed
- Semolina flour for dusting

FILLING:

- 3 Yukon Gold potatoes (about 1 ¼ pounds)
- 1 large egg, at room temperature, lightly beaten
- 4 tablespoons (½ stick) unsalted butter
- 3 medium yellow onions, diced
- Salt
- 4 ounces farmer's cheese or small-curd cottage cheese
- 1 ¼ teaspoons sweet paprika
- Freshly ground black pepper

TOPPING:

- 2 tablespoons unsalted butter
- 1 large onion, chopped
- Salt
- 3 slices bacon, chopped
- ½ cup sour cream

and, when cool enough to handle, remove their skins. While still very warm, pass the potatoes through a potato ricer into a large bowl. Alternatively, you can place them in a wide, shallow bowl and press them down with a potato masher until smooth. Add the egg and stir until well combined.

5 Heat a large skillet over medium-low heat for 2 to 3 minutes, then add the butter. When it melts and begins to foam, add the onions and a couple pinches of salt and cook, stirring occasionally, until completely softened, about 10 minutes. Turn the heat to medium and continue cooking until the onions have browned, stirring occasionally, about 12 minutes. Remove from the heat and let cool for 15 minutes.

6 Add the onions to the potatoes along with the farmer's cheese, paprika, and salt and pepper to taste, and mix well. Let cool to room temperature. The filling can be prepared a day ahead; cover and refrigerate, and bring back to room temperature before proceeding.

7 Make the pierogi. Cut the dough into four pieces. Set one on a lightly floured work surface and cover the others to prevent drying. Using a lightly floured rolling pin, flatten the dough to ½ inch. Continue rolling the dough, turning it 45 degrees every couple rolls, until it is ⅛ inch thick. (Alternatively, you can flatten the dough to ½-inch in thickness with a rolling pin, then run it through a pasta machine until the third to thinnest setting, typically notch 3) You don't want the dough too thin because it is quite delicate and can tear if too thin. Lightly dust each sheet of dough with flour and lay it on a surface lined with parchment paper or kitchen towels. Cover with a kitchen towel. Repeat until all the dough has been rolled out, stacking and separating the sheets with parchment or towels.

8 If you are using a metal pierogi form: Cut the pasta sheets so that they are approximately ½ inch wider—in all directions—than the pierogi form. Lightly flour the form and then center a sheet of pasta on top. Spoon a tablespoon of filling into the center of each semicircle, gently molding the filling to fit the shape. If you get filling on the pasta's border, carefully wipe it off with a finger. Should the dough have become a little dry during this process, lightly moisten the pasta border with a fingertip dipped in water.

Lay another sheet of dough, covering the filling, over the mold. As you do this, gently press down with the palm of your hand to push out any air within the pierogi. Run a rolling pin over the surface of the mold until the ridges of the pierogi beneath become visible. Remove excess dough from around the sides of the mold. Carefully flip the mold over to release the pierogi.

If you are making the pierogi by hand: Working with one sheet of dough at a time, lay it on a lightly floured work surface and, using a 3-inch biscuit or cookie cutter, cut out as many rounds as possible (you should end up with about 64 total).

Spoon 2 teaspoons of filling into the center of each round. Should the dough have become a little dry during this process, lightly moisten it with a fingertip dipped in water. Fold one edge of the pasta round over the filling, to create a half-moon, lining up the edges, and press down all along the edge to create a tight seal. As you do this, try to push out any air from inside. Press one more time to ensure the seal is tight.

9 Finally, regardless of the method used in making the pierogi, prick each pierogi once with a toothpick right in the center. This prevents the pierogi from exploding in the water due to vapor pressure. Repeat with the remaining dough. Gather any scraps together into a ball, roll it out to create additional pasta sheets, and use those as well.

10 Lightly dust the pierogis with flour, then arrange in a single layer on parchment paper-lined baking sheets heavily sprinkled with semolina flour. Let air-dry for 30

minutes on each side. At that point, cook or freeze on the baking sheets, transfer to freezer bags, and freeze up to 2 months. Do not thaw them prior to cooking (they will become mushy), and add an extra minute or two to their cooking time.

11 Prepare the topping. Heat a medium skillet over medium-low heat for 2 minutes, then add the butter. When it melts and begins to foam, add the onion and a couple pinches of salt and cook, stirring a few times, until completely softened, about 10 minutes. Turn the heat to medium and continue cooking until the onion has browned, about 12 minutes. Remove from the heat, cover, and keep warm.

12 Heat a separate medium skillet over medium-low heat for 2 minutes, then add the bacon. Cook for several minutes, stirring frequently, until all the bacon bits are crispy. Transfer the bacon to a paper towel to drain.

13 Cook the pierogis. Bring a large pot of water to a boil, add salt (1 tablespoon for every 4 cups water) and stir. Using a large slotted spoon, carefully lower the pierogi, a few at a time, into the boiling water. Stir for the first minute to prevent any sticking. Reduce the heat to medium (if the water is boiling furiously, it could cause the pierogi to burst). Cook until the pierogis float to the surface, 3 to 4 minutes. Take one of out of the water. If you don't see, upon slicing one in half, a starchy line in dough, it's done. Transfer the cooked pierogi to a colander to drain as they finish.

14 Arrange the pierogis on a warmed serving platter and top with the onions and bacon bits. Serve hot accompanied by the sour cream for diners to add themselves.

MUSHROOM *and* POTATO VARENYKY
with ZAZHARKA

YIELD: 6 TO 8 SERVINGS / ACTIVE TIME: 1 ½ HOURS / TOTAL TIME: 2 HOURS

Varenyky are Ukrainian dumplings shaped like half-moons that are similar to Polish pierogi. This savory version is accompanied by *zazharka,* a popular Ukrainian condiment consisting of savory browned onions and bacon.

1 Prepare the filling. Trim the stems of the mushrooms. Fill a large bowl with cold water and add the vinegar. Add the mushrooms and swirl them around in the water for 30 seconds or so. Transfer them to a colander and rinse under cold water. Drain well and transfer to a kitchen towel stem side down so they can drain. Let air-dry for 30 minutes, then mince.

2 Heat a large skillet over medium-low heat for 2 to 3 minutes. Add the butter and turn the heat up to medium. When it has melted and stopped foaming, add the onion, garlic, mushrooms, and a couple pinches of salt and stir. Cook, stirring occasionally, until they become very soft and brown, about 20 minutes. Remove from the heat.

3 While the onions cook, bring a large pot of water to a boil, then add the potatoes and cook until you can easily insert a knife through the potato, 30 to 45 minutes. Drain and, when cool enough to handle, remove the skins, cut into chunks, and run them through a potato ricer into a large bowl. Alternatively, you can place them in a wide, shallow bowl and press them with a potato masher until smooth. Add the onion mixture and salt and pepper to taste. Mix until well combined. Let cool to room temperature.

4 Prepare the dough. Place the flour and salt in a large bowl. Add the butter and sour cream and, using an electric mixer (with a paddle attachment if you have one), mix on medium speed until the dough has an even consistency, about 5 minutes (you can also mix it together by hand). Add the beaten egg to a measuring cup and add just enough water to measure ¾ cup. Beat the egg and water until well blended and pour into the bowl. Mix on medium speed until the dough holds together in a ball. If it's sticky, mix in more flour, a teaspoon at a time, until the dough is smooth and nonsticky.

INGREDIENTS:

FILLING:

½ pound cremini mushrooms

1 tablespoon distilled white vinegar

3 tablespoons unsalted butter

1 large yellow onion, minced

2 garlic cloves, minced

Salt

2 pounds (about 4) large russet potatoes

Freshly ground black pepper

DOUGH:

3 cups all-purpose flour, more as needed

4 tablespoons (½ stick) unsalted butter, at room temperature

⅔ cup sour cream, at room temperature

1 large egg, beaten

ZAZHARKA:

6 ounces bacon, minced

1 small yellow, minced

Salt

6 tablespoons (¾ stick) unsalted butter

TO COOK:

Salt

1 tablespoon vegetable oil

5 Transfer the dough to a lightly floured surface and, using a lightly floured rolling pin, roll out to ⅛ inch in thickness. Using a 3-inch stamp or biscuit or cookie cutter, cut it into as many rounds as possible. Place the rounds on a lightly floured parchment paper–lined baking sheet so they don't touch. When you have as many as you can fit in a single layer, cover them with another piece of parchment paper, sprinkle with flour, and keep arranging the rounds in the same way.

6 Make the *varenyky*. Place a round in the palm of your slightly cupped hand and hold it so that it takes the shape of a taco. Place 1 teaspoon of filling in the center. (Make sure to keep the filling in the middle. Once sealed, you will be able to evenly distribute the filling, but to facilitate making the *varenyky*, keep the filling away from the edges.) Using your thumb and index finger, firmly pinch the edges together, starting at one end of the "taco," to form a tight seal. You'll want this seal, or seam, to be between ¼ and ½ inch wide. Continue pinching and working your way to the other end until finished. Pat the sealed *varenyky* gently to evenly distribute the filling. Check for holes (patch them with a little bit of dough) and make sure the seal is tight. Cook or cover and refrigerate for up to 2 days. Or freeze on the baking sheets, transfer to freezer bags, and store in the freezer for 3 to 4 months. Do not thaw them prior to cooking (they will become mushy), and add an extra minute or two to their cooking time.

7 Prepare the *zazharka*. Heat a large skillet over medium-low heat for 2 to 3 minutes. Add the bacon and raise the heat to medium. Once the bacon renders its fat, add the onion and a pinch of salt, stir to combine, and cook until the onion is golden, about 20 minutes, stirring occasionally. Add the butter and stir until melted. Remove from the heat; keep warm.

8 To cook the *varenyky*, bring a large pot of water to a boil. Once it's boiling, add salt (1 tablespoon for every 4 cups water) and the oil (to prevent any sticking) and stir. Work in batches. Using a large slotted spoon, lower the *varenyky* into the boiling water. Alternatively, you can gently plop them in the water, though it increases the risk of tearing them. Once in the water, gently stir to keep them from sticking to the bottom. When the dumplings float to the surface, cook them for an additional 3 minutes.

9 Remove the *varenyky* from the water using a large slotted spoon and let them drain for a few seconds over the pot. Transfer to a warmed serving platter, drizzle with a teaspoon or two of *zazharka*, toss gently to combine, and tent with aluminum foil to keep warm as you cook the remainder.

10 Serve the *varenyky* piping hot topped with the remaining *zazharka*.

MANTI *with* BROWNED BUTTER, TOMATO "MARMALADE," *and* GARLIC YOGURT SAUCE

YIELD: 6 SERVINGS / ACTIVE TIME: 20 MINUTES / TOTAL TIME: 45 MINUTES

This very thick, caramelized sauce is typically paired with Turkish *manti* dumplings. What makes this tomato sauce particularly memorable is the use of *maraş* (or *marash*), a deep red chile pepper with medium but wonderfully lingering heat. In Turkey, you'll find it on every table, used as we do black pepper. Look for it in Middle Eastern food stores or online. You can use the somewhat more commonly available Aleppo pepper as a substitute. Sumac is slightly sour tasting and used in Turkish and many Middle Eastern cuisines as an ingredient, but also to be sprinkled over food at the table.

INGREDIENTS:

- 2 **garlic cloves, minced**
- ½ **teaspoon fresh lemon juice**
- 1 **cup whole-milk Greek yogurt**
- **Salt and freshly ground black pepper**
- 6 **tablespoons extra virgin olive oil, divided**
- 1 **14-ounce can diced tomatoes, drained**
- 2 ½ **tablespoons maraş pepper flakes**
- 1 **recipe Manti (page 312)**
- 4 **tablespoons (½ stick) unsalted butter**
- **Ground sumac for serving**

1 Put the garlic and lemon juice in a small bowl and let stand for 10 minutes. Add the yogurt and salt and pepper to taste and mix well. Set aside.

2 Heat a large skillet over medium-low heat for 2 to 3 minutes. Add 4 tablespoons of the olive oil, raise the heat to medium-high, and add the drained tomatoes, *maraş,* and a couple pinches of salt and stir. When the mixture begins to gently sizzle, turn the heat to low and cook, stirring frequently, until the mixture begins to resemble a soft marmalade, 12 to 15 minutes. Taste for seasoning and add salt if needed.

3 While the sauce cooks, bring a large pot of water to a boil. Once it's boiling, add salt (1 tablespoon for every 4 cups water) and stir. Add the *manti* and cook at a gentle boil until tender, 10 to 12 minutes.

4 While the *manti* cook, heat a small saucepan over medium-low heat for 2 to 3 minutes. Add the butter and turn the heat to medium. Cook the butter until the milk solids in the butter turn light brown, 8 to 9 minutes, stirring every few minutes. Remove from the heat, add the remaining 2 tablespoons oil and a couple pinches of salt, and whisk well. Cover to keep warm.

5 Drain the *manti* and return the pot to the stove. Immediately turn the heat to medium, add the manti and butter sauce, and gently toss to coat; continue to cook and toss until hot.

6 Divide the *manti* among six warmed bowls and dollop the tomato sauce and yogurt sauce on top. Serve piping hot with a sprinkling of sumac.

MANTI *with* SPICED MEAT FILLING
with GARLIC YOGURT SAUCE

YIELD: 6 SERVINGS ACTIVE TIME: 45 MINUTES TOTAL TIME: 1 ½ HOURS

These delicious Turkish dumplings are traditionally stuffed with a highly seasoned filling of beef or lamb. While there are many variations of the dumpling, this recipe pays homage to one of the most popular versions. Named *kayseri mantisi*, they are traditionally tiny (40 of them are supposed to fit on a spoon!) and are served with garlic-flavored yogurt and spiced tomato condiment, topped with a sprinkling of dried mint, *maraş* pepper flakes (a medium-hot chile from Turkey), and ground sumac, a Middle Eastern spice with a tangy, citrusy flavor.

1 Prepare the garlic yogurt sauce. Stir the yogurt, garlic, and salt to taste together in a small bowl. (This can be made a day ahead; cover and refrigerate.)

2 Prepare the spiced tomato condiment. Heat the oil in a small saucepan over low heat for a minute, then add the tomato paste, paprika, and salt and whisk well to incorporate. Cook, stirring a few times, for 5 minutes to heat through. Remove from the heat.

3 Prepare the manti filling. Heat a large skillet over medium heat for 2 to 3 minutes, then add the butter. When it has melted and stopped foaming, add the onion, a couple pinches of salt, and the spices, and stir. When the mixture starts to gently sizzle, reduce the heat to low, cover, and cook, until it becomes very soft and brown, about 20 minutes. Remove from the heat.

4 Once cool, transfer the onion mixture to a medium bowl, add the meat, parsley, and salt and pepper to taste, and mix until well combined. The filling can be prepared a day ahead; cover, refrigerate, and bring back to room temperature before proceeding.

5 Prepare the dough as directed on pages 131–133, rolling the dough to the thinnest setting (generally notch 5) for sheets that are about ¹⁄₁₆ inch thick. The sheets of dough will be so long that you will need to cut them in order to handle them more easily. Lay the cut sheets on lightly floured parchment paper-lined baking sheets. Should you run out of room,

INGREDIENTS:

GARLIC YOGURT SAUCE:

- 1 cup Greek whole milk yogurt
- 1 garlic clove, grated or minced
- Salt

SPICED TOMATO CONDIMENT

- 3 tablespoons extra virgin olive oil
- 3 tablespoons tomato paste
- 1 teaspoon sweet paprika
- ⅛ teaspoon salt

MANTI FILLING:

- 2 ½ tablespoons unsalted butter
- ½ large yellow onion, diced
- Salt
- ¾ teaspoon ground coriander
- ⅛ teaspoon ground cloves
- ½ pound ground lamb or beef
- 2 handfuls fresh parsley leaves, minced
- Freshly ground black pepper

MANTI DOUGH:

- ¾ cup plus 3 tablespoons all-purpose flour
- 1 teaspoon salt, plus more for the cooking water
- 2 large eggs, at room temperature
- 3 tablespoons warm water, more if needed

FOR SERVING:

- Dried mint
- Maraş or Aleppo pepper flakes
- Ground sumac

dust the pasta sheets lightly with flour, cover with parchment also lightly floured, and begin stacking vertically. Using a pastry wheel, cut each sheet of pasta into as many 1 ¼-inch squares as possible. Repeat with all the pasta sheets. Gather the scraps together into a ball, put it through the pasta machine to create additional pasta sheets, and cut those as well.

6 Make the *manti*. Form a small ball from 1 teaspoon of the meat mixture and place in the center of a square. Create a parcel by gently pulling two opposite corners away from one another and then over the filling to join them. Pinch firmly to create a tight seal. In a similar manner, gently pull the other two corners away from each other and then over the filling to join them, pinching firmly to create a tight seal (it's okay if some of the filling shows through along the edges of the pasta). Repeat with the remaining dough and filling. Set the *manti* on a well-floured parchment paper-covered baking sheet so they are not touching. Cook or cover and refrigerate the *manti* for up to 24 hours. Or freeze on the baking sheets, trans-

fer to freezer bags, and freeze up to 2 months. Do not thaw them prior to cooking (they will become mushy), and add an extra minute or two to their cooking time.

7 To cook the *manti,* bring a large pot of water to a boil. When it's boiling, add salt (1 tablespoon for every 4 cups water) and stir. Add the dumplings in batches of 15 or so and cook until tender, 7 to 8 minutes. Taste one to test it. Using a strainer, transfer them to a warmed serving bowl. Tent loosely with aluminum foil to keep warm. Repeat until all the *manti* are cooked. Reserve ¼ cup of the pasta water for the yogurt sauce.

8 When all the *manti* are cooked, whisk the reserved pasta water into the garlic yogurt sauce, which will warm it up a bit. Divvy the yogurt sauce among six warmed bowls, then arrange eight *manti* on top of the sauce. Serve piping hot, topped with a generous dollop of the tomato condiment and a light dusting of dried mint, *maraş* pepper flakes, and sumac.

SWEDISH STUFFED POTATO DUMPLINGS

YIELD: 8 SERVINGS / ACTIVE TIME: 1 HOUR / TOTAL TIME: 2 HOURS

These hefty, meat-filled potato dumplings known as *pitepalt* are part of the Swedish culinary tradition, possibly because their delicious heartiness can sustain the spirit during the coldest and grayest of winter months. Though they are made with different ingredients depending on geographic location, they typically are always filled with a salted pork product called *fläsk*. These hail from northern Sweden and are made from grated raw potatoes and wheat or barley flour. Its southern cousin, known as *kroppkakor*, is made from cooked potatoes and wheat flour. I've taken to replacing hard to find *fläsk* with pork belly or bacon and to adding minced rosemary to the filling, which makes its presence known the moment you bite into one. You can serve *pitepalt* with a range of accompaniments. The most common are melted butter, heavy cream, and lingonberry sauce, the last of which can be purchased at well-stocked international and gourmet food stores and, interestingly, at Ikea. One final note: Because *pitepalt* are made with raw potatoes, which quickly discolor, it is necessary to cook them as soon as possible after forming them. Once cooked, they can be refrigerated for a day before pan-frying.

1 Bring a small saucepan of water to a boil and add the pork belly dice. Once the water returns to a boil, cook for 5 minutes (doing this removes excess fat). Using a slotted spoon, transfer the pork belly to a paper towel-lined plate. Blot the top with paper towels to dry it as much as possible.

2 Heat a large skillet over low heat for a couple of minutes, add ½ tablespoon of the olive oil and half of the pork belly pieces and raise the heat to medium-low. Cook, stirring occasionally, until the pieces are nicely browned all over and have slightly shrunk, about 10 minutes (careful, the oil may spatter a bit). Using a slotted spoon, transfer the browned pieces to a bowl. Repeat with the remaining pork belly, adding the remaining ½ tablespoon oil if the pan looks too dry. Add the rosemary and mix well. Set aside.

3 Make the dumplings. Peel, wash, and, using the large holes of a grater, grate the potatoes directly into a large bowl of cold water. Soak for 5 minutes to remove excess starch, then drain the water from the bowl.

INGREDIENTS:

DUMPLINGS:

1	¾-pound slab pork belly, trimmed of skin if necessary and cut into ½-inch dice
½ to 1	tablespoon olive oil
	Leaves from 1 sprig fresh rosemary, minced
2	pounds (4 medium) Yukon Gold or russet potatoes
2	cups all-purpose flour, plus more for as needed
1 ½	tablespoons salt, plus more for the cooking water

TOPPING:

6	tablespoons (¾ stick) unsalted butter, warm and melted
	Lingonberry sauce

4 Add the flour and salt to the potatoes and mix well to form a thick dough. Using floured hands, shape the dough into golf ball-sized balls. Using your index finger, make a deep indentation in each ball and fill it with a tablespoon of pork belly dice. Smooth the dough over the hole to close it securely. Repeat with the remaining potatoes and pork belly; you'll end up having more pork belly than you need for the fillings.

5 Bring a large pot of water to a boil. Once it's boiling, add salt (1 tablespoon salt for every 4 cups water) and stir. Using a slotted spoon, gently lower the dumplings, one at a time, into the boiling water. Carefully stir for the first minute to prevent any sticking. Boil gently, making sure the water never reaches a furious and full-out boil, for 45 minutes.

6 Using a large slotted spoon, transfer the *pitepalt* to a warmed serving dish. Drizzle with the melted butter, sprinkle with the remaining pork belly dice, and serve with lingonberry sauce on the side.

BASIC DUMPLING WRAPPERS

YIELD: 32 3-INCH (MEDIUM) OR 24 4 ½-INCH (LARGE) DUMPLINGS OR 16 5 ½- TO 6-INCH (EXTRA LARGE) WRAPPERS (FOR *MANDU*) / ACTIVE TIME: 1 ½ HOURS / TOTAL TIME: 2 TO 3 ½ HOURS

This dough is suitable for potstickers, Korean *mandu,* Chinese *jiǎozi,* and Nepali *momo,* and the filled dumplings can be steamed, boiled, deep-fried, or pan-fried.

Important note: Have the dumpling filling ready before rolling out the dough in Step 6, as the dough sticks together best when it has not been exposed to air for too long.

INGREDIENTS:

- **2** cups all-purpose flour, plus more for dusting

- **⅔** cup + 1 tablespoon just-boiled water, more if needed

1 Mixing the dough by hand: Put the flour in a large bowl and make a well in the center. Add the water while stirring the flour with a spoon. Once all the water has been added, begin working the dough with your hands (the mixture will have cooled enough in the mixing process to be able to do so, but by all means do be careful by lightly touching it with one finger first to ensure that it has cooled enough that it won't burn you) to incorporate all the floury clumps into one mass. If the dough is too dry to come together, add additional hot water, 1 teaspoon at a time, until the dough sticks together in one firm mass (it is okay if it has some floury spots).

Mixing the dough in a stand mixer: Alternatively, use a stand mixer with the paddle attachment. Put the flour in the bowl and run the mixer on low speed while you add the water in a steady stream. Once the water has been added, stop the mixer and check the dough. If it is still too floury and clumpy, turn the mixer on medium speed and add more hot water, 1 teaspoon at a time, until the dough sticks together in one firm mass (it is okay if it has some floury spots).

2 Transfer the dough to a very lightly floured work surface. Knead it with the palm of your dominant hand, turning it 45 degrees with each pressing until the dough becomes uniformly smooth and it slowly bounces back when pressed with a finger, about 5 minutes. Wrap the dough tightly with clear food wrap and let rest at room temperature for anywhere between 30 minutes and 2 hours (the longer the better because time allows the gluten in the dough to relax so that it won't spring back when you try to roll it). Once rested, you can use the dough right away or refrigerate for 24 hours (bring it back to room temperature before using).

3 Cut two 5-inch squares of durable plastic (like the kind used in freezer bags) for the medium dumplings, 6-inch squares

for the large dumplings, and 8-inch squares for the extra large dumplings; you will need these to press the dough.

4 Transfer the dough to a lightly floured work surface. Cut in half and cover one half with clear food wrap.

5 With the palms of your hands, roll the other half of the dough into a 1-inch-thick log with flattened ends (no tapering). Cut it into 16 pieces (for medium dumplings) or 12 pieces (for large dumplings) or 8 pieces (for extra large dumplings). To ensure the pieces are the same size, start by cutting the log in half. Then cut both halves in half. Continue doing this until you've reached the number of pieces required. You want each piece to resemble a scallop, as it will make it easier to create a circle in the next step. Lightly flour each piece and cover with clear food wrap. Press down lightly on the dough to create a disk that is roughly ¼ inch thick. Repeat until all the pieces have been turned into disks. Repeat with the remaining dough.

6 Flattening the disks with a tortilla press: Place one of the two plastic squares on the bottom of the tortilla press plate. Place a dough disk, centered, on top and cover with the other plastic square. Close the press and turn the pressure handle to press down to create a disk that is roughly ⅛ inch thick. You may need to experiment a bit to see much pressure to use. Ultimately, you want to flatten the disks enough but still make it easy to peel the disks from the plastic squares.

Flattening the disks without a press: Place the disk between the two plastic squares and press down on it using a flat meat tenderizer or rolling pin until it is roughly ⅛ inch thick.

7 Transfer the flattened disk to a lightly floured work surface. Using a lightly floured rolling pin, gently apply pressure on the outer ½- to ¾-inch border of the disk, rotating it 45 degrees after each roll to ensure that the disk remains roughly round. (Leave the center of the disc, about 1 inch or the size of a quarter for medium wrappers, 1 ½ inches for large wrappers, and 2 inches for extra large wrappers, untouched. Doing this creates a more even distribution of dough once the wrapper has been bunched up around the filling.) Should any disks tear, roll them up in a ball and let them rest for a few minutes before pressing and rolling again. As you continue, you may need to reapply flour to the surface to prevent any sticking.

8 If any of the finished discs feels a little sticky, lightly dredge in flour. Place them in a single layer so they are not touching on a parchment paper-lined baking sheet, separating the layers with more parchment. Repeat with the remaining disks and dough. Fill the wrappers as directed in the particular dumpling recipe or freeze. If you are going to freeze them, separate the layers of wrappers with clear food wrap instead of parchment and freeze them on the baking sheets. You can then stack the frozen wrappers on top of each other, separated by plastic wrap, and store in a freezer bag for up to a month. To defrost, remove from the freezer and let defrost for 15 to 20 minutes, until they begin to bend.

EGG DOUGH WRAPPERS

Use this dough for making wontons or *siu mai,* which require a thin, delicate wrapper. The extra protein the egg provides gives the dough a bit more durability, which results in less tearing.

INGREDIENTS:

¼ cup water

1 large egg

1 ½ cups + 1 ¼ tablespoons unbleached all-purpose flour

¾ teaspoon salt

Potato starch or cornstarch for dusting

1 Whisk the water, salt, and egg together in a measuring cup.

2 Making and kneading the dough by hand: Put the flour and salt in a large bowl and make a well in the center. Add the egg mixture. Using a spoon, gradually bring the flour from the outer edges slowly toward the center, where the liquid is. Continue doing this until all the flour is mixed in with the liquid. A raggedy, sticky flour mass will soon form. Pick it up and start working it into a ball. If it's too sticky and wet, add ½ teaspoon flour at a time. Similarly, if it feels too dry and tough, add water, ½ teaspoon at a time, until it becomes more workable. Transfer the dough to a lightly floured work surface (with potato starch) and, using both hands, knead the dough until it is soft and smooth and, when pressed with a finger, springs back quickly, leaving no indentation, about 10 minutes.

Making and kneading the dough in a stand mixer: Put the flour and salt in the bowl of a stand mixer fitted with the paddle attachment. Turn the mixer on low speed and add the egg mixture in a steady stream. Once it has been added, stop the mixer and check the dough. If it is too crumbly, add water, 1 teaspoon at a time, until the dough sticks together in a firm mass. If too sticky (it won't leave the side the bowl), add more flour 1 tablespoon at a time, until it comes together. Swap the paddle attachment for the dough hook and knead on medium speed until the dough is soft and smooth and, when pressed with a finger, springs back quickly, leaving no indentation, about 10 minutes.

3 Cover the dough tightly with clear food wrap and let rest for 1 to 2 hours to relax the gluten.

4 Cut the dough into three even pieces. Set one piece on a lightly floured work surface and wrap up the rest in clear food wrap to prevent drying. Shape the dough into a ball, place it on the surface, and, with the palm of your hand, push down on it so that it looks like a thick pita. Using a rolling pin, roll the dough to ½ inch thickness. Try as much as possible to keep the thickness and width of the dough "patty" even, as it will help the dough fit through the pasta machine more easily.

5 Set the pasta machine for the flat roller (no teeth) on the widest setting (typically notch 1). (If using a stand mixer attachment, turn speed to medium-low.) Now feed the dough into the rollers. As a rather rough, thick sheet of pasta comes out the other end, make sure to support it with your hand or fingers. Fold it over itself twice, as you would a letter, and then turn it on its side (where you can see the layering of the folded dough) and feed it into the machine again. Repeat this folding and feeding it back into the machine three more times. This process is called "laminating" and it makes the dough more sturdy and manageable to handle.

6 Repeat Step 5 for the next two thinner notches (typically notch 2 and notch 3).

7 Set the machine to the second-thinnest setting (typically notch 4). Feed the pasta into the rollers. Again, support the pasta as it comes out the other side. At this point, there is no need to laminate the pasta.

8 Set the machine to the thinnest setting (typically notch 5). Again, support the pasta as it comes out the other side. This last setting makes the sheets so thin (about ¹⁄₁₆ inch/15 mm thick) that you can see light through them.

9 The just rolled pasta will be very delicate, so be gentle handling it. Lay each sheet of dough, which will roughly measure about 4 to 4 ½ inches in width, on a lightly floured flat work surface and, using a rolling pin, roll it out to increase its width to 6 inches, or as close to that as possible. Carefully transfer the sheet to a parchment paper-lined baking sheet. Repeat this process with the remaining dough.

10 To make the wrappers, lightly dust the work surface with potato starch or cornstarch. Lay a sheet of dough on top of it and dust it lightly as well.

Wontons: Cut the sheet into as many 4-inch squares as possible.

Siu mai: Using a 3-inch round stamp or biscuit or cookie, cut out as many rounds as possible. Dip the stamp in potato starch or cornstarch from time to time to prevent sticking.

11 After cutting out the wrappers, gather any scraps together into a ball, put it through the pasta machine to create additional sheets, and cut those as well.

12 As you cut the wrappers, you can pile them on top of each other, making sure they are well floured so they won't stick to one another. When you're done, wrap the pile in clear food wrap. Refrigerate, making sure wrappers are laying flat, for up to 3 days. Once refrigerated, wrappers may discolor a little but are otherwise still just as tasty.

CRYSTAL SKIN WRAPPERS

YIELD: 18 3-INCH WRAPPERS / ACTIVE TIME: 45 MINUTES / TOTAL TIME: 45 MINUTES

Perhaps nothing is more impressive than a steamed dumpling made from delicately transparent crystal skin wrappers. Made from two different types of starches, they are mixed with boiling water to prevent the dough from getting too elastic, creating, instead a smooth, malleable, and easy to roll dough. For all of their deliciousness and beauty, you unfortunately cannot buy these wrappers in a supermarket because they simply do not keep for long once made. Also for that reason, be sure to have your filling ready to go before making these. And if you're using a tortilla press to flatten them, cut two 5-inch squares of durable plastic (like the kind used in freezer bags) and have them ready. Wheat starch can be found in the baking and flour section of most well-stocked natural food stores or can be ordered online.

INGREDIENTS:

- 1 **cup wheat starch, plus more for dusting**
- ½ **cup cornstarch or tapioca starch**
- 1¼ **cups boiling water (add an additional 1 to 2 teaspoons in dryer climates)**
- 1 **tablespoon grapeseed or safflower oil**

1 Mix the wheat starch and cornstarch in a heatproof medium bowl. Add the boiling water and oil. Using a rubber spatula, mix the ingredients together until a loose dough forms. Turn the dough out onto a lightly floured (with wheat starch) work surface and knead the dough with the palm of your hand, turning it 45 degrees with each pressing, until the dough is smooth and it slowly bounces back when pressed with a finger; this will take about 10 minutes.

2 Transfer the dough to a work surface lightly dusted with wheat starch. With the palms of your hands, roll the dough into a 1 ½-inch-thick log. Cut it into 18 pieces To ensure the pieces are the same size, start by cutting the log in half. Then cut both halves in half. Continue doing this until you've got 18 pieces. You want each piece to resemble a scallop, as it will make it easier to create a circle in the next step. Lightly dust each piece with wheat starch and cover with clear food wrap. Press down lightly on the dough round to create a disk that is roughly ¼ inch thick. Repeat until all the pieces have been turned to disks.

3 Flattening the disks with a tortilla press: Place one of the two plastic squares on the bottom of the tortilla press plate. Place a dough disk, centered, on top and cover with the other plastic square. Close the press and turn the pressure handle to press down to create a disk that is roughly ⅛ inch thick. You may need to experiment a bit to see much pressure to use. Ultimately, you want to flatten the disks enough but still make

it easy to peel the disks from the plastic squares.

Flattening the disks without a press: Place the disk between the two plastic squares and press down on it using a flat meat tenderizer or rolling pin until it is roughly ⅛ inch thick.

4 Transfer the flattened disk to a work surface lightly dusted with wheat starch. Using a lightly floured rolling pin, gently apply pressure on the outer ½- to ¾-inch border of the disk, rotating it 45 degrees after each roll to ensure that the disk remains roughly round. (Leave the center of the disc untouched. Doing this creates a more even distribution of dough once the wrapper has been bunched up around the filling.) Should any disks tear, roll them up in a ball and let them rest for a few minutes before pressing and rolling again. As you continue, you may need to reapply wheat starch to the surface to prevent any sticking.

5 If any of the finished discs feels a little sticky, lightly dredge in wheat starch. Place them in a single layer so they are not touching on a parchment paper-lined baking sheet, separating the layers with more parchment. Repeat with the remaining discs. Fill the wrappers and cook them as directed in the particular dumpling recipe.

CHAI KUIH VEGETABLE DUMPLINGS

YIELD: 4 SERVINGS / ACTIVE TIME: 1 HOUR / TOTAL TIME: 2 HOURS

Almost transparent *chai kuih,* also known as "vegetable cakes," are sold by food vendors on the streets of many Chinese cities. Chewy and juicy, they feature jicama and dried shrimp. Look for dried shrimp in Asian markets or online; they are available in a variety of sizes and grades. Since this recipe requires the shrimp to be chopped, I recommend using the smaller and less expensive variety (as a bonus, they will require less time to soak in water to reconstitute). Not all jicamas are alike; I've noticed that some are juicy and release liquid when cooked, while others are dry and don't. If your jicama is too dry, add some water (up to ¼ cup) to moisten it. You want the jicama to be moist but not soaking in liquid; turn up the heat at the end to evaporate any excess liquid. Once assembled, these scrumptious dumplings can be consumed immediately or frozen for another day. Unfortunately, because their starchy wrappers begin to deteriorate quickly, it is not advisable to refrigerate them for any length of time.

INGREDIENTS:

- **10** dried shiitake mushrooms
- **½** of a 2-pound jicama
- **2** tablespoons peanut or grapeseed oil
- **⅓** cup dried shrimp
- **1** medium carrot, finely grated
- **2** tablespoons soy sauce
- **1** teaspoon sugar
- Salt and freshly ground black pepper
- **1** recipe Crystal Skin Wrappers (page 320)
- Cabbage leaves for steaming (optional)
- Thai Pepper Hot Sauce (page 743) or kecap manis (sweet soy sauce)

1 Put the dried shiitake mushrooms in a heatproof bowl and add just enough hot water to cover them by a few inches. Soak until the caps are soft, about 30 minutes. Drain and squeeze each mushroom tightly with your hand to remove excess water. (Reserve the mushroom water and add it to the filling for extra depth of flavor.) Discard the tough stems and thinly slice the caps.

2 Peel the jicama. Slice off the top and bottom of the vegetable with a sharp knife, then rest it on its widest cut end on a cutting board. Using the same knife (vegetable peelers are not strong enough for the job), rest the knife between the skin and the outermost part of the jicama and begin slicing it downward to remove pieces of skin. It is best to start at the top of the jicama and work your way down. Remove all the peel. Use a vegetable peeler to remove any remaining tough, fibrous sections on the surface of the jicama flesh. Keeping the jicama on its widest cut end, cut it from the top down into thick slabs. Grate the slabs using the largest holes of a box grater.

3 Heat a wok or large skillet over low heat for 2 to 3 minutes. Add the oil and turn the heat to medium. When it begins to swirl on the surface, add the shrimp and stir-fry until aromatic, 1 to 2 minutes. Add the jicama, mushrooms, and carrot and cook, stirring frequently, until the jicama is tender but still crunchy,

about 15 minutes. Add the soy sauce, sugar, and salt and pepper to taste and stir. Taste for seasoning and adjust if necessary.

4 Place a damp paper towel over the stack of wrappers (to keep them from drying out). Line a baking sheet with parchment paper. Also prepare a small fingerbowl of water for sealing.

5 Place a wrapper on your work surface and place 1 tablespoon of the filling in the center. Using your fingers, moisten the edge of the wrapper with water and fold the wrapper over to create a triangle. Take the edge of the wrapper that's furthest from you and gently fold it over the filling to meet the other edge. Using your thumb and index finger, pinch both edges together to create a tight seal, trying to push out as much air as you can as you do it. If you desire, crimp the folded edges with the tines of a small fork to create a pattern. Repeat with the remaining wrappers and filling. Place the finished dumplings on the prepared baking sheet so they aren't touching. Cook immediately or freeze on the baking sheet, transfer to a freezer bag, and freeze for up to a month. Do not thaw them prior to cooking (they will become mushy), and add an extra minute or two to their cooking time.

6 Bring 3 cups water to a boil in a large pot. Line a steamer with cabbage leaves or parchment paper cut to the size and shape of your steamer with lots of small incisions made in it to allow steam to circulate. Set the dumplings in the steamer spacing them ½ inch away from each other and the sides of the steamer. Place the steamer in the pot over the boiling water (it should not touch it), cover, and steam until the dumplings are tender but still chewy, about 10 minutes. Transfer to a warmed serving platter.

7 Serve the dumplings piping hot, accompanied by a small bowl of hot sauce or kecap manis.

HAR GOW SHRIMP DUMPLINGS

YIELD: 18 DUMPLINGS / ACTIVE TIME: 1 HOUR / TOTAL TIME: 1½ HOURS

A traditional dim sum offering, *har gow* are plump, juicy steamed dumplings whose savory shrimp and pork filling is visible through its almost transparent wrapper. Believed to have first originated in the sprawling Chinese port city of Guangzhou on the Pearl River, these delicate dumplings are often considered a confection on which the skill of dim sum chefs are assessed.

Traditionally, *har gow* need to have at least seven, and preferably ten or more, pleats imprinted on their wrapper. Personally, while I love the look of pleated dumplings, if I'm in a rush I will often just shape them in simple half-moons and seal the edges by crimping them with a fork.

Finally, if you can find it at the same market, pick up a bottle of Chinese black vinegar. Tasty and inexpensive, it is an aged, darkly colored, and fruity tasting vinegar that adds a nice touch of umami to the dish. If you cannot find it, use balsamic vinegar to approximate its flavor. Once assembled, these scrumptious dumplings can be consumed immediately or frozen for another day. Unfortunately, because their starchy wrappers begin to deteriorate quickly, it is not advisable to refrigerate them for any length of time.

INGREDIENTS:

- ¾ pound medium shrimp, deveined
- 1½ teaspoons baking soda
- 2 garlic cloves, grated or minced
- 1 2-inch piece fresh ginger, peeled and grated or minced
- 1 teaspoon Shaoxing rice wine or dry sherry
- 1 teaspoon chile oil
- ¾ teaspoon salt
- ½ teaspoon sugar
- 1 teaspoon cornstarch
- 1 recipe Crystal Skin Wrappers (page 320)
- Cabbage leaves for steaming (optional)
- Chinese black vinegar or balsamic vinegar for serving

1 Put the shrimp in a medium bowl and cover with just enough cold water to completely cover. Stir in the baking soda and refrigerate for 30 to 40 minutes (doing this helps keep the shrimp plump as they steam).

2 Drain the shrimp (dry the bowl), rinse under cold water, and pat dry with paper towels. Slice each shrimp into 5 to 6 pieces. Return to the bowl and add the garlic, ginger, rice wine, chile oil, salt, sugar, and cornstarch. Mix until thoroughly combined. The filling can be prepared a day ahead; cover, refrigerate, and bring back to room temperature before proceeding.

3 Place a damp paper towel over the stack of wrappers (to keep them from drying out). Line a baking sheet with parchment paper.

4 Cup a wrapper in your hand and add about 2 teaspoons of filling. Then, working your way around the outside edge of the wrapper, create pleats by folding a small section (¼-inch) of the wrapper over onto itself and then pinching it together.

Continue until you've made your way around the entire circumference of the wrapper. Finish by pinching the top of the dumpling together with your fingertips, resulting in a crown-like shape. Repeat with the remaining wrappers and filling. Place the finished dumplings on the prepared baking sheet so they aren't touching. Cook immediately or freeze on the baking sheet, transfer to a freezer bag, and freeze for up to a month. Do not thaw them prior to cooking (they will become mushy), and add an extra minute or two to their cooking time.

5   Bring 3 cups water to a boil in a large pot. Line a steamer with cabbage leaves

or parchment paper cut to the size and shape of your steamer with lots of small incisions made in it to allow steam to circulate. Set the *har gow* in the steamer spacing them ½ inch away from each other and the sides of the steamer. Place the steamer in the pot over the boiling water (it should not touch it), cover, and steam until the dumplings are tender but still chewy, about 7 minutes. Transfer to a warmed serving platter.

6   Serve the dumplings piping hot drizzled with the vinegar.

CHICKEN *and* KIMCHI POTSTICKERS

YIELD: 4 SERVINGS / ACTIVE TIME: 1 ½ HOURS / TOTAL TIME: 2 ¼ HOURS

Legend has it that these Chinese dumplings became potstickers, or *guōtiē*, when a chef forgot about them in the wok *(guō)* and discovered that they stuck *(tiē)* to the pan, forming a delightfully crusty and golden bottom. What a happy accident for us. Potstickers can sport a wide array of flavorful fillings; this particular one features kimchi and chicken.

1 Put the chicken, kimchi, soy sauce, ginger, sesame oil, rice wine, sugar, garlic, and scallion in a medium bowl and mix until thoroughly combined. Sprinkle the cornstarch over the top and mix again until well combined. Cover with plastic wrap and let sit at room temperature for 30 minutes or refrigerate overnight. Bring back to room temperature before proceeding.

2 Prepare the dumplings. Set up a small fingerbowl of water for sealing. Place a wrapper on your work surface and place a tablespoon of filling in the middle. Using your fingers, moisten the edge of the wrapper with water and fold the wrapper over to create a triangle. Press tightly to seal the edges, making sure to eliminate any air trapped inside. Transfer the dumpling to a parchment paper-lined baking sheet. Repeat with the remaining wrappers and filling. Place the finished dumplings on the prepared baking sheet so they aren't touching. Cook immediately or freeze on the baking sheet, transfer to a freezer bag, and freeze for up to 3 months. Do not thaw them prior to cooking (they will become mushy), and add an extra minute or two to their cooking time.

3 Whisk the dipping sauce ingredients together in a small bowl.

4 Heat a wok or large skillet over medium-high heat for a minute, then add 1 tablespoon of the peanut oil. When it begins to swirl on the surface, add the dumplings, leaving ample space between them. You will need to work in batches. Cook the dumplings until golden on the bottom, 2 to 3 minutes. Add 2 tablespoons water to the pan, cover, and steam until cooked through, about 4 minutes. Transfer to a warmed platter and tent loosely with aluminum foil to keep warm. Quickly dry the wok or skillet with a paper towel and repeat, adding more oil, until all the potstickers are cooked.

5 Serve warm with the dipping sauce.

INGREDIENTS:

DUMPLINGS:

- ½ pound ground chicken
- 1 cup kimchi, minced (store-bought is fine)
- 1 tablespoon soy sauce
- 1 3-inch piece fresh ginger, peeled and grated or minced
- 1 ½ teaspoons toasted sesame oil
- 1 ½ teaspoons Shaoxing rice wine or dry sherry
- 1 ½ teaspoons sugar
- 1 garlic clove, minced
- 1 scallion, trimmed and minced
- 1 tablespoon cornstarch
- 1 recipe Basic Dumpling Wrappers (page 316)
- 3 tablespoons peanut or grapeseed oil

DIPPING SAUCE:

- 3 tablespoons Chinese black vinegar or balsamic vinegar
- 2 teaspoons chile-garlic paste
- 1 teaspoon tamari or soy sauce
- ½ teaspoon toasted sesame oil
- ½ teaspoon sugar

PORK *and* ROASTED SQUASH POTSTICKERS

YIELDS: 6 SERVINGS / ACTIVE TIME: 1 ½ HOURS / TOTAL TIME: 1 ¾ HOURS

Once one gets the hang of making savory potstickers using easy peasy pre-made wrappers, the possibilities are almost limitless. Every day can bring a pleasantly crispy and chewy dumpling with an exciting and brand new filling to titillate the palate. This particular version marries aromatic spices and pork with butternut squash, though you can swap it out for kabocha with great results.

1 Put all the spices in a small skillet over medium heat and toast, stirring, until the spices are fragrant, 2 to 3 minutes. Transfer to a mini food processor or spice grinder and grind into a fine powder.

2 Preheat the oven to 350°F. On a baking sheet lined with parchment paper, toss the squash with the vegetable oil and 1 tablespoon of the spice mix until well coated with each. Place in the oven and bake, turning squash over after about 15 minutes, until lightly caramelized and soft, about 30 minutes. Transfer the squash to a large bowl and mash with a fork until smooth. Add the pork, ginger, rice wine, soy sauce, sesame oil, 3 of the scallions, the egg white, and 1 tablespoon of the spice mix and mix well until thoroughly combined.

3 Place a damp paper towel over the stack of wrappers (to keep them from drying out). Line a baking sheet with parchment paper. Also prepare a small fingerbowl of water for sealing.

4 Lay a wrapper in front of you and place a heaping teaspoon of filling in the middle of it. Dip your finger in the water and run it along the edges of the square. Fold one of the corners over the filling to create a triangle and tightly press the edges together to seal, trying to push out as much air as you can as you do it. Repeat with the remaining wrappers and filling. Place the finished dumplings on the prepared baking sheet so they aren't touching. Cook immediately or freeze on the baking sheet, transfer to a freezer bag, and freeze for up to a month. Do not thaw them prior to cooking (they will become mushy), and add an extra minute or two to their cooking time.

5 Bring a large pot of water to a boil. When it's boiling, add salt (1 tablespoon for every 4 cups water) and stir.

INGREDIENTS:

POTSTICKERS:

- 1 teaspoon coriander seeds
- 8 cloves
- ½ teaspoon Sichuan peppercorns
- ½ teaspoon black peppercorns
- 1 star anise
- 2 cardamom pods, crushed
- 2 bay leaves
- 2 cinnamon sticks, broke into bits
- 2 ½ pounds butternut squash, peeled, seeded, and cut into ½-inch cubes
- 2 tablespoons vegetable oil
- ½ pound ground pork
- 3 tablespoons minced fresh ginger
- 3 tablespoons Shaoxing rice wine or dry sherry
- 5 tablespoons soy sauce
- 1 tablespoon toasted sesame oil, plus more for drizzling
- 5 scallions, minced, divided
- 1 egg white, lightly beaten
- 1 recipe Basic Dumpling Wrappers (page 316) or 40 3-inch round wrappers

  Salt

DIPPING SAUCE:

- 2 tablespoons Chinese black vinegar or balsamic vinegar
- 2 tablespoons light soy sauce
- 2 teaspoons sugar
- 2 teaspoons hot chile oil

Carefully add the dumplings in batches and cook until they float to the surface and are cooked through, about 3 minutes. Remove carefully with a strainer and transfer to a warmed serving platter.

6 While the dumplings are cooking, whisk the vinegar, soy sauce, sugar, and chile oil together in a small bowl.

7 Drizzle the dumplings with a bit of sesame oil, sprinkle with the remaining scallions, and serve piping hot with the dipping sauce.

BEEF *and* CABBAGE JIAOZI

YIELD: 8 SERVINGS / ACTIVE TIME: 1½ HOURS / TOTAL TIME: 2 HOURS

Jiaozi dumplings, along with rice and noodles, are at the heart and soul of Chinese cooking. Filled with a variety of savory meat and vegetable fillings, they can be served as a meal or snack. They are also traditionally prepared to celebrate the New Year, becoming a social ritual as well, with family and friends gathering around the bowls of fillings and dough, rolling out the wrappers and stuffing them while visiting, until literally hundreds of the little morsels are ready to be cooked. They can be either steamed or boiled and this recipe covers both techniques. If making your own wrappers, prepare them first and then wrap them tightly with clear food wrap and refrigerate while you are preparing the filling and dipping sauce.

1 The day before making the *jiaozi,* put the meat, ginger, 2 tablespoons of the soy sauce, the cinnamon, sugar, 2 teaspoons salt, and pepper to taste in a medium bowl and mix until all the ingredients are thoroughly combined. Cover with clear food wrap and let sit at room temperature for 30 minutes before using or refrigerate overnight. Bring back to room temperature before using.

2 Bring a large pot of water to a boil. Separate the cabbage into leaves, trimming away the heavy stems. When the water is boiling, add salt (1 tablespoon for every 4 cups water) and stir. Add the cabbage leaves and cook until wilted, 2 ½ to 3 minutes. Using a strainer, remove them from the water, quickly run under cold water to stop the cooking process, drain well again, and, using your hands, squeeze to remove as much of their liquid as possible. Mince, then add to the filling mixture, along with the scallions, working them in thoroughly. To taste for seasoning, create a small little patty and fry it in a small skillet. Taste and add more salt, soy sauce, ginger, black pepper, and/or scallions, if needed.

3 Place a damp paper towel over the stack of wrappers (to keep them from drying out). Line a baking sheet with parchment paper. Also prepare a small fingerbowl of water for sealing.

4 Cup a wrapper in your hand and add about a heaping teaspoon of filling. Close your hand to close the dough around the filling. Using your thumb and index finger, pinch one fourth of the circumference of the wrapper, fold half of that circumference over itself in fan-like fashion to create a pleat, and then pinch that pleated edge together to form a tight seal. Repeat three more

INGREDIENTS:

DUMPLINGS:

2 **pounds ground beef chuck, not too lean**

2 **tablespoons soy sauce**

1 **2-inch piece fresh ginger, peeled and grated or minced**

2 **tablespoons ground cinnamon**

2 **teaspoons sugar**

Salt

Freshly ground black pepper

1 **pound cabbage**

6 **scallions, white and light green parts only, minced**

1 **recipe Basic Dumpling Wrappers (page 316) or 36 3-inch round wrappers**

DIPPING SAUCE:

2 **garlic cloves, minced**

⅓ **cup soy sauce**

2 ½ **tablespoons Shaoxing rice wine or dry sherry**

1 **teaspoon hot chile oil (optional)**

Minced fresh cilantro for garnish

times with the rest of the wrapper border until the dumpling resembles a rose about to bloom. Repeat with the remaining wrappers and filling. Place the finished dumplings on the prepared baking sheet so they aren't touching. Cook immediately or freeze on the baking sheet, transfer to a freezer bag, and freeze for up to a month. Do not thaw them prior to cooking (they will become mushy), and add an extra minute or two to their cooking time.

5 To steam the *jiaozi:* Bring 3 cups water to a boil in a large pot. Line a steamer with parchment paper cut to the size and shape of your steamer with lots of small incisions made in it to allow steam to circulate. Set the *jiaozi* in the steamer spacing them ½ inch away from each other and the sides of the steamer. Place the steamer in the pot over the boiling water (it should not touch it), cover, and steam until the dumplings are tender but still chewy, about 8 minutes.

To boil the *jiaozi:* Bring a large pot of water to a boil and carefully add the dumplings. Once the water starts boiling again, adding a cup of cold water to tame the boiling (this keeps the dumplings from breaking). Continue adding cold water in this way to prevent furious boiling. When the dumplings begin to float to the surface, cook for another 5 to 6 minutes. Remove carefully with a strainer.

6 While the *jiaozi* are cooking, make the dipping sauce. Put the garlic, soy sauce, the rice wine, and chile oil if using in a small bowl and whisk to combine.

7 Serve the *jiaozi* steaming hot on warmed small plates, garnished with cilantro and accompanied by the dipping sauce.

ZUCCHINI, SHIITAKE, *and* EGG JIAOZI

YIELD: 4 TO 5 SERVINGS / ACTIVE TIME: 1½ HOURS / TOTAL TIME: 2½ HOURS

In Chinese homes, *jiaozi* are a traditional offering on New Year's Eve menus because they symbolize longevity and wealth and serve as a savory omen of wonderful things to come. In fact, their half-moon shape resembles gold shoe-shaped ingots, an early form of Chinese currency. This vegetarian version features moist zucchini and earthy shiitake mushrooms. You can either steam or boil the dumplings; I've included the directions for both.

1 Coarsely grate the zucchini using the largest holes of a box grater. Toss the zucchini with 1½ teaspoons of the salt in a fine-meshed strainer set over a bowl and let stand for an hour. Transfer the zucchini to a kitchen towel (you'll have to do this in batches) and twist the towel, in tourniquet-like fashion, to squeeze out the excess moisture. Transfer to a large bowl.

2 Heat a large nonstick skillet over low heat for a minute. Add the peanut oil and turn the heat to medium-high. When the oil begins to swirl on the surface, add the eggs and cook, stirring continuously, until they just set (don't overcook the eggs so that they become dry). Transfer the eggs to a plate and cut into very small pieces. Transfer to the bowl with the zucchini and add the mushrooms, ginger, soy sauce, rice wine, sesame oil, pepper, sugar, and 1 teaspoon salt and mix well. Cover with clear food wrap and refrigerate for 2 to 3 hours. Right before making the *jiaozi,* stir in the scallions. To taste for seasoning, take a small amount of the mixture, flatten into a patty, and fry it in a small skillet. Taste and add more salt, soy sauce, ginger, or scallions to the mixture, if needed.

3 Place a damp paper towel over the stack of wrappers (to keep them from drying out). Line a baking sheet with parchment paper. Also prepare a small fingerbowl of water for sealing.

4 Place a wrapper in your cupped hand, mostly holding it on your fingers, and put about 1 tablespoon of filling in the center, leaving about ¾ inch of the wrapper clear all the way around it. Using the tip of the index finger of the other hand, lightly moisten that edge with water. Fold one edge of the wrapper over the filling into a half-moon and tightly press the edges together to seal, trying to push out as much air as you can as you do it. Repeat with the remaining wrappers and filling. Place the finished dumplings on the prepared baking sheet so they aren't

INGREDIENTS:

- 4 medium (about 1½ pounds) zucchini
- 1½ teaspoons salt, divided
- 2 tablespoons peanut oil
- 4 large eggs, lightly beaten
- 8 medium shiitake mushrooms, stems discarded and caps minced
- 1 2-inch piece fresh ginger, peeled and grated or minced
- 3 tablespoons soy sauce
- 3 tablespoons Shaoxing rice wine or dry sherry, divided
- 2 tablespoons toasted sesame oil
- 1 teaspoon freshly ground black pepper
- ½ tablespoon sugar
- 1 bunch (5 or 6) scallions, trimmed and thinly sliced
- 2 recipe Basic Dumpling Wrappers (page 316) or 40 3-inch round wrappers

  Cabbage leaves for steaming (optional)

DIPPING SAUCE:

- 2 garlic cloves, minced
- ⅓ cup soy sauce
- 2½ tablespoons Shaoxing rice wine or dry sherry
- 1 teaspoon chile oil (optional)

  Minced fresh cilantro for garnish

touching. Cook immediately, cover and refrigerate for up to 24 hours, or freeze on the baking sheet, transfer to a freezer bag, and freeze for up to a month. Do not thaw them prior to cooking (they will become mushy), and add an extra minute or two to their cooking time.

5 To steam the *jiaozi:* Bring 3 cups water to a boil in a large pot. Line a steamer with cabbage leaves or parchment paper cut to the size and shape of your steamer with lots of small incisions made in it to allow steam to circulate. Set the *jiaozi* in the steamer spacing them ½ inch away from each other and the sides of the steamer. Place the steamer in the pot over the boiling water (it should not touch it), cover, and steam until the dumplings are tender but still chewy, about 8 minutes.

To boil the *jiaozi:* Bring a large pot of water to a boil and carefully add the dumplings. Once the water starts boiling again, adding a cup of cold water to tame the boiling (this keeps the dumplings from breaking). Continue adding cold water in this way to prevent furious boiling. When the dumplings begin to float to the surface, cook for another 5 to 6 minutes. Remove carefully with a strainer.

6 While the *jiaozi* are cooking, make the dipping sauce. Put the garlic, soy sauce, rice wine, and chile oil if using in a small bowl and whisk to combine.

7 Serve the *jiaozi* steaming hot on warmed small plates, garnished with cilantro and accompanied by the dipping sauce.

PORK AND SHRIMP SIU MAI

YIELD: 28 TO 32 DUMPLINGS / ACTIVE TIME: 45 MINUTES / TOTAL TIME: 1½ HOURS

Dainty open-faced dumplings, *siu mai* are a requisite dim sum offering. But don't let their diminutive size fool you, as the filling peeking through its frilly wrappers is an unforgettably flavor-packed mixture of shiitakes, pork, shrimp, and scallions. Traditionally *siu mai* are served without a dipping sauce, though if you can't envision enjoying these moist morsels without one, mix together 2 tablespoons soy sauce, 1 teaspoon sesame oil, and 1 thinly sliced scallion in a small bowl and serve alongside.

You will need a bamboo steamer for this recipe.

1 Put the dried shiitake mushrooms in a heatproof bowl and add just enough hot water to cover them by a few inches. Soak until the caps soften, at least 30 minutes. Drain until they reconstitute and the caps become tender. Remove the water and gently squeeze each mushroom with your hands to remove excess water. Discard the stems and mince the caps. Transfer to a large bowl.

2 Put the bouillon cube in a snack-sized plastic bag and seal. Press down with a rolling pin to crush it into granules. Add to the bowl with the mushrooms along with the pork, shrimp, scallions, red pepper, egg whites, soy sauce, rice wine, fish sauce, sesame oil, cornstarch, sugar, and white pepper and mix until thoroughly combined. The filling can be prepared a day ahead; cover, refrigerate, and bring back to room temperature before proceeding.

3 Place a damp paper towel over the stack of wrappers (to keep them from drying out). Line a baking sheet with parchment paper.

4 Place a wrapper in your cupped hand and fill it with enough of the pork and shrimp mixture to fill the wrapper to the top, then flatten the filling with a butter knife. Gently tighten the wrapper around the filling with your closed hand, forming a rough cylinder-like shape with a flat bottom (the very top will show the filling). Repeat with the remaining wrappers and filling. Place the finished dumplings on the prepared baking sheet so they aren't touching. Cook immediately, cover and refrigerate for up to 24 hours, or freeze on the baking sheet, transfer to a freezer bag, and freeze for up to a month. Do not thaw them prior to cooking (they will become mushy), and add an extra minute or two to their cooking time.

INGREDIENTS:

- 8 dried shiitake mushrooms
- 1 cube chicken bouillon
- ¾ pound ground pork
- ½ pound shrimp, peeled and minced
- 4 scallions, white and light green parts, trimmed and thinly sliced, plus more for garnish
- ¼ red bell pepper, seeded and minced
- 2 egg whites
- 1 tablespoon soy sauce
- 1 tablespoon Shaoxing rice wine or dry sherry
- 1 teaspoon fish sauce
- 1 teaspoon toasted sesame oil
- 2 teaspoons cornstarch
- ½ teaspoon sugar
- ½ teaspoon freshly ground white pepper
- 1 recipe Basic Dumpling Wrappers (page 316) or 40 3-inch round wrappers

  Cabbage leaves for steaming (optional)

  Minced carrots for garnish

  Crab roe for garnish

5 Bring 3 cups water to a boil in a large pot. Line a steamer with cabbage leaves or parchment paper cut to the size and shape of your steamer with lots of small incisions made in it to allow steam to circulate. Set the *siu mai* in the steamer spacing them ½ inch away from each other and the sides of the steamer. Place the steamer in the pot over the boiling water (it should not touch it), cover, and steam until the dumplings are tender but still chewy, about 10 minutes.

6 Transfer the *siu mai* to a warmed platter and serve sprinkled with scallions and carrots, with each dumpling topped with a bit of crab roe.

TIBETAN BEEF *and* SICHUAN PEPPERCORN DUMPLINGS

YIELD: 4 SERVINGS / ACTIVE TIME: 45 MINUTES / TOTAL TIME: 1 ½ HOURS

One of the most beloved dishes of Tibet, *momos* are juicy, delicate filled dumplings shaped like half-moons or plump round purses. This recipe is a *sha momo*, which literally means "meat *momo*." The meat of choice in Tibet is yak, but I am substituting the much more procurable beef. If you are lucky enough to have any leftovers, they taste best when reheated in a frying pan with a little bit of oil.

1 Combine the beef, garlic, onion, scallions, ginger, and a couple pinches of salt in a medium bowl until thoroughly mixed together.

2 Toast the peppercorns in a small dry skillet over medium heat until fragrant, 2 to 3 minutes, then crush in a mortar or grind them into a powder in a spice grinder. Transfer to a small bowl, add the oil, water, and a couple pinches of salt and mix well. Pour over the meat mixture and mix thoroughly. The filling can be prepared a day ahead; cover, refrigerate, and bring back to room temperature before proceeding.

3 Place a damp paper towel over the stack of wrappers (to keep them from drying out). Line a baking sheet with parchment paper. Also prepare a small fingerbowl of water for sealing.

4 Place a wrapper in your cupped hand, mostly holding it on your fingers, and put about 1 tablespoon of filling in the center, leaving about ¾ inch of the wrapper clear all the way around it. Using the tip of the index finger of the other hand, lightly moisten that edge with water. Fold one edge of the wrapper over the filling into a half-moon and tightly press the edges together to seal, trying to push out as much air as you can as you do it. To pleat the sealed edges, start at one end of the half-moon and make small folds in the wrapper, pressing them flat as you work your way along the edge. In all, you'll be able to make 7 to 8 folds per dumpling. Repeat with the remaining wrappers and filling. Place the finished dumplings on the prepared baking sheet so they aren't touching. Cook or freeze on the baking sheet, transfer to a freezer bag, and freeze for up to a month. Do not thaw them prior to cooking (they will become mushy), and add an extra minute or two to their cooking time.

INGREDIENTS:

- ¾ pound ground beef
- 3 garlic cloves, minced
- ½ large yellow onion, finely diced
- 1 (5 or 6) bunch scallions, white and light green parts, trimmed and thinly sliced
- 1 2-inch piece fresh ginger, peeled and grated or minced
- Salt
- ½ heaping teaspoon Sichuan peppercorns
- 2 tablespoons safflower oil
- 5 tablespoons water
- 1 recipe Basic Dumpling Wrappers (page 316) or 36 3-inch round wrappers
- Cabbage leaves for steaming (optional)
- 1 cup Gingery Red Pepper Sauce (page 744)

5 Bring 3 cups water to a boil in a large pot. Line a steamer with cabbage leaves or parchment paper cut to the size and shape of your steamer with lots of small incisions made in it to allow steam to circulate. Set the *momos* in the steamer spacing them ½ inch away from each other and the sides of the steamer. Place the steamer in the pot over the boiling water (it should not touch it), cover, and steam until they have puffed out slightly and become slightly translucent, about 8 minutes. Transfer to a warmed plate and cover loosely with aluminum foil to keep warm. Repeat with the remaining dumplings.

6 Serve the dumplings piping hot, accompanied by the Gingery Red Pepper Sauce in a small bowl.

SICHUAN PEPPERCORNS

Toasting and crushing these peppercorns enhances their already unique and citrusy flavor, which pairs nicely with the ginger and garlic in this recipe. The fragrant Sichuan peppercorn is not spicy, and is entirely unrelated to the common black pepper we see often today. When eating this dish you may notice a slight tingling sensation in your mouth. Do not fret—the Sichuan peppercorn has a numbing property that is harmless. It is often favored in spicy dishes, because the numbness makes eating chile peppers less intense, and more enjoyable.

TOFU MOMO DUMPLINGS

YIELD: 5 TO 6 SERVINGS / ACTIVE TIME: ABOUT 1 HOUR / TOTAL TIME: ABOUT 1 ½ HOURS

Savory and brimming with aromatic vegetables, these steamed dumplings also contain pressed tofu. Known as *dòufu gān* or "dry bean curd" in Mandarin, pressed tofu has a dry, compact texture that lends itself wonderfully to dumpling fillings. You can even buy pre-seasoned varieties at most Asian markets for an extra wallop of flavor.

1 Put the dried shiitake mushrooms in a heatproof bowl and add just enough hot water to cover them by a few inches. Soak until the caps soften, at least 30 minutes. Drain until they reconstitute and the caps become tender. Remove the water and gently squeeze each mushroom with your hands to remove excess water. Discard the stems and mince the caps. Put the caps in a food processor, add a pinch of salt, then pulse 3 or 4 times to chop. Add the tofu, spinach, scallions, cilantro, and another pinch of salt and pulse until minced. Add the garlic and ginger and pulse a few times to mix in.

2 Transfer the mixture to a medium bowl. Add the carrots and soy sauce and, using your hands, mix until well combined. To taste for seasoning, take a small bit of the mixture, form into a patty, and fry in a small skillet. Taste and add more salt, soy sauce, ginger, cilantro, and/or scallions if needed. The filling can be prepared a day ahead; cover, refrigerate, and bring back to room temperature before proceeding.

3 Place a damp paper towel over the stack of wrappers (to keep them from drying out). Line a baking sheet with parchment paper. Also prepare a small fingerbowl of water for sealing.

4 Place a wrapper in your cupped hand, mostly holding it on your fingers, and put about 1 tablespoon of filling in the center, leaving about ¾ inch of the wrapper clear all the way around it. Using the tip of the index finger of the other hand, lightly moisten that edge with water. Fold one edge of the wrapper over the filling into a half-moon and tightly press the edges together to seal, trying to push out as much air as you can as you do it. To pleat the sealed edges, start at one end of the half-moon and make small folds in the wrapper, pressing them flat as you work your way along the edge. In all, you'll be able to make 7 to 8 folds per dumpling. Repeat with the remaining wrappers and filling. Place the finished dumplings on the prepared baking sheet so

INGREDIENTS:

7 fresh shittake mushrooms

Salt

½ pound pressed tofu, cubed

1 pound (about 2 cups) baby spinach

1 bunch (5 or 6) scallions, white and light green parts, trimmed and thinly sliced

2 handfuls fresh cilantro leaves

3 garlic cloves, grated or minced

1 2-inch piece fresh ginger, peeled and minced

2 medium carrots, coarsely grated on the largest holes of a box grater

3 tablespoons soy sauce

1 recipe Basic Dumpling Wrappers (page 316) or 36 3-inch round wrappers

Cabbage leaves for steaming (optional)

Tomato-Sesame Dipping Sauce (page 752)

they aren't touching. Cook immediately, cover and refrigerate for up to 24 hours, or freeze on the baking sheet, transfer to a freezer bag, and freeze for up to a month. Do not thaw them prior to cooking (they will become mushy), and add an extra minute or two to their cooking time.

5 Bring 3 cups water to a boil in a large pot. Line a steamer with cabbage leaves or parchment paper cut to the size and shape of your steamer with lots of small incisions made in it to allow steam to circulate. Set the *momos* in the steamer spacing them ½ inch away from each other and the sides of the steamer. Place the steamer in the pot over the boiling water (it should not touch it), cover, and steam until they have puffed out slightly and become slightly translucent, about 12 minutes. Transfer to a warmed plate and cover loosely with aluminum foil to keep warm. Repeat with the remaining dumplings.

6 Serve the dumplings piping hot, accompanied by the Tomato-Sesame Dipping Sauce in a small bowl.

FRIED WONTONS
with PORK *and* SHRIMP

YIELD: 48 WONTONS; 6 SERVINGS / ACTIVE TIME: 25 MINUTES / TOTAL TIME: 45 MINUTES

Literally "swallowing clouds" in Cantonese *zhá yúntun*, these fried wontons are a crispy dumpling typically filled with a mixture of pork, shrimp, and scallions. Andrea Nguyen, the author of the authoritative *Asian Dumplings: Mastering Gyoza, Spring Rolls, Samosas, and More,* counsels to use the thinnest wonton wrappers available, as they create airy, delicate wontons. If not making your own, this generally means a trip to your local Asian market to find Hong Kong-style wrappers.

1 Prepare the sweet and sour sauce. Whisk the cornstarch and water together in a small bowl; set aside. Combine the fruit juices, vinegar, sugar, ketchup, and soy sauce together in a medium saucepan and bring to a boil over medium heat. Stir in the cornstarch mixture and cook until it thickens, 2 to 3 minutes. Remove from the heat. Use immediately or let cool and store in an airtight container in the refrigerator for up to 1 week.

2 Make the wonton filling. Put the shrimp, pork, cornstarch, scallions, salt, sugar, and a few good cracks of black pepper in a medium bowl and mix until thoroughly combined. Let rest, covered, for 45 minutes at room temperature or overnight in the refrigerator.

3 Place a damp paper towel over the stack of wonton wrappers (to keep them from drying out). Line one baking sheet with parchment paper. Lightly dust a second baking sheet with cornstarch and set a wire rack on it. Cover the rack with paper towels. Also prepare a small fingerbowl of water for sealing.

4 Lay a wrapper in front of you and place a heaping teaspoon of filling in the middle of it. Dip your finger in the water and run it along the edges of the square. Fold one of the corners over the filling to create a triangle. As you tightly seal both sides, try to press out any air that may be inside (this will keep the wonton from coming apart in the oil). Bring the two longest corners of the triangle together to form a kerchief shape. Wet one of the corners with a dab of water and press tightly to seal. Repeat with the remaining wrappers and filling. Place the finished dumplings on the prepared baking sheet so they aren't touching. Cook immediately or cover and refrigerate for up to 2 days. Bring them back to room temperature before frying.

INGREDIENTS:

SWEET AND SOUR SAUCE:

- 1 ½ tablespoons cornstarch
- 1 ½ tablespoons water
- ⅓ cup pineapple juice
- ⅓ cup orange juice
- ⅓ cup rice vinegar
- ¼ cup light brown sugar
- 2 ½ tablespoons ketchup
- 1 ½ tablespoons soy sauce

WONTONS:

- 4 ounces medium shrimp, peeled and minced
- 4 ounces ground pork
- ¾ teaspoon cornstarch, plus more for dusting the baking sheet
- 3 scallions, trimmed and minced
- 1 teaspoon salt
- ½ teaspoon sugar
- Freshly ground black pepper
- 48 3-inch square wonton wrappers, homemade (page 318) or store-bought
- Safflower or peanut oil for frying

5 Pour oil in a large, deep skillet or 5-quart Dutch oven to a depth of 1 ½ to 2 inches. Heat over medium heat until it reaches 325°F on a deep-fryer thermometer.

6 Working in batches of 6 to 8, gently slip the wontons into the hot oil and fry until they are caramel-golden all over, about 1 minute per side. Transfer to the wire rack to drain. Repeat until all the wontons are fried.

7 Serve piping hot, accompanied by the dipping sauce.

KIMCHI MANDU

YIELD: 4 SERVINGS / ACTIVE TIME: 45 MINUTES / TOTAL TIME: 1 ½ HOURS

These succulent dumplings are filled with a garlic-spiked mixture of kimchi, tofu, and beans sprouts, for delicious morsels that deliver salty, sour, savory, spicy, crunchy, and creamy in every bite. They can be boiled, steamed, or pan-fried and you'll find directions for all three methods in the recipe. If you are buying wrappers, look for *mandu* wrappers, available in Asian or Korean markets and online.

1 Drain the tofu and cut into ½-inch cubes. Arrange them in a single layer on a paper-towel lined tray. Cover with paper towels and pat dry. Let them sit for 30 minutes, changing the paper towels after 15 minutes (to continue absorbing as much water as possible). Alternatively, use a tofu press, following the manufacturer's instructions, and cut into cubes. Once drained or pressed, mince the tofu.

2 While the tofu drains, bring a medium pot of water to a boil. While it comes to a boil, pick over the bean sprouts, discarding any discolored or spoiled ones. Put the remaining ones in a bowl of cold water. Discard the hulls that float to the top, then rinse them under cold water. Add the sprouts to the boiling water and cook for 2 minutes. Remove them from the water with a strainer and immediately run them under cold water to stop them from cooking further. Drain, mince, and transfer to a large bowl.

3 Put the kimchi in a double layer of cheesecloth. Gather the cheesecloth up at the top in a bundle and, over the sink, begin turning it, in tourniquet-like fashion, to squeeze as much liquid out of the kimchi as possible. Mince and add to the bowl with the bean sprouts. Add the tofu, garlic, shallots, egg, sesame oil, salt, and pepper to taste and mix until thoroughly combined. Use immediately or cover and refrigerate for up to a day (the garlic takes over the flavor of the filling after that). Bring back to room temperature before using.

4 Place a damp paper towel over the stack of wrappers (to keep them from drying out). Line a baking sheet with parchment paper. Also prepare a small fingerbowl of water for sealing.

5 Put a wrapper on your work surface and place 1 generous tablespoon of filling in the middle. Dip your finger in the water and run it along the edges of the square. Fold one of the

INGREDIENTS:

1   **pound extra firm tofu**

1 ½   **cups mung bean sprouts**

1 ½   **cups kimchi**

5   **garlic cloves, minced**

2   **large shallots, minced**

1   **large egg**

1 ½   **teaspoons toasted sesame oil**

2   **teaspoons salt**

   Freshly ground black pepper

1   **recipe Basic Dumpling Wrappers (page 316) or 40 3-inch round wrappers**

   Peanut or grapeseed oil if pan-frying

   Cabbage leaves if steaming (optional)

   Korean Dipping Sauce (page 753)

corners over the filling to create a triangle and tightly press the edges together to seal, trying to push out as much air as you can as you do it. Bring the two longest corners of the triangle together to form a kerchief shape. Wet one of the corners with a dab of water and press tightly to seal.

Repeat with the remaining wrappers and filling. Place the finished dumplings on the prepared baking sheet so they aren't touching. Cook immediately or freeze on the baking sheet, transfer to a freezer bag, and freeze for up to a month. Do not thaw them prior to cooking (they will become mushy), and add an extra minute or two to their cooking time.

6 To pan-fry the *mandu:* Heat a large skillet over medium-low heat for 2 to 3 minutes. Add enough oil to cover the bottom of the skillet with a film of oil and adjust the heat to medium-high. When the oil begins to swirl on the surface, add as many *mandu* as will fit in the skillet without overcrowding (you will need to work in batches). Cook until the bottoms are crisp and golden brown, 2 to 3 minutes. Reduce the heat to medium-low, add 2 tablespoons water, cover, and cook the *mandu* until most of the water disappears, about 5 minutes. Transfer the *mandu* to a warmed platter and tent loosely with aluminum foil to keep warm.

Wipe the skillet with paper towels until completely dry. Return to the stove and add enough oil to cover the bottom of the skillet with a film of oil. Repeat until all the *mandu* are cooked.

To steam the *mandu:* Bring 3 cups water to a boil in a large pot. Line a steamer with cabbage leaves or parchment paper cut to the size and shape of your steamer with lots of small incisions made in it to allow steam to circulate. Set the *mandu* in the steamer spacing them ½ inch away from each other and the sides of the steamer. Place the steamer in the pot over the boiling water (it should not touch it), cover, and steam until the dumplings are tender but still chewy, about 8 minutes.

To boil the *mandu:* Bring a large pot of water to a boil and carefully add the dumplings. Once the water starts boiling again, add a cup of cold water to tame the boiling (this keeps the dumplings from breaking). Continue adding cold water in this way to prevent furious boiling. When the dumplings begin to float to the surface, cook for another 5 to 6 minutes. Remove carefully with a strainer.

7 Serve the *mandu* piping hot with the dipping sauce.

SPICED LAMB BANSH DUMPLINGS

YIELD: 4 SERVINGS / ACTIVE TIME: 1½ HOURS / TOTAL TIME: 2 HOURS

These small dumplings can be found on dinner tables throughout Mongolia. *Bansh* are traditionally made with stronger tasting mutton, but lamb and beef both make for a tasty substitute. *Bansh* traditionally aren't served with a dipping sauce.

INGREDIENTS:

- ¾ pound ground lamb or beef
- 1 onion, cut into small dice
- 2 large garlic gloves, minced
- 1 tablespoon ground coriander
- Handful fresh parsley leaves, minced
- Salt and freshly ground black pepper
- 3 to 5 teaspoons water
- 1 recipe Basic Dumpling Wrappers (page 316) or 36 3-inch round wrappers
- Thinly sliced cucumber and radish rounds for serving

1 Mix the lamb, onion, garlic, coriander, parsley, and salt and pepper to taste together in a medium bowl. (To check the seasoning, take a bit of it, form into a patty, cook it in a small skillet, and taste to assess.) Add the water, 1 teaspoon at a time, mixing vigorously, until the filling is smooth. The filling can be prepared a day ahead; cover, refrigerate, and bring back to room temperature before proceeding.

2 Place a damp paper towel over the stack of wrappers (to keep them from drying out). Line a baking sheet with parchment paper.

3 Cup a wrapper in your hand and add about a heaping teaspoon of filling. Close your hand to close the dough around the filling. Using your thumb and index finger, pinch one fourth of the circumference of the wrapper, fold half of that circumference over itself in fan-like fashion to create a pleat, and then pinch that pleated edge together to form a tight seal. Repeat three more times with the rest of the wrapper border until the dumpling resembles a rose about to bloom. Repeat with the remaining wrappers and filling. Place the finished dumplings on the prepared baking sheet so they aren't touching. Cook immediately or freeze on the baking sheet, transfer to a freezer bag, and freeze for up to a month. Do not thaw them prior to cooking (they will become mushy), and add an extra minute or two to their cooking time.

4 To cook, bring a large pot of water to a boil and add salt (1 tablespoon for every 4 cups water). Once it's boiling, add the dumplings (they will sink to the bottom) and boil until they float to the surface, 8 to 10 minutes, stirring occasionally to prevent sticking.

5 Transfer to a warm platter and serve with the sliced cucumber and radish.

CRAB RANGOONS

YIELD: 6 SERVINGS / ACTIVE TIME: 25 MINUTES / TOTAL TIME: 45 MINUTES

Found on the menu of most American Chinese restaurants, super crispy crab rangoons contain an addictive creamy, sweet-savory filling. Once fried, do try and hold off devouring them until they've cooled slightly, as their filling can be scaldingly hot. I pair them with a spicy sweet-and-sour pineapple dipping sauce, which serves as the proverbial cherry on top.

1 Prepare the dipping sauce. Combine the pineapple, garlic, bell pepper, and red pepper flakes in a food processor or blender and pulse until minced. Pour the mixture into a small saucepan and add the vinegar, sugar, and water. Bring to a boil over medium heat. Reduce the heat to a simmer and continue cooking until the mixture thickens and becomes a clear, shiny red color, 10 to 12 minutes. Remove from the heat and let cool before serving. You can store in an airtight container in the refrigerator for up to a week.

2 Put the cream cheese, crabmeat, sugar, and salt in a medium bowl and cream together with a wooden spoon.

3 Place about 1 tablespoon of the cream cheese filling in the middle of a wonton wrapper. Dip a finger in a small bowl of water and moisten the outer edges of the wrapper. Gently pinch the two opposite corners of the wrapper and pull them together, over the filling. Repeat the step with the remaining opposite corners to create a tiny parcel. Pinch all the sealed sides together to create a tight seal that won't leak during frying. Repeat with the remaining wrappers and filling. Place the finished dumplings on a parchment paper-lined baking sheet so they aren't touching. Cook immediately or freeze on the baking sheet, transfer to a freezer bag, and freeze for up to 3 months. Do not thaw them prior to cooking(they will become mushy), and add an extra minute or two to their cooking time.

4 Pour oil in a large, deep skillet or Dutch oven to a depth of 1 ½ to 2 inches. Heat over medium heat until it reaches 325°F on a deep-fryer thermometer. Working in batches of 6 to 8, gently slip the wontons into the hot oil and fry until caramel-golden all over about 1 minute per side. Transfer to a wire rack set over paper towels to drain. Repeat with the remaining wontons.

5 Serve the wontons piping hot, accompanied by the dipping sauce.

INGREDIENTS:

SPICY PINEAPPLE DIPPING SAUCE:

½ cup chopped fresh pineapple

2 garlic cloves, peeled

½ red bell pepper, chopped

¼ teaspoon red pepper flakes (more if you prefer it to be spicy)

1 cup distilled white vinegar

¾ cup sugar

¼ cup water

CRAB RANGOONS:

2 8-ounce packages regular cream cheese, at room temperature

6 ounces fresh crabmeat

2 tablespoons confectioners' sugar

¼ teaspoon salt

40 3-inch wonton wrappers, homemade (page 318) or store-bought

Peanut or grapeseed oil for deep-frying

PAN-FRIED PORK *and* CABBAGE GYŌZA

YIELD: 8 SERVINGS / ACTIVE TIME: 1 HOUR / TOTAL TIME: 1 ¼ HOURS

Gyōza, savory dumplings traditionally filled with seasoned minced pork and shrimp, are a popular snack or side dish in Japan. Their name derives from that of their Chinese counterpart in the Shandong dialect, *jiaozi.* Indeed the dumplings are similar, though the Japanese *gyōza* has fewer choices of fillings, a subtler flavor, and thinner wrappers. Extremely versatile, they can be steamed, boiled, or pan-fried and are always served with a dipping sauce.

1 Toss the cabbage and 2½ teaspoons salt together in a fine-meshed strainer set over a bowl and let stand for 30 minutes. Transfer the cabbage to a kitchen towel and twist the towel, in tourniquet-like fashion, to squeeze out the excess moisture. Put the cabbage in a clean large bowl along with the garlic, ginger, pork, scallions, sugar, white pepper, and 1½ teaspoons salt and mix until thoroughly combined and slightly sticky to the touch. To check for seasoning, take a tablespoon of filling, form it in a small patty, and quickly cook it in a small nonstick skillet. Add more salt and/or pepper if needed. Use immediately or cover and refrigerate for up to a day (the garlic takes over the flavor of the filling after that). Bring back to room temperature before using.

2 Place a damp paper towel over the stack of wrappers (to keep them from drying out). Line a baking sheet with parchment paper. Also prepare a small fingerbowl of water for sealing.

3 Place a wrapper in your cupped hand, mostly holding it on your fingers, and put about 1 tablespoon of filling in the center, leaving about ¾ inch of the wrapper clear all the way around it. Using the tip of the index finger of the other hand, lightly moisten that edge with water. Fold one edge of the wrapper over the filling into a half-moon and tightly press the edges together to seal, trying to push out as much air as you can as you do it. To pleat the sealed edges, start at one end of the half-moon and make small folds in the wrapper, pressing them flat as you work your way along the edge. In all, you'll be able to make 7 to 8 folds per dumpling. Repeat with the remaining wrappers and filling. Place the finished dumplings on the prepared baking sheet so they aren't touching. Cook immediately, cover and refrigerate for up to 24 hours, or freeze on the baking sheet, transfer to a freezer bag, and freeze for up to a month. Do not thaw them prior to cooking (they will become mushy), and add an extra minute or two to their cooking time.

INGREDIENTS:

- ½ medium head (1 pound) Napa cabbage, cored and minced
- Salt
- 4 garlic cloves, minced
- 1 1-inch piece fresh ginger, peeled and grated or minced
- 1 pound ground pork shoulder
- 4 scallions, trimmed and thinly sliced
- 2 teaspoons sugar
- 1 ½ teaspoons white pepper
- 1 package round 3-inch dumpling wrappers (40 to 50 wrappers)
- Safflower oil for cooking
- ½ cup water
- ½ cup rice vinegar
- ¼ cup soy sauce
- 1 tablespoon hot chile oil

Heat a large nonstick skillet over low heat for a minute. Add just enough safflower oil to completely cover the bottom of the skillet in a thin film and turn the heat to medium. When it begins to swirl, add as many dumplings as will fit in a single layer, making sure they don't touch, and cook until evenly golden brown on the bottom, about 2 minutes.

Increase the heat to medium-high, add the water, cover, and steam the dumplings until cooked through, about 3 minutes, then remove the lid. Continue cooking, shaking the pan gently from time to time to make sure the dumplings are not sticking, until the water has completely evaporated and the dumplings have crisped again on the bottom, 2 to 3 minutes.

While the dumplings are steaming, whisk the vinegar, soy sauce, and chile oil together in a small bowl.

Slide the dumplings onto a warmed serving platter, arranging them crisped side up. Serving piping hot with the dipping sauce.

DUCK SPRING ROLLS
with SOUR CHERRY COMPOTE

YIELD: 4 SERVINGS / ACTIVE TIME: 45 MINUTES / TOTAL TIME: ABOUT 1 HOUR

Two things makes this spring roll shine. The first is duck rillettes, a pâté-like preparation made from braised duck meat mixed with Armagnac and spices. Depending on where you live, you may need to buy this online, or you can substitute the chopped meat from duck confit. The second, the sour cherry compote, perfectly offsets the richness of the duck.

1 Prepare the compote. The night (or for at least 8 hours) before preparing the compote, combine the dried cherries with enough rice wine or water to cover them by 2 inches in a small saucepan. Bring to a simmer over medium heat. Remove from the heat and let cool. Transfer to a small bowl and let them soak until plump and soft. Drain, reserving ¼ cup of the soaking liquid. Combine the remaining compote ingredients, including the reserved soaking liquid, in a medium saucepan and heat just until gently bubbling over medium heat. Using an immersion blender or transferring it to a food processor or blender, blend until smooth, then reheat to a gentle boil. Use immediately or let cool, cover, and refrigerate up to 3 days. Rewarm before serving.

2 Heat a small skillet over medium heat for 2 to 3 minutes. Add the truffle oil and turn the heat up to medium-high. When the oil begins to swirl on the surface, add the mushrooms and a pinch of salt and cook, stirring, until softened, 4 to 5 minutes. Add half of the ginger and all the garlic and cook, stirring, for another minute, until fragrant. Remove from the heat.

3 Put the duck rillettes, water chestnuts, chives, sesame oil, a few grinds of pepper, and the mushroom mixture in a medium bowl. Mix well to form a sticky filling.

4 Preheat the oven to 400°F. Line a baking sheet with parchment paper. Before starting, place a damp paper towel over the stack of wrappers (prevents them from drying out). Line a baking sheet with parchment paper. Also, prepare a small fingerbowl of water for sealing.

INGREDIENTS:

SOUR CHERRY COMPOTE:

1 cup dried sour cherries

Shaoxing rice wine as needed (optional)

2 garlic cloves, minced

2 shallots, minced

1 2-inch piece fresh ginger, peeled and grated or minced

1 8-ounce jar sour cherry jam

½ cup pomegranate juice

⅓ cup tamari or soy sauce

¼ cup hoisin sauce

1 teaspoon toasted sesame oil

WONTONS:

1 ½ tablespoons truffle oil

5 medium shiitake mushrooms, stems discarded and caps minced

Salt

1 2-inch piece fresh ginger, peeled and grated or minced

2 garlic cloves, minced

1 small tub (7 ounces) duck rillettes

½ cup water chestnuts, minced

Handful thinly sliced fresh chives

1 ½ teaspoon toasted sesame oil

Freshly ground black pepper

1 12-ounce package (25 sheets) 8-inch spring roll wrappers

Safflower oil for brushing the rolls

5 Treat each roll like a burrito. Position a wrapper with one corner pointing toward you. Place 2 heaping teaspoons of filling in the center of each wrapper. With a moistened finger, wet the edges of the wrapper. Fold the corner facing you over the filling, tucking it under a little bit to pull the ingredients closer together. Gently pull one side of the wrapper over the middle and then the other side. Finally, roll toward the last corner. Repeat with remaining wrappers and filling.

6 Place the rolls on the prepared baking sheet and lightly brush with safflower oil. Put on the center rack and bake until golden brown and crispy, 10 to 12 minutes, turning them over after about 5 minutes.

7 Serve warm, accompanied by the dipping sauce.

DUCK RILLETTES

This recipe takes a different take on duck rillettes than the typical French version, which is served on a baguette. In this recipe, the duck rillettes will add a distinct and rich flavor to your spring rolls. Though savory and fatty, duck is a much healthier option than the typical pork rillettes.

SOUPS & NOODLE BOWLS

---

*S*oup satisfies the soul. It is what mothers make for children when they are sick. It is what we bring to neighbors in times of need. Dress it up, and it welcomes dinner guests to an evening of relaxed conversation. There is nothing more restorative or comforting than fragrant steam rising from a bowl filled with diminutive, tender pasta shapes or long, springy noodles. Before you know it, in real Oliver Twist fashion, you will be holding up your bowl and murmuring, "Please, sir, I want some more."

PEA SOUP *with* PASTA *and* RICOTTA SALATA

YIELD: 4 SERVINGS / ACTIVE TIME: 25 MINUTES / TOTAL TIME: 40 MINUTES

This is the embodiment of simple, rustic food. Light and nourishing, it is the perfect choice when vegetable gardens and farmers' markets are brimming with fresh peas, tomatoes, and basil. The tart, slightly pungent taste of the ricotta salata beautifully complements the subtle sweetness of the ingredients.

Recommended pasta shapes: medium-size shells, ditalini, grattini

1 If using frozen peas, place them in a sieve and run warm water over them for 1 minute. Drain and keep in the sieve until ready to use.

2 Bring a small saucepan of water to a boil. Blanch the tomatoes in the boiling water for 1 minute. Use tongs to remove them to a cutting board and let cool until you can handle, then remove their skins. Cut them into quarters, remove the seeds, and chop into small pieces. Set aside.

3 Heat a large heavy-bottomed pot or Dutch oven over medium-low heat for 2 to 3 minutes. Add the olive oil, turn the heat up to medium-high, and let it heat for a couple of minutes. When the surface of the oil begins to swirl, add the onion and a couple pinches of salt and mix well. When the mixture begins to sizzle, adjust the heat to low, cover, and cook, stirring occasionally, until the onion becomes very soft, about 15 minutes.

4 Add the peas and a couple pinches of salt to the onion, raise the heat to medium-high, and cook, stirring frequently, for about 3 minutes. Add the tomatoes and any juices that have accumulated in their bowl, the sugar, broth, and 1½ teaspoons of salt and bring to a boil. Taste for seasoning and add more salt or pepper if needed. Add the pasta, stir, and cook, following the package instructions, until it is tender but pleasantly chewy.

5 Ladle the soup into four warmed bowls and serve piping hot, sprinkled with the cheese and basil.

INGREDIENTS:

- 3 cups fresh peas or 1 ½ 10-ounce bags frozen petite peas
- 8 very ripe plum tomatoes
- 3 tablespoons extra virgin olive oil
- 1 large yellow onion, chopped
- Salt
- ¼ teaspoon sugar
- 4 cups chicken or vegetable broth
- 1½ cups short pasta
- Salt and freshly ground black pepper
- ½ cup crumbled ricotta salata or feta cheese for garnish
- Handful fresh basil leaves, cut into thin slivers, for garnish

ZUPPA IMPERIALE

YIELD: 6 SERVINGS / ACTIVE TIME: 1 ½ HOURS / TOTAL TIME: 3 ¼ HOURS

A traditional dish from Emilia-Romagna, and the city of Bologna in particular, *pasta imperiale* is made from a roll of pasta dough that's wrapped in cheesecloth, simmered for hours in rich stock, then pressed overnight, diced, and reheated and served in the same stock in which it was cooked. This unusual dish (also known as *royale Bolognese*) is only as good as the meat broth used to make it. But don't take my word for it. Just ask any Italian from Emilia-Romagna. They know a thing or thirty-seven about flavorful cooking!

1 Put the Parmigiano, eggs, softened butter, flour, nutmeg, salt, and pepper in a large bowl and, using your hands, mix until the ingredients come together into a dough.

2 Transfer the dough to a large piece of cheesecloth and shape it into a 2-inch-wide roll. Wrap the cheesecloth tightly around the dough and tie it securely at both ends with kitchen string.

3 Put the broth and wrapped dough in a large pot. Bring to a boil, adjust the heat to low, cover, and cook at a bare simmer for 3 hours.

4 Transfer the roll to an aluminum foil-lined rimmed baking sheet (for easy clean up). Place another baking sheet on top of it and weigh it down with several books, water bottles, or large cans of tomatoes (this helps eliminate any broth or air bubbles trapped inside the dough). Let cool for an hour at room temperature, then refrigerate it, with the weights still on, for at least 6 hours (overnight is best). Refrigerate the broth separately after letting it cool for an hour or so first.

5 To serve, bring the broth to a gentle boil over medium-low heat. While it heats, remove the cheesecloth from the *pasta imperiale* and cut it into ½-inch cubes. Carefully add the cubes to the simmering broth and cook until the broth begins to gently simmer again, 7 to 10 minutes. Ladle into warmed soup bowls and top with a dusting of freshly grated nutmeg.

INGREDIENTS:

- 1 ½ cups freshly grated Parmigiano-Reggiano cheese

- 5 large eggs

- ½ cup (1 stick) unsalted butter, at room temperature

- 1 ½ cups + 3 tablespoons all-purpose flour

- 1 teaspoon freshly grated nutmeg, plus more for serving

- 1 teaspoon salt

- ½ teaspoon freshly ground white pepper

- 2 quarts full-bodied meat or chicken broth (see Mixed Meat Stock, page 750, or Capon or Chicken Stock, page 749)

VEGETABLE SOUP *with* MENIETTI PASTA

YIELD: 6 SERVINGS / ACTIVE TIME: 1 HOUR / TOTAL TIME: 1½ HOURS

Tiny lumps of wheat flour dough, *menietti* come from the coastal region of Liguria and are traditionally served in soups. It is a rustic pasta, not found in stores or online, and must be made from scratch to enjoy. Drizzle a little good quality extra virgin olive oil over the soup right before serving to add a fragrant touch.

INGREDIENTS:

2 large leeks

2 ½ tablespoons extra virgin olive oil, plus more for serving

2 carrots, diced

3 pale green inner celery stalks, diced

Salt

2 quarts Mixed Meat Stock (page 750)

2 bay leaves

1 sprig fresh rosemary

Freshly ground black pepper

1 recipe Menietti (page 251)

Freshly grated Parmigiano-Reggiano cheese

1 Prepare the leeks by trimming away the root ends and dark green leaves, keeping only the white and light green parts. With a sharp knife, cut each leek in half lengthwise and remove the two outer layers. Cut the halves vertically into thin slivers. Place them in a large bowl of water and swish them around to remove any dirt. Drain well, then transfer to a kitchen towel.

2 Heat a large stockpot over medium-low for 2 to 3 minutes. Add the olive oil and turn the heat up to medium-high. Once it begins to swirl on the surface but is not yet smoking, add the leeks, carrots, celery, and a couple pinches of salt, and cook, stirring occasionally, until the vegetables begin to gently sizzle. Turn the heat to medium-low, cover, and cook, stirring occasionally, until the vegetables are soft, about 15 minutes.

3 Add the stock, bay leaves, and rosemary, turn the heat to medium-high, and bring to a boil. Adjust the heat to low and cook for another 10 minutes. Taste for seasoning and add salt if needed and pepper. Discard the herbs.

4 If you want to cook the *menietti* right in the soup, bring the soup back to a boil and add them now. But keep in mind that pasta—even small pasta shapes—can absorb a lot of liquid. Your other alternative is to cook them separately: Bring a large pot of water to a boil. Once it's boiling, add salt (1 tablespoon for every 4 cups water) and stir. Add the pasta and stir for the first minute to prevent any sticking. Cook until it is tender but still chewy, 3 to 4 minutes. Drain. You have yet another choice; you can add them to the soup (where they will still absorb some of the broth—which does add flavor but will also make the pasta soft) or you can add the cooked *menietti* to each soup bowl and then top with the finished soup, storing any leftovers separate from the soup.

5 Ladle the soup into warmed soup bowls. Serve drizzled with good-quality extra virgin olive oil and topped with a dusting of Parmigiano (or pass the grated cheese at the table).

MOROCCAN-STYLE TOMATO *and* CHICKPEA SOUP *with* COUSCOUS

YIELD: 4 SERVINGS / ACTIVE TIME: 20 MINUTES / TOTAL TIME: 45 MINUTES

If you like warming spices, then this is the soup for you, as it contains *ras el hanout*, a coppery colored spice blend from North Africa that combines cumin, ginger, cinnamon, coriander, cayenne, allspice, cloves, black pepper, and salt. North Africa's equivalent to India's *garam masala*, it turns everyday ingredients into an exotic treat; it's available online. The heat from the dish comes from harissa, a fiery chile paste made from roasted red peppers, baklouti peppers (a super-hot but also flavorful chile from Tunisia), serrano peppers, spices, and herbs. Should you have difficulty finding it, use sriracha or sambal oelek (which is a bit less hot) in its place. Look for it in the hot sauce section of your supermarket or online.

1 Place the couscous in a heatproof bowl and add a couple of pinches of salt, a few good cracks of pepper, and 1 tablespoon of the oil. Mix well. Pour just enough of the hot broth over the couscous to cover it by ¼ inch. Mix well and cover with a plate. Set aside.

2 Heat a medium skillet over medium heat for 2 to 3 minutes. Add the remaining 2 tablespoons oil and heat for a minute or two. Add the onion, carrot, and a couple pinches of salt, stir, cover, and cook until the vegetables soften, about 15 minutes. Add the garlic and ginger, stir, and cook for 2 minutes. Add the harissa and *ras el hanout,* stir, and cook for another minute. Pour in the tomatoes, the remaining broth, the chickpeas, and a few more pinches of salt and stir. Bring to a boil, reduce the heat to low, and simmer, uncovered, until the liquid has somewhat thickened, about 25 minutes. Stir in the lemon juice.

3 Fluff the couscous with a fork. Ladle the soup into bowls and top with a small mound of couscous. Sprinkle the cilantro on top and serve piping hot, with more harissa in a small bowl for diners to stir into their soup, if they like.

INGREDIENTS:

- ½ cup couscous
- Salt and freshly ground black pepper
- 3 tablespoons extra virgin olive oil, divided
- 3 ¼ cups hot vegetable broth, divided
- 1 large onion, minced
- 1 carrot, cut into small dice
- 4 garlic cloves, minced
- 1 1-inch piece fresh ginger, peeled and grated or minced
- 1 tablespoon harissa, plus more for serving
- 1 ½ tablespoons ras el hanout
- 1 14-ounce can diced tomatoes, undrained
- 1 14-ounce can chickpeas, rinsed and drained
- Juice of ½ lemon
- Handful roughly chopped fresh cilantro for garnish

BRAISED VEGETABLES
with CAT'S EARS NOODLES IN BROTH

YIELD: 6 SERVINGS / ACTIVE TIME: 20 MINUTES / TOTAL TIME: ABOUT 3 HOURS

Hand-formed pasta shaped like an ear-shaped cone, *mao er duo* are the Chinese equivalent of Italian *orecchiette*. Unmistakably coarse, soft, and chewy, they are popular street food in the Chinese province of Hangzhou, where they are stir-fried in a rich sauce. This recipe serves them in a rich, savory broth brimming with vegetables.

1 Drain the tofu and cut it into ½-inch cubes. Arrange them in a single layer on a paper-towel lined tray. Cover with paper towels and pat dry. Let them sit for 30 minutes, changing the paper towels after 15 minutes (to continue absorbing as much water as possible). Alternatively, use a tofu press, following the manufacturer's instructions, then cut into cubes.

2 Place the dried shiitakes in a heatproof bowl and add just enough hot water to cover them by a few inches. Soak for at least 20 minutes, until they reconstitute and the caps are tender. Drain and squeeze each mushroom tightly in your hand to remove excess water. Cut away and discard the tough stems, and then dice.

3 Bring a large pot of water to a boil. Blanch the tomatoes in the boiling water for 1 minute. Use tongs to remove them to a cutting board and let cool enough to handle, then remove their skins. Cut them into quarters, remove the seeds, and dice.

4 Bring the water back to a boil and add salt (1 tablespoon for every 4 cups water) and stir. Add the *mao er duo*, stirring for the first minute to prevent sticking, and cook until tender but still chewy, about 3 minutes. Drain, transfer to a bowl, and toss with the grapeseed oil and toss to prevent any sticking.

5 While the pasta is cooking, heat a wok or large skillet over medium heat for 2 to 3 minutes. Add the peanut oil and turn the heat to high. When the oil begins to swirl on the surface, add, one at a time and stirring between the addition of each ingredient, the scallions, chiles, carrots, potatoes, and tomatoes. Add a couple pinches of salt and pepper and the soy sauce, and stir-fry until very fragrant, about 2 minutes. Add the tofu, both mushrooms, and a couple more pinches of salt and stir-fry for another 2 minutes. Add enough of the broth to immerse all the ingredients, stir, and bring to a boil. Add the cooked *mao er duo*,

INGREDIENTS:

1 **pound extra firm tofu**

4 **dried shiitake mushrooms**

4 **plum tomatoes**

Salt

¾ **pound Cat's Ear Noodles (page 211) or orecchiette, homemade (page 173) or store-bought**

½ **tablespoon grapeseed or safflower oil**

2 **tablespoons peanut oil**

1 **bunch (5 or 6) scallions, trimmed and sliced on the diagonal into ½-inch pieces**

3 **fresh red chiles, seeded and thinly sliced**

2 **medium carrots, thinly sliced**

2 **medium russet potatoes, peeled and diced**

Freshly ground black pepper

3 **tablespoons soy sauce**

1 **pound cremini mushrooms, diced**

4 **cups vegetable or chicken broth, more if needed**

6 **baby bok choy, quartered lengthwise**

¼ **cup water**

lower the heat to medium, cover, and simmer until heated through and the potatoes are tender, about 5 minutes.

6 While the sauce simmers, heat another large skillet over medium heat for 2 to 3 minutes. Add the bok choy, two pinches of salt, and the water and stir. Once the water starts to boil, cover and let steam for 2 minutes. Add the bok choy to the broth, stir well, and turn the heat off.

7 To serve, ladle the brothy braise into warmed soup bowls, making sure everyone gets an equal amount of pasta, tofu, mushrooms, and bok choy. Serve piping hot.

SARDINIAN SPINACH, CANNELLINI BEAN,
and FREGOLA SOUP

YIELD: 4 SERVINGS / ACTIVE TIME: 45 MINUTES / TOTAL TIME: 1 ¼ HOURS

A traditional Sardinian pasta, *fregola* consists of ⅛-inch round spheres of semolina dough. Besides its unique shape, it also distinguishes itself by being toasted, which gives it a nutty, earthy flavor and colors it varying shades of golden brown. Its rough surface and extremely porous texture makes it function more like couscous or rice than traditional pasta, and I've made my fair share of rustic and filling *fregola* "risottos." In this recipe, it is treated like rice and combined with a savory combination of spinach, cannellini beans, and a hint of plum tomatoes. No dish from Sardinia would be complete without the addition of a good dusting of spicy, pungent pecorino Sardo.

INGREDIENTS:

- 4 very ripe plum tomatoes
- 2 medium leeks
- ¼ cup extra virgin olive oil, plus more for drizzling
- 2 garlic cloves, crushed
- 1 small red onion, minced
- 4 pale green inner celery stalks, minced
- Salt
- 1 14-ounce can cannellini beans, rinsed and drained
- 1 tablespoon tomato paste
- Freshly ground black pepper
- 6 cups chicken or vegetable broth
- ⅔ cup fregola
- ½ pound fresh baby spinach
- Freshly grated pecorino Sardo cheese for serving

1 Bring a medium saucepan of water to a boil. Blanch the tomatoes in the boiling water for 1 minute. Use tongs to remove them to a cutting board and let cool until you can handle, then remove their skins. Cut them into quarters, remove the seeds, and roughly chop. Set aside.

2 Prepare the leeks by trimming away the root ends and dark green leaves, keeping only the white and light green parts. With a sharp knife, cut each leek in half lengthwise and remove the two outer layers. Place them in a large bowl of water and swish them around to remove any dirt. Drain well, then mince and transfer to a kitchen towel. Set aside.

3 Heat a large heavy-bottomed pot or Dutch oven over medium-low heat for 2 to 3 minutes. Add the oil and crushed garlic and turn the heat up to medium-high. Heat the oil and garlic for a couple of minutes, rubbing the bottom of the pot with the garlic using a wooden spoon. When the surface of the oil begins to swirl, remove and discard the garlic, add the onion, celery, leeks, and a couple pinches of salt, and mix well. When the mixture begins to sizzle, adjust the heat to low, cover, and cook, stirring occasionally, until the vegetables are very soft, about 15 minutes.

4 Turn the heat up to medium-high and add the cannellini beans, tomato paste, a couple pinches of salt, and pepper to taste. Cook, stirring frequently, until the cannellini beans begin to look slightly toasted, about 8 minutes.

5 Add the tomatoes, broth, and a couple pinches of salt and bring to a boil. Adjust the heat to low, cover, and simmer for 30 minutes to let the flavors blend. Taste for seasoning and add salt or pepper if needed.

6 Add the *fregola* and cook until it is tender but still pleasantly chewy, about 15 minutes. When it's almost done, add the spinach and stir.

7 Ladle the soup out into four warmed soup bowls and serve piping hot, topped with a drizzle of olive oil and a dusting of pecorino cheese (or pass the grated cheese at the table).

PASTA *and* BROCCOLI SOUP

YIELD: 4 SERVINGS / ACTIVE TIME: 20 MINUTES / TOTAL TIME: ABOUT 45 MINUTES

It doesn't get any more rustic than this humble pasta and broccoli soup. But don't let your taste buds know because they'll be too busy enjoying the rich, garlicky broccoli, chewy pasta, and savory broth to care. This soup is a take-off on one of my family's favorite weeknight go-to meals: Pasta with Broccoli and Garlic (page 502). While I enjoy the soup on its own, I think it is at its best when generously dusted with Parmigiano-Reggiano and lightly drizzled with a good quality extra virgin olive oil, as the subtle sweetness of the broccoli melds with the sharp, savory flavor of the cheese and the fruity pungency of the olive oil. The combination gives the palate so many flavors to hold on to and savor.

Recommended pasta shapes: large ditalini, fideos, small shells, orzo

INGREDIENTS:

- 1 ½ pounds broccoli florets
- 3 tablespoons extra virgin olive oil, plus more for serving
- 3 garlic cloves, minced
- 1 teaspoon salt

  Freshly ground black pepper
- 6 cups Capon or Chicken Stock (page 749) or good quality chicken broth
- ¾ pound small pasta shape

  Freshly grated Parmigiano-Reggiano for serving

1 Put a large pot of water on to boil. Once it's boiling, add salt (1 tablespoon for every 4 cups water) and stir. Add the broccoli florets and cook until just tender, 4 to 5 minutes. Drain well and transfer them to a medium heatproof bowl. Set aside. Dry the pot.

2 Heat the pot over medium heat for 2 to 3 minutes. Add the olive oil and garlic and heat for a minute or two. Once the garlic begins to gently sizzle, add the broccoli, salt, and a few good cracks of pepper and stir. Cook, stirring occasionally (and mashing some of the florets with a wooden spoon when they get soft enough), for about 5 minutes (this is to nicely flavor the broccoli). Add the stock and bring to a boil over medium-high heat. Add the pasta and stir for the first minute to prevent any sticking. Turn the heat down to medium, cover, and cook until the pasta is al dente.

3 Ladle the soup into four warmed bowls and serve piping hot, topped with a drizzle of olive oil and a sprinkle of Parmigiano (or pass the grated cheese at the table).

MUSHROOM *and* NOODLE SOUP

YIELD: 4 SERVINGS / ACTIVE TIME: 20 MINUTES / TOTAL TIME: 35 MINUTES

This very light soup is an excellent starter when you want something warm to begin an otherwise hearty and filling meal. The noodles play a supporting role to the mushrooms, though you would miss their pleasantly chewy texture if they were not there.

1 Cut the cucumber in half lengthwise. Scoop out the seeds, then cut each half across into thin slices. Set aside.

2 Heat a large skillet over medium heat for 2 to 3 minutes. Turn the heat to medium-high and add the oil. When it begins to swirl on the surface, add the scallions, garlic, and a couple pinches of salt and stir-fry until aromatic, about 1 minute. Add the mushrooms and stir-fry until they soften, 3 to 4 minutes. Add the broth and bring to a boil, stirring occasionally. Add the noodles and cook, following the package instructions, until tender but chewy. Add the cucumber slices and soy sauce and let cook until the broth returns to a boil. Taste for seasoning and add salt, soy sauce, and/or pepper as needed.

3 Ladle the soup into four warmed bowls and serve piping hot topped with the cilantro.

INGREDIENTS:

1 medium cucumber

2 tablespoons grapeseed or safflower oil

1 bunch (5 or 6) scallions, trimmed and thinly sliced

2 garlic cloves, thinly sliced

Salt

½ pound cremini mushrooms, stems removed and thinly sliced

6 cups chicken or vegetable broth

4 ounces flat, wide rice noodles

2 tablespoons soy sauce

Salt and freshly ground black pepper

2 handfuls chopped cilantro for garnish

PASTA, CHICKPEA, *and* SWISS CHARD SOUP

YIELD: 6 TO 8 SERVINGS / ACTIVE TIME: 45 MINUTES / TOTAL TIME: 1 ¾ HOURS

Warming and sustaining, this savory and slightly smoky soup is filled with vegetables and chickpeas and is ideal for nippy autumn and winter nights. While this recipe creates a rather liquid-y soup, feel free to decrease the amount of broth by 2 or 3 cups for a thicker consistency. Unless you are anticipating the whole soup to be consumed in one sitting, I would advise cooking the pasta separately to help the pasta maintain its texture (reduce the broth by a cup or so when preparing the soup). If you have made the soup in advance, add the cooked pasta when reheating the soup, as the pasta can become mushy if it stands too long in the soup.

Recommended pasta shapes: fideos, small shells, ditalini, orzo

1 If using dried beans, pick them over and discard any misshapen beans and stones. Place them in a large bowl and cover by 3 inches with water. Soak overnight. The next day, rinse the beans, drain, and place in a large stockpot. Add water to cover, 1 bay leaf, and the onion and bring to a boil over high heat. Add 1 tablespoon of salt and stir. Boil for 2 minutes, then remove from the heat, cover, and let stand for 1 hour. Discard the bay leaf and onion and drain. Rinse under cold water, drain again, and set aside.

2 Trim away the root ends and dark green leaves of the leeks, keeping only the white and light green parts. With a sharp knife, cut each leek in half lengthwise and remove the two outer layers. Cut the halves vertically into thin slivers. Place them in a large bowl of water and swish them around to remove any dirt. Drain well, then transfer to a kitchen towel to air-dry and mince.

3 Heat a large pot or Dutch oven over medium heat for 2 to 3 minutes. Add the olive oil, turn the heat up to medium-high, and heat for a minute or two. Add the pancetta and cook, stirring occasionally, until it turns golden caramel, 6 to 8 minutes. Turn up the heat to medium-high, add the leeks and a couple pinches of salt, and stir. the leeks, and a couple pinches of salt and stir. Once the leeks start to gently sizzle, adjust the heat to low, cover, and cook, stirring often, until they become very soft, about 20 minutes. Turn the heat to medium-high, add the garlic, stir, and cook until fragrant, about 1 minute. Add the carrots and a couple pinches of salt, and stir. Cook the carrots

INGREDIENTS:

1 cup dried chickpeas or 2 15-ounce cans chickpeas, drained and rinsed

1 bay leaf, if using dried beans

½ small white onion, if using dried beans

Salt

3 leeks

3 tablespoons extra virgin olive oil, plus more for serving

5 to 6 ounces chopped pancetta

4 large garlic cloves, minced

2 medium carrots, peeled and chopped

8 cups Capon or Chicken Stock (page 749) or good-quality chicken broth

1 14-ounce can peeled whole tomatoes (preferably San Marzano), with their juices, crushed very well by hand

Freshly ground black pepper

1 pound Swiss chard, stems discarded and leaves sliced into 1-inch-wide ribbons, or baby spinach leaves

½ pound pasta

Chopped fresh basil for garnish

Freshly grated pecorino Romano cheese for serving

for 3 minutes, stirring occasionally, to let them absorb some of the flavor. Add the stock, chickpeas, tomatoes, 1 teaspoon salt, and a few good cracks of pepper and bring to a boil. Cover, reduce the heat to low, and cook, stirring occasionally, until the chickpeas are very tender, about 1 hour.

4 To thicken the soup slightly, remove 2 cups of the cooked chickpeas and vegetables and puree in a blender or food processor. Return the puree to the pot and stir. Alternatively, use an immersion blender and pulse 3 or 4 times. Taste for seasoning and add salt or pepper if needed.

5 Stir in the Swiss chard ribbons and cook until softened, 5 to 6 minutes.

6 When the soup is almost ready, put a large pot of water on to boil for the pasta. Once it's boiling, add salt (1 tablespoon for every 4 cups water) and stir. Add the pasta and stir for the first minute to prevent any sticking. Cook according to the package instructions, draining the pasta 2 minutes short of the directed cooking time. The pasta should be soft but still very firm. Add it to the soup. Continue to cook until heated through, about 3 minutes. Remove the pot from the heat and taste for seasoning. Add salt or pepper if needed.

7 Ladle the soup into warmed soup bowls. Serve piping hot, topped with a drizzle of olive oil, basil, and pecorino (or pass the grated cheese at the table).

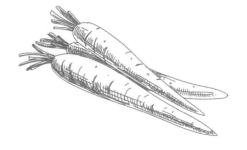

CALABRIAN RICOTTA DUMPLINGS
in CAPON BROTH

YIELD: 8 SERVINGS / ACTIVE TIME: 30 MINUTES / TOTAL TIME: 1 HOUR (WITHOUT MAKING THE STOCK)

This light yet filling soup incorporates two foods that are near and dear to the people of the southwestern Italian region of Calabria. The first are its feathery light ricotta dumplings, which reflect the Calabrian propensity of making meatballs or dumplings out of anything delicious. The second is pecorino cheese, which is considered the king of cheeses throughout the south but especially in Calabria. Many variations of this sharp, salty, and slightly spicy cheese exist. Chief among them are Calabria's locally produced pecorino, pecorino Crotonese, from the city of Crotone, and pecorino pepato, or "peppered pecorino," to which cracked black peppercorns are added. While most Calabrians would use pecorino cheese exclusively in this recipe, I find it contributes too strong of a sheep's milk flavor to the dumplings. For that reason, I have tempered it by adding Parmigiano. If you adore the flavor of pecorino cheese, I would encourage you to eliminate the Parmigiano and use ½ cup of pecorino instead.

INGREDIENTS:

- 1 ¼ cup whole milk ricotta
- ⅓ cup dry breadcrumbs
- 2 large eggs, room temperature
- 1 cup all-purpose flour, divided
- ¼ cup freshly grated Parmigiano-Reggiano cheese
- ¼ cup freshly grated pecorino Sardo
- 2 handfuls chopped fresh parsley, plus more for garnish
- Salt and freshly ground white pepper
- 2 ½ quarts Capon or Chicken Stock (page 749) or rich, good-quality chicken broth

---

1 Two hours prior to making the filling, line a medium sieve with cheesecloth and add the ricotta. Place the sieve on top of a bowl and let drain for 2 hours in the refrigerator. When finished, squeeze the cheesecloth, in tourniquet-like fashion, to remove any remaining water and transfer the ricotta to a large bowl. Add the breadcrumbs, eggs, ¼ cup of the flour, both cheeses, the parsley, 1 teaspoon of salt, and ½ teaspoon of white pepper and mix with a spoon until well integrated. Cover and refrigerate for 30 minutes.

2 Remove the ricotta mixture from the refrigerator and place the remaining flour in a pasta bowl. Pinch off 1 tablespoon of the ricotta mixture and roll it between the palms of your hands into a ball (it may be helpful to wet your hands occasionally to keep it from sticking to your hands). Toss the ball in the flour, tap off any excess, and set on a parchment paper-covered baking sheet. Repeat this step with the remaining ricotta mixture, making sure to arrange the floured dumplings so that they are not touching. Cook or refrigerate, uncovered, for up to 3 hours.

3 Place the stock in a large saucepan and bring to a boil over medium-high heat. Once it's boiling, adjust the heat to low so that it is gently simmering (you don't ever want it to boil because the delicate dumplings could fall apart in the turbulence). Carefully add the dumplings to the simmering stock, one at a time, and cook until they float to the surface, 3 to 4 minutes.

4 Ladle out the soup among eight warmed bowls and serve piping hot, topped with a sprinkling of parsley.

MISO SOUP *with* UDON NOODLES

YIELD: 4 SERVINGS / ACTIVE TIME: 20 MINUTES / TOTAL TIME: 35 MINUTES

Fans of Japanese food have undoubtedly tried miso soup, either prepared from miso paste and aromatized broth or in its instant version, which is ready in less than a minute and available in a variety of flavors. Miso paste, a savory and highly nutritional fermented soybean product, is available in many colors, thicknesses, and varieties. This recipe calls for red miso, which can be found in well-stocked supermarkets, natural food stores, and Asian markets. Along with soybeans, it also contains barley and other grains and is fermented longer, which yields rich, deep umami flavors, making it an ideal addition to hearty, sustaining soups as well as marinades for meat and poultry. If you cannot find red miso, you can substitute white miso. Made from soybeans and a high percentage of rice, it has a lighter, slightly sweeter taste but will approximate the flavor for this dish.

INGREDIENTS:

- ¾ pound fresh or frozen udon noodles, homemade (page 207) or store-bought
- 6 cups chicken or vegetable broth
- 3 tablespoons sake or rice wine
- 1 1½-inch piece fresh ginger, peeled and thinly sliced
- 4 medium cremini mushrooms, trimmed and thinly sliced
- 1 medium carrot, very thinly sliced at an angle
- 1½ tablespoons red miso paste
- 4 ounces silken tofu, cut into ½-inch cubes
- 1 bunch (5 to 6) scallions (dark green portion only), trimmed and thinly sliced lengthwise

1 Bring a large pot of water to a boil. When it's boiling, add the noodles and stir for the first minute to prevent any sticking. Cook until tender but still chewy, about 2 minutes. Drain and divide the noodles between four warmed soup bowls.

2 While the water is coming to a boil, combine the broth, sake, and ginger in a medium saucepan and bring to a boil over medium-high heat. Adjust the heat to medium-low and simmer for 5 minutes to let the flavors infuse. Using a strainer, remove the ginger slices and discard. Add the sliced mushrooms and carrot and simmer until the carrot just starts to soften, 4 to 5 minutes.

3 Put the miso in a small heatproof bowl and add ¼ cup of the hot broth. Stir until the miso dissolves and the liquid looks creamy, then pour it into the broth.

4 Warm up the tofu by placing it in a sieve and running a slow stream of hot tap water over it for 1 minute.

5 Divide the tofu among the soup bowls and ladle the hot broth on top. Serve piping hot, topped with the scallions.

SWEET *and* SOUR EGG DROP SOUP
with BLACK RICE NOODLES, MUSHROOMS, *and* TOFU

YIELD: 6 SERVINGS / ACTIVE TIME: 30 MINUTES / TOTAL TIME: 45 MINUTES

This tasty and nourishing soup, made more dramatic by the use of black rice noodles, may as well be an ancient doctor's curative. It combines the healing properties of chicken broth, the antiseptic qualities of vinegar, and the circulation-enhancing power of hot chile oil. Make a big pot, as the soup is even more delicious the following day.

1 Drain the tofu and cut into ½-inch cubes. Arrange them in a single layer on a paper-towel lined tray. Cover with paper towels and pat dry. Let them sit for 30 minutes, changing the paper towels after 15 minutes (to continue absorbing as much water as possible). Alternatively, use a tofu press, following the manufacturer's instructions, then cut into cubes.

2 While the tofu drains, bring a large pot of water to a boil and add the noodles. Cook according to the package instructions until tender but still chewy. Drain and rinse under cold water. Drain again, transfer to a medium bowl, and toss with ½ tablespoon of the sesame oil to prevent any sticking.

3 Heat a large skillet over low heat for 2 to 3 minutes. Add 1 tablespoon of sesame oil and turn the heat to medium. When the oil begins to swirl on the surface, add the garlic, ginger, sliced scallions, and a pinch of salt and cook until soft, stirring occasionally, about 5 minutes. Add the pork and break up any large pieces with a potato masher or wooden spoon. Cook, stirring occasionally, until the meat is no longer pink, 8 to 10 minutes. Add the broth and bring to a gentle boil. Add the tofu, mushrooms, vinegar, soy sauce, sugar, the remaining 1 tablespoon of sesame oil, and the chile oil if using and bring the soup back to a gentle boil over medium heat. Reduce the heat to a simmer, taste the soup, and adjust the seasoning with salt, sugar, or vinegar.

4 Whisk the eggs together in a small bowl until well blended. Slowly whisk them into the soup so they form strands. Bring the soup back to a simmer.

5 Divide the ramen among six warmed bowls and ladle the soup over it. Serve piping hot garnished with scallions pieces and toasted sesame seeds.

INGREDIENTS:

- 1 pound extra firm tofu
- 10 ounces black rice ramen noodles
- 2 ½ tablespoons toasted sesame oil, divided
- 3 garlic cloves, grated or minced
- 1 2-inch piece fresh ginger, peeled and grated or minced
- 6 scallions, trimmed and thinly sliced
- Salt
- ½ pound ground pork
- 8 cups chicken broth
- 8 medium cremini mushrooms, sliced
- ¼ cup rice vinegar or cider vinegar
- 3 tablespoons soy sauce
- 2 teaspoons sugar
- 1 tablespoon hot chile oil (optional)
- 2 large eggs
- 3 scallions, trimmed and cut into ¼-inch pieces for garnish
- Toasted sesame seeds for garnish

CHILEAN PASTA IN BROTH

YIELD: 4 TO 6 SERVINGS / ACTIVE TIME: 1 HOUR / TOTAL TIME: 1¼ HOURS

The sturdy flat pasta squares known as *pantrucas* are a beloved icon of Chilean home cooking and an invaluable food staple for the country's indigenous people, the Mapuche. Tasty and filling, this pasta dish differs based on where it is served in the country. In rural areas, *pantrucas* are made from wheat flour, water, and salt, boiled in water, and then pan-fried in a little oil. In more well to do urban areas, the dough includes eggs (which makes it incredibly pliable and easy to knead and roll by hand) and is served in a rich broth enriched with eggs yolks, Unlike most fresh pasta, *pantrucas* does not absorb much liquid when cooking.

1 Stir the flour and salt together in a large bowl. Add the lukewarm water, eggs, and oil and stir with a wooden spoon until the mixture starts to stick together. Switch to working the dough with your hands and knead it in the bowl until it becomes uniform, soft, and smooth in texture, about 10 minutes (the amount of water can vary, so add more, 1 teaspoon at a time, should the dough feel too dry).

2 Transfer the dough to a lightly floured work surface and roll it into a thick salami. Cut it into 10 medallions (the easiest way is to first cut the roll in half and continue cutting each piece in half until you have 10 pieces). Cover all the dough pieces with clear food wrap to prevent them from drying as you begin rolling out the piece of dough you are working with.

3 Shape the piece of dough into a ball and then, using the palm of your hand, flatten it into a round patty. Start rolling the dough with a lightly floured rolling pin, turning the patty 45 degrees with each roll, to ensure that it remains round. Once the dough has reached a thickness of ⅛ inch, cut the disc into strips 1½ inches wide, then cut the strips into 1½-inch pieces to create squares.

4 Arrange the pasta squares in a single layer on a lightly floured parchment paper-lined baking sheet so they don't touch. Once you run out of room on the sheet, cover the squares with another sheet of parchment paper, lightly dust with flour, and repeat. Repeat this process until all the dough is gone.

5 Whisk the egg yolks and 2 tablespoons water together in a small bowl. Set aside.

6 Bring the stock to a boil in a large pot. Taste for seasoning and add salt or pepper if needed. Once gently boiling, add the *pantrucas* and cook until tender yet chewy, about 10 minutes. Take the pot off the stove and add the whisked egg yolks. Stir well.

7 Ladle into soup bowls and serve piping hot topped with a sprinkle of fresh herbs.

INGREDIENTS:

- 2 cups all-purpose flour, plus more for dusting
- 1 teaspoon salt, plus more for seasoning
- ⅔ cup lukewarm water, or more if needed
- 2 large eggs
- 1 tablespoon vegetable oil
- 2 large egg yolks
- 2 tablespoons water
- 8 cups Capon or Chicken Stock (page 749)
- Freshly ground black pepper
- Handful chopped fresh cilantro, parsley, or chives for garnish

CURRY NOODLES *with* TOFU

YIELD: 4 SERVINGS / ACTIVE TIME: 30 MINUTES / TOTAL TIME: 45 MINUTES

This warming soup beautifully blends chewy noodles with the piquant flavor of red curry paste and the pleasant crunch of bean sprouts. This is an adaptation of a recipe from one of my favorite cookbooks, *Simple Thai Food* by Leela Punyaratabandhu. This version is vegetarian, though you can swap out the tofu for pieces of chicken breast if you are so inclined.

1 Drain the tofu and cut it widthwise into ½-inch-wide strips. Arrange them in a single layer on a paper-towel lined tray. Cover with paper towels and pat dry. Let them sit for 30 minutes, changing the paper towels after 15 minutes (to continue absorbing as much water as possible). Alternatively, use a tofu press, following the manufacturer's instructions, and then cut widthwise into ½–inch-wide strips.

2 Bring a large pot of water to a boil. While it comes to a boil, pick over the bean sprouts, discarding any discolored or spoiled ones. Put the remaining ones in a bowl of cold water. Discard the hulls that float to the top, then rinse them under cold water. Add the sprouts to the boiling water and cook for 2 minutes. Remove them from the water with a strainer and immediately run under cold water to stop them from cooking further. Drain well and set aside.

3 Bring the water back to a full boil and add the noodles. Cook until they are tender but still chewy, about 15 minutes. Drain, rinse the noodles under hot water to remove any starchy surface residue, and drain well again.

4 While the noodles are cooking, combine the oil, curry paste, and coconut cream in a large saucepan or Dutch oven over medium-high heat. Cook, stirring occasionally, for 3 to 4 minutes. Add the fish sauce, sugar, broth, and coconut milk, stir well, and bring to a simmer, 4 to 5 minutes. Add the curry powder and tofu and mix well. Turn the heat to low.

5 Divide the noodles evenly among four warmed soup bowls. Ladle over the piping hot soup, making sure everyone gets plenty of the tofu. Top with the bean sprouts and half an egg and serve. Offer the cilantro, peanuts, and shallots in bowls, along with the lime wedges, fish sauce, sugar, and red chile powder at the table for diners to add themselves.

INGREDIENTS:

1	pound extra-firm tofu
½	pound mung bean sprouts (about 4 cups)
½	pound dried rice sticks, 3 mm (about ⅛ inch) wide and 8 to 10 inches long
1	tablespoon shallot oil (page 747) or neutral oil of your choice
¼	cup red curry paste
3	tablespoons coconut cream (the thick layer at the top of a can of coconut milk; don't shake the can before opening it)
3	tablespoons fish sauce, plus more for serving
2	tablespoons light brown sugar
3	cups chicken broth
1½	cups unsweetened coconut milk
2	teaspoons curry powder

FOR SERVING:

2	medium-boiled eggs, peeled and cut in half
	Chopped fresh cilantro
	Minced peanuts
	Crispy Shallots (optional; page 747)
2 or 3	limes, cut into wedges
	Sugar
	Red Thai chile powder

UDON NOODLE SOUP
with BABY BOK CHOY, SHIITAKE MUSHROOMS, *and* POACHED EGGS

YIELD: 4 SERVINGS / ACTIVE TIME: 10 MINUTES / TOTAL TIME: 25 MINUTES

Soft, thick, almost slippery udon noodles lend their irresistible chewiness to this simple yet aromatic soup brimming with the earthy flavor of shiitake mushrooms and warming cinnamon. Try to use fresh udon noodles if at all possible, as their texture is unrivaled. The next best option is the frozen variety, which can be found in most well-stocked Asian supermarkets.

1 Bring the broth to a simmer in a large pot over medium-high heat. Add the star anise and cinnamon sticks, reduce the heat to low, and simmer for 10 minutes to infuse the broth with the flavor of the spices. Discard the spices.

2 Add the mushrooms to the simmering broth and stir.

3 Working quickly and with one egg at a time, crack it into a small bowl, then slide it into the broth. Cook for 2 minutes. Add the bok choy, gently pushing down to submerge them in the broth, being careful not to break the eggs. Cook for another 2 minutes, at which point the egg whites will be cooked. Cook for another minute or two if set yolks are desired.

4 While the broth is simmering, bring a large pot of water to a boil and add the noodles, stirring for the first minute to avoid any sticking. Cook until tender but still chewy, about 2 minutes. Drain and divide the noodles between four warmed soup bowls.

5 Take the pot off the stove and add the soy sauce and scallions. Stir gently to avoid breaking the eggs apart. Taste, adding more if needed.

6 Ladle the soup into the bowls, making sure each gets and egg and an even amount of the bok choy. Serve piping hot garnished with the sliced chiles.

INGREDIENTS:

- 8 cups chicken broth
- 3 star anise
- 2 cinnamon sticks
- 8 shiitake mushrooms, stems discarded and caps quartered
- 4 large eggs
- 4 baby bok choy, quartered lengthwise, then cut across into bite-size pieces
- 1 pound fresh or frozen udon noodles, homemade (page 207) or store-bought
- 6 tablespoons soy sauce
- 1 bunch (5 or 6) scallions, trimmed and thinly sliced
- 2 fresh red chiles, thinly sliced, for garnish

NORTH KOREAN COLD NOODLE SOUP

YIELD: **4 SERVINGS** / ACTIVE TIME: **35 MINUTES** / TOTAL TIME: **50 MINUTES**

Steaming summer days call for *mul naengmyun*, a salty and sweet soup made with buckwheat noodles and a cold, tangy broth topped with crisp cucumbers, pears, and even a few ice cubes for extra cooling. I have veered from tradition in this recipe by substituting the buckwheat noodles with noodles made from acorn flour. Koreans have been eating products made from the flour of ground red or white acorns flour since Neolithic times. One manifestation of this affinity for acorns comes to us in the form of *dotori guksu* or Korean acorn noodles. Made from a mixture of acorn flour, buckwheat or wheat flour, and salt, they are coarse and rustic-looking when dried, but turn smooth, nutty, subtly sweet, and wonderfully chewy once cooked and are terrific paired with a soup like *mul naengmyun*. Should you have a difficult time sourcing acorn noodles, feel free to use the less chewy but more readily Japanese soba noodles.

I have also bucked tradition by omitting *dongchimi* or "radish kimchi" juice from the broth, as it is a difficult ingredient to source. Finally, if you have access to an Asian market, consider purchasing a Korean radish. About 7 inches long, they are a light shade of green at their extremities and cream-colored in the middle, with a shiny skin. In comparison to their American counterparts, they are firmer and have a denser texture.

1 For the broth, combine the broth, vinegar, soy sauce, garlic, ginger, scallions, and sugar in a large stockpot and bring to a boil on medium heat. Once it's boiling, adjust the heat to low and simmer, uncovered, until it reduces by one quarter, about 30 minutes. Using a fine-meshed strainer, strain and let cool. Refrigerate until very cold, which will take at least an hour.

2 For the soup, put the cucumbers and radishes each in a medium bowl. Sprinkle each with ½ teaspoon each of the salt, sugar, and vinegar and toss to combine. Put the Asian pears in another medium bowl, sprinkle with the remaining ½ teaspoon salt and toss to combine. Let them all sit for 15 minutes.

3 Bring a large pot of water to a boil and add the noodles, stirring for the first minute to prevent any sticking. Cook until they are tender but chewy, 5 to 7 minutes. Drain, rinse under cold water, and drain again.

4 Divide the noodles among four bowls. Pour about 1¾ cups of the broth into each bowl. Add the crushed ice and arrange the radish, cucumber, egg halves, and pear toppings over the noodles. Sprinkle with sesame seeds and serve with the mustard on the side, for diners to add to taste.

INGREDIENTS:

BROTH:

- 8 cups beef broth
- ⅓ cup rice vinegar
- 1 ½ tablespoons soy sauce
- 2 garlic cloves, thinly sliced
- 1 2-inch piece fresh ginger, peeled and thinly sliced
- 4 scallions, trimmed and cut into ½-inch pieces on the diagonal
- 2 ½ tablespoons sugar

SOUP:

- 2 small cucumbers, peeled and cut into julienne
- ⅙ inch wide and 2 inches long
- ⅛ (about 6 ounces) of a Korean radish or 5 regular radishes, trimmed and very thinly sliced
- 2 small Asian pears, cut into julienne ⅙ inch wide and 2 inches long
- 1 ½ teaspoons salt, divided
- 1 teaspoon sugar
- 1 teaspoon rice vinegar
- ½ pound dotori guksu (Korean acorn noodles) or soba noodles
- 1 cup crushed ice
- 2 large hard-boiled eggs, peeled and sliced in half lengthwise
- Sesame seeds for garnish
- Korean mustard or other hot mustard as accompaniment

CHICKEN SOUP *with* CHICKEN MEATBALLS, FARFALLE, *and* SPINACH

YIELD: 8 SERVINGS / ACTIVE TIME: 35 MINUTES / TOTAL TIME: 1 HOUR

Here farfalle are paired with small, savory meatballs and vegetables to create a warming one-pot soup for the whole family.

1 Make the meatballs. Place the baguette pieces in a medium bowl and cover with water. Soak for 15 minutes, turning the pieces over twice. Squeeze as much of the liquid as possible from the bread and remove any hard pieces of crust that remain. Place the squeezed bread in a large bowl. Add the chicken, breadcrumbs, Parmigiano, tomato paste, parsley, eggs, and salt and pepper to taste. Mix well. The mixture should be rather firm and easy to shape. Form it into 45 to 50 half-inch balls.

2 Heat a large skillet over medium heat for 2 to 3 minutes, then add just enough oil to completely cover the bottom. Add the meatballs in a single layer (you'll have to cook them in batches) and cook until they are golden all over, 6 to 8 minutes. Transfer them to a paper towel-lined plate.

3 Prepare the leeks by trimming away the root ends and dark green leaves, keeping only the white and light green parts. With a sharp knife, lightly slice along the length of each leek to remove the two outer layers. Cut across into ¼-inch-thick rounds. Place them in a large bowl of water and swish them around to remove any dirt. Drain well, then transfer to a kitchen towel. Set aside.

4 Heat a large, heavy-bottomed pot over medium heat for 2 to 3 minutes. Add the olive oil and heat for a minute or two, then add the leeks, a couple pinches of salt, and pepper to taste. When the leeks start to sizzle, adjust the heat to low, cover, and cook, stirring occasionally, until very soft, about 15 minutes. Add the garlic and cook for another minute. Add the broth, carrots, and meatballs and bring to a gentle boil. Cook over medium-low heat for 15 minutes.

5 If you want to cook the farfalle right in the soup, add them now. But keep in mind that pasta can absorb a lot of liquid. Your other alternative is to cook them separately: bring a large pot of water to a boil. Once it's boiling, add salt (1 tablespoon for every 4 cups water) and stir. Add the pasta and stir for the first minute to prevent any sticking. Cook until it is tender but still

INGREDIENTS:

MEATBALLS:

	Half of a stale baguette, broken into pieces
1	pound ground chicken
½	cup soft breadcrumbs
1	cup freshly grated Parmigiano-Reggiano cheese
3	tablespoons tomato paste
	Handful fresh parsley leaves, chopped
3	large eggs
	Salt and freshly ground black pepper
	Peanut or grapeseed oil for frying

SOUP:

2	leeks
2	tablespoons extra virgin olive oil
	Salt and freshly ground black pepper
5	garlic cloves, thinly sliced
8	cups chicken broth
5	medium carrots, sliced into ½-inch-thick rounds
½	pound farfalle
2	handfuls baby spinach leaves, stems removed
¼	cup freshly grated Parmigiano-Reggiano cheese

chewy, 8 to 10 minutes. Drain. You have yet another choice; you can add them to the soup (where they will still absorb some of the broth—which does add flavor but will also make the cooked pasta soft) or you can add the pasta to each soup bowl and then top with the finished soup, storing any leftover pasta separate from the soup.

6 Either way, after the soup simmers for 15 minutes, remove from the heat and add the spinach and Parmigiano. Mix well. Let stand for 5 minutes to give the spinach leaves time to wilt and the Parmigiano time to melt into the soup. Give it another good stir, then ladle the soup into warmed bowls and dust with additional Parmigiano.

COCONUT CURRY CHICKEN NOODLE SOUP

YIELD: 4 SERVINGS / ACTIVE TIME: 30 MINUTES / TOTAL TIME: 45 MINUTES

I've always been a sucker for the combination of coconut milk and curry. So much so that my family has announced, well . . . demanded, a temporary moratorium on all coconut and curry dishes coming out of my kitchen. This recipe uses sambal oelek, Indonesia's favorite hot sauce. Made from a mixture of a variety of chile peppers and other seasonings, this dark red chile paste tends to add heat more than flavor; if you can't find it, substitute with sriracha (if you don't mind the inclusion of garlic, which it contains) or red pepper flakes. While the list of ingredients in this soup may seem eye-glazingly long, it's really just 20 minutes or so of prep work. A small price to pay for a bowlful of heaven.

1 Trim the top and base of the lemongrass stalk and use only the bottom 4 inches or so, as it is the most tender part. Peel off the dry or tough outer layer and then mince the tender inner core.

2 Bring a stockpot filled with water to a boil. While it comes to a boil, pick over the bean sprouts, discarding any discolored or spoiled ones. Put the remaining ones in a bowl of cold water. Discard the hulls that float to the top, then rinse them under cold water. Add the sprouts to the boiling water and cook for 2 minutes. Remove them from the water with a strainer and immediately run under cold water to stop them from cooking further. Drain well and set aside. Keep the water at a gentle simmer.

3 Heat a large skillet over medium-low heat for 2 to 3 minutes. Add the oil and turn the heat up to medium-high. When the oil begins to swirl on the surface, add the lemongrass, onion, ginger, and a pinch of salt and stir. When the mixture starts to gently sizzle, reduce the heat to low, cover, and cook, stirring occasionally, until softened, about 10 minutes (do not let it brown). Add the garlic and sambal oelek to the pan, stir, raise the heat to medium-high, and cook, stirring, until fragrant, about a minute. Add the chicken and a couple pinches of salt and stir-fry for 1 minute. Add the curry powder, stir to thoroughly coat the chicken with it, then add broth, coconut milk, cream, fish sauce, sugar, and turmeric if using and stir to combine. Bring to a boil, reduce the heat to low, and simmer until the chicken is completely cooked, 6 to 7 minutes.

INGREDIENTS:

1	stalk lemongrass
1	cup bean sprouts, plus more for serving
2	tablespoons safflower oil
1	small onion, minced
1	thumb-length piece fresh ginger, peeled and grated or minced
	Salt
2	garlic cloves, minced
1 to 2	teaspoons sambal oelek, to taste, plus more for serving
1	pound boneless, skinless chicken thighs, trimmed of any fat and cut into bite-size pieces
2 ½	tablespoons curry powder (preferably Malaysian)
4	cups chicken broth
11	4-ounce can unsweetened coconut milk
⅓	cup heavy cream
2 ½	tablespoons fish sauce
1 ½	tablespoons sugar, more to taste
½	teaspoon ground turmeric (optional)
½	pound long, thin dried rice or lai fun noodles
	Chopped fresh cilantro for serving
	Thinly sliced scallions for serving
	Fried Shallots for serving (optional; page 747)
	Lime wedges for serving

4 While the chicken is cooking, bring the pot of water back to a rolling boil, add the noodles, stir, and cook according to the package directions until they are tender but still chewy. Drain and rinse with hot water to remove any starchy surface residue. Drain well again.

5 Divide the hot noodles evenly among four warmed bowls. Ladle the piping hot soup over the noodles, being sure everyone gets an equal amount of the chicken. Top with a sprinkling of bean sprouts, cilantro, scallions, and fried shallots if using. Serve with lime wedges and additional sambal at the table.

CURRY

This recipe calls for Malaysian curry powder, which contains coriander seeds, cumin, fennel, chili powder, turmeric, clove, cinnamon, cardamom, and pepper. Many variations of curry powder exist to best complement an array of dishes. The assorted flavors in Malaysian curry powder will impeccably enrich this recipe.

PENICILLIN SOUP *with* EGG NOODLES
or MATZO BALLS

YIELD: 8 SERVINGS / ACTIVE TIME: 1 ¼ HOURS / TOTAL TIME: 2 HOURS

Whether you or your loved ones are sick, or whether you're just having one of those days where you wished you had stayed in bed, this soup can bring a smile to your face.

1 Prepare the stock. Remove the excess skin and fat from all chicken pieces. Heat a stockpot over medium heat for a few minutes and add the olive oil. As the oil heats, salt and pepper half of the chicken thighs. Once the oil begins to swirl, add them to the pan, skin side down. Adjust the heat so that you hear a happy sizzle. Cook for 5 minutes without moving them. Flip and cook the other side for another 5 minutes. Transfer the thighs to a platter. Repeat with the remaining thighs. Salt and pepper the chicken necks and add to the pot. Again, make sure you hear that happy sizzle. Cook for 5 minutes on one side, flip, and cook for another 5 minutes. Repeat this process with the chicken backs.

2 Add the vegetables and garlic to the pot and cook until browned, 12 to 15 minutes. Add ½ cup of the water and scrape up the browned bits from the bottom of the pot. Add all the chicken pieces back into the pot and the remaining water, along with the parsley, bay leaves, tomato paste, and peppercorns. Stir to mix in the tomato paste. Bring to a boil, then turn the heat down to a simmer. With a wide spoon, skim off the foam that comes up to the surface. Doing so will help create a nice, clear stock. Cook for 2 to 3 hours, depending on how much time you have. The longer you cook it, the more flavorful the stock becomes. Once cooled, strain the stock, using a large fine sieve, into another large stockpot. Separate the chicken meat from the bones and skin, then shred it.

3 Prepare the soup. Bring the stock to a low boil over medium heat. Add the chicken, carrots, and celery. Mix well. Cook until the carrots and celery are tender, about 15 minutes. Taste for seasoning and adjust by adding salt and pepper as necessary.

4 Place ½ cup of cooked egg noodles or two matzo balls into each warmed soup bowl. Ladle enough soup into almost fill the bowl, sprinkle with dill, and serve.

INGREDIENTS:

PENICILLIN STOCK:

- 5 pounds skin-on, bone-in chicken thighs (about 8 or 9)
- 12 chicken necks (or 4 chicken feet)
- 4 chicken backs
- 1 tablespoon olive oil
- Salt and freshly ground black pepper
- 3 stalks celery
- 2 medium carrots, cut into large pieces
- 1 leek, trimmed, washed well, and cut into pieces
- 1 medium yellow onion, sliced in half
- 3 garlic cloves, smashed and peel left on
- 3 quarts (12 cups) of water
- Handful fresh parsley, especially stems
- 2 bay leaves
- 3 tablespoons tomato paste
- 10 black peppercorns

SOUP:

- Shredded cooked meat from chicken used to make the stock
- 5 medium carrots, chopped into ¼-inch pieces
- 5 stalks celery, chopped into ¼-inch pieces
- Salt and freshly ground black pepper
- 4 cups warm cooked egg noodles or 16 matzo balls (page 263)
- Chopped fresh dill for garnish

INDONESIAN SPICY CHICKEN NOODLE SOUP

YIELD: 6 SERVINGS / ACTIVE TIME: 1 HOUR / TOTAL TIME: 1¼ HOURS

The rich, savory, fragrant Indonesian chicken soup known as *soto ayam* gives everyone a chance to enjoy the clear, herbal broth and chewy noodles while customizing a good number of garnishes, which are presented in small bowls in the middle of the table, for diners to add to their own liking.

1 Put the chicken breasts and thighs, salt, and 10 cups water in a large stockpot and bring to a boil over medium-high heat. Reduce the heat to medium and cook, uncovered, until the chicken is cooked through, 30 to 35 minutes. Transfer the chicken to a plate; when cool enough to handle, shred the chicken into thin strands and discard the bones. Reserve the shredded chicken and broth.

2 Place the vermicelli in a large bowl and add enough water to completely cover. Soak until tender but still chewy, 20 to 25 minutes. Drain, rinse under cold water, and drain again. Cut the noodles into 2- to 3-inch lengths and set aside.

3 Bring a medium saucepan of water to a boil. As it heats up, pick over the bean sprouts, discarding any discolored or spoiled ones. Put the remaining ones in a bowl of cold water. Discard the hulls that float to the top, then rinse them under cold water. Add the sprouts to the boiling water and cook for 1 minute. Remove them from the water with a strainer and immediately run under cold water to stop them from cooking further. Drain well and chop.

4 Trim the top and base of the lemongrass stalk and use only the bottom 4 inches or so, as it is the most tender part. Peel off the dry, tough outer layers and finely mince the tender inner core.

5 Put the jalapeños, ginger, garlic, lemongrass, shallots, coriander, turmeric, and 2 tablespoons water in a blender or mini food processor and process into a paste.

6 Heat a large, heavy-bottomed stockpot over medium-low heat for 2 to 3 minutes. Add the oil and turn the heat up to medium-high. Heat the oil for a couple of minutes, then add the flavor paste and sauté until fragrant, about 2 minutes. Pour the reserved broth through a fine-meshed sieve lined with cheese-

INGREDIENTS:

- **2 bone-in chicken breasts (about ¾ pound), skin removed**
- **2 bone-in chicken thighs (about ¾ pound), skin removed**
- **1½ tablespoons salt, plus more for seasoning**
- **10 cups + 2 tablespoons water**
- **¾ pound very thin rice vermicelli**
- **1½ cups mung bean sprouts**
- **1 stalk lemongrass**
- **2 jalapeño peppers, seeded and roughly chopped**
- **1 1-inch piece fresh ginger, peeled and roughly chopped**
- **3 garlic cloves, chopped**
- **4 shallots, roughly chopped**
- **¼ teaspoon ground coriander**
- **½ teaspoon turmeric**
- **2 tablespoons grapeseed or safflower oil**
- **2½ tablespoons fish sauce**
- **Juice of 1 juicy lime, 2 limes if on the dry side**
- **Freshly ground black pepper**

cloth into the pot and bring to a boil. Reduce the heat to low and simmer to let the flavors combine, about 15 minutes. Add the chicken, fish sauce, lime juice, and salt and pepper to taste, and simmer for 5 minutes. Taste for seasoning and add more salt and pepper if needed.

7 Place the garnishes in small bowls on the table. Divide the noodles among the six bowls and ladle the hot broth over the top. Serve immediately and let each guest assemble their soup to their taste.

FOR SERVING:

Handful fresh cilantro leaves, chopped

1 bunch (5 to 6) scallions, trimmed and sliced on the diagonal into ½-inch pieces

1 jalapeño pepper, seeded and cut into thin half-moon slices

3 hard-boiled eggs, halved lengthwise

½ recipe Crispy Shallots (page 747)

PASTA SOUP *with* CANNELLINI BEANS *and* MUSSELS

YIELD: 4 SERVINGS / ACTIVE TIME: 45 MINUTES / TOTAL TIME: 1¼ HOURS

This soup is inspired by a beloved dish in southern Italy, *pasta e fagioli co le cozze* or "pasta with beans (legumes) and mussels." To be ideal, it is said that the dish needs to be made from 50 percent mussels, 25 percent pasta, and 25 percent cannellini or borlotti (cranberry) beans and generously flavored with garlic, olive oil, white wine, plenty of red pepper flakes, and, if desired, only sun-kissed tomatoes. I have veered away from tradition by adjusting the amount of mussels and pasta in the dish, respectively decreasing and increasing them, and by turning the dish into a soup instead of the *"pastasciutta"*-like offering consisting of cooked pasta and sauce. Some southern Italian renditions use chickpeas, and you are certainly welcome to follow suit. I prefer the subtler flavor of the cannellini beans myself. If you can find wild-caught mussels, use them as they are much more flavorful than their farmed counterparts (though they will be more time-consuming to clean).

Recommended pasta shapes: cavatelli, ditalini, small ridged shells, short tubular pasta

INGREDIENTS:

- 8 very ripe plum tomatoes OR 1 15-ounce can diced tomatoes, with their juice
- 2 cups dry white wine
- 2 pounds mussels
- 1 15-ounce can cannellini beans, rinsed well and drained
- 2 tablespoons extra virgin olive oil
- 1 medium white onion, finely diced
- Salt
- 3 medium cloves garlic, minced
- 1 teaspoon red pepper flakes
- 1 tablespoon fish sauce
- 6 cups chicken or vegetable broth
- Leaves from 1 sprig fresh rosemary, chopped (reserve the stem)
- Freshly ground black pepper
- ½ pound pasta
- Handful fresh parsley leaves, chopped

1   If using plum tomatoes, bring a medium saucepan of water to a boil. Blanch the tomatoes in the boiling water for 1 minute. Use tongs to remove them to a cutting board and let cool until you can handle, then remove their skins. Cut them into quarters, remove the seeds, and finely chop. Set aside.

2   Bring the wine to a boil in a small saucepan and continue to boil until reduced almost by half (this will concentrate its flavor, including its acidity and sweetness), about 5 minutes. Remove from the heat and set aside.

3   Bring 2 cups of water to a boil in a large stockpot. Scrub the mussels under cold water, carefully cutting off any little fuzzy "beards" at the pointed ends. Add the mussels to the pot, cover, and turn the heat down to medium. They will quickly begin to open with the heat. As they do, pluck them out with tongs and transfer to a large bowl. When all the mussels have opened (discard the few that remain closed), strain the steaming liquid through a paper towel-lined fine-meshed strainer and reserve (you should have 1½ to 2 cups). Separate the meat of the mussels from shells, transferring the meat to a small bowl and

discarding the shells. Rinse and dry the stockpot and return to the burner.

4 Put the beans in a medium bowl and, using a potato masher, press down on them until approximately half of the beans are mashed. Set aside.

5 Heat the same stockpot over medium heat for 2 to 3 minutes. Add the olive oil and heat for a minute or two. Once it begins to swirl on the surface, add the onion and a couple pinches of salt and stir. Once the onion begins to sizzle, adjust the heat to low, cover, and cook, stirring occasionally, until very soft, about 20 minutes.

6 Add the garlic and pepper flakes, turn the heat up to medium-high, and cook until fragrant, about 1 minute. Stir in the fish sauce and cook for another minute to blend in the flavor. Add the broth, beans, tomatoes, rosemary stem, and the reserved mussel broth and stir. Taste for seasoning and add salt and/ or pepper if needed. Bring to a gentle boil, then add the pasta and stir. Cook the pasta according to package instructions until tender but chewy. Add the reserved mussel meat and stir until heated through.

7 Ladle into shallow soup bowls and serve with a good crack of pepper and the chopped rosemary and parsley sprinkled over the top.

SICILIAN SEAFOOD SOUP
with COUSCOUS

YIELD: 6 SERVINGS / ACTIVE TIME: 30 MINUTES / TOTAL TIME: 1 HOUR

Sicilian food has a strong Arab influence. In this traditional seafood soup, that cultural imprint is reflected by the addition of couscous and saffron threads, which are essentially the pollen-producing reproductive organ of the mercurial and high-maintenance crocus flower. One of the most revered of spices, saffron adds remarkable depth of flavor to any dish with its pungent, floral quality. Fortunately for us, while saffron is very expensive, we don't need much of it to add its unmistakable essence to a dish. The reason for its high price stems from the unreliable yields of the crocus flower and the extensive labor associated with its harvest (it takes 150 flowers to produce a single gram of saffron threads). When purchasing saffron, look for an Iranian or Spanish origin. While many believe Iranian saffron to be the best, it is difficult to find and typically prohibitively expensive for mere mortals. Spanish saffron is generally easier to find and slightly less expensive. Divided into grades, Spanish saffron comes in four main designations: coupe, superior, Rio, and La Mancha. Coupe is considered the best, as it contains the highest amount of crocin, one of the key essential oils in saffron, and is predictably the most expensive of the four. One final note about saffron: Don't buy it ground as it is often mixed with less expensive spices like turmeric and paprika.

The key to this soup is to make an intensely flavored base and then to add the seafood and cook it until just tender. I like to serve this accompanied by grilled slices of crusty Italian bread that have been rubbed lightly with fresh garlic and drizzled with olive oil. Heaven in a bowl. Finally, I don't add the couscous to the soup until I plate it because, if all of the soup is not consumed right away, the couscous will soak up a lot of the broth, turning it into more of a stew than a soup.

INGREDIENTS:

- **6** very ripe plum tomatoes OR 1 15-ounce can diced tomatoes with their juice
- **2** cups dry white wine
- **1** pound mussels
- **1** pound cleaned calamari
- **3** tablespoons extra virgin olive oil
- **1** medium yellow onion, minced
- **3** pale green inner celery stalks, minced
- Handful chopped fresh parsley, plus more for serving
- **1** teaspoon fish sauce
- Salt
- **1** medium zucchini, halved lengthwise and cut into ¼-inch-thick half-moons
- **2** tablespoons tomato paste
- **2** garlic cloves, minced
- **6 ½** cups seafood stock
- **¼** teaspoon Iranian or Spanish saffron threads, crumbled by hand
- **1** dried red chile pepper, broken into pieces
- Freshly ground black pepper
- **¾** pound medium shrimp, peeled and deveined
- **½** pound swordfish steak, cut into ¾-inch pieces
- **6** cups plain couscous, cooked according to package instructions and kept warm

1 If using plum tomatoes, bring a medium saucepan of water to a boil. Blanch the tomatoes in the boiling water for 1 minute. Use tongs to remove them to a cutting board and let cool until you can handle, then remove their skins. Cut them into quarters, remove the seeds, and roughly chop.

2 Bring the wine to a boil in a small saucepan and continue to boil until reduced almost by half (this will concentrate its flavor, including its acidity and sweetness).

3 Bring 2 cups of water to a boil in a large stockpot. Scrub the mussels under cold water, carefully cutting off any little fuzzy "beards" at the pointed ends. Add the mussels to the pot, cover, and turn the heat down to medium. They will quickly begin to open with the heat. As they do, pluck them out with tongs and transfer to a large bowl. When all the mussels have opened (discard the few that remain closed), strain the steaming liquid through a paper towel-lined fine-meshed strainer and reserve (you should have 1½ to 2 cups). Separate the meat of the mussels from the shells, transferring the meat to a small bowl and discarding the shells. Rinse and dry the stockpot and return to the burner.

Rinse the calamari under cold water. Cut the bodies across into ½-inch rings and cut the tentacles in half lengthwise.

4 Heat the stockpot over medium heat for 2 to 3 minutes. Add the olive oil and heat for a minute or two. Once it begins to swirl on the surface, add the onion, celery, parsley, fish sauce, and a couple pinches of salt and stir. Once the vegetables begin to sizzle, adjust the heat to low, cover, and cook, stirring occasionally, until very soft, about 20 minutes. Add the reduced wine and increase the heat to medium-high. Bring to a boil and cook, stirring frequently, until it reduces by a third, about 5 minutes. Add the tomatoes, zucchini, tomato paste, garlic, and 1 teaspoon salt, and stir. Cook, stirring occasionally, until the tomatoes and zucchini have softened, 5 to 6 minutes. Add the stock, saffron, chile, a couple pinches of salt, and pepper to taste and stir. Taste for seasoning and add more salt and/or pepper if needed.

5 Bring to a boil. Once it's boiling, reduce the heat to low and add the shrimp, swordfish, and calamari. Carefully ladle some of the soup on top of the seafood, cover the pot, and cook until the seafood has changed color and feels firm but not hard when pricked with a fork, about 10 minutes. After about 5 minutes, add the mussels to the pot. Shake the pot from time to time to prevent the sauce from sticking to the bottom (you don't want to stir at this point because you would risk breaking up the swordfish).

6 Divide the hot couscous among six warmed bowls and ladle the soup on top. Serve piping hot with a good crack of black pepper.

CURRY SHRIMP LAKSA

YIELD: 6 SERVINGS / ACTIVE TIME: 20 MINUTES / TOTAL TIME: 40 MINUTES

This Southeast Asian noodle soup (you can find versions of it in Singapore, Malaysia, the Philippines, and elsewhere) features a fantastic blend of creamy, spicy, sweet, and salty. The basis of it is flavor paste that I like to make from scratch but is also available ready made (sold as laksa paste) in most well-stocked Asian markets and online. Not surprisingly, homemade tastes best. Thankfully, most of its ingredients are easily procurable or have satisfying substitutes. Galangal, a rhizome similar in appearance to ginger with a piney flavor, may be the most challenging to find. Most often, if it's not available fresh, you'll find it in your Asian grocer's freezer.

1 Prepare the laksa paste. Put the chiles, galangal, ginger, garlic, turmeric, scallions, coriander, lemongrass, salt, and water in a blender or food processor and pulse into a smooth paste, adding more water, 1 teaspoon at a time, as needed to help the machine do its work. Transfer to a small bowl and stir in the oil.

2 Prepare the soup. Trim the top and base of the lemongrass stalks and use only the bottom 4 inches or so of each. Peel off the dry or tough outer layers and slice the inner core into ½-inch-thick pieces.

3 Bring a stockpot filled with water to a boil. While it comes to a boil, pick over the bean sprouts, discarding any discolored or spoiled ones. Put the remaining ones in a bowl of cold water. Discard the hulls that float to the top, then rinse them under cold water. Add the sprouts to the boiling water and cook for 2 minutes. Remove them from the water with a strainer and immediately run under cold water to stop them from cooking further. Drain well and set aside. Keep the water at a gentle simmer.

4 Heat a large skillet over medium heat for 2 to 3 minutes. Add the bok choy, two pinches of salt, and water and stir. When the water starts to boil, cover, and let steam for 2 minutes. Remove from the heat and set aside.

5 Heat another large skillet or a Dutch oven over medium-low heat for 2 to 3 minutes. Add ⅓ cup of the peanut oil and turn the heat to medium-high. When the oil begins to swirl on the surface, add the garlic, shallots, ginger, and a pinch of salt and stir. When the mixture sizzles, reduce the heat to low, cover, and cook, stirring occasionally, until very soft, about 15 minutes.

INGREDIENTS:

LAKSA PASTE:

6 dried Thai bird chiles, soaked in water to cover for 1 hour, drained, and roughly chopped (seeds removed for more moderate heat)

1 2-inch piece galangal, peeled and cut into small pieces

1 2-inch piece fresh ginger, peeled and cut into small pieces

4 garlic cloves, peeled

1 1-inch piece fresh turmeric, peeled, or 1 tablespoon ground turmeric

3 or 4 scallions, trimmed and roughly chopped

2 teaspoons ground coriander

1 stalk lemongrass, rough outer layers discarded, tender inner core cut into small pieces

1 teaspoon salt

3 tablespoons water, more if needed

1 tablespoon grapeseed or safflower oil

SOUP:

1/3 cup + ½ tablespoon peanut or grapeseed oil

3 garlic cloves, minced

5 large shallots, minced

6 Raise the heat to medium, add the laksa paste, and stir until very aromatic, about 1 minute. Add the lemongrass and cinnamon sticks, stir, and cook for 5 minutes. Add the broth, coconut milk, fish sauce, and salt and white pepper to taste and stir to combine. Bring to a boil, reduce the heat to medium-low, cover, and cook until all the flavors have sufficiently blended, about 15 minutes.

7 While the soup is simmering, bring the pot of water back to a rolling boil, add the noodles, and cook according to the package instructions until they are tender but chewy. Drain and transfer them to a medium bowl. Add the remaining ½ tablespoon peanut oil, toss well (this prevents the noodles from sticking together), and set aside.

8 Add the shrimp to the soup and cook until they are opaque and cooked through, about 5 minutes.

9 Divide the rice noodles among warmed bowls and place the bok choy on top of them. Ladle the piping hot soup over both, making sure everyone gets an equal amount of shrimp. Top with the bean sprouts and garnish with mint and fried shallots if using. Serve with lime wedges and sambal oelek at the table.

Half thumb-size piece fresh ginger, peeled and grated or minced

2 stalks lemongrass

2 cinnamon sticks

3 cups unsweetened coconut milk

8 cups chicken broth

2 tablespoons fish sauce

1 pound rice noodles

1 pound medium shrimp, peeled and deveined

Freshly ground white pepper

3 cups mung bean sprouts

Salt

¼ cup water

FOR SERVING:

¼ cup fresh mint leaves

Crispy Shallots (optional; page 747)

2 limes, quartered

Sambal oelek or sriracha for serving

PASTA E FAGIOLI

YIELD: 8 SERVINGS / ACTIVE TIME: 30 MINUTES / TOTAL TIME: 1 ¼ HOURS

In my heart of hearts, I must not be an engineer's daughter but an offspring of some hard-working, calloused-hand peasant because I consider this sort of traditional, rustic pasta and bean dish almost spiritual sustenance. There's nothing fancy about it, I'll grant you, and yet, with proper preparation and seasoning, it can be elevated to savory and satisfying heights. Ironically, *pasta e fagioli,* or *pasta fazool,* as it is sometimes referred to in Neapolitan dialect, has a prominent role in many Italian-American restaurants in the United States, while in Italy it is considered too simple a fare to be served to guests and is reserved for everyday, no-nonsense, nourishing family meals. Because it is a classic recipe, it varies greatly based on the region or town in which it is prepared. Sometimes *pasta e fagioli* has a soup consistency while other times it's more like a stew. I like it best as a soup, and hope you enjoy my rendition. It is almost exactly like the one my mother makes, though I have taken to adding a rind of Parmigiano for extra depth of flavor.

Recommended pasta shapes: ditalini, tubettini, conchigliette

1 If using dried beans, pick them over and discard any misshapen beans and stones. Place them in a large bowl and cover by 3 inches with water. Soak overnight. The next day, rinse the beans, drain, and place in a large stockpot. Add water to cover, the bay leaf, and ½ onion and bring to a boil over high heat. Add 1 tablespoon of salt and stir. Boil for 2 minutes, then remove from the heat, cover, and let stand for 1 hour. Discard the bay leaf and onion and drain. Rinse under cold water, drain again, and set aside.

2 Heat a large pot or Dutch oven over medium heat for 2 to 3 minutes. Add the olive oil, turn the heat up to medium-high, and heat for a minute or two. As the oil heats, blot the sparerib pieces with paper towels to absorb as much surface moisture as possible (it will help them to brown better). Salt and pepper them right before adding them to the pot. Once the oil begins to swirl on the surface, add the pancetta and sparerib pieces. Cook, turning the spareribs over every couple of minutes, until they are golden caramel, 6 to 8 minutes total. Transfer the spareribs to a plate. Lower the heat to medium.

INGREDIENTS:

- 1 ½ cups dried cannellini beans or 3 15-ounce cans cannellini beans, drained and rinsed
- 1 bay leaf, if using dried beans
- ½ onion, if using dried beans
- Salt
- 2 tablespoons extra-virgin olive oil, plus more for drizzling
- 1 pound pork spareribs, cut into 4 pieces along the bones
- 4 ounces pancetta or bacon, finely chopped
- Freshly ground black pepper
- 1 medium onion, minced (about 1 cup)
- 1 medium celery stalk, minced (about ⅔ cup)
- 3 medium carrots, chopped into ¼-inch pieces
- 3 medium garlic cloves, thinly sliced
- 3 oil-packed anchovy fillets
- 1 28-ounce can peeled whole tomatoes (preferably San Marzano), with their juices, crushed very well by hand
- 1 piece Parmigiano-Reggiano cheese rind, about 4 x 3 inches (optional)
- 6 ½ cups chicken broth
- ½ pound pasta
- ¼ cup chopped fresh parsley
- 1 cup freshly grated Parmigiano-Reggiano cheese

Add the onion, celery, carrots, and a couple pinches of salt, stir, and cook, stirring occasionally, until the vegetables begin to gently sizzle. Stir, cover, and cook, stirring occasionally, until the vegetables are very soft, about 20 minutes.

3 Add the garlic and anchovies and cook, stirring constantly, until fragrant and the anchovies dissolve, about 1 minute. Add the tomatoes and their juices and a couple pinches of salt and scrape up any browned bits from the bottom of the pot. Increase the heat to medium-high and add the cheese rind, beans, broth, and ½ teaspoon salt and bring to a boil. Reduce the heat to low and cook, stirring occa-

sionally, until the flavors blend together, about 45 minutes. Discard the cheese rind. Add the cooked spareribs back to the pot.

4 Add the pasta and cook until tender but still chewy, about 10 minutes (refer to the package instructions to better estimate pasta cooking time). Remove the pot from the heat and taste for seasoning. Add salt and/or pepper if needed.

5 Ladle the soup into warmed soup bowls. Serve piping hot, topped with a drizzle of olive oil, the parsley, and Parmigiano (or pass the grated cheese at the table).

PISAREI PASTA *and*
CRANBERRY BEAN SOUP

YIELD: 6 SERVINGS / ACTIVE TIME: 25 MINUTES / TOTAL TIME: ABOUT 1 HOUR

Nearly every region of Italy has its own tasty version of pasta and beans. In Emilia-Romagna, especially in the area around Piacenza, they turn their own rendition up a notch by making it with a fresh local pasta called *pisarei,* which are curled, almost dumpling-like pasta nubs, and creamy cranberry beans (also known as *borlotti* in Italian and as *fasö* in the local dialect), for a soup known simply as *pisarei e fasö.* The role of the *pisarei* pasta is so important that, in yesteryear, young women were assessed for marriage suitability based on the calluses on their right thumb, which was used in its preparation.

Other recommended pasta shapes or dumplings: orecchiette, cavatelli

1 Mince the *lardo* with the rosemary leaves to form a paste.

2 Heat a large pot or Dutch oven over low heat for 2 to 3 minutes. Add the *lardo* paste and turn the heat to medium. Once it's melted and slightly sizzling, add the onion, celery, and two pinches of salt, and cook, stirring a few times, until tender, 5 to 6 minutes (you do not want to brown the onion). Add the wine and cook until half of it has evaporated. Add the soaked beans, tomatoes, carrots, broth, nutmeg, cloves, a few pinches of salt, and bay leaf, stir well, raise the heat to medium-high, and bring to a boil. Adjust the heat down so the liquid is just simmering and cook until the beans are tender, about 45 minutes.

3 Raise the heat back up to medium-high, add the *pisarei,* Parmigiano, and parsley, stir, and cook until the pasta is heated through, about 6 minutes.

4 Ladle the soup into warmed soup bowls and top with a few good cracks of pepper and a sprinkling of Parmigiano (or pass the grated cheese at the table).

INGREDIENTS:

- ½ pound lardo (cured fatback) or pancetta
- Leaves from 2 sprigs fresh rosemary
- 1 medium yellow onion, chopped
- 2 tender celery stalks, chopped
- Salt
- 1 cup red wine
- 2 ½ cups dried cranberry beans, soaked in water overnight and drained
- 2 cups strained tomatoes or pureed chopped tomatoes
- 2 medium carrots, cubed
- 4 quarts (16 cups) beef broth or Mixed Meat Stock (see page 750)
- ¼ teaspoon freshly grated nutmeg
- 5 whole cloves
- 1 bay leaf
- 1 recipe Pisarei (page 249)
- 1 ¼ cups freshly grated Parmigiano-Reggiano cheese, plus more for serving
- Handful fresh parsley leaves, chopped
- Freshly ground black pepper

SPICY PORK, BABY KALE,
and SHIITAKE MUSHROOM SOUP

YIELD: 4 TO 5 SERVINGS / ACTIVE TIME: 30 MINUTES / TOTAL TIME: 30 MINUTES

Chock-full of vegetables and fragrant ground pork, this soup is almost as restorative as chicken noodle soup and makes a flavorful one-pot meal when the only medicine one needs is a full belly.

1 Place the dried noodles in a large bowl, cover with cold water, and let soak for 30 minutes.

2 While the noodles are soaking, heat the oil in a medium saucepan over medium-high heat until the surface is swirling but it is not yet smoking. Add the garlic, ginger, three quarters of the scallions, and a pinch of salt and stir. Once the mixture begins to sizzle, reduce the heat to low, cover, and cook, stirring occasionally, until soft, about 10 minutes.

3 Add the pork and another couple pinches of salt and raise the heat to medium-high. Break the meat up with a potato masher or wooden spoon and mix well so that aromatics are completely mixed with the meat. Cook until the meat is no longer pink, 8 to 10 minutes. Add the black bean paste and mix well. Add the broth, soy sauce, fish sauce, rice wine, and mushrooms. Bring to a gentle simmer and taste for seasoning, adding a little salt if necessary.

4 Drain the noodles in a colander and shake out as much excess water as possible. Gently separate any noodles sticking together with your fingers. Add them to the soup and bring the soup back to a gentle simmer. Add the kale, stir well, and take the pot off the heat. Let sit until the kale wilts, about 2 minutes.

5 Ladle the soup into warmed soup bowls and serve piping hot, garnished with the remaining scallions and cilantro leaves.

INGREDIENTS:

½ pound dried wide bánh *phở* rice sticks or flat rice noodles no wider than ¹⁄₁₆ inch

2 tablespoons peanut or grapeseed oil

4 garlic cloves, grated or minced

1 2-inch piece fresh ginger, peeled and grated or minced

8 scallions, trimmed and thinly sliced, divided

Salt

1 pound ground pork

¼ cup black bean chili paste

8 cups chicken broth

¼ cup soy sauce

2 teaspoons fish sauce

2 teaspoons Shaoxing rice wine or dry sherry

½ pound shiitake mushrooms, stems removed and caps thinly sliced

3 cups baby kale leaves

Chopped fresh cilantro for garnish

CAO LAU NOODLES
with SPICED PORK

YIELD: 6 SERVINGS / **ACTIVE TIME:** 1 HOUR / **TOTAL TIME:** 2 ½ HOURS, PLUS MARINATING TIME, AT LEAST 3 HOURS

Thick rice noodles, moist pork slices, and crispy bean sprouts make up one of Vietnam's most iconic dishes. Known as *cao lau*, it originates from the town of Hoi An in central Vietnam. The traditional dish uses *char siu* pork, a popular Cantonese method of preparing barbecued pork that yields meat with a sweet, shiny glaze, and dried *cao lau* noodles, which function like crunchy croutons. These noodles are the star of the show and what makes this dish unique to Hoi An. Made from the water of a specific well in the town and the alkalizing ash of a specific tree that grows on the Cham islands, off the coast of Hoi An, they are considered a local treasure and the recipe is protected like an ancient secret. About all the townspeople will definitely share with foreigners is that the noodles are steamed and not boiled.

This particular version takes a few liberties. The pork is not barbecued but braised until lusciously moist and tender, and it swaps out the squares of fried dough for easy to procure wonton wrappers. It's a satisfying mixture of textures and savory flavors that is sure to please. Serve with extra herbs, chiles, and lime and let everyone customize their own bowls.

1 Prepare the pork. Trim the top and base of the lemongrass stalks and use only the bottom 4 inches or so of each. Peel off the dry, tough outer layers and mince the inner core. Put in a large shallow bowl and mix together with the shallots, soy sauce, fish sauce, chile sauce, sugar, salt, cinnamon, cloves, peppercorns, and fennel seeds. Add the pork shoulder and toss to coat with the mixture. Cover and chill for at least 3 hours or preferably overnight. Remove the pork, scraping any excess marinade back into the bowl; reserve the marinade.

2 Heat a large heavy-bottomed pot or Dutch oven over medium-low heat for 2 to 3 minutes. Add the oil, raise the heat to medium-high, and let heat for a minute. When the surface of the oil begins to swirl, add the pork, turning occasionally, until nicely browned all over, about 12 minutes total. Transfer to a plate and set aside. Add the garlic and cook, stirring continuously, until fragrant but not at all colored, about 30 seconds. Add the water and reserved marinade, stir together, and bring to a boil. Add the browned pork, return the liquid to a boil, then reduce the heat to low. Cook, partially covered, turning the pork pieces over

INGREDIENTS:

PORK:

2 lemongrass stalks

3 medium shallots, minced

3 tablespoons soy sauce

1 ½ tablespoons fish sauce

1 tablespoon hot chile sauce (such as sambal oelek or sriracha)

2 teaspoons sugar

1 ½ teaspoons kosher salt

⅛ teaspoon ground cinnamon

⅛ teaspoon ground cloves

⅛ teaspoon ground Sichuan peppercorns or black peppercorns

⅛ teaspoon fennel seeds

2 pounds boneless pork shoulder, cut into 2 pieces

2 tablespoons grapeseed or safflower oil

4 garlic cloves, minced

4 cups water

TO FINISH:

8 3-inch wonton wrappers, cut into quarters

⅓ cup grapeseed or safflower oil

Salt

2 cups mung bean sprouts

1 pound thick, dried wide rice noodles

occasionally, until fork-tender but not falling apart, 1 to 1½ hours. Remove from the heat and let the pork cool in its liquid. The pork can be braised up to 2 days in advance (just cover and refrigerate).

3 Prepare the fried wonton wrappers (you will need to work in batches here). Heat a small skillet over medium-low heat for 2 to 3 minutes. Add the oil, raise the heat to medium-high, and let heat for a minute. When the surface of the oil begins to swirl, fry just enough wonton wrappers to fit in a single layer in the skillet. Cook until golden brown, about 30 seconds per side. Transfer to a paper towel-lined plate and sprinkle with salt. If you need to stack the fried wontons, separate them with paper towels. The wontons can be fried up to 5 days ahead. Let cool completely and store in an airtight container at room temperature.

4 Pick over the bean sprouts, discarding any discolored or spoiled ones. Put the remaining ones in a bowl of cold water. Discard the hulls that float to the top, then rinse them under cold water. Drain well and set aside.

5 Remove the pork from the braising liquid and cut into ⅛-inch-thick slices. Bring the braising liquid to a boil and add ⅔ cup water. Taste for seasoning; the flavor should still be concentrated and lightly salty. Simmer until the liquid begins gently boiling again, about 2 minutes. Remove from the heat and add the pork slices back in.

6 Bring a large pot of water to a boil. Add the noodles and cook according to the package directions until they are tender but still pleasantly chewy. Drain (reserving the cooking water), run under cool water, and drain again.

7 Divide the noodles among six warmed soup bowls. Place the bean sprouts in a large sieve and lower it in the noodle cooking water for 30 seconds. Drain well and divide among the bowls. Put several slices of pork on top of the noodles. Ladle some of the braising liquid over everything. Top with crispy wontons, a few slices of the pepper, a lime wedge, and a sprinkling of both herbs. Offer the hot sauce for diners to add their own.

1 **Fresno or jalapeño pepper, seeded and thinly sliced, for garnish**

1 **lime, cut into 6 wedges, for serving**

Handful fresh cilantro leaves for garnish

Handful fresh Thai or regular basil leaves for garnish

Hot chile sauce (such as sambal oelek or sriracha) for serving

UDON NOODLES *with* PORK *and* SHIITAKE MUSHROOMS

YIELD: 4 SERVINGS / ACTIVE TIME: 30 MINUTES / TOTAL TIME: 45 MINUTES

This recipe is a slight adaptation from one of my favorite Asian food blogs, *Woks of Life* (I know . . . what a great name!). It is unbelievably tasty, especially when you consider the limited number of ingredients it has, and comes together quickly enough to become a trusted and nourishing weeknight meal.

1 Cut the tenderloin into small, bite-sized strips. Transfer to a medium bowl, sprinkle with the cornstarch and salt and pepper to taste, and drizzle over 1 tablespoon of the oil. Mix well, until all the pieces of pork are coated with the cornstarch, seasonings, and oil.

2 Combine the broth, dashi, 1 tablespoon of the soy sauce, and the ginger in a large saucepan and bring to a simmer over medium heat. Cover, adjust the heat to low, and let continue to simmer as you prepare the rest of the dish.

3 Heat a wok or large skillet over medium-low heat for 2 to 3 minutes. Add the remaining 2 tablespoons oil and turn the heat to medium-high. Heat the oil until it begins to swirl on the surface, then add the garlic and cook, stirring frequently, until the cloves begin to crisp up on the outside, 2 to 3 minutes. Transfer the garlic to a medium bowl.

4 Add the pork strips in a single layer to the pan and turn the heat up to medium-high. Don't move the pieces for 2 minutes, so they brown nicely on one side, then stir-fry until they turn a golden color and feel firm all the way through, 4 to 5 minutes. Transfer the pork to the same bowl as the garlic. Tent loosely with aluminum foil to keep warm.

5 Add the mushrooms to the pan and cook, stirring occasionally, until just tender, 4 to 5 minutes. Stir in the mirin and remaining tablespoon soy sauce and cook for another minute. Return the pork and garlic to the pan and stir.

6 Right before you start to stir-fry, put a large pot of water on to boil. When it's boiling (and while you're stir-frying), add the noodles and stir for the first minute to avoid any sticking. Cook until tender but still chewy. Drain.

7 Divide the noodles among four warmed soup bowls. Divide the pork and mushroom mixture among the bowls, then ladle over the simmering broth. Serve piping hot, garnished generously with the scallions.

INGREDIENTS:

- 1 pound pork tenderloin
- 1 tablespoon cornstarch
- Salt and freshly ground black pepper
- 3 tablespoons grapeseed or safflower oil, divided
- 4 cups chicken broth
- 4 cups Dashi (page 751)
- 3 tablespoons soy sauce, divided
- 1 1-inch piece fresh ginger, cut into 6 thin slices
- 5 garlic cloves, smashed
- Salt and freshly ground black pepper
- 8 shiitake mushrooms, stems discarded and caps thinly sliced
- 2 ½ tablespoons mirin
- ¾ pound fresh or frozen udon noodles, homemade (207) or store-bought
- 1 bunch (5 or 6) scallions (white and green parts only), trimmed, thinly sliced lengthwise, then cut across into 2-inch lengths

AROMATIC BEEF SOUP
with HAND-PULLED NOODLES

YIELD: 4 SERVINGS / ACTIVE TIME: 35 MINUTES / TOTAL TIME: 4 ½ HOURS

Street vendors in Taiwan start selling this delicious soup the moment the weather turns cold. It's an easy job since you can smell its enticing fragrance a mile away. You can purchase Taiwanese noodles from well-stocked Asian markets, though flat egg noodles work just as well, or make your own.

1 Bring a stockpot filled with water to a boil. Blanch the tomatoes in the boiling water for 1 minute. Use tongs to remove them to a cutting board; keep the water boiling. Let the tomatoes cool so you can handle them, then remove their skins. Cut them into quarters, remove the seeds, and mince.

2 While waiting for the tomatoes to cool, add the noodles to the boiling water and cook until tender but chewy, 1 to 2 minutes. Drain, transfer to a bowl, add 1½ tablespoon of the peanut oil, and toss well (this prevents the noodles from sticking together). Set aside.

3 This step is optional but it helps yield a clearer broth. Bring a medium pot of water to a boil. Turn the heat off, add the beef shank, and soak for 10 minutes. Rinse the beef under cold water and pat dry with paper towels.

4 Heat a large pot over medium-low heat for 2 to 3 minutes. Add the remaining 1 tablespoon peanut oil and raise the heat to medium-high. When the oil begins to swirl on the surface, add the tomatoes, garlic, scallions, ginger, star anise, and a couple pinches of salt and stir. Cook until fragrant, stirring a few times, about 3 minutes. Add the black bean sauce, stir, and cook for 1 minute. Season the beef with salt and pepper and immediately add to the pot. Cook, undisturbed, until lightly browned, about 3 minutes. Turn and brown the other side. Add the soy sauce, stir, and cook for 3 minutes. Add the rice wine, carrots, and sugar and stir. Add enough broth to almost cover the soup ingredients in the pot and bring to a boil. Reduce the heat to low, cover, and simmer until the beef is falling apart tender, 2 ½ to 3 hours.

5 When you're just about ready to serve, heat a skillet over medium heat for 2 to 3 minutes. Add the quartered bok choy, two pinches of salt, and the water and stir. Once the water starts to boil, cover and let steam until you can easily pierce the root end of the bok choy with a knife, 2 to 3 minutes. Remove from the heat.

6 Divide the noodles and bok choy among four large warmed soup bowls. Ladle the soup on top (this will instantly reheat the noodles). Serve piping hot, accompanied by the chile oil for drizzling.

INGREDIENTS:

- 3 plum tomatoes
- ¾ pound flat egg noodles or 1 recipe Taiwanese Hand-Pulled Noodles (page 209)
- 1 ½ tablespoons peanut or grapeseed oil, divided
- 1 ½ pounds boneless beef shank, cut into 1-inch-thick pieces
- 5 garlic cloves, minced
- 4 scallions, sliced ¼ inch thick
- Half thumb-sized piece fresh ginger, peeled and grated or minced
- 2 star anise
- Salt
- 1 ½ tablespoons fermented black bean sauce
- Freshly ground black pepper
- ⅓ cup soy sauce
- ¼ cup Shaoxing rice wine or dry sherry
- 3 medium carrots, sliced at an angle into ⅛-inch-thick rounds
- 3 tablespoons sugar
- Beef or chicken broth, enough to cover soup ingredients in pot (about 2 ½ to 3 quarts)
- 6 baby bok choy, quartered lengthwise
- ¼ cup water
- Hot chile oil for serving

BEEF *and* LEEK UDON
NOODLE SOUP

YIELD: **4 SERVINGS** / ACTIVE TIME: **40 MINUTES** / TOTAL TIME: **50 MINUTES**

Hot and steamy comfort food in a bowl, this soup combines tender pieces of beef, leeks, and slippery udon noodles with the distinctive oceany essence of dashi broth, one of the culinary cornerstones of Japanese cuisine. This simple soup is topped with a tasty, eye-catching garnish called *narutomaki,* which can be found in the frozen section of well-stocked Asian markets. It is a cured seasoned fish paste that has been colored and rolled into a log such that, when you cut it across into slices, you end up with a beautiful pink spiral. Its name derives from that fact that the spiral calls to mind the whirlpools found in the Naruto Strait between Awaji Island and Shikoku in Japan.

1 Combine the dashi, 1 teaspoon of the sugar, and 1 tablespoon each of the mirin and soy sauce in a medium saucepan, mix well, and bring to a boil over medium heat. Taste the soup for seasoning, adding salt if needed. Reduce the heat to low and cover.

2 Wrap the meat in clear food wrap and put in the freezer for 20 minutes (this will make it easier to slice). Cut into the thinnest possible slices, then into bite-size pieces.

3 Trim away the root ends and dark green leaves of the leeks, keeping only the white and light green parts. With a sharp knife, cut each leek in half lengthwise and remove the two outer layers. Cut the halves vertically into thin slivers. Place them in a large bowl of water and swish them around to remove any dirt. Drain well, then transfer to a kitchen towel. Set aside.

4 Bring a large pot of water to a boil, add the noodles, and stir for the first minute to avoid any sticking. Cook until tender but still chewy, about 2 minutes. Drain and divide the noodles between four warmed soup bowls.

5 While the water is coming to a boil, heat a large skillet over low heat for 2 to 3 minutes. Add the oil and turn the heat to medium. When it begins to swirl on the surface, add the leeks and cook, stirring occasionally, until tender and slightly golden, about 10 minutes.

INGREDIENTS:

4   cups Dashi (page 751)

1   tablespoon + 1 teaspoon sugar

2   tablespoons mirin, divided

2   tablespoons soy sauce, divided

    Salt

1   pound top sirloin, tender petite medallions, or beef tenderloin

2   leeks

1   pound fresh or frozen udon noodles, homemade (page 207) or store-bought

2   tablespoons safflower oil

    Freshly ground black pepper

    Thin slices narutomaki for garnish

    Thinly sliced scallions for garnish

    Chopped fresh parsley for garnish

    Shichimi togarashi (Japanese 7-spice blend) for garnish

6 While the leeks cook, rub the meat pieces in paper towels to absorb as much surface moisture as possible (this will help them brown better). When the leeks are ready, raise the heat to medium-high, sprinkle the meat pieces with salt and pepper, and add them to the skillet. Cook, turning once, until the pieces are nicely browned on all sides, 3 to 4 minutes total. Add the remaining 1 tablespoon each sugar, soy sauce, and mirin and stir to combine. Continue to cook, stirring occasionally, until the sauce has caramelized and slightly thickened, 5 to 7 minutes. Remove from the heat.

7 Ladle the hot soup over the udon noodles in the bowls and place the meat and leeks on top. Arrange a few slices of *narutomaki* on each bowl, garnish with scallions and parsley, and serve with the *shichimi togarishi* in a small bowl for diners to sprinkle over their soup as they like.

MIRIN

In this recipe, mirin, a sweet rice wine, is used to balance out the saltier soy sauce. If you are unable to find or purchase mirin, you can substitute it for dry sherry, dry white wine, vermouth, or rice vinegar. If you replace the mirin, add ½ teaspoon of sugar per tablespoon of the substitute to create that same sweetness.

PHỞ

YIELD: 8 SERVINGS / ACTIVE TIME: 1 HOUR / TOTAL TIME: 5 ½ HOURS

This classic soup consisting of broth, *bánh Phở* rice noodles, fresh herbs, and thinly sliced meat is served in Vietnam at any time of the day, even breakfast. The best *Phở* vendors have long lines and sell out by 11 in the morning. One of the prerequisites for top-notch pho is its deeply flavored and intoxicatingly aromatic stock. Pre-cooking the meat and bones prior to making the stock goes a long way toward ensuring that the stock, like French consommé, is crystal clear.

1 Preheat the broiler, positioning the top rack as close as you can get it to the heating element. Put the onions and ginger on a parchment paper-lined baking sheet and broil until lightly blackened on all sides, turning the pieces every 30 seconds or so for even cooking; it should take about 3 minutes all together. (You can also do this on a grill, if you prefer.) Remove from the oven and when cool enough to handle, remove and discard all the burnt skin.

2 Place the beef shin and chuck in a large pot and add water to cover. Bring to a boil and cook for 20 minutes. Drain in a colander and thoroughly wash the pot. While this boiling is an extra step, I highly recommend it because it produces a much lighter and cleaner stock (in other words, no gunk). Once the meat and bones are cool enough to handle, rinse them under cold water, wiping away any debris or surface scum.

3 While the beef is cooling, toast the spices. Put the cloves, star anise, cinnamon stick, and fennel seeds in a small skillet over medium-low heat and toast until fragrant, 3 to 4 minutes, shaking the pan several times. Transfer them to a piece of cheesecloth and tie into a bundle.

4 Add 4 quarts fresh water to the pot and bring to a boil. Add the meat and bones, onions, ginger, toasted spice sachet, scallions, fish sauce, sugar, and salt and stir. Bring to a boil over high heat, then reduce the heat to low and simmer for 1½ hours, skimming the surface as needed to remove any fat and foam. Remove the piece of beef chuck to a small plate, tent with aluminum foil, and set aside. Once cooled, you can refrigerate until ready to use.

5 Continue to simmer the stock for at least another 3 hours, skimming any fat and foam as necessary. It should have a

INGREDIENTS:

SOUP:

2   small onions, cut in half

1   2-inch piece fresh ginger, cut in half lengthwise

4   pounds beef shin, some meat attached

1   pound boneless beef chuck

8   cloves

6   star anise

1   cinnamon stick

2   teaspoons fennel seeds

5   scallions, trimmed and cut into 4-inch lengths

¼   cup fish sauce

2 ½ tablespoons sugar

1   tablespoon salt

¾   pound dried bánh phở rice noodles or dried flat rice noodles no wider than ⅛ inch

⅓   pound beef eye round, slightly frozen, then sliced paper-thin against the grain

FOR SERVING:

Fresh cilantro leaves

Fresh basil leaves (preferably Thai or holy basil)

Thinly sliced fresh chiles

Thinly sliced scallions

Mung bean sprouts

Lime wedges

Sriracha

deep, highly spiced flavor; in fact, it should taste so good that you would happily drink it right then and there without adding any further ingredients. Strain through a fine-meshed strainer and discard the solids. Taste again and fine-tune, if necessary, by adding salt, sugar, and/or fish sauce.

6 While the stock simmers, prepare the noodles by soaking them in room temperature water until they are pleasantly chewy, 20 to 30 minutes. (If the noodles are much thicker than 1/8 inch, the soaking technique will not work and they will need to be cooked in plenty of boiling water like Italian pasta, though without added salt.) Drain the noodles and rinse to remove any starch. If not using them right away, cover and refrigerate. When ready to use, rinse under cold water if you find they are sticking together.

7 Slice the beef chuck into thin slices and the eye round into the thinnest possible slices.

8 *Phở* is the ultimate do-it-yourself meal. You can present all the elements on a platter or in individuals bowls for each diner to take as much or as little to put in their bowl— the noodles (if you made them ahead and they're cold, that's fine), slices of cooked beef chuck and raw beef round, fresh herbs, chiles, scallions, and bean sprouts. Noodles should go into the bowl first, topped with the beef. Bring the stock to a rolling boil, then ladle it directly into the bowls; it will cook the raw beef and reheat the noodles on contact. Diners can garnish their soup as they prefer. Have lime wedges and sriracha on hand for a final shot of flavor.

STIR-FRIES
& OTHER
NOODLE DISHES

*G*reater than the sum of their parts, stir-fries offer a satisfying sizzle at the stove and an endless variety of flavors, colors, textures and aromas on the plate. A perfect conduit for a parade of vegetables, meats, seafood, and starches, they fill the belly in the most savory and satisfying of ways—even when you don't have enough of any one ingredient to do the job. Best of all, once all the chopping and prepping is done, each satisfying dish comes together quickly and effortlessly.

SESAME SOBA NOODLES

YIELD: 4 SERVINGS / ACTIVE TIME: 25 MINUTES / TOTAL TIME: 30 MINUTES

These make a tasty side dish, brightly flavored with fresh herbs and the red pepper offering a bit of crunch. Many versions are served chilled, perfect for steamy summer days. This variation is more of a year-round offering, meant to be enjoyed even when snow blankets the ground. Soba noodles are made from buckwheat flour and offer a unique toasty, nutty flavor, though you can substitute whole wheat linguine if you can't find them.

1 Bring a large pot of water to a boil and add the noodles, giving them a good stir to ensure they all go under water. Once the water returns to a boil, reduce the heat just enough to keep the water at a very gentle boil. Cook until they are tender but still chewy, 4 to 5 minutes. Drain and immediately rinse thoroughly with cold water to stop the cooking process and remove excess starch. Drain again, place in a medium bowl, and toss with the grapeseed oil (this prevents the noodles from sticking together).

2 Heat a wok or large skillet over medium heat for 2 to 3 minutes. Add the sesame oil and turn the heat to medium-high. Heat the oil until it begins to swirl on the surface, add the noodles and toss continuously to heat them through. Add the sesame seeds, herbs, and red pepper and toss to thoroughly mix. Taste for seasoning, adding salt and pepper if necessary, toss again, and serve.

INGREDIENTS:

¾ **pound soba noodles**

½ **tablespoon grapeseed oil**

2 **tablespoons toasted sesame oil**

2 **tablespoons sesame seeds (preferably black)**

Handful fresh cilantro leaves, chopped

Handful fresh parsley leaves, chopped

½ **small red bell pepper, seeded and diced**

Salt and freshly ground black pepper

"RISOTTO-STYLE" RICE STICK NOODLES
with BEAN SPROUTS *and* CRISPY SHALLOTS

YIELD: 5 TO 6 SERVINGS / ACTIVE TIME: 30 MINUTES / TOTAL TIME: 40 MINUTES

Simple and rustic, this noodle dish breaks with the traditional approach of cooking the noodles separately and then combining them with their seasoning. Instead, the rice stick noodles are added directly to the broth and end up absorbing all of its flavor with super savory results. As a bonus, you will only need to use one pot. I particularly love the dish's subtle molasses-like flavor, which it acquires from the Indonesian *kecap manis*. Also known as sweet soy sauce or *ketjap manis*, it is thick, dark-hued, and syrupy sweet, from the generous addition of palm sugar. If you cook Asian food infrequently and don't want to invest money and shelf space on a bottle, you can approximate the flavor of *kecap manis* by combining ¼ cup soy sauce and ⅔ cup light brown sugar.

INGREDIENTS:

1 ½ cup mung bean sprouts

2 tablespoons grapeseed or safflower oil

4 garlic cloves, chopped

¼ cup soy sauce

4 cups unsalted chicken or vegetable broth

2 tablespoons kecap manis (sweet soy sauce)

1 teaspoon toasted sesame oil

½ teaspoon salt

Freshly ground white pepper

1 pound dried rice stick noodles

½ recipe Crispy Shallots (page 747)

1 Pick over the mung bean sprouts, discarding any discolored or spoiled ones. Transfer them to a bowl of cold water and discard the hulls that float to the top, then rinse them under cold water. Drain well and set aside.

2 Heat a wok or large skillet over low heat for 2 to 3 minutes. Add the oil and let it warm for 1 minute, then add the garlic and cook until aromatic, about 1 minute. (You don't want it to sizzle when it hits the pan. If it does, immediately remove the pan from the heat and, using a slotted spoon, push the garlic to the side and away from the source of the heat. Return to the heat once the oil has cooled and stopped sizzling.) Add the soy sauce and turn the heat to medium-high. Once it begins to sizzle, add the broth, *kecap manis,* sesame oil, salt, and white pepper to taste and stir to combine. Once the broth begins to boil, add the rice stick noodles, stirring continuously the first minute to prevent any sticking. Stir the noodles frequently as they cook in the broth (the broth will begin to disappear as it is absorbed by the noodles). Continue cooking until the noodles are tender but pleasantly chewy, 10 to 12 minutes.

3 Add the bean sprouts and toss well to combine with the noodles.

4 Divide the noodles among warmed shallow bowls and serve piping hot sprinkled with the shallots.

SOY *and* SCALLION NOODLES

YIELD: 6 SERVINGS / ACTIVE TIME: 15 MINUTES / TOTAL TIME: 25 MINUTES

Topped with crunchy flash-fried scallions, this vegetarian Taiwanese noodle dish known as *cong you ban mian* can be made in just about the same time it takes to order take-out. I like to top mine with sunny-side-up eggs for extra sustenance. This recipe calls for light soy sauce, also known as "fresh," "pure bean," or "thin" soy sauce, which can be found in most well-stocked Asian markets next to regular soy sauces. Despite its "light" designation, which reflects its lighter color, it is much saltier than regular soy sauce and consequently needs to be used sparingly.

INGREDIENTS:

- 3 bunches (5 to 6 per bunch) scallions
- 1 recipe Ding Ding Chao Mian Noodles (page 213)
- ¼ cup + ½ tablespoon peanut or grapeseed oil
- Salt
- 2 tablespoons dark soy sauce
- 1 tablespoon light soy sauce or 1 ½ tablespoons regular soy sauce
- 1 ½ teaspoons sugar

1 Julienne the scallions. Trim the root end and the top 1 inch of the green part of each scallion and remove the outermost layer. Rinse to remove any dirt, then pat dry. Slice each scallion into 3 to 4 pieces approximately 2 inches in length. Cut each piece in half lengthwise, then place both halves cut side down on a cutting board, and cut lengthwise again into thin, even slivers. Set aside.

2 Bring a large pot of water to a boil and add the noodles. Stir for the first minute to prevent any sticking. Reduce the heat to a gentle boil. Cook according to the recipe directions until tender but chewy, 3 to 4 minutes. Drain and rinse well under cold water to remove surface starch. Drain and transfer to a medium bowl. Drizzle with ½ tablespoon of the peanut oil (to prevent the noodles from sticking), toss, and cover to keep warm.

3 Heat a wok or large skillet over low heat for 2 to 3 minutes. Add the ¼ cup peanut oil and turn the heat to medium-high. When the oil begins to swirl on the surface, add the scallions and a couple pinches of salt and cook, occasionally stirring, until their edges begin to turn golden brown, 4 to 5 minutes. Transfer half the scallions to a small bowl and tent loosely with aluminum foil to keep warm.

4 Add both soy sauces and the sugar to the remaining scallions in the pan, turn the heat to low, and cook, stirring a few times, until mixture starts to bubble, 2 to 3 minutes. Add the noodles, turn the heat to medium-high, and toss until warmed through.

5 Divide the noodles among five or six warmed shallow bowls. Serve piping hot topped with the reserved scallions.

HOT OIL NOODLES

YIELD: 4 SERVINGS / ACTIVE TIME: 20 MINUTES / TOTAL TIME: 35 MINUTES

A rugged culinary ensemble typical of northern China, where wheat-based noodles, garlic, black vinegar, and dried chiles dominate, this one-pot vegetarian dish comes together easily and quicker than ordering take-out. It may seem a little unusual, since all it requires is adding some smouldering hot oil to cooked noodles, blanched vegetables, and a few seasonings. And yet, like a little miracle, it comes together into a simple yet delicious and filling meal that is not at all oily. Known as *you po mian,* it gets most of its intense flavor from raw garlic, one of the few power-packed flavoring agents used in northern China. If your love for garlic is less emphatic, feel free to scale back to 1 or 2 cloves. Also, any wide, dried wheat or egg "ribbon"-style Chinese noodle you find at your local Asian market will work nicely.

INGREDIENTS:

- 1 bunch (5 or 6) scallions
- 1 pound baby spinach
- ¾ pound fresh, frozen, or dried Chinese egg noodles, homemade (page 204–205) or store-bought
- 3 garlic cloves, minced
- 1½ tablespoons light soy sauce (also sold as "fresh," "pure bean," or "thin" soy sauce)
- 1 tablespoon dark soy sauce
- 2 teaspoons Chinese black vinegar (see page 446)
- Red pepper flakes
- 2 handfuls fresh cilantro leaves, chopped
- 7 tablespoons peanut or grapeseed oil

1 Julienne the scallions. Trim the root end and the top 1 inch of the green part of each green onion and remove the outermost layer. Rinse to remove any dirt, then pat dry. Slice each scallion into 3 to 4 pieces approximately 2 inches in length. Cut each piece in half lengthwise, then place both halves cut side down on a cutting board, and cut lengthwise again into thin, even slivers. Set aside.

2 Bring a large pot of water to a boil and add the spinach. Blanch for 30 seconds and remove with a strainer or large slotted spoon. Drain well and let cool enough so you can squeeze the spinach by the handful to remove as much water as possible from their leaves. Place them in a large heatproof bowl. Now add the noodles to the boiling water. Cook according to the package instructions until tender but still chewy. Drain and transfer them to the bowl with the spinach. Quickly add the scallions, garlic, both soy sauces, vinegar, red pepper flakes to taste, and the cilantro and toss well. Tent loosely with aluminum foil to keep warm.

3 Heat the oil in a small saucepan over medium heat until it starts to swirl on the surface. Carefully pour the hot oil over the bowl of noodles and vegetables and toss well. Serve piping hot.

GARDEN SESAME NOODLES

YIELD: 6 SERVINGS / ACTIVE TIME: 15 MINUTES / TOTAL TIME: 30 MINUTES

Few other Chinese dishes are as synonymous with take-out as sesame noodles. The irony is that it is so easy to prepare and so much more delicious when homemade, and it only takes about 15 minutes of prep. It makes a perfect light dinner when the heat of summer starts to take over and heavy, rich dishes lose their appeal. Should you not have Chinese sesame paste on hand, which is made from ground toasted seeds and oil, you can substitute tahini, which is made from untoasted sesame seeds and oil (just add a teaspoon of additional sesame oil to make up for any loss of toasted flavor). Finally, you can also swap out the Chinese egg noodles for flat, wide rice noodles for a gluten-free version.

1 Bring a large pot of water back to a boil. Add the noodles and stir for the first minute to prevent any sticking. Cook until tender but still chewy, 2 to 3 minutes. Drain and transfer the noodles to a large bowl. Add ½ tablespoon of the sesame oil and toss well (this prevents the noodles from sticking together).

2 Put the sesame paste and peanut butter in a small bowl. Add the soy sauce, vinegar, remaining 2 tablespoons sesame oil, sugar, chili-garlic sauce, ginger, and garlic and whisk together until smooth. Taste for seasoning and adjust the flavors according to your preference.

3 Add the sauce to the noodles and toss until well distributed. Arrange the noodles in a swirled knot in six bowls and top with the pepper slivers, cucumber slices, and snow peas. Garnish with the peanuts, sesame seeds, and scallions and pass a small bowl of chili-garlic sauce at the table.

INGREDIENTS:

- 1 pound fresh, frozen, or dried Chinese egg noodles, homemade (page 204-205) or store-bought
- 2 ½ tablespoons toasted sesame oil, divided
- 2 tablespoons Chinese sesame paste or tahini
- 1 ½ tablespoons smooth peanut butter
- ¼ cup soy sauce
- 2 tablespoons rice vinegar
- 1 tablespoon light brown sugar
- 2 teaspoons chili-garlic sauce (optional, or more or less depending on heat preference), plus more for serving
- 1 2-inch piece fresh ginger, peeled and grated or minced
- 2 garlic cloves, minced
- 1 yellow or orange bell pepper, seeded and cut into very thin strips
- 1 medium cucumber, peeled, seeded, and very thinly sliced
- 1 cup snow peas, trimmed
- ½ cup chopped roasted peanuts
- 2 tablespoons toasted black or regular sesame seeds
- 1 bunch (5 or 6) scallions (white and light green parts only), trimmed and sliced on the diagonal into ½-inch pieces

SOBA NOODLE STIR-FRY
with VEGETABLES

YIELD: 4 SERVINGS / ACTIVE TIME: 20 MINUTES / TOTAL TIME: 30 MINUTES

You don't need a side of vegetables with this savory soba noodle dish. Of course, this versatile stir-fry is just as satisfying with Chinese egg noodles and rice noodles, but I think soba's nutty flavor lends an additional welcomed dimension to the savory vegetables.

1 Combine the seasoning sauce ingredients in a small bowl.

2 Bring a large pot of water to a boil. When it's boiling, add the noodles and stir for the first minute to prevent any sticking. Cook until they are tender but chewy, 5 to 7 minutes. Drain, rinse under cold water, drain again, and place in a large bowl. Toss with the sesame oil to keep them from sticking.

3 Heat a wok or large skillet over medium heat for 2 to 3 minutes. Turn the heat to medium-high and add the grapeseed oil. When it begins to swirl on the surface, add the onion, carrots, asparagus, mushrooms, and salt. Stir-fry until the vegetables are tender and slightly colored, 4 to 5 minutes. Lower the heat to medium, add the garlic and pepper flakes if using and stir-fry until fragrant, about 1 minute. Add the soba noodles and edamame and continue to toss until heated through. Add the seasoning sauce and toss well.

4 Divide the noodles and vegetables among four warmed plates and serve immediately.

INGREDIENTS:
SEASONING SAUCE:

- ¼ cup soy sauce
- 3 tablespoons water
- 1 ½ tablespoons rice vinegar
- 2 teaspoons toasted sesame oil

STIR-FRY:

- ½ pound soba noodles
- 1 teaspoon toasted sesame oil
- 3 tablespoons grapeseed or safflower oil
- 1 medium yellow onion, thinly sliced into half-moons
- 2 medium carrots, peeled and cut into julienne ⅙ inch wide and 2 inches long
- 1 pound asparagus, ends trimmed, sliced on the diagonal into ¼-inch pieces
- 6 medium shiitake mushrooms, stems removed and caps cut into ⅙-inch-thick slices
- 1 teaspoon salt
- 2 garlic cloves, minced
- 1 teaspoon red pepper flakes or hot sauce (optional)
- ⅓ cup cooked shelled edamame

KOREAN NOODLES
with GOCHUJANG SAUCE

YIELD: 4 SERVINGS / ACTIVE TIME: 30 MINUTES / TOTAL TIME: 50 MINUTES

Simultaneously spicy, sweet, and tangy, *jjolmyeon* features one of the most popular noodles in Korea by the same name. Made from wheat flour and starch, the noodles are very elastic and chewy and fairly challenging to substitute for (a thick rice noodle is your best option). Found in the frozen noodle section of well-stocked Asian markets, the noodles need to be pried apart and separated under cold running water before adding them to boiling water. These unique noodles, combined with the sweet and savory sauce and refreshing vegetable toppings, create one of the most addictive bowls of noodles around. The main ingredient of the sauce is *gochujang*, a thick, sticky hot red chile paste that also contains fermented soybeans, salt, glutinous rice, and occasionally sweeteners. It adds a spicy and very concentrated flavor to the sauce (heat levels can vary between brands, so always taste it before deciding how much of it to add). This light and refreshing dish is particularly appealing on hot summer days.

1 Whisk all the sauce ingredients together in a medium bowl until smooth.

2 Bring a large pot of water to a boil.

3 While the water comes to a boil, pick over the bean sprouts, discarding any discolored or spoiled ones. Put the remaining ones in a bowl of cold water. Discard the hulls that float to the top, then rinse them under cold water. Add the sprouts to the boiling water and cook for 1 minute. Remove from the water with a strainer (you will use the water again to cook the noodles next) and immediately run them under cold water to stop them from cooking further. Drain well and set aside.

4 Add the *jjolmyeon* noodles to the boiling water and cook according to the package directions until tender but chewy, 3 to 5 minutes. Drain, rinse under cold water as you simultaneously rub down the noodles with both hands to eliminate excess starch (rinse for about 1 minute since these noodles are very starchy and tend to stick together), and drain completely.

5 Divide the noodles among four shallow bowls and then artfully arrange the sprouts, cabbage slivers, the julienned cucumber and carrots, and an egg half on top. Finally, add a few dollops of the sauce and serve.

INGREDIENTS:

SAUCE:

6 tablespoons rice vinegar

5 tablespoons water

¼ cup sugar

3 to 4 tablespoons gochujang (Korean red pepper paste), according to heat preference

2 tablespoons gochugaru (Korean red pepper flakes) or red pepper flakes

2 tablespoons toasted sesame oil

2 tablespoons toasted sesame seeds

3 garlic cloves, grated or minced

2 teaspoons salt, more to taste

TO ASSEMBLE:

2 cups mung bean sprouts

1½ pounds frozen jjolmyeon noodles, separated under cold running water

¼ of a 2-pound red cabbage, cored and thinly sliced

1 large cucumber, peeled and cut into julienne ⅛ inch wide and 2 inches long

2 medium carrots, peeled and cut into julienne ⅛ inch wide and 2 inches long

2 large hard-boiled eggs, cut in half lengthwise

HAKKA NOODLES *with* VEGETABLES

YIELD: 4 SERVINGS / ACTIVE TIME: 35 MINUTES / TOTAL TIME: 1 HOUR

Hakka noodles reflect the cuisine of the Hakka Chinese, a people from the provinces of Guangdong, Jiangxi, Guangxi, Sichuan, Hunan, and Fujian. Centuries ago they emigrated in large numbers to various parts of the world, and in particular to the area in India around Kolkata, a city that would come to be known as the Chinatown of India. The combination of local Bengali flavors and the simple, rustic Hakka approach towards cooking, which emphasizes an abundance of vegetables and sparse flavoring over expensive meats and oozy sauces, gave birth to what we now know as "Hakka noodles." This simple and flavorful dish consists of egg noodles that are stir-fried with a variety of vegetables. It makes a great one-dish meal. You have a lot of latitude in the choice of vegetables. I used scallions, green beans, mushrooms, carrots, celery, and red bell pepper, but you are free to substitute any of the vegetables except the scallions, which are a must. Once the vegetables are prepped, this satisfying meal comes together in minutes.

INGREDIENTS:

- ½ pound Hokkien noodles (round, fairly thick egg noodles are a good substitute)
- 2 ½ tablespoons peanut or grapeseed oil, divided
- 3 garlic cloves, minced
- 2 fresh red Thai bird chiles, minced (seeds removed for more moderate heat)
- 1 bunch (5 or 6) scallions, trimmed and thinly sliced, divided
- 4 ounces green beans, trimmed and thinly sliced across at an angle
- ½ pound cremini mushrooms, trimmed and sliced
- 1 medium carrot, julienned
- 1 celery stalk, thinly sliced
- 1 red bell pepper, seeded and cut into thin strips
- 2 tablespoons soy sauce
- ½ teaspoon rice vinegar
- Salt

1 Bring a large pot of water to a boil. Add the noodles, stirring for the first minute to prevent sticking. Cook according to the package instructions until they are tender but chewy. Drain and rinse under cold water to stop them from further cooking. Drain well, place in a medium bowl, and toss with ½ tablespoon of the oil to prevent sticking. Cover and set aside.

2 Heat a wok or large skillet over medium heat for 2 to 3 minutes. Add the remaining 2 tablespoons oil and heat until it begins to swirl on the surface. Add the garlic and chiles and cook, stirring, for 1 minute. Add two thirds of the scallions and the green beans and raise the heat to medium-high. Stir-fry for 2 to 3 minutes. Add the mushrooms, carrot, celery, and bell pepper and stir-fry until the vegetables begin browning slightly on the edges, about 4 minutes.

3 Add the soy sauce, vinegar, and salt to taste and stir. Add the noodles and toss well. Cook for a minute or two, until heated through.

4 Divide the noodles among four warmed shallow bowls. Serve piping hot, topped with the remaining scallions.

LO MEIN NOODLES
with MUSHROOMS *and* SNOW PEAS

YIELD: 4 SERVINGS / ACTIVE TIME: 20 MINUTES / TOTAL TIME: 35 MINUTES

Shiitake mushrooms add heft to this, but feel free to add a half pound of cubed tofu or some shredded leftover rotisserie chicken along with the mushrooms to make the dish even more substantial. While this book offers a recipe for homemade egg noodles, you can also use the fresh, frozen, or dried variety that can be found at your local Asian market. All three types will require boiling in water. Uncooked fresh or frozen noodles will need 30 to 60 seconds of boiling to become pleasantly chewy, while dried versions, usually sold as Hong Kong-style egg noodles, take a few minutes. Drain, rinse under cold water, and drain again before throwing them into your stir-fry. Be sure not to overcook any of these noodles because they will lose their chewy texture once they are also stir-fried. If you can find them, pre-cooked fresh lo mein noodles are sometimes available in the refrigerated section of some Asian markets and will be clearly labeled as such (you don't want to risk boiling precooked noodles or you'll end up with a mushy mess). People find the precooked version very convenient because they eliminate the need to boil them, making whipping up a weeknight meal particularly convenient.

INGREDIENTS:

- 1 bunch (5 or 6) scallions
- ¾ pound fresh, frozen, or dried Chinese egg noodles, homemade (page 204) or store-bought
- ½ tablespoon + 2 teaspoons peanut or grapeseed oil
- ½ cup low-sodium chicken broth
- 3 tablespoons soy sauce
- 1½ tablespoons oyster sauce
- 1 teaspoon toasted sesame oil
- 1 teaspoon chili-garlic sauce, plus more for serving
- 10 medium shiitake mushrooms, stems discarded, caps minced
- 2 garlic cloves, minced
- 1 2-inch piece fresh ginger, peeled and grated or minced
- ¾ pound snow peas, trimmed

1   Julienne the scallions. Trim the root end and the top 1 inch of the green part of each scallion and remove the outermost layer. Rinse to remove any dirt, then pat dry. Slice each scallion into 3 to 4 pieces approximately 2 inches in length. Cut each piece in half lengthwise, then place both halves cut side down on a cutting board, and cut lengthwise again into thin, even slivers. Set aside.

2   Bring a large pot of water to a boil and add the noodles. Stir for the first minute to prevent any sticking. Cook according to the package instructions until tender but chewy. Drain, rinse well under cold water, drain again, and transfer the noodles to a medium bowl. Add ½ tablespoon of the peanut oil and toss (this prevents the noodles from sticking). Set aside.

3   Combine the broth, soy sauce, oyster sauce, sesame oil, and chili-garlic sauce in a small bowl.

4   Heat a wok or large skillet over medium heat for 2 to 3 minutes. Add the remaining 2 teaspoons peanut oil and turn the

heat to medium-high. When it begins to swirl on the surface, add the mushrooms and stir-fry until tender and browned, about 5 minutes. Add the garlic and ginger and stir-fry until fragrant, about 1 minute. Add the noodles and snow peas and cook, tossing continuously, until the snow peas are just hot, about 2 minutes. Add the sauce and scallions and toss. Stir-fry until most of the sauce is absorbed, about 5 minutes.

5 Divide the lo mein among four warmed shallow bowls. Serve piping hot, with additional chili-garlic sauce on the side for diners to add.

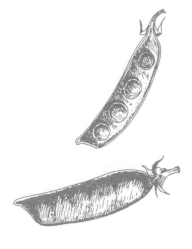

VIETNAMESE NOODLE SALAD

YIELD: 4 SERVINGS / ACTIVE TIME: 30 MINUTES / TOTAL TIME: 40 MINUTES

Vietnamese cuisine excels at contrasting flavors and textures in their dishes and this *bún,* which means "noodle salad" in Vietnamese, is no exception. Complete with chewy noodles, crunchy bean sprouts and peanuts, soft tofu, and a salty-sour-sweet sauce, it is delightfully complex flavor-wise yet remains incredibly simple to prepare. While I adore the crispy texture of fried tofu, you can always swap it out for marinated tofu or baked tofu if you prefer. This salad uses a traditional condiment called *nuoc cham,* which means "dipping sauce." A combination of sweet, sour, salty, savory, and spicy, the ingredients often include fish sauce, lime juice, and sugar. This dish does not, however, call for rice sticks, which are the traditional noodle for this sort of refreshing salad, but rather the equally chewy and tasty acorn noodles (but feel free to use rice sticks if you prefer). Finally, if you can find *rau răm,* or Vietnamese coriander, at your local Asian market, use it in this recipe. Donning dark green, maroon-blotched leaves with a burgundy underside, it is spicy and slightly musky, with a lemony bitterness.

1 Prepare the tofu. Drain and cut it into ½-inch strips. Arrange them in a single layer on a paper towel-lined tray. Cover with paper towels and pat dry. Let them sit for 30 minutes, changing the paper towels after 15 minutes (to continue absorbing as much water as possible). Alternatively, use a tofu press, following the manufacturer's instructions, then cut into strips. Cut the dried strips into ½-inch cubes and set aside.

2 Bring a large pot of water to a boil. As it heats up, pick over the bean sprouts, discarding any discolored or spoiled ones. Put the remaining ones in a bowl of cold water. Discard the hulls that float to the top, then rinse under cold water. Add the sprouts to the boiling water and cook for 1 minute. Remove them from the water with a strainer and immediately run under cold water to stop them from cooking further. Drain well and chop.

3 Add the noodles to the pot of boiling water and stir for the first minute to prevent any sticking. Cook until they are tender but chewy, 5 to 7 minutes. Drain, rinse under cold water, and drain again.

4 Combine all the *nuoc cham* ingredients in a small bowl, stirring until the sugar dissolves. This can be prepared up to 3

INGREDIENTS:

SALAD:

- 1 pound extra firm tofu
- 2 cups mung bean sprouts
- ½ pound dotori guksu (Korean acorn noodles) or dried rice sticks
- ¼ cup peanut oil
- Salt
- 2 ½ cups shredded romaine lettuce
- 2 handfuls mixed fresh herb leaves, coarsely chopped or torn (mint, cilantro, basil, or Vietnamese coriander; see right)
- 2 small cucumbers, peeled and cut into julienne ⅙ inch wide and 2 inches long
- 2 tablespoons chopped salted roasted peanuts for garnish

NUOC CHAM:

- ⅓ cup hot water
- ¼ cup fresh lime juice (from 4 small limes)
- ¼ cup fish sauce
- ¼ cup brown sugar
- 3 tablespoons rice vinegar
- 3 garlic cloves, minced
- 1 1-inch piece fresh ginger, peeled and grated
- 1 fresh hot chile pepper, such as Fresno or jalapeño, seeded and chopped

to 4 hours in advance and refrigerated; bring back to room temperature before using.

5 Heat a large, deep skillet over medium heat for 2 to 3 minutes. Add the oil, adjust the heat to medium-high, and let it warm up for a minute or two. As the oil heats up, gently press the tofu pieces with paper towels one more time to absorb as much surface moisture as possible (less moisture on surfaces allows the tofu to brown more effectively) and lightly sprinkle with salt. When the surface of the oil begins to swirl but is not yet smoking, add the tofu to the skillet in a single layer (you may need to work in two batches). Make sure there is plenty of room in the skillet, as the tofu pieces will cook better. Cook until golden on all sides, 4 to 6 minutes total. Transfer to a paper towel-lined platter to absorb oil.

6 Divide the noodles among four shallow bowls. Arrange the lettuce, herbs, cucumber, and tofu on top. Serve, drizzled with the *nuoc cham* and garnished with the peanuts.

MUGWORT SOBA NOODLE *and* CARROT SALAD *with* SESAME SEEDS *and* SCALLIONS

YIELD: 4 SERVINGS / ACTIVE TIME: 40 MINUTES / TOTAL TIME: 50 MINUTES

Cool, refreshing, and flavorful, this green-hued soba noodle dish is the equivalent of a Japanese pasta salad. It is a perfect side to grilled meats, fish, and tofu. The noodles' lovely shade of green comes from mugwort, an antimicrobial herb whose calming medicinal properties have been known for centuries. But mugwort doesn't just make the noodles look pretty, it also adds a deep nutty flavor to the dish and contributes to their firm texture. Look for the noodles in the macrobiotic section of your local natural food store and online.

INGREDIENTS:

- ½ pound mugwort soba noodles
- 2 ½ tablespoons toasted sesame oil, divided
- 2 tablespoons sesame seeds
- 3 tablespoons soy sauce
- 2 tablespoons rice vinegar
- ¾ teaspoon sugar
- 3 medium carrots
- 1 cucumber
- 1 bunch (5 or 6) scallions

1 Bring a large pot of water to a boil and add the noodles, stirring for the first minute to prevent any sticking. Cook until they are tender but chewy, 5 to 7 minutes. Drain, rinse under cold water, drain again, and place in a large bowl. Toss with ½ tablespoon of the sesame oil to keep them from sticking. If you want to serve chilled, cover and refrigerate.

2 Put the sesame seeds in a small skillet over medium heat and toast until golden brown, 8 to 10 minutes, occasionally shaking the pan. Transfer them to a plate to keep them from browning further.

3 Combine the soy sauce, the remaining 2 tablespoons sesame oil, the vinegar, and sugar in a small bowl, stirring until the sugar dissolves.

4 Peel the carrots thoroughly, then shave them with a vegetable peeler (this will generate about 3 cups of loosely packed carrot shavings). Slice the cucumbers into ¼-inch-thick rounds, and then quarter. Trim the scallions, then cut the light green and white parts into ½-inch pieces. Add them all to the bowl with the noodles

5 Pour the soy sauce mixture over the vegetables and noodles and toss until everything is well combined. Sprinkle with the toasted sesame seeds and serve chilled (it will keep in an airtight container for up to 3 days) or at room temperature.

SOBA NOODLE *and* MIXED MUSHROOM SALAD
with GINGERY LEMON DRESSING

YIELD: 4 SERVINGS AND ABOUT ¾ CUP OF DRESSING / ACTIVE TIME: 40 MINUTES / TOTAL TIME: 1 HOUR

This simple and flavorful noodle Japanese salad features two of the more exotic mushrooms in your supermarket's produce section, enoki and shimeji. They are, respectively, the second and third most popular mushrooms in Japan after shiitake. Long, thin, and tiny capped, enoki have a very crisp texture and a mild and somewhat fruity flavor, while shimeji, little, white, and topped with a taupe-colored cap, are buttery and nutty once cooked.

1 Prepare the dressing. Grate the lemon zest over a piece of wax paper. Cut the lemon in half on a cutting board and squeeze 2 teaspoons of juice into a small bowl. Put the lemon zest and juice, ginger, soy sauce, vinegar, honey, and Thai seasoning blend in a mini food processor or blender and process for 10 seconds, until well blended. Transfer to a small bowl, then whisk in the oils. Use or cover and refrigerate for up to 3 days.

2 Cut off the base of the cluster of shimeji and enoki to separate the mushrooms from each other. Discard the stems from the shiitakes. Fill a very large bowl with cold water and add the vinegar. Add the mushrooms and swirl them around in the water for 30 seconds or so. Drain and rinse them under cold water. Drain again and place on a kitchen towel, stem side down, so that any remaining water drains. Let air dry for 30 minutes. Mince the shiitakes.

3 Put the sesame seeds in a small skillet over medium heat and toast until golden brown, about 8 to 10 minutes, occasionally shaking the pan. Transfer them to a plate to keep them from browning further.

4 Bring a large pot of water to a boil and add the noodles, stirring for the first minute to prevent any sticking. Cook according to the package instructions until they are tender and chewy. Drain and rinse under cold water to remove excess surface starch. Drain again, transfer to a medium bowl, and toss with ½ tablespoon of the sesame oil to prevent any sticking. Set aside.

5 Heat a skillet large enough to hold the finished dish over medium heat for 2 to 3 minutes. Add the remaining 2 teaspoons sesame oil and the butter and let heat for a minute or two, then turn the heat up to high. Once the butter has melted and starts sizzling, add the mushrooms and 3 to 4 pinches of salt and stir. Cook, stirring continuously, for 2 to 3 minutes. Add the noodles, scallions, and ½ cup of the dressing, and toss well. Taste for seasoning and add more salt or dressing if needed. Transfer to a serving bowl, top with the basil leaves and sesame seeds, and serve warm or at room temperature.

INGREDIENTS:

GINGERY LEMON DRESSING:

- 1 lemon
- 1 2-inch piece fresh ginger, peeled and grated or minced
- ¼ cup soy sauce
- ¼ cup rice vinegar
- 1½ tablespoons honey
- ½ teaspoon Thai seasoning blend
- 3 tablespoons extra virgin or avocado oil
- 2 teaspoons toasted sesame oil

SALAD:

- 4 ounces shimeji mushrooms
- 4 ounces enoki mushrooms
- 2 medium shiitake mushrooms
- 1 tablespoon distilled white vinegar
- 2 tablespoons sesame seeds
- ½ pound soba noodles
- ½ tablespoon + 2 teaspoons toasted sesame oil, divided
- 1½ tablespoons unsalted butter
-   Salt
- 3 scallions, trimmed and thinly sliced
-   Handful fresh basil leaves, thinly slivered, for serving

SOBA NOODLE SALAD
with MARINATED EGGPLANT *and* TOFU

YIELD: 4 SERVINGS / ACTIVE TIME: 45 MINUTES / TOTAL TIME: 1 ¾ HOURS

The chewy noodles and crispy tofu make a satisfying backdrop for this salad's lightly caramelized eggplant and tangy ginger-soy dressing. I only recently started marinating tofu prior to cooking it and find that it brings the most flavorful dimension to an otherwise fairly bland food. The most effective way to make sure the tofu takes on as much flavor as possible is to drain it for at least an hour if not longer. If you are not up for tofu, this salad can be a great vehicle for using up leftover grilled steak or chicken.

1 Combine all the marinade ingredients in a small bowl. Combine all the dressing ingredients in another small bowl.

2 Trim both ends of the eggplants, slice them in half, and cut into ½-inch pieces. Put them in a medium bowl and toss with the marinade. Let stand for 1 hour at room temperature.

3 Drain the tofu and cut it into ½-inch strips. Arrange them in a single layer on a paper-towel lined tray. Cover with paper towels and pat dry. Let them sit for 30 minutes, changing the paper towels after 15 minutes (to continue absorbing as much water as possible). Cut the strips into ½-inch cubes. Alternatively, use a tofu press, following the manufacturer's instructions, then cut into ½-inch cubes.

4 Bring a large pot of water to a boil. When it's boiling, add the noodles and stir for the first minute to prevent any sticking. Cook until they are tender but chewy, 5 to 7 minutes. Drain, rinse under cold water, drain again, and place in a large bowl. Toss with the dressing and set aside.

5 Heat a wok or large skillet over medium heat for 2 to 3 minutes. Turn the heat to medium-high and add 2 tablespoons of the peanut oil. When it begins to swirl on the surface, add the eggplant cubes and a couple pinches of salt and stir-fry until they soften and turn golden, 5 to 6 minutes. Using a slotted spoon, transfer the eggplant to a paper towel-lined plate. Add the remaining tablespoon peanut oil to the wok and add the tofu cubes. Stir-fry until they turn golden all over, 4 to 5 minutes. Using a slotted spoon, transfer them to another paper towel-lined plate.

6 Divide the soba noodles among four bowls. Arrange the eggplant and tofu on top and serve topped with the scallions.

INGREDIENTS:

MARINADE:

2 tablespoons rice vinegar

3 tablespoons soy sauce

1 tablespoon toasted sesame oil

½ teaspoon sugar

2 garlic cloves, minced

DRESSING:

1 tablespoon rice vinegar

1 tablespoon peanut oil

1 teaspoon soy sauce

1 tablespoon toasted sesame oil

1 1-inch piece fresh ginger, peeled and grated

SALAD:

3 Chinese eggplants or regular eggplants (about 2 pounds)

¾ pound firm tofu

½ pound soba noodles

3 tablespoons peanut oil, divided

1 bunch (5 or 6) scallions, trimmed and sliced on the diagonal into ¼-inch pieces

Salt

RAMEN NOODLES *and* TOFU SAN BEI

YIELD: 4 SERVINGS / **ACTIVE TIME:** 30 MINUTES / **TOTAL TIME:** 1 HOUR

San bei, or "three cups" in Chinese, refers to the equal amounts of sesame oil, soy sauce, and rice wine traditionally used to make the extremely aromatic sauce for this Taiwanese dish. As it turns out, few people actually follow the original recipe and instead vary the ratios and other ingredients to suit their tastes. This recipe is no exception. It veers off the traditional path, which typically includes chicken and rice, by instead using ramen noodles and tofu.

1 Drain the tofu and cut it into ½-inch slices. Arrange them in a single layer on a paper-towel lined tray. Cover with paper towels and pat dry. Let them sit for 30 minutes, changing the paper towels after 15 minutes (to continue absorbing as much water as possible). Alternatively, use a tofu press, following the manufacturer's instructions, then cut into slices.

2 Heat the largest skillet you have over medium heat for 2 to 3 minutes. Add the peanut oil and heat until the surface starts to swirl but it is not yet smoking. Dredge the tofu slices in a shallow bowl filled with cornstarch, tapping off any excess. Working in batches, add the tofu in a single layer to the skillet. Turn the heat up to medium-high and cook until they are a golden caramel color, 3 to 4 minutes per side. Transfer to a paper towel-lined plate to drain.

3 Wipe the oil out of the skillet with paper towels, then add the sesame oil to the pan. Turn the heat to medium and, once the surface starts to swirl but it is not yet smoking, add the smashed garlic, ginger pieces, scallions, and two pinches of salt and cook, stirring a few times, until fragrant, about 2 minutes. Add the sugar and stir until melted. Add the ¾ cup water, the wine, and soy sauce and stir. Increase the heat to medium-high and bring to a boil. Reduce the heat to low, cover, and simmer, stirring occasionally, for 10 minutes, to let the flavors blend. Mix the remaining 1 ½ teaspoons cornstarch and 1 tablespoon water in a small bowl until smooth, then add to the sauce and stir until well mixed. Continue to cook, stirring occasionally, until the sauce slightly thickens, about 5 minutes. Add the tofu slices and cook until warmed through.

4 As the sauce simmers, bring a large pot of water to a boil. Add the ramen noodles and stir for the first minute to prevent any sticking. Cook according to the package instructions until tender and chewy. Drain.

5 Divide the noodles among four warmed shallow bowls. Top with the tofu slices, ladle over the sauce, garnish with the basil, and serve piping hot.

INGREDIENTS:

- 1   **pound extra-firm tofu**
- 3   **tablespoons peanut or grapeseed oil**
- 1 ½   **teaspoons cornstarch, plus extra for dredging the tofu**
- 3   **tablespoons toasted sesame oil**
- 8   **garlic cloves, peeled and smashed**
- 1   **2-inch piece fresh ginger, sliced into 8 pieces**
- 2   **bunches (10 or 12) scallions, trimmed and cut into ½-inch pieces**
-     **Salt**
- 3   **tablespoons sugar**
- ¾   **cup + 1 tablespoon water cup water**
- ¾   **cup Shaoxing rice wine or dry sherry**
- ⅓   **cup soy sauce**
- ⅓   **pound ramen noodles**
- 2   **handfuls fresh basil leaves (preferably Thai), thinly sliced, for garnish**

FRIED NOODLES

YIELD: 4 SERVINGS / ACTIVE TIME: 45 MINUTES / TOTAL TIME: 55 MINUTES

In Malaysia, this zesty dish known as *mee goreng* is often made with spicy squid, fried shrimp fritters, fried tofu pieces, and sometimes boiled potato wedges. This vegetarian version omits the seafood in favor of crispy, chewy yu choi sum. Anyone who has frequented an authentic Chinese restaurant has undoubtedly seen this leafy dark green vegetable served as a side dish. Also known as Chinese oil vegetable, it is slightly bitter, similar to mustard greens, and has an earthiness that nicely complements strong, spicy flavors. I've adapted this dish from a Yotam Ottolenghi recipe. I've had a soft spot for him ever since making the decadently rich and savory black pepper tofu from his wonderful cookbook *Plenty*.

While this book offers a recipe for homemade egg noodles, you can also use the fresh, frozen, or dried variety that can be found at your local Asian market. All three types will require boiling in water. Uncooked fresh or frozen noodles will need 30 to 60 seconds of boiling to become pleasantly chewy, while dried versions, usually sold as Hong Kong-style egg noodles, take a few minutes. Drain, rinse under cold water, and drain again before throwing them into your stir-fry. Be sure not to overcook any of these noodles because they will lose their chewy texture once they are also stir-fried. If you can find them, pre-cooked fresh lo mein noodles are sometimes available in the refrigerated section of some Asian markets and will be clearly labeled as such (you don't want to risk boiling precooked noodles or you'll end up with a mushy mess). People find the precooked version very convenient because they eliminate the need to boil them, making whipping up a weeknight meal particularly convenient.

1 Drain the tofu and cut it into ½-inch strips. Arrange them in a single layer on a paper towel-lined tray. Cover with paper towels and pat dry. Let them sit for 30 minutes, changing the paper towels after 15 minutes (to continue absorbing as much water as possible). Alternatively, use a tofu press, following the manufacturer's instructions, and cut into strips.

2 While the tofu is draining, bring a large pot of water to a boil. Cut off the bottom 2 inches of the choi sum's thick stems, then chop the leaves and remaining stems into large chunks. Wash well. When the water is boiling, add salt (1 tablespoon for every 4 cups water) and stir. Add the chopped choi sum and cook until

INGREDIENTS:

- ½ pound firm tofu
- 1 bunch yu choi sum (Chinese greens) or 6 baby bok choy
- Salt
- ¾ pound fresh, frozen or dried Chinese egg noodles, homemade (page 204) or store-bought
- 2 ½ tablespoons peanut or grapeseed oil, divided
- ½ cup mung bean sprouts
- 1 small onion, diced
- 1 ½ teaspoons ground cumin
- 1 teaspoon ground coriander
- ⅓ pound haricots vert, trimmed and cut in half on an angle
- 1 tablespoon dark soy sauce
- 1 ½ teaspoons light soy sauce (also sold as "fresh," "pure bean," or "thin" soy sauce)
- 1 ½ teaspoons sambal oelek or sriracha, plus more for serving

FOR SERVING:

- Lime wedges
- Handful thinly sliced iceberg lettuce
- Thinly sliced Thai bird chiles
- 2 tablespoons Crispy Shallots (page 747)

bright green, about 40 seconds. Remove from the water with a strainer and immediately rinse with cold water to stop the cooking process. Transfer to a kitchen towel to further drain. (If using bok choy, cut them in halves or quarters lengthwise, then cut across into bite-size pieces. Heat a large skillet over medium heat for 2 to 3 minutes. Add the bok choy, two pinches of salt, and ¼ cup water and stir. When the water starts to boil, cover and let steam for 2 minutes. Remove from the heat and set aside.)

3 Add the noodles to the boiling water and cook until tender but chewy. Using a strainer, transfer to a medium bowl, add ½ tablespoon of the oil, and toss well (this prevents sticking). Keep the water in the pot boiling.

4 Pick over the bean sprouts, discarding any discolored or spoiled ones. Put the remaining ones in a bowl of cold water. Discard the hulls that float to the top, then rinse them under cold water. Add the sprouts to the boiling water and cook for 2 minutes. Remove them from the water with a strainer and imme-

diately run under cold water to stop them from cooking further. Drain well and set aside.

5 Heat a wok or large skillet over medium heat for 2 to 3 minutes. Add the remaining 2 tablespoons oil and turn the heat to medium-high. When it begins to swirl on the surface, add the onion, cumin, coriander, and a pinch of salt and stir-fry until fragrant, about 1 minute. Add the tofu, haricots vert, and a pinch of salt, stirring gently so as to combine but not break up the tofu strips, and cook until the tofu turns a light golden color, 3 to 4 minutes. Add the choi sum (or bok choy) and stir-fry until it begins to lightly color, about 2 minutes. Add the noodles and cook, tossing gently, until warmed through. Add both soy sauces, the sambal oelek, and sprouts and stir-fry for a minute, until well mixed.

6 Divide among four warmed shallow bowls. Serve piping hot, accompanied by the lime wedges, lettuce, chiles, fried shallots if using, and more sambal oelek for diners to add to their bowl as they choose.

SPICY CELLOPHANE NOODLES
with GREEN BEANS *and* TOFU

YIELD: 4 SERVINGS / ACTIVE TIME: 40 MINUTES / TOTAL TIME: 1 HOUR

Also known as glass noodles, mung bean noodles, bean threads, crystal noodles, bean vermicelli, few noodles have as many aliases as the very thin, semi-translucent dried noodles made from mung bean starch and water known as cellophane noodles. They are used to good effect in this spicy vegetarian stir-fry. Brimming with summer grown-green beans, this recipe is an excellent vehicle for using them when they're bountiful and inexpensive at the farmers' market. If you have a hard time finding fresh Thai basil, pair fresh mint and basil to mimic its flavor.

1 Drain the tofu and cut it into ¾-inch-thick slices. Arrange them in a single layer on a paper-towel lined tray. Cover with paper towels and pat dry. Let them sit for 30 minutes, changing the paper towels after 15 minutes (to continue absorbing as much water as possible). Cut the slices into ¾-inch-wide strips. Alternatively, use a tofu press, following the manufacturer's instructions, then cut into strips.

2 Put the noodles in a large heatproof bowl and cover with 2 quarts of hot water. Let sit until the noodles become soft and pliable, about 15 minutes. Rinse with cold water and drain well.

3 Heat a wok or large skillet over medium heat for 2 to 3 minutes. Turn the heat to medium-high and add 2 tablespoons of the oil. When it begins to swirl on the surface, add one third of the tofu and cook until crispy and brown on all sides. Carefully transfer to a paper towel-lined plate. Add another tablespoon of oil and another third of the tofu, cook until crispy and brown on all sides, and transfer to the plate. Repeat with the remaining oil and tofu.

4 Add the shallots and a couple pinches of salt to the pan and cook until tender and golden brown, 3 to 4 minutes. Add the garlic, pepper flakes, and green beans and stir-fry until the beans are tender and bright green, 3 to 4 minutes. Add the tofu and brown sugar and cook until the tofu is heated through, about 3 minutes. Add the noodles, soy sauce, and fish sauce, and toss together until heated through, 2 to 3 minutes.

5 Remove from the heat and toss with the lime juice and half of the chopped herbs.

6 Divide among four warmed shallow bowls and serve piping hot, topped with peanuts and the remaining herb(s).

INGREDIENTS:

- 10 ounces (about ¾ of a block) extra-firm tofu
- ½ pound dry wide cellophane noodles
- 4 tablespoons peanut oil or grapeseed oil, divided, or more as needed
- 3 large shallots, minced
- Salt
- 2 garlic cloves, minced
- 1 teaspoon red pepper flakes
- 1 pound green beans, trimmed and cut on the diagonal into 2-inch pieces
- 2 tablespoons light brown sugar
- 2 tablespoons soy sauce
- 2 tablespoons fish sauce
- Juice of 2 limes (about 3 tablespoons)
- ½ cup coarsely chopped fresh Thai basil OR ¼ cup each coarsely chopped regular basil and fresh mint
- ⅓ cup coarsely chopped roasted peanuts

NOODLES *with* ROASTED SPICED CHICKEN *and* SWISS CHARD

YIELD: 4 SERVINGS / ACTIVE TIME: 40 MINUTES /
TOTAL TIME: 45 MINUTES WITHOUT MAKING NOODLES, 1¾ HOURS WHEN MAKING NOODLES

This recipe is an adaptation of a delicious rendition I found on one of my favorite food blogs, Alexandra Cooks. I particularly love the creaminess and richness that the cashew butter lends to the noodles and Swiss chard.

1 Preheat the oven to 400°F. Combine the spice mix ingredients in small bowl.

2 Whisk the sauce ingredients together in medium bowl until well mixed.

3 Heat a large ovenproof skillet (preferably cast iron) over medium heat for 2 to 3 minutes. Turn the heat to medium-high and add the grapeseed oil. As the oil heats up, pat the chicken with paper towels to absorb as much surface moisture as possible (eliminating surface moisture, along with the addition of sugar in the spice mix, will help the chicken to brown better), and then rub all over with the spice mix. When the oil begins to swirl on the surface, add the chicken and sear it, turning it over every 2 minutes or so, until nicely browned on both sides, 6 to 8 minutes total.

4 Transfer the skillet in the oven and roast until the meat reaches 165°F (if you don't have a meat thermometer, the chicken needs to feel firm and spring back when you press it with your finger and the juices run clear when poked with a knife), about 10 minutes; turn the chicken after 5 minutes. Remove from the oven and transfer the breasts to a plate to let cool. Once cool enough to handle, shred the chicken with your hands and set aside.

5 While the chicken it roasting, bring a large pot of water to a boil. Once it's boiling, add salt (1 tablespoon for every 4 cups water) and stir. Add the noodles and stir for the first minute to prevent any sticking. Once the noodles float to the top, continue to cook for 2 to 3 minutes more (it depends on thickness of your noodles), until they are cooked but still firm and very chewy. (You may want to taste test one to determine if they are ready. Alternatively, you can also test by removing one from the water

INGREDIENTS:

SPICE MIX FOR CHICKEN:
½	teaspoon salt
½	teaspoon cayenne paper
½	teaspoon brown sugar
½	teaspoon chili powder

SAUCE:
⅓	cup cashew butter
¼	cup soy sauce
1½	tablespoons rice vinegar
2½	teaspoons toasted sesame oil
2	teaspoons hot chile oil
¾	teaspoon sugar
¼ to 1	teaspoon cayenne pepper, to taste
2	garlic cloves, minced

CHICKEN, NOODLES, AND SWISS CHARD:
3	tablespoons grapeseed or safflower oil
2	medium (about 1 pound) bone-in chicken breasts
	Salt
1	recipe Ding Ding Chao Mian Noodles (page 213) or ¾ pound thick fresh Chinese noodles
1	pound Swiss chard, stems discarded and leaves sliced into 1-inch-wide ribbons, or baby spinach leaves
1	bunch (5 or 6) scallions, trimmed and thinly sliced

and slicing it in half; if you don't see a starchy line in the dough, they are done.)

6 One minute before you drain the noodles, add the Swiss chard ribbons to the water, stir, and drain. Transfer to a large bowl, add the shredded chicken and dressing, and toss to coat evenly. Serve immediately, topped with the scallions.

CHICKEN LO MEIN *with* BEAN SPROUTS, CABBAGE, *and* CARROTS

YIELD: 4 TO 6 SERVINGS / ACTIVE TIME: 45 MINUTES / TOTAL TIME: 45 MINUTES

Literally "stirred noodles" in Cantonese, lo mein noodles can be paired with an almost infinite number of meats and vegetables. A popular take-out dish found in every Chinese restaurant worth their noodles, lo mein dishes as easy to put together and, quite frankly, usually taste much better than what you can get in most restaurants. This recipe is sure to be a hit with even the pickiest eaters. While this book offers a recipe for homemade egg noodles, you can also use the fresh, frozen, or dried variety that can be found at your local Asian market. All three types will require boiling in water. Uncooked fresh or frozen noodles will need 30 to 60 seconds of boiling to become pleasantly chewy, while dried versions, usually sold as Hong Kong-style egg noodles, take a few minutes. Drain, rinse under cold water, and drain again before throwing them into your stir-fry. Be sure not to overcook any of these noodles because they will lose their chewy texture once they are also stir-fried. If you can find them, pre-cooked fresh lo mein noodles are sometimes available in the refrigerated section of some Asian markets and will be clearly labeled as such (you don't want to risk boiling precooked noodles or you'll end up with a mushy mess). People find the precooked version very convenient because they eliminate the need to boil them, making whipping up a weeknight meal particularly convenient.

INGREDIENTS:

- ½ pound boneless, skinless chicken breast, thinly sliced
- 2 teaspoons cornstarch
- 2 teaspoons water
- 2 teaspoons + 4 ½ tablespoons peanut or grapeseed oil
- 2 cups mung bean sprouts
- ½ pound fresh, frozen, or dried Chinese egg noodles, homemade (page 204) or store-bought
- 2 garlic cloves, minced
- 4 cups shredded cabbage
- 2 medium carrots, cut into into 1 ½-inch-long julienne
- Salt
- 1 tablespoon Shaoxing rice wine or dry sherry
- 1 ½ tablespoons dark soy sauce
- 1 tablespoon soy sauce
- 1 teaspoon toasted sesame oil
- ½ teaspoon sugar
- 4 scallions, trimmed and thinly sliced

1 Put the chicken in a medium bowl. Whisk the cornstarch, water, and 2 teaspoons of the peanut oil together in a small bowl until smooth. Add to the chicken and toss until the chicken is coated with the cornstarch slurry.

2 Bring a medium pot of water to a boil. While it comes to a boil, pick over the bean sprouts, discarding any discolored or spoiled ones. Put the remaining ones in a bowl of cold water. Discard the hulls that float to the top, then rinse them under cold water. Add the sprouts to the boiling water and cook for 2 minutes. Remove them from the water with a strainer and immediately run them under cold water to stop them from cooking further.

3 Bring a large pot of water back to a boil, then add the noodles. Cook until tender but still chewy, 2 to 3 minutes. Drain and transfer the noodles to a medium bowl. Add ½ tablespoon of the peanut oil and toss well (this prevents the noodles from sticking together). Set aside.

4 Heat a wok or large skillet over medium heat for 2 to 3 minutes. Add 2 tablespoons of the peanut oil and turn the heat to medium-high. Heat the oil until it begins to swirl on the surface, then add the chicken and cook, stirring occasionally, until the pieces become a golden caramel color, 2 to 3 minutes. Transfer them to a warmed plate and tent loosely with aluminum foil to keep warm.

5 Add the remaining 2 tablespoons peanut oil to the pan, and add the garlic, stirring.

After 15 seconds, add the cabbage, carrots, and a couple pinches of salt. Stir-fry for 2 minutes. Add the rice wine by pouring it around the perimeter of the pan and stir to mix. Add the noodles and chicken and toss well for 1 minute. Cover and let steam for 1 minute.

6 Remove the lid, add both soy sauces, sesame oil, and sugar, and stir. Cook for 1 minute. Add the bean sprouts and scallions and stir for 1 minute. Serve piping hot from the pan.

SHRIMP *and* TOFU PAD THAI

YIELD: 4 SERVINGS / ACTIVE TIME: 45 MINUTES / TOTAL TIME: 1 HOUR

Arguably the most well-known dish from Thailand, pad thai consists of rice noodles stir-fried in an aromatic mixture of seasonings. Aficionados insist that the key to a truly spectacular pad thai lies in cooking its stretchy, chewy white noodles, called *sen lek,* to firm yet tender perfection. In Thailand, respectable pad thai vendors always use *sen lek* that comes from the province of Chanthaburi, where they still dry their noodles in the open air instead of using drying machines. Should *sen lek* noodles prove difficult to find, use flat rice noodles no wider than ⅙ inch, preferably from Thailand, as a substitute. Also, no pad thai would be complete without a dollop of tamarind paste. Made from the sticky, sour-tasting fruit that grows in green pea-like pods on tamarind trees, it adds a hauntingly sweet and tart flavor to the dish. Look for it online or in Asian, Indian, or Hispanic food stores.

1 Drain the tofu and cut it into ½-inch strips. Arrange them in a single layer on a paper-towel lined tray. Cover with paper towels and pat dry. Let them sit for 30 minutes, changing the paper towels after 15 minutes (to continue absorbing as much water as possible). Alternatively, use a tofu press, following the manufacturer's instructions, then cut into strips. Cut the slices into matchsticks.

2 While the tofu drains, bring a medium saucepan of water to a boil. While it comes to a boil, pick over the bean sprouts, discarding any discolored or spoiled ones. Put the remaining ones in a bowl of cold water. Discard the hulls that float to the top, then rinse them under cold water. Add the sprouts to the boiling water and cook for 2 minutes. Remove them from the water with a strainer and immediately run under cold water to stop them from cooking further. Drain well and chop.

3 Soak the noodles in room temperature water (not hot, as the heat causes the noodles to release excess starch, which in turn causes them to stick together) until tender and chewy. Soaking time varies depending on the width of the noodles. (For ⅙-inch-wide noodles, 20 to 25 minutes should be sufficient, but always taste test.) Drain and transfer to a medium bowl. Toss with ½ tablespoon of the oil to prevent any sticking.

4 Combine the garlic, chiles, sugar, tamarind paste, and fish sauce in a small saucepan. Turn the heat to medium and

INGREDIENTS:

½ pound extra-firm tofu

1 cup mung bean sprouts

½ pound sen lek rice noodles

2 ½ tablespoons peanut or grapeseed oil, divided

2 garlic cloves, minced

2 Thai bird chiles, very thinly sliced (seeds removed if wishing only moderate heat)

⅓ cup packed light brown sugar

½ cup tamarind paste, pureed with 1 tablespoon water

5 tablespoons fish sauce

Juice of ½ lime

1 pound large shrimp, peeled and deveined

Salt

⅛ teaspoon red pepper flakes

3 large eggs, lightly beaten

2 scallions, trimmed and thinly sliced

2 medium carrots, cut into 1 ½-inch-long julienne

Chopped fresh cilantro for garnish

Chopped roasted peanuts for garnish

Lime wedges for serving

heat, stirring, until the sugar and paste have dissolved, 2 to 3 minutes. Remove from the heat and stir in the lime juice.

5 Heat a wok or large skillet over medium heat for 2 to 3 minutes. Once very hot (you can test by adding a drop of water; if it bounces off the surface, it's ready), add tthe remaining 2 tablespoons oil then add the shrimp, a couple pinches of salt, and the red pepper flakes and stir-fry until the shrimp begin to turn opaque and pink, about 3 minutes.

6 Add the eggs and cook without stirring until lightly set, about 30 seconds. Then, using a rubber spatula, stir well to scramble the eggs with the shrimp. Add one third of the garlic-chile sauce and all of the noodles and toss. Add a little more sauce if the noodles seem too dry. Add the tofu, bean sprouts, scallions, and carrots, and toss. Continue stir-frying until heated through and well mixed, 2 to 3 minutes.

7 Transfer to a warmed serving platter, garnish with the cilantro and peanuts, and serve piping hot with the lime wedges.

STIR-FRIED NOODLES
with MARINATED SALMON *and* COD

YIELD: 4 SERVINGS / ACTIVE TIME: 30 MINUTES / TOTAL TIME: 3 ½ HOURS

Wide rice noodles provide a satisfying backdrop to marinated morsels of fish and a savory and slightly spicy sauce.

1 Whisk 2 tablespoons of the oil, the green chiles, lime zest and juice, fish sauce, and sugar together in a medium bowl until the sugar dissolves. Add the cubed fish and toss until well coated with the marinade. Cover and refrigerate for 3 hours.

2 Place the rice noodles in a large heatproof bowl, cover with boiling water, and soak for the time specified in the package instructions, typically 8 to 10 minutes. Drain well.

3 Heat a wok or large skillet over medium heat for 2 to 3 minutes. Add the remaining 2 tablespoons oil, along with the shallots, garlic, and red chile and cook until very soft and just lightly brown, 8 to 10 minutes, stirring occasionally. Add the soy sauce and chile oil and stir. Add the marinated fish and cook, stirring a few times, until fully cooked (opaque all the way through), 2 to 3 minutes.

4 Add the drained noodles and carefully stir to mix in and coat with the sauce, taking care not to break the noodles in the process.

5 Divide the noodles and fish among four warmed plates and serve piping hot garnished with cilantro.

INGREDIENTS:

- 4 tablespoons peanut oil, divided
- 2 fresh green chiles, seeded and minced
- Grated zest and juice of 1 lime
- 1 ½ tablespoons fish sauce
- 1 tablespoon sugar
- ¾ pound skinless salmon fillet, cubed
- ¾ pound cod fillet, cubed
- ½ pound wide dried rice noodles
- 3 small shallots, minced
- 2 garlic cloves, thinly sliced
- 1 fresh red chile, seeded and minced
- 2 tablespoons soy sauce
- 1 to 2 tablespoons hot chile oil, to your taste
- Handful fresh cilantro leaves for garnish

CELLOPHANE NOODLE *and* SHRIMP SALAD *with* SPICY LIME DRESSING

YIELD: 6 SERVINGS / ACTIVE TIME: 35 MINUTES / TOTAL TIME: 45 MINUTES

This combination of refreshing herbs and spring mix lettuce, cool noodles, room-temperature grilled shrimp, and spicy lime dressing makes an easy and tasty salad that eats like a light meal. I love to make it when friends come over for a last-minute barbecue because the salad comes together in no time and we grill the shrimp instead of sautéing it for easier clean up. Depending on your preference, you can substitute an equal amount of marinated tofu, chicken, squid, or flank steak for the shrimp.

1. Combine all the lime dressing ingredients in a small bowl, stirring until the sugar dissolves. Put the shrimp in a medium bowl and toss with half of the dressing. Cover and refrigerate for 1 hour.

2. Put the noodles in a medium bowl and add enough room temperature water to cover. Let sit until the noodles become soft and pliable, 10 to 15 minutes. Rinse with cold water and drain well. Using kitchen scissors, cut the noodles into 2-inch pieces and return them to the now empty bowl.

3. Heat a large, deep skillet over medium heat for 2 to 3 minutes. Add the oil, adjust the heat to medium-high, and let warm up for a minute or two. As it heats, gently press the shrimp with paper towels to absorb as much surface moisture as possible and lightly sprinkle with salt (less moisture on the surface allows the shrimp to brown more effectively). When the surface of the oil begins to swirl but is not yet smoking, add the shrimp to the skillet in a single layer (you may need to work in two batches). Make sure there is plenty of room between the shrimp, as they will cook better. Cook them for 2 minutes on each side. Transfer to a large bowl and let cool for 10 minutes.

4. As the shrimp cool, divide the spring mix among six large salad plates.

5. To the bowl with the shrimp add the cellophane noodles, mint, scallions, basil, cilantro, a couple pinches of salt, and the remaining line dressing. Toss until well mixed. Mound the shrimp mixture onto the salad and sprinkle with the peanuts. Arrange a couple of lime wedges on each bowl and serve.

INGREDIENTS:

SPICY LIME DRESSING:

- 2 ½ tablespoons fish sauce
- Juice and zest of 1 juicy lime, 2 if on the "non-juicy" side, divided
- 1 ½ tablespoons grapeseed oil
- 1 ½ teaspoons oyster sauce
- 1 ½ tablespoons sugar
- 1 fresh chile, like Thai or jalapeño, sliced paper-thin

SALAD:

- 1 ½ pounds extra-large shrimp, shelled and deveined
- 6 ounces thin dried cellophane noodles
- 2 tablespoons grapeseed or safflower oil
- Salt
- 3 cups spring mix lettuce
- 1 cup loosely packed fresh mint leaves
- 1 bunch (5 or 6) scallions, trimmed and thinly sliced
- 2 handfuls fresh basil leaves, chopped
- 2 handfuls fresh cilantro leaves, chopped
- ⅔ cup salted roasted peanuts, chopped
- Lime wedges for serving

SINGAPORE RICE NOODLES
with SHRIMP *and* CURRY

YIELD: 8 SERVINGS / ACTIVE TIME: 50 MINUTES / TOTAL TIME: 1 ¼ HOURS

I recently fell in love with this dish. I first ordered it at a newly opened Chinese restaurant in my area and was immediately taken with its distinct yet unexpected curry flavor. When I asked the restaurant's pleasant but harried waitress about this dish, she quickly explained that we "Westerners" tended to think that curry dishes are exclusively from India. "If you look in the dictionary," she added, "you will see that the term 'curry' means a dish with a variety of spices, and not just curry powder. India has lots of curries that don't even contain curry powder." As it turns out, this dish actually contains curry powder. But not just any curry powder—Maharajah curry powder. Gorgeously colored and full-bodied in flavor, it contains some of the most prized spices in the world, including saffron, cardamom, cumin, fenugreek, ginger, nutmeg, fennel, cinnamon, white pepper, black pepper, cloves, and red pepper. The depth of flavor found in this dish comes from black garlic, a Korean preparation that is quickly becoming a seasoning darling among chefs in the United States. Black garlic is made by taking regular garlic heads and heating them at a relatively low temperature for 30 days. They are then left out to oxidize for another month or so. The result are black garlic cloves with a jellylike texture and deep umami flavor, described variously as reminiscent of soy sauce, balsamic vinegar, tamarind, and/or prunes. You can find black garlic online, as well as at Trader Joe's and Whole Foods.

INGREDIENTS:

- 2 packages (6 to 8 ounces each) rice stick noodles
- 8 ½ tablespoons peanut oil, divided
- 5 large eggs, lightly beaten
  Salt
- 2 tablespoons toasted sesame oil
- 1 pound pork tenderloin
- 1 pound shrimp, peeled, deveined, and tails removed
- 1 medium yellow onion, cut into thin half moons
- 2 jalapeño peppers, seeded and minced
- 1 2-inch piece fresh ginger, peeled and grated or minced
- 6 black garlic cloves, minced
- 2 red bell peppers, seeded and cut into thin slivers
- ½ cup green cabbage cut into thin slivers
- ½ pound cremini mushrooms, trimmed and thinly sliced
- 2 bunches (5 or 6 in each) scallions, trimmed and cut into 1 ½-inch sections
- 6 ounces snow peas, trimmed
- ½ teaspoon freshly ground white pepper
- ½ teaspoon ground coriander
- ½ teaspoon toasted sesame seeds
- ¼ cup Maharajah curry powder
- 1 cup chicken broth
  Handful chopped fresh cilantro for garnish

1 Soak the noodles in a medium bowl of warm water until softened, about 20 minutes. Drain well, wipe the bowl with a paper towel, and return the noodles to it. Toss with ½ tablespoon of the peanut oil to prevent sticking.

2 Heat a wok or large skillet over medium heat for 2 to 3 minutes. Turn the heat to medium-high and add 1 tablespoon of the peanut oil. When it begins to swirl on the surface, add the eggs and two pinches of salt and cook, without stirring, until set, 2 to 3 minutes. Transfer to a plate. Once cool, slice into thin, 2-inch-long slivers.

3 Add the sesame oil to the pan. Wipe down the pork with paper towels to remove as much surface moisture as possible (it will brown better). Once the oil begins to swirl on the surface, sprinkle the surface of pork with salt and add it (cut in

half widthwise if using a wok) to the pan, lowering the heat to medium. Cook, turning occasionally, until completely cooked, with no pink in the center, 6 to 10 minutes total. Transfer it to a cutting board. When it's cool enough to handle, cut it into strips ¼ inch thick and 1 ½ inches long

4 Pat the shrimp dry with paper towels. Heat the pan again and add 1 tablespoon of the peanut oil. When the surface of the oil begins to swirl, increase the heat to medium-high, add the shrimp and a couple pinches of salt, and stir-fry until firm and cooked through, 4 to 5 minutes. Transfer to the cutting board with the pork.

5 Add 2 tablespoons of the peanut oil to the pan. When it shimmers on the sur-face, add the onion, jalapeños, ginger, and garlic and cook until the onion is translucent, 6 to 7 minutes. Add red cabbage, mushrooms, scallions, snow peas, white pepper, coriander, toasted sesame seeds, and ½ teaspoon salt and stir-fry for 1 minute.

6 Combine the curry, broth, and the remaining 4 tablespoons peanut oil in a small bowl and mix. Pour over the vegetables in the pan and let gently steam for 3 to 4 minutes, until they are slightly softened. Add the chicken, shrimp, eggs, cilantro, and rice stick noodles and toss until coated. Taste for seasoning and add a little additional salt if needed.

7 Divide the stir-fry among eight warmed plates and serve piping hot.

SHANGHAI STIR-FRIED NOODLES
with PORK *and* CHINESE BROCCOLI

YIELD: 4 TO 6 SERVINGS / ACTIVE TIME: 25 MINUTES / TOTAL TIME: 40 MINUTES

This is traditionally made with Shanghai-style noodles known as *cu mian*. The more commonly known and available Japanese udon noodles can be used as a substitute. Delightfully thick and chewy, they provide satisfying heft to this simple yet tasty dish. For a vegetarian version, replace the pork with tofu or more mushrooms.

1 Place the dried shiitakes in a heatproof bowl and add just enough hot water to cover them by a few inches. Soak for at least 20 minutes, until they reconstitute and the caps are tender. Drain and squeeze each mushroom gently in your hand to remove excess water. Cut off and discard the tough stems, and thinly slice the caps. Set aside.

2 While the mushrooms soak, remove any remaining silverskin from the pork tenderloin. Slice across into thin medallions, then slice the medallions into ½-inch-wide strips. Whisk the light soy sauce, 1 tablespoon of the dark soy sauce, the cornstarch, ¼ teaspoon of the sugar, and the rice wine together in a medium bowl until smooth. Add the pork strips and toss until they are evenly coated with the soy mixture.

3 Bring a large pot of water to a boil. Cut off and discard the bottom 2 inches of the choi sum's thick stems, then chop the leaves and remaining stems into large chunks. Wash well. When the water is boiling, add salt (1 tablespoon for every 4 cups water) and stir. Add the chopped choi sum and cook until bright green, about 40 seconds. Remove from the water with a strainer and immediately rinse with cold water to stop the cooking process. Transfer to a kitchen towel to further drain. (If using bok choy, cut them in halves or quarters lengthwise, then cut across into bite-size pieces. Heat a large skillet over medium heat for 2 to 3 minutes. Add the bok choy, two pinches of salt, and ¼ cup of water and stir. When the water starts to boil, cover, and let steam for 2 minutes. Remove from the heat and set aside.)

4 Bring the water back to a boil, add the noodles, and cook according to the recipe or package instructions until tender but still chewy, generally about 3 minutes for fresh, 8 minutes for dried. Drain, rinse under water to remove excess surface starch, drain again and transfer to a bowl.

INGREDIENTS:

8 dried shiitake mushrooms

½ pound pork tenderloin

1 tablespoon light soy sauce (also sold as "fresh," "pure bean," or "thin" soy sauce)

1 tablespoon + 2 ½ teaspoons dark soy sauce

1 teaspoon cornstarch

¾ teaspoon sugar, divided

1 ½ teaspoons Shaoxing rice wine or dry sherry

1 bunch (1 ½ pounds) choi sum or 6 baby bok choy

Salt

1 pound fresh or frozen udon noodles, homemade (page 207) or store-bought

4 tablespoons peanut or grapeseed oil, divided

2 ½ teaspoons soy sauce

Chinese black vinegar for serving (page 446)

CHINESE BLACK VINEGAR

In this recipe, Chinese black vinegar is used to add a final touch of umami flavor to the finished dish. Also known as Chinkiang or Zhenjiang vinegar, it is an aged vinegar made by adding acetic acid and bacteria typically to glutinous rice, though it can also be made from wheat, millet, sorghum, or a combination of the four. Darkly colored and fruity tasting, Chinese black vinegar is reminiscent of balsamic vinegar, though it is less sweet, less acidic, and has a strong, fragrant flavor that is almost spicy in nature. Found in well-stocked Asian markets, it is also quite tasty as a dipping sauce, on its own or when mixed with soy sauce, and adds depth when added to marinades and sauces for stir-frying.

5 Heat a wok or large skillet over medium heat for 2 to 3 minutes. Add 2 tablespoons of the oil and turn the heat to high. When the oil begins to swirl on the surface, add the pork (try to do it to maximize initial surface contact with the hot skillet) and stir-fry until browned. Turn the heat to medium, transfer the pork to a warmed plate, and tent loosely with aluminum foil.

6 Add the remaining 2 tablespoons oil to the pan, heat for a minute, then add the mushrooms and a pinch of salt. Stir-fry for about 2 minutes. Add the noodles and toss to coat well with the mixture. Add the regular soy sauce and the remaining 2 ½ teaspoons dark soy sauce and ½ teaspoon sugar and stir-fry until the noodles turn an even deep brown color. Add the choi sum (or bok choy) and pork and stir-fry until heated through, about 2 minutes.

7 Divide the mixture among four heated plates and serve piping hot with Chinese black vinegar at the table for drizzling.

RICE NOODLES *with* BEEF IN BLACK BEAN SAUCE

YIELD: 4 SERVINGS / ACTIVE TIME: 30 MINUTES / TOTAL TIME: 45 MINUTES

This recipe fully utilizes the flavor-packed powers of Chinese black bean sauce, which is a paste-like condiment made from fermented black soybeans, called *douche* in Chinese. Inoculated with a special mold spore, *Aspergillus oryzae*, the soybeans are then dried in the sun, where they develop a flavor that is simultaneously sharp, pungent, salty, spicy, and slightly sweet. Once dried, the beans are combined with other ingredients to make black bean sauce, an important flavoring agent in Chinese cuisine, especially in Cantonese and Sichuan cooking. In China, it is as common and everyday as ketchup is in the United States. When added to dishes, the paste adds a meaty and robust note to anything it touches. Just as importantly, it flavors dishes almost instantly, without requiring lengthy marinating.

1 Wrap the meat in clear food wrap and put in the freezer for 20 minutes (will make it easier to slice). Cut into the thinnest possible 2-inch slices.

2 Bring a large pot of water to a boil. When it's boiling, add the noodles and stir for the first minute to prevent any sticking. Cook until they are tender but still chewy, about 15 minutes. Drain, rinse the noodles under hot water to remove any starchy surface residue, and drain well again. Set aside.

3 While the noodles are cooking, combine the dark soy sauce, rice wine, sugar, and white pepper in a medium shallow bowl. Add the sliced meat and mix to ensure it is completely coated.

4 Heat a wok or large skillet over medium heat for 2 to 3 minutes. Turn the heat to medium-high and add the oil. When it begins to swirl on the surface, add the beef and stir-fry until it begins to brown on its edges and surface, about 3 minutes. Quickly remove the beef slices to a warmed bowl. Tent them loosely with aluminum foil to keep warm.

5 Add the scallions and peppers to the pan and stir-fry until the peppers begin to brown on their edges, 2 to 3 minutes. Add the black bean sauce and continue stir-frying until you no longer see it, then add the light soy sauce. Add the drained rice noodles and toss until fully mixed with the vegetables and sauce, 1 to 2 minutes. Return the beef to the pan and stir-fry until all the ingredients are warmed through, 2 to 3 minutes.

6 Divide the stir-fry among four warmed bowls and serve piping hot.

INGREDIENTS:

- ½ pound rump steak, thinly sliced
- ½ pound dried rice sticks, 3 mm (about ⅛ inch) wide and 8 to 10 inches long
- 1 tablespoon dark soy sauce
- 2 teaspoons Shaoxing rice wine or dry sherry
- 1 teaspoon sugar
- ½ teaspoon freshly ground white pepper
- 3 tablespoons peanut or grapeseed oil
- 1 bunch (5 or 6) scallions, trimmed and thinly sliced
- 1 red bell pepper, seeded and cut into thin strips
- 1 green bell pepper, seeded and cut into thin strips
- 2 tablespoons black bean sauce
- 3 tablespoons light soy sauce (also sold as "fresh," "pure bean," or "thin" soy sauce)

KOREAN-CHINESE NOODLES
with PORK *and* BLACK BEAN SAUCE

YIELD: 4 SERVINGS / ACTIVE TIME: 25 MINUTES / TOTAL TIME: 40 MINUTES

Sweet and savory, *jajangmyeon*, or *jjajangmyeon*, is a popular Korean-Chinese noodle dish. Traditionally served by parents to celebrate their children's birthdays, exam days, and graduations, it has become deeply embedded in the culinary fabric of Korea. More recently, *jajangmyeon* has also become "the" noodle dish that single South Koreans eat while commiserating with their other single friends every April 14th on what is called Black Day.

While ramen or Chinese egg noodles work well in this recipe, I would recommend searching for the fresh noodles called *junghwa-myeon* (typically found in the frozen section of Asian markets), as they have a remarkably springy and chewy texture. They are typically sold in slightly twisted bunches and look like lightly golden strands covered in white flour. Because they are always sold frozen, you will need to have them sit out on the counter for 15 minutes, at which point you can separate them. Look for Korean black bean sauce in well-stocked supermarkets and Asian markets; it is first fried in oil to tame its subtle bitter taste and a bit of sugar is added as well. While pork is the classic option for this dish, beef, chicken, or even shrimp can be substituted.

1 Combine the pork cubes, rice wine, ginger, ½ teaspoon salt, and pepper in a medium bowl and mix well. Let marinate at room temperature as you cut up the vegetables.

2 Put the black bean paste, 2 tablespoons of the oil, and the sugar in a small saucepan and cook over medium heat for 2 to 3 minutes, stirring constantly, until it becomes a runny paste, 3 to 4 minutes. Set aside.

3 Bring a large pot of water to a boil.

4 Heat a wok or a large skillet over medium heat for 2 to 3 minutes. Turn the heat to medium-high, add the remaining 2 tablespoons oil, and let heat for 1 minute. When it begins to swirl on the surface, add the pork and stir-fry until it is no longer pink and begins to brown on the edges and surface, 3 to 4 minutes. Transfer to a warmed bowl and tent loosely with aluminum foil to keep warm.

INGREDIENTS:

- ½ pound pork loin or tenderloin, cut into ½-inch cubes
- 2 tablespoons Shaoxing rice wine, mirin or dry sherry
- 1 1-inch piece fresh ginger, peeled and grated
- Salt
- ½ teaspoon freshly ground black pepper
- ½ cup Korean black bean paste (chunjang or jjajang)
- 4 tablespoons grapeseed or safflower oil, divided
- 2 tablespoons sugar
- 1 large onion, diced
- 1 ½ cups cabbage cut into ½-inch pieces
- 1 large zucchini, cut into ½-inch cubes
- 2 cups chicken or vegetable broth
- 2 tablespoons cornstarch, dissolved in ¼ cup water
- 1 ½ pounds jung-hwa-myeon, ramen, or Chinese egg noodles
- 1 small cucumber, peeled, seeded, and cut into julienne ⅛ inch wide and 2 inches long

5 Add the onion, cabbage, zucchini, and a couple pinches of salt to the pan and cook, stirring occasionally, until soft, 5 to 6 minutes. Add the pork and the black bean mixture and toss until everything is well coated with the paste. Add the broth and bring to a boil. Cook for 3 to 4 minutes. Add the cornstarch slurry, mix well, and cook until the sauce thickens, 1 to 2 minutes. Taste for seasoning and add more salt or sugar if needed.

6 When the water for the noodles is boiling, add the noodles and stir for the first minute to prevent any sticking. Cook according to the package directions until they are tender but still chewy. Drain and rinse with warm water to remove any starchy surface residue. Drain well and set aside.

7 Divide the noodles among four warmed shallow bowls. Spoon the sauce over the noodles and garnish with the cucumber julienne.

ANTS CLIMBING A TREE

YIELD: 4 SERVINGS / ACTIVE TIME: 20 MINUTES / TOTAL TIME: 45 MINUTES

A Sichuan classic. Its unusual name comes from an imaginative estimation that the noodles, chopped scallions, and ground meat resemble, respectively, tree branches, green leaves, and ants. Very thin thread-like cellophane noodles, also known as bean threads, give this dish a unique shimmery appearance. Made from mung bean flour and water, they become almost transparent when soaked in water before cooking and don a unique slippery texture that, when stir-fried, easily picks up the flavors of the other ingredients. If you like your dishes very saucy, consider increasing the chicken broth to 1 cup, as cellophane noodles are very absorbent and will dry out the dish.

INGREDIENTS:

- ½ pound cellophane noodles
- 2 ½ tablespoons peanut oil, divided
- 4 ounces ground pork
- 4 ounces ground beef
- 1 ½ tablespoons soy sauce, divided
- ⅛ teaspoon salt
- 1 ½ tablespoons chili bean paste
- 1 teaspoon dark soy sauce
- ¾ cup chicken broth, hot
- 3 scallions, white and light green parts only, trimmed and thinly sliced

1 Soak the noodles in a medium bowl of warm water until softened, about 20 minutes. Drain well, wipe the bowl with a paper towel, and return the noodles to it. Toss with ½ tablespoon of the oil to prevent them from sticking together.

2 Combine both ground meats, ½ tablespoon of the soy sauce, and the salt in another medium bowl and mix well.

3 Heat a wok or large skillet over medium heat for 2 to 3 minutes. Turn the heat to high and add the remaining 2 tablespoons oil. When it begins to swirl on the surface, add the ground meat mixture and cook, stirring and pressing down on it often, until it begins to brown, 5 to 7 minutes. Add the chili bean paste and mix well. Add the dark soy sauce and mix well again. Add the noodles, broth, and remaining 1 tablespoon soy sauce and toss to thoroughly coat the noodles. Lower the heat to medium-low, cover, and simmer until there is very little moisture in the bottom, 8 to 10 minutes.

4 Carefully shake the wok, without stirring, and sprinkle the scallions over the top. Serve piping hot.

MONGOLIAN BEEF
with CRISPY CHOW MEIN NOODLES

YIELD: 4 SERVINGS / ACTIVE TIME: 45 MINUTES / TOTAL TIME: 55 MINUTES, PLUS 3 HOURS TO MARINATE

This gingery and subtly sweet dish is a delightful combination of textures. The crunchy noodles contrast nicely with the fried beef strips that, thanks to the tenderizing beer in which it has been marinated, are tender and chewy. Bok choy balances out the ingredients by adding a fresh element. While this book offers a recipe for homemade egg noodles, you can also use the fresh, frozen, or dried variety that can be found at your local Asian market. All three types will require boiling in water. Uncooked fresh or frozen noodles will need 30 to 60 seconds of boiling to become pleasantly chewy, while dried versions, usually sold as Hong Kong-style egg noodles, take a few minutes. Drain, rinse under cold water, and drain again before throwing them into your stir-fry. Be sure not to overcook any of these noodles because they will lose their chewy texture once they are also stir-fried. If you can find them, pre-cooked fresh lo mein noodles are sometimes available in the refrigerated section of some Asian markets and will be clearly labeled as such (you don't want to risk boiling precooked noodles or you'll end up with a mushy mess). People find the pre-cooked version very convenient because they eliminate the need to boil them, making whipping up a weeknight meal particularly convenient.

1 Put the flank steak and beer to a large ziplock plastic bag. Place in a shallow pan and marinate in the refrigerator for 3 hours, turning the bag over a few times. Let the steak come to room temperature before cooking.

2 Heat a small saucepan over medium heat for 1 minute. Add the sesame oil, heat for a minute, then add the garlic and ginger and cook, stirring, until fragrant, about 1 minute. Add the soy sauce and ½ cup of the water and bring to a boil. Add the molasses, sriracha, and brown sugar and cook, stirring frequently, until the sauce lightly thickens, about 5 minutes. Remove from the heat and set aside.

3 Bring a large pot of water to a boil and add the noodles. Cook according to the package or recipe instructions until they are tender but chewy. Drain and place them on a kitchen towel to absorb as much moisture as possible before frying. You will need to work in two batches for the crispiest results.

INGREDIENTS:

- 1 **pound flank steak**
- 1 **12-ounce bottle beer**
- 1 **tablespoon toasted sesame oil**
- 3 **garlic cloves, thinly sliced**
- 1 **2-inch piece fresh ginger, peeled and grated or minced**
- ½ **cup soy sauce**
- ¾ **cup water, divided**
- 1 ½ **tablespoons molasses**
- 1 **teaspoon sriracha, more to taste**
- ⅔ **cup firmly packed brown sugar**
- ¾ **pound fresh, frozen or dried Chinese egg noodles, homemade (page 204) or store-bought**
- 2 **cups + 4 tablespoons peanut or grapeseed**
- 2 **tablespoons cornstarch**
- 8 **baby bok choy, quartered lengthwise**
- **Salt**

4 Line two plates with paper towels and begin crisping the noodles. Heat a medium skillet over low heat for 2 to 3 minutes. Add 2 tablespoons of the peanut oil and raise the heat to medium-high. Allow the oil to heat for 1 to 2 minutes until it begins to swirl on the surface but is not yet smoking and then add half of the air-dried noodles and evenly distribute them over the bottom of the pan. Cook the noodles, without touching them, until they are golden brown and crispy on the bottom, 3 to 4 minutes. (Using a spatula or rubber-coated tongs, carefully lift up the noodles to check the color after 3 minutes.) Once the noodles are golden brown and crisp, carefully flip the disc over with the assistance of both a spatula and tongs. Cook the other side for 3 minutes undisturbed. Transfer the crisped noodles to one of the paper towel-lined plate.

5 Add 2 more tablespoons of the peanut oil to the pan and repeat the process with the remaining noodles. Once cooked, transfer to the other paper towel-lined plate.

6 Remove the steak, now at room temperature, from its marinade; discard the bag of marinade. Pat dry with paper towels and transfer to a cutting board. Slice into thin strips, cutting against the grain. Place the strips in a medium bowl and toss with the cornstarch until all pieces are evenly coated.

7 Line a serving platter with paper towels and begin cooking the steak. Heat a medium, deep saucepan over low heat for 2 minutes. Add the remaining 2 cups peanut oil and turn the heat to medium-high. Using a candy or deep-fry thermometer, measure the heat of the oil. Once it reaches 360°F, carefully add 4 steak slices. Cook for 1 ½ minutes and remove with a slotted spoon. Transfer to the paper towel-lined platter and tent loosely with aluminum foil to keep warm. Repeat with the remaining steak slices. You want to maintain the temperature between 360° and 375°F at all times, so keep your eye on the thermometer and adjust the heat up or down as necessary.

8 As the steak slices cook, heat a large skillet over medium heat for 2 minutes. Add the quartered bok choy, two pinches of salt and the remaining ¼ cup water and stir. Once the water starts to boil, cover and let steam for 2 minutes. Remove from the heat and set aside.

9 Transfer the cooked steak slices to a medium bowl, add ¾ cup of the sauce, and toss. Cut both crispy noodle circles in half and place them on four plates. Top with the steak slices and bok choy. Serve piping hot, accompanied by a bowl containing the remaining sauce for drizzling.

NOODLES *with* SEARED BEEF *and* PEANUTS

YIELD: 6 SERVINGS / ACTIVE TIME: 45 MINUTES / TOTAL TIME: 1 HOUR

Stir-fried marinated slices of beef offset rich and savory egg noodles in this fast and tasty recipe. Feel free to add snap peas for an extra splash of color. Also, freezing the steak for 30 minutes makes it much easier to slice. While this book offers a recipe for homemade egg noodles, you can also use the fresh, frozen, or dried variety that can be found at your local Asian market. All three types will require boiling in water. Uncooked fresh or frozen noodles will need 30 to 60 seconds of boiling to become pleasantly chewy, while dried versions, usually sold as Hong Kong-style egg noodles, take a few minutes. Drain, rinse under cold water, and drain again before throwing them into your stir-fry. Be sure not to overcook any of these noodles because they will lose their chewy texture once they are also stir-fried. If you can find them, pre-cooked fresh lo mein noodles are sometimes available in the refrigerated section of some Asian markets and will be clearly labeled as such (you don't want to risk boiling precooked noodles or you'll end up with a mushy mess). People find the precooked version very convenient because they eliminate the need to boil them.

1 Trim any fat from the meat. Slice in half lengthwise and then, cutting across the grain, cut each half into ⅙-inch-thick slices.

2 Combine 3 tablespoons of the soy sauce, 1 tablespoon of the vinegar, and 1 teaspoon of the sugar in a medium bowl, stirring until the sugar dissolves. Add half the scallions, 2 teaspoons of the sesame oil, and a good couple cracks of black pepper. Add the beef slices and stir to coat well. Marinate for 30 minutes at room temperature.

3 Put the remaining scallions, 2 tablespoons soy sauce, 1 tablespoon vinegar, and 1 teaspoon sugar, 1 tablespoon of the sesame oil, the peanut butter, ginger, red pepper flakes, and boiling water in a food processor or blender. Process until well blended and smooth. Set aside.

4 Bring a large pot of water to a boil. Once it's boiling, add salt (1 tablespoon for every 4 cups water) and stir. Add the noodles, stirring for the first minute to prevent any sticking, and cook according to the package or recipe instructions until they are tender but still chewy.

INGREDIENTS:

- 1 **pound boneless beef top sirloin**
- 5 **tablespoons soy sauce, divided**
- 2 **tablespoon rice vinegar, divided**
- 2 **teaspoons sugar, divided**
- 6 **scallions (white and light green parts), trimmed and thinly sliced**
- 1 ½ **tablespoons + 2 teaspoons toasted sesame oil**

  Freshly ground black pepper
- ⅓ **cup creamy natural peanut butter**
- 1 **2-inch piece fresh ginger, peeled and chopped**
- ¾ **teaspoon red pepper flakes**
- 3 **tablespoons boiling hot water**

  Salt
- ¾ **pound fresh, frozen or dried Chinese egg noodles, homemade (page 204) or store-bought**
- 2 ½ **tablespoons peanut or grapeseed oil, divided**
- 1 **red bell pepper, seeded and cut into thin strips**

  Handful chopped fresh cilantro for garnish

  Chopped roasted peanuts for garnish

5 Warm the peanut sauce in the microwave for 30 to 45 seconds.

6 Drain the noodles, rinse briefly with hot water, and drain. Place in a warmed serving bowl along with the remaining ½ tablespoon sesame oil and the peanut sauce and toss to coat. Taste for seasoning, adding salt and pepper if needed. Cover and keep warm.

7 Heat a wok or large skillet over medium heat for 2 to 3 minutes. Once it's very hot (you can test by adding a drop of water; if it bounces off the surface, the pan is ready), add 2 tablespoons of the peanut oil and let heat up for 30 seconds. Working in batches so as to not overcrowd the pan, sear a few pieces of meat in a single layer for about 30 minutes per side. Transfer to a warmed plate and tent loosely with aluminum foil to keep warm. Once finished cooking the meat, add the remaining ½ tablespoon peanut oil to the pan, followed by the pepper slivers and a pinch of salt. Stir and cook for a minute. Transfer to the plate with the cooked meat.

8 Divide the noodles among six warmed bowls and top with the beef and pepper slices. Serve immediately, topped with cilantro and peanuts.

RICE NOODLES *with* BEEF *and* CHINESE BROCCOLI

YIELD: 4 SERVINGS / ACTIVE TIME: 30 MINUTES / TOTAL TIME: 45 MINUTES

This is a wonderful one-pot meal to add to your weeknight repertoire. It features wide rice noodles, in all of their chewy and springy glory, and Chinese broccoli, or gai lun, which looks like elongated Swiss chard but actually tastes like bolder and slightly more bitter broccoli. While you can swap it out for regular broccoli, if you can find it in your local food store, I encourage you to give it a try. The steak should be sliced as thin as you can manage; putting it in the freezer for a half hour to firm it up helps, if you have the time. Finally, this recipe calls for Korean fermented soybean paste. Called *doenjang*, it adds a distinctive flavor that is simultaneously earthy, salty, and incredibly savory. While it is found in the Korean section of well-stocked Asian markets, it can also be substituted with the more readily available red or brown Japanese miso paste, which will lend an approximate essence to the dish.

1 Slice the steak against the grain as thinly as you can. Combine the baking soda, 3 tablespoons of the soy sauce, and the pepper in a medium bowl and whisk together until smooth. Add the steak slices and toss until the beef is evenly coated with the soy mixture. Cover and set aside (the meat needs to be room temperature to cook at its best).

2 Trim each stalk of broccoli about 1½ inches from the bottom. Keep the stalks and leafy parts separate as you prep them. Cut the stalks into approximately ½-inch-thick slices and chop the green leafy sections into 2-inch pieces. (If using regular broccoli, cut the stems in the same way and the florets into bite-size pieces.)

3 Combine 6 tablespoons of the broth and the cornstarch in a medium bowl and whisk until smooth, with no lumps. Whisk in the oyster sauce and fermented soybean paste, then gradually whisk in the rest of the broth to keep any lumps from forming. Set aside.

4 Bring a large pot of water to a boil and add the noodles. Cook according to the package instructions until they are tender but chewy. Drain, rinse under cold water, drain again, and place them on a kitchen towel to absorb as much moisture as possible before frying. You will need to work in two batches for the crispiest results.

INGREDIENTS:

1 **pound rib-eye steak**

2 **teaspoons baking soda**

4 **tablespoons soy sauce, divided**

¾ **teaspoon freshly ground black pepper**

1 ¾ **pounds Chinese broccoli**

6 **cups chicken broth**

6 **tablespoons cornstarch**

2 **tablespoons oyster sauce**

2 **teaspoons fermented soybean paste (doenjang) or red or brown miso paste**

¾ **pound wide rice noodles**

6 **tablespoons peanut or grapeseed oil, divided**

2 **tablespoons dark soy sauce, divided**

6 **garlic cloves, minced**

Fish sauce for serving (optional)

5 Line two plates with paper towels and begin crisping the noodles. Heat a medium skillet over low heat for 2 minutes. Add 2 tablespoons of the oil and raise the heat to medium-high. Let the oil heat up for 1 to 2 minutes, until it starts to swirl on the surface but is not yet smoking. Add half of the noodles and 1 tablespoon each of the soy sauce and the dark soy sauce and toss to mix. Evenly distribute the noodles over the bottom of the skillet, turn the heat to high, and let the noodles sit undisturbed until browned and crispy on the bottom, 2 to 3 minutes. (Using a spatula or rubber-coated tongs, carefully lift a side to check the color after 2 minutes.)

6 Once the noodles are golden brown and crisp, carefully flip the noodles over with the spatula and tongs. Cook the other side until golden and crisp, another 3 minutes. Remove the crisped noodles from the pan and transfer to one of the paper towel-lined plates.

7 Add another 2 tablespoons oil to the pan and repeat the process with the remaining noodles, adding the remaining 1 tablespoon each soy sauce and dark soy sauce. Once cooked, transfer to the other paper towel-lined plate.

8 Return the skillet to high heat, add the remaining 2 tablespoons oil and the garlic and stir-fry for about 30 seconds. Add the beef and broccoli stalks and cook, stirring frequently, until the meat is almost fully cooked (they will still have a few pink spots), 2 to 3 minutes. Add the leafy parts of the broccoli and cook for an additional minute. Pour the sauce over all the ingredients and cook, stirring occasionally, until the sauce thickens, about 2 minutes.

9 Break each noodle cake in half and place on a plate. Ladle the broccoli mixture in equal amounts over the noodles and serve piping hot, with fish sauce on the table for diners to drizzle on top.

VIETNAMESE BEEF *and* VERMICELLI NOODLE SALAD

YIELD: 4 SERVINGS / ACTIVE TIME: 1 HOUR / TOTAL TIME: 1 ¼ HOURS

Bun bo xao xa is a popular Vietnamese dish that combines stir-fried lemongrass-marinated beef strips, chewy rice noodles, and a variety of fresh, crunchy vegetables and herbs. It is a terrific main-course lunch or dinner option, particularly in the summertime, when this lukewarm salad offers us a cooling bowl of food with lots of fabulous flavors. In addition to the tasty and slightly crispy browned beef, this salad gets another wallop of flavor from *nuoc cham*. A general Vietnamese term used to describe "dipping sauces," *nuoc cham* come in different flavorings, though their combination of sweet, sour, salty, savory and spicy flavors typically contain fish sauce, lime juice, and sugar.

1   Put all the *nuoc cham* ingredients in a medium bowl and whisk until the sugar dissolves. Set aside.

2   Place the noodles in a large bowl or pan and cover with cold water. Let them sit for 30 minutes. Drain, rinse them under cold tap water, and drain again. Transfer to a medium bowl, cover, and place in the refrigerator to chill.

3   Wrap the meat in clear food wrap and put in the freezer for 20 minutes (this will make it easier to slice). Slice the beef against the grain into ⅙-inch slices.

4   Prepare the lemongrass by peeling off the tough, dry outer layers. Bash the whole length with a rolling pin or knife handle to release the aromatics. Slice the lemongrass into thin rounds and mince. Mix the sliced beef, lemongrass, fish sauce, garlic, and sugar together in a small medium bowl and let marinate at room temperature for 30 minutes.

5   Bring a medium saucepan of water to a boil. While it comes to a boil, pick over the bean sprouts, discarding any discolored or spoiled ones. Put the remaining ones in a bowl of cold water. Discard the hulls that float to the top, then rinse them under cold water. Add the sprouts to the boiling water and cook for 2 minutes. Remove them from the water with a strainer and immediately run under cold water to stop them from cooking further. Drain and set aside.

6   Heat a wok or large skillet over medium heat for 2 to 3 minutes. Once very hot (you can test by adding a drop

INGREDIENTS:

NUOC CHAM:

3   tablespoons hot water

2   tablespoons brown sugar

1   cup bean sprouts

3   tablespoons grapeseed or safflower oil

2   tablespoons fresh lime juice (from 2 small limes)

2   tablespoons fish sauce

3   tablespoons rice vinegar

3   garlic cloves, minced

1   1-inch piece fresh ginger, peeled and grated

1   red chile, such as Fresno or jalapeño, seeded and chopped

SALAD:

¾   pound thin rice vermicelli noodles

1   pound rib-eye, sirloin, rump, or flank steak

1   stalk lemongrass

2   tablespoons fish sauce

3   garlic cloves, minced

1   tablespoon brown sugar

1   head butter lettuce, pulled apart into leaves and cut across into ribbons

2   handfuls fresh cilantro leaves, chopped

2   handfuls fresh basil leaves, chopped

water; if it bounces off the surface, it's ready), add 1 tablespoon of the oil. Raise the heat to medium-high and add one third of the beef so that it is in a single layer (leaving some room between slices so that the beef doesn't steam). Don't move it for 2 minutes, so that it can develop a nice golden brown color. Flip over and cook for another 2 minutes without moving. Transfer to a warmed plate. Tent loosely with aluminum foil to keep warm. Repeat this step, adding 1 tablespoon of oil each time, two more times until all the meat is cooked.

7 Divide the lettuce and herbs among four shallow bowls. Divide the noodles into four portions and place on top of the greens. Top each bowl, on one side with the cooked beef and, on the other side, with bean sprouts, carrots, and cucumbers. Sprinkle generously with the peanuts and shallots. Finally, drizzle a couple of spoonfuls of *nuoc cham* all over (diners will then be the ones to toss everything together before eating).

2	handfuls fresh mint leaves, chopped
1	medium carrot, cut into thin julienne 3 inches long
1	medium cucumber, peeled, seeded, and cut into thin julienne 3 inches long
⅓	cup roasted peanuts, crushed
½	cup Crispy Shallots (page 747)

FRIED NOODLES IN LAMB TOMATO SAUCE

YIELD: 4 SERVINGS / ACTIVE TIME: 35 MINUTES / TOTAL TIME: 1¼ HOURS

Ding ding chao mian is a signature dish from Xinjiang, a region located in the far west of China, adjacent to Kazakhstan and Mongolia. Literally "stir-fried noodle cubes," the short, fat noodles in this hearty, bold-flavored noodle dish are also known as *soman* and *din din soman* in Central Asia. It consists of hand-pulled noodles the thickness of chopsticks stir-fried with lamb, tomatoes, and red bell and jalapeño peppers in a ginger-garlic sauce. Make sure to cut every ingredient into small cubes, as this dish is meant to be eaten with a spoon. Should you not be up for making the *ding ding chao mian* noodles, I recommend using the thickest and widest fresh noodles you can find and simply chop them into shorter pieces before boiling them to approximate the traditional noodle experience.

1 Put the lamb, rice wine, 1 teaspoon salt, cornstarch, and pepper in a medium bowl and mix well. Set aside for 15 to 20 minutes. Bring a small saucepan filled with water to a boil. Add the plum tomatoes and cook for 1 minute. Immediately transfer them to a plate (leave the water boiling on the burner). Once cooled enough to handle, remove their skins. Cut them into quarters, remove the seeds, and mince.

2 Heat a wok or large skillet over medium-low heat for 2 to 3 minutes. Add the oil and turn the heat to medium-high. When the oil begins to swirl on the surface, add the onion, garlic, ginger, and a pinch of salt and cook, stirring a few times, until the onion turns slightly golden, about 3 minutes.

3 Using a spatula or wooden spoon, move the onion mixture to one side of the pan. Add the lamb mixture and a couple pinches of salt on the empty side and spread it out over the bottom. Leave it like that for 2 minutes to let it brown slightly. Then stir and continue cooking until it is entirely cooked through. Mix the lamb and onion mixture together. Add the tomatoes and a pinch of salt and stir. Add the cooked noodles and stir. Taste for seasoning and add salt if needed. Add the chopped tomatoes, red pepper, jalapeño, soy sauce, sugar and a couple pinches of salt and stir-fry for 2 to 3 minutes. Add the vinegar and stir to combine.

4 Divide the stir-fry among four warmed plates and serve piping hot.

INGREDIENTS:

- ¾ pound ground lamb
- 2 tablespoons Shaoxing rice wine or dry sherry
- Salt
- 1 teaspoon cornstarch
- ¼ teaspoon ground Sichuan peppercorns or black pepper
- 2 plum tomatoes
- 2 tablespoons grapeseed or peanut oil
- ½ medium yellow onion, chopped
- 4 garlic cloves, minced
- Half thumb-sized piece fresh ginger, peeled and grated or minced
- ½ cup strained tomatoes
- 1 recipe Ding Ding Chao Mian Noodles (page 213) OR ¾ pound thick fresh egg Chinese noodles, cooked and cut into 2-inch lengths
- 1 red bell pepper, seeded and cut into small dice
- 1 jalapeño pepper, seeded and chopped
- 2 tablespoons soy sauce
- 1 teaspoon sugar
- 2 tablespoons Chinese black vinegar (page 466)

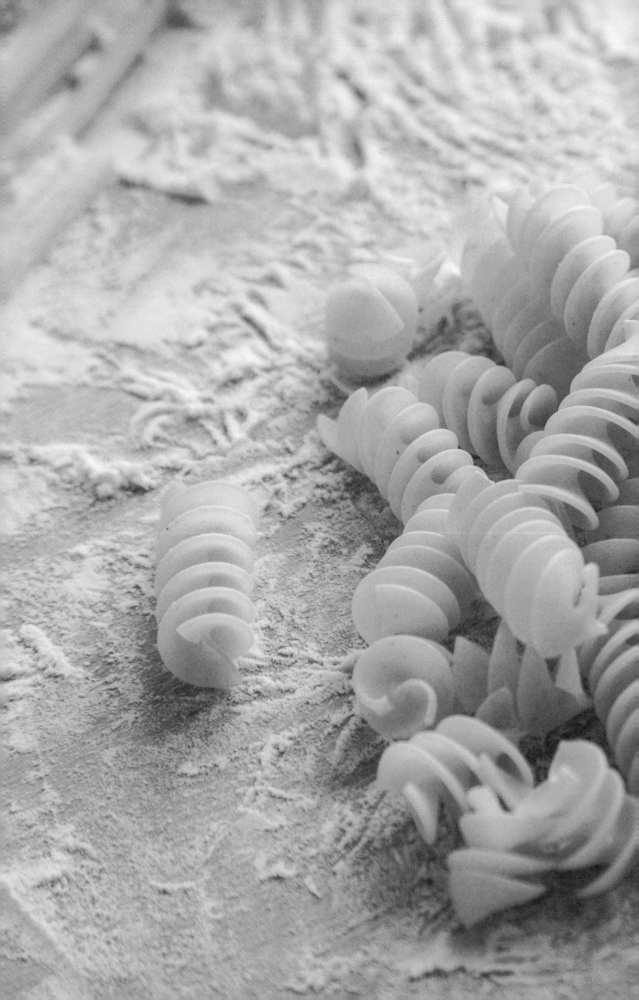

FAST & FURIOUS

*S*ocrates warned, "Beware the barrenness of a busy life." Despite his caution, however, we often find ourselves short of time to smell the roses. Although these fast and furious recipes may not lead you to higher meaning, they will fill your tummy and lift your spirits. Best of all, they don't require many ingredients and come together in the time it takes the water to come to a boil and the pasta to cook.

SPAGHETTI *with* GARLIC, OIL, *and* RED PEPPER

YIELD: 4 SERVINGS / ACTIVE TIME: 10 MINUTES / TOTAL TIME: 25 MINUTES

A typical first course from the central Italian region of Lazio and the city of Rome in particular, *spaghetti all' aglio, olio e peperoncino* is a simple and classic example of *cucina povera*, which refers to humble or rustic cooking. I like to call this the "I just got back from vacation" dish, because it comes together quickly using pantry ingredients and fills the belly in the most savory and piquant way. While you can use red pepper flakes, I recommend whole dried chiles, as they pack a greater punch heat-wise. The seeds are very hot, however, so you may want to use them sparingly until you figure out the heat index that is right for you. Also, if you happen to have some parsley on hand, mince a handful and sprinkle on top for a dash of pungent brightness. Finally, unlike what many recipes—even in this book—call for, add the garlic to the olive oil while everything is still cold. Then be watchful as the oil begins to heat that the garlic doesn't sizzle aggressively. In this recipe, we want the garlic flavor to infuse the oil but without having it color, which lends a slightly burnt and bitter taste to the dish.

INGREDIENTS:

- ⅓ cup + ½ tablespoon extra virgin olive oil, divided
- 3 garlic cloves, thinly sliced
- 1 to 2 dried red chiles, broken into pieces, with or without seeds, depending on your heat preference
- Salt
- ¾ pound spaghetti
- Handful fresh parsley leaves, chopped (optional)

1 Put a large pot of water on to boil for the pasta.

2 While the water comes to a boil, put ⅓ cup of the olive oil, the garlic, and chiles in a medium skillet and heat over medium-low heat. Let everything warm up together, with the garlic gently sizzling but not coloring at all; if need be, turn the heat down to low or turn it off entirely.

3 Once the pasta water is boiling, add salt (1 tablespoon for every 4 cups water) and stir. Add the pasta, stirring for the first minute to prevent any sticking. Cook according to the package instructions, draining the pasta 2 minutes short of the directed cooking time. The pasta should be soft but still very firm. Right before draining the pasta, reserve ¼ cup of the pasta water. Return the pot to the stove. Immediately turn the heat to high, add the remaining ½ tablespoon oil and reserved pasta water. Add the drained pasta and toss. Pour in the garlic oil and cook, tossing continuously, for 2 minutes.

4 Divide the pasta among four warmed bowls. Serve piping hot sprinkled with the parsley if using.

BROWNED BUTTER
and SAGE SAUCE

YIELD: 4 SERVINGS / ACTIVE TIME: NEGLIGIBLE / TOTAL TIME: 10 MINUTES

Piney and aromatic sage is the star in this classic pan sauce for a seemingly endless list of filled pastas, gnocchi, and dumplings. Browning the butter gives it a delicious toasty flavor. Use the crisp fried sage leaves as a garnish.

Recommended pasta shapes or dumplings: meat-, vegetable-, and cheese-filled ravioli, spätzle, agnolotti, and vegetable- and cheese-based gnocchi

1 Bring a large pot of water to a boil.

2 While the water comes to a boil, heat a skillet large enough to hold the finished pasta over medium-low heat for 2 to 3 minutes, then add the butter. Turn the heat up to medium and, once the butter melts and stops foaming, add the sage leaves. Cook, stirring occasionally, until the butter begins to brown on the bottom and the sage leaves become crispy. You will need to be very attentive during this step, as butter can burn in a blink of an eye. You want to make sure the sage is sizzling very gently so that

INGREDIENTS:

6 tablespoons (¾ stick) unsalted butter, cut into several pieces, plus 1 tablespoon for seasoning the pasta

8 fresh sage leaves

Salt

¾ pound filled pasta like ravioli, dumplings, or gnocchi

Freshly ground black pepper

Freshly grated Parmigiano-Reggiano cheese for serving

it gets nice and crisp when finished, while monitoring it carefully to ensure it does not burn in the process. If sizzling too much, lower the heat and take the skillet off the stove for 30 seconds or so before returning it to the burner. Take the pan off the heat once the sage leaves are done. Remove the leaves from the butter and reserve as a garnish.

3 When the water is boiling, add salt (1 tablespoon for every 4 cups water) and stir. Add the pasta, stirring for the first minute to prevent any sticking. Cook according to the package (or recipe) instructions. Right before draining the pasta, reserve ½ cup of the pasta water. Return the empty pot to the stove. Immediately turn the heat to high, add the remaining 1 tablespoon butter and reserved pasta water. Add the drained pasta and toss. Now add the browned butter and cook, tossing continuously, for 1 to 2 minutes.

4 Serve piping hot on warmed plates, each serving topped with two fried sage leaves, a few good cracks of black pepper, and Parmigiano (or pass the grated cheese at the table).

PASTA WITH BROWNED BUTTER, SAGE, AND PROSCIUTTO

This is great with gnocchi, spätzle, penne, campanelle, gemelli, trenette, and tagliatelle. The shreds of prosciutto get wonderfully crispy. Two minutes after you add the sage to the skillet, add 10 very thin slices prosciutto (about 5 ounces), sliced across into 1-inch ribbons, increase the heat to medium-high, and cook, stirring a few times, until the sage is crisp and the prosciutto caramel colored. Take off the heat and continue with the recipe as directed.

CLASSIC BUTTERED NOODLES

YIELD: 4 SERVINGS AS MAIN DISH OR 6 TO 8 SERVINGS AS SIDE DISH
ACTIVE TIME: 10 MINUTES / TOTAL TIME: 20 MINUTES

A simple, speedy, and tasty first course or side dish, buttered noodles require just a handful of ingredients and satisfy children of all ages, even adult ones. For the tastiest results, serve it piping hot and generously dusted with white pepper. For extra flavor, omit salting the pasta water and add a couple bouillon cubes instead.

1 Bring a large pot of water to a boil. Once it's boiling, add salt (1 tablespoon for every 4 cups water) and stir. Add the noodles and stir for the first minute to prevent any sticking. Cook according to the package instructions, draining the pasta 2 minutes short of the directed cooking time. The pasta will be soft but still very firm. Right before draining the pasta, reserve ¼ cup of the pasta water. Return the pot to the stove. Immediately turn the heat to high, add ½ tablespoon of the butter and the reserved pasta water. Add the drained pasta and toss. Add the remaining 5 tablespoons butter, the Parmigiano, parsley, and pepper to taste and cook, tossing continuously, for 2 minutes.

2 Transfer to a large bowl, sprinkle with more Parmigiano (or pass the grated cheese at the table) and serve.

INGREDIENTS:

- Salt
- ¾ pound flat egg noodles
- 5 ½ tablespoons room temperature unsalted butter, divided
- ½ cup freshly grated Parmigiano-Reggiano cheese, plus more for serving
- Handful fresh parsley leaves, chopped
- Freshly grated white pepper

MALTAGLIATI *with* CREAMY LEMON SAUCE

YIELD: 4 SERVINGS / ACTIVE TIME: 10 MINUTES / TOTAL TIME: 25 MINUTES

Ideal for hot summer days, this refreshing pasta dish makes you feel as though you are having a lovely meal in Sorrento, the enchanting coastal town located on the Amalfi Coast. The lemon, so representative of the gigantically bumpy and canary yellow citrus fruits that grow abundantly on the area's spectacular cliffs, breaks up the richness of the cream with its acidity, making the sauce piquant and feathery light. Because the sauce is so light, this dish is at its best when paired with a delicate pasta shape since larger pasta shapes would overwhelm it.

Other recommended pasta shapes: tagliatelle, angel hair, vermicelli

INGREDIENTS:

Grated zest and juice of 1 lemon

5 tablespoons unsalted butter, divided

½ cup heavy cream, more if needed

¼ teaspoon freshly ground white pepper, or more, to taste

Salt

¾ pound maltagliati, homemade (page 183) or store-bought

½ cup freshly grated Parmigiano-Reggiano cheese, plus more for serving

1 Put a large pot of water on to boil for the pasta.

2 Put the lemon zest and juice in a 2-cup Pyrex measuring cup along with 4 tablespoons of the butter cut into small pieces, the cream, pepper, and a few generous pinches of salt. Put the measuring cup in a microwave and heat on high for 45 to 60 seconds, until the butter is fully melted. Cover and set aside.

3 When the pasta water is boiling, add salt (1 tablespoon for every 4 cups water) and stir. Add the pasta, stirring for the first minute to prevent any sticking. Cook according to the package (or recipe) instructions, draining the pasta 2 minutes short of the directed cooking time. The pasta should be soft but still very firm. Right before draining the pasta, reserve ¼ cup of the pasta water. Return the empty pot to the stove. Immediately turn the heat to high, add the remaining 1 tablespoon butter and reserved pasta water. Add the drained pasta and toss. Add the warm lemon cream mixture and the Parmigiano and cook, tossing continuously, for 2 minutes.

4 Divide the pasta among four warmed bowls and serve piping hot dusted with Parmigiano (or pass the grated cheese at the table).

FETTUCCINE ALFREDO

YIELD: 4 SERVINGS / ACTIVE TIME: 15 MINUTES / TOTAL TIME: 20 MINUTES

This iconic Italian-American pasta dish was invented in 1914 by a Roman restaurateur named Alfredo di Lelio. Desperate to have his pregnant and nauseous wife eat something, he cooked up some fettuccine and seasoned it with butter and Parmigiano-Reggiano. When his creation got his wife eating again, he decided to put the simple dish on his restaurant's menu and named it, very humbly, after himself. (Why not after the woman carrying his child, I'll never know.) Shortly thereafter, Mary Pickford and Douglas Fairbanks, two Hollywood silent film stars in Rome on their honeymoon, wandered in for a bite to eat and fell in love again . . . with this dish. It didn't take long for word to get out in the States, bringing Mr. di Lelio a parade of vacationing movie starlets along with troupes of well-heeled tourists intent on rubbing elbows with Hollywood royalty. Ironically, despite its birthplace, fettuccine Alfredo has become a much more popular dish in the United States than it ever has been in Italy. This is perhaps because, unlike the plainer Italian version, which contains only butter and Parmigiano and is served predominantly to young children and convalescing adults, the Italian-American version added lavish amounts of heavy cream somewhere along the way. This particular version stays faithful to its Italian origins, and gets its creaminess from the emulsion between the melted butter, grated cheese, and starchy pasta water.

INGREDIENTS:

4 ½ tablespoons unsalted butter, divided

Salt

¾ pound fettuccine or other long pasta

1 cup freshly grated Parmigiano-Reggiano cheese, plus more for serving

Freshly ground black pepper

1 Cut the 4 tablespoons of butter into 4 pieces and set aside to soften as you cook the pasta.

2 Bring a large pot of water to a boil. Once it's boiling, add salt (1 tablespoon for every 4 cups water) and stir. Add the fettuccine and stir for first minute to prevent any sticking. Cook according to the package instructions, draining the pasta 2 minutes short of the directed cooking time. The pasta should be tender but still very firm.

3 About 4 minutes before you will need to drain the fettuccine, transfer 1 cup pasta water to a skillet large enough to hold the finished pasta dish. Bring to a gentle simmer, then whisk in the butter, a piece at a time, until emulsified. Whisking constantly, gradually add the Parmigiano, making sure what you've added is completely melted and incorporated into the sauce before adding more (caution: rushing this part creates globs of cheese in the sauce).

4   Drain the pasta, reserving ½ cup of the pasta water (though you will most likely not need all of it). Return the empty pot to the stove and immediately turn the heat to high. Add the remaining ½ tablespoon butter and ¼ cup of the pasta water. Quickly add the drained pasta and toss until all the liquid at the bottom of the pot has been absorbed.

5   Transfer the pasta to the skillet with the cheese sauce and toss to coat, adding more of the pasta water as needed, until the noodles are evenly coated.

6   Divide the fettuccine among four warmed bowls. Serve piping hot, dusted with a good crack or two of pepper and more Parmigiano (or pass the grated cheese at the table).

FONDUTA

YIELD: 4 SERVINGS / ACTIVE TIME: 12 MINUTES / TOTAL TIME: 25 MINUTES

I have a friend who always says "Check your health concerns at the door" when sitting down communally to a rich and creamy dish such as this. I would have to agree because this sauce is delightfully decadent, and really should only be indulged in occasionally. What makes *fonduta* particularly delicious is the fontina cheese, a mild, nutty-flavored semi-soft cow's milk cheese from the Valle d'Aosta region of Italy. Because it is added to the sauce right before serving, it hasn't had the time to fully melt and thus creates a stringy consistency reverently referred to as *alla bava* or "drool-worthy."

Recommended pasta shapes or dumplings: gnocchi, spätzle, penne, campanelle, gemelli, trenette, tagliatelle

INGREDIENTS:

Salt

¾ pound pasta

1 garlic clove, cut in half

6 ounces Val D'Aosta Fontina cheese, grated, divided

½ cup freshly grated Parmigiano-Reggiano cheese, plus more for serving

1 ¼ cups heavy cream

4 large egg yolks

4 ½ tablespoons unsalted butter, at room temperature

2 teaspoons Worcestershire sauce

1 teaspoon freshly grated nutmeg

Freshly ground white pepper

Chopped fresh parsley for garnish

1 Bring a large pot of water to a boil. Once it's boiling, add salt (1 tablespoon for every 4 cups water) and stir. Add the pasta and stir for the first minute to prevent any sticking. Cook following the package (or recipe) instructions, though you will drain the pasta 2 minutes prior to the directed cooking time. The pasta should be soft but still very firm. Right before draining the pasta, reserve ¼ cup of the pasta water.

2 While the pasta is cooking, rub the inside of a medium metal bowl with the cut garlic, then discard. Make a double boiler by placing the garlic-rubbed bowl over a medium saucepan that has been filled one third of the way with boiling water; the bowl should not touch the water. Set the saucepan over the lowest heat possible. Add half the fontina, the Parmigiano, and the cream to the bowl and heat, stirring continuously, until the cheeses melt and the mixture becomes thick enough to coat the back of a spoon, about 6 minutes.

3 Put the egg yolks and ¼ cup of the cheese mixture in a small bowl and whisk until well combined. (This step, called tempering, brings up the temperature of the eggs so that they can be added to the rest of the hot cheese sauce without scrambling them.) Add this mixture, along with 4 tablespoons of the butter and the Worcestershire, to the cheese sauce and stir continuously until the butter has melted and the sauce looks slightly foamy, about 6 minutes. Season with the nutmeg and salt and white pepper to taste. Add the remaining fontina and give the sauce a good stir.

4 Drain the pasta and return the empty pot to the stove. Immediately turn the heat to high and add the remaining ½ tablespoon butter and reserved pasta water. Add the pasta and toss until the water is absorbed. Add the cheese sauce and cook, mixing continuously, for 1 to 2 minutes.

5 Ladle the pasta into four warmed bowls and serve piping hot with a few good cracks of white pepper and sprinkled with parsley and Parmigiano (or pass the grated cheese at the table).

GORGONZOLA CREAM SAUCE
with PAN-TOASTED SPICED WALNUTS

YIELD: 4 SERVINGS / ACTIVE TIME: 12 MINUTES / TOTAL TIME: 25 MINUTES

While my husband has never met a wheel of gorgonzola he hasn't absolutely adored, I sometimes find its distinctively sharp bite a little too, well . . . biting. That's why I love this particular version of gorgonzola cream sauce, because it contains gorgonzola dolce, or "sweet gorgonzola" in Italian. Developed in the north of Italy after World War II, this white to pale yellow creamy cheese came about in response to the demand for a milder version of the cheese. While it still sports gorgonzola's defining greenish-blue veins of mold, it is aged less than regular gorgonzola and consequently develops a much milder flavor.

Recommended pasta shapes or dumplings: gnocchi, spätzle, penne, campanelle, gemelli, trenette, tagliatelle

INGREDIENTS:

- 1 tablespoon olive oil
- 1 teaspoon Chef Paul Prudhomme's Magic Seasoning Blend for Meat or seasoning blend of your choice
- 1 tablespoon honey
- ½ tablespoon water
- 1 cup walnut halves
- 1 tablespoon sugar
- Salt
- ⅛ teaspoon cayenne pepper
- ¾ pound pasta
- 2 cups heavy cream
- 4 ounces gorgonzola dolce cheese, cut into pieces
- ⅔ cup freshly grated Parmigiano-Reggiano cheese
- 1 teaspoon freshly grated nutmeg
- Freshly ground white pepper
- ½ tablespoon unsalted butter

1 Heat a large nonstick skillet over low heat for a minute. Add the olive oil and seasoning blend, stir, and raise the heat to medium. Once the oil begins to gently sizzle, stir for 30 seconds, then add the honey, stir, add the water, and stir again. Add the walnuts and toss to coat them well with the mixture. Sprinkle them with the sugar, 1 teaspoon salt, and the cayenne and cook, stirring frequently, until they are lightly browned, 2 to 3 minutes. Transfer to a parchment paper-lined baking sheet so they are in a single layer and let cool completely. They will keep in an airtight container up to a month.

2 While the nuts cool, bring a large pot of water to a boil. Once it's boiling, add salt (1 tablespoon for every 4 cups water) and stir. Add the pasta and stir for first minute to prevent any sticking. Cook following the package (or recipe) instructions, though you will drain the pasta 2 minutes prior to the directed cooking time. The pasta should be soft but still very firm. Right before draining the pasta, reserve ¼ cup of the pasta water.

3 While the pasta cooks, heat the cream and cheeses together in a medium saucepan over medium heat until the cream is gently simmering, whisking occasionally until the sauce is smooth. Continue to simmer the sauce until it is thick enough to coat the back of a spoon (the sauce will reduce by about a third), 8 to 9 minutes. Season with the nutmeg and salt and white pepper to taste.

4 Drain the pasta and return the empty pot to the stove. Immediately turn the heat to high and add the butter and reserved pasta water. Add the pasta and toss until the water is absorbed. Add the sauce and cook, mixing continuously, for 1 to 2 minutes.

5 Ladle the pasta into four warmed bowls and serve piping hot with a few good cracks of white pepper and topped with the walnuts.

WALNUT, BLACK GARLIC, *and* MASCARPONE SAUCE

YIELD: **4 SERVINGS** / ACTIVE TIME: **10 MINUTES** / TOTAL TIME: **15 MINUTES**

This rich, earthy-tasting sauce features black garlic, a preparation that was developed in Korea and is quickly becoming a darling among chefs in the United States. Black garlic is made by taking regular garlic heads and heating them at a relatively low temperature for 30 days. They are then left out to oxidize for another month or so. The result are black garlic cloves with a jelly-like texture and deep umami flavor, described variously as reminiscent of soy sauce, balsamic vinegar, tamarind, and/or prunes. You can find it online, as well as at Trader Joe's and Whole Foods. While I recommend serving this sauce with chocolate pasta, mostly for dramatic effect and for the subtle flavor of unsweetened chocolate, this dish firmly remains in the savory category and generates many "ohs!" and "ahs!" when served to dinner guests.

Recommended pasta shapes or dumplings: angel hair, fettuccine, gnocchi

INGREDIENTS:

- 3 tablespoons pine nuts
- Salt
- ½ cup walnut pieces
- 2 black garlic cloves
- ½ cup mascarpone
- 3 ½ tablespoons whole milk
- 3 tablespoons freshly grated Parmigiano-Reggiano cheese
- Freshly ground white pepper
- ¾ pound chocolate pasta, homemade (fettuccine, homemade (page 715) or store-bought
- 3 tablespoons unsalted butter

1 Bring a large pot of water to a boil.

2 While the water comes to a boil, heat a small skillet over medium-low heat for 2 minutes. Add the pine nuts and cook, stirring frequently, until they turn golden in spots, 3 to 4 minutes. Remove from the heat, add ⅛ teaspoon salt, and stir well.

3 Put the walnuts and garlic cloves in a mini food processor and process until grainy. Transfer the mixture to a small saucepan and add the mascarpone, milk, Parmigiano, and salt and white pepper to taste, and stir. Heat the mixture over medium-low heat until it becomes very warm (but do not boil). Remove from the heat and cover.

4 When the water for the pasta is boiling, add salt (1 tablespoon for every 4 cups water) and stir. Add the pasta and stir for the first minute to prevent any sticking. Cook following the recipe or package instructions until the pasta is soft but still very firm. Right before draining the pasta, reserve ¼ cup of the pasta water. Return the empty pot to the stove. Immediately turn the heat to high and add the butter and reserved pasta water. Add the drained pasta and toss until the water is absorbed. Add the sauce and cook, mixing continuously, for 1 to 2 minutes.

5 Divide the pasta between four warmed bowls and serve piping hot topped with the toasted pine nuts.

PIZZOCCHERI DELLA VALTELLINA

YIELD: 4 SERVINGS / ACTIVE TIME: 15 MINUTES / TOTAL TIME: 25 MINUTES

A unique dish from the Valtellina, the foothills of the Italian Alps, this little known dish marries buckwheat pasta with potatoes, cabbage, butter, and the local cheeses of the region. Infinitely rich and hearty, it is enjoyed best when the bitter chill of winter is in the air and you're craving warming sustenance. To prepare it without sourcing the harder-to-get cheeses traditional to the dish, I've included a selection of more easily procurable ones from which to choose that will deliver delicious results.

INGREDIENTS:

- 4 ½ ounces Gruyere, Fontina, or Taleggio, grated
- ½ cup freshly grated Parmigiano-Reggiano cheese
- Salt and freshly ground black pepper
- 2 medium russet potatoes, peeled and cut into ½-inch cubes
- ¾ pound Pizzoccheri (page 161)
- ¾ cup slivered Savoy cabbage
- 4 tablespoons (½ stick) unsalted butter
- 1 garlic clove, lightly smashed
- 5 to 6 fresh sage leaves, minced

1 Combine the cheeses in a medium bowl with a few good cracks of pepper. Mix well and place the bowl by the stove.

2 Bring a large pot of water to a boil. Once it's boiling, add salt (1 tablespoon for every 4 cups water) and stir. Add the potatoes and cook for 10 minutes, stirring occasionally. Add the *pizzoccheri* and cook until they are soft but still firm (the cooking time may vary depending on its thickness and size). Add the cabbage slivers and cook for 1 more minute.

3 While the potatoes, pasta, and cabbage cook, heat a small skillet over medium heat for 2 to 3 minutes. Add the butter and turn the heat down to medium-low. When it's melted, add the garlic and sage and cook, stirring occasionally, until the butter starts to brown, 5 to 7 minutes. Discard the garlic, remove the pan from the heat, and cover to keep warm.

4 When the pasta is ready and the potatoes and cabbage are soft, using a strainer or large slotted spoon, transfer them to a warmed serving platter. (You want some of the pasta water to come along, so don't spend too much time draining them over the pot before moving them over to the skillet.) Scatter a handful of cheese over the top of each batch of drained *pizzoccheri* and vegetables you add to the platter. Repeat the process until all the pasta and vegetables have been transferred to the platter and layered with cheese. Pour the sage butter over the top and give it a couple good cracks of pepper. Serve from the platter, without stirring everything together.

PASTA *with* HAZELNUTS *and* TRUFFLE BUTTER

YIELD: 5 TO 6 SERVINGS/ ACTIVE TIME: 20 MINUTES / TOTAL TIME: 30 MINUTES

I would not be a born and bred Piedmontese if I didn't include a recipe that celebrated one of the region's agricultural jewels: the truffle. Considered one of the most prized food items in the world, truffles belong to the fungus family and come in a black and white (more valued) variety. Because they grow underground, they are challenging to find and require specialized hunting methods that often include highly trained sniffing dogs (or pigs). Fresh truffles can often be found at high-end gourmet stores or can be sourced online (once purchased, bury them under rice in a jar with a tight-fitting lid and refrigerate for up to 3 days; it'll perfume the rice wonderfully). Because fresh truffles are very expensive, you can substitute less pricey oil-packed jars of sliced or minced truffles or use good quality, authentic truffle oil made from real truffles. In this recipe, the earthy truffle blends beautifully with the creamy richness of butter and Parmigiano, while the contrasting crunch of toasted hazelnuts serves as the proverbial "cherry on top."

Recommended pasta shapes or dumplings: potato or butternut squash gnocchi, maltagliati, fettuccine and other long somewhat wide ribbons, ricotta ravioli

INGREDIENTS:

- ⅔ cup blanched hazelnuts, slightly crushed
- 6 tablespoons (¾ stick) unsalted butter, divided
- ½ ounce fresh black or white truffle, grated, or minced jarred truffle, or 1 tablespoon truffle oil
- Salt and freshly ground white pepper
- ¾ pound pasta
- 1 cup freshly grated Parmigiano-Reggiano cheese

1 Heat a large skillet over medium-low heat for 2 to 3 minutes. Add the hazelnuts and cook, stirring continuously, until they turn a golden caramel color and give off the most wonderful toasty aroma. Remove from the heat and let cool.

2 Bring a large pot of water to a boil.

3 While the water is coming to a boil, heat a small saucepan over medium-low heat for 2 to 3 minutes, then add 5 tablespoons of the butter. Once it's melted and stops foaming, add half of the truffle if using, at least ¾ teaspoon salt, and a pinch of white pepper and stir. Adjust the heat to low and cook for an additional minute, just until heated through. Remove from the heat and cover to keep warm.

4 Once the water is boiling, add salt (1 tablespoon for every 4 cups water) and stir. Add the pasta and stir for the first minute to prevent any sticking. Cook following the package (or recipe) instructions, though you will drain the pasta 2 minutes

prior to the directed cooking time. The pasta will be soft but still very firm. Right before draining the pasta, reserve ½ cup of the pasta water. Return the empty pot to the stove. Immediately turn the heat to high, add the remaining tablespoon butter and the reserved pasta water, and stir. Add the drained pasta and toss until the water is absorbed. Add the truffle butter (or the melted butter and truffle oil if using), the Parmigiano, white pepper to taste, and the remaining grated truffle if using and cook, tossing continuously, for 2 minutes.

5 Divide the pasta among four warmed bowls and serve piping hot topped with the toasted hazelnuts.

PICI PASTA
with PECORINO CHEESE *and* PEPPER

YIELD: 4 SERVINGS / ACTIVE TIME: 10 MINUTES / TOTAL TIME: 30 MINUTES

Known as pici cacio e pepe, this is essentially high-end Italian maca-roni and cheese. Like its eggier cousin *spaghetti alla carbonara,* it is a relative newcomer to the repertoire of Roman cuisine, appearing around the middle of the twentieth century. It has remained a classic first course in Rome and the neighboring region of Lazio, and has recently begun showing up at highbrow restaurants in the United States and England. That's because few dishes exem-plify the rewards of pan sauce precision like this rich, creamy, and slightly piquant dish made only from three ingredients: cheese, pasta, and pepper. You can substitute *pici* with a pasta that is potentially easier to source, but the satisfying meaty chew in this pasta dish comes only from using spaghetti's corpulent cousin.

Other recommended pasta shapes or dumplings: tagliolini, bucatini, spaghetti

---

1 Heat a skillet large enough to hold the finished dish over medium heat for 2 to 3 minutes. Add the olive oil and turn the heat up to medium-high. When the oil is swirling on the sur-face but not yet smoking, add the pepper and cook for 2 minutes. Remove from the heat.

2 Bring a large pot of water to a boil. Once it's boiling, add salt (1 tablespoon for every 4 cups water) and stir. Add the pasta, stirring for the first minute to prevent any sticking. Cook accord-ing to the recipe (or package) instructions, draining the pasta 2 minutes short of the directed cooking time. The pasta should be soft but still very firm. Right before draining the pasta, reserve ½ cup of the pasta water.

3 Using tongs, transfer the *pici* to the skillet (do not drain in a colander). Immediately turn the heat to high and toss it with the oil and pepper until coated with the mixture. Add the cheeses and 3 tablespoons of the pasta water and continue to toss until the pasta is coated evenly with the cheese. Add another tablespoon or two of pasta water if the dish seems too dry.

4 Divide the pasta among four warmed bowls and serve pip-ing hot topped with a few cracks of pepper and a good dust-ing of Parmigiano (or pass the grated cheese at the table).

INGREDIENTS:

- **7** tablespoons extra virgin olive oil

- **2 ½** teaspoons freshly ground black pepper

- Salt

- **¾** pound pici, homemade (page 169) or store-bought

- **1** cup freshly grated grana Padano or Parmigiano-Reggiano cheese, plus more for serving

- **½** cup freshly grated pecorino cheese (pecorino Sardo preferably)

CAPER *and* LEMON SAUCE

YIELD: 4 SERVINGS / ACTIVE TIME: 10 MINUTES / TOTAL TIME: 15 MINUTES

This light sauce, full of the citrusy flavor of lemon, pairs perfectly with very fine and delicate strands of pasta and makes a terrific side dish for grilled fish. The wine is integral to the flavor of this recipe. If you can find sea salt-packed capers, instead of the brined variety, use them. To remove their excess saltiness, see below.

Recommended pasta shapes or dumplings: cappellini, angel hair, tajarin

1 Bring a large pot of water to a boil.

2 While the water comes to a boil, bring the wine to a gentle boil in a small saucepan over medium heat and let continue to boil until reduced by half, about 5 minutes. Add the lemon juice and broth and heat until gently bubbling. Remove from the heat and let cool slightly.

3 When the water for the pasta is boiling, add salt (1 tablespoon for every 4 cups water) and stir. Add the pasta and stir for first minute to prevent any sticking. Cook following the package (or recipe) instructions, though you will drain the pasta 2 minutes prior to the directed cooking time. The pasta should be soft but still very firm. Right before draining the pasta, reserve ¼ cup of the pasta water.

INGREDIENTS:

- 1 cup dry white wine
- Juice and grated zest of 1 lemon
- ⅓ cup chicken broth
- Salt
- ¾ pound pasta
- 4 tablespoons (½ stick) unsalted butter, at room temperature
- 1 ½ tablespoons all-purpose flour
- 3 tablespoons capers, rinsed and minced
- Handful fresh parsley leaves, chopped
- Freshly ground white pepper
- Freshly grated Parmigiano-Reggiano cheese for serving

CAPERS

If you can find sea salt-packed capers, use them. They have a fresher taste than brined, an almost floral aroma, and they keep their shape and firmness during cooking. To remove their excess saltiness, place them in a bowl and cover with warm water. Carefully remove any salt stuck to them, then let them sit for a minute. Rinse them under cold water and taste. If they are still too salty, repeat the process.

4 While the pasta cooks, heat another small saucepan over medium-low heat for 1 to 2 minutes and add the butter. When it's melted and stops foaming, whisk in the flour until a thick paste forms. Continue to cook, still whisking, until the paste stops foaming and the mixture begins to turn a slight golden color. Very slowly pour in the wine mixture in an even stream, whisking continuously. Once the sauce thickens, remove from the heat and stir in the capers, lemon zest, and parsley. Taste for seasoning, adding salt and pepper if needed.

5 Drain the pasta and return the empty pot to the stove. Immediately turn the heat to high and add the reserved pasta water. Add the pasta and toss until the water is absorbed. Add the caper sauce and cook, mixing continuously, for 1 to 2 minutes.

6 Divide the pasta between four warmed bowls and serve piping hot with a few cracks of white pepper and a sprinkling of Parmigiano (or pass the grated cheese at the table).

BASIL PESTO

YIELD: 4 SERVINGS / ACTIVE TIME: 25 MINUTES / TOTAL TIME: 25 MINUTES

The seaside region of Liguria has made many delectable contributions to Italian cooking, including *focaccia* and *farinata*, the thin unleavened chickpea pancake. But the most famous of all is pesto or, to be more precise, *pesto alla Genovese*. Canonically served with boiled green beans and cubed potatoes and paired with linguine or short, thin, twisted *trofie,* pesto is now typically served alone on pasta. It's a pity, though, as that combination is quite delicious and even more nourishing. This recipe also adheres to its traditional roots by calling for two different kinds of cheeses, mellower Parmigiano and the slightly sharper pecorino. If you can find it, use pecorino Sardo, as it is slightly milder than pecorino Romano and creates a more balanced, less sharp pesto sauce. If you end up using pecorino Romano, increase the amount of Parmigiano-Reggiano as indicated in the ingredients list to balance its extra sharpness. Finally, in order to be authentic, pesto needs to be made with Genoese basil. I've known die-hard cooks who grow this precious herb from seedlings just to have access to its bright mint green color and unminty flavor. The rest of us can make do, though, and still create a delicious pesto, by using the freshest basil we can buy at the farmers' market. While pesto is traditionally prepared using a mortar and pestle, I've also included directions for making it with a food processor or blender.

Recommended pasta shapes or dumplings: linguine, trofie

INGREDIENTS:

- ¼ cup toasted walnuts or pine nuts
- 2 large cloves garlic, peeled
- Sea salt
- 2 cups tightly packed fresh basil leaves
- ½ cup + 1 teaspoon extra virgin olive oil
- ¼ cup freshly grated Parmigiano-Reggiano and ¼ cup freshly grated pecorino Sardo, plus extra Parmigiano for serving

OR

- ¼ cup each freshly grated Parmigiano-Reggiano and Pecorino Sardo cheese, plus more Parmigiano for serving
- ¾ pound pasta
- Freshly ground black pepper

1 Heat a small skillet over low heat for a minute. Add the nuts and cook, stirring frequently, until they begin to give off a toasty fragrance if using walnuts (because of their skin, they will not change color) or until the pine nuts become lightly golden brown, 2 to 3 minutes. Transfer to a plate to cool completely.

2 Making the pesto by hand: Put the garlic and a pinch of sea salt in a mortar and use the pestle to crush them together into a paste. Add the basil leaves a few at a time, crushing them along the side and bottom of the mortar until they become paste-like. Continue like this until you have crushed them all. Add the nuts and firmly pound them until they break into little pieces. Add ½ cup of the olive oil in a thin stream as you quickly whisk it in (if your mortar isn't big enough, first transfer it to a medium bowl, then add the oil).

Making the pesto by machine: Put the garlic, salt, and nuts in a food processor or blender and pulse until crushed and crumbly looking. Add the basil and pulse until finely minced. Transfer the basil mixture to a medium bowl and add the oil in a thin stream as you quickly whisk it in (mixing oils in the food processors turns them bitter).

3 Regardless of the method you've used, add the cheeses and thoroughly mix with a spoon. Use or store in an airtight container, covered with a thin film of olive oil, in the refrigerator for up to 4 days or the freezer for up to 3 months. (While some recipes call for freezing pesto without the cheese, I have found that it freezes beautifully, without any impact on its flavor or coloring, with the cheese.)

4 Bring a large pot of water to a boil. Once it's boiling, add salt (1 tablespoon for every 4 cups water) and stir. Add the pasta and stir for the first minute to prevent any sticking. Cook following the package (or recipe) instructions, though you will drain the pasta 2 minutes prior to the directed cooking time. The pasta will be soft but still very firm. Right before draining the pasta, reserve 1 cup of the pasta water. Return the pot to the stove. Immediately turn the heat to high, add the remaining teaspoon oil and ½ cup of the reserved pasta water, and stir. Add the drained pasta and toss until the water is absorbed. Add the pesto and the remaining ½ cup reserved pasta water and cook, tossing continuously, for 2 minutes.

5 Divide the pasta among four warmed bowls and serve piping hot topped with a few good cracks of pepper and additional grated Parmigiano (or pass the grated cheese at the table).

HAZELNUT BASIL PESTO

YIELD: 4 SERVINGS/ ACTIVE TIME: 10 MINUTES / TOTAL TIME: 15 MINUTES

This aromatic, basil-filled condiment is inspired by pesto, one of Italy's most well-known and beloved sauces. It contains hazelnuts, whose nutty flavor is enhanced by pan-toasting, and manchego, a delicious cheese made from sheep's milk. Made in the La Mancha region of Spain, it has a distinctive creamy and slightly piquant flavor and can be purchased fresh, semi-aged, and aged, all of which offer a variation of textures and flavors. This recipe requires the aged version, called manchego viejo, known for its sharp and peppery flavor, rich yellow color, and crumbly texture, which makes it easy to grate. This condiment also makes a tasty sandwich spread. Store any leftovers in an airtight container, completely covered with a film of oil, in the refrigerator; it will keep for up to a week.

Recommended pasta shapes or dumplings: tagliatelle, paglia e fieno, taglierini

INGREDIENTS:

- ½ cup blanched hazelnuts
- Salt
- 1 garlic clove, peeled
- 1 cup tightly packed fresh basil leaves
- 1 cup grated aged manchego cheese, plus more for serving
- Freshly ground black pepper
- ⅓ cup + 1 teaspoon hazelnut or walnut oil
- ¾ pound pasta

1 Heat a small skillet over medium-low heat for 2 to 3 minutes. Add the hazelnuts and raise the heat to medium. Stir continuously with a wooden spoon until they start looking slightly toasted and you can smell a most wonderful hazelnut aroma. Add a pinch of salt and stir. Remove from the heat and let cool.

2 Put the garlic and hazelnuts in a food processor and process until the mixture resembles breadcrumbs. Add the basil and pulse until not quite a smooth puree (you should still be able to see very small pieces of basil). Transfer the mixture to a medium bowl and add the cheese, along with salt and pepper to taste. It will become an aromatic paste. Whisk in ⅓ cup of the olive oil until thoroughly blended with the other ingredients. Set aside.

3 Bring a large pot of water to a boil. Once it's boiling, add salt (1 tablespoon for every 4 cups water) and stir. Add the pasta and stir for the first minute to prevent any sticking. Cook following the package (or recipe) instructions, though you will drain the pasta 2 minutes prior to the directed cooking time. The pasta will be soft but still very firm. Right before draining the pasta, reserve 1 cup of the pasta water. Return the empty pot to the stove. Immediately turn the heat to high, add the remaining teaspoon oil and ½ cup of the reserved pasta water, and stir. Add the pasta and toss until the water is absorbed. Add the pesto and remaining ½ cup reserved pasta water. Cook, tossing continuously, for 2 minutes.

4 Divide the pasta among four warmed bowls and serve piping hot, topped with a few good cracks of pepper and additional grated manchego (or pass the grated cheese at the table).

PISTACHIO, MANCHEGO, *and* CHIPOTLE PESTO

YIELD: 4 SERVINGS / ACTIVE TIME: 15 MINUTES / TOTAL TIME: 30 MINUTES

Two years ago my husband's work brought us to Portland, Oregon, for a week. Considered one of the food and restaurant meccas of the United States, it regaled us with one delightful meal after another (even their food carts are outstanding!). While grabbing a light lunch at a vegetarian eatery one day, I had the good fortune of ordering a pasta dish with a gorgeously red-hued pesto-like condiment containing chipotle peppers. One piquant bite and I was hooked. Upon returning home, I created my own spin on the delicious sauce, including two of my favorite ingredients, pistachios and manchego cheese (though you could easily substitute walnuts or pecans and Parmigiano if you so desire). The sauce, as you might expect, is robust and needs to be paired with a hefty pasta shape. I chose *trofie,* a traditional pasta from the northwestern region of Liguria. Two-inch-long twisted strands with tapered ends, they remain quite chewy once cooked and the creases on their surface zealously hold onto the sauce.

Recommended pasta shapes: trofie, penne, gemelli

INGREDIENTS:

- **4 canned chipotle peppers in adobo sauce**
- **3 cloves garlic, peeled**
- **⅔ cup shelled salted pistachios**
- **⅓ cup + 1 teaspoon grapeseed or avocado oil**
- **1 cup freshly grated manchego cheese, plus more for serving**
- **Salt**
- **¾ pound pasta**
- **fresh cilantro sprigs for garnish**

1 Open up each chipotle pepper and remove all the seeds (or keep some or all of them if you are looking for more heat). Put the chipotles and garlic in a food processor or blender and process into a a smooth puree. Add the pistachios and pulse 5 or 6 times to crush them a bit. Transfer to a medium bowl. While whisking continuously, add ⅓ cup of the oil in a slow, steady stream, then stir in the cheese. Taste for salt.

2 Bring a large pot of water to a boil. Once it's boiling, add salt (1 tablespoon for every 4 cups water) and stir. Add the pasta and stir for the first minute to prevent any sticking. Cook following the package (or recipe) instructions, though you will drain the pasta 2 minutes prior to the directed cooking time. The pasta will be soft but still very firm. Right before draining the pasta, reserve 1 cup of the pasta water. Return the pot to the stove. Immediately turn the heat to high, add the remaining teaspoon oil and ½ cup of the reserved pasta water, and stir. Add the drained pasta and toss until the water is absorbed. Add the pesto and the remaining ½ cup reserved pasta water and cook, tossing continuously, for 2 minutes.

3 Divide the pasta among four warmed bowls and serve piping hot garnished with cilantro and additional grated manchego (or pass the grated cheese at the table).

ROSE SAUCE

YIELD: 4 SERVINGS / ACTIVE TIME: 15 MINUTES / TOTAL TIME: 30 MINUTES

Thick, creamy, and comforting, this sauce has never met a child it hasn't mesmerized with its deliciousness. Reducing the cream really makes a difference, as it adds an even greater level of flavor and richness to the sauce.

Recommended pasta shapes: tagliatelle, tagliolini, bavette, penne, bigoli, sedani, tortelloni

INGREDIENTS:

- 4 pounds very ripe plum tomatoes
- 4 ½ tablespoons unsalted butter, divided
- 1 very small or ½ medium white or Vidalia onion, cut into quarters
- Salt
- 1 teaspoon sugar (optional)
- 2 cups heavy cream
- Freshly ground black pepper
- ¾ pound pasta
- Freshly grated Parmigiano-Reggiano cheese for serving
- Handful fresh basil or parsley leaves, thinly sliced

1 Bring a medium pot of water to a boil. Blanch the tomatoes in the boiling water for 1 minute. Use tongs to remove them to a cutting board and let cool until you can handle, then remove their skins. Cut them into quarters and remove the seeds. Use a food processor, blender, or food mill to puree them.

2 Heat a medium saucepan over medium-low heat for 2 to 3 minutes. Add 4 tablespoons of the butter and turn the heat to medium. Once it melts and stops foaming, add the onion and a pinch of salt and stir. When it begins to gently sizzle, adjust the heat to low, cover, and cook, stirring occasionally, until the onion has softened, about 10 minutes.

3 Add the pureed tomatoes and a couple pinches of salt (and the sugar if the tomatoes are not in season) and stir. Bring to a boil, then adjust the heat to low and simmer, uncovered, for 20 minutes. The rather liquidy sauce should thicken during this time. If not, raise the heat to medium-low and cook for another 10 minutes or so. Remove the onion pieces with a slotted spoon.

4 As the tomato sauce cooks, add the cream to a small saucepan and cook over low heat until it has reduced by about half. Remove from the heat. Once the tomato sauce has thickened, add the reduced cream and stir. Taste for seasoning, adding salt if needed.

5 Bring a large pot of water to a boil. Once it's boiling, add salt (1 tablespoon for every 4 cups water) and stir. Add the pasta and stir for first minute to prevent any sticking. Cook following the package (or recipe) instructions, though you will drain the pasta 2 minutes prior to the directed cooking time. The pasta should be soft but still very firm. Right before draining the pasta, reserve ¼ cup of the pasta water. Return the empty pot to the stove. Immediately turn the heat to high and add the remaining ½ tablespoon butter and reserved pasta water. Add the pasta and toss until the water is absorbed. Add the tomato sauce and cook, mixing continuously, for 1 to 2 minutes.

6 Divide the pasta between four warmed bowls and serve piping hot topped with the basil and a sprinkling of Parmigiano (or pass the grated cheese at the table).

ARRABBIATA

YIELD: 4 SERVINGS / ACTIVE TIME: 10 MINUTES / TOTAL TIME: 25 MINUTES

Arrabbiata translates to "angry," and this spicy sauce is sure to get your taste buds agitated, but in a good way. I recommend purchasing your olives from the olive bar in your local supermarket, as they are more flavorful and have a firmer texture than canned. Also, if you can find sea salt-packed capers, use them. They have a fresher taste, an almost floral aroma, and they keep their shape and firmness during cooking. To remove their excess saltiness, see page 481.

Recommended pasta shapes: linguine, bucatini, rigatoni, casarecce, fusilli, spaghetti, sedani

INGREDIENTS:

- 2 ½ tablespoons extra virgin olive oil, divided
- 3 garlic cloves, crushed
- 2 dried chiles, broken in pieces
- 1 24-ounce can peeled whole plum tomatoes (preferably San Marzano)
- Salt
- ¾ pound pasta
- Handful fresh parsley leaves, chopped
- Freshly ground black pepper
- Freshly grated Parmigiano-Reggiano cheese for serving

1 Heat a large, deep skillet over low heat for 1 to 2 minutes. Add 2 tablespoons of the olive oil, the garlic, and chiles, raise the heat slightly to medium-low, and let the oil heat up. When the garlic begins to gently sizzle, cook until it begins to turn golden in color, 1 to 2 minutes. Remove the garlic and as much of the crushed chiles as possible, then add the tomatoes, breaking them up with your hand as you add them to the skillet (also add any liquid from the can). Raise the heat to medium-high and bring to a boil. Reduce the heat to medium-low and cook, stirring occasionally, until the sauce is thick and shiny and the oil has separated from the sauce and is on the surface, about 20 minutes.

2 While the sauce is simmering, bring a large pot of water to a boil. Once it's boiling, add salt (1 tablespoon for every 4 cups water) and stir. Add the pasta and stir for first minute to prevent any sticking. Cook following the package instructions, though you will drain the pasta 2 minutes prior to the directed cooking time. The pasta should be soft but still very firm. Right before draining the pasta, reserve ¼ cup of the pasta water. Return the empty pot to the stove. Immediately turn the heat to high, add the remaining ½ tablespoon oil and reserved pasta water. Add the pasta and toss until the water is absorbed. Add the tomato sauce and cook, mixing continuously, for 1 to 2 minutes.

3 Divide the pasta between four warmed bowls and serve piping hot topped with the parsley, a few good cracks of pepper, and a sprinkling of Parmigiano (or pass the grated cheese at the table).

BUCATINI ALL'AMATRICIANA

YIELD: 4 SERVINGS / ACTIVE TIME: 15 MINUTES / TOTAL TIME: 30 MINUTES

This flavorful dish from the town of Amatrice, located in the mountainous area of the Italian region of Lazio, derives its depth of flavor from guanciale, salt-cured pork jowl, and its fieriness from a combination of black pepper and red chiles. Many opinions are liberally shared about what makes an authentic *Amatriciana,* and judgments are often based on whether it is made with bucatini or spaghetti, guanciale or pancetta, and pecorino or Parmigiano. I'll let the purists fight it out because, in my estimation, any *Amatriciana* not made with tomatoes grown in Italy's magical Mediterranean climate offers only an approximation of the flavor of the original dish. But thankfully for us, even an approximation is gloriously satisfying. On a final note, because this sauce benefits from the addition of some starchy pasta water, it is important to prepare the sauce while you simultaneously cook the pasta. Just make sure to have all the ingredients already prepped and ready to go because time is of the essence in this recipe.

Other recommended pasta shapes: spaghetti, pici, pizzocotti

INGREDIENTS:

- 2 ½ pounds very ripe plum tomatoes
- 4 ounces sliced guanciale or pancetta
- 1 tablespoon + 1 teaspoon extra virgin olive oil, plus more for drizzling
- 2 dried red chiles, broken into bits (with or without seeds, depending on your heat preference)
- ½ cup dry white wine
- 2 pinches sugar
- Salt and freshly ground black pepper
- ¾ pound bucatini
- ½ cup freshly grated pecorino Romano cheese, or more to taste
- Handful fresh parsley leaves, chopped

1 Bring a large pot of water to a boil. Blanch the tomatoes in the boiling water for 1 minute. Use tongs to remove them to a cutting board and let cool until you can handle, then remove their skins. Cut them into quarters, remove the seeds, and roughly chop. Reserve the water for cooking the pasta, keeping it at a simmer.

2 If using guanciale, cut into ¼- to ½-inch-wide strips 1 inch long. If using pancetta, cut into ⅓-inch-wide strips 1 inch long.

3 Bring the large pot of water back up to a boil. As the water heats up, heat a skillet large and deep enough to hold the finished pasta dish over medium-low heat for 2 to 3 minutes, then add 1 tablespoon of the olive oil and let heat for a couple of minutes. Turn the heat to medium and add the guanciale and red chile pieces. Cook, stirring a few times, until the guanciale turns a light golden caramel color (don't let it crisp), 5 to 6 minutes. Transfer the guanciale to a small dish.

4 Once the water comes to a roaring boil, add salt (1 tablespoon for every 4 cups water) and stir. Add the pasta, stirring for the first minute to prevent any sticking. Cook according to the package (or recipe) instructions, draining the pasta 2 minutes short of the directed cooking time.

5 Raise the heat under the skillet to medium-high and add the wine. Scrape up all the browned bits stuck to bottom of the pan with a wooden spoon. Cook for 5 minutes to reduce the wine a bit. Add the tomatoes, sugar, and salt and pepper to taste. Cook for 10 minutes; the bubbling of the sauce should be lively. Every so often add a few spoonfuls of the pasta water, if it looks as though the sauce is thickening up too much. It's important to add the pasta water because it contains some of the starch from the pasta and that's what's going to help bind the sauce. Taste and add salt or pepper if necessary.

6 Once pasta is 2 minutes short of its completed cooking time (it should be soft but still very firm), reserve ¼ cup of the pasta water before draining. Return the empty pot to the stove. Immediately turn the heat to high, add the remaining 1 teaspoon oil and the reserved pasta water. Add the drained pasta and toss for a minute.

7 Transfer the pasta to the skillet with the sauce, sprinkle over the pecorino and guanciale, and cook, tossing continuously, for 2 minutes.

8 Divide the pasta among four warmed bowls and top with a little more sauce. Serve piping hot sprinkled with parsley and more grated pecorino (or pass the grated cheese at the table).

PASTA *with* ARUGULA *and* POTATOES

YIELD: 4 SERVINGS / ACTIVE TIME: 20 MINUTES / TOTAL TIME: 30 MINUTES

Light and very flavorful, this weeknight dish comes together quickly and, served with a salad, makes a complete and nourishing meal. I recommend purchasing your olives from the olive bar in your local supermarket, as they are more flavorful and have a firmer texture than canned.

Recommended pasta shapes: orecchiette, radiatori, gemelli, armoniche

INGREDIENTS:

- 1 teaspoon nonpareil (small) capers
- ½ cup green pitted olives
- 2 large russet potatoes
- 6 tablespoons + 1 teaspoon extra virgin olive oil
- 2 garlic cloves, cut in half
- ⅛ teaspoon cayenne pepper
- Salt
- ¾ pound pasta
- ½ pound baby arugula
- ¼ cup freshly grated pecorino cheese, plus more for serving
- Freshly ground black pepper

1 Rinse the capers and drain on a paper towel. Using a sharp paring knife, remove the flesh from around the olive pits. Mince the capers and olives together.

2 Peel the potatoes and cut into ½-inch cubes.

3 Heat a large, deep skillet over low heat for 2 to 3 minutes, then add the 6 tablespoons olive oil, garlic, minced capers and olives, and cayenne and cook, stirring occasionally, for 5 minutes; you want the garlic to infuse its flavor into the oil and become light golden—don't let it burn. Discard the garlic and turn off the burner.

4 Bring a large pot of water to a boil. Once it's boiling, add salt (1 tablespoon for every 4 cups water) and stir, then add the potatoes. Once the water begins to boil again, add the pasta and stir for the first minute to prevent any sticking. Cook the pasta according to the package (or recipe) instructions. One minute prior to draining the pasta, add the arugula. Right before draining the pasta, reserve ½ cup of the pasta water and turn the burner under the olive and caper sauce to medium-high. Return the empty pot to the stove. Immediately turn the heat to high and add the remaining 1 teaspoon oil and reserved pasta water. Transfer the drained pasta, potatoes, and arugula to the pot and toss for a minute, then pour it all into the skillet and cook, tossing continuously, for 2 minutes. Add the pecorino and toss to mix it in.

5 Divide the pasta among four warmed bowls and serve piping hot topped with a good crack of pepper and a light dusting of pecorino cheese (or pass the grated cheese at the table).

PUTTANESCA SAUCE

YIELD: 4 SERVINGS / ACTIVE TIME: 15 MINUTES / TOTAL TIME: 30 MINUTES

This traditional southern Italian spicy pasta sauce is reputed to have been invented by "ladies of the night" wishing to lure unwitting customers to their lairs. One whiff of this aromatic sauce and the legend seems more than plausible. I recommend purchasing olives from the olive bar in your local supermarket or upscale grocer, as they are more flavorful and have a firmer texture. Likewise, if you can find sea salt-packed capers, use them. They have a fresher taste, an almost floral aroma, and they keep their shape and firmness during cooking; see page 481 for how to remove their excess saltiness. The same holds true for anchovies, whose flavor and texture is far superior when canned in crystallized salt and salty brine. Just carefully pry them out of the salt, so as to not break them, and then rinse them under cold running water. Some of the skin may wash off, but the goal is to keep the anchovy intact. Soak them in water for 20 to 30 minutes, after which they should be soft and malleable enough to fillet the anchovy. Separate the fillets by gently inserting the index and middle fingers of one hand where the stomach is and gently wiggling them until the anchovy opens. Remove any viscera and silverskin from the cavity and then carefully pull the spine away from the fillet it is sticking to. Separate the fillets and inspect them with your eyes and by running your fingers over the fillets, removing tiny fins or hard bony parts. Any hair-like bones are too soft to be a nuisance and can be left alone. Rinse each fillet under cold running water, transfer to fresh paper towels to absorb excess water, and then use as desired.

Recommended pasta shapes (egg varieties): penne, sedani, fettuccine, maltagliati, other long somewhat wide ribbons

INGREDIENTS:

- ½ cup extra virgin olive oil
- 3 garlic cloves, minced
- 1 28-ounce can peeled whole plum tomatoes (preferably San Marzano)
- ½ pound black olives, pitted
- ¼ cup nonpareil capers
- 5 oil-packed anchovy fillets OR 2 whole salt-packed anchovies
- 1 teaspoon red pepper flakes
- Salt and freshly ground black pepper
- ¾ pound pasta
- Handful chopped fresh parsley
- Freshly grated Parmigiano-Reggiano cheese for serving

1 Heat a large, deep skillet over low heat for 2 minutes. Add the olive oil and garlic and increase the heat to medium-low. Cook the garlic until it begins to sizzle gently. Add the tomatoes and their juice (crush each tomato by hand before adding it to the skillet), olives, capers, and anchovies and stir, pressing down on the anchovies to break them up. Add the red pepper flakes and salt and black pepper to taste, stir to combine, and increase the heat to medium. Let simmer, stirring occasionally, until the sauce thickens a little. Remove from the heat and cover to keep warm.

2 While the sauce simmers, bring a large
pot of water to a boil. Once it's boiling,
add salt (1 tablespoon for every 4 cups water)
and stir. Add the pasta and stir for first minute to prevent any sticking. Cook following
the package (or recipe) instructions, though
you will drain the pasta 2 minutes prior to the
directed cooking time. The pasta should be soft
but still very firm. Right before draining the
pasta, reserve ¼ cup of the pasta water. Return
the pot to the stove. Immediately turn the heat
to high and add the reserved pasta water. Add
the pasta and toss until the water is absorbed.
Add the sauce and cook, mixing continuously,
for 1 to 2 minutes.

3 Divide the pasta between four warmed
bowls and serve piping hot topped with
a few good cracks of black pepper and a sprinkling of the parsley and Parmigiano (or pass the
grated cheese at the table).

PINA'S SPAGHETTI
with POMODORINI *and* PESTO

YIELD: 4 SERVINGS / ACTIVE TIME: 10 MINUTES / TOTAL TIME: 30 MINUTES

This simple and fresh-tasting dish comes straight from the kitchen of my dear friend Pina, whom I miss dearly since moving away from New Jersey. I helped her prepare it one weekend when our families visited together and it has since become a family favorite. If you have pesto on hand, you can prepare it in the time it takes to cook the spaghetti. Filled with tomatoes and aromatic fresh herbs as it is, one may not even need a salad to make it a complete meal. *Pomodorini* is the diminutive of *pomodoro*, or tomato, and refers to mini versions, like cherry or grape tomatoes.

Other recommended pasta shapes: linguine, bucatini, spaghetti alla chitarra

INGREDIENTS:

- **3 garlic cloves**
- **Salt**
- **¾ pound spaghetti**
- **2 tablespoons + 1 teaspoon extra virgin olive oil**
- **1 pint grape or cherry tomatoes, cut in half**
- **½ cup tomato sauce of your choice**
- **⅓ cup pesto, homemade (page 483) or store-bought**
- **2 handfuls fresh parsley leaves, chopped**
- **Freshly grated Parmigiano-Reggiano cheese for serving**

1 Bring a large pot of water to a boil for the pasta.

2 While the water comes to a boil, chop the garlic into large pieces if you like a subtler garlic flavor; mince them if you want more kick.

3 Once the pasta water is boiling, add salt (1 tablespoon for every 4 cups water) and stir. Add the pasta, stirring for the first minute to prevent any sticking. Cook according to the package (or recipe) instructions, draining the pasta 2 minutes short of the directed cooking time. The pasta should be soft but still very firm. Right before draining the pasta, reserve ¼ cup of the pasta water.

4 While the pasta cooks, heat a large skillet over medium heat for 2 to 3 minutes. Add 2 tablespoons of the olive oil and heat for a minute or two, then add the garlic. Cook, stirring, until the garlic turns golden, 2 to 3 minutes. Add the tomatoes, tomato sauce, and a couple pinches of salt. Cook until the tomatoes soften but still retain their shape, about 5 minutes. Taste for seasoning, adding more salt if needed.

5 Drain the pasta and return the pot to the stove. Immediately turn the heat to high, add the remaining 1 teaspoon oil and reserved pasta water. Add the drained pasta and toss. Add the tomato sauce, pesto, and parsley and cook, tossing continuously, for 2 minutes.

6 Divide the pasta among four warmed bowls. Serve piping hot, dusted with Parmigiano (or pass the grated cheese at the table).

ASPARAGUS *and* RICOTTA SAUCE

YIELD: 4 SERVINGS / ACTIVE TIME: 12 MINUTES / TOTAL TIME: 25 MINUTES

I ate this refreshing combination for the first time years ago in the East Village in New York City, at a small—and now closed—place called Cremecaffe. It was mostly a coffee shop, though it also offered a handful of delicious pasta dishes and salads in the evening (no surprise, since the owner was from Bologna, a city known for its culinary prowess). One evening he came over to say hello and, upon seeing my enthusiasm for the dish, was kind enough to share his recipe. I believe its deliciousness comes from combining fresh, in-season asparagus, in all of their bright-tasting and earthy glory, with the comforting creaminess of ricotta.

Recommended pasta shapes: penne, campanelle, gemelli, mezze maniche, linguine, trenette

INGREDIENTS:

About 2 pounds thin or medium-thick asparagus

6 tablespoons water, divided

2 cups whole-milk ricotta

Grated zest of ½ lemon

1 tablespoon extra virgin olive oil

Salt

¾ pound pasta

6 tablespoons (¾ stick) unsalted butter, divided

Freshly grated Parmigiano-Reggiano cheese for serving

1 Bring a large pot of water to a boil.

2 While the water comes to a boil, bend each asparagus spear toward the bottom; it will snap at the point where the spear goes from tender to tough. It usually means you lose about a third of the spear, which seems sad except that it's tough and woody and no fun to eat.

3 Lay the trimmed asparagus in a shallow microwave-friendly bowl (I use a Pyrex pie pan). Add 1 tablespoon of the water. Cover the dish with plastic wrap, leaving a small section loose to allow steam to escape. Microwave for 3 minutes (the formula is to nuke asparagus at 1 minute per pound if you like them to have a nice snap when you eat them. For this pasta sauce, I need them to be softer, so I cook them a little longer).

4 Quickly transfer the asparagus to a large bowl filled with ice water or rinse until cool. Cut off the asparagus tips and set them aside. Place the remainder of the cooked spears, cut into half or thirds, in a food processor with the remaining 5 tablespoons water and process into a smooth puree.

5 In a small microwave-friendly bowl, mix the ricotta, lemon zest, olive oil, and a couple pinches of salt together.

6 When the water for the pasta is boiling, add salt (1 table-spoon for every 4 cups water) and stir. Add the pasta and stir for first minute to prevent any sticking. Cook following the package instructions, though you will drain the pasta 2 minutes prior

to the directed cooking time. The pasta should be soft but still very firm. Right before draining the pasta, reserve ¼ cup of the pasta water.

7 While the pasta cooks, heat a medium skillet over medium heat for 2 to 3 minutes. Add 2 tablespoons of the butter and turn the heat up to medium-high. Once it's melted and gently bubbling, add the asparagus tips and a couple pinches of salt. Cook, stirring a few times, until they develop a nice toasted color, about 2 minutes. Transfer them to a small warmed bowl with a slotted spoon, leaving as much of the butter as possible behind in the skillet. Tent the bowl with aluminum foil to keep warm.

8 To the same skillet add another 3 tablespoons butter. Once it's melted and gently bubbling, add the asparagus puree and a couple pinches of salt, stir, and cook, stirring a few times, until the puree starts gently bubbling, about 3 minutes. Adjust the heat to low and cover.

9 When the pasta is just about ready, place the bowl with the ricotta mixture in the microwave and heat for 1 minute, until very warm. Mix well to ensure it is uniformly warm.

10 Drain the pasta and return the empty pot to the stove. Immediately turn the heat to high and add the remaining tablespoon butter and the reserved pasta water. Add the pasta and toss until the water is absorbed. Add the asparagus puree and cook, mixing continuously, for 1 to 2 minutes.

11 Divide the pasta among four warmed bowls and top each one with ½ cup of the warm ricotta mixture. Artfully arrange the cooked asparagus tips on top and around the ricotta. Serve piping hot with a sprinkling of Parmigiano (or pass the grated cheese at the table).

PASTA *with* BROCCOLI RABE

YIELD: 4 SERVINGS / ACTIVE TIME: 15 MINUTES / TOTAL TIME: 25 MINUTES

A staple of southern Italian cuisine, this dish can be put together in the time it takes to bring a pot of water to a boil and cook the pasta. The star of the dish is broccoli rabe, also known as *rapini* in Italy, which has a mildly bitter flavor that mellows out significantly when boiled in salted water. This is often prepared with a lot of garlic; I like the garlic flavor to be subtler, so I keep the cloves whole and remove them before serving. Pancetta adds savory unctuousness, red pepper flakes provide heat, and pecorino cheese a sharp and welcome tanginess.

Recommended pasta shapes or dumplings: orecchiette, gemelli, gnocchetti Liguri, any type of short, chunky pasta

INGREDIENTS:

- 3 pounds broccoli rabe
- ⅓ cup + 2 tablespoons extra virgin olive oil
- 3 garlic cloves, peeled
- 6 ounces pancetta (bacon is fine to substitute), diced
- 1 teaspoon red pepper flakes
- Salt
- ¾ pound pasta
- Freshly ground black pepper (optional)
- ½ cup freshly grated pecorino cheese, plus more for serving

1 Bring a large pot of water to a boil.

2 Fill a large bowl with cold water. Immerse the broccoli rabe in the bowl and swish it about with your hand to dislodge any dirt in the leaves. Remove from the bowl and shake off the excess water. Using a sharp knife, trim off the thick stems and any discolored leaves. Slice across into ½-inch-wide strips.

3 Heat a small skillet over low heat for 2 to 3 minutes. Add ⅓ cup of the oil and turn the heat up to medium. Add the garlic, pancetta, and red pepper flakes. Stir, breaking up the pieces of pancetta that are sticking together with a fork. Continue cooking for 3 to 4 minutes, stirring frequently, until the pancetta and garlic both turn lightly golden. Take off the heat, discard the garlic, and set the pan aside.

3 Once the pot of water is boiling, add salt (1 tablespoon for every 4 cups water) and stir. Add the broccoli rabe and pasta and stir for the first minute to prevent any sticking. Cook following the package (or recipe) instructions, though you will drain the pasta 2 minutes prior to the directed cooking time. The pasta should be soft but still very firm. Right before draining the pasta and broccoli rabe, reserve ½ cup of the cooking water. Return the empty pot to the stove. Immediately turn the heat to high, add the remaining 2 tablespoons oil and reserved pasta water, and stir. Add the drained broccoli rabe and pasta and toss until the water is absorbed. Now add the pancetta mixture along with a few good cracks of black pepper if you like and the pecorino. Cook, tossing continuously, for 2 minutes.

4 Divide the pasta among four warmed bowls. Serve piping hot, dusted with additional pecorino (or pass the grated cheese at the table).

PASTA *with* BROCCOLI *and* GARLIC

YIELD: 4 SERVINGS / ACTIVE TIME: 10 MINUTES / TOTAL TIME: 25 MINUTES

This dish, found throughout Italy, is one of the easiest and fastest answers to "What's for dinner?" particularly on weeknights. The combination of olive oil and broccoli becomes delightfully pleasing because some of the florets break up in the cooking process and, once joined with the garlicky oil and a little pasta water, turn into a savory and pasta-clinging sauce. This recipe belongs on everyone's weeknight rotation menu.

Recommended pasta shapes: fusilli, penne, gemelli, radiatori

1 Bring a large pot of water to a boil. When it's boiling, add salt (1 tablespoon for every 4 cups water) and stir. Add the pasta and stir for first minute to prevent any sticking. When the pasta is 6 minutes shy of its designated cooking time (according to package instructions), add the broccoli florets and stir. (For instance, if your pasta will take 12 minutes to cook, add the broccoli 6 minutes into its cooking time.)

2 As the pasta and broccoli cook, heat ⅓ cup of the olive oil, the garlic, and red pepper flakes if using in a small skillet over medium-low heat until the garlic starts to gently sizzle. Reduce the heat to low and let it cook for 4 minutes to infuse the flavors, making sure that the garlic doesn't color at all. Remove from the heat.

3 Drain the pasta and broccoli when the pasta is soft but still very firm and return the empty pot to the stove. Immediately turn the heat to high, add the remaining ½ tablespoon oil and reserved pasta water. Add the drained pasta and broccoli and toss. Add the oil and cook, tossing continuously, for 2 minutes.

4 Divide the pasta among four warmed bowls. Serve piping hot sprinkled with Parmigiano (or pass the grated cheese at the table).

INGREDIENTS:

Salt

¾ **pound pasta**

1 ½ **pounds broccoli crowns, cut into small, evenly sized florets**

⅓ **cup + ½ tablespoon extra virgin olive oil, divided**

3 **garlic cloves, chopped**

½ **teaspoon red pepper flakes, or more to taste (optional)**

Freshly grated Parmigiano-Reggiano cheese for serving

CREAMY LEEK SAUCE

YIELD: 4 SERVINGS / ACTIVE TIME: 12 MINUTES / TOTAL TIME: 25 MINUTES

Have you cooked with leeks? Did you know they are just a very mild sweet onion? Sort of like a giant scallion, except they don't make you cry when you chop them. Leeks are wonderful and so easy to work with and simply wonderful in this rich sauce.

Recommended pasta shapes or dumplings: penne, campanelle, gemelli, mezze maniche, linguine, trenette

INGREDIENTS:

4   leeks

2 ½   tablespoons unsalted butter, divided

    Salt

1   cup heavy cream

¼   cup whole milk

½   teaspoon freshly ground white pepper, plus more for serving

¾   pound pasta

    Freshly grated Parmigiano-Reggiano cheese for serving

1   Prepare the leeks by trimming away the root ends and dark green leaves, keeping only the white and light green parts. With a sharp knife, cut each leek in half lengthwise and remove the two outer layers. Cut the halves vertically into thin slivers. Place them in a large bowl of water and swish them around to remove any dirt. Drain well, then transfer to a kitchen towel. Set aside.

2   Heat a large skillet over low heat for 2 to 3 minutes. Add 2 tablespoons of the butter and turn the heat up to medium. Once it's melted and stopped foaming, add the leeks and a couple pinches of salt and stir. Once they begin to gently sizzle, adjust the heat to low, cover, and cook, stirring occasionally, until the leeks become very soft and turn a slightly darker shade of green, about 20 minutes.

3   Raise the heat to medium-high and add the cream, milk, white pepper, and salt to taste and bring to a boil. Reduce the heat to low and cook, uncovered, for 5 minutes.

4   While the sauce simmers, bring a large pot of water to a boil. Once it's boiling, add salt (1 tablespoon for every 4 cups water) and stir. Add the pasta and stir for first minute to prevent any sticking. Cook following the package instructions, though you will drain the pasta 2 minutes prior to the directed cooking time. The pasta should be soft but still very firm. Right before draining the pasta, reserve ¼ cup of the pasta water. Return the pot to the stove. Immediately turn the heat to high, add the remaining ½ tablespoon butter and reserved pasta water. Add the pasta and toss until the water is absorbed. Add the leek sauce and cook, mixing continuously, for 1 to 2 minutes.

5   Divide the pasta between four warmed bowls and serve piping hot topped with a couple cracks of white pepper and a sprinkling of Parmigiano (or pass the grated cheese at the table).

SOPA SECA DE FIDEO

YIELD: 5 TO 6 SERVINGS / ACTIVE TIME: 15 MINUTES / TOTAL TIME: 30 MINUTES

Sopa seca de fideo is a classic Mexican noodle dish especially common in the central part of the country. The dish requires toasting very thin, short pasta strands called *fideos* in oil before cooking them in a savory broth. *Sopa seca* translates to "dry soup," and alludes to how the noodles absorb all the water in which they are cooked, much like rice pilaf, instead of swimming in liquid as they would in a regular soup. As with many culinary classics, *sopa seca de fideo* has as many variations as people preparing this simple and tasty dish. Some cooks add more flavor by first roasting the tomatoes, onion, and garlic, or by adding ancho (dried poblanos) or a variety of chile powder, like chipotle or cayenne. My girls prefer this more basic version, which is especially delicious when made with a rich chicken stock. If unable to find the *fideo* variety of pasta, substitute thin spaghetti, breaking it into approximately 2-inch pieces. For a more dramatic presentation, you can also substitute *fideos* with angel hair nests, which look like Van Gogh clouds once cooked.

INGREDIENTS:

- **4** plum tomatoes
- **2** canned chipotle peppers in adobo sauce, plus 1 tablespoon of sauce
- **2** garlic cloves, roughly chopped
- Salt and freshly ground black pepper
- **¼** cup extra virgin olive oil
- **½** pound fideo pasta
- **1** large yellow onion, minced
- **2** cups Capon or Chicken Stock (page 749)
- **1** ripe avocado, peeled, pitted, and cubed
- Handful fresh cilantro leaves

1 Bring a medium pot of water to a boil. Blanch the tomatoes in the boiling water for 1 minute. Use tongs to remove them to a cutting board and let cool until you can handle, then remove their skins. Open up each chipotle pepper and remove all the seeds (or keep some or all of the seeds if you want more heat). Put the tomatoes, chipotle and sauce, garlic, 1 teaspoon salt, and a few good cracks of black pepper in a food processor or blender and process into a smooth puree.

2 Heat a large, deep skillet over medium-low heat for 2 to 3 minutes. Add the olive oil and turn the heat to medium. When the surface of the oil begins to swirl but is not yet smoking, add the *fideo* nests, working in batches, and fry them on both sides in the hot oil until golden caramel in color, 2 to 4 minutes per side. Transfer to a paper towel-lined plate as they finish.

3 Add the onion and a couple pinches of salt to the skillet and cook, stirring occasionally, until the onion begins to sizzle. Turn the heat to medium-low and cook until the onion is lightly browned, about 20 minutes. Add the stock and tomato mixture, stir, and turn the heat up to medium-high. Once the mixture begins gently boiling, add the toasted *fideo* nests in a single layer, tightly nestled deep into the broth; reduce the heat to its lowest

setting. Turn the nests over in the broth to moisten them on both sides. Cover and cook until the nests have soaked up all the liquid, about 5 minutes. (If after 5 minutes you see the tops of the nests are dry, flip them over and cook for another minute.) Remove from the heat and let sit, covered, for 5 more minutes before serving.

4 Divide the nests among warmed serving plates, top with the avocado and cilantro leaves, and serve piping hot.

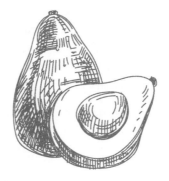

EGG NOODLES *with* BROWNED ONIONS *and* CABBAGE

YIELD: 4 SERVINGS / ACTIVE TIME: 20 MINUTES / TOTAL TIME: 30 MINUTES

It doesn't get much simpler than this cabbage, onion, and noodle dish called *haluski* that is found throughout central and eastern Europe. The combination may sound plain, but the deeply browned vegetables have a subtle smoky sweetness, while the sturdy egg noodles provide a satisfying chew. It is pure comfort food. Some versions also include caraway seed or salt pork.

1 Heat a large skillet over medium heat for 1 minute. Add the oil and turn the heat to medium high. When the oil starts swirling but is not yet smoking, add the kielbasa and cook until the cubes start to brown and crisp, stirring a few times; it'll take 3 to 5 minutes. Using a slotted spoon, transfer them to a small bowl.

2 Add 3 tablespoons of the butter to the skillet. When it has melted and stopped foaming, add the onions and a couple pinches of salt and cook, stirring frequently, until softened, 8 to 10 minutes. Add another 3 tablespoons butter, the cabbage, a few more pinches of salt, and a good few cracks of pepper and mix well. When the mixture starts sizzling, cover and reduce the heat to medium-low. Cook, stirring occasionally, until very soft and brown, 12 to 15 minutes.

3 As the onions and cabbage cook, bring a large pot of water to a boil. When it's boiling, add salt (1 tablespoon for every 4 cups water) and stir. Add the egg noodles and stir for the first minute to prevent any sticking. Cook them according to the package instructions. Reserve ¼ cup of the pasta water, then drain the noodles.

4 Return the pot to the stove. Immediately turn the heat to high and add the remaining ½ tablespoon butter and reserved pasta water. Quickly add the drained noodles and toss. Once the added water has been absorbed by the noodles, add the kielbasa and onion-and-cabbage mixture and toss well. Cook for 1 to 2 minutes, mixing continuously but gently, so as to not break the noodles. Taste for seasoning and add more salt and pepper if needed (lots of black pepper is traditional).

5 Divide the pasta among four warmed bowls and serve piping hot.

INGREDIENTS:

2 tablespoons extra virgin olive oil

½ pound kielbasa sausage, cut into small cubes

6 ½ tablespoons unsalted butter, divided

2 large yellow onions, diced

Salt

1 ½ pounds green cabbage, cored and cut into bite-sized pieces

Freshly ground black pepper

¾ pound wide egg noodles

HERBED COUSCOUS PILAF
with CRANBERRIES *and* PINE NUTS

YIELD: 8 SERVINGS AS SIDE DISH / ACTIVE TIME: 15 MINUTES / TOTAL TIME: 20 MINUTES

This tasty and aromatic side dish pairs beautifully with grilled meats and fish; I also like it as a side for a frittata. It's a big hit with kids too.

1 Heat a small saucepan over medium heat for 2 to 3 minutes. Add the olive oil and let heat for a minute. Add the shallots and a pinch of salt and cook, stirring a few times, until tender, about 5 minutes.

2 Raise the heat to medium-high, stir in the couscous, and cook for a minute. Add just enough broth to cover the couscous by ¼ inch. Add salt to taste, stir, and bring to a boil. Cover, remove from the heat, and let rest for 5 minutes.

3 As the couscous rests, toast the pine nuts. Put them in a skillet over medium heat. Stir continuously with a wooden spoon until they acquire a golden color, 4 to 5 minutes. Add a pinch of salt and stir well. Remove from the heat and let cool.

4 Fluff the couscous with a fork and transfer to a serving bowl. Stir in the parsley, thyme, cranberries, and pine nuts until well combined and serve.

INGREDIENTS:

- 1 tablespoon extra virgin olive oil
- 4 shallots (about 5 ounces), minced (about 1 cup)
- Salt
- 1 cup couscous
- 1 ¼ cups chicken or vegetable broth
- ½ cup pine nuts
- Handful chopped fresh parsley
- Leaves from 2 sprigs fresh thyme, chopped
- ¼ cup dried cranberries

PICI *with* CRISPY ANCHOVY BREADCRUMBS

YIELD: 4 SERVINGS / ACTIVE TIME: 10 MINUTES / TOTAL TIME: 25 MINUTES

Popular throughout southern Italy, this anchovy-filled pasta dish known as *pici ammuddicata* reflects a time when the working poor often had little more than stale bread and a few anchovies to eat. Dialect for *mollica, ammuddicata* refers to the soft, airy insides of fresh crusty bread. In this recipe, the *mollica* needs to be from day-old bread that is not rock hard; you want it to be easy to break up into crumbs using a food processor, blender, or even your fingers. Given the limited number of ingredients in this dish, consider using salt-packed anchovies if you can find them (see page 574 for how to prep them), as both their taste and texture are superior to that of oil-packed varieties. Be sure not to heat the oil too much before adding the anchovies, as you don't want to risk inadvertently frying them and turning them into a frazzled mess in the pan.

Other recommended pasta shapes: spaghetti

INGREDIENTS:

⅓ cup + 2 ½ tablespoons extra virgin olive oil

10 anchovy fillets

2 cups soft breadcrumbs

Salt

¾ pound Pici (page 169)

2 handfuls chopped fresh parsley

2 teaspoons freshly ground 5-peppercorn medley or black pepper

1 Put a large pot of water on to boil for the pasta.

2 Heat a heavy-bottomed skillet over medium heat for 2 to 3 minutes. Add ⅓ cup of the olive oil and let heat for just a minute or two. Add the anchovy fillets, mashing them with a fork until they disintegrate, 2 to 3 minutes. Turn the heat up to medium-high and add the breadcrumbs. Fry them, stirring often, until they are golden brown, 2 to 3 minutes. Remove from the heat and taste for seasoning, adding salt if needed. Tent loosely with aluminum foil to keep warm (don't use a lid because it will create steam and make the breadcrumbs mushy).

3 Once the pasta water is boiling, add salt (1 tablespoon for every 4 cups water) and stir. Add the pasta, stirring for the first minute to prevent any sticking. Cook according to the recipe (or package) instructions, draining the pasta 2 minutes short of the directed cooking time. The pasta should be soft but still very firm. Right before draining the pasta, reserve ½ cup of the pasta water. Return the empty pot to the stove. Immediately turn the heat to high, add the remaining

2 ½ tablespoons oil and reserved pasta water. Add the drained pasta and toss. Cook, tossing continuously, for 2 minutes.

4 Transfer the pasta to a warm serving bowl. Top with the warm anchovy-breadcrumb mixture and toss well. Sprinkle with the parsley and pepper and serve piping hot in warmed bowls.

TUNA, OLIVE, *and* CAPER SAUCE

YIELD: 4 SERVINGS / ACTIVE TIME: 10 MINUTES / TOTAL TIME: 25 MINUTES

Zesty and fragrant, this olive oil-based sauce comes from the volcanic Lipari islands, located in the Tyrrhenian Sea, north of Sicily. The culinary pride of the islands' cuisine, it features tuna and capers, both of which are found in abundance in the surrounding sea and on land. This recipe is based on a dish my mother made when we vacationed yearly by the ocean in our family's beloved pop-up camper, where a two-stove burner required simplicity. When my father's fishing exploits were fruitful, we ate this sauce with the fillets of freshly caught snapper, croaker, flounder, or sea trout. When they weren't, we ate it with canned tuna. Either way, it was delicious and remains so.

Recommended pasta shape: spaghetti, linguine, busiata

INGREDIENTS:

- ½ cup pitted black olives
- 3 tablespoons nonpareil capers, rinsed and drained
- 3 small garlic cloves, peeled
- Salt
- ¾ pound pasta
- ⅔ cup + 1 teaspoon extra virgin olive oil
- 1 17-ounce jar imported olive oil-packed tuna, well drained and roughly crumbled
- Freshly ground black pepper
- Handful fresh parsley leaves, chopped

1 Mince the olives, capers, and garlic together.

2 Bring a large pot of water to a boil. When it's boiling, add salt (1 tablespoon for every 4 cups water) and stir. Add the pasta, stirring for the first minute to prevent any sticking. Cook according to the package instructions, draining the pasta 2 minutes short of the directed cooking time. The pasta should be soft but still very firm. Right before draining, reserve ½ cup of the pasta water.

3 While the pasta water is heating up, start the sauce. Heat a large, deep skillet over medium heat for 2 to 3 minutes, add ⅔ cup of the olive oil and let heat for a couple of minutes. Add the olive mixture and cook for 3 to 4 minutes. Add the tuna and a generous amount of pepper and mix well. Cook for another 5 minutes and take the skillet off the heat. Cover to keep warm.

4 Drain the pasta and return the pot to the stove. Immediately turn the heat to high and add the remaining 1 teaspoon oil and reserved pasta water. Add the drained pasta and toss. Add the tuna and olive mixture and cook, tossing continuously, for 2 minutes.

5 Divide the pasta among four warmed bowls. Serve piping hot topped with the parsley.

PACCHERI *with* CLAMS *and* CALAMARI

YIELD: 4 SERVINGS / ACTIVE TIME: 25 MINUTES / TOTAL TIME: 30 MINUTES

In contrast to American renditions of this dish, which often feature a heavy tomato sauce, the Italian version includes tomatoes merely for a splash of color and a hint of flavor. In fact, its sauce isn't saucy at all. The real stars of the dish are the pasta, always paccheri and always al dente and the unforgettable briny clams. In Italy, the clams most often used for this classic dish are small carpet-shells, though in the United States they can be substituted with more readily available littleneck clams or cockles.

INGREDIENTS:

- 1 **pound small uncleaned squid or ¾ pound cleaned bodies and tentacles**

   Salt and freshly ground black pepper

- 3 **large plum tomatoes**

- ¼ **cup + 1 teaspoon extra virgin olive oil**

- 2 **garlic cloves, thinly sliced**

   Salt

- 3 ½ **pounds small hard-shell clams, scrubbed with a wire brush and rinsed; discard any that won't close**

- ¾ **pounds paccheri**

- 2 **handfuls chopped fresh parsley**

1 Clean the squid, if necessary. Remove their tentacles by making a straight cut right below the eyes. Hold the tentacles and remove the mouth, or beak, in the central part of the body (it will look like a little bulb and just pops out when you apply a little pressure from the opposite direction). Then run your thumb and index finger down each tentacle to remove the majority of the suction cups (which tend to be a little crunchy once cooked). If the tentacles are big, slice in half or even quarter them. Remove the insides from the tubular section of the squid, making sure to get the ink sack and the clear cartilage that serves as the squid's backbone. Slip off the thin layer of dark skin from the body, then gently tear off the two back fins located at the pointy tip of the body. Lay the body flat on a cutting board and, using a very sharp knife, slice across into ¼-inch-wide rings. Place the prepped calamari in a colander, rinse well, and drain. Sprinkle with salt and pepper and mix well with your hands.

2 Bring a medium saucepan of water to a boil. Blanch the tomatoes in the boiling water for 1 minute. Use tongs to remove them to a cutting board and let cool until you can handle, then remove their skins. Cut them into quarters and remove the seeds, then roughly chop.

3 Bring a large pot of water to a boil to cook the pasta.

4 As the water heats up, heat a large, deep skillet over medium-low heat for 2 to 3 minutes. Add ¼ cup of the olive oil, raise the heat to medium-high, and let heat for a minute. Add the tomatoes, garlic, calamari, and a couple pinches of salt, stir, and cook for 5 minutes. Add the clams and cook, stirring occasionally, until a few begin to open. Remove from the heat and cover the skillet.

5 Once the pasta water is boiling, add salt (1 tablespoon for every 4 cups water) and stir. Add the pasta and stir for first minute to prevent any sticking. Cook according to the package instructions, draining the pasta 2 minutes short of the directed cooking time. The pasta will be soft but still very firm. Right before draining the pasta, reserve ½ cup of the pasta water. Return the pot to the stove. Immediately turn the heat to high, add the remaining 1 teaspoon oil and reserved pasta water. Add the drained pasta and toss. Add the clam sauce and cook, tossing continuously, for 2 minutes.

6 Divide the paccheri among four warmed bowls. Serve piping hot topped generously with the parsley and a good crack of pepper.

SPAGHETTI *with* MUSSELS, PARSLEY, *and* GARLIC

YIELD: 4 SERVINGS / ACTIVE TIME: 10 MINUTES / TOTAL TIME: 25 MINUTES

This simple spaghetti dish is a riff on a classic Venetian soup, *zuppa de' peoci*. Awash with the flavors of garlic, ripe tomatoes, and, of course, seafood, the soup was served with thick slices of crusty bread. In this recipe, spaghetti replaces the bread, though you may still want to dip bread slices in any remaining sauce to absorb what is left of the delicious sauce. For a more sophisticated presentation you can remove the mussels from their shell, though I've never heard any complaints when serving it in its gloriously rustic state.

INGREDIENTS:

- 3 very ripe plum tomatoes
- ½ cup dry white wine
- 2 cups water
- 2 pounds mussels
- ¼ cups + 1 teaspoon extra virgin olive oil
- 3 garlic cloves, thinly sliced
- Salt and freshly ground black pepper
- 2 handfuls fresh parsley leaves, roughly chopped
- ¾ pound spaghetti

1 Bring a medium saucepan of water to a boil. Blanch the tomatoes in the boiling water for 1 minute. Use tongs to remove them to a cutting board and let cool until you can handle, then remove their skins. Cut them into quarters, remove the seeds, and roughly chop.

2 Bring the wine to a boil in a small saucepan and continue to boil until reduced almost by half (this will concentrate its flavor, including acidity and sweetness).

3 Bring the water to a boil in a large pot. Scrub the mussels under cold water, carefully cutting off any little fuzzy "beards" at the pointed ends. Add the mussels to the pot, cover, and turn the heat down to medium. They will quickly begin to open with the heat. As they do, pluck them out with kitchen tongs and transfer to a large bowl. When all the mussels have all opened (discard the few that remain closed), strain the mussel liquid through a paper towel-lined fine-meshed strainer. Set the mussels and strained liquid aside.

4 Put a large pot of water on to boil for the pasta.

5 Heat a skillet large enough to accommodate all the mussels over medium-low heat for 2 to 3 minutes. Add ¼ cup of the olive oil and let heat for a couple of minutes. Add the garlic, tomatoes and, a couple generous pinches of salt, raise the heat to medium-high, and cook for 5 minutes, stirring a few times. Stir in a few good cracks of pepper and the parsley. Add the mussels and their strained juices and the reduced wine, cover, and cook until the liquid on the bottom of the pot starts boiling, about 8 minutes.

6 When the pasta water is boiling, add salt (1 tablespoon for every 4 cups water) and stir. Add the pasta, stirring for the first minute to prevent any sticking. Cook according to the package instructions, draining the pasta 2 minutes short of the directed cooking time. The pasta will be soft but still very firm. Right before draining pasta, reserve ¼ cup of the pasta water. Return the pot to the stove.

Immediately turn the heat to high, add the remaining 1 teaspoon oil and reserved pasta water. Add the drained pasta and toss. Add the mussels and cook, tossing continuously, for 2 minutes.

7 Divide the pasta among four warmed bowls. Serve piping hot topped with more pepper.

PASTA *with* MUSSELS *and* COCONUT MILK

YIELD: 4 SERVINGS / ACTIVE TIME: 15 MINUTES / TOTAL TIME: 30 MINUTES

Ever since eating a deliriously delicious combination of braised rabbit and coconut milk at the now sadly defunct New York City restaurant Vong, I have made it a point to pair rich-tasting coconut milk with a variety of protein sources. Mussels are by far my favorite. Cheap, lightly briny, and plump, they brilliantly complement the fragrant coconut milk infused with Thai-influenced aromatics. Few dishes prepared in just 30 minutes are so flavorful.

Recommended pasta shapes: spaghetti, round rice noodles

INGREDIENTS:

1	stalk lemongrass
2	cups water
2	pounds mussels
2 ½	tablespoons safflower oil
1	1-inch piece fresh ginger, peeled and grated or minced
2	garlic cloves, minced
2	shallots, minced
1 to 2	red Thai chiles, seeded and thinly sliced
	Salt
1	14-ounce can unsweetened coconut milk
¾	pound pasta
	Grated zest of ½ lemon
¾	teaspoon fish sauce
½	cup fresh cilantro leaves, chopped

1 Trim the lemongrass by cutting off its ends and the outermost layers, and grate the tender inner core.

2 Bring the water to a boil in a large pot. Scrub the mussels under cold water, carefully cutting off any little fuzzy "beards" at the pointed ends. Add the mussels to the pot, cover, and turn the heat down to medium. They will quickly begin to open with the heat. As they do, pluck them out with kitchen tongs and transfer to a large bowl. When all the mussels have all opened (discard the few that remain closed), strain the mussel liquid through a paper towel-lined fine-meshed strainer. Set the mussels and strained liquid aside.

3 Heat a skillet large enough to accommodate the mussels over medium heat for 2 to 3 minutes. Add 2 tablespoons of the oil and heat for a couple of minutes. Add the ginger, garlic, lemongrass, shallots, chile(s), and a couple pinches of salt. When they sizzle, adjust the heat to low, cover, and cook, stirring occasionally, until very soft, about 15 minutes.

4 While the aromatics cook, bring a large pot of water to a boil. Once it's boiling, add salt (1 tablespoon for every 4 cups water) and stir. When the aromatics have cooked and you are ready to add the mussels (see next step), add the pasta to the water, stirring for the first minute to prevent any sticking. Cook according to the package instructions, draining the pasta 2 minutes short of the directed cooking time. The pasta will be soft but still very firm. Right before draining pasta, reserve ¼ cup of the pasta water.

5 When the aromatics are ready, add the opened mussels, their strained liquid, and the coconut milk to the skillet. Cover with a tight-fitting lid and cook until the liquid on the bottom of the pot starts boiling, 7 to 8 minutes. Remove from the heat but keep warm.

6 Drain the pasta and return the empty pot to the stove. Immediately turn the heat to high and add the remaining ½ tablespoon oil and reserved pasta water. Add the mussel mixture and cook, tossing continuously, for 2 minutes.

7 Divide the pasta and mussels among four warmed bowls. Serve piping hot topped with the cilantro.

THAI CHILE PEPPER

The Thai chile pepper in this recipe adds heat to this dish, while the coconut milk balances out the spice. There is a wide variety of Thai chile peppers, but they all possess great flavor and some zest. If the chile peppers are too strong for your palate, try cayenne pepper. It adds a mild heat, but will not overpower the flavor of the dish.

SPICY TUNA SAUCE *with* TOMATOES

YIELD: 4 SERVINGS / ACTIVE TIME: 15 MINUTES / TOTAL TIME: 30 MINUTES

This is a wonderful pantry sauce that you can pull together in a matter of minutes. My parents used to make it when we returned, tired and hungry, from vacation and our refrigerator was empty. For the tastiest results, use tuna that's been packed in olive oil (versus water). When I make this sauce, I buy the "fancy" and more expensive tuna in the glass jars because I find it to be generally more flavorful and to have chunkier and firmer pieces of tuna.

Recommended pasta shapes: spaghetti, penne, bucatini, ziti

1 Heat a large, deep skillet over medium-low heat for 2 to 3 minutes. Add 2 tablespoons of the olive oil and heat for a couple of minutes. Add the garlic, capers, and olives and cook until the mixture just starts to sizzle (you don't want it to color at all). Add the tuna and chile oil and stir. Adjust the heat to low and cook for 5 minutes, stirring a few times. Add the tomatoes and a pinch of salt, stir, increase the heat to medium-high, and bring to a gentle boil. Cover, reduce the heat to medium-low, and simmer until thickened, about 15 minutes.

2 While the sauce simmers, bring a large pot of water to a boil. Once it's boiling, add salt (1 tablespoon for every 4 cups water) and stir. Add the pasta and stir for first minute to prevent any sticking. Cook following the package instructions, though you will drain the pasta 2 minutes prior to the directed cooking time. The pasta should be soft but still very firm. Right before draining the pasta, reserve ¼ cup of the pasta water. Return the empty pot to the stove. Immediately turn the heat to high and add the remaining ½ tablespoon of olive oil and reserved pasta water. Add the pasta and toss until the water is absorbed. Add the tuna sauce and cook, mixing continuously, for 1 to 2 minutes.

3 Divide the pasta between four warmed bowls and serve piping hot with a few cracks of black pepper and a sprinkling of parsley.

INGREDIENTS:

- 2 ½ tablespoons extra virgin olive oil, divided
- 2 garlic cloves, chopped
- 1 teaspoon nonpareil capers, rinsed
- 6 black olives, pitted and chopped
- 2 6-ounce cans oil-packed tuna, drained
- 1 teaspoon hot chile oil or red pepper flakes
- 1 14-ounce can crushed tomatoes
- Salt
- ¾ pound pasta
- Freshly ground black pepper
- Chopped fresh parsley for garnish

PASTA *with* HOT-SMOKED SALMON

YIELD: 4 SERVINGS / ACTIVE TIME: 15 MINUTES / TOTAL TIME: 25 MINUTES

Hot-smoked salmon, a specialty of the Pacific Northwest, has a firm, flaky texture, very different from cold-smoked (or lox-style) salmon. I like to keep a package on hand in the refrigerator for days when I'm not inspired to spend a lot of time at the stove but still crave something savory and a little out of the ordinary. You can halve the amount of hot-smoked salmon in this recipe; it will still be delicious. I like to use a larger portion because it makes the dish even more substantial.

Recommended pasta shapes or dumplings: linguine, spaghetti, busiata, trofie

INGREDIENTS:

- 1 **cup dry white wine, preferably Chardonnay**
- ⅓ **cup pine nuts**
- **Salt**
- ¾ **pound pasta**
- ¾ **cup heavy cream**
- 1 **tablespoon unsalted butter**
- 1 **pound hot-smoked salmon, any skin removed and flaked**
- ¼ **cup freshly grated Parmigiano-Reggiano cheese**
- **Handful arugula leaves, stemmed and thinly sliced**

1 Bring the wine to a boil in a medium saucepan and continue to boil until reduced almost by half (this will concentrate its flavor, including acidity and sweetness). Remove from the heat.

2 Put the pine nuts in a small skillet and turn the heat to medium. Stir continuously with a wooden spoon until they start to acquire a golden color, 4 to 5 minutes. Add a pinch of salt and stir well. Remove from the heat.

3 Bring a large pot of water to a boil. Once it's boiling, add salt (1 tablespoon for every 4 cups water) and stir. Add the pasta, stirring for the first minute to prevent any sticking. Cook according to the package (or recipe) instructions, draining the pasta 2 minutes short of the directed cooking time. The pasta should be soft but still very firm. Right before draining the pasta, reserve ¼ cup of the pasta water.

4 While the pasta cooks, add the cream and a couple pinches of salt to the reduced wine and bring to a gentle simmer over low heat.

5 Drain the pasta and return the pot to the stove. Immediately turn the heat to high, add the butter and reserved pasta water. Add the drained pasta and toss. Add the cream sauce, flaked salmon, and Parmigiano and cook, tossing continuously, for 2 minutes.

6 Divide the pasta among four warmed bowls and serve piping hot topped with the toasted pine nuts and arugula.

PERCIATELLI *with* BOTTARGA

YIELD: 4 SERVINGS / ACTIVE TIME: 10 MINUTES / TOTAL TIME: 25 MINUTES

Bottarga is the salted and pressed fish roe of tuna or gray mullet, and popular in coastal areas of Italy like Sardinia, Sicily, Liguria, and Calabria. The best is rumored to come from the Sardinian lagoons of Cabras, on the coast facing Spain, where it has its own "delimited area of production" designation, or DOC, just like wine. Reminiscent of a time when no part of the fish went unused, *bottarga* is now a pricey but worthwhile treat that adds a memorable maritime flavor to a dish. I have to resort to buying it online because the supermarkets in my area don't carry it. Depending on the type of fish, it can be powerful and pronounced or more subdued. Here it is combined with *perciatelli*, thick, long tubes of pasta whose heft can stand up to the pungency of the sauce. This is a very quick recipe; you can pretty much put it together in the time it takes the water to boil and the pasta to cook.

Other recommended pasta shapes or dumplings: spaghetti, bucatini, pici, culurgiones

INGREDIENTS:

- 5 ½ tablespoons extra virgin olive oil, divided
- 1 cup dry breadcrumbs
- Freshly ground white pepper
- Handful fresh parsley leaves, minced
- 1 ounce bottarga, cut into paper-thin slivers
- Salt
- ¾ pound perciatelli

1 Put a large pot of water on to boil.

2 While the water comes to a boil, heat the largest skillet you have over medium heat for 2 to 3 minutes. (The width of the skillet is important because it allows more of the breadcrumbs to have direct contact with the heat.) Add 2 tablespoons of the olive oil and turn the heat up to medium-high. Once it begins to swirl on the surface but is not yet smoking, add the breadcrumbs and ½ teaspoon white pepper (don't add salt as the bottarga is plenty salty). Cook, stirring frequently, until the crumbs are a deep golden color, about 8 minutes. Transfer the breadcrumbs to a bowl and toss with the parsley and a third of the *bottarga*.

3 When the pasta water is boiling, add salt (1 tablespoon for every 4 cups water) and stir. Add the pasta and stir for the first minute to prevent any sticking. Cook according to the package (or recipe) instructions, draining the pasta 2 minutes short of the directed cooking time. The pasta will be soft but still very firm. Right before draining the pasta, reserve ¼ cup of the pasta water.

4 Without wiping it out, heat the large skillet again over medium heat for 1 minute, then add 3 tablespoons of the oil and raise the heat to medium. Once the oil begins to swirl on the surface, add the remaining *bottarga*. Let it sizzle in the oil for a minute, then immediately take the skillet off the heat.

5 Drain the pasta and return the empty pot to the stove. Immediately turn the heat to high, add the remaining ½ tablespoon oil and reserved pasta water. Add the drained pasta and toss. Add the *bottarga* and oil from the skillet and cook, tossing continuously, for 2 minutes.

6 Divide the pasta among four warmed bowls and serve piping hot topped with the breadcrumbs.

PAPPARDELLE *with* WILD BOAR SAUSAGE SAUCE

YIELD: 4 SERVINGS / ACTIVE TIME: 15 MINUTES / TOTAL TIME: 30 MINUTES

Boar is immensely popular in Tuscany, where it can be found in the wild (only a limited number are allowed to be killed each year), as well as in sausages and turned into prosciutto and salami. Here boar sausage is crumbled and married to Marsala, butter, and sage in a delicious sauce that is paired with *pappardelle*, whose very broad ribbons beautifully capture the light yet substantial sauce. Look for the sausage in local specialty food stores or butchers, or purchase it online.

Other recommended pasta shapes: strozzapreti, malfade

1 Bring the Marsala to a boil in a small saucepan and continue to boil until reduced almost by half (this will concentrate its flavor, including acidity and sweetness). Remove from the heat.

2 Remove the casings from the sausages and crumble the sausage into very small pieces.

3 Heat a large skillet over medium-low heat for 2 to 3 minutes, then add 6 tablespoons of the butter. Once it has melted and stopped foaming, add the crumbled sausage and sage. Raise the heat to medium-high and cook, stirring a few times, until the meat is golden brown, 5 to 7 minutes. Add the reduced Marsala and broth, adjust the heat to low so that the sauce simmers gently, and let cook until it visibly thickens and the oil has separated from the sauce and is on the surface, about 15 minutes. Remove the sage leaves.

3 While the sauce simmers, bring a large pot of water to a boil. Once it's boiling, add salt (1 tablespoon for every 4 cups water) and stir. Add the pasta, stirring for the first minute to prevent any sticking. Cook according to the package (or recipe) instructions, draining the pasta 2 minutes short of the directed cooking time. The pasta should be soft but still very firm. Right before draining the pasta, reserve ¼ cup of the pasta water. Return the pot to the stove. Immediately turn the heat to high, add the remaining ½ tablespoon butter and reserved pasta water. Add the drained pasta and toss. Add the sauce and Parmigiano and cook, tossing continuously, for 2 minutes.

4 Divide the pasta between four warmed bowls and serve piping hot topped with a few good cracks of pepper and a sprinkling of Parmigiano (or pass the grated cheese at the table).

INGREDIENTS:

1 cup dry Marsala wine

1 pound wild boar sausage (you can substitute bratwurst)

6 ½ tablespoons unsalted butter, divided

6 fresh sage leaves

½ cup chicken broth

Salt

¾ pound pappardelle, homemade (page 155) or store-bought

¾ cup freshly grated Parmigiano-Reggiano cheese, plus more for serving

Freshly ground black pepper

SPAGHETTI ALLA CARBONARA

YIELD: 4 SERVINGS / ACTIVE TIME: 15 MINUTES / TOTAL TIME: 30 MINUTES

Possibly the most entertaining description of this wonderfully indulgent pasta dish was in a *New York Times* article Ian Fisher wrote about it. He called *spaghetti alla carbonara* "a deli egg-bacon-and-cheese-on-a-roll that has been pasta-fied, fancified, fetishized and turned into an Italian tradition." Like its creamy cousin *pici cacio e pepe* (see page 480), it is a relative newcomer, having become part of the Roman culinary repertoire around the middle of the last century. Beloved for its satisfyingly savory flavor, it may also have earned its popularity because it can be prepared in the time it takes to boil water and cook spaghetti. While true carbonara has no cream, it develops a cream-like sauce when eggs and cheese are tossed with the hot spaghetti, which cooks them on contact into a velvety "sauce" that coats the pasta.

INGREDIENTS:

- 2 ½ tablespoons extra virgin olive oil, divided
- 4 ounces guanciale (cured pork jowls) or pancetta, cut into ¼-inch dice
- Freshly ground black pepper
- 2 large eggs, room temperature
- ¾ cup freshly grated Parmigiano-Reggiano cheese, plus more for serving
- Salt
- ¾ pound spaghetti

1 Put a large pot of water on to boil for the pasta. While the water comes to a boil, heat a medium skillet over medium-low heat for 2 to 3 minutes. Add 2 tablespoons of the oil and let heat for a couple of minutes. Turn the heat to medium and add the guanciale and a few cracks of pepper. Cook, stirring occasionally, until the cubes render their fat and start turning golden brown, 4 to 5 minutes (in this recipe, you do not want to cook the guanciale until it is crisp). Remove from the heat and partially cover with a lid or loosely tent with aluminum foil to keep warm.

2 While the guanciale cooks, break the eggs into a small bowl and whisk well. Add the Parmigiano and salt and pepper to taste and whisk well again.

3 Once the pasta water is boiling, add salt (1 tablespoon for every 4 cups water) and stir. Add the pasta, stirring for the first minute to prevent any sticking. Cook according to the package instructions, draining the pasta 2 minutes short of the directed cooking time. The pasta should be soft but still very firm. Right before draining the pasta, reserve ¼ cup of the pasta water. Return the pot to the stove. Immediately turn the heat to high, add the remaining ½ tablespoon oil and reserved pasta water. Add the drained pasta and toss. Take the pot off the heat, add the egg and Parmigiano mixture, and toss well to coat all the strands of the pasta with it.

4 Divide the pasta among four warmed bowls. Serve piping hot dusted with a dusting of Parmigiano cheese (or pass the grated cheese at the table) and more pepper.

SPAGHETTI ALLA GRICIA

YIELD: 4 SERVINGS / ACTIVE TIME: 10 MINUTES / TOTAL TIME: 30 MINUTES

Gricia is a classic sauce from the central Italian region of Lazio, particularly around the city of Rome. Considered the "white *amatriciana*" for its absence of coloring tomato, it is made with three ingredients: salty pecorino, copious amounts of black pepper, and, perhaps most importantly, guanciale, cured pork jowl. Guanciale (the word derives from *guancia* or "cheek" in Italian) comes from the pig's jowls, versus bacon and pancetta, which both come from the belly. Cured (but not smoked) for three weeks with salt, pepper, and rosemary, it has a more pronounced flavor than bacon; if you can't find it locally, order it online. You can substitute pancetta, though you will only get an approximation of the desired taste.

Other recommended pasta shapes: linguine, spaghetti alla chitarra, tonnarelli

INGREDIENTS:

½ pound guanciale, cut into ¼-inch dice

½ teaspoon + pinch freshly ground black pepper

Salt

¾ pound spaghetti

1 teaspoon extra virgin olive oil

⅓ cup freshly grated pecorino Romano, plus more for serving

1 Heat a large, deep skillet over medium-low heat for 2 to 3 minutes. Add the guanciale, raise the heat to medium, and cook, stirring occasionally, until it starts to render its fat and some of the cubes are golden brown while others are still translucent, about 20 minutes. Add ½ teaspoon of the pepper, stir well, and remove from the heat.

2 While the guanciale cooks, bring a large pot of water to a boil. Once it's boiling, add salt (1 tablespoon for every 4 cups water) and stir. Add the pasta, stirring for the first minute to prevent any sticking. Cook according to the package (or recipe) instructions, draining the pasta 2 minutes short of the directed cooking time. The pasta should be soft but still very firm. Right before draining the pasta, reserve ¾ cup of the pasta water. Return the pot to the stove. Immediately turn the heat to high and add the olive oil and reserved pasta water. Add the drained pasta and toss. Add the guanciale and its rendered fat and the pecorino and cook, tossing continuously, for 2 minutes.

3 Divide the pasta among four warmed bowls and serve piping hot dusted with pecorino (or pass the grated cheese at the table).

PASTA *with* PANCETTA, HAZELNUTS, ORANGE, *and* SAGE

YIELD: 4 SERVINGS / ACTIVE TIME: 10 MINUTES / TOTAL TIME: 25 MINUTES

The combination of hazelnuts and pancetta is perhaps far less familiar than peanut butter and jelly, Laurel and Hardy, and camping and bug spray, but it nevertheless merits serious consideration. The toasty, meaty flavors of the unlikely duo meld well in this pasta sauce, particularly when joined by the tart brightness of citrus and the warming, pine-like aroma of sage. Regular bacon does not make a good substitute for the pancetta in this recipe because its smokiness overshadows the toffee-like taste of the hazelnuts.

Recommended pasta shapes or dumplings: spaghetti, linguine, fettuccine, gnochetti, ricotta gnocchi

INGREDIENTS:

1	cup dry white wine
2	tablespoons + 1 teaspoon extra virgin olive oil
4	thick slices (⅓ pound) pancetta, diced
½	cup blanched hazelnuts, roughly chopped
4	tablespoons (½ stick) cold unsalted butter
5 to 7	fresh sage leaves (leave them whole)
	Grated zest of ½ orange
	Salt
¾	pound pasta
¾	cup very hot chicken broth
	Freshly ground black pepper

1 Bring the wine to a gentle boil in a small saucepan and let continue to boil until reduced by half, about 5 minutes. Take off the heat and let cool slightly.

2 Heat a large skillet over low heat for 2 to 3 minutes. Add 2 tablespoons of the olive oil and increase the heat to medium. Once the oil begins to swirl on the surface but is not yet smoking, add the pancetta and cook, stirring every few minutes, until it turns a golden caramel color, about 8 minutes.

3 Add the hazelnuts and toast for 2 to 3 minutes, stirring. Using a slotted spoon, transfer the pancetta and hazelnuts to a small bowl. Turn the heat up under the skillet to medium and wait for a minute. Add the reduced wine and cook for 5 minutes. Add the butter, sage leaves, and orange zest, stir, and bring to a gentle boil. Take off the heat and cover to keep warm.

4 Bring a large pot of water to a boil. Once it's boiling, add salt (1 tablespoon for every 4 cups water) and stir. Add the pasta and stir for the first minute to prevent any sticking. Cook following the package (or recipe) instructions, though you will drain the pasta 2 minutes prior to the directed cooking time. The pasta will be soft but still very firm. Drain the pasta and return the empty pot to the stove. Immediately turn the heat to high, add the remaining teaspoon oil and the broth, and stir. Add the drained pasta and toss until the broth is absorbed. Add the pancetta mixture and cook, tossing continuously, for 2 minutes.

5 Divide the pasta among four warmed bowls and serve piping hot topped with a few good cracks of pepper and the toasted hazelnuts.

HERBED MADEIRA CREAM SAUCE
with PANCETTA

YIELD: 4 SERVINGS / ACTIVE TIME: 10 MINUTES / TOTAL TIME: 20 MINUTES

If I were feeling silly, I would call this sauce "Witch's Brew" since it contains a little of this, a little of that, and a little of the other thing as well. And despite the hodgepodge of ingredients, it comes together, as if by magic, into a lightly creamy and remarkably fragrant sauce. I think it goes without saying the success in this sauce rests on using fresh herbs.

Recommended pasta shapes: farfalle, lagane, maltagliati, trofie

INGREDIENTS:

- 1 cup Madeira wine
- 4 fresh sage leaves
- 1 sprig fresh rosemary
- 1 tablespoon extra virgin olive oil
- 4 ounces pancetta, chopped
- 2 ½ tablespoons unsalted butter, divided
- 1 small Vidalia onion, chopped
- Salt and freshly ground white pepper
- ¾ pound pasta
- ½ cup heavy cream
- Freshly grated manchego cheese for serving

1 Bring the Madeira to a boil in a small saucepan and continue to boil until reduced almost by half (this will concentrate its flavor, including acidity and sweetness). Remove from the heat.

2 Set 3 sage leaves aside and very thinly slice (paper thin!) the fourth one. Set aside. Remove one third of the leaves from the sprig of rosemary and mince. Leave the rest of the rosemary sprig as is and set aside.

3 Heat a large skillet over medium-low heat for 2 to 3 minutes. Add the olive oil and increase the heat to medium. Once the oil begins to swirl on the surface but is not yet smoking, add the pancetta and cook, stirring occasionally, until it renders its fat and turns a golden caramel color, about 8 minutes. Using a slotted spoon, transfer the pancetta to a small bowl.

4 Add 2 tablespoons of the butter to the skillet and raise the heat to medium-high. Once it melts and stops foaming, add the onion, a couple pinches of salt, the 3 sage leaves, the rosemary sprig, and white pepper to taste, and stir. When the onion starts to sizzle, adjust the heat to low, cover, and cook, stirring occasionally, until very soft, about 20 minutes.

5 While the onion cooks, put a large pot of water on to boil for the pasta. Once it's boiling, add salt (1 tablespoon for every 4 cups water) and stir. Add the pasta, stirring for the first minute to prevent any sticking. Cook according to the package (or recipe) instructions, draining the pasta 2 minutes short of the directed cooking time. The pasta should be soft but still very firm. Right before draining the pasta, reserve ¼ cup of the pasta water.

6 When the onion is cooked and you've added the pasta to the water, remove the sage leaves and rosemary sprig from the onion mixture. Raise the heat to medium-high under the skillet and add the cream and reduced Madeira. Cook, stirring a few times, until the sauce thickens a bit, about 8 minutes.

7 Drain the pasta and return the pot to the stove. Immediately turn the heat to high and add the remaining ½ tablespoon butter and reserved pasta water. Add the drained pasta and toss. Add the onion mixture and cook, tossing continuously, for 2 minutes.

8 Divide the pasta among four warmed bowls. Serve piping hot topped with the crispy pancetta bits, the slivered sage, the mincedrosemary, and a good dusting of man-chego cheese (or pass the grated cheese at the table).

KIRA'S GARGANELLI PASTA
with CREAM, HAM, *and* PEAS

YIELD: 4 SERVINGS / ACTIVE TIME: 10 MINUTES / TOTAL TIME: 30 MINUTES

Typically, this toothsome triumvirate of heavy cream, ham, and peas is paired with ridged, golden tubes of *garganelli*, especially in the region of Emilia-Romagna. However, the sauce is so delicious that it works just as well with twirly fusili and other shapes. Many recipes I've seen cook the ham with the shallots, but this version crisps the strips up separately so that they become a crunchy and savory garnish. Should you desire to use fresh peas, add them to the boiling water at the same time as the pasta, as they require more time to cook. My daughter Kira loves this pasta dish so much that she asks me to make it often, especially when one of her sweet friends comes over for dinner. Invariably, these little girls go home and proceed to hound their moms to ask me for the recipe. The excitement around this dish is understandable . . . it is pretty darn delicious.

Other recommended pasta shapes: penne, rigatoni, sedani

INGREDIENTS:

- 6 ounces thick-sliced unsmoked ham
- 1 tablespoon extra virgin olive oil
- 4 ½ tablespoons unsalted butter, divided
- 3 shallots, minced

  Salt
- ¾ pound garganelli, homemade (page 191) or store-bought
- 1 ½ cups frozen peas
- ¾ cup heavy cream
- 1 teaspoon freshly grated nutmeg

  Freshly ground white pepper

  Freshly grated Parmigiano-Reggiano cheese for serving

1 Cut the ham slices into thin strips. Then cut the strips across into 1-inch pieces.

2 Heat a large, deep skillet over medium heat for 2 to 3 minutes. Add the olive oil and raise the heat to medium-high. Add the ham and cook, stirring a few times, until it turns golden and crisp, about 5 minutes. Using a slotted spoon, transfer the ham to a small bowl.

3 Add 4 tablespoons of the butter to the skillet. Once it has melted and stopped foaming, add the shallots and a pinch of salt and stir. Adjust the heat to low, cover, and cook, stirring occasionally, until they are very soft and golden brown, about 15 minutes.

4 While the shallots are cooking, bring a large pot of water to a boil. When it's boiling, add salt (1 tablespoon for every 4 cups water) and stir. Add the pasta, stirring for the first minute to prevent any sticking. About 5 minutes into the cook time, add the peas, if using frozen. Cook the pasta according to the package (or recipe) instructions, draining it 2 minutes short of the directed cooking time. The pasta should be soft but still very firm. Right before draining the pasta, reserve ¼ cup of the pasta water.

5 When the shallots are ready, add the cream, nutmeg, and pepper to taste to the pan. Taste for seasoning and add more salt if needed. Bring to a gentle simmer. Simmer for 3 minutes to let the flavors infuse, and, then take the skillet off the heat.

6 Drain the pasta and return the empty pot to the stove. Immediately turn the heat to high, add the remaining ½ tablespoon but-

ter and reserved pasta water. Add the drained pasta and peas and toss. Add the cream sauce and cook, tossing continuously, for 2 minutes.

7 Divide the pasta among four warmed bowls. Serve piping hot topped with the crisped ham and a good dusting of Parmigiano-Reggiano (or pass the grated cheese at the table).

SAUCES & RAGÙS

"From thence, the sauce to meat is ceremony; Meeting were bare without it." Lady Macbeth knew that sauce turns a meal into a celebration. It is an expression of love that carries the heart and soul of the cook to the guests who sit at the table. It says, Welcome, good friends, I honor you tonight. While this sort of reverence can sometimes entail hours to coax just the right flavor from a long-simmered sauce, other times it can be a faster and more effortless endeavor that can take less than an hour.

ROASTED ROOT VEGETABLE
and RICOTTA SALATA CONDIMENT

YIELD: 4 SERVINGS / ACTIVE TIME: 40 MINUTES / TOTAL TIME: 1 ¼ HOURS

This recipe resembles many tasty Asian stir-fry recipes: most of the work is up front and involves vegetable prepping. For the effort, diners get to enjoy the earthy taste of roasted root vegetables juxtaposed with the salty tanginess of ricotta salata and the springy texture of egg pasta. For the best carrot flavor, buy smaller, thinner ones sold in bunches with their green tops still on; they're sweeter than the carrots you buy in bags. I like to serve this dish directly from the baking pan because it looks marvelously rustic and also saves every last drop of the precious condiment in which the vegetables have cooked.

Recommended pasta shapes: tagliolini, taglierini, angel hair

INGREDIENTS:

- **3** small golden beets
- **3** small red beets
- **8** tablespoons extra virgin olive oil, divided
- **8** thin carrots
- **½** red onion
- **Leaves from handful fresh thyme sprigs, minced, plus a couple sprigs for serving**
- **Salt**
- **¾** pound pasta
- **¼** cup chicken broth, very hot
- **4 ounces ricotta salata, crumbled**
- **Freshly ground black pepper**

1 Preheat the oven to 400°F.

2 Prep the beets by cutting off both ends and slicing them in half lengthwise. If not organic, peel the beets as well. Cut the red beets on a separate board, as they tend to stain the other vegetables with their crimson hue.

3 Place the golden beets cut side down and slice each half into ½-inch-thick slivers. Transfer them to a large bowl and toss with 1 tablespoon of the olive oil until well coated, then arrange in a single layer on a baking sheet.

4 Slice each carrot in half, making sure to include part of the fresh green leaves on each half. Rub them with 1 tablespoon of the oil until completely coated and arrange in a single layer next to the golden beets.

5 Place the onion cut side down on the cutting board and slice into ⅓-inch-thick half moons. Toss with another 1 tablespoon of the oil, then arrange alongside the golden beets and carrots.

6 Lastly, cut the red beets into slivers as you did the golden beets, toss with 1 tablespoon of the oil, and arrange in the single layer on a separate small baking sheet. Sprinkle all the vegetables with the thyme.

7 Put the baking sheets in the oven and lower the temperature to 375°F. Roast for 20 minutes, turning the vegetables over once.

8 While the vegetables are roasting, bring a large pot of water to a boil. Once it's boiling, add salt (1 tablespoon for every 4 cups water) and stir. Add the pasta, stirring for the first minute to prevent any sticking. Cook following the package (or recipe) directions but drain the pasta 2 minutes prior to the directed cooking time. The pasta will be soft but still very firm.

9 Take the baking sheets out of the oven and drizzle 3 tablespoons of the oil evenly over the vegetables. Return them to the oven, increase the temperature to 450°F, and roast until the vegetables are lightly browned in spots and a knife can be easily inserted through the thickest part of the carrots, 10 to 12 minutes. Remove the sheets from the oven and generously salt the vegetables.

10 Drain the pasta and return the pot to the stove. Immediately turn the heat to high and add the remaining 1 tablespoon oil and the broth. Add the drained pasta and cook, 1 to 2 minutes, tossing until the broth is absorbed.

11 Add the pasta to the baking sheet with the golden beets, carrots, and onion and toss well. Using tongs, individually place the red beets on top of the tossed pasta and vegetables. Sprinkle with the ricotta salata and a few sprigs of thyme and add a few good cracks of black pepper. Serve immediately from the baking sheet.

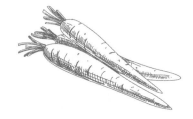

AROMATIC WALNUT SAUCE

YIELD: 4 SERVINGS / ACTIVE TIME: 20 MINUTES / TOTAL TIME: 50 MINUTES

Thick and creamy, this decadent sauce hails from the herb-laden hills of Liguria, in northwestern Italy. Not often seen on the menu at Italian restaurants, I urge you to indulge in it as often as possible.

Recommended pasta shapes or dumplings: spaghetti (and very nice with whole wheat spaghetti), farfalle, linguine, spinach or Swiss chard ravioli

1 Place the bread cubes in a small bowl, cover with warm water, and let soak for 30 minutes. Drain, then tightly squeeze the bread to remove as much water as possible. Set aside.

2 Bring a small saucepan of water to a boil, then add the walnuts, cook for 2 minutes, drain, and let cool enough to handle. Rub off their skins and place on paper towels to dry. Place in a small ziptop bag and break them up with a rolling pin. Transfer to a small bowl.

3 Place the squeezed bread cubes, walnuts, garlic, breadcrumbs, parsley, and half the marjoram in a food processor or blender. Pulse until you have a smooth paste. Transfer to a medium bowl, add the walnut oil, and whisk until it is thoroughly incorporated. Add the cream, 3 tablespoons of the butter, and a couple generous pinches of salt and whisk well to combine.

4 Bring a large pot of water to a boil. Once it's boiling, add salt (1 tablespoon for every 4 cups water) and stir. Add the pasta and stir for first minute to prevent any sticking. Cook following the package (or recipe) instructions, though you will drain the pasta 2 minutes prior to the directed cooking time. The pasta should be soft but still very firm. Right before draining the pasta, reserve ¼ cup of the pasta water. Return the empty pot to the stove. Immediately turn the heat to high and add the remaining 2 tablespoons butter and reserved pasta water. Add the drained pasta and toss until the water is absorbed. Add the walnut sauce and cook, mixing continuously, for 1 to 2 minutes.

5 Divide the pasta among four warmed bowls and serve piping hot topped with crumbled gorgonzola and the remaining marjoram.

INGREDIENTS:

- 1 cup ½-inch cubes day-old country bread
- 1 cup walnuts
- 1 garlic clove, thinly sliced
- ¼ cup dry breadcrumbs
- Handful fresh parsley leaves, chopped
- Leaves from 2 sprigs fresh marjoram, chopped, divided
- 3 tablespoons walnut oil
- 3 tablespoons heavy cream
- 5 tablespoons unsalted butter, at room temperature, divided
- Salt
- ¾ pound pasta
- Crumbled gorgonzola cheese for serving

PASTA PRIMAVERA

YIELD: 6 SERVINGS / ACTIVE TIME: 35 MINUTES / TOTAL TIME: 1 HOUR

Supposedly invented in the late 1970s by the chefs at Le Cirque, the celebrated French restaurant in New York City, this dish is a delicious amalgam of fresh vegetables and rich cream and Parmigiano. How could it not be good? I make it when I know finicky eaters will be joining us for dinner (and I am referring to children and "adult" children alike here). I don't know if it is the creaminess of the sauce or the buttery crunchiness of the panko breadcrumbs that wins them over . . . maybe it's the combination. My secret ingredient is adding a smidge of Worcestershire to the cream sauce. While I can never pronounce it and certainly have trouble spelling it, I often add this fermented concoction to my cream-based dishes because it magically brightens them up. Should you desire a lighter version, skip the sauce and use extra virgin olive oil, freshly grated Parmigiano, and the fresh parsley and basil.

Recommended pasta shapes: gemelli, fusilli, cavatelli

1 Preheat the oven to 400°F. Cover two 9 x 13-inch baking sheets with parchment paper.

2 Heat a large skillet over medium-low heat for 2 to 3 minutes, then add 2 tablespoons of the butter. Once it has melted and stopped foaming, add the panko and cook, stirring constantly, until they are dark golden brown, 4 to 5 minutes. Remove from the heat, pour into a bowl so they don't darken any further, sprinkle generously with salt and pepper, and stir.

3 Add the zucchini and bell peppers to a large bowl, drizzle with 2 tablespoons of the oil, and toss until evenly coated. Transfer to one of the prepared baking sheets and spread them out in a single layer. Add the carrots to the same large bowl, drizzle with the remaining 1 tablespoon oil, and toss until evenly coated. Transfer to the other prepared baking sheet and spread them out in a single layer. Place both baking sheets in the oven. Roast the zucchini and peppers, stirring once about halfway through, until softened and browned, 10 to 12 minutes. Roast the carrots, stirring once about halfway through, until fork-tender and lightly browned, 15 to 18 minutes. Remove from the oven, sprinkle with salt and pepper, mix well, and set aside.

4 While the vegetables are roasting, bring a large pot of water to a boil.

INGREDIENTS:

6 ½ tablespoons (¾ stick) unsalted butter, divided

1 cup panko breadcrumbs

Salt and freshly ground black pepper

1 medium zucchini, halved lengthwise and cut across into ⅓-inch-thick half-moons

1 red bell pepper, seeded and cut into ½-inch-wide and 1 ½-inch long strips

1 yellow bell pepper, seeded and cut into ½-inch-wide and 1 ½-inch long strips

3 tablespoons olive oil, divided

2 medium carrots, cut into thin slices on the diagonal

1 ½ cups heavy cream

¼ teaspoon Worcestershire sauce

1 ½ cups freshly grated Parmigiano-Reggiano cheese, plus more for serving

1 teaspoon freshly grated nutmeg

¾ pound pasta

2 handfuls chopped fresh parsley for garnish

2 handfuls chopped fresh basil for garnish

5 Stir the cream, Worcestershire, and 4 tablespoons of the butter together in a medium saucepan over medium-low heat until the butter melts and is fully incorporated. Gently stir in the cheese, then season with salt, pepper, and the nutmeg. Bring the sauce to a gentle simmer and cook until it lightly thickens, 2 to 3 minutes. Remove from the heat, cover, and set aside.

6 Once the pasta water is boiling, add salt (1 tablespoon for every 4 cups water) and stir. Add the pasta and stir for first minute to prevent any sticking. Cook according to the package instructions, draining the pasta 2 minutes short of the directed cooking time.

The pasta should be tender but still very firm. Right before draining the pasta, reserve ¼ cup of the pasta water. Return the empty pot to the stove. Immediately turn the heat to high, add the remaining ½ tablespoon butter and reserved pasta water. Add the drained pasta and toss until all the liquid at the bottom of the pot has been absorbed. Add the cream sauce and roasted vegetables and gently toss continuously for 2 minutes.

7 Divide the pasta among four warmed bowls. Serve piping hot topped with the toasted breadcrumbs, a generous sprinkling of parsley and basil, and additional Parmigiano (or pass the grated cheese at the table).

PASTA *with* CHICKPEAS

YIELD: 4 SERVINGS / ACTIVE TIME: 20 MINUTES / TOTAL TIME: 1 HOUR

The Italian combination of pasta and chickpea is ancient. Horace, the leading Roman lyric poet during the rule of Augustus, was recorded as writing, in Latin, of course, "I am going home to a bowl of leeks and chickpeas and lasagne." The tradition has continued in Italy to this day, most commonly in soups. But this recipe delivers the duo "*pastasciutta* style," which means cooked pasta seasoned with a condiment or sauce. It's the only way I've ever enjoyed this combination of pasta and legume. But I can't take credit for it. My grandmother taught it to my mother, who then taught it to me . . . as frequently happens with tasty family recipes.

Recommended pasta shapes: gemelli, rigatoni, sedani, or other stout tubular pasta

INGREDIENTS:

4 medium yellow onions

6 tablespoons + 1 teaspoon extra virgin olive oil

Salt and freshly ground black pepper

1 tablespoon balsamic vinegar

¾ pound pasta

1 14-ounce can chickpeas, rinsed and well drained

1 Trim the tip and root from the onions, cut them in half, and remove the skins. Slice each onion vertically, from root to stem, into thin slivers. Make sure the slivers are similar in size, as it will help them to cook and eventually brown more evenly.

2 Heat a large skillet over medium heat for 2 to 3 minutes. Add 6 tablespoons of the olive oil and heat for a minute or two, then add the onions. Stir them gently to make sure all the slivers are thoroughly coated with oil. Turn the heat up to medium-high and cook just until they begin to soften, about 5 minutes; they will also begin to release some of their moisture at this point. Reduce the heat to medium-low (low if you have a powerful stove) and cook, stirring frequently, until the onions are deeply browned and slightly sticky, about 40 minutes. During this process, reduce the heat further if the onions are sizzling or scorching or raise the heat if the onions are not browning at all after 15 minutes or so. The onions are fully browned when they develop a molasses-like color and flavor. Add at least ¼ teaspoon each of salt and pepper (or more, to taste) and the vinegar and mix well. Remove from the heat and cover to keep warm.

3 Bring a large pot of water to a boil. Once it's boiling, add salt (1 tablespoon for every 4 cups water) and stir. Add the pasta and chickpeas, stirring for the first minute to prevent any sticking. Cook according to the package instructions, draining the pasta 2 minutes short of the directed cooking time. The pasta will be soft but still very firm. Right before draining pasta, reserve ¼ cup of the pasta water. Return the empty pot to the stove. Immediately turn the heat to high, add the remaining 1 teaspoon oil and reserved pasta water. Add the drained pasta and toss. Add the caramelized onions and cook, tossing continuously, for 2 minutes.

4 Divide the pasta among four warmed bowls and serve piping hot.

TRAHANA *with* GREEN BEANS *and* TOMATOES

YIELD: 4 SERVINGS / ACTIVE TIME: 30 MINUTES / TOTAL TIME: 45 MINUTES (WITH STORE-BOUGHT TRAHANA)

This dish is an adaptation of a recipe from prolific cookbook author and *New York Times* food section contributor Martha Rose Shulman. I knew I had to make it the moment I saw her recipe because its combination of stewed green beans and tomatoes immediately reminded me of one of my favorite childhood vegetable dishes. My mother only prepared it in the summer, when my dad's vegetable garden was awash with petite green beans and sun-kissed tomatoes. She would get upset with me every time she made it too, because I would completely ignore the meat dish she had prepared to accompany the meal. But I was all too happy devouring the vegetables and dipping endless pieces of crusty bread in its sumptuously tasty oil-based sauce to be bothered with anything else. While my mother would just serve the vegetables by themselves, this recipe calls for adding the granular Greek pasta called *trahana*. You can either make it from scratch, which is a laborious but worthwhile process, or buy it. Depending on where you live, you may need to buy it online.

Other recommended pasta shapes: mini farfalle, spätzle

INGREDIENTS:

- **6** very ripe plum tomatoes
- **3** tablespoons extra virgin olive oil, plus more for drizzling
- **1** medium yellow onion, finely diced
- Salt
- **1** garlic clove, minced
- **1½** pounds fresh green beans, ends trimmed
- **1½** cups chicken or vegetable broth, more if needed
- **⅔** cup dried sour trahana, homemade (page 198) or store-bought
- **¼** cup fresh basil leaves, cut into thin slivers
- Freshly ground black pepper

1 Bring a medium saucepan of water to a boil. Blanch the tomatoes in the boiling water for 1 minute. Use tongs to remove them to a cutting board and let cool until you can handle, then remove their skins. Cut them into quarters, remove the seeds, and mince.

2 Heat a large, deep skillet over medium-low heat for 2 to 3 minutes. Add the olive oil and increase the heat to medium. When it begins to swirl on the surface, add the onion and a couple pinches of salt and cook, stirring occasionally, until the onion begins to gently sizzle, then turn the heat to low, cover, and cook until very soft, about 15 minutes. Add the garlic and cook, stirring continuously, for 1 minute, until fragrant. Add the tomatoes and a couple pinches of salt and stir. Raise the heat to medium-high. Once the sauce begins to sizzle, adjust the heat to low, cover, and cook, stirring occasionally, until the tomatoes soften and start breaking down, about 10 minutes.

3 Add the green beans, broth, ¼ teaspoon salt, and the *trahana*. Raise the heat to medium-high and bring to a gentle simmer. Reduce the heat to medium-low and cook, stirring occasionally, until both the green beans and *trahana* are tender, 15 to 20 minutes. Add more broth, if necessary, to ensure that the beans are halfway covered. Taste for seasoning and add salt if needed.

4 Remove from the heat and stir in the basil and a few cracks of black pepper. You can serve this hot or at room temperature. Drizzle a thin film of olive oil onto each bowl before serving.

CREAMY MUSHROOM SAUCE

YIELD: 4 SERVINGS / ACTIVE TIME: 20 MINUTES / TOTAL TIME: 40 MINUTES

A fast and tasty sauce for mushroom lovers. For additional warmth and aroma, you can add ½ teaspoon freshly grated nutmeg to the cream.

Recommended pasta shapes or dumplings: canederli, tagliatelle, maltagliati, gemelli, sedani, rigatoni, penne

INGREDIENTS:

- **1 pound cremini mushrooms**
- **1 tablespoon distilled white vinegar**
- **3 tablespoons unsalted butter**
- **3 garlic cloves, minced**
- **Salt**
- **3 small sprigs fresh thyme**
- **¾ pound pasta**
- **1 cup heavy cream**
- **Freshly ground white pepper**
- **¾ cup freshly grated Parmigiano-Reggiano cheese, plus more for serving**
- **Handful chopped fresh parsley**

1 Trim the bottoms of the mushroom stems. Fill a large bowl with cold water and add the vinegar. Add the mushrooms and swirl them around in the water for 30 seconds or so. Drain and rinse them under cold water. Drain again and place on a kitchen towel, stem side down, so that any remaining water drains. Let air dry for 10 minutes, then thinly slice.

2 Bring a large pot of water to a boil.

3 Heat a large skillet over medium-low heat for 2 to 3 minutes. Add the butter and turn the heat up to medium. Once it's melted and stops foaming, add the garlic. Cook for 30 seconds, stirring continuously, then add the mushrooms and a couple pinches of salt. Cook, stirring occasionally, until they lose their water, the water evaporates, and the mushrooms are tender and browned, about 10 minutes. Add the thyme and cook, stirring continuously, for 1 minute.

4 When the water for the pasta is boiling, add salt (1 tablespoon for every 4 cups water) and stir. Add the pasta and stir for the first minute to prevent any sticking. Cook following the package instructions, though you will drain the pasta 2 minutes prior to the directed cooking time. The pasta should be soft but still very firm. Right before draining the pasta, reserve ¼ cup of the pasta water.

5 While the pasta cooks, add the cream and salt and pepper to taste to the mushrooms and stir. Slowly bring to a gently boil over medium heat, then reduce the heat to low and simmer until slightly reduced and thickened, about 8 minutes. Add the Parmigiano and stir until melted.

6 Drain the pasta and return the empty pot to the stove. Immediately turn the heat to high and add the reserved pasta water. Add the drained pasta and toss until the water is absorbed. Add the mushroom sauce and cook, mixing continuously, for 1 to 2 minutes.

7 Divide the pasta between four warmed bowls and serve piping hot topped with the parsley and a sprinkling of Parmigiano (or pass the grated cheese at the table).

FRESH MUSHROOM SAUCE

YIELD: 4 SERVINGS/ ACTIVE TIME: 30 MINUTES / TOTAL TIME: 45 MINUTES

We so often see mushroom sauces containing copious amounts of cream that it's easy to forget how delicious they can be without it. This sauce is a case in point. My apologies to the purists who do not agree with washing mushrooms. While I wish I had the patience to brush the dirt off each individual mushroom, I fear I would go insane in the process. Washing them quickly, as I do here, prevents the mushrooms from absorbing water (or at least, the amount they absorb is negligible) and it keeps me sane, which I think my girls and husband especially appreciate.

Recommended pasta shapes: lumachelle, maltagliati, trofie, fettuccine, linguine

1 Trim the bottoms of the mushroom stems. Fill a very large bowl with cold water and add the vinegar. Add the mushrooms and swirl them around in the water for 30 seconds or so. Drain and rinse them under cold water. Drain again and place on a kitchen towel, stem side down, so that any remaining water drains. Let air dry for 10 minutes. Cut into ⅓-inch slices.

2 Bring a large pot of water to a boil.

3 While the water comes to a boil, heat a skillet large enough to hold finished pasta over low heat for 2 to 3 minutes. Add 4 tablespoons of the butter and the olive oil and raise the heat to medium. When the butter stops foaming, add the garlic and cook until it begins to turn golden, about 3 minutes. Discard the garlic.

4 Add the mushrooms and salt and white pepper to taste, mixing well. Raise the heat to medium-high and cook until the mushrooms release their water, about 6 minutes. Continue to cook until their water has evaporated and the mushrooms are nice and soft but haven't turned brown yet, 4 to 5 minutes Remove from the heat and cover to keep warm.

5 When the water for the pasta is boiling, add salt (1 tablespoon for every 4 cups water) and stir. Add the pasta and stir for first minute to prevent any sticking. Cook following the package (or recipe) instructions, though you will drain the pasta 2 minutes prior to the directed cooking time. The pasta should be soft but still very firm. Right before draining the pasta, reserve ¼ cup of the pasta water.

INGREDIENTS:

- 2 pounds fresh porcini or an assortment of fresh mushrooms (a mixture is best—white button, cremini, shiitakes, and/ or chanterelles, if you can find them)

- 1 tablespoon distilled white vinegar

- 4 ½ tablespoons unsalted butter, divided

- ½ cup extra virgin olive oil

- 3 garlic cloves, crushed

  Salt and freshly ground white pepper

- ¾ pound pasta

- 2 sprigs fresh thyme

- 2 handfuls fresh parsley leaves, minced

  Freshly grated Parmigiano-Reggiano cheese for serving

6 While the pasta cooks, measure out a cup of cooked mushrooms and puree (using an immersion blender is fastest but you can use a regular blender or mini food processor). Return the puree to the skillet, along with the thyme and two thirds of the parsley, and stir. Heat the mixture to a gentle boil over medium heat, then adjust the heat to low and cover.

7 Drain the pasta and return the empty pot to the stove. Immediately turn the heat to high and add the remaining ½ tablespoon butter and reserved pasta water. Add the drained pasta and toss until the water is absorbed. Add the mushroom sauce and cook, mixing continuously, for 1 to 2 minutes.

8 Divide the pasta between four warmed bowls and serve piping hot topped with a few good cracks of pepper and sprinkled with the remaining parsley and Parmigiano (or pass the grated cheese at the table).

TRUFFLED MUSHROOM *and* PINE NUT SAUCE

YIELD: 6 SERVINGS / ACTIVE TIME: 1 HOUR / TOTAL TIME: 1 HOUR

This luxurious smelling and tasting dish is positively swoon-worthy company fare. Should you have access to fresh truffles, feel free to garnish the dish with a few paper-thin slices. Truffles, a type of fungus that grows on tree roots in parts of Italy, France, and Spain, have an earthy, woodsy mushroom-like flavor and enticing aroma that help dishes "jump off the plate." Unfortunately, they are persnickety and have proven impossible to farm. To this day they must to be "sniffed out" from the ground, usually with the help of trained dogs, and dug up individually, which makes them very expensive. So expensive that, in 2007, a Macau casino owner set a record by paying $330,000 for 3.3 pounds of truffles unearthed in Tuscany!

Given the difficulty in procuring them and their high prices, it follows that the nominally priced bottles of truffle oil you find in gourmet stores and supermarkets are unlikely to contain any significant, if at all, amount of real truffle. In fact, if the bottle's label mentions truffle "essence" or "aroma," what it contains is a mixture of olive oil and chemical additives, flavorings, and aromas. I recently found an all-natural truffle oil online that contains truffles grown in Oregon and is reasonably inexpensive, considering that it is actually made with the "real deal." While it may not be from Tuscany, it is fragrant and delicious and I will be ordering it again.

Recommended pasta shapes: corzetti, mafalde, maltagliati, pappardelle, tagliatelle

INGREDIENTS:

- 1 **pound cremini mushrooms**
- 1 **tablespoon distilled white vinegar**
- ¼ **cup pine nuts**
- **Salt**
- 2 **tablespoons unsalted butter**
- 4 **tablespoons white truffle oil, divided**
- 2 **garlic cloves, lightly crushed**
- **Freshly ground white pepper**
- 1 **teaspoon freshly grated nutmeg**
- ½ **cup heavy cream**
- ¾ **pound pasta**

1 Trim the bottom of each mushroom stem. Fill a large bowl with cold water and add the vinegar. Add the mushrooms and swirl them around in the water for 30 seconds or so. Drain and rinse them under cold water. Drain again and place on a kitchen towel, stem side down, so that any remaining water drains. Let air dry for 10 minutes. Cut into ⅓-inch slices.

2 Heat a small skillet over medium-low heat for 2 minutes. Add the pine nuts and cook, stirring frequently, until they appear golden in spots, 3 to 4 minutes. Remove from the heat and add ⅛ teaspoon salt. Stir well and set aside.

3 Put a large pot of water on to boil for the pasta.

4 Heat a skillet large enough to hold the finished pasta over medium heat for 2 to 3 minutes. Add the butter and 2

tablespoons of the truffle oil. When the butter melts and stops foaming, add the garlic and cook, stirring a few times, until it begins to turn golden, about 3 minutes. Discard the garlic.

5 Add the mushrooms, a couple pinches of salt, and pepper to taste to the pan, mixing well. Raise the heat to medium and cook, stirring occasionally, until the mushrooms release their water, about 6 minutes. Continue to cook until their water has evaporated and the mushrooms are nice and soft but haven't browned yet, about 8 minutes. Add the nutmeg, stir, and taste, adding more salt if needed. Add the cream, stir, and heat through. Remove from the heat, cover, and keep warm until the pasta is ready.

6 When the pasta water is boiling, add salt (1 tablespoon for every 4 cups water) and stir. Add the pasta while the mushrooms are cooking, stirring for the first minute to prevent any sticking. Cook according to the package (or recipe) instructions, draining the pasta 2 minutes short of the directed cooking time. The pasta will be soft but still very firm. Drain and transfer directly to the skillet with the mushroom sauce. Immediately turn the heat to high and cook, mixing continuously, for 2 minutes.

7 Divide the pasta and sauce among four warmed bowls and serve piping hot topped with a drizzle of the remaining 2 tablespoons truffle oil and the toasted pine nuts.

RED BELL PEPPER *and* SHALLOT PESTO

YIELD: 4 SERVINGS / ACTIVE TIME: 25 MINUTES / TOTAL TIME: 50 MINUTES

Love bell peppers? If so, this sauce, in all of its delightful summer sweetness, is for you. Feel free to substitute yellow and orange bell peppers for the red if you are so inclined, though they won't be quite as sweet as the red. The secret flavor weapon in this sauce is the umami-packed Worcestershire sauce. Made from anchovies, vinegar, onions, molasses, sugar, salt, garlic, tamarind, cloves, chili powder, and water, it brightens the flavor of the cooked peppers and shallots and contrasts nicely with the tanginess of the feta cheese.

Recommended pasta shapes: penne, gemelli, rigatoni, bavette, linguine

INGREDIENTS:

- **3** very firm red bell peppers
- **3** tablespoons + 1 teaspoon extra virgin olive oil,
- **3** shallots, diced
- Salt
- **¾** pound pasta
- **1** tablespoon Worcestershire sauce
- **¾** cup crumbled feta cheese for serving
- Handful chopped fresh parsley
- Handful chopped fresh basil

1 Preheat the oven to 500°F, then turn on the broiler. Place a wire rack on top of a parchment paper-lined baking sheet and set the peppers on top. Broil the peppers until their skins are black and charred all around, turning them several times (you will need to babysit them during this process: wear sturdy oven gloves to avoid burning yourself). Once charred on all sides, place the peppers in a paper bag until cool enough to handle (the steam inside will help the skin fall off). Remove from the bag, peel off any remaining skin, and discard the stems, seeds, and internal membranes.

2 Heat a small skillet over medium-low heat for 2 to 3 minutes. Add 3 tablespoons of the olive oil and turn the heat up to medium. Once the oil begins to swirl on the surface but is not yet smoking, add the shallots and a couple pinches of salt and stir. When they begin to sizzle, reduce the heat to medium-low and cook, stirring every few minutes, until soft and beginning to turn golden, about 10 minutes.

3 Put the peppers and shallots in a food processor or blender and process until very smooth. Transfer back to the skillet in which the shallots were cooked, cover and, keep warm. (At this point, you can cool, cover, and refrigerate for up to 2 days.)

4 Bring a large pot of water to a boil. Once it's boiling, add salt (1 tablespoon for every 4 cups water) and stir. Add the pasta and stir for the first minute to prevent any sticking. Cook following the package instructions, draining it 2 minutes before its directed cooking time. Right before draining the pasta, reserve ¼ cup of the pasta water. Return the pot to the stove. Immediately turn the heat to high and add the remaining teaspoon oil and reserved pasta water. Add the drained pasta and toss until the pasta water gets absorbed. Add the pepper puree and Worcestershire and cook, tossing continuously, for 1 to 2 minutes.

5 Divide the pasta among four warmed bowls and serve piping hot sprinkled with the feta and herbs.

ROASTED RED PEPPER, CREAMY CORN, *and* HERB SAUCE

YIELD: 4 SERVINGS / ACTIVE TIME: 30 MINUTES / TOTAL TIME: ABOUT 1 HOUR

This Mexican-inspired pasta sauce celebrates the bounty of a happy summer garden brimming with fresh red peppers, corn, parsley, and cilantro.

Nicknamed the "Parmesan of Mexico," Cotija is a hard, salty cheese made from cow's milk. If you can't find it, use Parmigiano cheese or, for extra sharpness, pecorino Romano.

Recommended pasta shapes or dumplings: tagliatelle, pappardelle, maltagliati, gemelli, gnocchetti toscani

INGREDIENTS:

- 2 large red bell peppers
- 2 ½ tablespoons unsalted butter, divided
- 1 bunch (5 or 6) scallions, trimmed and thinly sliced
- Salt
- Kernels cut from 4 ears corn
- Ground ancho chile powder
- 2 tablespoons extra virgin olive oil
- Freshly ground black pepper
- 2 handfuls minced fresh parsley, divided
- 2 handfuls minced fresh cilantro, divided
- ¼ cup heavy cream
- ¾ pound pasta
- ¾ cup crumbled Cotija cheese

1 Preheat the oven to 500°F, then turn on the broiler. Place a wire rack on top of a parchment paper-lined baking sheet and set the peppers on top. Broil the peppers until their skins are black and charred, turning them several times to achieve this effect on all sides (you will need to babysit them during this process; wear sturdy oven gloves to avoid burning yourself). Once charred on all sides, place the peppers in a paper bag until cool enough to handle (the steam bag will help the skin fall off). Remove from the bag, peel off any remaining skin, and discard the stems, seeds, and internal membranes. Roughly chop.

2 Heat a large skillet over medium-low heat for 2 to 3 minutes. Add 2 tablespoons of the butter and heat for a minute or two, then add the scallions and a couple pinches of salt and stir. Cook until soft but not brown, 3 to 4 minutes, stirring a few times. Add two thirds of the corn kernels, a couple more pinches of salt, and a pinch of ancho powder, and stir. Cook until the kernels become soft, about 4 minutes. Remove from the heat and let cool for 10 minutes, then transfer to a food processor and pulse several times to create a rough puree.

3 Heat a separate skillet over medium heat for 2 to 3 minutes. Add the olive oil and heat for a minute or two, then add the peppers, the remaining corn, and salt and black pepper to taste, and stir. Turn the heat up to medium-high and cook until the corn begins turning golden brown in places, 5 to 6 minutes. Add half of the parsley and cilantro and mix well, cooking for another 30 seconds or so. Add the roughly pureed corn mixture and cream and stir. Turn the heat down to low. Taste for seasoning, adding salt or pepper if needed. Slowly and gently bring the mixture to a gentle simmer, then remove from the heat and cover to keep warm.

4 While the sauce comes to a simmer, bring a large pot of water to a boil. Once it's boiling, add salt (1 tablespoon for every 4 cups water) and stir. Add the pasta and stir for the first minute to prevent any sticking. Cook following the package (or recipe) instructions, though you will drain the pasta 2 minutes prior to the directed cooking time. The pasta should be soft but still very firm. Right before draining the pasta, reserve ¼ cup of the pasta water. Return the empty pot to the stove. Immediately turn the heat to high and add the remaining ½ tablespoon butter and reserved pasta water. Add the drained pasta and toss until the water is absorbed. Add the sauce and cook, mixing continuously, for 1 to 2 minutes.

5 Divide the pasta between four warmed bowls and serve piping hot topped with the remaining parsley and cilantro and the Cotija (or pass the cheese at the table).

SMOKED MOZZARELLA *and* ROASTED YELLOW BELL PEPPER CONDIMENT

YIELD: 4 SERVINGS / ACTIVE TIME: 30 MINUTES / TOTAL TIME: 50 MINUTES

I created this combination when I had a surplus of gorgeous peppers on my kitchen counter and a smoked mozzarella burning a hole in my refrigerator. I would call it a very happy accident.

Recommended pasta shapes or dumplings: gemelli, strangolapreti, garganelli, radiatori

1 Preheat the oven to 400°F. Place the peppers, onion, half the thyme, and 5 tablespoons of the olive oil in a large bowl and toss until everything is coated with the oil. Pour into a 9 x 13-inch baking dish. Put on the center rack of the oven and roast, turning the vegetables twice, until they begin turning a caramel brown color, 35 to 40 minutes. Remove from the oven, season with salt and pepper to taste, and gently stir. Tent loosely with aluminum foil and return to the oven. Turn the oven off.

2 While the vegetables are roasting, bring a large pot of water to a boil. Once it's boiling, add salt (1 tablespoon for every 4 cups water) and stir. Add the pasta and stir for first minute to prevent any sticking. Cook following the package instructions, though you will drain the pasta 2 minutes prior to the directed cooking time. The pasta will be soft but still very firm. Right before draining the pasta, reserve ¼ cup of the pasta water. Return the empty pot to the stove. Immediately turn the heat to high and add the remaining tablespoon oil and reserved pasta water. Add the drained pasta and toss until the water is absorbed by the pasta. Transfer the pasta to the baking dish containing the roasted vegetables and toss for a minute.

3 Divide the pasta among four warmed bowls and serve piping hot topped with the smoked mozzarella, parsley, and a couple cracks of pepper.

INGREDIENTS:

- 2 yellow bell peppers, seeded and thinly sliced lengthwise

- 2 orange bell peppers, seeded and thinly sliced lengthwise

- 1 Vidalia (preferable) or white onion, thinly sliced into half-moons

- Leaves from 4 sprigs fresh thyme, chopped, divided

- 6 tablespoons extra virgin olive oil, divided

- Salt and freshly ground black pepper

- ¾ pound pasta

- 8 ounces smoked mozzarella, cut into small dice

- Handful chopped fresh parsley for garnish

ROASTED POBLANO PEPPER
and MEXICAN SOUR CREAM SAUCE

YIELD: 4 SERVINGS / ACTIVE TIME: 1 HOUR / TOTAL TIME: 1 ½ HOURS

In Mexico, dark green and mildly spicy poblano peppers are often roasted and combined with *crema,* a thinner, slightly less sour version of sour cream. *Crema* and other dairy products are frequently paired with chiles because they contain milk proteins that neutralize the capsaicin molecules responsible for the peppers' hotness. The strategic union of the two enables diners to enjoy a dish's zestiness without any lingering discomfort.

This recipe fuses the subtle smoky quality of *rajas,* or roasted poblanos, the sweetness of corn and caramelized onions, and the soothing creaminess of *crema.* Look for *crema* in the refrigerated section of the supermarket with other Hispanic dairy products. If you can't find it, substitute it with crème fraîche or sour cream.

Recommended pasta shapes: tagliatelle, pappardelle, mafalde

INGREDIENTS:

- 3   poblano peppers
- 4 to 5 tablespoons extra virgin olive oil, as needed
- 2   large Vidalia onions, halved and thinly sliced
- Salt
- Kernels cut from 3 ears corn
- 1   cup Mexican crema
- ¾   cup grated freshly grated manchego cheese, plus more for serving
- 1 to 2 tablespoons water or milk, if needed
- ¾   pound pasta
- Freshly ground black pepper
- 2   handfuls chopped fresh cilantro for serving

1   Preheat the oven to 450°F. For the easiest possible clean-up, line a small sheet pan with aluminum foil, including the sides, and then with parchment paper trimmed to fit the pan's bottom. Put the poblanos on the sheet. Place on the center rack of the oven and bake, turning the chiles 3 to 4 times during that time to promote even roasting, until the skins are completely wrinkled and charred, 25 to 30 minutes. Remove from the oven, transfer the chiles to a large sheet of foil, and wrap them up in it. Let cool, then remove their skins by rubbing them lightly with your fingers; the skins will flake off. Slice the chiles in half and remove the seeds and stems. Cut into quarters lengthwise.

2   Heat a large, deep skillet over low heat for 2 to 3 minutes. Add 3 tablespoons of the olive oil and heat for a couple of minutes. Raise the heat to medium-low, add the onions and a couple pinches of salt, and cook until the onions are brown and are very soft, about 45 minutes, stirring occasionally to keep them from scorching. Transfer ½ cup of the cooked onions to a small bowl and set aside.

3   Add the corn and a couple pinches of salt to the onions remaining in the skillet (if the pan looks really dry, add another tablespoon olive oil when you add the corn). Increase the heat to medium, and cook until the corn starts to brown in spots, about 10 minutes, stirring occasionally. Transfer the mixture to a bowl.

4 While the corn browns, put the poblanos, the reserved ½ cup caramelized onions, *crema,* the Manchego, and 3 to 4 pinches of salt in a food processor. Process until the mixture resembles a smoothie, adding 1 to 2 tablespoons of water or milk if it seems too thick.

5 Reheat the same skillet (no need to wipe, as the skillet contains a little of the tasty condiment from cooking the corn and onions) in which the onions were cooked in for 2 to 3 minutes over medium-low heat. Add another tablespoon oil and heat for a minute or two, then add the poblano puree. Cook until heated through, then adjust the heat to low to keep it simmering. Taste for salt and pepper, then cover.

6 Bring a large pot of water to a boil. Once it's boiling, add salt (1 tablespoon for every 4 cups water) and stir. Add the pasta and stir for the first minute to prevent any sticking. Cook according to the package (or recipe) instructions, draining it about 2 minutes before directed, when it is a tender but still very firm. A minute before draining the pasta, turn the heat up under the poblano puree so that it starts bubbling. Using a pasta fork or tongs, quickly transfer the pasta—still dripping with pasta water—to the skillet with the poblano puree. Toss until the sauce generously coats the pasta.

7 Divide the pasta among four warmed bowls. Top with the onion-corn mixture, garnish with the cilantro and more manchego, and serve piping hot.

CLASSIC FRESH TOMATO SAUCE

YIELD: 4 SERVINGS / ACTIVE TIME: 20 MINUTES / TOTAL TIME: 45 MINUTES

I've seen recipes for fresh tomato sauce that use up to 50 pounds of plum tomatoes only to then instruct readers to freeze it in batches. I figure that if I go to the trouble of making sauce from fresh tomatoes, I don't want my freezer involved, so I only make enough for a meal or two. When dealing with such a small quantity of fresh tomatoes, the sauce doesn't take that long to make.

Recommended pasta shapes: spaghetti, penne, rigatoni, radiatori, farfalle, ruote, ricotta cavatelli

INGREDIENTS:

- 4 pounds very ripe plum tomatoes
- 2 tablespoons extra virgin olive oil or unsalted butter
- 1 medium onion, grated or thinly sliced
- Salt
- Handful fresh basil leaves (optional)
- ¾ pound pasta
- Chopped fresh basil for serving (optional)
- Freshly grated Parmigiano-Reggiano cheese for serving

1 Bring a medium pot of water to a boil. Blanch the tomatoes in the boiling water for 1 minute. Use tongs to remove them to a cutting board and let cool until you can handle, then remove their skins. Cut them into quarters and remove the seeds. Use a food processor, blender, or food mill to puree them.

2 Heat a skillet large enough to hold the finished pasta over low heat for 2 to 3 minutes. Add the olive oil, raise the heat to medium, and heat for a minute or two. Add the onion and a pinch of salt and cook, stirring frequently, until softened, about 10 minutes. Add the tomatoes and two pinches of salt, and stir. Bring to a boil, then adjust the heat to low, cover, and simmer until thickened, about 20 minutes.

3 Once the sauce is done, you can place the whole basil leaves on its surface if you like and close the lid for 5 minutes. The basil will gently perfume the sauce.

4 While the sauce simmers, bring a large pot of water to a boil. Once it's boiling, add salt (1 tablespoon for every 4 cups water) and stir. Add the pasta and stir for first minute to prevent any sticking. Cook following the package (or recipe) instructions, though you will drain the pasta 2 minutes prior to the directed cooking time. The pasta should be soft but still very firm. Right before draining the pasta, reserve ¼ cup of the pasta water. Return the empty pot to the stove. Immediately turn the heat to high and add the reserved pasta water. Add the pasta and toss until the water is absorbed. Add the tomato sauce and cook, mixing continuously, for 1 to 2 minutes.

5 Divide the pasta between four warmed bowls and serve piping hot topped with a sprinkling of chopped basil if you like and Parmigiano (or pass the grated cheese at the table).

CLASSIC CANNED TOMATO SAUCE

YIELD: 9 TO 10 SERVINGS / ACTIVE TIME: 25 MINUTES / TOTAL TIME: 55 MINUTES

At its best, plain tomato sauce is . . . well, plain, and made only with tomatoes, olive oil, salt, and a small grated onion. Really. That's it. While I love garlic and use it in many, MANY dishes, I don't include it in this basic tomato sauce because its pungency detracts from the sweetness of the tomatoes. I usually do make it in fairly large batches and freeze several containers to keep on hand. They come in handy not just when I'm desperate for a quick-fix meal (who doesn't love the occasional spaghetti with tomato sauce and meatballs?), but they also serve as the foundation for other recipes such as eggplant parmigiana or broiled chicken breasts with tomato sauce and mozzarella. If you've never had truly plain, five-ingredient tomato sauce, please give this one a try. Its brightness, freshness, and sweetness will make you smile as you taste it. If you prefer a slightly creamier flavor, you can replace the oil with butter, as Marcella Hazan so famously did. Be sure to offer grated Parmigiano-Reggiano cheese at the table for sprinkling.

Recommended pasta shapes: Just about any shape under the sun—spaghetti, penne, gemelli, rigatoni, rotini, fusilli, and sedani work particularly well

INGREDIENTS:

- 3 tablespoons extra virgin olive oil
- 1 medium white or Vidalia onion, grated
- Salt
- 2 28-ounce cans whole peeled plum tomatoes (preferably San Marzano)
- 1 teaspoon sugar
- Handful fresh basil leaves (optional)

1 Heat a heavy-bottomed pot or cast-iron Dutch oven over low heat for 2 to 3 minutes. Add the olive oil and turn the heat up to medium. When it begins to swirl on the surface but is not yet smoking, add the onion and a couple pinches of salt and mix well. Once the onion begins to sizzle, reduce the heat to low and give it a stir. Cover and cook, stirring occasionally, until the onion becomes very soft and translucent, about 20 minutes.

2 While the onion cooks, use a food processor, blender, or food mill to puree the tomatoes, working with one can of tomatoes at a time.

3 Pour the very liquidy tomatoes into the pot with the onion, along with a few more pinches of salt and the sugar (to tame the acidity of the tomatoes). Raise the heat to medium-high and bring to a boil. Adjust the heat to medium-low and simmer, uncovered, until thickened, about 30 minutes, stirring every 10 minutes or so. You should see a gentle bubbling in the pot.

4 Once the sauce is done, you can place the basil leaves on its surface if you like and close the lid for 5 minutes. The basil will gently perfume the sauce.

5 Use or let cool, transfer to an airtight container, and refrigerate for up to 3 days or freeze up to 2 months.

SIMPLE ROASTED TOMATO *and* GARLIC SAUCE

YIELD: 4 SERVINGS / ACTIVE TIME: 15 MINUTES / TOTAL TIME: 2 HOURS

This sauce is perfect for people who are not partial to heavy garlic flavors in their tomato sauce. I understand. I too find garlic a bit overpowering in most simple tomato sauces. The earthy sweetness of the roasted garlic in this recipe, however, is a tasty exception.

Recommended pasta shapes: tagliatelle, bavette, penne, sedani, rigatoni, maltagliati, malfatti

INGREDIENTS:

- 3 pounds very ripe plum tomatoes, halved lengthwise
- ¼ cup + ½ tablespoon extra virgin olive oil, plus more as needed
- 5 large garlic cloves

  Salt and freshly ground black pepper
- ¾ pound pasta

  Handful fresh basil leaves, left whole, plus 5 basil leaves, thinly sliced

  Freshly grated Parmigiano-Reggiano cheese for serving

1 Preheat the oven to 350°F. Place the tomatoes on a large parchment paper-lined rimmed baking sheet and drizzle with ¼ cup of the olive oil. Using your fingers, mix well to ensure an even coating. Arrange the tomatoes cut side down, then put the sheet on the center rack, lower the temperature to 325°F, and roast for 1 hour.

2 Place the garlic cloves in a small bowl and add just enough oil to lightly coat them. Add the garlic to the baking sheet and roast for another 30 minutes. At this point, the tomatoes will be soft and have a golden caramel color and the garlic should be soft to the touch. Remove from the oven, season with salt and pepper to taste, and let cool. Once cooled, remove the skins from the garlic cloves (just squeeze them from the root end).

3 When the tomatoes and garlic are just about cooled, bring a large pot of water to a boil. Once it's boiling, add salt (1 tablespoon for every 4 cups water) and stir. Add the pasta and stir for the first minute to prevent any sticking. Cook following the package (or recipe) instructions, though you will drain the pasta 2 minutes prior to the directed cooking time. The pasta should be soft but still very firm. Right before draining the pasta, reserve ¼ cup of the pasta water.

4 While the pasta is cooking, put the roasted tomatoes and garlic and basil leaves in a food processor and puree until smooth. Transfer to a medium saucepan over medium heat and heat until gently bubbling.

5 Drain the pasta and return the empty pot to the stove. Immediately turn the heat to high and add the remaining ½ tablespoon oil and reserved pasta water. Add the drained pasta and toss until the water is absorbed. Add the sauce and cook, mixing continuously, for 1 to 2 minutes.

6 Ladle the pasta into warmed bowls and serve piping hot with a few good cracks of pepper and sprinkled with the basil ribbons and Parmigiano (or pass the grated cheese at the table).

TOMATO *and* EGGPLANT SAUCE ALLA NORMA

YIELD: 4 SERVINGS / ACTIVE TIME: 40 MINUTES / TOTAL TIME: 1 ½ HOURS

From Sicily's ancient port city of Catania, this traditional dish features a trifecta of the island's renowned ingredients: tomatoes, eggplant, and ricotta. Some people like to use mildly pungent ricotta salata, essentially drained and dried ricotta, but I revel in ricotta's milky freshness. I find it perfectly balances out the natural acidity in the tomatoes.

Recommended pasta shapes: ziti, cavatelli, gemelli, fusilli, penne

1 Peel and quarter the eggplants. If their centers are overly seedy or spongy, remove those sections, as they will not help the texture and flavor of the sauce. Cut the eggplant quarters into 1-inch cubes, put in a colander set in the sink or a large bowl, and sprinkle with 2 tablespoons of salt. Let drain for 30 minutes. Thoroughly pat the cubes dry with paper towels.

2 Preheat the oven to 400°F. For the easiest possible clean up, line a large baking pan with aluminum foil, including the sides, and then with parchment paper (to prevent sticking) trimmed to fit the pan's bottom. Place the eggplant cubes in the pan, add 5 tablespoons of the olive oil and, using your hands, toss the eggplant and oil together until all the cubes are evenly coated. Spread the cubes out into an even layer. Place the pan on the center rack and roast, gently stirring twice during roasting, until they are tender and golden brown, about 25 minutes. Remove from the oven and cover with foil to keep warm.

3 Bring a large pot of water to a boil. Once it's boiling, add salt (1 tablespoon for every 4 cups water) and stir. Add the pasta and stir for the first minute to prevent any sticking. Cook according to the package (or recipe) instructions, draining the pasta 2 minutes short of the directed cooking time. The pasta will be soft but still very firm. Right before draining the pasta, reserve ¼ cup of the pasta water. Return the empty pot to the stove. Immediately turn the heat to high, add the remaining ½ tablespoon oil and reserved pasta water. Quickly add the drained pasta and toss. Add a few ladlefuls of the tomato sauce and cook, tossing continuously, for 2 minutes.

4 Divide the pasta among four warmed bowls and top with a little additional sauce. To each serving add a few dollops of ricotta, a fourth of the roasted eggplant cubes, the basil, a crack of pepper, and a good dusting of Parmigiano to each bowl (or pass the grated cheese at the table). Serve piping hot.

INGREDIENTS:

2 large firm eggplants (about 2 pounds total)

Salt

5 ½ tablespoons extra virgin olive oil

¾ pound pasta

5 cups plain tomato sauce, like Classic Canned Tomato Sauce (page 566), piping hot

1 cup ricotta cheese

Freshly ground black pepper

Freshly grated Parmigiano-Reggiano cheese for serving

Handful fresh basil leaves, thinly sliced, for serving

TOMATO SAUCE *with* RICOTTA *and* CRISPY EGGPLANT BALLS

YIELD: 4 SERVINGS / ACTIVE TIME: 45 MINUTES / TOTAL TIME: 1 ½ HOURS

A recipe for fried eggplant balls inspired me to create this spin-off of *pasta alla norma,* the classic Sicilian pasta dish of sautéed eggplant in tomato sauce (see page 569). While making the "meat" balls takes a not insignificant amount of time, they also add a satisfyingly meaty texture that sautéed eggplant, however delicious, can't replicate. If you are more partial to piquant flavors, you can swap out fresh-tasting ricotta for the salty tanginess of its pressed and dried cousin, ricotta salata.

Recommended pasta shapes: penne, fusilli, gemelli, rigatoni

1 Preheat the oven to 400°F. Cover two baking sheets with parchment paper.

2 Bring a medium pot of water to a boil. Blanch the tomatoes in the boiling water for 1 minute. Use tongs to remove them to a cutting board and let cool until you can handle, then remove their skins. Cut them into quarters, remove the seeds, and roughly chop.

3 Peel and quarter the eggplants. Cut away any overly seedy or spongy parts, then cut into 1-inch cubes. Divide the cubes between the two prepared baking sheets and toss the cubes on each sheet with 2 tablespoons of the olive oil until well coated. Put the sheets in the oven and roast, turning occasionally and swapping the positions of the sheets once, until golden brown, about 20 minutes. Take one sheet out of the oven, add the garlic, return to the oven, and bake until the skins of the garlic have turned a very light brownish color and have opened, about another 15 minutes. When done, remove from the oven, season with salt and pepper to taste, and mix well. When cool enough to handle, remove the skins from the garlic cloves and roughly chop everything up.

4 To make the sauce, heat a large, deep skillet over medium heat for 2 to 3 minutes. Add 2 tablespoons of the oil and heat for a minute or two, then add the onion, a pinch of salt, and the red pepper flakes and cook, stirring frequently, until softened, about 10 minutes. Add the tomatoes, two pinches of salt, and the sugar and bring to a boil. Adjust the heat to maintain a simmer, cover, and cook until it reaches the consistency of tomato sauce, about 30 minutes.

INGREDIENTS:

4 pounds ripe plum tomatoes

2 large eggplants

8 garlic cloves

6 tablespoons + 1 teaspoon extra virgin olive oil

8 garlic cloves

Salt and freshly ground black pepper

1 medium onion, grated or thinly sliced into half-moons

¼ teaspoon red pepper flakes

1 teaspoon sugar

2 ¼ cups panko breadcrumbs, divided

1 cup freshly grated Parmigiano-Reggiano cheese, plus more for serving

2 handfuls fresh parsley leaves, chopped

2 large eggs, lightly beaten

Grapeseed or safflower oil for frying

¾ pound pasta

¾ cup whole milk ricotta

Leaves from 3 sprigs fresh oregano, chopped

5 As the sauce cooks, make the eggplant balls by combining the chopped eggplant-garlic mixture, 1½ cups of the panko, the Parmigiano, two thirds of the parsley, the eggs, and salt and pepper to taste. Mix well, then roll the eggplant mixture into balls about ¾ inch in diameter. Place the remaining panko in a small bowl and roll each ball in the breadcrumbs to coat evenly. Set on a plate or tray.

6 Pour enough frying oil into a large skillet to cover the bottom by ½ inch. Turn the heat to medium and when the oil begins to swirl on the surface but is not yet smoking, carefully add the balls. Work in batches to prevent overcrowding. Fry, turning them gently as needed, until browned all over, 3 to 5 minutes total per batch. Remove with a slotted spoon to a paper towel-lined plate. Tent with aluminum foil to keep them warm.

7 Bring a large pot of water to a boil. Once it's boiling, add salt (1 tablespoon for every 4 cups water) and stir. Add the pasta, stirring for the first minute to prevent any sticking. Cook according to the package instructions, draining the pasta 2 minutes short of the directed cooking time. The pasta will be soft but still very firm. Right before draining the pasta, reserve ¼ cup of the pasta water. Return the empty pot to the stove. Immediately turn the heat to high and add the remaining 1 teaspoon oil and reserved pasta water. Add the drained pasta and toss. Add a few ladlefuls of the tomato sauce and cook, tossing continuously, for 2 minutes.

8 Divide the pasta among four warmed bowls and top with a little more sauce. Add a few dollops of ricotta and 6 eggplant balls, sprinkle with the oregano and a dusting of Parmigiano (or pass grated cheese at the table), and serve piping hot.

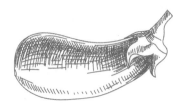

SPICY ANCHOVY, CARAMELIZED ONION, *and* TOASTED BREADCRUMB SAUCE

YIELD: 4 SERVINGS / ACTIVE TIME: 40 MINUTES / TOTAL TIME: ABOUT 1 HOUR

Long strands of pasta are paired with an umami-loaded sauce of briny anchovies, deep brown onions, and crunchy breadcrumbs. You can reduce the amount of red pepper flakes, though a little heat perfectly contrasts with the salty and sweet elements of this filling pasta dish.

Recommended pasta shapes: bigoli, spaghetti, bucatini, perciatelli

INGREDIENTS:

- ¼ cup + 5 ½ tablespoons extra virgin olive oil
- 2 cups soft breadcrumbs (preferably from rustic crusty bread, crusts removed)
- Salt and freshly ground black pepper
- ¼ cup minced fresh basil
- 1 ½ pounds (about 2) large red onions, thinly sliced and then cut into slivers
- 2 2-ounce cans oil-packed flat anchovy fillets, well drained and minced
- 1 ½ teaspoons red pepper flakes
- ¾ pound pasta

1 Heat the largest skillet you have over medium heat for 2 to 3 minutes (the width is important because it allows more of the breadcrumbs, and the onion slivers to come, to have direct contact with the heat.) Add ¼ cup of the olive oil and turn the heat up to medium-high. Once the oil begins to swirl on the surface but is not yet smoking, add the breadcrumbs and ¼ teaspoon each salt and black pepper. Cook, stirring frequently, until the crumbs are a deep golden color, about 8 minutes. Transfer them to a bowl and toss with the basil.

2 Wipe out the skillet with a paper towel and heat over medium-high for 2 to 3 minutes. Add 5 tablespoons of the oil. When it once again begins to swirl on the surface but is not yet smoking, add the onions. Stir gently to make sure all the slivers are thoroughly coated with oil and cook, stirring a few times, until they begin to soften and start to release some of their moisture to the pan, about 5 minutes. Reduce the heat to medium-low and cook until the onions are deeply browned and sticking slightly to the pan, about 40 minutes. During this process, reduce the heat if the onions start to sizzle or scorch or raise the heat if the onions are not browning at all after 15 minutes or so. Be sure to check on them and give them a stir every 10 minutes or so. (The exact cooking time can vary depending on the size of the onions, their liquid and sugar content, and their age, which is why it's important to check in on them regularly. Also, be sure not to stir the onions too often, as they need enough time over direct heat to brown properly.) The onions are perfectly done when they develop a molasses-like color and flavor. Add at least ¼ teaspoon each salt and black pepper (or more, to taste) and mix well. Add the anchovies and red pepper flakes and cook, mashing them into the cooked onions, until they dissolve.

ANCHOVIES

If you can find sea salt-packed anchovies, use them in the recipes where I call for them. Their flavor and texture are far superior to those canned in salty brine. Just carefully pry them out of the salt, so as to not break them, then rinse them under cold running water. Some of the skin may wash off, but the goal is to keep the anchovy intact. Soak them in water for 20 to 30 minutes, after which they should be soft and malleable enough to fillet. Separate the fillets by gently inserting the index and middle fingers of one hand where the stomach is and gently wiggling them until the anchovy opens. Remove any viscera and silverskin from the cavity and then pull the spine away from the fillet it is sticking to it. Separate the fillets and inspect them with your eyes and by running your fingers over them, removing tiny fins or hard bony parts. Any hair-like bones are too soft to be a nuisance and can be left alone. Rinse each fillet under cold running water, transfer to paper towels to absorb excess water, and then use as directed.

3 Meanwhile, bring a large pot of water to a boil. Once it's boiling, add salt (1 tablespoon for every 4 cups water) and stir. Add the pasta and stir for the first minute to prevent any sticking. Cook according to the package instructions, draining the pasta 2 minutes short of the directed cooking time. The pasta will be soft but still very firm. Right before draining the pasta, reserve ¼ cup of the pasta water. Return the pot to the stove. Immediately turn the heat to high, add the remaining ½ tablespoon oil and reserved pasta water. Add the drained pasta and toss. Add the onion mixture and cook, tossing continuously, for 2 minutes. Add half of the toasted breadcrumbs and toss to coat.

4 Divide the pasta among four bowls and serve piping hot topped with the remaining bread crumbs.

BROCCOLI, RAISIN, *and* PINE NUT SAUCE

YIELD: 4 SERVINGS / ACTIVE TIME: 30 MINUTES / TOTAL TIME: 45 MINUTES

Broccoli gets a Sicilian treatment in this recipe, paired with pine nuts and raisins, two ingredients so commonly used in that island's cuisine that they are often sold already mixed together. If you prefer a stronger and more astringent flavor, you can substitute broccoli rabe for the broccoli.

Recommended pasta shapes: orecchiette, shells, gemelli, or any other short, thick pasta

---

1 Heat a small skillet over medium-low heat for 2 minutes. Add the pine nuts and cook, stirring frequently, until they turn golden in spots, 3 to 4 minutes. Remove from the heat and add ⅛ teaspoon salt. Stir well and set aside.

2 Add the raisins to a small bowl and cover with warm water. Soak for 10 minutes. Drain and transfer to a paper towel-lined plate to absorb any surface water.

3 Slice off the bottom third of the broccoli stalks and cut off the florets. Cut really large florets in half so they will cook evenly with the smaller ones. Peel the remaining stalks, then slice into ¼-inch-thick medallions.

4 Bring a large pot of water to a boil. Once it's boiling, add salt (1 tablespoon for every 4 cups water) and stir. Add the broccoli, bring the water back to a boil, and cook for 3 minutes. Remove the broccoli with a strainer and transfer to a colander placed in a large bowl. Take to the sink and run the broccoli under cold water to stop the cooking. Drain and set aside. Keep the water boiling for the pasta.

5 Heat a skillet large enough to hold the finished pasta dish over low heat for 1 to 2 minutes. Add 3 tablespoons of the olive oil and raise the heat to medium. Once the surface of the oil begins to swirl, add the onion and a pinch of salt and stir. Cook until very soft, stirring occasionally, about 10 minutes.

6 Heat a small saucepan over low heat for 1 to 2 minutes. Add 2 tablespoons of the oil and let it heat for a couple of minutes. Add the anchovies and cook for a minute, pressing down on them with a fork or wooden spoon until they disintegrate and combine with the oil into a paste.

INGREDIENTS:

¼ cup pine nuts

Salt

⅓ cup golden raisins

1 pound broccoli

6 tablespoons extra virgin olive oil

1 large yellow onion, very thinly sliced

5 oil-packed canned anchovies, chopped

Freshly ground black pepper

¾ pound pasta

7 Add the raisins, broccoli, and a couple pinches of salt to the onion and stir. Cook for 8 minutes to heat through. Add the anchovy oil and a few good cracks of pepper and stir. Taste for seasoning, adding salt or pepper if needed.

8 Add the pasta to the boiling water and stir for the first minute to prevent sticking. Cook following the package (or recipe) instructions, though you will drain the pasta 2 minutes prior to the directed cooking time. The pasta will be soft but still very firm. Right before draining the pasta, reserve ½ cup of the pasta water. Return the empty pot to the stove. Immediately turn the heat to high, add the remaining tablespoon oil and reserved pasta water, and stir. Add the drained pasta and toss until the water is absorbed. Add the broccoli mixture, along with a few good cracks of pepper, and cook, tossing continuously, for 2 minutes.

9 Divide the pasta among four warmed bowls and serve piping hot.

SALMON, LEEK,
and FETA CONDIMENT

YIELD: 6 SERVINGS / ACTIVE TIME: 25 MINUTES / TOTAL TIME: 40 MINUTES

This delicious company-worthy dish comes together quickly and easily. The sweetness of the leeks contrasts nicely with the sharp tanginess of feta.

Recommended pasta shapes or dumplings: spaghetti, tagliarini, linguine

INGREDIENTS:

- 4 leeks
- 6 tablespoons (¾ stick) unsalted butter, divided
-   Leaves from 3 sprigs fresh thyme
- 1 pound salmon fillet
-   Salt and freshly ground white pepper
- ¾ pound pasta
-   Crumbled feta cheese for serving
-   Chopped fresh dill for serving

1 Prepare the leeks by trimming away the root ends and dark green leaves, keeping only the white and light green parts. With a sharp knife, cut each leek in half lengthwise and remove the two outer layers. Thinly slice the leeks across into crescents. Place them in a large bowl of water and swish them around to remove any dirt. Drain well, then transfer to a kitchen towel. Set aside.

2 Heat a large, deep skillet over medium heat for 2 to 3 minutes. Add 2 tablespoons of the butter and turn the heat to medium-high. Once it melts and starts bubbling, add the thyme and cook for 2 minutes.

3 As the butter heats, pat the salmon dry with paper towels, then season with salt and pepper on both sides. Add the salmon to the skillet, skin side up. You should hear a happy sizzle when the salmon hits the pan. Cook the salmon, undisturbed, for 2 minutes, then turn it over and cook, undisturbed, for another 2 minutes. At this point, the salmon should be nicely browned on both sides and completely cooked through. Transfer the salmon to a warmed plate. Break it into large flakes with a fork, discarding the skin; tent it with aluminum foil to keep warm.

4 Add another 2 tablespoons butter to the skillet. Once it melts and stops foaming, add the leeks, a couple pinches of salt, and pepper to taste, and mix thoroughly. Cook until the leeks start to sizzle, then lower the heat to medium-low; cover and continue to cook, stirring occasionally, until the leeks are completely soft, about another 15 minutes.

5 While the leeks are cooking, bring a large pot of water to a boil. Once it's boiling, add salt (1 tablespoon for every 4 cups water) and stir. Add the pasta, stirring for the first minute to prevent any sticking. Cook according to the package instructions, though you will drain the pasta 2 minutes prior to the directed

cooking time. The pasta will be soft but still very firm. Right before draining the pasta, reserve ¼ cup of the pasta water. Return the empty pot to the stove. Immediately turn the heat to high and add the remaining 2 tablespoons butter and reserved pasta water. Add the pasta, then the leeks and salmon, and cook, mixing continuously, for 1 to 2 minutes.

6 Divide the pasta among six warmed bowls and serve piping hot sprinkled with crumbled feta cheese and dill.

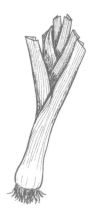

SMOKED SALMON
and ASPARAGUS SAUCE

YIELD: 4 SERVINGS / ACTIVE TIME: 20 MINUTES / TOTAL TIME: 45 MINUTES, PLUS UP TO 3 HOURS TO MARINATE

I've adapted this recipe from one of my favorite go-to sources for cooking inspiration, *The New York Times'* food section. This particular jewel was developed by Florence Fabricant, the longtime and long-acclaimed contributor to *The New York Times* and prolific cookbook author. Pleasantly creamy and smoky, the sauce comes together quickly and yet still makes for a company-worthy elegant dish. Use fresh pasta and freshly grated nutmeg for the best results.

Recommended pasta shapes: paglia e fieno, linguine, fettuccine, tagliatelle, angel hair

INGREDIENTS:

- **2** leeks
- **4** ounces sliced smoked salmon (lox type)
- **¾** cup heavy cream
- **1** teaspoon freshly grated nutmeg
- **1** pound asparagus
- **2** tablespoons water
- **3** tablespoons unsalted butter, divided
- Salt
- **¾** pound pasta
- **6** fresh chives, thinly sliced

1 Trim the leeks by removing the root end and their dark green leaves, keeping only the white and light green parts of the vegetable. With a sharp knife, lightly slice along the length of the leeks and remove the first two outer layers and discard. Cut each leek in quarters and then slice the quarters into thin slivers. Place them in a large bowl of water and swish the water around with your hand to remove any dirt. Pour into a colander and rinse under cold water. Drain again and transfer to a kitchen towel to air dry until needed.

2 Cut the salmon in very small, thin strips. Transfer to a small bowl and add the cream and nutmeg. Mix, cover, and marinate for 2 to 3 hours in a cool place (but not the refrigerator).

3 Snap the tough ends off the asparagus (the spear will know where to break; just follow its lead when you bend it). Place the asparagus in a microwave-friendly dish and add the water. Cover with clear food wrap and microwave (1 minute for thin asparagus and 1 ½ to 2 minutes for thick asparagus). Remove it from the microwave and rinse under cold water to stop it from cooking further. Drain well, then pat dry. Cut off the asparagus tips. Cut each spear in half lengthwise, then, keeping the halves together, cut them across on the diagonal into ½-inch pieces.

4 Heat a large skillet over medium-low heat for 2 to 3 minutes. Add 1 ½ tablespoons of the butter and raise the heat to medium-high. When it's melted, add all the asparagus pieces and a couple pinches of salt and stir. Cook, stirring occasionally, until they just begin to turn golden, 4 to 5 minutes. Transfer them with

a slotted spoon to a small warmed plate and tent with aluminum foil to keep warm. (Optionally, you can pick out half the cooked asparagus tips and set them aside as a garnish.)

5 Add the leeks and a pinch of salt to the skillet, stir, and cover. Cook, stirring occasionally, until they are soft and translucent, about 15 minutes. Add the asparagus and salmon and cream mixture and stir well. Adjust the heat to low and heat through, about 5 minutes.

6 While the leeks cook, bring a large pot of water to a boil. Once it's boiling, add salt (1 tablespoon for every 4 cups water) and stir. Add the pasta and stir for the first minute to prevent any sticking. Cook following the package (or recipe) instructions, though you will drain the pasta 2 minutes prior to the directed cooking time. The pasta should be soft but still very firm. Right before draining the pasta, reserve ¼ cup of the pasta water. Return the empty pot to the stove. Immediately turn the heat to high and add the remaining 1 ½ tablespoons butter and reserved pasta water. Add the drained pasta and toss until the water is absorbed. Add the sauce and cook, mixing continuously, for 1 to 2 minutes.

7 Divide the pasta between four warmed bowls and serve piping hot topped with the chives and the asparagus tips if you set them aside.

SWORDFISH *and* CAPER SAUCE

YIELD: 4 SERVINGS / **ACTIVE TIME:** 15 MINUTES / **TOTAL TIME:** 3 ¼ HOURS

This simple and flavorful pasta dish exemplifies Sicily's penchant for combining seafood with tomatoes. Here the tomatoes serve as a colorful and subtly sweet backdrop to the dish's real star—the swordfish. A spectacular meal when accompanied with a crisp salad, sliced blood oranges and fennel bulb, and black olives.

Recommended pasta shapes: cavatelli, fusilli, busiata, orecchiette, spaghetti

1 Bring a medium saucepan of water to a boil. Blanch the tomatoes in the boiling water for 1 minute. Use tongs to remove them to a cutting board and let cool until you can handle, then remove their skins. Cut them into quarters and remove the seeds, then roughly chop.

2 Using a sharp paring knife, remove the flesh from around the olive pits and set flesh aside.

3 Place the fish on a paper towel-lined plate and thoroughly blot it dry with paper towels. You want the pieces to have as little surface moisture as possible so that they will brown better.

4 Heat a large skillet over low heat for 2 to 3 minutes. Add 5 tablespoons of the olive oil and the garlic, turn the heat to medium, and cook, stirring a few times until the garlic turns golden, 2 to 3 minutes. Discard the garlic. Raise the heat to medium-high. Right before adding the swordfish pieces, season lightly with salt and pepper. Add to the pan in a single layer and don't touch them for 2 minutes (they should be lightly browned at this point). Flip them over to cook on the other side, again, without touching them, for 2 minutes, or until lightly browned. Transfer to a warmed plate and tent loosely with aluminum foil to keep warm. Add the capers to the now empty skillet and cook for a minute. Add the tomatoes and a couple pinches of salt and stir. Bring to a boil, then adjust the heat to low, cover, and simmer for 10 minutes. At this point, the sauce should look slightly shiny and will have reduced a bit. Return the fish to the skillet and cook for just a minute or two to heat through.

5 While the sauce simmers, put a large pot of water on to a boil. Once it's boiling, add salt (1 tablespoon for every 4 cups water) and stir. Add the pasta and stir for the first minute to

INGREDIENTS:

6 very ripe plum tomatoes

½ cup green olives

1 pound swordfish, cut into ¾-inch pieces

5 tablespoons + 1 teaspoon extra virgin olive oil

3 garlic cloves, cut in half

Salt and freshly ground black pepper

2 tablespoons nonpareil capers, rinsed and drained

¾ pound pasta

2 handfuls minced fresh parsley, divided

prevent any sticking. Cook according to the package (or recipe) instructions, draining the pasta 2 minutes short of the directed cooking time. The pasta will be soft but still very firm. Right before draining the pasta, reserve ½ cup of the pasta water. Return the pot to the stove. Immediately turn the heat to high, add the remaining 1 teaspoon oil and reserved pasta water. Add the drained pasta and toss. Add the sauce, a few good cracks of pepper, and half the parsley and cook, tossing continuously, for 2 minutes.

6 Divide the pasta among four bowls and serve piping hot topped with the remaining parsley.

SCALLOP *and* VIDALIA ONION SAUCE

YIELD: 4 SERVINGS / ACTIVE TIME: 25 MINUTES / TOTAL TIME: 45 MINUTES (PLUS 3 HOURS MARINATING)

Brimming with the flavor of sweet Vidalia onions, this light yet tasty seafood sauce is wonderful with the Sardinian spiraled pasta ribbons called *busiate*. The name derives from the Arab word *bus*, a plant whose stem was used to form the pasta and it reflects the lasting culinary influence of the Arab occupation of parts of Italy and the wider Mediterranean in the 9th century. Today, *bus* has been replaced with the *ferretto,* a metal rod around which the ribbons are twirled to give them their irresistibly charming shape. *Busiate* are available in short or long form; I personally prefer the short version for this dish.

Other recommended pasta shapes: linguine, fettuccine, spaghetti

INGREDIENTS:

- 6 very ripe plum tomatoes
- 1 ½ pounds large sea scallops
- ⅓ cup + 2 ½ tablespoons extra virgin olive oil
- Salt and freshly ground black pepper
- 1 Vidalia onion, thinly sliced lengthwise into slivers
- ¾ pound pasta
- Handful fresh basil leaves, cut into thin slivers
- Handful fresh parsley leaves, chopped
- Lemon wedges for serving

1 Bring a medium saucepan of water to a boil. Blanch the tomatoes in the boiling water for 1 minute. Use tongs to remove them to a cutting board and let cool until you can handle, then remove their skins. Cut them into quarters, remove the seeds, and roughly chop.

2 When ready to make the pasta dish, remove the scallops from the refrigerator so that they reach room temperature when you are ready to use them. Rinse the scallops under cold water and pat them dry. You may find side muscles, or little rectangular tags of tissue, on the side of some scallops. Since they are tough, remove them by pinching them between your thumb and index finger and tearing them away. Put the scallops in a shallow medium bowl, add ⅓ cup of the olive oil and salt and pepper to taste.

3 Heat a large skillet over medium-low heat for 2 to 3 minutes. Add 2 tablespoons of the oil and increase the heat to medium. When it begins to swirl but is not yet smoking, add the onion slivers and a couple pinches of salt and stir. Cook, stirring occasionally, until the onion becomes very soft, about 12 minutes. Add the tomatoes and a couple pinches of salt and stir. When the sauce begins to sizzle, lower the heat to a gentle simmer and cook until the tomatoes soften and start breaking down, about 10 minutes.

4 When you add the tomatoes to the skillet, put a large pot of water on to boil. Once it's boiling, add salt (1 tablespoon for every 4 cups water) and stir. Add the pasta, stirring for the first

minute to prevent any sticking. Cook according to the package (or recipe) instructions, draining the pasta 2 minutes short of the directed cooking time. The pasta will be soft but still very firm. Right before draining the pasta, reserve ¼ cup of the pasta water.

5 Heat another large skillet over medium-low heat for 2 to 3 minutes. Raise the heat to medium-high and let the skillet heat for a minute or two. Add the scallops and their oil in the skillet and let them sear without moving them until they turn golden brown, about 3 minutes. Flip them over and cook for another 3 minutes, without moving, until golden brown.

Remove from the heat and tent loosely with aluminum foil to keep them warm.

6 Drain the pasta and return the empty pot to the stove. Immediately turn the heat to high, add the remaining ½ tablespoon oil and reserved pasta water. Add the drained pasta and toss. Add the tomato and onion sauce and cook, tossing continuously, for 2 minutes.

7 Divide the pasta among four warmed bowls and serve piping hot, topped with the seared scallops, the herbs, a few good cracks of pepper, and a spritz of lemon juice.

SHRIMP *and* PISTOU SAUCE

YIELD: 4 SERVINGS / ACTIVE TIME: 35 MINUTES / TOTAL TIME: 1 HOUR

Ink squid-hued spaghetti adds an unexpected and impressive element of presentation to what is otherwise a fairly simple and straightforward plate of pasta. Surprisingly, for its startling color, it tastes just like regular spaghetti, with no "fishy" taste. I have been unable to find it in my local supermarkets and have had to resort to ordering it online (make sure you get the thicker spaghetti for this, not the thin). Pistou, the recipe's flavor powerhouse, is an olive oil-based condiment from Provence. It closely resembles pesto, but for the absence of pine nuts. While traditional pistou is green and made predominantly from basil, garlic, and Parmigiano, this version contains tomato paste for extra depth of flavor and umami (it yields about ¾ cup). With regards to the tomato sauce in this recipe: it needs to be plain, plain, plain (just onion, oil, strained tomatoes, and salt). If the tomato sauce is too burdened with strong flavors, it will compete with the pistou. I recommend using Classic Canned Tomato Sauce (page 566) or Classic Fresh Tomato Sauce (page 565). If you have any leftover spaghetti, save it and make the super easy and dramatic SLeftover Spaghetti Frittata Cake (page 682).

Recommended pasta shapes or dumplings: squid ink spaghetti, spaghetti, linguine, spaghetti alla chitarra

INGREDIENTS:

- 1 ½ pounds medium to large shrimp, peeled and deveined
- 4 garlic cloves, peeled
- 5 tablespoons tomato paste
- Salt
- ½ cup freshly grated Parmigiano-Reggiano cheese
- 2 handfuls fresh basil leaves, torn or cut into ribbons
- 6 ½ tablespoons extra virgin olive oil
- 3 cups plain tomato sauce
- ½ cup water
- Freshly ground black pepper
- ¾ pound pasta
- Lemon wedges
- Handful chopped fresh parsley for serving

1 Drain the shrimp on a paper towel-lined plate while you prep everything else, as they will cook better when they are at room temperature.

2 Making the pistou in a food processor: Put the garlic, tomato paste, and a generous pinch of salt in a mini food processor and pulse until well combined. Add the Parmigiano and pulse until integrated. Add the basil and pulse for just a few seconds; you want to see pieces of the basil in the mixture—it shouldn't be a smooth puree. Transfer the mixture to a small bowl and whisk in 4 tablespoons of the olive oil until fully integrated.

Making the pistou in a mortar: This is my preferred method. Put the garlic and a generous pinch of salt in a mortar and mash it into a paste with the pestle. Add the tomato paste, 4 tablespoons of the olive oil, and a little more salt and pound it thoroughly with the pestle. Once fully integrated, add the Parmigiano and mix again. Add the basil and mash with the pestle to break up the leaves. Either way you make it, pistou can be stored in an airtight container in the refrigerator for a week and the freezer for 3 months.

3 Heat a large, deep skillet over medium heat for 2 to 3 minutes. Add 2 table-spoons of the oil and heat for a minute or two. As it heats up, gently pat the shrimp with a paper towel to absorb as much surface moisture as possible and lightly sprinkle with salt. When the surface of the oil begins to swirl but is not yet smoking, add the shrimp to the skillet in a single layer; make sure there is plenty of room between them, as they will cook better. You will likely have to cook them in several batches. Sear the shrimp for 2 minutes on each side. Transfer to a warmed plate and loosely tent with aluminum foil to keep warm.

4 Add the tomato sauce and water to the skillet and heat over medium-high until the sauce begins to bubble. Add the pistou and stir until well mixed. Taste the seasoning and correct with salt and pepper if necessary. Once the sauce starts bubbling again, adjust the heat to low, cover, and keep warm. Remove 1 cup of the sauce to a small bowl right before adding the whole batch to the cooked pasta in Step 6.

5 Bring a large pot of water to a boil, add salt (1 tablespoon for every 4 cups), and stir. Add the pasta, stirring for the first minute to prevent any sticking. Cook following the package (or recipe) instructions, though you will drain the pasta 2 minutes prior to the directed cooking time. The pasta will be soft but still very firm. Right before draining the pasta, reserve ¼ cup of the pasta water. Return the empty pot to the stove. Immediately turn the heat to high, add the remaining ½ table-spoon oil and reserved pasta water. Add the drained pasta and toss. Now add the tomato sauce (minus the 1 reserved cup) and cook, tossing continuously, for 2 minutes.

6 Divide the pasta among four warmed bowls, dollop with the reserved sauce, and arrange the shrimp over the top. Spritz each plate with lemon juice and sprinkle with the parsley. Serve piping hot.

BRAISED SWISS CHARD
and SQUID SAUCE

YIELD: 5 TO 6 SERVINGS / ACTIVE TIME: 40 MINUTES / TOTAL TIME: 1 ¼ HOURS

This recipe is a slight adaptation of a recipe I discovered on one of my favorite (and extremely authentic) Italian food blogs, *Memorie di Angelina*. *In zimino* is a term that refers to a class of dishes in which the main ingredient, typically seafood, is braised with leafy greens like spinach or Swiss chard. In order to reach earthy perfection in this dish, the greens need to be braised for an unusually long time, until they literally begin to break down in the skillet and lose their nice green color. When cooked this way, they complement the brininess of the calamari beautifully.

Recommended pasta shapes: fettuccine, maltagliati, or other long and somewhat wide ribbons

INGREDIENTS:

- **2** pounds small uncleaned squid or 1 ½ pounds cleaned bodies and tentacles
- Salt and freshly ground black pepper
- **2** pounds Swiss chard
- **3** tablespoons + 1 teaspoon extra virgin olive oil
- **2** garlic cloves, minced
- **1** small white onion, minced
- **2** inner pale green celery stalks, minced
- Handful fresh parsley leaves, minced, plus more for serving
- **2** tablespoons tomato paste
- Pinch of red pepper flakes (optional)
- **1** pound pasta

1 Clean the squid, if necessary. Remove their tentacles by making a straight cut right below the eyes. Hold the tentacles and remove the mouth, or beak, in the central part of the body (it will look like a little bulb and just pops out when you apply a little pressure from the opposite direction). Then run your thumb and index finger down each tentacle to remove the majority of the suction cups (which tend to be a little crunchy once cooked). If the tentacles are big, slice in half or even quarter them. Remove the insides from the tubular section of the squid, making sure to get the ink sack and the clear cartilage that serves as the squid's backbone. Slip off the thin layer of dark skin from the body, then gently tear off the two back fins located at the pointy tip of the body. Lay the body flat on a cutting board and, using a very sharp knife, slice across into ¼-inch-wide rings. Place the prepped calamari in a colander, rinse well, and drain. Sprinkle with salt and pepper and mix well with your hands.

If you have bought already cleaned squid, cut the bodies into rings and if any of the tentacles are large, cut them as described above.

2 Prepare the Swiss chard. Cut the leaves away from the stems (you can save the stems to cook in another dish). Bring a large pot of water to a boil. Once it's boiling, add salt (1 tablespoon for every 4 cups water) and stir. Add the chard leaves and cook until wilted, about 3 minutes. Using a strainer, transfer them to a colander set in a large bowl (don't drain the chard; you're going to use their cooking water to cook the pasta). Take the bowl to the sink and quickly run the chard under cold water to cool

them down. Drain well and, using your hands, squeeze as much liquid out of them as possible. Transfer to a kitchen towel and set aside.

3 Heat a large, deep skillet over low heat for 2 to 3 minutes. Add 3 tablespoons of the oil, turn the heat to medium, and let it heat for a couple of minutes. When the surface of the olive oil begins to swirl but is not yet smoking, add the garlic, onion, celery, parsley, and a couple pinches of salt and stir. When the mixture begins to gently sizzle, turn the heat down to low, cover, and cook, stirring occasionally, until the vegetables have softened and turned translucent, about 20 minutes.

4 Add the squid, turn the heat up to medium, and cook, stirring occasionally, for 5 minutes. Add the tomato paste and red pepper flakes if using and stir until well mixed. Add the chard, a couple pinches of salt, and ¼ cup of the chard cooking water and mix well.

Bring to a gentle boil, then reduce the heat to low, cover, and cook for 25 minutes. Check the mixture occasionally and add a little water if it seems too dry (you want it to be a bit brothy).

5 After the chard and squid have been cooking 10 to 15 minutes, bring the chard cooking water back to a boil. Once it's boiling, add the pasta, stirring for the first minute to prevent any sticking. Cook the pasta according to the package (or recipe) instructions. Right before draining the pasta, reserve ¼ cup of the pasta water. Return the empty pot to the stove. Immediately turn the heat to high and add the remaining 1 teaspoon oil and reserved pasta water. Transfer the drained pasta to the pot and toss until it absorbs all the pasta water. Pour the pasta into the skillet with the chard and squid and cook, tossing continuously, for 2 minutes.

6 Serve piping hot with a sprinkling of parsley and a few good cracks of pepper.

SPAGHETTI *with* CALAMARI FRA DIAVOLO

YIELD: 6 SERVINGS / ACTIVE TIME: 40 MINUTES / TOTAL TIME: 1 HOUR

Typically, classic Italian-American *fra diavolo* sauce, which means "Brother devil" in Italian, consists of succulent shrimp smothered in a devilishly spicy tomato sauce. While I enjoy the shrimp version, I like this sauce best when combined with the small and tender rings and tentacles of baby squid. I just love their springy—but not chewy—texture. And most markets in the United States sell squid already cleaned. Should you find them "fresh off the boat," you can refer to step 1 on page 589 to learn how to clean and prepare them for cooking.

1 Bring the wine to a boil in a small saucepan and continue to boil until reduced almost by half, about 5 minutes (this will concentrate and deepen its flavor). Remove from the stove and set aside.

2 Cut the squid bodies across into ½-inch rings and slice the tentacles in half lengthwise. Wash the squid thoroughly and drain well. Transfer to a paper towel-lined plate to drain as much as possible. Blot the squid with paper towels to absorb as much surface moisture as possible (they will brown better this way).

3 Heat a large, deep skillet over medium heat for 2 to 3 minutes, then add 3 tablespoons of the olive oil, garlic, ½ teaspoon of the red pepper flakes, and a pinch of salt and let heat for a couple of minutes. Once the garlic begins to gently sizzle, turn the heat up to medium-high and add the calamari, anchovies, and half the parsley. Cook, stirring occasionally, until the anchovies dissolve and the calamari begins to turn a golden caramel color, about 5 minutes. Add the reduced wine and continue to cook, stirring occasionally, until it reduces by about a third, about 5 minutes. Add the tomatoes, a couple pinches of salt, the broth, and the remaining ½ teaspoon red pepper flakes and stir. Bring to a boil, then reduce the heat to medium-low and simmer until the sauce is lightly thickened and the flavors have blended, about 20 minutes.

4 While the sauce is simmering, bring a large pot of water to a boil. Once it's boiling, add salt (1 tablespoon for every 4 cups water) and stir. Add the pasta and stir for the first minute to prevent any sticking. Cook according to the package instructions, draining the pasta 2 minutes short of the directed cooking time. The pasta should be tender but still very firm. Right before

INGREDIENTS:

- 1 cup dry red wine such as Cabernet Sauvignon, Pinot Noir, or Sangiovese
- 2 pounds cleaned squid
- 3 ½ tablespoons extra virgin olive oil
- 4 garlic cloves, minced
- 1 teaspoon red pepper flakes, divided

  Salt
- 3 oil-packed anchovy fillets
- 2 handfuls chopped fresh parsley, divided
- 1 28-ounce can peeled whole plum tomatoes (preferably San Marzano), pureed in a food mill or blender
- ½ cup fish broth or bottled clam juice
- 1 pound spaghetti

  Leaves from 1 sprig fresh oregano, chopped, for garnish

draining the pasta, reserve ¼ cup of the pasta water. Return the empty pot to the stove. Immediately turn the heat to high and add the remaining ½ tablespoon oil and reserved pasta water. Add the drained pasta and toss until all the liquid at the bottom of the pot has been absorbed. Ladle three quarters of the sauce into the pot and toss continuously for 2 minutes.

5 Divide the pasta among six warmed bowls. Serve piping hot topped with a couple spoonfuls of the remaining sauce and a generous sprinkling of the remaining parsley and the oregano.

CHICKEN SPAGHETTI ALLA SERENA

YIELD: 4 SERVINGS / ACTIVE TIME: 45 MINUTES / TOTAL TIME: 1 ¼ HOURS

I had never heard of this dish until a wonderful neighbor named Corrie dropped it off for my family on the day we moved to our new home. I couldn't believe her generosity and thoughtfulness, especially when you consider she had four children below the age of six and was seven months pregnant at the time. Her dinner, which tasted as scrumptious as it smelled, was so abundant with chicken and vegetables that we were also able to feed one of my daughter's friends who was over at the time. My girls, now big fans, ask me to make it on a regular basis.

Out of curiosity, I tried to learn more about this dish, but even the late *New York Times* food editor and restaurant critic Craig Claiborne shared that its lineage was unclear. From what I can tell, it seems to be a Midwestern dish, birthed right along the time Campbell soup started inspiring myriad casserole dinners. I have also learned that chicken spaghetti is usually baked or prepared in a crockpot, though, in my "Italian-ness," I have turned my version into a straightforward pasta dish that requires cooking the pasta separately and making a sauce. It's savory, filling, and completely kid-friendly.

1 Bring the wine to a boil in a small saucepan and continue to boil until reduced almost by half, about 5 minutes (this will concentrate and deepen its flavor). Remove from the stove and set aside.

2 Cook the mushrooms, which requires working in two batches. Heat a skillet large enough to hold the finished dish over medium-low heat for 2 to 3 minutes, then add 2 tablespoons of the butter. Once it has melted and stopped foaming, turn the heat to medium-high, add half of the mushrooms, and a pinch of salt and cook, stirring occasionally, until softened and until the edges of the mushrooms begin to color slightly, 6 to 8 minutes. Transfer to a warmed bowl and cover loosely with aluminum foil to keep warm. Add 2 more tablespoons of the butter to the same pan, add the remaining mushrooms and another pinch of salt, and cook in the same way. Add to the other mushrooms in the bowl.

3 Heat the same skillet over medium-low heat for 2 to 3 minutes. Add the olive oil, raise the heat to medium, and let heat for a minute. When the surface of the oil begins to swirl, add the onion and a pinch of salt and cook, stirring occasionally, until

INGREDIENTS:

- ⅔ cup Madeira wine
- 8 ½ tablespoons unsalted butter, divided
- 1 pound cremini mushrooms, cleaned and quartered, divided
- Salt
- 2 tablespoons extra virgin olive oil
- 1 small yellow onion, grated
- 1 red bell pepper, seeded and cut into thin strips
- 1 cup whole milk
- 6 ounces Gruyère cheese, grated
- 2 cups shredded rotisserie chicken breast
- Large handful fresh parsley leaves, chopped, plus more for garnish
- Freshly ground white pepper
- ¾ pound spaghetti
- Freshly grated Parmigiano-Reggiano for serving

they become translucent, about 5 minutes. Add the pepper strips and a pinch of salt and cook, stirring occasionally, until they are tender, 8 to 10 minutes. Raise the heat to medium-high and cook until the edges of the strips begin to color, 4 to 5 minutes.

4 Return the mushrooms to the skillet and mix well. Add the reduced wine and the milk, bring to a boil, and reduce the heat to low. Add 4 tablespoons of the butter and the Gruyère and stir until melted. Add the chicken, parsley, and ½ teaspoon each of salt and white pepper and mix. Continue to cook on low, stirring occasionally, until the chicken is heated through.

5 As the vegetables cook, bring a large pot of water to a boil. Once it's boiling, add salt (1 tablespoon for every 4 cups water) and stir. Add the spaghetti, stirring for the first minute to prevent any sticking. Cook according to the package instructions, draining the pasta 1 minute short of the directed cooking time. The pasta will be tender but still very firm. Right before draining the pasta, reserve ½ cup of the pasta water. Return the empty pot to the stove. Immediately turn the heat to high, add the remaining ½ tablespoon butter and reserved pasta water. Add the drained pasta and toss until all the pasta water on the bottom has been absorbed, then transfer the spaghetti to the skillet and toss until well combined. Taste for seasoning, adding more salt or pepper if needed.

6 Divide the pasta among four warmed bowls and serve piping hot topped with more parsley and a sprinkling of Parmigiano (or pass the grated cheese at the table).

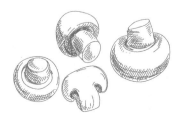

TRAHANA *with* CHICKEN, RED PEPPER, *and* THYME

YIELD: 6 SERVINGS / ACTIVE TIME: 40 MINUTES / TOTAL TIME: 1 HOUR

The petite, granular Greek pasta called *trahana* functions similarly to Arborio or Carnaroli rice in this tasty and filling risotto-like dish. By releasing starch as it cooks, *trahana*'s granules thicken the broth to create that coveted velvety, creamy consistency for which risotto is known. When preparing it, be careful to add smaller and smaller ladlefuls of broth when the *trahana* is almost completely cooked, as you don't want to end up with a "wet" dish when the pasta has finished cooking. You can make this tasty and unusual pasta from scratch, which is a laborious but worthwhile process, or buy it. Depending on where you live, you may need to order it online.

1 Warm the broth in the microwave or on stovetop.

2 Heat a large skillet over medium heat for 2 to 3 minutes, and then add 2 tablespoons of the butter. While the butter melts, blot the chicken pieces with paper towels to remove as much surface moisture as possible (doing this will help them brown better). Once the butter has melted and stopped foaming, turn the heat up to medium-high and add a sprinkling of salt to half the chicken strips. Add them to the pan in a single layer (you should hear a happy sizzle when it hits the pan). Cook for 2 minutes, then add half the thyme and a good crack of pepper and mix for a few seconds. Continue to cook, stirring occasionally, until the strips are lightly browned, about 2 more minutes. Transfer the chicken to a medium bowl and tent loosely with aluminum foil to keep warm. Add 1 tablespoon of butter to the pan and repeat the process with the remaining chicken strips and thyme, transferring it to the bowl when done.

3 Return the skillet to the stove and add the pepper strips and a pinch of salt. Cook, stirring a few times, over medium-high heat until they begin to soften and start lightly browning on their edges, 5 to 6 minutes. Transfer to the bowl with the chicken.

4 Add the olive oil to the skillet, add the onion and a pinch of salt, and stir. Once it begins to sizzle, adjust the heat to low, cover, and cook until softened, about 10 minutes. Add the *trahana* and stir until every granule is coated with oil; toast for a

INGREDIENTS:

4 cups chicken broth

5 tablespoons unsalted butter, divided

1 pound boneless, skinless chicken breasts, cut into thin strips

Salt

Leaves from 2 sprigs fresh thyme, chopped, plus more for garnish

Freshly ground black pepper

1 red bell pepper, seeded and cut into thin strips

2 tablespoons extra virgin olive oil

1 small Vidalia or white onion, grated

1½ cups sour trahana, homemade (page 198) or store-bought

¾ cup dry white wine

¾ cup crumbled feta cheese for garnish

couple of minutes. Add the wine and raise the heat to medium. Cook, stirring almost continuously, until the wine has been completely absorbed. Begin adding the warm broth, a ladleful at a time, and cook, stirring frequently, until the broth has been almost completely absorbed before adding the next ladleful. Continue in this manner until the *trahana* is tender but still chewy, 15 to 20 minutes. Taste for seasoning and add salt or pepper if needed. Add the remaining 2 tablespoons butter, and return the peppers and chicken to the skillet. Mix thoroughly but gently, to ensure the peppers are not damaged.

5 Remove from the heat and allow the *trahana* to rest, covered with a kitchen towel, for 5 minutes.

6 Spoon into six warmed bowls and serve piping hot topped with the feta cheese and a sprinkling of fresh thyme.

CHICKEN LIVER, GUANCIALE,
and PORCINI MUSHROOM SAUCE

YIELD: 6 SERVINGS / ACTIVE TIME: 45 MINUTES / TOTAL TIME: 1½ HOURS

Years ago my girlfriend dated a nice guy named Luigi who owned a trattoria in Italy and who, as you might expect, knew his way around the kitchen. One night he regaled us with a bottle of Barolo wine and this spectacularly savory sauce with the enticing aroma of porcini mushrooms. As we complimented him in between ravenous bites, he admitted that it had taken him awhile to nail this sauce because for a long time he had just been using chicken livers. "I thought they would be flavorful enough on their own," he shared, "but the sauce didn't come together until I added guanciale." The guanciale (cured pig jowl) added flavor and—more importantly—fat, as the livers always ended up turning out rather dry and pasty on their own. Smart guy, that Luigi. Too bad he didn't stick around.

Recommended pasta shapes or dumplings: potato or butternut squash gnocchi, maltagliati, fettuccine or other long somewhat wide ribbons, ravioli

1 Bring the wine to a boil in a small saucepan and let boil until reduced by half, about 5 minutes. Remove from the heat.

2 Place the porcini in a small bowl with enough warm water to cover them and let soak until softened, about 15 minutes. Lightly run your fingers across all the pieces to dislodge any dirt or debris. Gather them in your hand and gently squeeze over the bowl to remove excess water, then chop. Strain the soaking liquid through a small paper towel-lined strainer; set aside.

3 Rinse the chicken livers, then trim away any remaining filaments or connective tissue. Pat dry, then chop.

4 Heat a large, deep skillet over medium-low heat for 2 to 3 minutes. Add 2 tablespoons of the olive oil, turn the heat to medium, and heat until the oil starts swirling but is not yet smoking. Add the guanciale and cook, stirring occasionally, until brown and crisp, about 8 minutes. Add the porcini, onion, celery, and a couple pinches of salt and stir well. When the mixture starts to sizzle, adjust the heat to low, cover, and cook, stirring occasionally, until the vegetables are very soft, about 20 minutes.

5 Add the chicken livers and a couple more pinches of salt to the skillet, raise the heat to medium-high, and cook, stirring a few times, until they turn a grayish color, with no pink apparent.

INGREDIENTS:

1	cup Madeira wine
1	ounce dried porcini mushrooms
½	pound chicken livers
2 ½	tablespoons extra virgin olive oil, divided
3	ounces guanciale or pancetta, very finely diced
1	medium yellow onion, minced
2	inner pale green celery stalks, minced
	Salt
2	tablespoons tomato paste
5 to 6	fresh sage leaves, stacked and cut across into thin strips
6	canned San Marzano tomatoes
¼	cup freshly grated Parmigiano-Reggiano cheese, plus more for serving
	Freshly ground black pepper
1	pound pasta
	Handful minced fresh parsley for serving

Add the tomato paste, stir well, and cook for 2 to 3 minutes. Add the reduced wine, reserved mushroom soaking liquid, sage, tomatoes (crush them in your hand before adding them to the skillet), and a couple more pinches of salt and stir. Bring to a gentle boil. Reduce the heat to low, cover, and simmer for 15 minutes. Uncover the skillet and cook for another 20 minutes, stirring occasionally. Remove from the heat, add the Parmigiano and a couple of good cracks of pepper, and stir.

6 While the sauce simmers, bring a large pot of water to a boil. Once it's boiling, add salt (1 tablespoon for every 4 cups water) and stir. Add the pasta and stir for the first minute to prevent any sticking. Cook following the package (or recipe) instructions, though you will drain the pasta 2 minutes prior to the directed cooking time. The pasta should be soft but still very firm. Right before draining the pasta, reserve ¼ cup of the pasta water. Return the empty pot to the stove. Immediately turn the heat to high and add the remaining ½ tablespoon oil and reserved pasta water. Add the drained pasta and toss until the water is absorbed. Add the sauce and cook, mixing continuously, for 1 to 2 minutes.

7 Ladle the pasta into six warmed bowls and serve piping hot with a sprinkling of parsley and Parmigiano (or pass the grated cheese at the table).

DUCK RAGÙ

YIELD: 4 SERVINGS / ACTIVE TIME: 20 MINUTES / TOTAL TIME: ABOUT 3 HOURS

I once sat next to someone at a dinner party who shared that he often used chicken meat in sauces meant to be prepared with duck and found the end result just as delicious. I nodded politely at the time, but I fervently disagree. Duck has a deep, rich flavor that chicken just can't match. This is a long-simmered sauce and requires time. While you can prepare it in 3 hours, it's even better if it simmers all day. Duck legs, especially wild duck legs, require at least 3 hours to tenderize, while domesticated ones only need 2. For best results, get a good sear on the duck, as the thick layer of crusty bits on the bottom of the pan will add intense flavor. You can prepare this sauce up to 3 days ahead and freeze it for up to 3 months.

Recommended pasta shapes: pappardelle, tagliatelle, bavette, penne, bigoli, sedani, rigatoni

INGREDIENTS:

- **1** cup dry red wine
- **2 ½** tablespoons + 1 teaspoon extra virgin olive oil
- **1** tablespoon unsalted butter
- **4** duck legs

  Salt and freshly ground black pepper
- **2** garlic cloves, minced
- **1** small onion, chopped
- **2** cups chicken broth
- **2** teaspoons ground cinnamon
- **2** bay leaves

  Leaves from 1 small sprig fresh rosemary, minced (reserve the stems)
- **1** 28-ounce can peeled whole plum tomatoes (preferably San Marzano)
- **¾** pound pasta

  Freshly grated Parmigiano-Reggiano cheese for serving

1 Bring the wine to a boil in a small saucepan and let boil until reduced by half, about 5 minutes. Remove from the heat.

2 Heat a large, deep skillet over medium heat for 2 to 3 minutes. Add 2 tablespoons of the olive oil and the butter. As the butter and oil heat up, thoroughly pat dry the duck legs with paper towels and sprinkle with ½ teaspoon each salt and pepper. When the butter stops foaming, turn the heat to medium-high. Add the duck legs and cook on both sides until golden brown and some of fat has rendered, about 10 minutes. Transfer to a plate.

3 Drain just enough of the duck fat from the skillet that you only see a thin film covering the entirety of the skillet bottom. (Drain it in a small bowl if you're concerned you will drain too much and want to add some in.) Add the garlic, onion, and a couple pinches of salt. When the mixture starts to sizzle, adjust the heat to low, cover, and cook, stirring occasionally, until very soft, about 20 minutes.

4 Add the reduced wine, stir, turn the heat up to medium-high, and cook for 2 minutes. Return the duck legs to the skillet, along with any juices that might have accumulated on the plate. Add the broth, cinnamon, bay leaves, two pinches of salt, the rosemary stems, and the tomatoes and their juices, crushing the tomatoes by hand before adding them to the skillet. Bring to a boil, then reduce the heat to low, cover, and gently simmer for 2 hours. You'll know the sauce is done when it has visibly thickened and the fat has separated and is bubbling on the surface.

5 Transfer the duck legs to a cutting board and remove the bay leaves and rosemary stems from the sauce. Puree the sauce with an immersion blender. Alternatively, you can carefully blend it in batches in a food processor or blender (don't overfill the container and keep your hand on the lid of the blender when you do this). Return the sauce to the skillet, turn the heat to medium-high, and cook until slightly reduced, stirring occasionally, 8 to 10 minutes.

6 While the sauce reduces, remove the skin from the duck legs and thinly slice. Set aside. Using a fork, finely shred the duck meat. Return the shredded duck to the sauce, add the minced rosemary, and season with salt and pepper to taste. Reduce the heat to a simmer.

7 Bring a large pot of water to a boil. Once it's boiling, add salt (1 tablespoon for every 4 cups water) and stir. Add the pasta and stir for the first minute to prevent any sticking. Cook following the package (or recipe) instructions, though you will drain the pasta 2 minutes prior to the directed cooking time. The pasta should be soft but still very firm. Right before draining the pasta, reserve ¼ cup of the pasta water.

8 While the pasta is cooking, crisp up the duck skin by warming a small skillet over medium-high heat along with 1 teaspoon of the oil. Add the skin and cook, turning frequently, until it becomes crispy, then transfer to a folded paper towel to drain and chop.

9 Drain the pasta and return the empty pot to the stove. Immediately turn the heat to high and add the remaining ½ tablespoon oil and reserved pasta water. Add the pasta and toss until the water is absorbed. Add the sauce and cook, mixing continuously, for 1 to 2 minutes.

10 Ladle the pasta into four warmed bowls and serve piping hot topped with the crispy duck skin and a sprinkling of Parmigiano (or pass the grated cheese at the table).

RABBIT RAGÙ

YIELD: 4 SERVINGS / ACTIVE TIME: 1 HOUR / TOTAL TIME: 2 ¾ HOURS

When many people think of rabbits they think of pets not pans. But, unfortunately for rabbits, they are as delicious as they are cute and furry. Folks in Italy and France certainly think so, as those two countries account for the highest production and consumption of rabbit in Europe. For best results, use 15- to 20-week-old rabbits, called roasters, which are less pricey and benefit most from the rather long braise in this recipe. Finally, this sauce is considered a "white ragù," because it is traditionally tomato-less. I cheat a little by including a bit of tomato paste, which colors the final sauce a lovely shade of rose.

Recommended pasta shapes or dumplings: pappardelle, lagane, casarecce, strangolapreti, tortiglioni, tagliatelle, spätzle, potato gnocchi, casarecce

1 Heat a large, deep, heavy-bottomed pot or a cast-iron Dutch oven over medium-low heat for 2 to 3 minutes. Add 3 tablespoons of the olive oil and turn the heat up to medium. Add the pancetta and cook, stirring every few minutes, until golden brown, about 8 minutes. Transfer to a small plate using a slotted spoon. Add the onion, celery, carrot, tomato paste, and a couple of pinches of salt to the hot rendered fat in the pot and stir. When the mixture starts to sizzle, turn the heat down to low, cover, and cook, stirring occasionally, until the vegetables are very soft, about 30 minutes. Add the garlic and cook another minute, until fragrant. Turn the heat to medium-high, add the rabbit, and cook, stirring occasionally, until it looks gray and is completely cooked. Add the wine, stir, and cook for 5 minutes. Add the broth, salt to taste, the pancetta along with any fat that might be on the plate, and the rosemary stems and bring to a boil. Reduce the heat to low and simmer, stirring occasionally, for 2 hours, adding more broth if the sauce starts looking a little dry. Once finished cooking, remove the rosemary stems and discard.

2 Add the minced rosemary and oregano and stir well. Taste and adjust seasonings as needed. Transfer the rabbit to a large plate. Using two forks, remove the meat from the bones and return it to sauce. Stir and cover.

INGREDIENTS:

- 3 ½ tablespoons extra virgin olive oil, divided
- 3 ounces pancetta (or substitute bacon), finely diced
- 1 small onion, minced
- 2 inner pale green celery stalks
- 1 small carrot, finely diced
- 3 tablespoons tomato paste

  Salt
- 2 garlic cloves, minced
- 1 3- to 3 ½-pound skinned rabbit, cut into 8 pieces and patted dry
- 1 ½ cups dry white wine
- 1 ½ to 2 cups chicken broth, or more as needed

  Leaves from 2 small sprigs fresh rosemary, minced (reserve the stems)

  Leaves from 1 sprig fresh oregano, minced
- ¾ pound pasta

  Freshly ground black pepper

  Generous handful fresh parsley leaves, minced, for serving

  Freshly grated Parmigiano-Reggiano cheese for serving

3 Bring a large pot of water to a boil. Once it's boiling, add salt (1 tablespoon for every 4 cups water) and stir. Add the pasta and stir for the first minute to prevent any sticking. Cook following the package (or recipe) instructions, though you will drain the pasta 2 minutes prior to the directed cooking time. The pasta should be soft but still very firm. Right before draining the pasta, reserve ¼ cup of the pasta water. Return the empty pot to the stove. Immediately turn the heat to high and add the remaining ½ tablespoon oil and reserved pasta water. Add the drained pasta and toss until the water is absorbed. Add the sauce and cook, mixing continuously, for 1 to 2 minutes.

4 Ladle the pasta into four warmed bowls and serve piping hot with a few good cracks of the pepper and a sprinkling of the parsley and Parmigiano (or pass the grated cheese at the table).

PENNE ALLA VODKA

YIELD: 6 SERVINGS / ACTIVE TIME: 40 MINUTES / TOTAL TIME: 1 HOUR

Quintessential comfort food, *penne alla vodka* is a beloved Italian-American pasta dish brimming with the finely tuned flavors of tomatoes, cream, Parmigiano, and pancetta. Ironically, the only ingredient you don't taste is its namesake. It's not an oversight either, as the vodka is meant to be imperceptible. It nevertheless plays an integral role by bringing out the flavors in tomatoes that are alcohol soluble and otherwise inaccessible to the palate. In doing so, vodka makes the tomatoes taste brighter, richer, and more vibrant, very similarly to how red and white wines release the flavors of the ingredients with which they are cooked. This is an excellent dish to make for a large group of people, since short pasta like penne cook much more easily than long strands.

INGREDIENTS:

- **4 to 5 ounces pancetta, diced**
- **2 ½ tablespoons unsalted butter, divided**
- **3 shallots, minced**
- **Salt**
- **1 28-ounce can peeled whole plum tomatoes (preferably San Marzano), pureed in a food mill or blender**
- **1 teaspoon red pepper flakes**
- **1 cup heavy cream**
- **1 ¼ pounds penne**
- **½ cup vodka, room temperature**
- **1 cup freshly grated Parmigiano-Reggiano cheese, plus more for serving**
- **2 handfuls chopped fresh parsley for garnish**

1 Heat a skillet large enough to hold the finished past dish over medium-low heat for 2 to 3 minutes, then add the pancetta. Raise the heat to medium and slowly cook, stirring occasionally, until the pieces become crisp, 8 to 10 minutes. Using a slotted spoon, remove the pieces and transfer to a small bowl. Add 2 tablespoons of the butter to the skillet. Once it has melted and stopped foaming, add the shallots and a pinch of salt. Once they begin to gently sizzle, adjust the heat to low, cover, and cook, stirring occasionally, until soft, about 10 minutes.

2 Add the tomatoes, red pepper flakes and a couple pinches of salt, stir, and raise the heat to medium-high. Once the mixture begins to gently boil, adjust the heat to low and cook, partially covered and stirring occasionally, until the sauce slightly thickens, 15 to 20 minutes. Add the cream and heat through until the sauce gently bubbles. Remove from the heat and cover.

3 While the sauce is simmering, bring a large pot of water to a boil. Once it's boiling, add salt (1 tablespoon for every 4 cups water) and stir. Add the penne and stir for first minute to prevent any sticking. Cook according to the package instructions, draining the pasta 2 minutes short of the directed cooking time. The pasta should be tender but still very firm. Right before draining the pasta, reserve ¼ cup of the pasta water. Return the empty pasta pot to the stove. Immediately turn the heat to high, add the remaining ½ tablespoon butter, the reserved pasta water, and the vodka. Add the drained penne and toss until all the liquid at the bottom of the pot has been absorbed. Add three quarters of the sauce to the pot and the Parmigiano and toss continuously for 2 minutes.

4 Divide the penne among six warmed bowls. Serve piping hot topped with a couple spoonfuls of the remaining sauce and a generous sprinkling of parsley, the crisped pancetta, and grated Parmigiano (or pass the grated cheese at the table).

"FAKE" SAUCE

YIELD: 4 SERVINGS / ACTIVE TIME: 15 MINUTES / TOTAL TIME: 45 MINUTES

Literally "fake sauce," *sugo finto* is a mostly meatless sauce that is essentially considered the poor man's ragù and reflects a time when working people could only afford to eat meat on Christmas and at a handful of religious holidays. While the traditional recipe includes carrots, I have excluded it, finding it lends too much sweetness to the sauce.

Recommended pasta shapes: gigli, strangolapreti, tagliatelle, fusilli, ziti

1 Heat the broth and tomato paste in a small saucepan over medium-high heat. Stir until the paste dissolves. Remove from the heat.

2 Heat a large, deep skillet ample enough to hold the finished pasta dish over low heat for 2 to 3 minutes. Add the *lardo* and cook, stirring occasionally, until it starts to render, 5 to 6 minutes. Turn the heat to medium and add the celery, scallions, a few pinches of salt, and a good crack of pepper. Cook until the vegetables are completely wilted, about 15 minutes. Add the broth mixture and simmer until the sauce becomes quite dense, 10 to 15 minutes, stirring occasionally. Taste for seasoning and add salt and pepper if needed.

3 While the sauce simmers, bring a large pot of water to a boil. Once it's boiling, add salt (1 tablespoon for every 4 cups water) and stir. Add the pasta, stirring for the first minute to prevent any sticking. Cook according to the package (or recipe) instructions, draining the pasta 2 minutes short of the directed cooking time. The pasta will be soft but still very firm. Right before draining the pasta, reserve ¼ cup of the pasta water. Return the empty pot to the stove. Immediately turn the heat to high and add the olive oil and reserved pasta water. Add the drained pasta and pecorino and toss to combine well. Add a few ladlefuls of the sauce and toss. Cook, tossing continuously, for 2 minutes.

4 Divide the pasta among four warmed bowls and top with a little more sauce. Serve piping hot sprinkled with the parsley and a dusting of pecorino (or pass the grated cheese at the table).

INGREDIENTS:

- ¾ cup chicken or vegetable broth
- 2 tablespoons tomato paste
- 3 ounces lardo (pork fatback) or fatty parts of bacon, finely diced
- 4 inner pale green celery stalks, minced
- 1 bunch (5 or 6) scallions (white and pale green parts), trimmed and minced
-    Salt and freshly ground black pepper
- ¾ pound pasta
- 1 teaspoon extra virgin olive oil
- ⅓ cup freshly grated pecorino Romano cheese, plus more for serving
-    Handful fresh parsley leaves, minced, for serving

PASTA *with* CARAMELIZED LEEKS *and* PANCETTA

YIELD: 4 SERVINGS / ACTIVE TIME: 20 MINUTES / TOTAL TIME: 1 HOUR

Browned leeks lend just the right amount of mellow, earthy sweetness to balance the richness of the pancetta and aromatic pineyness of the rosemary.

Recommended pasta shapes or dumplings: passatelli, spätzle, gemelli, farfalle, trofie, tagliolini

1 Bring the Marsala to a boil in a small saucepan, then continue to boil until reduced by half. Remove from the heat.

2 Prepare the leeks by trimming away the root ends and dark green leaves, keeping only the white and light green parts. With a sharp knife, cut each leek in half lengthwise and remove the two outer layers. Cut the halves vertically into thin slivers. Place them in a large bowl of water and swish them around to remove any dirt. Drain well, then transfer to a kitchen towel to air dry and mince.

3 Heat a large skillet over low heat for 2 to 3 minutes. Add 3 tablespoons of the butter and turn the heat up to medium. Once it melts and stops foaming, add the pancetta and cook, stirring almost constantly, until it turns golden brown, 7 to 8 minutes. Using a slotted spoon, transfer the pancetta bits to a small bowl. Add the leeks and a couple pinches of salt to the skillet, stir, and cook until the leeks are very soft and have lightly browned in spots, 18 to 20 minutes. Add the reduced Marsala and reserved rosemary stem, stir, and bring to a boil. Reduce the heat to low, cover, and cook until the sauce acquires a fairly chunky consistency, about 20 minutes. Discard the rosemary stem and add the chopped rosemary leaves and white pepper to taste and stir. Taste for seasoning, adding salt and more pepper if needed.

4 Bring a large pot of water to a boil and then add salt (1 tablespoon for every 4 cups water) and stir. Add the pasta and stir for the first minute to prevent any sticking. Cook following the package (or recipe) instructions, draining it 2 minutes before its directed cooking time. Right before draining the pasta, reserve ½ cup of the pasta water. Return the pot to the stove. Immediately turn the heat to high and add the remaining tablespoon butter and reserved pasta water. Transfer the drained pasta to the pot. Toss well until the pasta water is absorbed. Add the leek mixture and cook, tossing continuously for 2 minutes.

5 Ladle out into four warmed pasta bowls and serve piping hot, topped with a good crack of fresh pepper, the crispy pancetta bits, and a light dusting of Parmigiano (or pass the grated cheese at the table).

INGREDIENTS:

1 cup dry Marsala wine

2 large leeks

4 tablespoons (½ stick) unsalted butter, divided

4 ounces pancetta, diced

Salt

Leaves from 1 sprig fresh rosemary, minced (reserve the stem)

Freshly ground white pepper

¾ pound pasta

Freshly grated Parmigiano-Reggiano cheese for serving

FAVA BEAN, PANCETTA,
and PECORINO CONDIMENT

YIELD: 4 SERVINGS / ACTIVE TIME: 15 MINUTES / TOTAL TIME: 50 MINUTES

Fresh fava beans mean springtime and lend a beautiful light green color to this tasty and nourishing sauce. Also known as broad beans, fava beans are smoother, sweeter, and creamier than most other beans and would probably be more popular if they didn't need to be peeled twice before using. If you purchase them still in their pods, you will need to first shell them as you would peas. Secondly, you will need to remove the thick, whitish skin that envelops each bean. I've found the easiest way to do this is to blanch them in a large pot of salted boiling water for 1 minute, drain, and cool under cold running water, then squeeze each bean out of its skin with your fingers. To add a splash of vibrant color and aromatic, savory flavor, I roast the cherry tomatoes with thyme.

Recommended pasta shapes or dumplings: maltagliati, farfalle, lagane, Ligurian gnocchetti, gnocchi, spätzle, penne, campanelle, gemelli, trofie

1 Preheat the oven to 450°F. Toss the tomatoes with the thyme, 2 tablespoons of the olive oil, a couple pinches of salt, and a good crack of black pepper on a parchment paper–lined baking sheet. Place the sheet on the center rack and roast, turning once, until the tomatoes are blistered and beginning to burst, about 20 minutes. Remove from the oven and tent loosely with aluminum foil to keep warm.

2 Bring a medium saucepan of water to a boil. Once it's boiling, add salt (1 tablespoon for every 4 cups water) and stir. Add the fresh fava beans, bring the water back to a boil, and cook for 3 minutes. Drain, rinse under cold water, then pop the beans out of their skins by squeezing them at one end. (If using frozen peeled beans, skip this step.)

3 Heat a large, deep skillet over low heat for 2 to 3 minutes. Add 2 tablespoons of the oil and turn the heat up to medium. Once the oil begins to swirl on the surface but is not yet smoking, add the scallions, pancetta, and red pepper flakes and cook, stirring every few minutes, until the scallion whites are golden brown and the pancetta has rendered its fat, about 12 minutes. Add the fava beans, broth, and a couple pinches of salt. Stir and bring to a boil over medium-high heat. Once gently boiling, reduce the heat to low and cook until the broth reduces by half and the fava beans are tender, about 20 minutes. Transfer two ladlefuls of fava beans

INGREDIENTS:

1	pint cherry tomatoes
	Leaves from 2 sprigs fresh thyme
5	tablespoons extra-virgin olive oil, divided
	Salt and freshly ground black pepper
3	cups shelled (not peeled) fava beans, 2 ½ pounds fava bean pods, or 1 cup frozen peeled fava beans
4 to 5	scallions, trimmed and thinly sliced
4	ounces pancetta (or substitute bacon), finely diced
½	teaspoon red pepper flakes
1	cup chicken broth
¾	pound pasta
6	tablespoons freshly grated pecorino Romano cheese

to a blender or food processor and reduce them to a puree. Stir the puree back into the skillet and taste for seasoning, adding salt if needed. Keep warm over very low heat

4 While the favas are cooking, bring a large pot of water to a boil. Once it's boiling, add salt (1 tablespoon for every 4 cups water) and stir. Right before removing the favas to the blender, add the pasta to the water and stir for the first minute to prevent any sticking. Cook following the package (or recipe) instructions though you will drain the pasta 2 minutes prior to the directed cooking time. The pasta will be soft but still very firm. Right before draining the pasta, reserve ½ cup of the pasta water. Return the empty pot to the stove. Immediately turn the heat to high, add the remaining tablespoon oil and reserved pasta water, and stir. Add the drained pasta and toss until the water is absorbed. Add the fava bean and pancetta mixture and cook, tossing continuously, for 2 minutes, then gently stir in the tomatoes and pecorino cheese.

5 Divide the pasta among four warmed bowls and serve piping hot sprinkled with a dusting of pecorino (or pass the grated cheese at the table).

FONTINA SAUCE *with* ROASTED CAULIFLOWER, MUSHROOMS, *and* BACON

YIELD: 4 SERVINGS / ACTIVE TIME: 40 MINUTES / TOTAL TIME: 1 ¼ HOURS

I call this savory autumn dish a perfect shoo-in for adult mac and cheese. While the fontina cheese sauce is of course delicious (how could it not be?), I believe what makes this dish so satisfying is the balance between the nutty butteriness of the sauce and the intense flavor of the aromatic roasted vegetables, especially the mushrooms. The key to coaxing out that coveted deep, earthy flavor is to roast the mushrooms until they are browned and quite crisp on their edges. It gives them a nice texture to bite into to boot. Should you not be able to find fontina, you can substitute it with Gruyère or Emmental cheese.

Recommended pasta shapes: gigli, fusilli, penne, rigatoni, sedani

INGREDIENTS:

- 1 head (about 2 pounds) cauliflower
- 6 ½ tablespoons extra virgin olive oil, divided
- Salt and freshly ground black pepper
- 1 pound cremini mushrooms
- Leaves from 3 small sprigs fresh thyme
- 6 ounces bacon, chopped into ½-inch pieces
- 1 large yellow onion, grated
- ½ cup chicken or vegetable broth
- 4 ounces fontina cheese, grated
- ¾ cup heavy cream
- ½ tablespoon Worcestershire sauce
- ¾ pound pasta
- Handful chopped fresh parsley leaves for serving

1 Preheat the oven to 450°F.

2 Trim the outer leaves from the cauliflower, then cut the head in half and then into quarters. Separate the florets from the core center and cut any large florets in half to create a flat surface. Add them to a large bowl along with 2 tablespoons of the olive oil and rub gently to coat with the oil. Place cut side down on a parchment paper–lined rimmed baking pan. Season with salt and pepper to taste and cover the pan tightly with aluminum foil. Place it in the oven and roast for 15 minutes.

3 As the cauliflower roasts, wipe the mushrooms clean, trim their stems, and quarter them. Add to the same bowl you used for the cauliflower, along with another 2 tablespoons oil, and mix well. Arrange on another parchment paper–lined rimmed baking sheet, season with salt and pepper, and sprinkle with the thyme.

4 Remove the pan with the cauliflower from the oven and carefully remove the foil (the released steam will be hot). Using a narrow spatula, carefully turn the cauliflower over and return to the oven, uncovered. Lower the temperature to 400°F. Add the mushroom tray to the oven. Roast for 15 minutes, at which point the mushrooms will have released some liquid. Remove that tray from the oven, carefully drain the liquid, and return the pan to the oven. Roast for another 25 minutes. The vegetables are done when they are soft and lightly browned on their edges. Remove from the oven.

5 Heat a large skillet over medium-low heat for 2 to 3 minutes. Add 2 tablespoons of the oil and raise the heat to medium. Add the bacon and cook, stirring a few times, until it turns golden and crisp, 8 to 10 minutes. Using a slotted spoon, transfer it to a small bowl and set aside.

6 Return the same skillet to the stove, add the grated onion and a couple pinches of salt to the rendered bacon fat and stir. Cook over medium-high heat, stirring frequently, until the onion starts to gently sizzle. Adjust the heat to low, cover, and cook, stirring occasionally, until it becomes very soft, about 15 minutes. Turn the heat up to medium-high, add the broth, cheese, and cream, and stir until the cheese is melted and the mixture is bubbly. Stir in the Worcestershire. Remove from the heat and cover to keep warm.

7 While the sauce is simmering, bring a large pot of water to a boil. Once it's boiling, add salt (1 tablespoon for every 4 cups water) and stir. Add the pasta and stir for first minute to prevent any sticking. Cook following the package instructions, though you will drain the pasta 2 minutes prior to the directed cooking time. The pasta will be soft but still very firm. Right before draining the pasta, reserve ¼ cup of the pasta water. Return the now empty pot to the stove. Immediately turn the heat to high and add the remaining ½ tablespoon oil and reserved pasta water. Quickly add the drained pasta and toss until the water is absorbed. Add the sauce and cook, mixing continuously, for 1 to 2 minutes.

8 Divide the pasta among four warmed bowls. Serve piping hot topped with plenty of roasted vegetables, the crispy bacon bits, a generous crack of black pepper, and the parsley.

BROCCOLI RABE *and* HAM SAUCE

YIELD: 4 SERVINGS / ACTIVE TIME: 25 MINUTES / TOTAL TIME: 40 MINUTES

This recipe is a somewhat gussied up twist on an old classic from southern Italy and the region of Puglia in particular, *pasta e broccoletti*. The original, made with pasta, garlic, and red chiles, celebrates Italy's beloved winter vegetable, broccoli rabe. This version goes a step further by adding onion for a touch of sweetness and capers for pungency. Make sure to aggressively trim the broccoli rabe to just the florets, the smaller (and more tender) leaves, and the thinnest stems. Only then can you eliminate the bitterness for which broccoli rabe is known.

Recommended pasta shapes: orecchiette, maccherroni, garganelli, ziti

1 Bring a large pot of water to a boil. Once it's boiling, add salt (1 tablespoon for every 4 cups) and stir. Add the broccoli rabe and boil for 6 minutes. Remove using a fine-meshed strainer and rinse under cold water. You will use the same pot of water to cook the pasta; keep the water at a low simmer until the sauce is almost done, then ratchet up the heat. Drain the broccoli rabe well, squeeze to remove excess water, then chop.

2 Heat a large skillet over low heat for 2 to 3 minutes. Add 4 tablespoons of the olive oil and turn the heat to medium. Once it begins swirling but is not yet smoking, add the onion, garlic, and a pinch of salt and stir. Cook, stirring a few times, until the onion turns translucent, 4 to 5 minutes. Add the capers and ham and cook, stirring frequently, until the mixture becomes very soft, 5 to 6 minutes. Add the broccoli rabe and a couple pinches of salt, stir well to combine, and cook for another 5 minutes. Remove from the heat, cover, and keep warm.

3 Add the pasta to the boiling water, stirring for the first minute to prevent any sticking. Cook according to the package (or recipe) instructions, draining the pasta 2 minutes short of the directed cooking time. The pasta will be soft but still very firm. Right before draining the pasta, reserve ½ cup of the pasta water. Return the pot to the stove. Immediately turn the heat to high, add 1 teaspoon of the oil and the reserved pasta water. Quickly add the drained pasta and toss. Add the sauce, a few good cracks of pepper, and the remaining 2 tablespoons oil and cook, tossing continuously, for 2 minutes.

4 Divide the pasta among four warmed bowls. Serve piping hot topped with the pecorino (or pass the grated cheese at the table).

INGREDIENTS:

Salt

1 ½ pounds broccoli rabe, trimmed as described

6 tablespoons + 1 teaspoon extra virgin olive oil

1 small yellow onion, finely diced

3 garlic cloves, thinly sliced

1 tablespoon nonpareil capers, rinsed

4 ounces sliced ham, julienned

¾ pound pasta

Freshly ground black black pepper

⅓ cup freshly grated pecorino Sardo or pecorino Romano cheese for serving

SAUSAGE RAGÙ

YIELD: 4 SERVINGS / ACTIVE TIME: 20 MINUTES/ TOTAL TIME: 2 ½ HOURS

This is a real stick-to-your-ribs kind of sauce, mostly because of the considerable fat content in sausage. It's the type of dish that nourishes both body and soul, especially after a day of gardening or hiking in the mountains. I like to keep a container of it in my freezer for those days when I am too harried to cook. For best results, prepare this sauce when you have time on your hands. To be at its finest, it needs to cook for at least 2 hours, as its flavor is enhanced with each additional minute that the ingredients bubble together. Once prepared, it keeps 3 days when refrigerated and up to 3 months in the freezer.

Recommended pasta shapes: malloreddus, cavatelli, cavatappi, ziti, sedani, fusilli, chifferi

INGREDIENTS:

- 3 ½ tablespoons extra virgin olive oil, divided
- 4 sweet Italian sausages, casings removed
- 1 small onion, minced
- 2 garlic cloves, thinly sliced
- ½ teaspoon paprika
- Salt and freshly ground black pepper
- 2 sprigs fresh thyme
- 1 28-ounce can peeled whole plum tomatoes (preferably San Marzano)
- ¾ pound pasta
- Handful chopped freshly parsley for serving
- ½ cup freshly grated pecorino cheese for serving

1 Heat a medium heavy-bottomed pot or Dutch oven over medium-low heat for 2 to 3 minutes. Add 3 tablespoons of the olive oil and raise the heat to medium-high. Once it begins to swirl but is not yet smoking, add the sausage, onion, garlic, and paprika and, using a potato masher or wooden spoon, press down to crumble the sausage and mix it with vegetables. Add a couple pinches of salt and a good crack of pepper and cook, stirring occasionally, for 10 minutes. Add the thyme and tomatoes with their juices, crushing the tomatoes by hand before adding them to the pot. Bring to a boil, then lower the heat to low and simmer for 2 hours. The sauce is done when it has visibly thickened and the oil has separated and is bubbling on the surface.

2 While the sauce simmers, bring a large pot of water to a boil. Once it's boiling, add salt (1 tablespoon for every 4 cups water) and stir. Add the pasta and stir for first minute to prevent any sticking. Cook following the package (or recipe) instructions, though you will drain the pasta 2 minutes prior to the directed cooking time. The pasta should be soft but still very firm. Right before draining the pasta, reserve ¼ cup of the pasta water. Return the empty pot to the stove. Immediately turn the heat to high and add the remaining ½ tablespoon oil and reserved pasta water. Add the drained pasta and toss until the water is absorbed. Add the sauce and cook, mixing continuously, for 1 to 2 minutes.

3 Ladle the pasta into four warmed bowls and serve piping hot with a few good cracks of pepper and sprinkled with the parsley and pecorino (or pass the grated cheese at the table).

BROCCOLINI *and*
SAUSAGE MEATBALL SAUCE

YIELD: 4 SERVINGS / ACTIVE TIME: 15 MINUTES (40 MINUTES IF MAKING MEATBALLS) /
TOTAL TIME: 35 MINUTES (1 ¼ HOURS IF MAKING MEATBALLS)

Short, chewy pasta shapes are paired with broccolini, broccoli's sweeter and more tender cousin, and savory sausage meatballs in this satisfying dish. I usually triple the meatball sausage recipe and freeze the extra, which allows me to reap the rewards of my labor (and clean up) for two future meals. Once the pan-fried morsels are defrosted, they help weeknight dinners come together in a flash.

Recommended pasta shapes: farfalle, garganelli, penne, fusilli, orecchiette

1 Prepare the meatballs. Grind the bacon in a food processor until it resembles ground meat. Set aside. Crush the garlic and 1 teaspoon of the salt together into a paste in a mortar. Add the vinegar and mix well. Combine the pork, bacon, garlic paste, parsley, nutmeg, red pepper if using, and remaining 1 teaspoon salt until well mixed. Shape the mixture into cherry tomato-sized balls.

2 Heat a large, deep skillet over medium-low heat for 2 to 3 minutes. Add just enough olive oil to cover the bottom of the skillet, raise the heat to medium-high, and let the oil heat for a minute. Add the meatballs (you will need to work in at least two batches to make sure they have enough room to cook properly). Cook them until they are golden brown on all sides and no longer pink in the middle, 5 to 10 minutes. Transfer to a paper towel-lined plate to drain. Use or let them fully cool, cover, and refrigerate for up to 2 days or freeze for up to a month.

3 Bring a large pot of water to a boil. Once it's boiling, add salt (1 tablespoon for every 4 cups).

4 While the water is heating, remove the bottom third of each stalk of broccolini (it's too tough to eat). Cut the thicker stems lengthwise so that they match size-wise with the thinner ones. This will ensure they cook evenly. Wash them well, plunge them in the now boiling salted water, and cook for 2 minutes. Using a strainer or large slotted spoon, transfer to a colander placed over a large bowl and run under cold water to cool. Drain well. Keep the pot of water at a low simmer; you will use it to cook the pasta.

INGREDIENTS:
SAUSAGE MEATBALLS:

5 slices (6 ounces) hickory-smoked bacon

2 garlic cloves, peeled

2 teaspoons salt, divided

2 teaspoons cider vinegar

1 pound ground pork

½ cup chopped fresh parsley

1 teaspoon freshly grated nutmeg

½ teaspoon red pepper flakes (optional)

Olive oil for frying

BROCCOLINI AND PASTA:

Salt

1 pound broccolini (2 small bunches)

5 tablespoons + 1 teaspoon extra virgin olive oil

4 garlic cloves, thinly sliced

½ teaspoon red pepper flakes (optional)

¾ pound pasta

Freshly grated Parmigiano-Reggiano or pecorino Romano cheese for serving

5 Heat a large, deep skillet over medium-low heat for 2 to 3 minutes. Add 3 tablespoons of the olive oil, the garlic, and red pepper flakes if using and cook for 2 to 3 minutes, stirring occasionally. The garlic should be gently sizzling but not color at all. Add the well-drained broccolini and sausage meatballs and cook, stirring occasionally, until heated through.

6 Bring the broccolini water back to a full boil. Add the pasta and stir for the first minute to prevent any sticking. Cook according to the package (or recipe) instructions, draining the pasta 2 minutes short of the directed cook-ing time. The pasta will be soft but still very firm. Right before draining the pasta, reserve ¼ cup of the pasta water. Return the empty pot to the stove. Immediately turn the heat to high, teaspoon of the oil and reserved pasta water. Add the drained pasta and toss. Add the meatballs, broccolini, and remaining 2 tablespoons oil and cook, gently tossing so as to not break apart the the meatballs, for 2 minutes.

7 Divide the pasta among four warmed bowls. Serve piping hot topped with a good dusting of Parmigiano or pecorino (or pass the grated cheese at the table).

SIGNORA SOFIA'S SPICED PORK SAUCE

YIELD: 6 TO 8 SERVINGS / ACTIVE TIME: 20 MINUTES / TOTAL TIME: ABOUT 1 HOUR

This is the kind of aromatic meat sauce for which ridged pasta was created, allowing the sauce to adhere to each individual piece. But I can't take credit for this sauce. It was the creation of the now sadly departed Signora Sofia, my grandmother's best friend, who graciously shared it with us years ago.

Recommended pasta shapes or dumplings: pappardelle, tagliatelle, bavette, penne, sedani, rigatoni, potato gnocchi

1 Heat a large heavy-bottomed pot or cast-iron Dutch oven over medium-low heat for 2 to 3 minutes. Add 3 tablespoons of the butter and turn the heat up to medium-high. When it's melted, add the onion, celery, and a couple pinches of salt and mix well. When the mixture starts to sizzle, reduce the heat to low and give it a stir. Cover and cook, stirring occasionally, until the vegetables are very soft, about 30 minutes.

2 Add the ground pork to the pot and turn the heat up to medium-high. With a potato masher or wooden spoon, press down on the meat as it is cooking to break it up and mix it with the vegetables. Add a couple pinches of salt and mix well. When the meat has turned a grayish brown, add the milk. Continue cooking, stirring occasionally, until the milk has completely evaporated, about 10 minutes. Add the cloves and cook for a couple of minutes. Add the broth, tomato paste, and bay leaves and bring to a boil. Adjust the heat to low, cover and simmer for 45 minutes, stirring occasionally. You'll know the sauce is done when the fat has separated and is bubbling on the surface. Remove the bay leaf from the sauce and discard.

3 When the sauce is ready, melt 3 tablespoons of the butter in a small skillet over medium-low heat. Once it starts to bubble, add the sage leaves. Cook for a few minutes, until the leaves lightly crisp up and darken in color. Do not allow the butter to brown; you want to cook it just enough so that the sage leaves release their oil into the butter. Discard the sage, pour the butter into the meat sauce, and mix very well. Use or cool, transfer to an airtight container, and refrigerate for 3 days or freeze for up to 3 months.

4 As you are melting the butter, also put a large pot of water on to boil. Once it's boiling, add salt (1 tablespoon for every 4 cups water) and stir. Add the pasta and stir for the first minute to

INGREDIENTS:

6 ½ tablespoons butter, divided

1 medium yellow onion, grated

2 pale green inner celery stalks, stringed and grated

Salt

1 ½ pounds ground pork

1 cup milk

5 cloves or ½ teaspoon ground cloves

1 cup chicken broth

2 tablespoons tomato paste

2 bay leaves

6 fresh sage leaves

1 pound pasta

Freshly grated Parmigiano-Reggiano cheese for serving

prevent any sticking. Cook following the package (or recipe) instructions, though you will drain the pasta 2 minutes prior to the directed cooking time. The pasta should be soft but still very firm. Right before draining, the pasta, reserve ¼ cup of the pasta water. Return the empty pot to the stove. Immediately turn the heat to high and add the remaining ½ tablespoon butter and reserved pasta water. Add the drained pasta and toss until the water is absorbed. Add the sauce and cook, mixing continuously, for 1 to 2 minutes.

5 Divide among warmed bowls and serve piping hot topped with a sprinkling of Parmigiano (or pass the grated cheese at the table).

WILD BOAR RAGÙ

YIELD: 6 SERVINGS / ACTIVE TIME: 1 HOUR / TOTAL TIME: 4 HOURS, PLUS OVERNIGHT FOR MARINATING

It's widely accepted that wild pigs, which roam freely and graze on a variety of forageable food, taste better than pigs kept in pens. Their meat has the sort of darker and richer color that suggests a deeper and more satisfying porcine flavor. It's also leaner than its domesticated counterpart and, as such, is ideal for long-simmering dishes like this rich ragù. Granted, it's not exactly easy to purchase at your local supermarket, but I've been able to find a handful of small and reputable online companies that sell it. You can, of course, substitute it with regular pork—use the more flavorful heritage pork breeds if possible—though the sauce will have a subtler flavor. Regardless of the type of meat you use, be sure to always include the slightest hint of fish sauce in this sauce. While it may seem like a curious addition, it has become one of my flavoring weapons because of the touch of umami brings to whatever I add it to.

Recommended pasta shapes or dumplings: pappardelle, fettuccine, mafalde, bavette, rigatoni, potato gnocchi

INGREDIENTS:

- 2 pounds wild boar shoulder or leg, cut into 1 ½- to 2-inch cubes
- 10 black peppercorns
- 2 sprigs fresh rosemary, cut into several pieces
- 4 garlic cloves, crushed
  Full-bodied red wine, enough to cover boar
- 2 tablespoons extra virgin olive oil
- 3 inner pale green celery stalks, minced
- 3 inner celery stalks, minced
- 1 onion, grated
  Salt and freshly ground black pepper
- 1 14-ounce can crushed tomatoes
- 1 cinnamon stick
- 5 cloves
- 1 ½ teaspoons fish sauce
- 3 cups chicken or vegetable broth, divided
- ¾ pound pasta
  Freshly grated Parmigiano-Reggiano cheese for serving

1 The night before making the ragù, place the meat in a very snug-fitting shallow bowl or baking dish along with the peppercorns, rosemary, and garlic. Pour in enough wine to fully cover the meat. Mix well, cover, and refrigerate.

2 The next day, remove the meat from the bowl, shaking it slightly to remove any surface liquid, and place on a paper towel-lined plate to drain. Discard the aromatics from the bowl; reserve the wine.

3 Heat a large, heavy-bottomed pot or Dutch oven over low heat for 2 to 3 minutes. Add the olive oil, turn the heat up to medium, add the celery, onion, and a couple pinches of salt, and stir. When the mixture starts to sizzle, reduce the heat to low, cover, and cook until the vegetables are soft, about 20 minutes.

4 Gently press the cubes of meat with paper towels to absorb more surface moisture (less moisture on the surface allows the hot oil to do its job and brown what you are cooking—too much moisture and the meat will steam rather than brown). Season the meat with salt and pepper on all sides. Add the meat to the skillet and raise the heat to medium-high. Cook, stirring frequently, until all the liquid released by the meat has evaporated and the meat is browned on all sides, 10 to 12 minutes. Add the

reserved wine and continue to cook, stirring frequently, until most of the wine has evaporated, about 10 minutes. Add the tomatoes, cinnamon stick, cloves, fish sauce, 1 ½ cups of the broth, and a couple pinches of salt and bring to boil. Reduce the heat to very low and cook, partially covered, for 45 minutes.

5 Add the remaining 1½ cups broth and continue to simmer, stirring occasionally, for another 2½ hours. At this point, the meat should fall apart when touched by a fork. Remove from the heat and break the meat up into fine shreds with a fork into the sauce. Cover to keep warm.

6 Bring a large pot of water to a boil. Once it's boiling, add salt (1 tablespoon for every 4 cups water) and stir. Add the pasta and stir for the first minute to prevent any sticking. Cook following the package (or recipe) instructions, though you will drain the pasta 2 minutes prior to the directed cooking time. The pasta should be soft but still very firm. Right before draining the pasta, reserve ¼ cup of the pasta water. Return the empty pot to the stove. Immediately turn the heat to high and add the reserved pasta water. Add the drained pasta and toss until the water is absorbed. Add the sauce and cook, mixing continuously, for 1 to 2 minutes.

7 Ladle the pasta into six warmed bowls and serve piping hot with a few good cracks of black pepper and sprinkled with Parmigiano (or pass the grated cheese at the table).

HEARTY MEAT SAUCE *with* BRACCIOLE *and* SPARE RIBS

YIELD: 8 SERVINGS / ACTIVE TIME: 35 MINUTES / TOTAL TIME: ABOUT 5 HOURS

I believe this is the sauce Italian Americans lovingly refer to as "Sunday gravy." And no wonder, since this sauce takes half a day to make! But as with most things, the effort you're willing to expend gives back tenfold. I encourage you, if at all possible, to cook this rich and savory sauce one to two days before you plan on serving it, as the flavors will have a chance to amalgamate and the sauce will taste even better. Just cover the sauce, complete with *bracciole,* and refrigerate. On the day you serve, bring the sauce to room temperature and then gently reheat it in a covered pot before cooking the pasta. One final, semi-serious note: If you are interested in following the cultural norms of Italians, you will absolutely never combine this sauce with spaghetti. Italians don't have a good reason to explain this rather arbitrary rule, unless you consider "because it's just not done!" valid, but they will nevertheless judge you if they see you doing so. The same is true of Bolognese sauce.

Recommended pasta shapes: ziti, bucatelli, rigatoni, maltagliati.

INGREDIENTS:

- ½ cup freshly grated Parmigiano-Reggiano cheese, plus more for serving
- ⅓ cup chopped fresh parsley
- 4 garlic cloves, minced
- 1 ½ pounds beef top round
- Salt and freshly ground black pepper
- 2 ½ tablespoons extra virgin olive oil, divided
- 1 ½ pounds pork spare ribs
- 2 medium onions, minced
- 2 inner pale green celery stalks and fronds, minced
- 2 tablespoons tomato paste
- 2 28-ounce cans peeled whole plum tomatoes (preferably San Marzano)
- 2 bay leaves
- ¾ pound pasta

1 Make the *bracciole.* Mix the Parmigiano, parsley, and half of the garlic together in a small bowl. Set aside. Pat the beef dry with paper towels, wrap tightly in clear food wrap, and put in the freezer for 20 minutes (this will make it easier to slice). Remove from the freezer, remove the wrap, place on a cutting board, and cut into ½-inch-thick medallions Working with one slice at a time, place it on the cutting board and cover with a sheet of parchment paper. Using a flat meat pounder, pound on the slice until it is ¼ inch thick. Season each slice on both sides with salt and pepper and divvy the cheese mixture between the slices, spreading it over one side. Roll up each slice tightly and secure with toothpicks. Gently wrap each *bracciola* (singular) in paper towels to absorb as much surface moisture as possible (this will help them brown better later on).

2 Heat a large heavy-bottomed pot or cast-iron Dutch oven over medium-low heat for 2 to 3 minutes. Add 2 tablespoons of the olive oil and turn the heat up to medium-high. Once it's swirling on the surface but not yet smoking, add the *bracciole* to the pot in a single layer (you may have to do this in batches). Don't move them for 2 minutes to allow them the time to properly brown. Turn the *bracciole* and continue to cook in this manner until browned on

all sides, 6 to 8 minutes. Transfer to a plate when done.

3 As the *bracciole* brown, cut the pork into individual ribs. Season with salt and pepper. When the *bracciole* are done, add the ribs to the pot and brown on all sides in the same way, 4 to 6 minutes. Transfer to the plate holding the *bracciole*. Cover with aluminum foil to keep from drying.

4 Add the onions, celery, the remaining garlic, the tomato paste, a couple of pinches of salt, and a few good cracks of pepper to the pot. When the mixture starts to sizzle, mix well, and reduce the heat to low. Cover and cook, stirring occasionally, until the vegetables are very soft, about 30 minutes.

5 Turn the heat up to medium-high, add the tomatoes and their juice, crushing the tomatoes by hand as you add them to the pot, and stir. Add a couple pinches of salt, the bay leaves, and browned *bracciole* and spare ribs (making sure to add any juices left behind on the plate). Mix well. Bring to a boil, reduce the heat to low, and simmer, stirring occasionally, until the meat is very tender, about 4 hours. Taste for seasoning, adding salt and pepper if necessary.

6 Transfer the *bracciole* and spare ribs to two warmed plates. Remove the toothpicks from the *bracciole* and tent with foil to keep warm. Remove the bones from the spare ribs, shred the meat, and return it to the pot.

7 Bring a large pot of water to a boil. Once it's boiling, add salt (1 tablespoon for every 4 cups water) and stir. Add the pasta and stir for first minute to prevent any sticking. Cook following the package (or recipe) instructions, though you will drain the pasta 2 minutes prior to the directed cooking time. The pasta should be soft but still very firm. Right before draining the pasta, reserve ¼ cup of the pasta water. Return the empty pot to the stove. Immediately turn the heat to high, add the remaining ½ tablespoon oil and reserved pasta water. Add the drained pasta and toss until the water is absorbed. Add the sauce and cook, mixing continuously, for 1 to 2 minutes.

8 Divide the pasta between warmed bowls and serve piping hot with a few good cracks of pepper and topped with the one or two *bracciole* and a sprinkling of Parmigiano (or pass the grated cheese at the table).

ALEXIA'S MEAT
and TORTELLINI SKILLET DISH

YIELD: 4 TO 5 SERVINGS / ACTIVE TIME: 20 MINUTES / TOTAL TIME: 45 MINUTES

My daughter offered to start cooking Sunday dinners when she was thirteen. What a treat! I love watching her negotiating skillets, measuring cups, and onion chopping-induced tears. It makes this mamma bear proud. I stay close so she can ask me questions, but pretty much try to stay out of her way (also because it hurts my feelings when my daughter indignantly chases me out of my own kitchen). This is one of the dishes she regaled us with on one particular occasion, accompanied by a Caesar salad and a lot of pomp and circumstance. It was so tasty that I suggested she make it the following Sunday night, when a girlfriend and her son were expected for a casual dinner. That evening, when the boy tasted it, he chewed it thoughtfully for a minute before blurting out, "It tastes like Hamburger Helper . . .but a gazillion times better!" I have to say I agree.

INGREDIENTS:

- 1 **10-ounce bag frozen petite peas**
- 2 **tablespoons extra virgin olive oil**
- 1 **large yellow onion, minced or grated**
- **Salt**
- ½ **pound ground beef**
- ½ **pound ground pork**
- 2 **tablespoons tomato paste**
- 1 ½ **teaspoons Worcestershire sauce**
- 1 ¼ **cups beef or chicken broth**
- 1 **20-ounce package cheese tortellini**
- 1 **cup freshly grated Parmigiano-Reggiano, plus more for serving**
- **Freshly ground black pepper**

1 Place the peas in a medium sieve and run warm water over them for 1 minute. Drain and keep in the sieve until ready to use.

2 Heat a large heavy-bottomed pot or Dutch oven over medium-low heat for 2 to 3 minutes. Add the oil and turn the heat up to medium-high. Heat for a couple of minutes until it begins to swirl on the surface, then add the onion and a couple pinches of salt and mix well. When it begins to sizzle, adjust the heat to low and give it a stir. Cover and cook, stirring occasionally, until the onions are very soft, about 30 minutes.

3 Turn the heat up to medium-high and add the ground meats and 1 teaspoon of salt. With a potato masher or wooden spoon, press down on the meat as it cooks to break up any large chunks. Continue to cook until the meat has turned a grayish brown, indicating that it is completely cooked, 8 to 10 minutes. Add the tomato paste and Worcestershire, stir, and cook for 1 minute. Add the broth, peas, and ½ teaspoon salt, stir, and bring to a boil. Add the tortellini, stir, and reduce the heat to medium. Cover and cook, stirring occasionally, until the tortellini are tender but chewy, 3 to 4 minutes. Remove from the heat, add the Parmigiano, and stir well.

4 Divide the tortellini among four warmed bowls. Serve piping hot topped with a few cracks of black pepper and a good dusting of Parmigiano (or pass the grated cheese at the table).

BOLOGNESE SAUCE

YIELD: ENOUGH SAUCE FOR 10 SERVINGS / ACTIVE TIME: 20 MINUTES / TOTAL TIME: 4 ½ HOURS

Recipes for this rich and savory meat sauce from the beautiful city of Bologna often include carrots. I used to as well, until I learned from one of my best friends' mom, an excellent cook from Emilia-Romagna, that it is better to omit them because they add too much sweetness to the sauce. After a comparison test, I agreed with her and have left them out ever since. For extra depth of flavor—and I am definitely bucking tradition here—I often add 1 ½ teaspoons Asian fish sauce along with the pureed tomatoes.

Because this sauce takes several hours to prepare, it makes sense to make a large batch and freeze it. It will keep refrigerated for 3 days and frozen for up to 3 months. One final, semi-serious note: If you are interested in following the cultural norms of Italians, you will absolutely never combine this sauce with spaghetti. Italians don't have a good reason to explain this rather arbitrary rule, unless you consider "because it's just not done!" valid, but they will nevertheless judge you if they see you doing so.

Recommended pasta shapes: tagliatelle, pappardelle, maltagliati, fettuccine

INGREDIENTS:

- 3 tablespoons extra virgin olive oil
- 1 medium yellow onion, grated
- 2 inner pale green celery celery stalks and fronds, grated

  Salt
- 2 pounds ground meat (a blend of pork, veal, and beef gives wonderful flavor)
- 2 cups whole milk
- 2 28-ounce cans peeled whole tomatoes (preferably San Marzano tomatoes), pureed in a food mill, food processor, or blender
- 2 bay leaves
- 7 cloves or 1 teaspoon ground cloves

1 Heat a large heavy-bottomed pot or cast-iron Dutch oven over medium-low heat for 2 to 3 minutes. Add the oliveoil and turn the heat up to medium-high. Heat the oil for a couple of minutes, then add the onion, celery, and a couple pinches of salt and mix well. When the vegetables begin to sizzle, lower the heat to low and give it another stir. Cover and cook for 30 minutes, stirring occasionally. (It may seem like a long cooking time, but don't be tempted to turn up the flame to make this process go faster. This step slowly brings out the natural sweetness of the onion and celery, and rushing it can make them taste bitter instead.)

2 Turn the heat up under the pot to medium-high and add the ground meat. With a potato masher or wooden spoon, press down on it to break up large chunks. When the meat has turned a grayish brown and there is no pink remaining, add the milk. Continue cooking, stirring occasionally, until the milk has completely evaporated. (The milk acts as a meat tenderizer here.)

3 Add the tomatoes to the pot, along with the bay leaves, cloves, and a few pinches of salt, stir, and bring to a boil. Adjust the heat to low and cook, uncovered, for 4 hours, stirring every 30 minutes or so. You should see a gentle bubbling in the pot. You can choose to cook it even longer if you have the time, because the longer it cooks, the better it tastes. You'll know the sauce is done when it has visibly thickened and the fat has separated and is bubbling on the surface. Discard the bay leaves. Use or cool, transfer to an airtight container, and refrigerate or freeze.

SAUERKRAUT *and* MASCARPONE SAUCE
with CRISPY CORNED BEEF STRIPS

YIELD: 4 SERVINGS / **ACTIVE TIME:** 45 MINUTES / **TOTAL TIME:** 1 HOUR 10 MINUTES

This recipe is my attempt at creating a pasta experience similar to downing a delicious corned beef on rye sandwich, as I do so miss New York City's excellent Jewish delis. You may think the combination odd for a pasta dish, but I love how the savory crisped corned beef strips contrast with the creaminess of the mascarpone and the chewiness of the pasta. I hope you do too.

Recommended pasta shapes: rye mafalde, pizzoccheri, cencioni, garganelli

1 Whisk the mascarpone, mustard, ground caraway, and salt and white pepper to taste together in a small bowl. Set aside.

2 Heat a large skillet over medium-low heat for a couple minutes. Turn the heat to medium and add the caraway seeds. Cook, stirring frequently, until they are fragrant, 3 to 4 minutes. Transfer to a small bowl.

3 Cut the corned beef into thin strips. Heat the same skillet over medium heat for a minute. Turn the heat to medium-high and add 1 tablespoon of the olive oil. Let it heat for a minute, then add the coriander. When it starts to sizzle, add the corned beef and cook, stirring a few times, until the slivers turn golden brown, 3 to 5 minutes. Remove with a slotted spoon to a small bowl.

4 Return the skillet to the stove. Add 2 tablespoons of the oil and the butter. When the butter has melted, add the onion and a couple pinches of salt and stir. When the onion starts to sizzle, adjust the heat to low and give it a stir. Cover and cook, stirring occasionally, until the onion is very soft, about 30 minutes, stirring occasionally.

5 Add the sauerkraut and white pepper to taste to the skillet, stir, and raise the heat again to medium-high. When the mixture begins to sizzle, adjust the heat to low and cover. Cook, stirring occasionally, until the sauerkraut softens, 12 to 15 minutes. Taste for seasoning and add salt and white pepper if needed. Remove from the heat and keep warm.

6 While the sauce cooks, bring a large pot of water to a boil. Once it's boiling, add salt (1 tablespoon for every 4 cups water) and stir. Add the pasta and stir for the first minute to prevent

INGREDIENTS:

½ cup mascarpone cheese

1 ½ tablespoons whole-grain mustard

1 teaspoon ground caraway seeds

Salt and freshly ground white pepper

2 teaspoons caraway seeds

4 ⅛-inch-thick slices corned beef

3 ½ tablespoons extra virgin olive oil, divided

⅛ teaspoon ground coriander

2 tablespoons unsalted butter

1 medium yellow onion, thinly sliced into half-moons

2 cups good-quality sauerkraut, well drained

¾ pound pasta

any sticking. Cook following the package (or recipe) instructions, though you will drain the pasta 2 minutes prior to the directed cooking time. The pasta should be soft but still very firm. Right before draining the pasta, reserve ¼ cup of the pasta water. Return the empty pot to the stove. Immediately turn the heat to high, add the remaining ½ tablespoon oil and reserved pasta water. Add the drained pasta and toss until the water is absorbed. Add the sauce and cook, mixing continuously, for 1 to 2 minutes.

7 Ladle the pasta into four warmed bowls and serve piping hot topped with a dollop of the flavored mascarpone, some crispy corned beef slivers, and a few toasted caraway seeds.

TOMATO-VEAL *and* ROASTED BUTTERNUT SQUASH SAUCE

YIELD: 6 SERVINGS / ACTIVE TIME: 1 HOUR / TOTAL TIME: 2 ¾ HOURS

I normally don't cook veal, finding calves far too cute and their fate far too tragic. But once or twice a year, I make this veal and roasted butternut squash pasta dish my only exception. Yes, it's THAT good. I typically pair it with the very narrow, rolled and twisted tubes of pasta called *casarecce*. Sicilian in origin, they have crevices that perfectly capture this dish's rich, unctuous sauce. But what I like best about this dish are the caramelized cubes of butternut squash used to garnish it; their subtle sweetness perfectly complements the savoriness of the sauce.

Recommended pasta shapes: casarecce, penne, fusilli, gemelli

1 Heat a large, deep skillet over medium heat for 2 to 3 minutes. Add 4 tablespoons of the olive oil and heat for 2 to 3 minutes. Once it begins to swirl but is not yet smoking, add the onion, celery, and a couple pinches of salt and cook until the onion is translucent, stirring occasionally, about 20 minutes. Add the garlic and cook for another 2 minutes, stirring frequently.

2 As the vegetables cook, pat the veal cubes with paper towels to absorb surface moisture, then sprinkle with salt. Turn the heat up to medium-high and add them to the pan in a single layer, pushing the vegetables out of the way so they make full contact with the bottom. Cook, stirring occasionally, until lightly browned all over. Add the tomatoes, sage, and a couple pinches of salt and stir. Add the broth and bring to a boil. Cover, reduce the heat to low, and simmer, stirring occasionally, until the sauce is thick and shiny and the oil has separated from the sauce and is on the surface, about 1 hour.

3 While the sauce simmers, roast the squash. Preheat the oven to 400°F. Slice off the top and bottom off the squash. Rest it on its widest end and, using a heavy kitchen knife, slice down vertically. If it's difficult to do (it is for me), use a rubber mallet to tap gently on the pointy side of the blade. Work as slowly as you need to and wedge the knife all the way to the base of the squash. When you have the two separated squash halves, use a spoon to scrape out the seeds and fibrous insides. Peel the squash, cut into ½-inch-thick slices, then cut the slices into ½-inch dice. Put the dice on a parchment paper-lined baking sheet and toss with the remaining 2 tablespoons oil (I use my hands to do this). Place on the

INGREDIENTS:

6 ½ tablespoons extra virgin olive oil, divided

1 medium Vidalia onion, diced

2 inner pale green celery stalks, minced

Salt

2 garlic cloves, thinly sliced

1 ½ pounds lean boneless veal, cut into 1 ½-inch cubes

6 very ripe plum tomatoes, diced (about 1 cup)

1 sprig fresh sage

3 ½ cups warm veal or chicken broth

1 2-pound butternut squash

¾ pound pasta

Freshly grated Parmigiano-Reggiano for serving

center rack of the oven and roast until the squash is tender and browned, about 30 minutes. Sprinkle lightly with salt and tent loosely with aluminum foil.

4 When the sauce and squash are almost ready, bring a large pot of water to a boil. Once it's boiling, add salt (1 tablespoon for every 4 cups water) and stir. Add the pasta and stir for the first minute to prevent any sticking. Cook according to the package instructions, draining the pasta 2 minutes short of the directed cooking time. The pasta will be soft but still very firm. Right before draining the pasta, reserve ¼ cup of the pasta water. Return the pot to the stove. Immediately turn the heat to high, add the remaining ½ tablespoon oil and reserved pasta water. Add the drained pasta and toss. Add several ladles of the veal sauce and cook, tossing continuously, for 2 minutes.

5 Divide the pasta among six warmed bowls and top with a little more sauce. Divide the butternut squash cubes between the bowls. Serve piping hot topped with a good dusting of Parmigiano (or pass the grated cheese at the table).

ROMAN-STYLE TRIPE SAUCE

YIELD: 5 TO 6 SERVINGS / ACTIVE TIME: 1½ HOURS / TOTAL TIME: 5½ HOURS

There's no doubt about it, tripe (the muscle wall of a cow's stomach) is an acquired taste. It's a pity, because when properly prepared, tripe is wonderful. In Rome, it's served as a one-pot meal with crusty bread, but it's also delicious as a sauce for short tubular pastas like ziti or rigatoni. This recipe uses honeycomb tripe, the meatiest and most tender part of the stomach, which means it doesn't require as much cooking. Be prepared, however, because it will shrink considerably as it cooks. Find a source for tripe that steams it clean rather than treating it with food-grade bleach; it's much more flavorful.

Recommended pasta shapes: ziti, garganelli, rigatoni, pennoni (large penne)

1 Rinse the tripe under cold running water. Soak it in a large bowl of fresh water for 1 hour, then rinse it again until it is free of grit. Fill a large pot with water, add the tripe, and bring it to a boil. Drain and rinse the tripe again. Refill the pot with fresh water, add the tripe, and bring it to a boil again. Adjust the heat to low and simmer until the tripe is tender (a sharp knife should pierce it with no resistance), about 3 hours, checking on the tripe regularly and adding more water if it's no longer covering the tripe. Drain and let cool. Trim any remaining fat from the tripe and cut it into short strips.

2 Bring the wine to a boil in a small saucepan and let boil until reduced by half, about 5 minutes. Remove from the heat.

3 Heat a large skillet over medium-low heat for 2 to 3 minutes. Add 3 tablespoons of the olive oil and raise the heat to medium. When it begins to swirl but is not yet smoking, add the pancetta and red pepper flakes and stir. Cook the pancetta, stirring every few minutes, until it renders its fat and is lightly browned. Add the onion, celery, a couple pinches of salt, and a good crack of black pepper and stir. Once the mixture begins to sizzle, adjust the heat to low, cover, and cook, stirring occasionally, until the vegetables are very soft, about 20 minutes, (If necessary, add a tablespoon of water every now and again to ensure that the mixture cooks thoroughly but doesn't brown.)

4 Add the tripe to the skillet, turn the heat to medium-high, and cook, stirring, for 5 minutes. Add the reduced wine

INGREDIENTS:

2   **pounds honeycomb tripe**

1   **cup dry white wine**

3 ½ **tablespoons extra virgin olive oil, divided**

4   **ounces pancetta, diced**

1   **teaspoon red pepper flakes**

1   **medium yellow onion, diced**

3   **inner pale green celery stringed and minced**

    Salt and freshly ground black pepper

2   **24-ounce cans strained tomatoes**

    Salt and freshly ground black pepper

¾   **pound pasta**

    Handful chopped fresh mint or parsley for serving

    Freshly grated pecorino cheese for serving

and the tomatoes, stir, and bring to a boil, then cover and reduce the heat to low. Simmer it until the sauce is well reduced, 40 to 45 minutes.

5 While the sauce simmers, bring a large pot of water to a boil. Once it's boiling, add salt (1 tablespoon for every 4 cups water) and stir. Add the pasta and stir for the first minute to prevent any sticking. Cook following the package (or recipe) instructions, though you will drain the pasta 2 minutes prior to the directed cooking time. The pasta should be soft but still very firm. Right before drain-ing the pasta, reserve ¼ cup of the pasta water. Return the empty pot to the stove. Immediately turn the heat to high, add the remaining ½ tablespoon oil and reserved pasta water. Add the drained pasta and toss until the water is absorbed. Add the tripe sauce and cook, mixing continuously, for 1 to 2 minutes.

6 Ladle the pasta into warmed bowls and serve piping hot topped with a few good cracks of black pepper and sprinkled with the mint and pecorino (or pass the grated cheese at the table).

PANCETTA

Pancetta is cut from pork belly and cured, like bacon. However, unlike its American counter-part, pancetta is not smoked, and has a subtler flavor. Find pancetta at your grocery store's deli or gourmet food isle. If it is unavailable you can substitute it for bacon. To maintain the desired taste, simply boil the bacon for 2-3 minutes to eliminate the smoky flavor.

MEAT RAGÙ *with* BÉCHAMEL SAUCE

YIELD: 5 TO 6 SERVINGS / ACTIVE TIME: 15 MINUTES / TOTAL TIME: 30 MINUTES (INCLUDES MAKING THE BÉCHAMEL)

The only way you can beat the heavenly comfort of a rich and savory meat ragù is if you add the creamy embrace of béchamel sauce. The speediness of this dish requires having batches of frozen Bolognese sauce on hand. But if you don't have it and still want a comforting dish, swap out the Bolognese sauce for tomato sauce.

Recommended pasta shapes or dumplings: garganelli, gnocchi, spätzle, penne, campanelle, gemelli, trenette, tagliatelle

1 Combine the Bolognese, béchamel, broth, and 1 tablespoon of the butter in a medium saucepan and bring to a gentle simmer over medium heat, stirring several times.

2 While the sauce heats up, bring a large pot of water to a boil. Once it's boiling, add salt (1 tablespoon for every 4 cups water) and stir. Add the pasta and stir for the first minute to prevent any sticking. Cook following the package (or recipe) instructions, though you will drain the pasta 2 minutes prior to the directed cooking time. The pasta should be soft but still very firm. Right before draining the pasta, reserve ¼ cup of the pasta water. Return the empty pot to the stove. Immediately turn the heat to high and add the remaining tablespoon butter and reserved pasta water. Add the drained pasta and toss until the water is absorbed. Add the sauce and cook, mixing continuously, for 1 to 2 minutes.

3 Divide the pasta between warmed bowls and serve piping hot topped with a few good cracks of black pepper and a sprinkling of parsley and Parmigiano (or pass the grated cheese at the table).

INGREDIENTS:

3 cups Bolognese Sauce (page 629)

1 ½ cups Aromatic Béchamel Sauce (page 742)

¼ cup beef broth

2 tablespoons unsalted butter, divided

Salt

¾ pound pasta

Freshly ground black pepper

Handful chopped fresh parsley for serving

Freshly grated Parmigiano-Reggiano for serving

SWEETBREAD, CORN, *and* JALAPEÑO SAUCE

YIELD: 4 SERVINGS / ACTIVE TIME: 30 MINUTES / TOTAL TIME: 1 ½ HOURS

The story behind this savory sauce is a timeless one. Looking for absolution from a misguided moment of over-the-top Mediterranean temper, I made this dish for my husband, who absolutely adores sweetbreads. I was forgiven. The end.

Recommended pasta shapes or dumplings: culurgiones, tagliatelle, busiata

INGREDIENTS:

- ½ **pound sweetbreads (preferably thymus)**
- 1 **tablespoon distilled white vinegar**
- **Salt and freshly ground black pepper**
- ½ **cup (1 stick) unsalted butter**
- **Kernels cut from 4 ears corn**
- 2 **jalapeño peppers, seeded and minced**
- ¾ **pound pasta**
- 4 **ounces Cotija cheese (or substitute goat or feta cheese), crumbled**
- **Thinly sliced fresh chives**

1 Rinse the sweetbreads under cold water and soak them in a bowl of ice water for 3 hours. Transfer them to a medium saucepan, cover with water, and add the vinegar. Bring to a boil over medium-high heat and let boil for 1 minute (if you are using the larger-sized heart sweetbreads, cook for 3 minutes). Drain and rinse under cold water to stop the cooking process. Using a sharp paring knife, peel away the membrane, tubes, gristle, and anything else that doesn't look like white sweetbread tissue, then mince. Transfer to a plate and season them well with salt and pepper.

2 Heat a large skillet over medium-low heat for 2 to 3 minutes, add the butter, and raise the heat to medium. Once it has melted and stops foaming, add the sweetbreads, corn, jalapeños, and a couple of pinches of salt and stir. Cook until the mixture turns caramel brown, stirring occasionally, about 10 minutes. Remove from the heat and cover to keep warm.

3 While the sauce cooks, bring a large pot of water to a boil. Once it's boiling, add salt (1 tablespoon for every 4 cups water) and stir. Add the pasta, stirring for the first minute to prevent any sticking. Cook according to the package (or recipe) instructions, draining the pasta 2 minutes short of the directed cooking time. The pasta should be soft but still very firm.

4 Divide the pasta among four warmed bowls, spoon over the sauce, sprinkle with the cheese and chives, and serve piping hot.

SWEETBREAD, TOMATO, *and* CAPER SAUCE

YIELD: 4 SERVINGS / ACTIVE TIME: ABOUT 1 HOUR / TOTAL TIME: 1 ½ HOURS,
PLUS 6 TO 24 HOURS TO SOAK THE SWEETBREADS

Tender, almost creamy, sweetbreads are often called the "supreme offal" and come from the pancreas (heart sweetbread) and thymus glands (throat sweetbread) of a calf, lamb, or pig. Thymus sweetbreads are preferred in this dish because they are slightly milder tasting. The acidity of the tomatoes and capers contrasts nicely with the richness of the sweetbreads.

Recommended pasta shapes: cappellacci dei briganti, maltagliati, penne, campanelle, gemelli, mezze maniche

1 Rinse the sweetbreads under cold water and soak them in a bowl of ice water for 3 hours. Transfer them to a medium saucepan, cover with water, and the vinegar. Bring to a boil over medium-high heat and let boil for 1 minute (if you are using the larger-sized heart sweetbreads, cook for 3 minutes). Drain and rinse under cold water to stop the cooking process. Using a sharp paring knife, peel away the membrane, tubes, gristle, and anything else that doesn't look like white sweetbread tissue, and then mince. Transfer to a plate and season them well with salt and pepper.

2 Bring a medium pot of water to a boil. Blanch the tomatoes in the boiling water for 1 minute. Use tongs to remove them to a cutting board and let cool until you can handle, then remove their skins. Cut them into quarters, remove the seeds, and roughly chop. Set aside.

3 Heat a large, deep skillet over medium-low heat for 2 to 3 minutes. Add 2 tablespoons of the olive oil and turn the heat up to medium-high. Add the onion, garlic, a pinch of salt, and a good crack of pepper, and stir. When the onion starts to sizzle, reduce the heat to low and give it a stir. Cover and cook, stirring occasionally, until the onion is very soft, about 20 minutes.

4 Add the capers and lemon zest, increase the heat to medium, and cook for 3 minutes, stirring a few times. Add the tomatoes, tomato paste, and a couple pinches of salt and stir. Cook until the tomatoes soften, about 7 minutes.

5 Season the sweetbreads with salt and pepper and add them to the skillet, along with the milk and a pinch of salt. Stir and bring the mixture to a gentle boil. Adjust the heat to low and

INGREDIENTS:

½ pound sweetbreads (preferably thymus)

1 tablespoon distilled white vinegar

Salt and freshly ground black pepper

6 very ripe plum tomatoes

2 ½ tablespoons extra virgin olive oil, divided

1 small yellow onion, diced

2 garlic cloves, lightly smashed

2 teaspoons nonpareil capers, rinsed

Grated zest of ½ lemon

1 tablespoon tomato paste

¾ cup whole milk

¾ pound pasta

¼ cup freshly grated Parmigiano-Reggiano cheese for serving

¼ cup freshly grated pecorino cheese for serving

cook until the sauce thickens, about 30 minutes, stirring occasionally. Taste for seasoning, adding salt and pepper if needed.

6 While the sauce cooks, bring a large pot of water to a boil. Once it's boiling, add salt (1 tablespoon for every 4 cups water) and stir. Add the pasta and stir for the first minute to prevent any sticking. Cook following the package (or recipe) instructions, though you will drain the pasta 2 minutes prior to the directed cooking time. The pasta should be soft but still very firm. Right before draining the pasta, reserve ¼ cup of the pasta water. Return the empty pot to the stove. Immediately turn the heat to high and add the remaining ½ tablespoon oil and reserved pasta water. Add the drained pasta and toss until the water is absorbed. Add the sauce and cook, mixing continuously, for 1 to 2 minutes.

7 Divide the pasta between four warmed bowls and serve piping hot sprinkled with the cheeses (or pass the grated cheeses at the table).

LAMB RAGÙ

YIELD: 6 TO 8 SERVINGS / ACTIVE TIME: 35 MINUTES / TOTAL TIME: ABOUT 4 HOURS

A perfect choice for dinner on a cold winter's night. This is quite easy to make, as it uses ground lamb; it just requires time to simmer. The resulting sauce is deliciously aromatic and goes particularly well with egg-based pasta, though it works just as well with dried pasta. Lamb does tend to be fatty, however, and that can transfer into the sauce. If you're interested in removing some of it, plan on making the sauce a day ahead and refrigerating it (it freezes beautifully for up to 3 months as well). The fat will congeal on the top and is very easy to remove with a spoon, though I have to confess that I save that fat and use it to top baked potatoes. One note about ground lamb: Only buy it if you can access high-quality lamb, preferably locally raised. There is absolutely no comparison in flavor between that and the pink stuff you buy in plastic packaging in the supermarket.

Recommended pasta shapes or dumplings: pappardelle, fregnacce, tagliatelle, bavette, penne, sedani, tortiglioni, rigatoni, potato gnocchi

INGREDIENTS:

- 2 ½ tablespoons extra virgin olive oil, divided
- 2 small onions, minced
- 2 inner pale green celery stalks, minced
- Salt
- 2 pounds ground lamb
- 1 cup dry red wine
- Leaves from 3 to 4 small sprigs fresh thyme, minced
- 2 small sprigs fresh marjoram, minced
- 1 small dried chile pepper
- 2 28-ounce cans peeled whole plum tomatoes (preferably San Marzano)
- 1 pound pasta
- Minced fresh chile pepper or red pepper flakes for serving
- Shaved Parmigiano-Reggiano or pecorino Romano cheese for serving

1 Heat a large heavy-bottomed pot or cast-iron Dutch oven over medium-low heat for 2 to 3 minutes. Add 2 tablespoons of the olive oil and turn the heat up to medium-high. After it's heated for a minute, add the onions, celery, and a couple pinches of salt and mix well. When the mixture starts to sizzle, adjust the heat to low and give it a stir. Cover and cook, stirring occasionally, until the vegetables are very soft and turn slightly darker in color, about 30 minutes.

2 Add the meat to the pot and cook, breaking it apart with a wooden spoon, until it is no longer pink. Raise the heat to medium-high, add the wine, and cook, stirring occasionally, for 5 minutes. Add the thyme, marjoram, and chile, stir, and cook for 2 minutes. Add the tomatoes, crushing them by hand as you place them in the pot, and their juices, along with a few generous pinches of salt and stir again. Bring to a boil, then reduce the heat to medium-low. Cover and gently simmer, stirring occasionally, for 2 hours. You'll know the sauce is done when it has visibly thickened and the fat has separated and is bubbling on the surface.

3 Bring a large pot of water to a boil. Once it's boiling, add salt (1 tablespoon for every 4 cups water) and stir. Add the pasta and stir for the first minute to prevent any sticking. Cook following

the package (or recipe) instructions, though you will drain the pasta 2 minutes prior to the directed cooking time. The pasta should be soft but still very firm. Right before draining the pasta, reserve ¼ cup of the pasta water. Return the pot to the stove. Immediately turn the heat to high and add the remaining ½ tablespoon oil and reserved pasta water. Add the drained pasta and toss until the water is absorbed. Add the sauce and cook, mixing continuously, for 1 to 2 minutes.

4 Ladle the pasta into warmed bowls and serve piping hot topped with a sprinkling of minced chile or red pepper flakes and shavings of cheese.

MUTTON RAGÙ

YIELD: 4 SERVINGS / ACTIVE TIME: 45 MINUTES / TOTAL TIME: 2 ¼ HOURS

Mutton doesn't seem to make the culinary scene very often. In fact, its place in Western diets has dropped precipitously since World War II, when soldiers were fed mutton stew ad nauseam. A pity for those who love the flavor of lamb meat since mutton, essentially a lamb older than two years, possesses a similar but stronger flavor. While difficult to locally source for most folks, I encourage lamb lovers to try this meat by special ordering it through a local butcher or buying direct online from reputable farms.

This sauce benefits flavor-wise from the inclusion of *lardo*, or cured pork fatback. Considered a cold cut like prosciutto or mortadella, *lardo* is often served in Italy as an appetizer on a tray with other cured meats. Two of Italy's most well known *lardi* are *lardo di Colonnata*, from the central Italian region of Tuscany, and *lardo di Arnad*, from the northern region of Valle D'Aosta. Both are delicious and literally melt in your mouth. While you can use pancetta or bacon in lieu of *lardo* in this recipe, your sauce will not benefit from its more delicate flavor and fat content, which lends compelling unctuousness.

Recommended pasta shapes or dumplings: sorcetti, potato gnocchi, pappardelle, tagliatelle, bavette, penne, rigatoni

INGREDIENTS:

- 1 cup dry white wine
- 10 very ripe plum tomatoes
- 4 ounces lardo (or substitute pancetta or bacon, though the flavor won't be the same), diced
- 1 medium yellow onion, finely diced
- Salt
- ¾ pound boneless mutton shoulder or leg, cut into small pieces
- Leaves from 1 sprig fresh rosemary, chopped (reserve the stem)
- ¾ pound pasta
- ½ tablespoon extra virgin olive oil
- Freshly ground black pepper
- Freshly grated pecorino cheese for serving

1 Bring the wine to a boil in a small saucepan and let boil until reduced by half, about 5 minutes. Remove from the heat.

2 Bring a large pot of water to a boil. Blanch the tomatoes in the boiling water for 1 minute. Use tongs to remove them to a cutting board and let cool until you can handle, then remove their skins. Cut them into quarters and remove the seeds, then mince. Transfer the tomatoes and any juices to a bowl. Set aside.

3 Heat a medium heavy-bottomed skillet or cast-iron Dutch oven over low heat for 2 to 3 minutes. Add the *lardo* and turn the heat up to medium. Heat until it begins rendering its fat, then add the onion and a couple pinches of salt and stir. Once the mixture starts to sizzle, stir, adjust the heat to low, cover, and cook, stirring occasionally, until very soft, about 25 minutes.

4 Add the meat and a couple pinches of salt to the pot and turn the heat to medium-high. Cook, stirring frequently, until the meat develops a nice golden color on all sides. Add the reduced wine and reserved rosemary stem, cover, and cook for 10 minutes. Add the tomatoes and their juice and a couple pinches

of salt and stir. Bring to a gentle boil, then adjust the heat to low, cover, and cook about 1½ hours, stirring occasionally. You'll know the sauce is done when it has visibly thickened and the fat has separated and is bubbling on the surface. Remove the rosemary stems and add the chopped rosemary, stir, and cover the sauce until ready to use.

5 Bring a large pot of water to a boil. Once it's boiling, add salt (1 tablespoon for every 4 cups water) and stir. Add the pasta and stir for the first minute to prevent any sticking. Cook following the package (or recipe) instructions, though you will drain the pasta 2 min-utes prior to the directed cooking time. The pasta should be soft but still very firm. Right before draining the pasta, reserve ¼ cup of the pasta water. Return the pot to the stove. Imme-diately turn the heat to high and add the olive oil and reserved pasta water. Add the drained pasta and toss until the water is absorbed. Add the sauce and cook, mixing continuously, for 1 to 2 minutes.

6 Divide the pasta between warmed bowls and serve piping hot topped with sev-eral good cracks of pepper and a sprinkling of pecorino (or pass the grated cheese at the table).

BAKED LAMB *and* TOMATO SAUCE

YIELD: 6 SERVINGS / ACTIVE TIME: 45 MINUTES / TOTAL TIME: 1 ½ HOURS

Lamb lovers are sure to adore this tasty dish brimming with the flavor of roasted tomatoes and aromatic oregano. It makes for a stunning presentation as well, and is therefore ideal for dinner parties and special occasions. If you can find it, I recommend using grated kefalotiri cheese. Also known as kefalotyri, it is a hard, salty, and yellowish Greek cheese made from sheep or goat's milk that dates back to the Byzantine era and tastes like a saltier, tangier version of Gruyère. If possible, purchase kefalotiri that has been aged for at least a year, as it has a stronger, sharper flavor. Add any leftover cheese to cheeseboards or grate it over sauces, pizzas, stews and salads.

1   Preheat the oven to 350 °F.

2   Bring a large pot of water to a boil. Blanch the tomatoes in the boiling water for 1 minute. Use tongs to remove them to a cutting board and let cool until you can handle, then remove their skins. Cut them into quarters and remove the seeds, then roughly chop. Transfer the tomatoes and any juices to a bowl. Set aside.

3   Rinse the lamb chops under cold water (helpful in removing any potential bone splinters from the chopping) and thoroughly pat dry with paper towels.

4   Heat a shallow, heavy-bottomed skillet over medium heat for 2 to 3 minutes, then add 4 tablespoons of the olive oil. Raise the heat to medium-high and wait until the oil begins to swirl on the surface but is not yet smoking (you will need to cook them in two batches to ensure that each chop browns properly.) Add a pinch of salt and pepper to each lamb chop immediately before placing it in the skillet. Let the chops brown for 2 minutes without moving them. Flip and brown other side for another 2 minutes, again without moving them. If necessary, use tongs to stand the chops on their side so the sides can brown as well. Once fully browned, transfer the chops to a baking dish.

5   Add the tomatoes and a couple pinches of salt to the skillet and mix well with the condiment left over in the pan. Be sure to scrape the crispy bits stuck to the bottom of the pan, as they are full of flavor. Add the garlic and oregano stems and cook for another minute. Carefully pour the tomato mixture over the

INGREDIENTS:

- 2 pounds ripe plum tomatoes
- 3 pounds lamb shoulder round bone chops
- 5 tablespoons extra virgin olive oil, divided
- Salt and freshly ground black pepper
- 5 garlic cloves, thinly sliced
- Leaves from 3 sprigs fresh oregano, roughly chopped (reserve the stems)
- 2 chicken, vegetable, or beef bouillon cubes (optional)
- 2 tablespoons tomato paste (optional)
- ½ pound orzo
- Freshly grated Parmigiano-Reggiano or kefalotiri for serving

lamb chops. With tongs, rearrange the chops so that some of the tomato mixture in on the bottom of the baking dish and some on top of the chops.

6 Loosely cover with aluminum foil, place in the oven, and bake for 15 minutes. Take the lamb out of the oven and remove the foil. Flip each chop and return, uncovered, to the oven. Bake for 15 more minutes, occasionally basting the meat and turning it over once in the baking process.

7 As the lamb bakes, bring a medium saucepan of water to a boil. Add either salt or the optional bouillon cubes and tomato paste, mix well, and then add the orzo. Cook following the directions on the package instructions. Once soft but still firm, drain the orzo and transfer it to a warmed serving bowl. Add the remaining tablespoon of oil and mix well (doing so prevents the orzo from sticking together as it cools) and tent with foil to keep warm.

8 Remove the baking dish from the oven (the lamb should have an internal temperature of 170°F). Transfer the chops on a warmed plate and remove the oregano stems from the tomato mixture in the baking dish. Add half of the juices from the baking dish, including some of the cooked tomatoes, to the orzo and mix well. Arrange the lamb chops on top and pour over the rest of the tomato mixture from the baking dish. Serve piping hot sprinkled with the chopped oregano and grated cheese.

RADICCHIO CREAM SAUCE

YIELD: 8 SERVINGS / **ACTIVE TIME:** 20 MINUTES / **TOTAL TIME:** 40 MINUTES

There are four varieties of radicchio, but the one most commonly found in the United States is Chioggia. It resembles a small, dark crimson cabbage and is available at most well-stocked supermarkets throughout the year. Of all the radicchio, it has the strongest flavor. If you prefer a little less boldness, consider using the Treviso variety. It looks like a larger, awkwardly shaped crimson Belgian endive, and lends mellower astringency to the sauce.

1 Heat a large skillet over medium heat for 2 to 3 minutes, then add the butter. When it melts and stops foaming, add the radicchio, a couple pinches of salt, and white pepper to taste and stir. Cook, stirring a few times, until the radicchio wilts, about 5 minutes.

2 Add the warm water and cook until the radicchio softens, another 4 to 5 minutes. Using a slotted spoon, transfer the radicchio to a bowl and cover to keep warm. Add the cream to the skillet and bring to a gentle boil. Reduce the heat to low and cook until the sauce is thick and reduced, about 15 minutes.

INGREDIENTS:

- 3 tablespoons unsalted butter
- 1 large head radicchio, cored and shredded
- Salt and freshly ground white pepper
- 1½ cups heavy cream
- Juice of ½ lemon
- 3 tablespoons warm water
- ½ cup loosely packed fresh parsley leaves, chopped

IMPOSTER NOODLES

*T*he words "pasta" and "noodles" are synonymous with versatility. To twirl your fork or chopsticks around their flavors, textures, and aromas, you do not even need pasta in its traditional grain-based form. Spaghetti squash, squid, tofu, zucchini, and a host of other tasty (and gluten-free!) stand-ins may just entice you to forget the original!

EGG "FETTUCCINE"
with GINGERY RED PEPPER SAUCE *and* LEEKS

YIELD: 4 SERVINGS / ACTIVE TIME: 30 MINUTES / TOTAL TIME: 45 MINUTES

INGREDIENTS:

- 4   leeks
- 2   tablespoons peanut or grapeseed oil
- 1   tablespoon toasted sesame oil
-     Salt
- 8   large eggs
- ¼   cup thinly sliced fresh chives
- 2   handfuls chopped fresh cilantro, plus more for serving
- 2   tablespoons soy sauce
- 2   tablespoons dry sherry
- 1   recipe warm Gingery Red Pepper Sauce (page 744), warm

1 Prepare the leeks by trimming away the root ends and dark green leaves, keeping only the white and light green parts. With a sharp knife, cut each leek in half lengthwise and remove the two outer layers. Quarter each leek and then cut each quarter into thin slivers. Place them in a large bowl of water and swish them around to remove any dirt. Drain well, then transfer to a kitchen towel. Set aside.

2 Heat a large skillet over medium-low heat for 2 to 3 minutes. Add both oils and turn the heat up to medium. When the oil is swirling on the surface but not yet smoking, add the leeks and a couple pinches of salt and stir. When the leeks start to sizzle, reduce the heat to low, cover, and cook, stirring occasionally, until very soft and browned in some spots, about 20 minutes. Remove from the heat, let cool slightly, and, using a fine-mesh strainer, strain.

3 Whisk the eggs, cooked leeks, chives, cilantro, soy sauce, sherry, and a couple pinches of salt together in a medium bowl until well blended. Heat the skillet that contained the leeks (don't wipe it out) over medium-high heat. If there is enough oil leftover from cooking the leeks (you want a film of oil over the bottom), you are set. If not, add a tablespoon of peanut or grapeseed oil. Pour enough of the egg mixture into the skillet so that it just covers the bottom. Swirl the skillet continuously as you add the egg mixture so it covers the bottom evenly. Cook until the egg sets. Gently slide it onto a large plate, flip it, and then slide it back into the skillet and cook another 20 to 30 seconds. Transfer to to a parchment paper-covered surface. Repeat the process three more times with the rest of the egg mixture, adding a small bit of oil between cooking when needed. As you finish, you can pile the rounds of cooked egg on top of one another. When all of the egg mixture has been cooked, slice the stack into thin strips and then gently separate them into strands.

4 Divide the egg strips among four warmed bowls, top with the warm red pepper sauce and a sprinkling of cilantro, and serve piping hot.

SESAME STIR-FRIED CARROT "NOODLE SPIRALS"

YIELD: 4 SERVINGS / ACTIVE TIME: 30 MINUTES / TOTAL TIME: 30 MINUTES

Delicious and beautifully colored, this carrot "noodle" stir-fry incorporates the flavors of peanut butter, sesame oil, ginger, and soy sauce to make a tasty side dish. For a fun and whimsical presentation, consider cutting the carrots with a spiralizer, a fairly inexpensive kitchen tool that slices vegetables into long, curled ribbons that resemble noodles. It's not necessary, however. This dish will taste just as delicious with carrots grated on the large holes of a sturdy grater. For best results, it is important not to overcook the carrots; you want to remove them from the heat when they are bendable but still have a little pleasant crunch to them.

1 Put the sesame seeds in a small skillet over medium heat and toast until golden brown and aromatic, about 8 minutes. Transfer them to a small bowl and set aside.

2 Whisk the peanut butter, water, vinegar, soy sauce, sugar, sesame oil, chili bean sauce, and ginger, together in a small saucepan over medium-low heat until thoroughly combined and bring to a gentle boil. Continue cooking, stirring frequently, until the sauce thickens, 4 to 5 minutes. Set aside.

3 Heat a wok or large skillet over medium heat for 2 to 3 minutes. Turn the heat to medium-high and add the peanut oil (you will need to cook the carrots in two batches). When the oil begins to swirl on the surface, add half of the carrots and a pinch of salt and stir-fry until the carrots have softened, about 2 minutes. Transfer the carrots to a bowl and set aside. Repeat the process, adding a drizzle of peanut oil if necessary, with the remaining carrots.

4 Add the peanut butter mixture to the bowl and toss with the carrots until they are evenly coated with it. Served hot topped with the sesame seeds and scallions.

INGREDIENTS:

2	teaspoons sesame seeds
2	tablespoons smooth peanut butter
2	tablespoons water
2	tablespoons seasoned rice vinegar
1	tablespoon soy sauce
1	tablespoon light brown sugar
2	teaspoons toasted sesame oil
1	teaspoon chili bean sauce, more if additional heat is desired
1	1-inch piece fresh ginger, peeled and grated
2	tablespoons peanut oil
4 to 6	very large carrots, peeled and either spiralized or grated on the large holes of a grater
	Salt
1	bunch (5 to 6) scallions, trimmed and sliced on the diagonal into ½-inch pieces, for serving

CUCUMBER "NOODLES" *with* COCONUT, LIME, *and* CUMIN DRESSING

YIELD: 4 SERVINGS / ACTIVE TIME: 30 MINUTES / TOTAL TIME: 40 MINUTES

This refreshing spiced cucumber salad is a perfect accompaniment to grilled meats and fish in the summer. I personally find the combination of warming, pungent cumin, sweet and soothing coconut, and crispy cucumbers absolutely satisfying. It is fairly easy to assemble as well, though it does require opening up a young Thai coconut, whose very sturdy surface requires a little bravery to crack. Found in most well-stocked Asian markets, young Thai coconuts are as large as melons, resemble a whitish yurt, and have a moist, aromatic internal pulp that is very different from the solid flesh of mature coconuts. If this is your first time opening one, I encourage you to avail yourself of the numerous instructional videos online. Sometimes an image is truly worth a thousand words of instruction.

INGREDIENTS:

- 5 large cucumbers
- 1 young Thai coconut
- Juice and grated zest from 2 juicy limes, divided
- ¼ cup coconut water (from the young Thai coconut)
- 1 teaspoon chili garlic sauce, more if desired
- 1 teaspoon grated peeled fresh ginger
- 1 teaspoon sugar
- 1 teaspoon cumin
- 1 teaspoon salt
- ½ cup chopped salted roasted peanuts for serving
- 1 bunch (5 or 6) scallions, trimmed and thinly sliced, for serving

1 Peel the cucumbers. Cut each in half lengthwise and, using a small scoop or spoon, remove the seeds from the center. Cut each cucumber half lengthwise into as many ⅛-inch slices as possible. Then cut the slices into "noodles" that are ⅛ inch wide. Place the cucumber strands on paper towels to absorb as much of their liquid as possible.

2 Place the coconut of a work surface, holding it steady near the bottom with your hand. You will need a mallet and a very large, sharp knife for the following steps. To make your first cut, place the bottom corner of the knife blade about 1½ inches below the tip of the coconut. Now gently strike the knife with a mallet to create a small indentation on the surface. Making sure the bottom corner of the blade is placed in the indentation you have just created, strike down harder on the mallet until you crack the outer shell and break through to the inner shell of the coconut.

3 Make your second cut, using the same technique, so that the two combined incisions create a 90 degree angle. Continue this process with the third cut, which will create a "U" shape and then the fourth cut, which will create a square shape at the top of the coconut.

4 Using the bottom corner of your knife blade, pry open the square you've created at the top of the coconut. If the square doesn't release easily, it means you'll need to go over the cuts you've made and give them another crack, this time using more force.

Once pried open, invert the coconut and pour the delicious coconut water into a glass or cup; reserve (young coconuts typically contain 1¼ cups of water, so you will need a tall glass or large cup).

5 Open the coconut by turning it over so that its opening is now on its side. Place the bottom corner of the knife blade halfway along the length of the coconut. Now gently strike the knife with a mallet to create a small indentation on the surface. Making sure the bottom corner of the blade is placed in the indentation you have just created, strike down harder on the mallet until you split the coconut open. Using a spoon, scrape out the coconut flesh inside and transfer it to a small bowl.

6 Put the coconut flesh, lime juice, ¼ cup of the coconut water (drink the remaining cup in good health!), chili garlic sauce, ginger, sugar, cumin, and salt in a small food processor or a blender and process until smooth.

7 Transfer the cucumber "noodles" to a large serving bowl. Top with the sauce and toss well to evenly coat them. Chill for at least 15 minutes and up to 2 hours in the refrigerator.

8 To serve, sprinkle over the lime zest, scallions, and peanuts.

BAKED "SPAGHETTI" SQUASH *with* TOMATO SAUCE, BÉCHAMEL, *and* RICOTTA

YIELD: 4 TO 6 SERVINGS / ACTIVE TIME: 40 MINUTES / TOTAL TIME: 1 ¾ HOURS

You'll never miss the noodles in this "Italian-ized" spaghetti squash dish. The key to enjoying the brightness of the tomato sauce and creaminess of the béchamel is to remove as much of the moisture from the spaghetti squash as possible, since it can literally water down the flavors of this simple, tasty dish.

INGREDIENTS:

- 2 spaghetti squash (about 2 pounds each)
- 1 ½ teaspoons salt
- ¾ cup Classic Canned Tomato Sauce (page 566) or plain tomato sauce
- ½ recipe Béchamel Sauce (page 741)
- 1 tablespoon unsalted butter for greasing baking dish
- ½ cup whole milk ricotta

  Handful fresh basil leaves, sliced into thin slivers, for serving

1 Preheat the oven to 425°F. Line a large baking pan, including the sides, with aluminum foil (for easy clean up) and trim parchment paper to fit snugly in the bottom. Slice off and discard the ends of the squash. Using a spoon, scrape out the seeds. Cut each squash widthwise into four medallions and set in the prepared pan. Put in the oven, lower the temperature to 400°F, and bake until the strands are tender but still firm, 50 to 60 minutes. Remove from the oven and let cool for 10 minutes. Using a fork, pull the strands into the center of each round (this technique creates long strands of "spaghetti"). Working in two batches, transfer half of the squash to a kitchen towel and gently squeeze, in tourniquet-like fashion, to remove as much water from the squash as possible. Transfer the squash to a large bowl. (You can do this up to a day ahead; cover and refrigerate.)

2 Preheat the oven to 375°F. When ready to bake, add the salt, tomato sauce, and béchamel to the strands and mix gently but thoroughly to fully coat the squash. Butter a 3-inch-deep 5 x 9-inch baking dish and transfer the squash mixture to it. Place in the oven and bake until bubbly and heated through, about 25 minutes. Remove from the oven and dot the top with the ricotta. Turn on the broiler and adjust the oven shelf to its top level. Return the dish to the oven and broil until dark golden caramel spots develop on the ricotta and squash, 2 to 3 minutes.

3 Serve piping hot topped with the basil slivers.

HOT *and* GARLICKY EGGPLANT "NOODLES"

YIELD: 4 SERVINGS / ACTIVE TIME: 45 MINUTES / TOTAL TIME: 45 MINUTES

This gluten-free "noodle" dish uses eggplant to fill the carbohydrate void and chili garlic paste to add heat and pungent garlicky flavor. The only time-consuming aspect of preparing this dish is needing to work in two batches in order to perfectly brown the eggplant strands. Alternatively, you can use two frying pans for speedier results.

1 Cut off the stem ends from each eggplant and peel completely. Using the julienne attachment of a mandoline, carefully cut the eggplant into thin noodles. Alternatively, cut each eggplant into ¼-inch-thick slices, then cut each slice into ¼-inch-wide strips.

2 Combine the garlic chili paste and water in a small bowl until well mixed.

3 You will need to work in batches to cook the eggplant. Heat a large nonstick frying pan over medium heat for 1 minute. Add half of the olive oil, sesame oil, and chili garlic mixture and turn the heat up to medium-high. When the oil begins to swirl on the surface but is not yet smoking, add half of the eggplant noodles and a couple pinches of salt. Cook, stirring frequently, until the strands have softened and started turning a golden caramel color, about 5 minutes. Transfer to a warmed serving platter and tent loosely with aluminum foil to keep warm. Wipe the pan with a paper towel and repeat the process using the remaining eggplant, olive oil, sesame oil, and chili garlic mixture.

4 Serve piping hot topped with the cilantro and almonds.

INGREDIENTS:

- 4 pounds (4 medium) eggplant
- 2 tablespoons chili garlic paste, or more to taste
- 2 teaspoons water
- 3 tablespoons extra virgin olive oil, divided
- 1 tablespoon toasted sesame oil, divided
- Salt
- 2 handfuls fresh cilantro leaves, thinly sliced, for serving
- ½ cup almonds (preferably tamari almonds), coarsely chopped, as garnish (if using regular almonds, toast them on a baking sheet in a 350°F oven for 10 to 12 minutes first)

MUSHROOM *and* GOAT CHEESE EGGPLANT ROLLS

YIELD: 6 TO 8 SERVINGS / ACTIVE TIME: 45 MINUTES / TOTAL TIME: 1¼ HOURS

If you're looking to wow your crowd of loved ones, consider making these very pretty eggplant rolls. They are so delicious that even the most unabashed pasta lover will not feel short-changed by this pasta-free offering. For a lighter version, you can substitute whole milk ricotta for the whipped goat cheese but do keep the savory mixture of mushrooms, garlic, and thyme, as it complements the earthy taste of the eggplants beautifully. Best of all, this dish can also be served as an appetizer by omitting the hint of tomato sauce and adding a simple salad of arugula, cherry tomatoes, and crispy bacon bits. For best results, do not use the ends of the eggplant slices, which consist of one side of skin. Instead, slice them into thin slivers and combine them with chopped fresh parsley, 1 minced garlic clove, and a drizzle of olive oil and serve as a tasty side dish.

1 Place the porcini mushrooms in a medium bowl, cover with warm water, and soak until softened, about 30 minutes. Run your fingers across each piece to remove any grit. Transfer the cleaned porcini to a cutting board and chop. Strain the soaking water through a small cheesecloth-lined strainer.

2 Slice the bottom off each cremini mushroom stem. Fill a very large bowl with cold water and add the vinegar. Add the mushrooms and swirl them around in the water for 30 seconds or so. Transfer them to a colander in the sink and rinse under cold water. Drain well and place them on a kitchen towel stem side down, so that any remaining water drains. Let air dry for 30 minutes. Chop and set aside.

3 Preheat the oven to 400°F. Salt the sliced eggplant on both sides and let stand in a colander, separated in layers by paper towels, to draw out the bitter juices, about 15 minutes. Rinse under cold water and pat dry with paper towels. Brush the slices with olive oil and place on a parchment paper-lined baking sheet. Place on the center rack of the oven, lower the temperature to 375°F, and bake until slices turn golden on the bottom, about 20 minutes. Remove from the oven, season with pepper, and let cool. (Alternatively, you can grill the eggplant slices, turning them over when they start to become golden in color and develop grill marks on each side.) Turn the temperature back up to 400°F (or turn it on if you grill the eggplants).

INGREDIENTS:

- 2 ounces dried porcini mushrooms
- 1 pound cremini mushrooms
- 1 tablespoon distilled white vinegar

  Salt

- 4 eggplants, sliced ¼ inch thick (don't peel)
- 3 tablespoons extra virgin olive oil, plus more for brushing the eggplants

  Freshly ground black pepper

- 5 garlic cloves, minced
- 1 sprig fresh thyme
- 1 poun herbed goat cheese, at room temperature
- 2 cups Classic Canned Tomato Sauce (page 566), warm

  Handful baby arugula, for serving

  Shaved Parmigiano-Reggiano cheese for serving

5 Heat a large skillet over medium-low heat for 2 to 3 minutes. Add the 3 tablespoons olive oil and the garlic and turn the heat up to medium. Cook until the garlic softens (but don't let it color), then add the cremini and porcini mushrooms, the thyme, a couple pinches of salt, and a good crack of pepper. Stir well and cook, stirring occasionally, until the mushrooms release their liquid and the liquid then evaporates, 10 to 12 minutes. Remove from the heat and discard thyme. Taste for seasoning, and add salt and pepper if needed. Let cool.

6 Place the goat cheese in a small bowl and whisk until whipped and spreadable.

7 Assemble the eggplant rolls by laying each roasted or grilled eggplant slice on a work surface. Spread the goat cheese on top. Spoon the mushroom mixture over the cheese and spread in a thin, even layer. Roll each slice up from a short end and, if needed, secure with a toothpick. Place the eggplant rolls on a parchment paper-lined baking sheet, put on the center rack of the oven, and bake for 15 minutes (to warm up the eggplant rolls). Turn on the oven broiler and broil until they begin to turn slightly golden brown on top, 2 to 3 minutes.

8 To serve, ladle a dollop of the tomato sauce on warmed plates. Place two or three rolls on the sauce and top with arugula leaves and some Parmigiano shavings.

PORCINI MUSHROOMS

Porcini mushrooms will add a rich, nutty, flavor to this dish. Dried porcini mushrooms, specifically, have an intensified flavor, and a great deal of protein, so they are a valuable addition to most meals. If you buy too many porcini, throw the leftovers in an airtight container, and store them in a dark place. They should last for about six months.

SPAGHETTI SQUASH "NOODLES"
with SWISS CHARD *and* TOASTED SPICED PECANS

YIELD: 4 SERVINGS / ACTIVE TIME: 30 MINUTES / TOTAL TIME: 1¼ HOURS

A perfect offering when vegan or vegetarian friends and family come to visit, or just when you are in the mood to eat something delicious, wholesome, and sustaining. The colors are beautiful to boot. I serve it with homemade focaccia bread and braised rosemary cannellini beans and everyone gets up from the table happy and smiling.

INGREDIENTS:

- 2 spaghetti squash (about 2 pounds each)
- 1 large bunch Swiss chard (about 1 pound)
- Salt
- ½ cup pecans
- 3 tablespoons + 2 teaspoons extra virgin olive oil, divided
- 1 teaspoon chili powder
- 1 teaspoon sugar
- 2 garlic cloves, minced
- ½ teaspoon red pepper flakes
- Leaves from 1 small sprig fresh rosemary, minced
- 1 teaspoon Chinese black vinegar
- Freshly ground white pepper
- ¾ cup freshly grated Parmigiano-Reggiano cheese

1 Preheat the oven to 400°F. Line a large baking pan, including the sides, with aluminum foil (for easy clean up) and trim parchment paper to fit snugly in the bottom of the pan. Slice off and discard the ends of each squash. Using a spoon, scrape out the seeds. Cut each squash widthwise into four medallions and set in the prepared pan. Put in the oven, and bake until the strands are tender but still firm, 50 to 60 minutes. Remove from the oven and let cool for 10 minutes. Using a fork, pull the strands into the center of each round (this technique creates long strands of "spaghetti"). Working in two batches, transfer half of the strands to a kitchen towel and gently squeeze in tourniquet-like fashion, to remove as much water from the squash as possible. Transfer the squash to a large bowl and repeat this step with the other half of the squash. Set aside.

2 While the squash is roasting, prepare the Swiss chard. Trim the leaves from their stems (if you like, save the stems for another preparation). Bring a large pot of water to a boil. Once it's boiling, add salt (1 tablespoon for every 4 cups water) and stir. Add the chard leaves and cook until wilted, about 2 minutes. Using a strainer, transfer to a colander and run under cold water until cool. Drain well, then, using your hands, squeeze the chard to remove as much liquid as possible and mince.

3 Place the pecans in a small ziptop bag and gently crush into pieces using a rolling pin. Heat a skillet for 2 to 3 minutes over low heat. Add 2 teaspoons of the olive oil, the chili powder, and sugar and stir. Once the mixture starts to gently sizzle, add the pecans and stir until coated. Continue to cook and stir until you begin to smell the nuts' toasty fragrance, about 2 minutes. Add salt to taste and mix well. Transfer to a plate and let cool.

4 Heat a large skillet over low heat for 2 to 3 minutes. Add 1 tablespoon of the oil and heat for a minute or two, then add

the garlic, red pepper flakes, rosemary, and a pinch of salt. Cook until the garlic just starts to turn golden, 2 to 3 minutes. Turn the heat up to medium-high, add the chard and a pinch of salt, stir to combine, and cook for 3 minutes. Transfer the chard to a warmed bowl and tent to keep warm. Add the remaining 2 tablespoons olive oil and let it heat for a minute or two. Add the spaghetti squash strands and two pinches of salt and toss to coat. Sprinkle the vinegar over the top, add white pepper to taste, and toss again. Taste for seasoning, adding more salt if needed. Remove from the heat, add the Parmigiano, and toss to coat.

5 Divide the squash noodles among four warmed bowls and top with the spiced pecans.

ZUCCHINI "NOODLES" *with* OVEN-ROASTED STILTON, RADICCHIO, *and* PEACHES

YIELD: 4 SERVINGS / ACTIVE TIME: 30 MINUTES / TOTAL TIME: 45 MINUTES

Having grown up in a "salad is just lettuce, tomato, and a few thin slices of red onion" kind of family, I take great pride in pushing the envelope when it comes to putting leafage together. I take it as a positive sign that the salad bowl always returns empty to the kitchen when this particular ensemble is on the menu.

1 Bring a large pot of water to a boil. Once it's boiling, add salt (1 tablespoon of salt for every 4 cups of water).

2 Trim both ends from each zucchini. Using the julienne attachment of a mandoline or a vegetable spiralizer, carefully slice the zucchini into thin noodles. Blanch the zucchini for 2 minutes in the boiling salted water. Drain and run under cold water until cool. Drain again and set aside.

3 Put the pine nuts in a small skillet over medium heat and cook, stirring continuously, until they start to turn golden, 4 to 5 minutes. Remove from the heat and let cool.

4 Slice the peach in half, remove the pit, and cut each half lengthwise into wedges.

5 Preheat the oven to 500°F.

6 Put the pine nuts, basil, and lemon juice in a mortar or mini food processor and crush or process until you have a fairly smooth puree. Transfer the mixture to a large bowl, add the olive oil and a couple pinches of salt and cracks of pepper, and whisk well for a minute. Add the blanched zucchini and toss well to coat with the mixture.

7 Put the cheese, lemon zest, honey, a pinch of salt, and a couple of cracks of pepper in a small bowl and toss gently to mix. Transfer the cheese mixture to a parchment paper-lined baking sheet, put on the center rack of the oven, turn the broiler on, and broil until the top of the mixture turns golden, 2 to 3 minutes. Remove from the oven and let cool for a minute or two.

8 Arrange the shredded radicchio leaves on a platter and top with the zucchini, peach wedges, toasted cheese crumbles, and cranberries. Serve at room temperature.

INGREDIENTS:

- Salt
- 4 medium zucchini
- ⅓ cup pine nuts
- 1 ripe but not soft peach
- 2 handfuls fresh basil leaves
- Grated zest and juice of 1 lemon
- 2 tablespoons extra virgin olive oil
- Freshly ground black pepper
- 4 ounces Stilton cheese, crumbled
- 1½ tablespoons honey
- 2 cups shredded radicchio leaves
- 1 tablespoon dried cranberries

SQUID "PASTA"
with GARLIC SAUCE

YIELD: **4 SERVINGS** / ACTIVE TIME: **45 MINUTES** / TOTAL TIME: **1 HOUR**

This gluten-free "pasta" dish is a slight adaptation of one by Japanese chef and restaurateur Nobuyuki "Nobu" Matsuhisa. The unmistakable flavor of *shichimi togarashi* (also known as Japanese seven-spice powder, it contains red pepper flakes, orange peel, sesame seeds, Sichuan pepper, ginger, and seaweed) lends just the right amount of aromatic seasoning to this exotic combination of ingredients. It's increasingly available in stores but if you can't find it locally, buy it online.

---

1 Fill a small bowl with cold water and add the vinegar. Add the mushrooms and swirl them around in the water for 30 seconds or so. Transfer them to a colander and rinse under cold water. Drain well and place them on a kitchen towel with the stem end facing down, so that any remaining water drains. Let air dry for 15 minutes. Thinly slice and set aside.

2 Clean the squid if necessary. First remove their tentacles by cutting them right below the eyes (you won't need them for this recipe but consider dredging them in some flour and pan-frying them for a delicious treat). Using kitchen scissors, cut each body lengthwise to open up the tubes so that they can lie flat on the counter. Rinse under cold water, removing any leftover dark skin that may be lingering on the surface, and pat dry with paper towels. Lay them flat on a cutting board and, with a very sharp knife, incise the surface very lightly (do not cut all the way through) with parallel lines about ¼ inch apart that run across the shorter side of the squid. Doing this creates ridges that will grab the sauce. Now cut the squid perpendicular to those incisions into ½-inch-wide strips. Sprinkle the strips with salt and pepper.

3 Mix the mirin and soy sauce together in a small bowl.

4 Heat a large skillet over medium heat for 2 to 3 minutes. Add the butter. Once it melts and has stopped foaming, add the garlic, stir, and cook until it starts to sizzle. Increase the heat to medium-high, add

INGREDIENTS:

- **1** tablespoon distilled white vinegar
- **4** large shiitake mushrooms, stems removed
- **¾** pound squid (about 6)

  Salt and freshly ground black pepper
- **5** tablespoons mirin
- **2** tablespoons tamari or soy sauce
- **3** tablespoons unsalted butter
- **3** garlic cloves, thinly sliced
- **16** thin asparagus spears, cut into 2-inch pieces on a diagonal

  Shichimi togarashi (Japanese seven-spice powder)

the mushrooms, and cook for 1 minute. Add the squid strips, asparagus, a couple pinches of salt, and a few good cracks of black pepper. Cook until the squid strips turn opaque and begin curling, about 2 minutes. Drizzle the mirin mixture over everything and toss well to combine.

5 Divide among four warmed plates, evenly apportioning the squid and asparagus, sprinkle with *shichimi togarashi* to taste, and serve piping hot.

SQUID

Squid is eaten across the world, and each culture brings a unique approach to its preparation. The Mediterranean favors fried squid, while Australians serve it as fish and chips. Being high in protein and low in fat and calories, squid is a healthful and tasty choice for a pasta substitute. In this recipe, pay attention to the short cook time, because if you cook squid for too long it may become rubbery.

TOFU "NOODLES"
with CHICKEN *and* MIXED PEPPERS

YIELD: 4 SERVINGS / **ACTIVE TIME:** 35 MINUTES / **TOTAL TIME:** 35 MINUTES

This spicy mock noodle dish features tofu skins, also known as yuba or bean curd skins, widely used in Chinese and Japanese cooking. Ideal for the gluten intolerant, they are made from the thin skin that forms on the surface of boiling soy milk. Once dried into a sheet, it can be thinly sliced and looks just like egg noodles. Try making this with shishito peppers, which can be found in most well-stocked Asian markets. They are unfortunately somewhat unpredictable in their heat index, sometimes mild and delicious and sometimes excessively hot. I suggest tasting a very small piece before deciding, based upon preference, how many you want to include in the recipe. Should they prove hard to find in your area, substitute jalapeño peppers.

1 Whisk the rice wine, soy sauce, and sesame oil together in a medium bowl. Add the chicken and toss until well coated.

2 Heat a large wok or skillet over medium-high heat for 2 to 3 minutes and add 2 tablespoons of the peanut oil. Once it begins to shimmer but is not yet smoking, add the chicken and marinade and stir-fry until cooked through, 3 to 4 minutes. Transfer to a warmed plate. Add the remaining 2 tablespoons peanut oil. Let the oil heat for a minute or two, until it begins to swirl on the surface but is not yet smoking, then add the peppers and stir-fry until soft, about 3 minutes. Add the garlic and scallions and stir-fry until they soften and start turning slightly golden brown, about 2 minutes.

3 Return the chicken to the wok, add the tofu "noodles," and stir-fry until everything's heated through, about 5 minutes.

4 Divide the mixture among four warmed plates and serve piping hot.

INGREDIENTS:

2 tablespoons Shaoxing rice wine or dry sherry

1 tablespoon soy sauce

2 teaspoons toasted sesame oil

½ to ¾ pound boneless skinless chicken breast, sliced across into thin strips

4 tablespoons peanut or grapeseed oil, divided

1 to 3 long hot green peppers, seeded and thinly sliced

1 red bell pepper, seeded and cut into thin strips

2 garlic cloves, thinly sliced

2 scallions, trimmed and cut into 2-inch lengths

1 9-ounce package tofu sheets, cut into thin strips

BAKED PASTA DISHES

*S*ometimes food comes wrapped like a present. And there is no better gift than baked pasta. It arrives as a gorgeous parcel of crispy dough with sumptuous ribbons of toasted cheese, sauce, or breadcrumbs. Like little children, we sit with eager anticipation of the treasures within. A meatball? Or perhaps a chewy noodle? Maybe some creamy goodness that will make us feel loved.

PORCINI MUSHROOM *and* BÉCHAMEL LASAGNA

YIELD: 6 SERVINGS / ACTIVE TIME: 1 HOUR / TOTAL TIME: 2 HOURS

If I were forced, at gunpoint, to choose my absolute, hands-down favorite pasta dish, it would have to be this one. I would feel like a ghastly coward and turncoat, because in truth I am in love with so, so many delicious pasta dishes. But in this imaginary moment of urgency, the truth would inevitably come out. I am powerless before this bewitching and earthy combination of porcini mushrooms, sumptuous and velvety béchamel sauce, and the brightening lemony, minty notes of thyme. While you are, of course, welcome to prepare this dish with no-boil lasagna noodles, with wonderful results, I will say that the tender texture of the egg pasta, which lends itself so marvelously here, can only be captured by an hour's worth of work to make the lasagna sheets from scratch.

1 If making with fresh pasta, prepare the dough as directed on pages 137–139, rolling the dough to the thinnest setting (generally notch 5) for pasta sheets that are about 1⁄16 inch thick. Cut the pasta sheets into approximately 12-inch-long pieces. Lay the cut pasta sheets on lightly floured parchment paper-lined baking sheets. Allow them to dry for at least 15 minutes before boiling, as it will prevent the pasta from sticking together when boiling in the water.

2 Place the porcini in a small bowl with the water and let soak until softened, about 15 minutes. Lightly run your fingers across all the pieces to dislodge any dirt or debris. Gather them in your hand and gently squeeze over the bowl to remove excess water, then chop. Strain the soaking liquid through a small paper towel-lined strainer, measure out 1 ½ cups of the soaking liquid, and set aside.

3 Bring the wine to a boil in a small saucepan and continue to boil until reduced almost by half, about 5 minutes (this will concentrate and deepen its flavor). Remove from the heat and set aside.

4 Heat a large, deep skillet (you will be adding the béchamel sauce later in the recipe) over medium heat for 2 to 3 minutes and add the butter. When the butter melts and stops foaming, add the shallots and a pinch of salt and stir. Once the shallots begin to gently sizzle, adjust the temperature to low, cover, and cook, stirring occasionally, until softened, about 10 minutes. Stir

INGREDIENTS:

- ½ recipe All Yolk Pasta Dough (p. 137) or ½ pound lasagna noodles
- 1 ounce (about 1 cup) dried porcini mushrooms
- 2 cups warm water
- 1 cup dry red wine such as Cabernet Sauvignon, Pinot Noir, or Sangiovese
- 2 tablespoons unsalted butter
- 3 medium shallots, minced

  Salt
- 2 garlic cloves, minced
- 1 pound cremini mushrooms, trimmed and cut into ⅛-inch slices

  Leaves from 2 sprigs fresh thyme, chopped, plus more for garnish

  Freshly ground black pepper
- ½ recipe Béchamel Sauce (page 741)
- 1 ½ cups grated Parmigiano-Reggiano cheese

in the garlic and cook until it becomes fragrant, 30 to 60 seconds. Turn the heat up to medium-high, add the porcini and cremini mushrooms, thyme, and a couple pinches of salt, and stir. Cook, stirring frequently, until the mushrooms begin to soften and release their water, about 6 minutes. Add the reduced wine, the porcini soaking liquid, and a pinch of salt and bring to a gentle boil. Continue to cook on medium-high heat, stirring occasionally, until the mushrooms are tender and the liquid has reduced by half, 12 to 15 minutes. Remove from the heat and taste for seasoning, adding salt or pepper if needed. Add the béchamel sauce and stir until well combined.

5 Preheat the oven to 350°F.

6 Bring a large pot of water to a boil. Once it's boiling, add salt (1 tablespoon for every 4 cups water) and stir. Add the pasta sheets, only one or two at a time, and boil them until still very firm, 1 to 2 minutes for fresh pasta and about three quarters of the time directed on the package for dried pasta. Once ready, using a slotted spoon (the larger the better), transfer them to a large bowl of cold water. Allow them to completely cool, then arrange them in a single layer on clean, damp kitchen towels. Continue this process with the remaining lasagna sheets.

7 Assemble the lasagna. Spoon in enough of the mushroom sauce to cover the bottom of a deep (about 3 inches) 9 x 13-inch baking dish. Arrange a single layer of noodles lengthwise, making sure they are slightly overlapping one another. Then spoon enough sauce to cover the first layer of noodles evenly and sprinkle with ½ cup of the Parmigiano. Repeat this layering two more times, ending with a layer of the mushroom sauce topped with the remaining Parmigiano. Cover loosely with aluminum foil, place in the oven, and bake 35 minutes. Remove the foil and continue to bake until the edges of the lasagna sheets are lightly browned, about 12 minutes. For nice, clean slices, allow the lasagna to rest for at least 20 minutes before slicing.

BAKED ZITI

YIELD: 6 SERVINGS / ACTIVE TIME: 40 MINUTES / TOTAL TIME: 1½ HOURS

While ricotta is the traditional addition to baked Italian-American ziti, I prefer this version with a creamy Parmigiano béchamel and a tangy, slightly spicy tomato sauce. I find that ricotta has a tendency to get dry and grainy when baked, which is why I prefer to add it fresh to pasta dishes. The inclusion of fish sauce is perhaps unusual and certainly not at all traditional, but it adds the most wonderful deeply savory note to the sauce. For an extra crispy top, add the pasta to the baking dish without pressing it down. This allows more open space between the pasta at the top, which enables the heat to crisp everything up that much more.

Other recommended pasta shapes: penne, rigatoni

INGREDIENTS:

- 1 28-ounce can peeled whole tomatoes (preferably San Marzano)
- 1 14-ounce can peeled whole tomatoes (preferably San Marzano)
- 2 tablespoons extra virgin olive oil
- 2 ounces pancetta, diced
- 1 large yellow onion, chopped
- Salt
- 2 teaspoons red pepper flakes
- 1 tablespoon tomato paste
- 1 tablespoon fish sauce or 2 oil-packed anchovy fillets
- ¼ teaspoon sugar
- 1½ tablespoons unsalted butter for greasing the baking dish
- ½ recipe Béchamel Sauce (page 741)
- 1 pound room-temperature fresh mozzarella cheese, cut into ½-inch cubes
- 1 pound ziti
- 2½ cups freshly grated Parmigiano-Reggiano cheese, divided
- Handful chopped fresh basil for serving

1 Run the tomatoes through a food mill or puree them in a blender with their juices.

2 Heat a large skillet over medium-low heat for 2 to 3 minutes. Add the olive oil and increase the heat to medium. When the oil begins to swirl but is not yet smoking, add the pancetta. Cook, stirring often, until golden brown, 4 to 5 minutes. Turn the heat up to medium-high and add the onion, a couple pinches of salt and the red pepper flakes. When the mixture begins to gently sizzle, reduce the heat to low, cover, and cook, stirring occasionally, until the onion has become very soft, about 15 minutes.

3 Turn the heat up to medium-high, stir in the tomato paste and fish sauce, and cook, stirring continuously, until the mixture has slightly darkened, about 2 minutes. Add the tomatoes, sugar and a couple pinches of salt and stir. Bring the sauce to a gentle boil. Adjust the heat to low, cover, and cook, stirring often, until the sauce is slightly reduced and thickened, about 30 minutes. Taste for seasoning and add more salt if needed.

4 Preheat the oven to 350°F. Butter the sides and bottom of 9 x 13-inch baking dish. Combine the béchamel and mozzarella cubes in a large bowl.

5 Bring a large pot of water to a boil. Once it's boiling, add salt (1 tablespoon for every 4 cups water) and stir. Add the pasta and stir for the first minute to prevent any sticking. Cook for half of the time instructed on the package. The pasta will be somewhat softened but still very firm and clearly not cooked through. Drain and immediately add to the bowl the béchamel along with 1 cup of the Parmigiano, and toss to combine and coat the pasta

fully. Add all but 1 ½ cups of the tomato sauce to the bowl and gently fold the mixture a few times, leaving streaks of béchamel.

6 Transfer the mixture to the prepared baking dish and top with the remaining tomato sauce and Parmigiano. Bake or cover and refrigerate for up to 2 days or freeze for up to 1 month (defrost it overnight in the refrigerator before baking it). Place the dish in the oven and bake until the sauce is bubbling and the mozzarella has melted, 15 to 20 minutes (if it's cold going into the oven, cook time will be longer, about 30 minutes). Turn the broiler on and broil the pasta, without adjusting the oven shelf, until dark caramel-colored spots begin to develop on the surface, about 4 minutes.

7 Remove from the oven and let sit for 15 minutes before serving on warmed plates, topped with a sprinkling of basil.

CANNELLONI *with* BUTTERNUT SQUASH, RICOTTA, *and* SAGE

YIELD: 9 TO 10 SERVINGS / ACTIVE TIME: 1 HOURS / TOTAL TIME: 1 ½ HOURS

Literally "large reeds" in Italian, cannelloni are thin sheets of pasta rolled around a savory filling. In this recipe, they encase the classic combination of butternut squash and sage, enriched by creamy ricotta cheese.

Suggested sauces: Browned Butter and Sage Sauce or its variation (page 466)

1 Preheat the oven to 400°F. Slice the top and bottom off the squash. Rest it on its widest end and, using a heavy kitchen knife, slice down vertically. If it's difficult to do (it is for me), use a rubber mallet to tap gently on the pointy side of the blade. Work as slowly as you need to and wedge the knife all the way to the base of the squash. When you have the two separated squash halves, use a spoon to scrape out the seeds and fibrous insides. Prick the flesh with a fork. Brush all the cut surfaces lightly with 1 tablespoon of the olive oil (I use my hands to do this) and place, cut side down, on a parchment paper-lined baking sheet. Place on the center rack of the oven, lower the temperature to 375°F, and roast until you can easily pierce the squash with a fork, 40 to 45 minutes. Remove from the oven and let cool, then scoop the soft flesh off the skins with a large metal spoon. Run the squash flesh through a potato ricer directly over a medium bowl. Alternatively, you can place it in a wide, shallow bowl and press on it with a potato masher until smooth.

2 Heat a large skillet over low for 2 to 3 minutes. Add 2 tablespoons of the oil and the garlic and turn the heat up to medium. Once it just starts to turn golden, take the skillet off the heat and transfer the garlic and oil to the bowl with the pureed squash. Add the cheeses, half the slivered sage, the nutmeg, 2 teaspoons salt, and pepper to taste and mix well. Use or cover and refrigerate for up to 3 days. Bring back to room temperature before proceeding.

3 Mix and prepare the dough following the directions on pages 137–139, rolling the dough to the thinnest setting (generally notch 5 or 6) for pasta sheets that are about ¹⁄₁₆ inch thick. Lay the cut pasta sheets on a lightly floured parchment paper-lined baking sheets, separating them with more lightly floured sheets of parchment. Make sure to work quickly to keep the pasta sheets from drying out and becoming brittle.

INGREDIENTS:

FILLING:

- 1   2-pound butternut squash
- 5   tablespoons extra virgin olive oil, divided
- 5   garlic cloves, minced
- 1 ½ cups whole-milk ricotta cheese
- 1   cup freshly grated Parmigiano-Reggiano cheese
- 12   fresh sage leaves, thinly slivered, divided
- 1   teaspoon freshly grated nutmeg

     Salt

     Freshly ground white pepper

DOUGH:

- 1   recipe All Yolk Pasta Dough (page 137)

     Semolina flour for dusting

- ½   tablespoon olive oil

     Salt

4 Working with one sheet at a time, place it on a lightly floured work surface in front of you. Using a pastry cutter, cut each sheet into as many 4 ½- to 5-inch squares as possible. Place the finished squares on another lightly floured parchment-lined baking sheet so they don't touch. As you run out of room, lightly dust them with flour, cover with another sheet of parchment, and arrange more squares on top of that. Repeat with all the pasta sheets. Gather any scraps together into a ball, put it through the pasta machine to create additional pasta sheets, and cut those as well.

5 Bring a large pot of water to a boil. Once it's boiling, add salt (1 tablespoon for every 4 cups water) and stir. Add the squares and carefully stir for the first minute to prevent any sticking. Cook until they are just tender, about 2 minutes. Drain, rinse under cold water, and toss with ½ tablespoon oil to prevent sticking.

6 Generously coat with oil a baking dish large enough to fit all the filled cannelloni in a single layer. To fill the cannelloni, place a pasta square in front of you. Place ¼ cup of the squash mixture in the center of the square and shape it into a rough cylinder. Roll the pasta square around the filling into a tube and transfer to the prepared baking dish, seam side down. Repeat with remaining sheets and filling. When the baking dish is filled, brush the cannelloni tops with the remaining 2 tablespoons oil. Bake or cover and refrigerate for up to 4 hours. If using a ceramic or glass baking dish, bring back to room temperature before baking (sudden temperature changes can make them crack unless very thick and strong).

7 Preheat the oven to 375°F. Put the baking dish on the center rack and bake until the cannelloni are very hot and begin to turn golden in color, about 20 minutes. Serve directly from the baking dish, topped with a drizzle of the sauce of your choice and the remaining slivered sage leaves.

LEFTOVER SPAGHETTI FRITTATA CAKE

YIELD: 4 TO 6 SERVINGS / ACTIVE TIME: 15 MINUTES / TOTAL TIME: 45 MINUTES

I created this dramatic-looking Bundt frittata when I was trying to figure out how to recycle leftover Shrimp and Pistou Sauce (page 587) that I had tossed with squid ink spaghetti. Wanting to inspire my girls to eat the rather ominous looking—but delicious!—black pasta, I decided to make its presentation fun, as if I were preparing a savory cake. It worked! When I served them each a slice of black-dotted Bundt frittata "cake," along with a generous dollop of sweet tomato sauce and a heavy-handed dusting of pan-toasted breadcrumbs, they lapped it up in seconds flat. You can, of course, use any leftover spaghetti that has been seasoned in tomato sauce and use a springform pan, though it will not look as show-stopping.

INGREDIENTS:

8 large eggs

Salt and freshly ground black pepper

4 cups leftover spaghetti with tomato sauce

¾ cup freshly grated Parmigiano-Reggiano cheese

Handful fresh parsley leaves, roughly chopped

1 tablespoon unsalted butter

1 tablespoon extra virgin olive oil

¼ cup panko breadcrumbs

1 cup warm tomato sauce of your choice for serving

1 Preheat the oven to 350°F.

2 Break the eggs into a large bowl and whisk, along with a couple pinches of salt and pepper to taste, until well combined. Add the leftover pasta, Parmigiano, parsley, and more salt and pepper to taste and mix well.

3 Grease a Bundt pan with the butter, making sure the entire surface is covered. Pour the pasta mixture into the pan and flatten the surface down with the back of a large spoon. Place the pan on the center rack and bake for 30 minutes. Increase the oven temperature to 425°F and bake until a tester inserted in the center comes out clean and the top is golden brown, 8 to 10 minutes. Remove from the oven and let cool for 10 minutes.

4 As the frittata bakes, toast the breadcrumbs. Heat the olive oil in a small skillet over medium heat. Add the panko and cook, stirring constantly, until it's dark golden brown, 4 to 5 minutes. Remove from the heat, pour into a bowl so it doesn't darken any further, sprinkle generously with salt and pepper, and stir.

5 Run a knife around the edge of the cake pan to loosen the frittata. Place a large plate over the pan, then invert the two together to unmold the frittata. Cut into wedges and serve each with a generous dollop of warm tomato sauce and a sprinkling of toasted breadcrumbs.

VEGETABLE *and* TOFU-STUFFED ROTOLO *with* GINGERY RED PEPPER SAUCE

YIELD: 4 TO 5 SERVINGS / ACTIVE TIME: 1 ¼ HOURS / TOTAL TIME: 1 ½ HOURS

This is my own personal mash-up, combining pasta with aromatic and delicious Asian flavors. If you would prefer to not make your own pasta, purchase boxed dried pasta sheets, overlapping them slightly as you roll them to achieve 15 inches in length. The recipe for the dough makes four 15-inch-long pasta sheets.

1 Clean the mushrooms. Slice off the bottom of each mushroom stem. Fill a very large bowl with cold water and add the vinegar. Add the mushrooms and swirl them around in the water for 30 seconds or so. Transfer them to a colander and rinse under cold water. Drain well and place them on a kitchen towel, stem side down, so that any remaining water drains. Let air-dry for 30 minutes, then mince.

2 Drain the tofu and cut it into ½-inch slices. Arrange them in a single layer on a paper towel-lined tray. Cover with paper towels and pat dry. Let them sit for 30 minutes, changing the paper towels after 15 minutes (to continue absorbing as much water as possible). Alternatively, use a tofu press, following the manufacturer's instructions. Chop the tofu into small pieces.

3 Heat a large skillet over medium heat for 2 to 3 minutes. Add the peanut oil and heat for a minute or two. When it begins to swirl but is not yet smoking, add the scallions and a pinch of salt and stir. Cook, stirring a few times, until soft, 3 to 4 minutes. Raise the heat to medium-high, add the mushrooms, tofu, cabbage, carrots, and a couple more pinches of salt, and stir. Cook, stirring frequently, until all the vegetables have softened and the cabbage has slightly wilted and looks translucent, about 5 minutes.

4 While the vegetables cook, whisk the soy sauce, 2 tablespoons of the water, the sugar, pepper, and sesame oil together in a small bowl. In another small bowl, whisk the cornstarch with the remaining 1 tablespoon water until smooth, then whisk it into the soy mixture. Stir this into the vegetables and raise the heat to high. Cook until the liquid evaporates from the bottom of the skillet and the vegetables are cooked through, about 2 minutes. You should see a slight thickening of the vegetable mixture at this point. Remove from the heat and let cool slightly, then transfer to a food processor. Pulse several times until you have a rough puree;

INGREDIENTS:

FILLING:

1 pound cremini mushrooms

1 tablespoon distilled white vinegar

1 pound extra firm tofu

5 tablespoons peanut or grapeseed oil

2 bunches scallions, trimmed and thinly sliced

Salt

4 cups shredded cabbage

4 carrots, peeled and grated

3 tablespoons soy sauce

3 tablespoons water, divided

2 tablespoons sugar

1 teaspoon freshly ground white pepper

4 teaspoons toasted sesame oil, plus more for greasing the pan

4 teaspoons cornstarch

DOUGH:

1 recipe All Yolk Pasta Dough (page 137)

TO ASSEMBLE:

2 handfuls chopped fresh cilantro

FOR SERVING:

2 cups Gingery Red Pepper Sauce (page 744), piping hot, for serving

Chopped fresh cilantro for garnish

you don't want it to be super smooth. Taste for seasoning, add salt and/or pepper if needed, and pulse one last time to mix. Use or cover and refrigerate for up to 2 days.

5 Mix and prepare the dough as directed on pages 137–139, rolling the dough to the thinnest setting (generally notch 5) for pasta sheets that are about 1/16 inch thick. At this point, the pasta sheets will be so long you will need to cut it into 15-inch lengths in order to handle them more easily.

6 Bring a large pot of water to a boil. Once it's boiling, add salt (1 tablespoon for every 4 cups water) and stir, then add a single sheet of pasta. Cook for a minute, then carefully retrieve the sheet using two large slotted spoons. Transfer to a kitchen towel laid out flat on the kitchen counter and let cool. Repeat the process until all the pasta sheets are cooked and draining, in a single layer, on kitchen towels.

7 Assemble the dish. Preheat the oven to 475°F. Generously grease a 10 x 14-inch baking dish with sesame oil. Work with one pasta sheet at a time. Lay it on a work surface covered with parchment paper. Using a rubber spatula, spread the filling over the sheet and sprinkle with a small amount of the cilantro. Starting at one short end, roll the sheet up tightly. Once you are done rolling, rest it on its seam to keep it from unrolling, or you can secure the end with a couple of toothpicks. Repeat with the remaining pasta sheets, filling, and cilantro.

8 Using a very sharp knife, slice each pasta roll into 1¼-inch-thick rounds. Arrange them, cut side down in the prepared baking dish, leaving ¼ inch between them. Put the dish on the center rack and bake until lightly browned on top and heated through, 10 to 12 minutes.

9 To serve, pool 2 to 3 tablespoons of piping hot Gingery Red Pepper Sauce on each warmed plate; with the back of the spoon, push the sauce out from the center to the sides of the plate to create a rough circle of sauce. Arrange three rotolo slices on top, sprinkle with cilantro, and serve.

SCALLOP *and* ZUCCHINI-STUFFED CANNELLONI *with* GARLIC-THYME CREAM SAUCE

YIELD: 4 SERVINGS / ACTIVE TIME: 1½ HOURS, IF NOT MAKING THE PASTA / TOTAL TIME: 2 HOURS, IF MAKING THE PASTA

In Italy, cannelloni (or manicotti, as many know it in the United States) is a Sunday lunch or holiday dish. When people used to spend more time in the kitchen, cannelloni was always prepared with homemade egg pasta. Now we have a choice of whether to make and roll out our own dough or buy the dried tubes, ready to be stuffed. Either way you decide to go, this dish, infused with the scent of the sea and the subtle fragrance of garlic and thyme, is remarkable. For best results, do not overcook the pasta so that it can retain a pleasing, firm texture once baked.

1 Rinse the scallops under cold water and pat dry. You may find side muscles, or little rectangular tags of tissue, on the side of some scallops. Since they are tough, remove by pinching them between your thumb and index finger and tearing them away. Chop the scallops.

2 Heat a large skillet over low heat for 2 to 3 minutes. Add the olive oil and raise the heat to medium-high. Once it begins to swirl on the surface, add the Old Bay. Stir for a minute, until fragrant, then add the zucchini, one third of the thyme, and two pinches of salt and stir. Cook until the zucchini starts to soften, about 5 minutes, stirring occasionally, then lower the heat to medium-low and cook, stirring occasionally, until softened, about 5 minutes. Add the scallops and stir. Cook, stirring occasionally, until the scallops feel firm but not hard, about 4 minutes. Remove from the heat. Use or cover and refrigerate for up to 1 day.

3 Mix and prepare the dough following the directions on pages 137–139, rolling the dough to the thinnest setting (generally notch 5) for pasta sheets that are about ¹⁄₁₆ inch thick. Lay the cut pasta sheets on a lightly floured parchment paper-lined baking sheets, separating them with more lightly floured sheets of parchment. Make sure to work quickly to keep the pasta sheets from drying out and becoming brittle.

4 Working with one sheet at a time, place it on a lightly floured work surface in front of you. Using a pastry cutter, cut each sheet into as many 4-inch squares as possible. Place the finished squares on another lightly floured parchment paper-lined baking sheet so they don't touch. As you run out of room, lightly dust them with flour, them, cover with another sheet of parchment,

INGREDIENTS:

FILLING AND SAUCE:

1   pound sea scallops

2   tablespoons extra virgin olive oil

¼   teaspoon Old Bay seasoning

3   small zucchini, diced

     Leaves from 2 small sprigs fresh thyme, minced

     Salt

⅔   cup fish stock, divided

1   cup heavy cream

2   garlic cloves, lightly crushed

     Freshly ground white pepper

DOUGH:

1   recipe All Yolk Pasta Dough (page 137)

     Semolina flour for dusting

     Salt

½   tablespoon olive oil, plus more for the baking dish

and arrange more squares on top of that. Repeat with all the pasta sheets. Gather any scraps together into a ball, put it through the pasta machine to create additional pasta sheets, and cut those as well.

5 Bring a large pot of water to a boil. Once it's boiling, add salt (1 tablespoon for every 4 cups water) and stir. Add the squares and carefully stir for the first minute to prevent any sticking. Cook until they are just tender, about 2 minutes. Drain, rinse under cold water, and toss with ½ tablespoon oil to prevent sticking.

6 Generously coat with oil a baking dish large enough to fit all the filled cannelloni in a single layer. To fill the cannelloni, place a pasta square in front of you. Place ¼ cup of the filling mixture in the center of the square and shape it into a rough cylinder. Roll the pasta square around the filling into a tube and transfer to the prepared baking dish, seam side down. Repeat with remaining sheets and filling. When the baking dish is filled and you are ready to bake, pour over ⅓ cup of the stock.

7 Preheat the oven to 425°F. Put the baking dish on the center rack and bake until the cannelloni are very hot and begin to turn golden in color, about 20 minutes.

8 While the cannelloni bake, make a quick sauce. Put the cream, garlic, remaining thyme and stock, and a pinch of salt and white pepper in a small saucepan and cook over low heat until it has reduced by about half. Remove the garlic with a slotted spoon and discard. Taste for seasoning, adding salt or white pepper if needed. Keep hot.

9 Serve the cannelloni directly from the baking dish, topped with a drizzle of the garlic-thyme cream sauce.

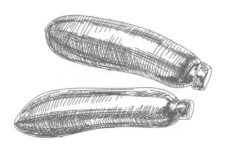

PASTA *with* FRESH SARDINES

YIELD: 4 SERVINGS / ACTIVE TIME: 45 MINUTES / TOTAL TIME: 1 ½ HOURS

Possibly no other pasta dish defines the savory-sweet flavor combination of Sicilian cuisine better than *pasta con le sarde*. Throughout Sicily, and especially in Palermo, the capital, dishes often blend the taste of the sea with the sweetness of golden raisins. In this recipe, sardines, so plentiful in the surrounding waters that they may as well jump right into this dish, are combined with raisins and fennel fronds. Should fresh sardines not be available, use (thawed) frozen or canned sardines. While they will lack slightly in texture and flavor, they will still yield magnificent results.

Recommended pasta shapes: bucatini, penne, spaghetti, ziti

1 You can ask your fishmonger to clean the sardines or do it yourself: Place the sardine on a work surface with the belly facing you. Using your thumbnail and starting where the anal fin meets the belly, separate the flesh from the bone. Do so by working your thumb under the flesh as you slide your thumb toward the tail of the fish. At this point, you will have separated the top fillet from the spine. Now slide your thumb on top of the backbone, toward the head of the fish, to separate the ribs from the fillet. Pinch the backbone of the sardine between your thumb and index finger and gently pull it away from the flesh (doing so will bring many of the smaller bones along with it). When you get to the head of the sardine, snap it and then slice it off. You now have two sardine fillets. Wash them well under cold water and pat dry with paper towels. Chop half of the fillets into 1-inch pieces and leave the remainder whole.

2 Put the raisins in a small bowl, cover with warm water, and soak for 10 minutes. Drain and transfer to a paper towel-lined plate to absorb any excess water.

3 Heat a small skillet over medium-low heat for 2 minutes. Add the pine nuts and cook, stirring frequently, until they appear golden in spots, 3 to 4 minutes. Remove from the heat and add ⅛ teaspoon of salt. Stir well and set aside.

4 Bring a large pot of water to a boil. When it's boiling, add the fennel fronds and boil for 1 minute. Remove them from the water using a strainer, drain well, pat dry with paper towels, and chop. You will use this pot of water to cook the pasta later on; keep it at a low simmer.

INGREDIENTS:

1 ½ **pounds fresh sardines**

½ **cup golden raisins**

⅓ **cup pine nuts**

Salt

Handful fresh feathery fennel fronds

5 **tablespoons extra virgin olive oil, plus more for the baking dish**

1 **small yellow onion, thinly sliced into half-moons**

5 **oil-packed anchovy fillets, chopped**

½ **teaspoon fennel seeds**

¾ **pound ziti**

Freshly ground black pepper

5 Heat a skillet large enough to hold the finished pasta dish over low heat for 1 to 2 minutes. Add 3 tablespoons of the olive oil and raise the heat to medium. Once it begins to swirl on the surface, add the onion and a couple pinches of salt and cook, stirring occasionally, until soft but not golden, about 10 minutes. Add the raisins and pine nuts, stir, and cook for another 3 minutes. Add the blanched fennel and a pinch of salt and stir. Adjust the heat to low, cover, and cook, stirring occasionally, until the onion becomes very soft, about another 15 minutes. If the mixture begins to look too dry, add a tablespoon or two of the fennel blanching water.

6 At this point, preheat the oven to 400°F and grease a deep baking dish with oil.

7 Add the anchovies, chopped sardines, and fennel seeds to the skillet with the onion mixture and cook, stirring frequently, until the anchovies have completely disintegrated into the sauce, about 10 minutes. Add more fennel blanching water, a tablespoon or two at a time, if the mixture begins to look too dry.

8 While that cooks, bring the fennel blanching water back to a boil. Once it's boiling, add salt (1 tablespoon for every 4 cups) and stir. Add the pasta and stir for the first minute to prevent any sticking. Cook according to the package instructions, draining the pasta 2 minutes short of the directed cooking time and reserving ¼ cup of the pasta water. The pasta will be soft but still very firm. Immediately transfer the pasta to the skillet with the sardine mixture. Add the reserved pasta water and toss well. Transfer the mixture to the prepared baking dish. Lay the sardine fillets on top, drizzle with the remaining 2 tablespoons oil, and give it a few good cracks of pepper. Cover with aluminum foil, place on the center rack, and bake until the sardines have turned a beige color, about 15 minutes. Serve piping hot.

SPAGHETTI *with* SEAFOOD *in* PARCHMENT PARCELS

YIELD: 4 SERVINGS / ACTIVE TIME: 35 MINUTES / TOTAL TIME: 1 HOUR

Classic southern Italian *spaghetti al cartoccio* is one of the more awe-inspiring pasta presentations on a plate. Delivered in a neatly wrapped package, the diner may feel like their birthday has come early as they unwrap their seafood-scented parcel. I have pieces of advice. First, make sure to cook the spaghetti only three quarters of the way through before finishing it in the oven with the seafood, otherwise you will end up with pasta mush. Secondly, I strongly urge you to precook the mussels. It does require an extra step and pot to clean, but it also goes a long way toward ensuring grit-free mussels. I've eliminated this step many times and have been lucky enough to enjoy a delicious and grit-free meal. On a few occasions I wasn't as fortunate, and couldn't enjoy the meal because of the frequent "crunch" between my teeth. I love mussels so much that now I don't take any chances.

Other recommended pasta shapes: linguine

INGREDIENTS:

- 1 **pound ripe plum tomatoes OR 1 14-ounce can peeled whole tomatoes (preferably San Marzano)**
- ¾ **cup dry white wine**
- 2 **cups water**
- 1 **pound fresh mussels**
- 3 ½ **tablespoons extra virgin olive oil, divided**
- 2 **garlic cloves, minced**

  Salt and freshly ground black pepper
- ¾ **pound pasta**
- 1 **pound medium shrimp, peeled and deveined**

  Handful fresh parsley leaves, chopped

1 If using fresh tomatoes, bring a medium pot of water to a boil. Blanch the tomatoes in the boiling water for 1 minute. Using tongs, transfer them to a cutting board and let cool until you can handle, then remove their skins. Cut them into quarters, remove the seeds, and roughly chop. If using canned tomatoes, pour into a small bowl and crush the whole tomatoes with your hand into pulp.

2 Bring the wine to a boil in a small saucepan and continue to boil until reduced almost by half (this will concentrate its flavor, including acidity and sweetness).

3 Bring the water to a boil in a large pot. Scrub the mussels under cold water, carefully cutting off any little fuzzy "beards" at the pointed ends. Add the mussels to the pot, cover, and turn the heat down to medium. They will quickly begin to open with the heat. As they do, pluck them out with kitchen tongs and transfer to a large bowl. When all the mussels have all opened (discard the few that remain closed), strain the mussel liquid through a paper towel-lined fine-meshed strainer. Set the mussels and strained liquid aside.

4 Preheat the oven to 300°F and put on a large pot of water on to boil for the pasta. Cut four pieces of parchment paper into 12x18-inch rectangles and place each sheet in a shallow bowl.

5 Heat a medium saucepan over medium-low heat for 2 to 3 minutes, add 3 tablespoons of the olive oil and the garlic. When the garlic gently starts to sizzle, add the tomatoes and a couple generous pinches of salt and raise the heat to medium-high. Cook for 5 minutes, stirring a few times, then add 1 cup of the reserved mussel liquid and a few good cracks of pepper, mix well, and cook for 10 minutes. Taste for seasoning, adding a bit more salt if necessary. Remove from the heat and cover to keep warm.

6 Bring a large pot of water to a boil. When it's boiling, add salt (1 tablespoon for every 4 cups) and stir. Add the pasta, stirring for the first minute to prevent any sticking. Cook the pasta three quarters of the time directed on the package and drain, reserving ¼ cup of the pasta water. The pasta will still be too hard to eat. Return the empty pot to the stove. Immediately turn the heat to high and add the remaining ½ tablespoon oil and reserved pasta water. Add the drained pasta and toss well. Add the tomato sauce and mix until well coated well.

7 Divide the pasta between the four parchment-lined bowls, then top with the mussels, shrimp, and parsley. Fold each side of the parchment, one at a time, over the pasta filling. Twist the ends together, like the wrapper for an old-fashioned candy. Place the parcels on an aluminum foil-lined baking sheet and place on the center rack of the oven. Bake for 10 minutes.

8 Place the parcels on individual serving plates and caution guests to be careful when opening them, as the steam can be scalding hot.

VINCISGRASSI

YIELD: 6 TO 8 SERVINGS / ACTIVE TIME: 2 HOURS / TOTAL TIME: 2 HOURS

While lasagna is the signature dish of the northern region of Emilia-Romagna, *vincisgrassi* is the traditional lasagna-like offering from picturesque Macerate, a town nestled in the low-rising hills of Le Marche in central Italy. Legend has it that this dish was created by a local chef for a banquet held to honor the Austrian general Prince Windischgrätz, who was commandeering in the region during the Napoleonic Wars. As with so many dishes from long ago, it is hard to know whether the prince was truly the inspiration behind this dish. Historical records also show that a similar sauce by the name of *Pringsgras* appeared in a 1779 book by Antonio Nebbia titled *Il Cuoco Maceratese* or "The Cook from Macerate." Regardless of its origin, this memorable baked dish features the region's prized ham, *prosciutto di Parma*, and *Boletus brisa*, a species of porcini mushroom that grows mainly in the Apennines near Parma and in other mountain areas. The epitome of elegant rusticity, *vincisgrassi* is rich and filling, and some versions are even more so, with the inclusion of sweetbreads and a pasta dough enriched with a fortified wine like *vin santo* or Marsala.

1 Bring the Marsala to a boil in a small saucepan and continue to boil until reduced almost by half (this will concentrate its flavor, including its acidity and sweetness). Remove from the heat.

2 Place the porcini mushrooms in a medium bowl and cover with warm water. Soak for 30 minutes. Once reconstituted, run your fingers across each piece and gently remove any dirt. Transfer the cleaned porcini to a cutting board and strain the porcini water through a small cheesecloth-lined sieve; reserve it. Chop the porcini and set aside.

3 Cut a 5-inch square of cheesecloth and place the cloves, bay leaves, rosemary, and thyme in the center. Gather the cheesecloth together to form a bundle and secure it shut with kitchen string. Once sealed, cut off any excess string and cheesecloth. You now have an aromatic *bouquet garni*.

4 Heat a large heavy-bottomed pot or Dutch oven over medium-low heat for 2 to 3 minutes, then add 2 tablespoons of the butter. Turn the heat up to medium-high and, once the butter has melted and stopped foaming, add the prosciutto and cook until it starts to brown, stirring a few times, 5

INGREDIENTS:

- 3 cups dry Marsala
- 1 ounce dried porcini mushrooms
- 8 cloves
- 2 bay leaves

  Leaves from 1 small sprig fresh rosemary
- 1 sprig fresh thyme
- 7 tablespoons unsalted butter, divided
- 1 1 ¼-inch-thick slice (7 to 8 ounces) prosciutto (preferably di Parma), diced
- 1 large yellow onion, minced
- 4 inner pale green celery stalks, minced

  Salt
- 1 tablespoon tomato paste
- 2 pounds boneless veal shoulder, trimmed of fat and cut into ¼-inch dice
- 5 tablespoons extra virgin olive oil, divided

  Freshly ground black pepper
- 8 cups Capon or Chicken Stock (page 749) or 8 cups chicken broth
- 4 cups heavy cream
- 1 large egg, at room temperature
- ½ teaspoon freshly ground white pepper
- 1 pound cremini mushrooms, trimmed and minced
- ½ recipe All Yolk Pasta Dough rolled to second-thinnest setting (page 137) or 5 sheets fresh pasta for lasagna, each about 9 x 12 inches

  2 cups freshly grated Parmigiano-Reggiano cheese

  Shaved truffles for garnish (optional)

to 6 minutes. Add the onion, celery, and two pinches of salt and stir. When the vegetables begin to sizzle, adjust the heat to low, cover, and cook, stirring occasionally, until the vegetables are very soft, about 20 minutes. Stir in the tomato paste and cook for another 5 minutes.

5 Heat a large, heavy skillet over medium-low heat for 2 to 3 minutes. As the skillet heats, wipe the surface of the veal with paper towels to absorb as much surface moisture as possible (doing this will help it brown better). Add 3 tablespoons each of the butter and olive oil and turn the heat up to medium-high. As the fats are heating, sprinkle salt and black pepper over half of the veal dice. When the butter has melted and the surface of the oil begins to swirl, add the salted half of the veal dice. Cook stirring frequently, until it starts to brown. Using a slotted spoon, transfer it to the pot. Repeat this step with the remaining half of the veal.

6 Pour out any fat remaining in the skillet and return it to the stove over medium-high heat. Add the reduced Marsala and cook, loosening the crispy bits stuck to the bottom of the pan with a wooden spoon, until reduced by a third, 3 to 4 minutes. Pour into the pot. Add 4 cups of the stock, the browned veal, and the *bouquet garni*. Partially cover the pot and simmer for 2 hours, stirring occasionally, until the sauce has slightly thickened. Taste for seasoning and add salt and/or pepper if needed. Set aside.

7 Combine the cream and remaining 4 cups stock in a medium saucepan. Bring to a simmer over medium heat, then adjust the heat to low and cook, stirring occasionally, until the mixture thickens and reduces to about 2 cups, about 1 hour.

8 Lightly beat the egg in a small bowl and add a few tablespoons of the reduced cream mixture. Mix well, then add a few more tablespoons of the mixture and whisk well to integrate. Pour the egg mixture back into the cream mixture, season with white pepper, and whisk thoroughly. Taste for seasoning and add salt if necessary. Set aside to cool.

9 Heat a large skillet over medium-low heat for 2 to 3 minutes. Add the remaining 2 tablespoons oil and turn the heat up to medium-high. Heat the oil for a couple of minutes. When the surface of the oil begins to swirl, add the porcini and cremini mushrooms and a couple pinches of salt and cook, stirring frequently, until the cremini mushrooms have lost their water, 8 to 10 minutes. Add to the veal mixture, stir, and set aside.

10 Bring a large pot of water to a boil. Once it's boiling, add salt (1 tablespoon for every 4 cups water) and stir. Have a large bowl of ice water next to the stove. Add the pasta sheets, one or two at a time, and boil until still very firm, 1 to 2 minutes. Once the pasta sheets are done, carefully remove them with a slotted spoon (the larger the better) and transfer to the bowl of cold water. Let them sit for 15 seconds, remove, and place them on a kitchen towel to dry. Repeat this process with all the pasta sheets.

11 Preheat the oven to 350°F and grease a 9 x 13-inch baking dish with 3-inch sides with the remaining 2 tablespoons butter. Lay a sheet of pasta in the pan. Spread about one third of the veal ragù over the pasta. Spread with ½ cup of the cream sauce and sprinkle with ¼ cup of the Parmigiano. Repeat this layering two more times, then cover with the last sheets of pasta. Spread the remaining cream sauce and Parmigiano on top.

12 Place the dish in the oven and bake until bubbling, about 30 minutes. Turn on the broiler and continue to cook (without moving the oven shelving) until the top of the dish turns a nice dark golden caramel color in spots, 3 to 4 minutes. Remove from the oven and let sit for 20 minutes before cutting into squares and serving with shavings of truffle if you like.

CLASSIC LASAGNA
with BOLOGNESE *and* BÉCHAMEL

YIELD: 10 SERVINGS / ACTIVE TIME: 2 HOURS / TOTAL TIME: 3 HOURS

It seems like everyone in Italy and in many parts of the world has a favorite version of this. Though it appears that the precursor of this fabled dish dates back to ancient Greek civilization and that it had traveled as far as Great Britain in the late 14th century, it is indisputable that the Italians need to be credited for perfecting the layers and layers of deliciousness that represent lasagna in its current form.

Variations on the lasagna theme are endless, though my personal favorite contains béchamel sauce, which I consider one of the secrets to making this filling dish unforgettable. Outside of a few regions of northern Italy, however, the tendency is for most cooks and restaurants to use ricotta. With all due respect to ricotta users, I believe béchamel to be an essential ingredient. Requiring only a little extra effort to prepare, this luxurious white sauce adds intoxicating creaminess without cheese. When it is layered between thin sheets of egg pasta, a savory meat sauce, and grated Parmigiano-Reggiano, it creates a lasagna that is both stick-to-your-ribs satisfying and surprisingly light.

Granted, this is not a last-minute type of dish. Since it requires making Bolognese sauce and béchamel, a little planning goes a long way. I suggest spreading the task over a couple of days by making the Bolognese two days ahead and the béchamel the day before you assemble the dish. Finally, while you can always use store-bought dried lasagna sheets, fresh egg pasta always tastes better and is more tender than dried versions.

INGREDIENTS:

- 1½ pounds dried lasagna strips or 1 recipe All Yolk Pasta Dough (page 137)
- Salt
- 1 recipe Bolognese Sauce (page 629)
- 1 recipe Béchamel Sauce (page 741)
- 2 cups freshly grated Parmigiano-Reggiano cheese

1 If using fresh pasta, prepare the dough as directed on pages 137–139, rolling the dough to the thinnest setting (generally notch 5) for pasta sheets that are about 1⁄16 inch thick. Cut the pasta sheets into approximately 12-inch-long pieces. Lay the cut pasta sheets on lightly floured parchment paper-lined baking sheets. Allow them to dry for at least 15 minutes before boiling, as it will prevent the pasta from sticking together when boiling in the water.

2 Bring a large pot of water to a boil. Once it's boiling, add salt (1 tablespoon for every 4 cups water) and stir. Add the pasta sheets, only one or two at a time, and boil them until still very firm (1 to 2 minutes for fresh pasta and about three quarters of the way for dried lasagna strips, typically 5 to 6 minutes). Once ready,

using a slotted spoon (the larger the better), transfer them to a large bowl of cold water. Allow them to completely cool, then arrange them in a single layer on clean, damp kitchen towels.

3 To assemble the lasagna, ladle enough Bolognese sauce over the bottom of a 15 x 10-inch baking dish with 3-inch sides to completely cover it. Arrange a single layer of the cooked noodles lengthwise over the sauce, making sure they are slightly overlapping one another. Then spoon enough meat sauce to cover the noodles evenly. Dollop a quarter or so of the béchamel sauce on the Bolognese and gently spread it over the meat sauce. Evenly sprinkle over ½ cup of the cheese. Repeat this layering until the lasagna is about ½ inch or so from the top of the baking dish. Spread a thin layer of meat sauce over the top layer of noodles and sprinkle with the remaining cheese. Cover loosely with aluminum foil and bake or refrigerate for up to a day, bringing it back to room temperature before baking.

4 Preheat the oven to 375°F. Put the lasagna in the oven and bake 45 minutes. Remove the foil and continue baking until the top is crusty around the edges, about another 20 minutes or so. For nice, clean slices, allow the lasagna to rest for at least 30 minutes.

SANGE CHJNE

YIELD: 10 TO 12 SERVINGS / ACTIVE TIME: 3 HOURS / TOTAL TIME: 4 HOURS

Typical of the rustic and robust cuisine found in the southern Italian region of Calabria, *sange chjne* is a delectable layering of pasta squares, small meatballs, hard-boiled eggs, and cheese. It is so unique that it has become Calabria's signature lasagna. Very labor-intensive to prepare, mostly due to the almost infinite number of marble-sized meatballs the dish requires, *sange chjne* typically graces the table only on the day after Easter, which is called *la Pasquetta*, or "little Easter." When purchasing the mozzarella, it is important to buy the block of cheese in the rectangular plastic packaging and not the water-packed variety, which releases too much water into the dish.

---

1 Put the pork, breadcrumbs, cheese, parsley, salt, pepper, and egg in a large bowl and work them thoroughly together with a wooden spoon or with your hands (which I think is the most effective way).

2 Heat the olive oil in a small skillet. When the oil starts swirling but is not yet smoking, shape 1 tablespoon of the mixture into a patty and fry for a minute on each side. Remove the skillet from the stove and let the sample cool. Taste it and determine whether you need to add more salt and/or pepper to the meatball mixture. When the seasoning is right, make the meatballs. Nip a little of the mixture from the bowl, roll it between the palms of your hands into a ½-inch ball, and set on a platter. Repeat until all of the mixture has been rolled into meatballs.

3 Return the skillet to the stove and let the oil heat for a couple of minutes. When it starts swirling but is not yet smoking, add about one third of the meatballs to the pan. (You don't want to add too many at once because they'll drop the temperature of the oil too much and then they won't brown as well. You also risk having them steam-cook instead of pan-fry if you don't give them a little room to breathe.) Stir them around with a wooden spatula until they are nice and golden on all sides, 5 to 6 minutes total. Transfer to a plate lined with paper towels to absorb any excess oil. Repeat with the remaining meatballs.

4 Put the tomato sauce in a large heavy-bottomed pot or Dutch oven over medium heat, add the meatballs, bring to a gentle simmer, and cook for 10 minutes, stirring occasionally. Ladle out 1 ½ cups of the sauce (no meatballs) and reserve. Add

INGREDIENTS:

MEATBALLS:

- 1 pound ground pork
- ⅔ cup dry breadcrumbs
- ⅓ cup freshly ground pecorino Romano cheese
- 2 handfuls fresh parsley leaves, chopped
- 2 teaspoons salt
- 1 teaspoon freshly ground black pepper
- 1 large egg
- 1 tablespoon extra virgin olive oil

SAUCE:

- 1 recipe Classic Canned Tomato Sauce (page 566) or 8 cups other tomato sauce
- 1 pound frozen petite peas

TO ASSEMBLE:

- 1 recipe All Yolk Pasta Dough (page 137) or 1 pound store-bought fresh egg pasta sheets
- Salt
- 6 hard-boiled eggs, thinly sliced
- 1 pound mozzarella cheese, thinly sliced
- 1 ½ cups freshly grated pecorino Romano cheese

the frozen peas to the pot and cook until they are tender, about 5 minutes (if the sauce has become a little too thick, add up to ½ cup of water and stir). Remove from the heat.

5 Prepare the dough following the directions on pages 137–139, rolling the dough to the thinnest setting (generally notch 5) for pasta sheets that are about ¹⁄₁₆ inch thick. Lay the cut pasta sheets on lightly floured parchment paper-lined baking sheets. Place each sheet on a lightly floured work surface in front of you and, using a pastry cutter, cut into 12-inch lengths. Repeat with all the pasta sheets.

6 Bring a large pot of water to a boil. Once it's boiling, add salt (1 tablespoon for every 4 cups water) and stir. Cook in batches, adding 2 or 3 pasta sheets at a time, and carefully stir to prevent any sticking. Cook until they are just tender, about 1 ½ minutes. Drain, rinse under cold water, and lay out on a kitchen towel so they are not touching (they will stick).

7 Grease the bottom and sides of a 9 x 13-inch baking dish with 3-inch sides with a little tomato sauce. Line the bottom and sides of the pan with pasta sheets, arranging them so that part of the sheets are hanging over the side of the baking dish by 5 inches (they will be eventually folded over the top layer of filling). Ladle one quarter of the meatball and tomato mixture evenly over the bottom of the dish. Layer one quarter of the egg slices on top, followed by the mozzarella slices and then by ¼ cup of the pecorino. Cover the filling (leaving the sides of the dish alone) with more pasta sheets and repeat the layering. Repeat the entire process two more times.

8 Place a final pasta sheet on top. Fold over all the overhanging pasta sheets (they will overlap), making sure that the filling is completely covered. Spread the reserved tomato sauce over the top and dust with the remaining ¼ cup pecorino. Bake or cover and refrigerate for up to 1 day, bringing it back to room temperature before baking.

9 Preheat the oven to 425°F. Place the dish in the oven and bake until it is bubbling and lightly puffed out in the center, about 40 minutes. To be able to cut clean slices, let the dish rest for 30 minutes. Cut into slices and serve on warmed plates.

BACON MACARONI *and* CHEESE

YIELD: 6 SERVINGS / ACTIVE TIME: 40 MINUTES / TOTAL TIME: 1¼ HOURS

While some may think macaroni and cheese is an American classic, this gooey, cheesy baked pasta dish actually has its roots in Europe. Spotty historic records make it difficult to ascertain its specific origin, but early versions of this dish can be found in various 14th-century cookbooks, including the anonymously written Italian book titled *Liber de Coquina* or "Book of Cooking," and in Elizabeth Raffald's 1769 book *The Experienced English Housekeeper*, in which Ms. Raffald gives instructions for béchamel sauce and advises readers to top the casserole with breadcrumbs and Parmigiano. The combination of pasta and cheese proved so bewitching that it eventually sailed over the Atlantic Ocean to America. Thomas Jefferson, who was introduced to pasta during his travels and work in Europe, was among its earliest champions. He served it proudly, often himself, to guests attending his dinner parties at Monticello.

Mac and cheese's appeal is easy to see, and taste. Incredibly simple, its name pretty much amounts to the sum of its parts, pasta and cheese. . . until a cook wants to turn this classic up a notch by adding other savory flavors, that is. This recipe takes full advantage of the smoky unctuousness of bacon and subtle kick of jalapeños, as it simultaneously tips its hat to R&B singer Patti LaBelle, who uses pepper jack cheese instead of traditional white cheddar in her recipe.

When preparing this, be sure to undercook the pasta until it is almost still a little crunchy, lest it become a pasta mess once baked. Also, rinse the cooked pasta under cold water before combining it with the cheese sauce. While one would think that the added starch on the pasta would assist in further thickening the cheese sauce, it merely adds an unappealing floury texture.

INGREDIENTS:

- **6** tablespoons unsalted butter, divided, plus more for the baking dish
- **1** cup panko breadcrumbs
- Salt and freshly ground black pepper
- **¼** cup fresh parsley leaves, minced
- **5 to 6** ounces bacon, diced
- **2** jalapeño peppers, seeded and minced
- **¼** cup all-purpose flour
- **2¾** cups whole milk
- **¼** teaspoon freshly grated nutmeg
- **¼** teaspoon cayenne pepper
- **2** cups (about 8 ounces) grated pepper jack cheese, divided
- **1** cup (about 6 ounces) grated Gruyère cheese, divided
- **1¼** cups (about 5 ounces) grated Parmigiano-Reggiano cheese, divided
- **1** pound elbow macaroni

1 Preheat the oven to 375°F. Butter a 3-quart casserole dish and set aside.

2 Heat the largest skillet you have over medium heat for 2 to 3 minutes (the width is important because it allows more of the breadcrumbs to have direct contact with the heat). Add 2 tablespoons of the butter and turn the heat up to medium-high. Once it has melted and stopped foaming, add the breadcrumbs and ¼ teaspoon each salt and pepper. Cook, stirring frequently, until the crumbs are a deep golden color, about 6 minutes. Transfer them to a bowl. Once cooled, toss with the parsley.

3 Return the same skillet to the stove and turn the heat to medium. Add the bacon and cook until its fat renders and it turns crispy, about 8 minutes. Using a slotted spoon, transfer the bacon bits to a small bowl. Drain all the fat from the skillet into a Pyrex measuring cup, then return just enough to it to cover the entire bottom of the skillet in a thin film. Add the jalapeños and cook, scraping up any browned bits from the bottom of the pan, until they soften, about 5 minutes. Remove from the heat.

4 Melt the remaining 4 tablespoons butter in a medium saucepan over medium heat. Once it has melted and stopped foaming, add the flour and whisk into a paste. Cook, stirring continuously, until the mixture begins to turn a slightly golden color, 2 to 3 minutes. Very slowly pour the milk into the pan, whisking continuously to combine it with the roux. Once it has all been added, cook, whisking constantly, until the mixture thickens, about 5 minutes. Add 1 teaspoon salt, ¼ teaspoon black pepper, the nutmeg, cayenne pepper, 1 cup of the pepper jack, and ¾ cup each of the Gruyère and Parmigiano and stir until the cheeses are melted. Remove from the heat and set aside.

5 Bring a large pot of water to a boil. Once it's boiling, add salt (1 tablespoon for every 4 cups water) and stir. Add the pasta, stirring for the first minute to prevent any sticking. Cook the pasta 4 fewer minutes than directed on the package, at which point the pasta will still be too firm to eat. Drain the pasta, rinse under cold water, and drain well. Return the pasta to its pot, add the cheese sauce, bacon bits and jalapeños, and any remaining oil in the skillet, and toss well.

6 Pour the mixture into the prepared baking dish. Sprinkle the remaining cheddar, Gruyère, and Parmigiano over the top. Bake until bubbling and slightly browned on top, about 30 minutes. Remove the dish from the oven and turn on the broiler. Sprinkle the breadcrumbs evenly over the top and return to the oven until the breadcrumbs are warmed through, 1 to 2 minutes. Remove the dish from the oven and let cool for 10 minutes before serving.

BAKED SHELLS *with* ZUCCHINI, HAM, *and* AROMATIC BÉCHAMEL SAUCE

YIELD: 6 SERVINGS / ACTIVE TIME: 1 HOUR / TOTAL TIME: 1 ¾ HOURS

Savory and moist, this baked dish stars *lumaconi*, the hefty seashell-shaped pasta so large that three or four are generally all you will need for a filling dish. What makes this dish particularly appetizing is the inclusion of scamorza, an Italian semi-soft white cheese made from sheep and/or cow's milk. Elastic and stringy, it resembles a drier version of mozzarella, though its flavor is spicier and creamier. A smoked version of the same cheese is also sold, but I wouldn't recommend it for this, as the ham already adds a subtle note of smokiness. The key to success is not overboiling the pasta, so that it retains a pleasant chew once baked.

1 Heat a large skillet over medium heat for 2 to 3 minutes, then add the olive oil. When the oil begins to swirl but is not yet smoking, add the onion and a couple pinches of salt. Cook until translucent, about 10 minutes, stirring occasionally. Add the zucchini and a couple more pinches of salt and cook, stirring occasionally, until it is thoroughly cooked but not falling apart, about another 10 minutes. Remove from the heat and let cool.

2 Bring a large pot of water to a boil. Once it's boiling, add salt (1 tablespoon for every 4 cups water) and stir. Add the pasta and stir for the first minute to prevent any sticking. Cook for three quarters of the time instructed on the package. The pasta will have softened a bit but still be very firm and clearly not cooked through. Drain, rinse under cold water, and drain well again. Drain in a single layer on kitchen towels.

3 Preheat the oven to 375°F.

4 Combine the zucchini mixture, breadcrumbs, cheese, ham, 1 cup of the béchamel sauce, and pepper to taste in a large bowl. Mix gently but thoroughly. Taste and adjust for seasonings. Carefully, using a small spoon, fill each shell with the filling.

5 Spread ¾ cup of the béchamel sauce over the bottom of a baking dish large enough to accommodate the pasta in a single layer. Add the filled shells. Pour the remaining béchamel sauce over the top, making sure to cover each shell. Sprinkle evenly with the Parmigiano and cover the dish with aluminum foil.

6 Place the dish in the oven and lower the temperature to 350°F. Bake for 20 minutes. Remove the foil and bake until the tops of the shells just start to turn a golden caramel color, about 10 minutes. If desired, run it under the broiler for a couple of minutes so that it barely browns on top. Serve piping hot.

INGREDIENTS:

- 2 tablespoons extra virgin olive oil
- 1 small yellow onion, thinly sliced
- Salt
- ¾ pound large shell pasta
- 3 medium zucchini, cut into small dice
- ¼ cup plain dry breadcrumbs
- ½ pound unsmoked scamorza, scamorzarella, or mozzarella cheese, grated
- ½ pound thickly sliced honey ham, cut into small dice
- 1 recipe Aromatic Béchamel Sauce (page 742)
- Freshly ground black pepper
- 1 ½ cups freshly grated Parmigiano-Reggiano cheese

BAKED RIGATONI *with* MUSHROOMS, LEEKS, *and* SAUSAGE

YIELD: 6 TO 8 SERVINGS / ACTIVE TIME: 1 ½ HOURS / TOTAL TIME: 2 ½ HOURS

The only possible way to make this rustic rigatoni dish even more delicious would be to use fresh porcini mushrooms instead of cremini. Thankfully, the small amount of dried porcini required by the recipe adds a nice measure of that fungi's irresistible woodsy flavor. The leeks, mushrooms, and sausage need to be cooked separately, so this dish requires a bit of time to prepare, but it is worth every second of it.

1 Bring a large pot of water to a boil. Once it's boiling, add salt (1 tablespoon for every 4 cups) and stir. Add the pasta, stirring for the first minute to prevent any sticking. Cook for three quarters of the time instructed on the package. The pasta have softened a bit but still very firm and clearly not cooked through. Drain, rinse under cold water, and drain well again. Transfer to a bowl and add ½ tablespoon of the olive oil (this keeps the pasta from sticking), mix well, and cover.

2 Place the porcini in a small bowl with enough warm water to cover them and let soak until softened, about 15 minutes. Lightly run your fingers across all the pieces to dislodge any dirt or debris. Gather them in your hand and gently squeeze over the bowl to remove excess water, then chop. Strain the soaking liquid through a small paper towel-lined strainer; set aside.

3 While the mushrooms soak, prepare the leeks by trimming away the root ends and dark green leaves, keeping only the white and light green parts. With a sharp knife, cut each leek in half lengthwise and remove the two outer layers. Cut the halves vertically into thin slivers. Place them in a large bowl of water and swish them around to remove any dirt. Drain well, then transfer to a kitchen towel. Set aside.

4 Heat a large skillet over medium-low for 2 to 3 minutes, then add 2 tablespoons each of the butter and oil. Once the butter has melted and stopped foaming, add the leeks and a few good pinches of salt and stir. Raise the heat to medium and cook, stirring occasionally, until the leeks are soft, about 15 minutes. Remove from the heat and season with a few cracks of pepper and the nutmeg. Transfer to a bowl and set aside.

INGREDIENTS:

Salt

1 pound rigatoni

5 ½ tablespoons extra virgin olive oil, divided

1 ounce dried porcini mushrooms

5 large leeks

4 tablespoons (½ stick) unsalted butter, divided

Freshly ground black pepper

2 teaspoons freshly grated nutmeg

1 pound cremini mushrooms, chopped

1 pound bratwurst sausage (preferably Wisconsin style), casings removed

2 ½ cups Aromatic Béchamel Sauce (page 742)

1 ¼ cups freshly grated Parmigiano-Reggiano cheese

5 Wipe the skillet out with a paper towel and return to the stove. Heat over medium-low for 2 to 3 minutes, then add 2 tablespoons each of the butter and oil. Once the butter has melted and stopped foaming, add the porcini mushrooms and a pinch of salt and stir. Cook for 1 minute, then add the sliced cremini mushrooms along with a couple pinches of salt and turn the heat to medium-high. Cook, stirring occasionally, until the mushrooms begin to give off their liquid, about 6 minutes. Continue to cook to evaporate their liquid.

6 While the mushrooms cook, heat a medium skillet over medium-low for 2 to 3 minutes, then add the remaining tablespoon oil and increase the heat to medium-high. Once it begins to swirl on the surface but is not yet smoking, add the crumbled sausage. Cook until no longer pink and the crumbles begin to brown slightly and turn a caramel color.

Transfer, using a slotted spoon, to a bowl and set aside.

7 Preheat the oven to 350°F.

8 Once their liquid has evaporated, transfer the mushrooms to a very large bowl and add the béchamel sauce and the porcini and their strained soaking water. Mix well and taste for seasoning, adding salt, pepper, and/or nutmeg if necessary. Add the leeks and sausage, ¾ cup of the Parmigiano, and the cooked pasta. Toss to coat evenly.

9 Transfer the mixture to a large baking dish or, alternatively, divide the pasta among 10 buttered ramekins. Sprinkle with the remaining ½ cup Parmigiano. Place on the center rack and bake until it is bubbling, about 20 minutes. Run it under the broiler for a few minutes if you want the top to be nice and golden. Serve piping hot.

BRATWURST

This dish takes a new approach to bratwurst, unlike the typical charcoal grilled version you may have seen before. Historically, Wisconsin bratwurst is served in a bun with mustard, but this recipe will rival the traditional style. Mixed with rigatoni and mushrooms, the crumbled sausage will add a savory element to this dish.

PACCHERI *with* LAMB RAGÚ, BROWNED ONIONS, *and* MINT

YIELD: 6 SERVINGS / ACTIVE TIME: 1 ¼ HOURS / TOTAL TIME: 1 ¾ HOURS (LAMB RAGÚ ADDS AN ADDITIONAL HOUR OF ACTIVE TIME AND 2 TO 3 HOURS OF PASSIVE TIME)

Very large pasta tubes originating from the southern Italian regions of Campania and Calabria, *paccheri* can be treated like any ordinary boxed pasta and seasoned with tasty pasta sauces. I believe they are at their best, however, when stuffed and baked. Here I fill them with a sumptuous mixture of lamb, caramelized onions, and mint and assemble them in a springform pan, standing them up on their ends side by side. Once baked and slightly cooled, this dish is unmolded and served as a "pasta cake." Because this dish requires two fairly time-consuming components, the onions and lamb ragú, I suggest spreading out the tasks over a couple of days to make the process of preparing it more manageable.

Other recommended pasta shapes: cannelloni/manicotti

INGREDIENTS:

- 1 ½ tablespoons unsalted butter, at room temperature
- 1 cup fresh mint leaves
- Salt
- ¾ pound paccheri
- 4 cups Lamb Ragú (page 641)
- 1 ½ cups freshly grated Parmigiano-Reggiano cheese, plus extra for dusting
- 1 recipe Browned Onions (page 746)
- Freshly ground black pepper

1 Line a 12-inch springform pan by cutting a strip of parchment paper long enough to wrap around the pan and 2 inches taller than the height of the pan. Place the pan on a sheet of parchment and, using a pencil, trace around it. Cut the round out. Butter the side of the pan with half the butter and line the inner rim of the pan with the strip. (Temporarily use paper clips to fix it into place if necessary and then remove once the pasta is in the pan.) Grease the bottom of the pan with the remaining butter and place the parchment round on top. Press on the side and bottom of the pan to fix the parchment in place.

2 As the onions are browning, blanch the mint leaves. Bring a medium saucepan of water to a boil. Add the mint, blanch for 10 to 15 seconds (until their color brightens), drain in a fine-meshed strainer, and rinse under cold water. Drain well and place on a paper towel-lined plate to dry. Reserve 20 of the smallest leaves for garnish and mince the rest.

3 Bring a large pot of water to a boil. Once it's boiling, add salt (1 tablespoon for every 4 cups water) and stir. Add the pasta, stirring for the first minute to prevent any sticking. Cook for half of the time instructed on the package. The pasta will be somewhat soft but still very, very firm and clearly not cooked through. Drain, rinse under cold water to cool, and drain well again. Transfer in a single layer to a kitchen towel to air-dry.

4 Preheat the oven to 350°F.

5 Assemble the dish. Ladle in enough lamb ragú to completely cover the bottom of the prepared pan and add a generous dusting of the Parmigiano.

6 Fill the *paccheri*. You'll do this by standing them upright in the pan as you fill them with sauce. Make sure to gently press the *paccheri* down against the bottom of the pan as you fill them, as it will ensure that the sauce remains in each tube of pasta and not end up on the bottom of the pan. Using a very small teaspoon, fill each *pacchero* (singular) halfway with ragú, then add ½ teaspoon of browned onions, a small pinch of minced mint, and fill the rest of the way up with sauce. Continue in this way until you fill all the *paccheri*. Once they are filled, evenly sprinkle 1 cup of the Par-

migiano in between all the pasta tubes (this will enable the *paccheri* to stick together once the ring of the springform pan is removed). If you have sauce left, use it to fill any spaces between the *paccheri*. Sprinkle with the remaining ½ cup Parmigiano and season with pepper. Bake or cover and refrigerate for up to a day.

7 Place the pan on the center rack and bake until the tops of the pasta tubes are golden, about 40 minutes (about 10 minutes longer if you cook it straight out of the refrigerator). If you'd like it to be a bit more browned, broil it for 1 to 2 minutes. Remove from the oven and let rest for 10 minutes.

8 Unfasten the side of the pan and carefully remove it. Place 4 to 5 *paccheri* on each warmed plate, sprinkle with the reserved mint, and serve.

PASTITSIO

YIELD: 8 TO 10 SERVINGS / ACTIVE TIME: 1 ½ HOURS / TOTAL TIME: 3 ½ HOURS

The word *pastitsio* comes from the Italian word *pasticcio*, meaning "big mess," and refers to a large family of baked savory pies that spans several countries. In Italy a *pasticcio* pretty much refers to anything that's baked together, but a Greek *pastitsio* and its Egyptian counterpart *ma'karonah bil béchamel* traditionally contain meat, typically beef or lamb, pasta, an egg-enriched béchamel sauce, and, in a *pastitsio*, tomato sauce. As with any culinary classic, every Greek and Egyptian cook will tweak the ingredients, particularly the spices and aromatics, to make it their very own. *Pastitsio* is a substantial and nourishing meal that is often prepared around holidays and special occasions because it can, quite literally, feed a small army. This particular version plays up the role of the baked ziti and béchamel sauce and treats the sauce as an attractive plating mechanism that also adds savory moistness to the dish. Depending on how much of the sauce you ladle when plating the dish, you will probably have three to four cups of leftover sauce, which can be frozen and used for an easy peasy pasta dish. When making the ragù, feel free to use a dry red wine instead of milk, though I prefer to use the latter because it acts as an effective meat tenderizer. Finally, traditional *pastitsio* calls for kefalotyri, a hard, salty Greek cheese made from sheep or goat's milk. If you have a hard time sourcing it, substitute Parmigiano.

1 Prepare the meat sauce. Heat a large, deep skillet over medium heat for 2 to 3 minutes. Add the olive oil and heat for a minute or two, then add the onions and a couple pinches of salt. Stir and adjust the heat to low. Cover and cook until the onions become very soft and look translucent, about 20 minutes, stirring occasionally. Add the garlic, stir, and cook for 1 minute. Increase the heat to medium-high and add the lamb, pressing it down with a potato masher or wooden spoon to break it up. Cook, stirring occasionally, until the meat is brown and completely cooked, 8 to 10 minutes. Add the milk and cook until all the liquid has evaporated, about 15 minutes. The meat will look lighter in color and a bit plumper and feel more tender when you stir it. Add the tomatoes, thyme, spices, 1 tablespoon salt, and a

INGREDIENTS:

MEAT SAUCE:

- 2 tablespoons extra virgin olive oil
- 2 medium onions, minced
  Salt
- 4 large garlic cloves, minced
- 2 pounds ground lamb
- 2 cups whole milk
- 1 26-ounce container strained tomatoes or 1 28-ounce can tomato puree
- 4 sprigs fresh thyme
- 1 ½ teaspoons grated nutmeg
- 1 teaspoon ground cinnamon
- 10 whole cloves
  Freshly ground black pepper

BÉCHAMEL SAUCE:

- 8 tablespoons (1 stick) unsalted butter
- ½ cup + 2 tablespoons all-purpose flour
- 4 cups whole milk
- 1 ½ teaspoons freshly grated nutmeg
- 1 ½ teaspoons salt
- 1 cup freshly grated kefalotyri or Parmigiano-Reggiano cheese
- 3 large egg yolks

TO FINISH:

- 1 ½ tablespoons unsalted butter for the baking dish
  Salt
- 1 pound ziti
- 1 cup panko breadcrumbs
- ⅓ cup freshly grated kefalotyri or Parmigiano-Reggiano cheese

few good cracks of black pepper. Mix well and bring to a boil. Reduce the heat to low, cover, and cook, stirring every half hour or so, for 2 hours. If the sauce looks too watery after 1½ hours of cooking, let it cook uncovered for the last half hour. Discard the thyme sprigs and let cool.

2 Prepare the béchamel. Melt the butter in a medium saucepan over medium heat. Add the flour and whisk until a paste forms. Continue to stir and cook until the roux turns a pale shade of caramel, 6 to 8 minutes. Pour in the milk, very slowly at first (if you add it too fast, the roux will end up as little lumps floating around in the milk), whisking the whole time until all the milk has been added. Bring the sauce to a boil over medium heat, whisking frequently, then continue to cook until the sauce thickens. Remove from the heat and let cool for 10 to 15 minutes. Stir in the nutmeg, salt, and cheese..

3 Whisk the egg yolks in a medium bowl until fully combined. Slowly add one ladle of the béchamel to the eggs while whisking vigorously. Add another ladle while continuing to whisk until the mixture is slightly warm. Add the egg mixture to the béchamel sauce and whisk until fully incorporated. Lay a piece of plastic wrap directly on the surface of the sauce to keep a skin from forming.

4 Preheat the oven to 400°F. Grease the bottom and sides of a 9 x 13-inch baking dish with the butter.

5 Bring a large pot of water to a boil. Once it's boiling, add salt (1 tablespoon for every 4 cups water) and stir. Add the ziti, stirring for the first minute to prevent any sticking. Cook the pasta for three quarters of the time instructed on the package. The pasta should be somewhat soft and able to bend but still very, very firm. Drain well, transfer to the prepared baking dish along with 2 cups of the béchamel, and toss to evenly coat the ziti. (It is important to mix enough of the béchamel in with the cooked pasta because it is what is going to help keep the ziti in place when you slice portions.) Once cooled just enough to handle, arrange the ziti so that they are all lined up next to each other, side by side. Continue arranging them so that they are evenly spread throughout the dish, particularly around the edges. Spread the remaining béchamel evenly on top.

6 Put the dish on the center rack and lower the oven temperature to 375°F. Bake until the sauce is bubbling, 40 to 45 minutes. (You can also cover and refrigerate the uncooked dish for up to 2 days or freeze for up to a month; thaw it before baking and in both cases bring back to room temperature.) While the ziti bake, reheat the the meat sauce.

7 Toss the breadcrumbs and cheese together in a medium bowl. Quickly take the dish out of the oven and sprinkle evenly with the crumb mixture. Return to the center rack and turn on the broiler. Remove the dish when the crumb topping turns golden brown. Let cool for 15 minutes before plating.

8 Ladle enough of the meat sauce on the bottom of each warmed bowl and then top with a slice of *pastitsio*.

PASTA &
NOODLE DESSERTS

Kahlil Gibran once said, "In the sweetness of friendship let there be laughter, and sharing of pleasures." Such as the delectable, indulgent pleasures of pasta and noodle desserts. A touch of cheese and a sprinkle of sugar combine for a sweet, farewell kiss to end the meal.

CHOCOLATE PASTA DOUGH

YIELD: 1 ¼ POUNDS; 10 SERVINGS / **ACTIVE TIME:** 1 HOUR / TOTAL TIME 1 ½ HOURS

Do not be concerned about the amount of cocoa powder in this recipe, as the resulting dark brown pasta tastes delightfully of chocolate but contains no hint of bitterness. Best suited for long strands of delicate pasta, like *tagliatelle, taglierini*, fettuccine, and angel hair.

INGREDIENTS:

- 1 ½ cups all-purpose flour, or more as needed
- ½ cup unsweetened cocoa powder, plus more for dusting
- 3 large eggs
- 1 tablespoon water
- 1 tablespoon extra virgin olive oil

1 Mixing and kneading the dough by hand: On a flat work surface combine the flour and cocoa and form it into a mountain-like mound. Create a well in the center, then add the eggs, water, and olive oil. Using a fork or your fingertips, gradually start pulling the flour into the pool of egg, beginning with the flour at the inner rim of the well. Continue to gradually add flour until the dough starts holding together in a single floury mass, adding more water—1 tablespoon at a time—if the mixture is too dry to stick together. Once the dough feels firm and dry, and can form a craggy looking ball, it's time to start kneading.

Begin by working the remaining flour on the work surface into the ball of dough. Using the heel of your hand, push the ball of dough away from you in a downward motion. Turn the dough 45 degrees each time you repeat this motion, as doing so incorporates the flour more evenly. As you continue to knead, you'll notice the dough getting less and less floury. Eventually it will have a smooth, elastic texture. If the dough still feels wet, tacky, or sticky, dust it with flour and continue kneading. If it feels too dry and is not completely sticking together, wet your hands with water and continue kneading. Wet your hands as many times as you need in order to help the flour shape into a ball.

Knead for 8 to 10 minutes. It seems like a long time, but it accomplishes two things.

1. It creates a dough that is smooth and springy.

2. It eliminates any air bubbles and bits of unincorporated flour in the dough.

The dough has been sufficiently kneaded when it is very smooth and gently pulls back into place when stretched.

Mixing and kneading the dough with a mixer: Put the flour and cocoa in a large bowl and stir well with a spoon. Create a well in the center. Using a hand-held or stand mixer fitted with the dough (spiral) attachment, set the speed to 1 or 2 and slowly add half of the eggs and oil and the tablespoon water while mixing. Mix until the wet ingredients have been fully incorporated into the flour, then add the remaining eggs and oil and continue to mix on low speed until fully incorporated Soon the dough will begin coming together in a single floury mass. Add water—1 tablespoon at a time—if the mixture is too dry to stick together. Add flour—1 teaspoon at a time—if the mixture is too wet and sticky. Once the dough feels firm and dry, and can be formed into a coarse looking and slightly tacky ball, it's time to start kneading.

Turn the speed on the mixer to medium-high, typically notch 4, and mix for 8 to 10 minutes. The dough has been sufficiently kneaded when it is very smooth and gently pulls back into place when stretched.

2 Resting the dough: Wrap the ball of dough tightly in clear food wrap and let rest for 1 hour—2 hours is even better if you have the time. If using within a few hours, leave it out on the kitchen counter, otherwise refrigerate it (it will keep for up to 3 days.) If you do refrigerate it, however, the dough may experience some discoloration (but it won't affect the flavor at all).

3 Rolling the dough: Cut the dough into four even pieces. Set one piece on a smooth work surface and wrap up the rest in clear food wrap to prevent drying. Shape the dough into a ball, place it on the surface, and, with the palm of your hand, push down on it so that it looks like a thick pita. Using a rolling pin, roll the dough to ½ inch thick. Try as much as possible to keep the thickness and width of the dough "patty" even, as it will help the dough fit through the pasta machine more easily.

Set the pasta machine for the flat roller (no teeth) on the widest setting (typically notch 1). Now feed the dough into the rollers. As a rather rough, thick sheet of pasta comes out the other end, make sure to support it with your hand or fingers. Fold the sheet of dough over itself twice, as you would a letter, and then turn the folded dough on its side and feed it back into the machine again. Repeat this folding and feeding it back into the machine three more

times. This process is called "laminating" and it makes the dough more sturdy and manageable to handle.

Set the machine to the second-widest setting (typically notch 2) and feed the dough into the rollers. Again, support the pasta as it comes out the other side. Again fold it as you would a letter and feed it into the rollers on its short side; repeat this three more times.

Set the machine to the third-widest setting (typically notch 3) and feed the dough into the rollers. Again, support the pasta as it comes out the other side. Again fold it as you would a letter and feed it into the rollers on its short side; repeat this three more times.

Set the machine to the second-thinnest setting (typically notch 4). Feed the pasta into the rollers. Again, support the pasta as it comes out the other side. At this point, there is no need to laminate the pasta.

Set the machine to smallest setting (typically notch 5). Cut the pasta sheet in half and feed it into the rollers. Again, support the pasta as it comes out the other side.

This last setting makes pasta sheets so thin (about ¹⁄₁₆ inch/1.5 mm thick) that you can see light through them. It is ideal for filled pastas like ravioli, whose fillings can easily be overshadowed by too much surrounding dough. Also, the perfect thickness for angel hair. If you like your fettuccine, pappardelle, and tagliatelle very thin, then this is the setting for you.

The just rolled pasta will be very delicate, so be gentle handling it. If the pasta sheet is too long to easily handle, carefully cut it in half. Lightly dust each sheet with cocoa and lay it on a surface lined with wax or parchment paper. Repeat the preceding steps with the remaining pieces of dough.

4 Drying the sheets of dough: Pasta dough needs to be allowed to dry for approximately 15 minutes after it has been rolled out and before it is cut into strands or other shapes. This drying time makes the dough less sticky and easier to handle. Keep in mind that when

the pasta is very thick or wide it will need to be turned over to ensure thorough and even drying (not necessary for thin noodles). Pasta sheets are now ready to be shaped or cut according to recipe requirements.

The notable exception to this rule is if you are making stuffed pasta. In this case, not letting the dough dry is best because the slight stickiness helps the pasta adhere better and creates a better seal.

5 Drying the cut pasta before cooking: Once fresh pasta has been cut (see the individual recipes), toss it with cocoa flour and then place it on a surface lightly dusted with cocoa and allow to dry for at least 15 minutes before cooking. This drying period is impor-

tant because it allows the pasta to dry enough to become firmer and less sticky, which prevents the pasta from sticking together as it cooks (shaped pasta also holds its shape better when allowed to dry slightly before cooking). More specific drying times are indicated in individual pasta recipes. Just note that the drying process can be fickle. Depending on temperature, humidity levels, and the size of the noodles or pasta, the process may take a longer or shorter period of time than stated in the recipes. It is probably best to avoid making pasta on very humid days. If you can't avoid it, turn on the air conditioning or even a movable fan to help the air circulate more effectively.

CHOCOLATE FETTUCCINE *with* PAN-TOASTED PECAN *and* CARAMEL SAUCE

YIELD: 6 TO 8 SERVINGS / ACTIVE TIME: 15 MINUTES / TOTAL TIME: 20 MINUTES (USING ALREADY MADE PASTA)

While the combination of chocolate pasta and caramel may not exactly shout out "traditional" when it comes to pasta dishes, it certainly makes for an occasional and unexpected treat, particularly when children and chocoholics are involved. My girls loved it so much that I will keep this recipe in my back pocket for those inevitable times when, as older teens, they will temporarily hate me for one reason or another. Make the chocolate pasta yourself or shop for it online.

INGREDIENTS:

- ⅔ cup pecans
- 4 ½ tablespoons unsalted butter, divided
- Salt
- ¾ cup packed light brown sugar
- ½ cup heavy cream
- 1 teaspoon vanilla extract
- ¾ pound Chocolate Pasta Dough (page 715), rolled out to ⅟₁₆ inch and cut into fettuccine (see page 155), or store-bought
- Shaved chocolate and fresh raspberries for serving

1 Put the pecans in a small ziptop bag and gently crush into pieces using a rolling pin. Heat a small skillet for 2 to 3 minutes over low heat. Add 1 tablespoon of the butter and raise the heat to medium. Once it's melted, add the pecans and cook, stirring continuously, until you smell their toasty fragrance, about 2 minutes. Add 2 pinches of salt and mix well. Transfer to a plate and let cool. Wipe out the skillet with a paper towel.

2 Put a large pot of water on to boil for the pasta.

3 While the water heats, put the skillet you toasted the pecans in over low heat for a minute. Add 3 tablespoons of the butter, the brown sugar, cream, and a pinch of salt and raise the heat to medium-low. Cook, whisking gently, until the sauce thickens, 5 to 7 minutes. Stir in the vanilla and cook another minute. Stir in the toasted pecans. Remove from the heat and cover to keep warm.

4 When the pasta water is boiling, add salt (1 tablespoon for every 4 cups water) and stir. Add the pasta and stir for the first minute to prevent any sticking. Cook following the package (or recipe) instructions until the pasta is soft but still very firm. Right before draining the pasta, reserve ¼ cup of the pasta water. Return the empty pot to the stove. Immediately turn the heat to high and add the remaining ½ tablespoon butter and reserved pasta water. Add the drained pasta and toss until the water is absorbed. Add the sauce and cook, mixing continuously, for 1 to 2 minutes.

5 Ladle the pasta into warmed bowls and serve piping hot topped with shavings of chocolate and a handful of raspberries.

CHOCOLATE FETTUCCINE *with* PEARS, CANDIED GINGER, *and* GORGONZOLA CHEESE

YIELD: 6 TO 8 SERVINGS / **ACTIVE TIME:** 20 MINUTES / **TOTAL TIME:** 35 MINUTES (USING ALREADY MADE PASTA)

Filling enough to qualify as a main course, this fettuccine dish combines the sweet richness of ripe lush pears with pungently spicy candied ginger and sharp gorgonzola. It requires flambéing, a technique that involves spritzing food with alcohol and lighting it briefly. Often performed for dramatic effect, flambéing also infuses the rich flavor of the liquor. The recommended alcohol content for this technique is 80-proof. Weaker proofs don't contain enough alcohol to properly flambé while stronger liquors like 120-proof varieties are considered highly flammable and dangerous. You can, of course, skip the alcohol and flambéing, and the dish will still be delicious.

1 Slice the pears in half lengthwise, then into quarters; cut away the core. Cut each quarter into three lengthwise slices. Place the slices on paper towels to absorb as much surface moisture as possible so that they brown properly in the next step.

2 Heat a large skillet over medium heat for 2 to 3 minutes, then add the butter. Once it has melted and stopped foaming, turn the heat to medium-high and add the pear slices. Let them cook for 2 to 3 minutes, undisturbed, to brown properly. Gently turn them over, so as to not break them, and cook until the other side has browned, another 2 minutes.

3 Add the liquor to the pan and light with a long match, making sure to stand back from the stove when you do this (don't be alarmed by the flames, which will rise from the skillet for a few seconds). When the flames have subsided, swirl the skillet to move the pears around. Add the ginger and cook 2 more minutes. Remove from the heat, cover, and keep warm.

4 Bring a large pot of water to a boil. Once it's boiling, add salt (1 tablespoon for every 4 cups water) and stir. Add the pasta, stirring for the first minute to prevent any sticking. Cook according to the package (or recipe) instructions. Right before draining the pasta, reserve ¼ cup of the pasta water. Return the pot to the stove. Immediately turn the heat to high and add the reserved pasta water. Add the drained pasta and gorgonzola crumbles and toss. Cook, tossing continuously, until the crumbles warm and begin to melt, about 2 minutes.

5 Divide the pasta among four warmed bowls. Divide the pears among the bowls, arranging them on top of the pasta, then pour over the ginger sauce. Serve piping hot, garnished with the chocolate shavings and hazelnuts.

INGREDIENTS:

- 4 red pears (like Comice or Anjou)
- 4 tablespoons (½ stick) unsalted butter
- 2 tablespoons brandy (preferably pear), cognac, or pear vodka
- ⅓ cup chopped candied ginger
- ¾ pound Chocolate Pasta Dough (page 715), rolled out to ¹⁄₁₆ inch thick and cut into fettuccine (see page 155), or store-bought
- ⅓ cup crumbled gorgonzola cheese
- 3 tablespoons chocolate shavings for serving
- 3 tablespoons toasted chopped hazelnuts for serving

KATAIFI PUDDING

YIELD: 8 SERVINGS / ACTIVE TIME: 30 MINUTES / TOTAL TIME: 1 HOUR

Kataifi, like the more well-known baklava, is a popular Greek dessert made with an angel hair-like pastry dough by the same name. This particular recipe bypasses *kataifi* dough of using easier to find angel hair pasta. Once baked, its pudding-like consistency is a satisfying mixture of sweet chewiness and crunch.

1 Preheat the oven to 325°F and butter a 9-inch square baking dish.

2 Bring a large pot of water to a boil. When it's boiling, add salt (1 tablespoon for every 4 cups of water) and stir. Add the pasta and stir for the first minute to prevent any sticking. Cook according to the package instructions, draining the pasta 3 minutes short of the directed cooking time. You want the pasta somewhat softened but still very, very firm. Reserve ¼ cup of the pasta water.

3 Return the pot to the stove, turn the heat to high, and add 4 tablespoons of the butter and reserved pasta water. Quickly add the drained pasta and mix well. Add the cinnamon and toss until it evenly coats the pasta. Cook, mixing continuously, for 1 to 2 minutes. Remove from the heat.

4 Transfer one third of the cooked pasta to the prepared baking dish. Sprinkle over half the almonds, raisins, pistachios, and sugar. Add another third of the cooked pasta and sprinkle with the remaining almonds, raisins, pistachios, and sugar. Top with the remaining pasta. Dot the top with the remaining 3 tablespoons butter cut into pieces. Put on the center rack of the oven, reduce the temperature to 300°F, and bake for 25 minutes.

5 While it bakes, make the caramel sauce. Put the sugar in a small saucepan over low heat and stir until it melts and turns golden brown. Remove from the heat and very slowly and carefully (it will splatter a bit) add the water. Return to the heat and stir until the mixture thickens, 4 to 5 minutes.

6 At 25 minutes, remove the dish from the oven and pour the sauce evenly over the top. Return to the oven to bake until the topping is golden brown, about another 5 minutes.

7 Serve warm directly from the pan, topped with whipped cream.

INGREDIENTS:

PUDDING:

7 tablespoons unsalted butter, divided, plus more for the dish

Salt

½ pound angel hair pasta

1 teaspoon ground cinnamon

¾ cup slivered almonds

¾ cup raisins

¾ cup unshelled pistachios, shelled and chopped

3 ½ tablespoons superfine (caster) sugar

CARAMEL SAUCE AND TOPPING:

½ cup superfine (caster) sugar

¼ cup ice water

Whipped cream for serving

BAKED SWEET RAVIOLI

YIELD: 8 SERVINGS / ACTIVE TIME: 1 ½ HOURS / TOTAL TIME: 3 ½ HOURS

Good things come in small packages, and Italian ravioli are no exception. Diminutive casings of pasta dough filled with an impressively vast array of fillings, ravioli are generally associated with sumptuously savory fillings made with veal, pumpkin, pancetta, Parmigiano, spinach, ricotta, and/or nutmeg. Thankfully, their stuffings aren't limited to savory flavors, as this recipe can attest. Filled with a tantalizing cannoli-like mixture of ricotta flavored with cinnamon, vanilla, and lemon zest and studded with petite dark chocolate chips, it becomes a perfect snack or ending to a wonderful meal, especially when dusted with a little powdered sugar for good measure.

1 Prepare the filling. Two hours prior to making the filling, line a medium sieve with cheesecloth and add the ricotta. Place the sieve on top of a bowl and let drain for 2 hours in the refrigerator. When finished, squeeze the cheesecloth, in tourniquet-like fashion, to remove any remaining water and transfer the ricotta to a large bowl. Add the confectioners' sugar, vanilla, cinnamon, zest, and chocolate chips and mix with a spoon until well combined. This can be prepared up to a day ahead; cover and refrigerate.

2 Form the ravioli. Place a sheet of dough on a work surface lightly dusted with cocoa and fold it in half lengthwise. Lightly tap on the folded edge to create a guideline. Unfold the dough so that it's laying flat, the fold line now delineating two pasta strips that are still connected. Place balls of filling about the size of hazelnuts in the center of one pasta strip, spacing the mounds, from the top to the bottom of the strip, about 1¾ inches apart. Should the dough have become a little dry during this process, lightly moisten the pasta border with a fingertip dipped in water (it's helpful to have a small bowl near you for this purpose). Cover the filling with the other half of the sheet of dough. Using your fingertips, gently but firmly press down the dough around each filling mound. As you do this, try to push out any air from around the filling (this keeps the ravioli from coming apart in the water when boiling due to vapor pressure). Press one more time to ensure you have a tight seal. Using a ridged pastry cutter, slice between the mounds to create squares about 1 ¾ inches in size.

3 Set the finished ravioli on parchment paper-covered baking sheets lightly dusted with cocoa so they are not touching. Because they are being baked, they will not need to be dried like regular ravioli. Cook or cover and refrigerate for up to a day.

4 Preheat the oven to 350°F. Bake the ravioli until golden brown, about 20 minutes. Remove from the oven and let cool completely. Serve at room temperature, lightly dusted with confectioners' sugar.

INGREDIENTS:

- 2 cups ricotta cheese, preferably fresh

- ⅓ cup confectioners' sugar, plus more for dusting

- ½ teaspoon vanilla extract

- ¼ teaspoon ground cinnamon

- Grated zest of ½ lemon

- 2 ounces mini dark chocolate chips

- 1 recipe Chocolate Pasta Dough (page 715), rolled out to ¹⁄₁₆ inch thick or 5 sheets fresh pasta for lasagna, each about 9 x 12 inches

- Unsweetened cocoa powder for dusting

- Confectioners' sugar for dusting

ANGEL HAIR *in* CHOCOLATE SAUCE

YIELD: 8 SERVINGS / **ACTIVE TIME:** 15 MINUTES / **TOTAL TIME:** 30 MINUTES, PLUS SEVERAL HOURS TO CHILL

One of Italy's few authentic pasta desserts, this sweet, chocolaty treat comes straight from Orvieto, a lovely city in the central Italian region of Umbria. I discovered this recipe in Anna Del Conte's wonderful book *On Pasta*. I adapted it slightly to honor my Piedmontese roots by replacing the walnuts and blanched almonds that her recipe calls for with copious amounts of toasted hazelnuts. You can make it with regular sugar but superfine dissolves more easily and will yield a smoother sauce. Once baked, it will need to be refrigerated, though be sure to remove it from the refrigerator at least 1 hour before serving, as it is at its best when served at room temperature.

1 Combine the chocolate, sugar, and cream in a small saucepan over low heat. Stir until the chocolate melts and the mixture is smooth. Remove from the heat.

2 Heat a small skillet over medium-low heat for 2 to 3 minutes. Add the hazelnuts and raise the heat to medium. Stir continuously with a wooden spoon until they look slightly toasted and you can smell a most wonderful hazelnut aroma. Add a pinch of salt and stir. Remove from the heat and let cool.

3 Combine the hazelnuts, orange zest, honey, allspice, and a couple pinches of salt in another small saucepan over low heat and stir until the honey has melted and everything is well mixed. Remove from the heat.

4 Bring a large pot of water to a boil. Once it's boiling, add salt (1 tablespoon for every 4 cups water) and stir. Add the pasta, stirring for the first minute to prevent any sticking. Cook according to the package instructions, draining the pasta 2 minutes short of the directed cooking time. The pasta should be soft but still very firm. Right before draining the pasta, reserve ¼ cup of the pasta water.

5 Drain the pasta and return the pot to the stove. Immediately turn the heat to high and add the butter and reserved pasta water. Quickly add the drained pasta and toss. Add the chocolate sauce and cook, tossing continuously, until the pasta is completely coated with the sauce. Remove from the heat.

6 Transfer half the angel hair to a buttered 1-quart baking dish. Pour the honey mixture over it, then spread evenly with a rubber spatula. Top with the rest of the angel hair. Cover and refrigerate for 2 to 3 hours to allow the noodles to set. Remove from the refrigerator at least one hour before serving. Cut into slices and serve topped with a dollop of whipped cream if you like.

INGREDIENTS:

3 ½ ounces 70% cocoa solids dark chocolate, chopped

3 tablespoons superfine (caster) sugar

⅔ cup heavy cream

1 ¼ cups chopped hazelnuts

Salt

1 tablespoon unsalted butter

Grated zest of 1 orange

¼ cup honey

¼ teaspoon ground allspice

½ pound angel hair pasta

½ tablespoon butter, plus softened butter for the baking dish

Whipped cream for serving (optional)

FRIED ANGEL HAIR NESTS
with HONEY, DATES, *and* PISTACHIOS

YIELD: 4 TO 5 SERVINGS / ACTIVE TIME: 30 MINUTES / TOTAL TIME: 45 MINUTES

Pasta has been one of Italy's favorite dishes for centuries, so it is not surprising that resourceful Italian cooks have found ways to incorporate it into desserts. In fact, the idea of pasta as a dessert has been in existence since the Renaissance, when court chefs would top pasta, which at that time was considered an expensive and luxurious ingredient, with sugar, grated nutmeg, and Parmigiano. In time, with the country's increasing prosperity, sweetened pasta could be found in most all Italian homes. This dessert uses nests of angel hair to provide a crunchy backdrop for moist and chewy dates. Feel free to substitute the dates with the candied fruit of your choice if you so desire.

INGREDIENTS:

Salt

Sugar

½ pound angel hair pasta

1 tablespoon sesame or safflower oil

⅓ cup honey

3 tablespoons minced dates

Vegetable oil for frying

Finely crushed pistachios for serving

Ground cinnamon for serving

1 Bring a large pot of water to a boil. Once it's boiling, add salt and sugar (1 tablespoon of each for every 4 cups water) and stir. Add the pasta, stirring for the first minute to prevent any sticking. Cook according to the package instructions, draining the pasta 2 minutes short of the directed cooking time. The pasta will be soft but still very firm. Drain the pasta, rinse under cold water, and drain again. Transfer to a bowl, add the sesame or safflower oil, and toss to coat (this prevents any sticking and makes it easier to twirl it, as required in Step 3).

2 While the pasta cooks, place the honey in a microwave-friendly bowl and heat on high until it liquefies and becomes easy to pour, 20 to 30 seconds. Remove from the microwave and stir in the dates.

3 Pour enough vegetable oil in a large skillet to cover the bottom by ¼ inch. Turn the heat to medium-high. You will need to work in batches in order to cook all the pasta without crowding the skillet. Once the surface of the oil begins to swirl but is not yet smoking, add the pasta to the skillet by twirling it around a fork to create small nests. Carefully place them in the hot oil and cook until golden and crisp at the edges, 30 to 60 seconds on each side. Transfer the crisp nests to a paper towel-lined plate to absorb excess oil. Repeat until all the pasta has been cooked.

4 Arrange the crisp pasta nests on serving plates. Serve warm,drizzled with the honey-date mixture and topped with a sprinkle of pistachios and cinnamon.

PORTUGUESE VERMICELLI PUDDING

YIELD: 4 SERVINGS / ACTIVE TIME: 10 MINUTES / TOTAL TIME: 30 MINUTES

Aletria has a special place on the Portuguese Christmas dinner table. Much like rice pudding, this noodle pudding is a sweet, soothingly soft, and creamy treat that everybody loves. It is best served warm, as that is when it's at its creamiest.

1 Wash the lemon, then, using a sharp paring knife or vegetable peeler, slice off the rind. (Make the slivers as long and large as possible so that you can easily remove them from the milk mixture in the next step; try to get only yellow rind, none of the white underneath.)

2 Put the milk, vanilla, rum if using, butter, cinnamon stick, sugar, and lemon rind in a medium saucepan over medium heat and stir until the sugar dissolves. Slowly bring to a gentle boil, then reduce the heat to low, cover, and simmer for 5 minutes to let the lemon and cinnamon flavors infuse the milk.

3 Discard the lemon rind and cinnamon stick, increase the heat to medium-high, and bring the milk back to a boil. Add the pasta and cook, stirring occasionally, for 10 minutes (you want to slightly overcook the pasta in this recipe). When the pasta is very soft and most of the liquid has been absorbed, remove the pan from the heat and let cool for 10 minutes.

4 Whisk the egg yolks together in a medium bowl until fully combined. Slowly add one spoonful of the warm pasta mixture and mix well to combine. Add another spoonful and mix until well combined. Add the egg mixture back into the pasta mixture and mix until fully incorporated (if it seems too thick, add more milk, 1 tablespoon at a time, until the thickness is similar to that of rice pudding).

5 Transfer the pudding to four shallow serving bowls and let diners sprinkle their own with ground cinnamon. Serve warm, at room temperature, or cold.

INGREDIENTS:

1 lemon

2 cups whole milk

2 teaspoons vanilla extract

1 teaspoon dark rum (optional)

3 tablespoons unsalted butter

1 cinnamon stick

½ cup sugar

4 ½ ounces angel hair pasta, vvermicelli or angel hair pasta, broken into 2-inch pieces

3 large egg yolks

Ground cinnamon for serving

LOKSHEN KUGEL

YIELD: 10 TO 12 SERVINGS / ACTIVE TIME: 20 MINUTES / TOTAL TIME: 1 ½ HOURS

Lokshen kugel, a baked egg noodle-based pudding or casserole, is a traditional Ashkenazic dish and is often served on Shabbat and for Jewish holidays. To know a sweet and moist slice of kugel is to know the simplicity of lightly sweet comfort food. Very filling and versatile, you can serve it as a side dish, for breakfast, or as a nutritious snack.

1 Preheat the oven to 375°F. Butter a 9 x 13 inch baking dish.

2 Add the wine to a 4-cup Pyrex measuring cup and heat in the microwave for 30 seconds, until warm. Add the raisins and let plump up for 20 minutes. Drain them (drink the Marsala, it's darn delicious!) and place them on a paper towel to absorb any excess liquid.

3 Bring a large pot of water to a boil. Once it's boiling, add salt (1 tablespoon for every 4 cups water) and stir. Add the noodles, stirring for the first minute to prevent any sticking. Cook for three quarters of the time directed on the package. Drain, rinse under cold water to stop the cooking, and drain well again. Return the cooked noodles to the pot.

4 While the noodles cook, put the eggs, cream cheese, sour cream, cottage cheese, melted butter, sugar, and ½ teaspoon salt in a food processor and process until well blended and creamy. Have the mixture ready to add to the hot just-drained noodles.

5 Immediately add the cheese mixture to the pot with the drained noodles and toss until well combined. Add the soaked raisins and dates and toss again. Pour the noodle mixture into the prepared baking dish. If not ready to bake the kugel, cover and refrigerate for up to 48 hours (bring it back to room temperature before proceeding).

6 Place the dish on the center rack. Lower the oven temperature to 350°F. Bake until the middle of the kugel has set and the noodles sprouting out of the kugel have turned a caramel color, about 1 hour. Remove from the oven and let rest for 30 minutes before slicing. Serve warm or at room temperature.

INGREDIENTS:

- 4 tablespoons (½ stick) unsalted butter, melted, plus softened butter for the baking dish
- ½ cup Marsala wine
- ½ cup raisins
- Salt
- 1 pound wide egg noodles
- 6 large eggs
- ½ pound cream cheese, softened
- 1 ½ cups sour cream
- 1 ½ cups cottage cheese
- 1 cup sugar
- 10 large dried dates, seeds removed and minced

SWEET SEMOLINA DUMPLINGS

YIELD: 8 SERVINGS / ACTIVE TIME: 40 MINUTES / TOTAL TIME: 2 ¾ HOURS

From the northern region of Piedmont, *frittelle di semolina dolce* are lightly sweetened dumplings that are breadcrumb-crispy on the outside and moist and tender on the inside. They are traditionally served during Carnevale, an Italian celebration resembling New Orleans' Mardi Gras festivities in its exuberance and use of costumes. They are also included in one of Piedmont's culinary classics, *fritto misto*. Intimately tied to folk tradition, *fritto misto* features a wide array of fried meat. In olden days, the dish was linked to the ritual slaughter of pigs and the need to not to waste any part of the animal, so originally it included some of the funkier parts of the animal, such as the liver and lungs. Over time, with the increasing prosperity of the region, the dish began including richer ingredients, such as macaroons and sweet semolina. I have fond childhood memories of eating slices of these morsels every time I went to visit my mother's dear friend Domenica. To this day, I have not tasted a version as delicious as hers.

INGREDIENTS:

- 1 tablespoon extra virgin olive oil
- 2 lemons
- 4 cups whole milk
- ⅓ tablespoon sugar
- ¼ teaspoon salt
- 1 cup semolina flour
- 1½ cups dry unseasoned regular or fine breadcrumbs
- 2 tablespoons unsalted butter

  Grapeseed or safflower oil for frying
- 3 large eggs, well beaten

1 Line a 9 x 12-inch baking sheet with parchment paper, making sure the paper extends over the rims (to prevent any sticking). Using a pastry brush, coat the sheet with the olive oil.

2 Wash the lemons, then, using a sharp paring knife or vegetable peeler, slice off the rind. Try to get only yellow rind, none of the white underneath. Tie the zest up in a piece of cheesecloth and secure with kitchen string. Trim the top and excess string. Place the lemon sachet in a medium saucepan and add the milk, sugar, and salt. Bring to a gentle boil over medium-high heat, stirring constantly. Remove the lemon sachet and lower the heat to medium. Add the semolina to the milk in a steady stream, stirring continuously to keep lumps from forming. Cook, stirring constantly, until the mixture becomes creamy but firm, 9 to 10 minutes. Remove from the heat but keep stirring for another few minutes to help cool it down.

3 Pour the mixture onto the prepared baking baking sheet and use a rubber spatula to spread it in an even layer. Let fully cool at room temperature, then refrigerate for 2 to 3 hours or overnight (the best).

4 When ready to fry, return the sweet semolina to room temperature (if it's cold, it will affect the temperature of the oil

too much and not fry properly). Carefully flip the pan over onto a cutting board and remove the parchment. Cut into diamond shapes of a similar size. Place the breadcrumbs in a wide, shallow dish.

5 Heat a large skillet over medium heat for 2 to 3 minutes. Add the butter and enough frying oil to cover the bottom of the skillet. Increase the heat to medium-high.

6 As the butter melts and the oil heats, beat the eggs in a wide, shallow bowl. Dip the cut semolina diamonds in the beaten eggs, then dredge them gently in the breadcrumbs, completely coating them on all sides. When the surface of the oil begins swirling but the oil is not yet smoking, begin adding them to the pan a few pieces at a time. You will need to work in batches to avoid overcrowding. Fry until golden, about 2 minutes, then turn them over and cook the other side until golden, another 1 to 2 minutes. Drain the fritters on paper towels to absorb any extra oil. Repeat until all the semolina pieces are cooked. Serve piping hot or warm.

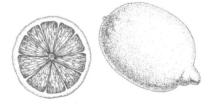

BLUEBERRY VARENYKY

YIELD: 36 *VARENYKY* / ACTIVE TIME: 1 ¼ HOURS / TOTAL TIME: 1 ½ HOURS

A staple Slavic dish for centuries, *varenyky* are filled Ukrainian dumplings shaped like half-moons. Similar to Polish pierogis, they can be filled with meat, potatoes, sauerkraut, cheese, or fruit, though, unlike pierogis, they are boiled and not sautéed in butter. This sweet fruity version makes for a most satisfying snack or dessert.

1 Prepare the filling. Put two thirds of the blueberries in a medium saucepan. Add the sugar and lemon zest and stir. Turn the heat to medium and cook, stirring a few times, until the blueberries burst and release their juice, about 4 minutes. Reduce the heat to low and simmer, uncovered, for 18 to 20 minutes, stirring frequently to prevent sticking on the bottom. The mixture should be very thick, resembling warm marmalade, at this point. Stir the reserved raw blueberries into the filling. Remove the saucepan from the heat and let cool completely.

2 Prepare the dough. Put the flour and salt in a large bowl. Add the butter and sour cream and, using a stand mixer (with a paddle attachment if you have one), mix on medium speed until the dough looks evenly crumbly, about 5 minutes (you can also mix it together by hand). Add the beaten egg to a measuring cup and add just enough water to measure ¾ cup. Beat the egg and water until well blended and pour into the bowl. Mix on medium speed until the dough holds together in a ball. If it's sticky, mix in more flour, a teaspoon at a time, until the dough is smooth and nonsticky.

3 Transfer the dough to a lightly floured work surface and, using a lightly floured rolling pin, roll it out to ⅛ inch in thickness. Using a 3-inch stamp or biscuit or cookie cutter, cut it into as many rounds as possible. Place the rounds on a lightly floured parchment paper-lined baking sheet so they don't touch. When you have as many as you can fit in a single layer, cover them with another piece of parchment, sprinkle with flour, and keep arranging the rounds in the same way.

4 Make the *varenyky*. Place a round in the palm of your slightly cupped hand and hold it so that it takes the shape of a taco. Place 1 teaspoon of filling in the center. (Make sure to keep the filling in the middle. Once sealed, you will be able to evenly distribute the filling, but to facilitate making the *varenyky*, keep the filling away from the edges.) Using your thumb and index finger,

INGREDIENTS:

FILLING:

- 1 pound fresh blueberries, picked over for stems and rinsed
- 1 tablespoon sugar

  Grated zest of 1 lemon

DOUGH:

- 3 cups all-purpose flour, or more as needed
- ½ teaspoon salt
- 4 tablespoons (½ stick) unsalted butter, at room temperature
- ⅔ cup sour cream, at room temperature
- 1 large egg, beaten

TO COOK:

  Salt
- 1 tablespoon vegetable oil

FOR SERVING:

- 5 tablespoons unsalted butter, cut into small pieces

  Confectioners' sugar

firmly pinch the edges together, starting at one end of the "taco," to form a tight seal. You'll want this seal, or seam, to be between ¼ and ½ inch wide. Continue pinching and working your way to the other end until finished. Pat the sealed *varenyky* gently to evenly distribute the filling. Check for holes (patch them with a little bit of dough) and make sure the seal is tight. If you have any filling leftover, save it. Cook or cover and refrigerate for up to 2 days. Or freeze them on the baking sheet, transfer to freezer bags, and freeze for 3 to 4 weeks. There is no need to thaw; they will just take an extra few minutes to cook.

5 Bring a large pot of water to a boil. Once it's boiling, add salt (1 tablespoon for every 4 cups water) and the oil (to prevent any sticking) and stir. You will need to cook the *varenyky* in batches. Using a rounded slotted spoon, lower the *varenyky* into the boiling water. Alternatively, you can gently plop them

in the water, though it increases the risk of tearing them. Gently stir for the first minute to keep them from sticking to the bottom. When the dumplings float to the surface, cook them for another 3 minutes.

6 While the first batch of *varenyky* boils, melt the butter in a microwave or over low heat. If you have any leftover blueberry filling, also warm that up very gently.

7 Remove the *varenyky* from the water using a large slotted spoon, and let them drain for a few seconds over the pot. Transfer to a warmed platter, top them with a tablespoon or so of melted butter, and gently toss. Tent loosely with aluminum foil to keep them warm while you cook the remaining dumplings.

8 Serve the *varenyky* piping hot dusted with confectioners' sugar and topped with warm leftover blueberry filling (if any).

USEFUL RECIPES

These preparations are called for in multiple recipes throughout the book. Workhorse preparations to the core, they lend indispensable flavor to the dishes they touch.

BÉCHAMEL SAUCE

YIELD: 2 ½ CUPS / ACTIVE TIME: 5 MINUTES / TOTAL TIME: 15 MINUTES

When properly prepared, béchamel adds a creamy texture, a light buttery taste, and moistness to baked dishes and stretches or renews leftovers (I've been known to make some when I only have enough leftover Bolognese sauce for two people in my family of four.) I see many recipes that insist that the milk used in making béchamel be hot when added to the mixture of butter and flour, lest you get lumps. I don't find that to be the case at all. For the past 20 years I've been using milk right out of the refrigerator and getting creamy and consistent results. What I find makes a difference is adding just enough milk to the roux (butter and flour) to completely cover the bottom of the pot by a half inch and stirring vigorously until incorporated. Then I add the rest of the milk all at once and stir continuously for the first minute.

INGREDIENTS:

- 8 tablespoons (1 stick) unsalted butter
- ½ cup all-purpose flour
- 4 cups whole milk
- ½ teaspoon freshly grated nutmeg
- Salt and freshly ground white pepper

1 Melt the butter in a medium saucepan over medium heat (don't let it brown at all). Add the flour all at once and quickly whisk until the mixture becomes velvety smooth. Whisking all the while, cook the flour and butter mixture (called roux) for about 5 minutes. You will notice that it will start to foam slightly as it bubbles. Continue whisking. Eventually the foaming will subside and the mixture will turn golden in color.

2 Pour in ½ cup or so of the milk and whisk vigorously until you've loosened the thick flour mixture. Add the rest of the milk, whisking constantly. Within minutes the mixture will start to thicken. Add the nutmeg, salt to taste, and white pepper if you like. Mix thoroughly and use immediately or let cool, cover, and refrigerate for up to 2 days. Bring back to room temperature before using.

THE ORIGINS OF BÉCHAMEL

The Italians and French each want to take credit for inventing béchamel, understandably. Historical records on the subject are spotty, which means we'll never really know for sure, though they do offer two likely scenarios. The first suggests that the chefs in the kitchens of the court of Louis XIV created it, the second that its birthplace was Tuscany and that it was introduced to France by Italian noblewoman Caterina de' Medici of Florence. Of the two, my favorite is Caterina, who seemed like quite the pragmatist. Married off to French royalty for political gain, this wealthy child bride arrived in France with full-on insurance against home sickness. In addition to her governess, she brought several pastry chefs, three cooks, and a gelato-maker. Imagine! She also brought the flavors and scents of Tuscan cuisine along with the entourage. One specialty in particular was béchamel, though at the time it had the unfortunate name of *colla* or glue. Not surprisingly, the name was changed to béchamel, in all likelihood after a French courtier and patron of the arts by the same name.

AROMATIC BÉCHAMEL SAUCE

YIELD: 3 CUPS / ACTIVE TIME: 10 MINUTES / TOTAL TIME: 30 MINUTES

While regular béchamel sauce, made from butter, flour, and milk, adds a creamy texture, a light buttery taste, and moistness to everything it touches, aromatic béchamel brings the added subtle flavor of mild-tasting white onions to pasta dishes.

INGREDIENTS:

- **4** cups whole milk
- **2** bay leaves
- **½** medium white onion
- **10** black peppercorns
- **8** tablespoons (1 stick) unsalted butter
- **½ c** up all-purpose flour

Salt and freshly ground white pepper

1 Put the milk, bay leaves, onion half, and peppercorns in a medium saucepan over low heat. Stirring it occasionally, let it heat just until it's about to boil, then take it off the heat. Let it cool for 20 minutes so the flavors of the bay leaves, onion, and peppercorns can infuse the milk. Strain.

2 Melt the butter in a medium saucepan over medium heat (don't let it brown at all). Add the flour all at once and quickly whisk until the mixture becomes velvety smooth. Whisking all the while, cook the flour and butter mixture (called roux) for about 5 minutes. You will notice that it will start to foam slightly as it bubbles. Continue whisking. Eventually the foaming will subside and the mixture will turn golden in color.

3 Pour in ½ cup or so of the milk and whisk vigorously until you've loosened the thick flour mixture. Add the rest of the milk, whisking constantly. Within minutes the mixture will start to thicken. Add salt to taste, and white pepper if you like. Mix thoroughly and use immediately or let cool, cover, and refrigerate for up to 2 days. Bring back to room temperature before using.

THAI PEPPER HOT SAUCE

YIELD: ABOUT 2 CUPS / ACTIVE TIME: 10 MINUTES / TOTAL TIME: 40 MINUTES

This recipe yields a sauce that is similar to sriracha, though a little thinner and smoother, with a slightly deeper flavor. This is my go-to sauce for any Asian-style food and pizza. Yes, pizza! If you like hot sauce on your pizza, I got the goods right here!

INGREDIENTS:

- 1 pound (about 4 cups) Thai chile peppers
- 4 garlic cloves, unpeeled
- ¼ cup packed brown sugar
- 1 teaspoon hoisin sauce
- ¾ cup water
- ¾ cup rice vinegar
- ¾ cup cider vinegar

1 Preheat the oven to 300°F. Line two baking sheets with parchment paper and arrange the chiles on them in a single layer. Add the garlic cloves. Bake, turning the chiles over 3 to 4 times during that time to promote even roasting, until the skins begin to slightly char. Remove from the oven and let cool. Squeeze the roasted flesh out of the garlic peels and, wearing disposable plastic gloves, cut the stems from the chiles.

2 Put the chiles, garlic, sugar, hoisin, and water in a blender or food processor and blend until smooth. Add both the vinegars and blend to combine.

3 Pour the mixture into a fine-meshed strainer set over a medium saucepan and strain. Turn the heat to medium-high and heat until the sauce registers 180°F on an instant-read thermometer.

4 Remove from the heat and immediately (and carefully) pour into heatproof bottles. Let cool, then cover and refrigerate for up to 6 months.

GINGERY RED PEPPER SAUCE

YIELD: 1 ¾ CUPS / ACTIVE TIME: 10 MINUTES / TOTAL TIME: 10 MINUTES

Beautiful on the plate and packed with flavor. Makes a nice dipping sauce for dumplings.

1 Put all the ingredients in a food processor and pulse into a smooth puree.

2 Transfer to a small saucepan and cook over medium heat until it has the consistency of a nice, thick tomato sauce, about 20 minutes. You can prepare this sauce in advance and refrigerate for up to 3 days.

INGREDIENTS:

2 red bell peppers, seeded and roughly chopped

1 1-inch piece fresh ginger, peeled and roughly chopped

4 garlic cloves, peeled

3 tablespoons raw or regular sugar

2 generous tablespoons tomato paste

1 tablespoon extra virgin olive oil

1 tablespoon cider vinegar

1 tablespoon soy sauce

BROWNED ONIONS

YIELD: 1 CUP / ACTIVE TIME: ABOUT 50 MINUTES / TOTAL TIME: ABOUT 50 MINUTES

Browned onions add a deep, savory, and subtly sweet flavor to any dish. Consider it an umami boost, if you will. Depending on the amount of these mouthwatering onions you will need for a given recipe, you may have leftovers, which will feel like a gift when you add them to grilled meats and sandwiches.

INGREDIENTS:

- 5 tablespoons extra virgin olive oil

- 2 large red onions, thinly sliced (3 cups)

- Salt and freshly ground black pepper

- 1 tablespoon balsamic vinegar

1 Heat the largest skillet you have over medium heat for 2 to 3 minutes. Add the olive oil and turn the heat up to medium-high. Once the oil begins to swirl on the surface but before it starts to smoke, add the onion slices. Stir them gently to make sure all the onions are thoroughly coated in oil. Cook until they begin to soften and start to release some of their moisture to the pan, about 5 minutes.

2 Reduce the heat to medium-low and cook, uncovered, until the onions are deeply browned and slightly sticky, about 40 minutes. Be sure to check on the onions and give them a stir every 10 minutes or so, but no more than that. The onions need to have direct contact with the heat to brown properly, so you don't want to stir them too much. Also, the exact cooking time can vary depending on the size of the onions, their moisture and sugar content, and their age. That's why it's important to check on them regularly as they cook. During this process, reduce the heat if the onions are sizzling or in danger of scorching or raise the heat if they haven't browned at all after 15 minutes or so. The onions are perfectly done when they have a molasses-like color and flavor.

3 Stir in ¼ teaspoon each of salt and pepper and the vinegar. Taste for seasoning and add more salt and/or pepper if needed.

CRISPY SHALLOTS

YIELD: ABOUT 2 CUPS / ACTIVE TIME: 15 TO 20 MINUTES / TOTAL TIME: 15 TO 20 MINUTES

A common garnish in Indian and Asian cooking, crispy shallots add subtle and savory sweetness and a pleasant crunch to finished dishes. If you're not in the mood to make them yourself, you can purchase them in Indian food stores, much like French's fried onions. For best results, use a neutral flavored oil to prepare them. While I love olive oil and use it in so much of my cooking, I find its flavor too strong for this condiment. The key to creating perfectly crispy shallots is to have all the ingredients at room temperature when you start preparing them.

INGREDIENTS:

1   cup sunflower, safflower, or non-GMO canola oil

2   cups (about 9 ounces) thinly sliced shallots

1   Before you start, set a fine-meshed strainer over a heatproof bowl and place next to the stove so that it is handy when the shallots are ready to be drained.

2   Put the sliced shallots in a large skillet set on a cold burner. Break them up with your fingers to separate them into rings and slivers. Add the oil and mix around with a fork to continue separating the shallot slices as much as possible. Turn the heat to medium. Cook, stirring occasionally, until the shallots start to gently sizzle, about 5 minutes. Lower the heat to medium-low and continue to cook, stirring every couple of minutes to ensure even cooking, as the shallot slices at the edge of the pan tend to cook faster than those in the middle. Cook until the shallots are golden, 8 to 10 minutes. If they aren't at that point, reduce the heat to low and cook until they are, which should take another 2 to 3 minutes.

3   Once the shallots are golden, quickly and carefully pour the skillet contents into the prepared strainer. Allow both the shallots and oil to cool completely and place them in two separate airtight containers and refrigerate. The shallot oil will keep for 2 months and the crispy shallots for 3 weeks.

CHICKEN SCHMALTZ

YIELD: ½ TO ¾ CUP / **ACTIVE TIME:** 30 MINUTES / **TOTAL TIME:** 2 HOURS

I grew up nestled in the comforting cuisine of Italy, so I didn't discover the magical flavoring potion known, quite unbecomingly, as schmaltz until I moved to New York City in my early twenties. One of the first friends I made, an avid cook with a kitchen the size of a dishwasher, taught me how to make her grandmother's version and it is so flavorful that I have never felt the need to expand my schmaltz repertoire. It is wonderfully simple to boot. While not the most appetizing thing to look at in its jar, it sure contributes a wallop of flavor to anything it touches, like matzo balls, latkes (potato pancakes), savory kugel (baked egg noodle pudding), and pan-fried potatoes and onions. One final note: This recipe's yield depends largely on how lean or fatty your chicken is.

An added boon here is that you also end up with delicious chicken broth you can use to cook your matzo balls.

INGREDIENTS:

- 1 **4-pound whole chicken**
- 1 **small onion, peeled and cut in half**
- 2 **garlic cloves, peeled**
- 1 **celery stalk, broken in two**
- 3 **sprigs fresh parsley**
- 2 **teaspoons salt**
- 1 **small onion, minced**

1 Put all the ingredients except the minced onion in a stockpot and add enough water to cover everything, typically between 2 to 3 quarts of water. Bring to a slow boil over medium-low heat and let continue to bubble until the meat falls off the bones, 3 to 4 hours. Let cool enough so you can strain through a fine-meshed strainer without burning yourself.

2 Pick the meat from the bones. Save the skin in a small bowl. Cover the broth. Refrigerate everything.

3 The next day, the fat will have solidified on top of the broth and you can skim it off with a spoon and transfer it to a small saucepan, along with the reserved skin and the onion. Cook over low heat until the liquid is golden and the pieces of skin and onion look caramelized, about 1½ hours. Strain it through a cheesecloth-lined strainer directly into an airtight container. It will keep in the refrigerator for up to a week or the freezer up to 3 months.

CAPON *or* CHICKEN STOCK

YIELDS: 2 QUARTS / ACTIVE TIME: 30 MINUTES / TOTAL TIME: 2 ½ HOURS

Capons are a special strain of chicken that are neutered, which prevents the bird from going through puberty and becoming tough as it grows over 12 weeks. They have the more delicate flavor of younger chickens but are significantly larger, generally 6 to 10 pounds instead of the average 3 to 5 pounds for their younger counterparts. If capon is hard to find in your area, you can use regular chicken and still make a delicious homemade broth. This stock freezes beautifully for up to 3 months, so you can always have it on hand when a dish you're preparing requires an especially flavorful stock.

INGREDIENTS:

1 8-pound capon or 2 4-pound chickens, cut into pieces and excess fat removed

2 carrots, roughly chopped

2 garlic cloves, unpeeled, lightly smashed

1 onion, roughly diced

4 stalks celery, coarsely chopped

2 plum tomatoes, coarsely chopped

½ tablespoon tomato paste

1 tablespoon black peppercorns

Stems from 1 bunch fresh parsley

Salt

1 Put all the ingredients, except the salt in a stockpot and cover with cold water. Bring to a boil over medium-high heat, reduce the heat to low, cover, and cook for 2 hours, at which point the meat will be tender. As the stock cooks, periodically skim off any foam that forms on the surface. Remove the stock from the heat and let cool.

2 Remove the poultry pieces with a strainer or large slotted spoon. Pour the broth and vegetables into a fine-meshed strainer set over a large bowl. Press on all the solids with the back of a large spoon, or with your hand, to squeeze as much liquid from the vegetables as possible. Taste for seasoning and add salt as needed.

3 Cover and refrigerate overnight to allow the fat to solidify on the surface. The next day, remove the hardened fat with a slotted spoon. The stock will keep in the refrigerator up to 3 days or freezer for 3 months.

MIXED MEAT STOCK

YIELD: 2 QUARTS / ACTIVE TIME: 20 MINUTES / TOTAL TIME: 4 HOURS

"Good broth will resurrect the dead," goes an old South American proverb. Indeed. A rich stock made with plenty of bones is the magic elixir for making cure-all warming soups and sauces with a delicious depth of flavor. Best of all, if freezes beautifully for up to 3 months.

1 Preheat the oven to 450°F. Completely line, including the raised sides, a rimmed baking sheet with aluminum foil (for easy clean up). Then line the bottom with a sheet of parchment paper. Place the beef bones on the sheet and place on the center rack. Roast until browned, 40 to 45 minutes.

2 Add the roasted bones and remaining ingredients to a stockpot. Be sure to scrape the brown bits on the parchment paper directly into the stockpot, as they are packed with flavor. Fill with enough water to cover everything. Bring to a gentle boil over medium heat, then adjust the heat to low and cook for 3 hours. Remove from the heat, let cool, and strain using a large fine sieve. Then strain again, this time lining the sieve with cheesecloth. Cover and refrigerate overnight.

3 Skim the fat off the top of the stock (by now it should have congealed into a hard cap that is easy to remove in pieces). It will keep for up to 5 days in the refrigerator.

INGREDIENTS:

- **3** pounds beef bones, with a little meat attached
- **3** pounds chicken backs, necks, and wings
- **1** celery stalk
- **1** leek, greens trimmed and discarded, split and washed
- **1** tablespoon tomato paste
- **8** sprigs fresh parsley
- **3** garlic cloves, unpeeled and lightly smashed
- **2** bay leaves
- **1** teaspoon black peppercorns
- **4** cloves
- **2 ½** quarts water

DASHI

YIELD: ABOUT 1 QUART / **ACTIVE TIME:** 5 MINUTES / **TOTAL TIME:** 10 MINUTES

One of the culinary cornerstones of Japanese cooking, *dashi* is a clear, simple broth that tastes like the essence of the sea and comes together in about 10 minutes. In addition to water, it requires only two ingredients. The first is the kelp seaweed called kombu, whose surface crystals of glutamic acid gives the broth much of its savoriness. You can find it in the macrobiotic section of your local natural food store. Be sure not to boil the kombu, as it will impart an unpleasantly slimy texture and bitter flavor to the broth. The second are bonito flakes. Known as *katsuobushi* in Japanese, they are finely shaved flakes of dried bonito fish and add an ocean-like flavor.

INGREDIENTS:

4   cups water

1   4-inch piece kombu

1   cup loosely packed dried bonito flakes (*katsuobushi*)

1   Add the water and kombu to a medium saucepan and slowly bring to a gentle simmer over medium heat.

2   Immediately remove the pan from the heat, add the bonito flakes, and stir. Let steep for 5 minutes.

3   Strain through a fine-meshed strainer and discard the kombu and bonito or store in the refrigerator for up to a week and make another batch of *dashi* with it, though the *dashi* will be weaker. Use the *dashi* or cool, transfer to an airtight container, and refrigerate for up to 1 week, or store in the freezer for up to 3 months.

TOMATO-SESAME DIPPING SAUCE

YIELD: 1 CUP/ **ACTIVE TIME:** 10 MINUTES / **TOTAL TIME:** 10 MINUTES

1 Bring a small saucepan of water to a boil. Blanch the tomatoes in the boiling water for 1 minute. Use tongs to remove them to a cutting board and let cool until you can handle, then remove their skins. Cut them into quarters, remove the seeds, and roughly chop.

2 Heat a small saucepan over medium-low heat for 2 to 3 minutes. Add the oils and let them warm up for a minute. Add the onion, garlic, pepper flakes, chili powder, and a pinch of salt. Cook until the onion starts to soften, about 6 minutes. Add the tomatoes, water, and soy sauce, bring to a boil, and reduce the heat to medium-low. Simmer until the pieces of tomato are soft and the sauce has thickened, about 15 minutes.

3 Stir in the vinegar and black pepper to taste. Purée the mixture with an immersion blender or in a food processor or blender. Transfer to a serving bowl and serve at room temperature. You can prepare this sauce in advance and refrigerate for up to 3 days.

INGREDIENTS:

3 very ripe plum tomatoes

1 tablespoon toasted sesame oil

1 tablespoon peanut oil

1 small red onion, roughly diced

2 garlic cloves, roughly chopped

½ teaspoon red pepper flakes

¼ teaspoon chili powder

Salt

¼ cup water

1 ½ tablespoons soy sauce

2 tablespoons rice vinegar

Freshly ground black pepper

KOREAN DIPPING SAUCE

YIELD: ABOUT ½ CUP / **ACTIVE TIME:** 5 MINUTES / **TOTAL TIME:** 5 MINUTES

Mix all the ingredients together in a small bowl, stirring until the sugar dissolves. Use or cover and refrigerate for up to 2 hours. Allow to come to room temperature before serving.

INGREDIENTS:

3 tablespoons soy sauce

1 ½ tablespoons water

½ tablespoon rice vinegar or 1 tablespoon cider vinegar

½ tablespoon toasted sesame oil

½ tablespoon sugar

¼ teaspoon freshly ground black pepper

1 garlic clove, crushed

3 scallions, trimmed and chopped

METRIC EQUIVALENTS

Weights
1 ounce = 28 grams
4 ounces (¼ pound) = 113 grams
8 ounces (½ pound) = 227 grams
16 ounces (1 pound) = 454 grams

Volume Measures
¼ teaspoon = 1.25 ml
½ teaspoon = 2.5 ml
1 teaspoon = 5 ml
1 tablespoon (3 teaspoons) = 1/2 fluid ounce = 15 ml
2 tablespoons = 1 fluid ounce = 29.5 ml
¼ cup (4 tablespoons) = 2 fluid ounces = 59 ml
⅓ cup (5 ⅓ tablespoons) = 2.6 fluid ounces = 79 ml
½ cup (8 tablespoons) = 4 fluid ounces = 118 ml
⅔ cup (10 ⅔ tablespoons) = 5 1/3 fluid ounces = 158 ml
¾ cup (12 tablespoons) = 6 fluid ounces = 177 ml
1 cup (16 tablespoons) = 8 ounces = 237 ml

Length Measures
¹⁄₁₆ inch = 1.5 mm
1/8 inch = 3 mm
¼ inch = 6.25 mm
½ inch = 1.25 cm
¾ inch = 2 cm
1 inch = 2.5 cm

Temperatures Equivalents

°F	°C	Gas Mark
250	120	½
275	135	1
300	150	2
325	165	3
350	175	4
375	190	5
400	205	6
425	220	7
450	230	8
475	245	9
500	260	10

ADDITIONAL READINGS

For further reading, find below some of the inspirations behind Cosmo's cooking and this cookbook.

BOOKS

Oretta Zanini de Vita
Encyclopedia of Pasta

This reference book captures the history of pasta, including the geography, key ingredients, and preparation of authentic Italian pasta. This is a great read for anyone who wants to dig deeper into one of America's beloved cuisines.

Oretta Zanini de Vita
Pasta the Italian Way: Sauces & Shapes

This work is more than just a cookbook—it is a guide into the Italian way of cooking, serving, and eating pasta. Here you can learn how to become an authentic Italian cook from the comfort of your home.

Marc Vetri
Mastering Pasta

Continue your study of fresh handmade pasta with Vetri's cookbook, containing over 100 recipes, with more than 30 varieties of pasta dough. In *Mastering Pasta*, Vetri shares his wealth of knowledge from 10 years of research.

Leela Punyaratabandhu
Simple Thai Food

This book contains 100 authentic Thai food recipes inspired by street food, classic Thai dishes, and family recipes. Punyaratabandhu provides an overview of key Thai food ingredients and tools for cooking, along with varied recipes, desserts, and more.

Andrea Quynhgiao Nguyen
Asian Dumplings: Mastering Gyoza, Spring Rolls, Pot Stickers, and More

Nguyen provides a comprehensive guide to the varied techniques of how to shape, fill, cook, and serve dumplings in this cookbook. A beginner to Asian dumpling cooking will be delighted to also find information on key ingredients, necessary equipment, and more.

Kantha Shelke
Pasta and Noodles: A Global History

Shelke digs deep into pasta's past, making this work much more than a cookbook. Here you will not only find a variety of recipes, but you will also learn about fascinating folklore, the evolution of pasta, and other little known facts.

Silvano Serventi and Francoise Sabban
Pasta: The Story of a Universal Food

Pasta delves into the history of the titular cuisine, exploring its origins and evolution. Serventi and Sabban debunk myths and explain how pasta grew to have the global presence that it maintains today.

Anna Del Conte
On Pasta

On Pasta is complete with 120 recipes that originate from all regions of Italy, and includes dishes with a variety of focuses: meat, dairy, vegetables, soups, stuffed pasta and baked pasta. Del Conte also includes an overview of the history and different types of pasta included in this book, and how to properly cook pasta for a novice in the kitchen.

Harold McGee
On Food and Cooking: The Science and Lore of the Kitchen

This is a classic for anyone who wants to learn about the science and history of food and cooking. McGee explains key information about ingredients and cooking methods for anyone from a novice to an experienced chef.

Aliza Green
Making Artisan Pasta: How to Make a World of Handmade Noodles, Stuffed Pasta, Dumplings, and More

Become an artisan pasta maker yourself with Green's easy to follow instructions on rolling, shaping, and stuffing dough for dozens of styles of pasta. Learn the best ingredients, techniques, and recipes for your pasta, including how to make your own hand-stretched dough.

Jenn Louis
Pasta By Hand: A Collection of Italy's Regional Hand-Shaped Pasta

Explore over 65 recipes from the regions of Italy, including gnocchi, orecchiette, spatzli, and more. Louis also offers the best sauces to pair with your hand-shaped pasta and dumplings.

Francine Segan
Pasta Modern: New & Inspired Recipes from Italy

Segan's cookbook stands out amongst the rest of the works on this list that are rooted in the history and tradition of pasta. Instead, Segan offers 100 recipes that highlight and celebrate the new, unusual, and contemporary pasta dishes being made today.

Micol Negrin
Rustico: Regional Italian Country Cooking

Negrin delves into each of Italy's 20 regions, providing a narrative of the region's culinary influences, its local lifestyle, and so much more. Each region has its own chapter including 10 recipes that encompass an entire meal: from appetizers to desserts and everything in between.

Yotam Ottolenghi
Plenty: Vibrant Vegetable Recipes from London's Ottolenghi

Ottolenghi explores the diverse food culture of London in *Plenty*. Here you will find 120 delicious recipes, all vegetarian, and all based on the freshness of the dish.

Elizabeth Raffald
The Experienced English Housekeeper

Though published in 1769, this book stands the test of time, and is cited by many well-known chefs today. Raffald includes 900 recipes in this piece, with easy to follow instructions.

BLOGS

Serena Cosmo
Rustic Plate
rusticplate.com

If you haven't had enough of this cookbook yet, stop by our author's own blog! Here she focuses on rustic cuisine that is comforting, simple, and appealing to all family members. She has tried all of her own recipes, and provides easy to follow and thorough instructions.

Leela Punyaratabandhu
She Simmers
shesimmers.com

Explore Punyaratabandhu's favorite Thai recipes on her blog, including a multitude of rice dishes, Pad Thai varieties, salads and vegetables, desserts, and more. She even includes information on ingredients and helpful equipment, an assortment of "how to's", and blog posts on different restaurants and bakeries she recommends.

Simona Carini
Briciole
pulcetta.com

When visiting *Bricole*, you will find recipes for breads, pizzas, pastas, cured meats, desserts, and more. Carini's blog is a place where she embraces her Italian heritage, and shares her stories and delicious meals with her readers.

The Leung Family
The Woks of Life
thewoksoflife.com

This blog began as a way to reconnect a family of four when the parents, Bill and Judy, relocated to Beijing, and the daughters, Sarah and Kaitlin, stayed back in the United States. They used this site as a way to share meals, and now it is a great place for anyone looking to learn authentic Chinese dishes. Their recipes include a variety of appetizers, beverages, bread, breakfast, chicken, beef, seafood, eggs, tofu, baked goods, take out, and much more.

Alexandra Stafford
Alexandra's Kitchen
alexandracooks.com

Stafford shares simple and seasonal dishes on her blog Alexandra's Kitchen. Here you can learn how to make your own bread, and cook a wide variety of appetizers, soups, and dinners.

Frank Fariello
Memorie di Angelina
memoriediangelina.com

Fariello's food advice derives from years of his Italian grandmother's cooking, and the ten years he spent in Rome exploring the food and culture. The emphasis of the blog is to educate readers on the technique and experience of authentic Italian cooking through many enticing recipes.

GLOSSARY OF COOKING TERMS

Al dente: pasta and rice that is tender, but firm, and ready to be drained. Vegetables prepared al dente tend to keep more nutrients.

Arrabbiata: translates to "angry." Typically penne or pasta in a spicy tomato sauce. Also, a term for cooking rabbit, chicken, and other meats in a skillet with spices.

Arrowroot: a powdered root that is similar to cornstarch and used for thickening sauces.

Baccala: dried or salted cod, usually has to soak for several days before cooking.

Béchamel sauce: a creamy sauce used in baked dishes, usually alongside Bolognese sauce.

Bed: a layer of greens, vegetables, or starch that a dish is served on.

Blanche: to partially cook vegetables in boiling water. This helps them peel easier or soften.

Blend: to combine ingredients until smooth.

Boil: to cook pasta or other ingredients in boiling water.

Bolognese: relating to the city, Bologna. Also, refers to classic Emilian dishes made of ground beef, tomato, onion, and herbs, such as ragù.

Bone: to remove bones from fish or meat.

Bouillon cubes and powder: cubes used for seasoning, made from concentrated stock. Typically used to flavor sauces, gravies, meat, vegetables, and soups.

Braise: to stew in a covered container over a long period of time. This technique is best used for red meat and poultry.

Bread crumbs: small pieces of bread. Meat, fish, or vegetables are dipped in beaten eggs, and then coated with bread crumbs before frying.

Broil: to cook meat, fish or vegetables through direct contact, similar to grilling.

Broth: stock made from meat, fish, or vegetables.

Brown: to cook meat or vegetables until they reach a golden brown color. In a pan, cook in oil or butter over low heat. In an oven, cook until top of dish is desired color.

Caramelize: to create caramel by the process of heating sugar with water until it melts. This technique can also be used with food, such as onions.

Chitarra: a rectangular pasta maker used for square-shaped spaghetti alla chitarra (also known as maccheroni alla chitarra).

Chop: to cut ingredients with a knife.

Clean: refers to the preparation of food prior to cooking. For example, to gut a fish, or to rinse shellfish in water to wash away sand.

Cook over low heat: to cook ingredients over the lowest setting of heat. For example, stews are cooked over low heat to reach the desired level of tenderness.

Cover: to put a lid or foil over a pot, pan, or dish. This practice can help boil water and cook food faster, or prevent food from becoming dry.

Crush: to flatten or grind ingredients, such as garlic or pepper.

Curry: refers to a sauce made from a variety of spices and turmeric, originating from India. Also refers to a meat or vegetable dish cooked in curry.

Deep-fry: to immerse ingredients in hot oil or fat, cooked over high heat.

Dice: to cut ingredients into small, cube-shaped pieces.

Dilute: to add water, or any other appropriate liquid, to a sauce or seasoning to make it thinner.

Dissolve: the act of putting a dry ingredient in a liquid to make a solution. For example, putting salt in water to create salt water.

Durum: a type of hard wheat. Found in arid regions, durum produces the flour used in most pasta.

Dust: to lightly coat, typically with flour. Ingredients can be dusted prior to frying, or cooking surfaces can be dusted to avoid dough sticking to them.

Evaporate: to dry out. In cooking, evaporating an additional liquid can add extra flavor to the meal.

Fill: a chocolate, cream, custard, or jelly used to fill a puff or to use between layers of a cake.

Fillet: to use a knife to separate and remove the fleshy piece of a fish from its bones.

Flambé: to spritz food with alcohol and ignite it briefly to burn off the alcohol. Suggested alcohol content is 80-proof for this technique.

Flavor: to add herbs or vegetables to enhance taste and aroma to a dish.

Fry: to cook ingredients in oil or butter over heat.

Garnish: a decorative technique to make a dish more appealing. Typical garnishes are herb sprigs and lemon slices.

Grease: to coat the baking dish, pan, or other cooking surface with oil or butter to prevent the ingredients from sticking to the dish or pan.

Grind: to use a food processor or grinder to crush ingredients finely. Meat can be grinded for ground meat, or spices can be ground to make a fine powder.

Heaping: when making pasta, assembling flour into a pyramid like shape with a hollow center. After heaping, add the egg into the hollow center.

Julienne: to cut vegetables into thin sticks.

Knead: to work flour that has been moistened with water, or other solid and liquid mixtures, into dough with hands or an electric mixer.

Lard: fat from a pig's belly, used in cooking. Or, the process of inserting fat, bacon, pancetta, or cured ham into a piece of meat prior to cooking, which tenderizes and seasons the meat.

Line: to cover the surface of a cooking container with a layer of wax or parchment paper, to prevent sticking; or, with a layer of pastry, vegetables, or other ingredients to be set for a filling.

Marinate: to immerse meat, fish, or other food in a sauce made typically of oil, vinegar, herbs and spices. Marinating can take as few as 30 minutes, or up to 3 hours, depending on the desired level of flavor and tenderization.

Pancetta: cured pork from the belly of a pig. It is similar to bacon, but it is not smoked.

Poach: a method of cooking eggs. Crack eggs into boiling water, and let them cook for a few minutes, longer if a set yolk is desired. Poach fish, meat, and poultry by lightly simmering them in water or stock.

Prosciutto: Uncooked, dry-cured ham, typically produced in Parma. In Italy, all varieties of cured ham are called prosciutto.

Purée: to create a liquid or smooth blend using a food processor or blender. For example, tomatoes can be pureed into a tomato puree or paste. Fruits are another common substance to be pureed.

Ragù: a classic Italian sauce made from ground meat, onions, tomato, spices, and red wine.

Reduce: to thicken a liquid by heating it for a period of time. If a sauce is too runny, you can reduce it by keeping it on the heat for longer.

Ribbon: a long, flat strand of pasta, in a variety of lengths and thickness. Typical ribbon pastas are fettuccine, lasagne, linguine, pappardelle, and tagliatelle.

Rice: small grains used for cooking. A typical type of rice used for Italian risotto is Arborio, a short-grain white rice. Rice can also be used to make rice flour, which is utilized when making rice noodles.

Roast: to cook meat, fish or vegetables through extended contact with heat in an oven, a pan, or over a fire.

Roll out: to flatten dough, typically using a rolling pin, until it reaches an even and desired thickness.

Salt: to sprinkle salt on an ingredient, like eggplant, to extract its juices.

Sauté: to cook meat, fish, or vegetables in butter or olive oil on a heated skillet or pan until golden brown. Pasta and risotto are also sautéed in certain circumstances.

Season: to use spices, such as salt or pepper, to add flavor to a dish.

Shred: to cut or grate ingredients into thin shreds.

Sift: to shake ingredients through a sifter. It is common to sift flour, if mixing with oil or melted butter, because it is prone to form lumps if it is not sifted.

Simmer: to cook gently below the boiling point.

Skim: to remove excess fat or froth that rises to the surface of stock, or other liquids, while cooking. Small amounts can be removed with a skimmer or slotted spoon, while thicker layers of fat may need to be chilled in the refrigerator and removed once the fat has solidified.

Soak: to immerse dehydrated or dried foods, such as fruits and vegetables, in water or another liquid to add volume and freshness.

Soften: to make chilled food, such as butter, softer and easier to handle by allowing it to sit at room temperature.

Spiralize: to cut or peel vegetables in a spiral shape, sometimes with the help of a kitchen tool called a spiralizer. Spiralized vegetables such as zucchini are often used as a replacement for pasta noodles.

Sprinkle: to scatter small amounts of liquid, spices, or garnishes over a dish for even distribution and additional flavor.

Steam: to use the steam that rises from boiling water to cook food such as vegetables.

Steep: to soak ingredients such as coffee or tea in liquid to infuse the liquid with the flavor of the ingredient.

Stew: a combination of solid ingredients cooked in a small amount of liquid over low heat. Also, to cook ingredients, such as vegetables or meat, by the same method.

Stock: a liquid made by simmering vegetables, fish, or meat in water or wine. The resulting liquid is usually used as the base for soups or sauces.

Stuff: to insert a mixture of ingredients into a main ingredient. In pasta dishes, shell-shaped pasta is commonly stuffed with mixtures of meat, cheese, and sauce.

Thicken: to add flour or other ingredients to a sauce and heat the mixture, which causes the sauce to become thicker.

Tofu: an block-shaped ingredient made from the curds of soybean milk. It absorbs other flavors well. Also known as beancurd, this popular Asian ingredient has become common as a vegetarian substitute.

Whisk: to quickly combine or beat ingredients with a handheld or electric mixer. Whisking ingredients such as cream or egg whites adds air and volume.

WHEN SHAPE MATTERS

Both pasta and sauce making are a labor of love, and if you deny your sauce the right pasta pairing, you will miss out on a crucial step. For your robust ragù-type sauces, we recommend the following durable pasta shapes, which will be able to handle the heavy and flavorful meat sauce you have prepared.

TOP TEN NOODLES
FOR MEAT SAUCES

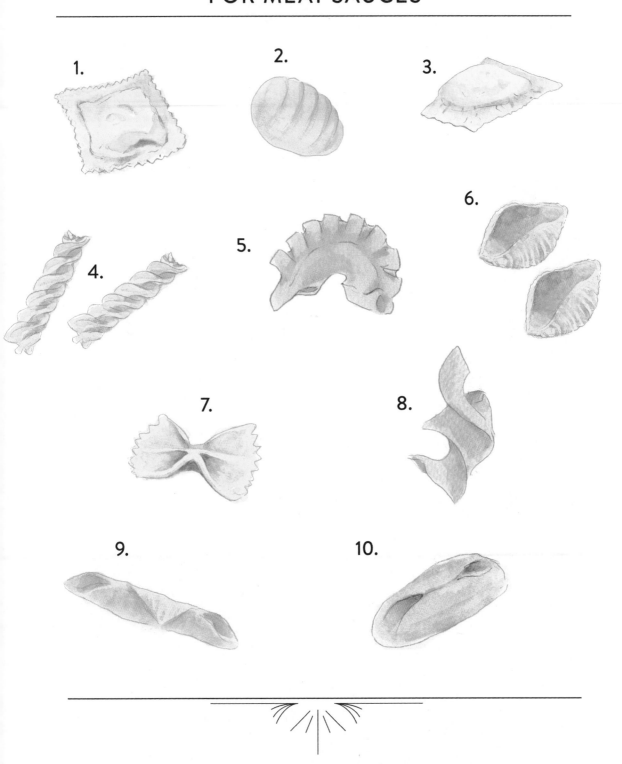

1. Ravioli 2. Gnocchi di Patate 3. Tortelli 4. Fusilli 5. Creste di Gallo
6. Conchiglie 7. Farfalle 8. Nuvole 9. Garganelli 10. Cavatelli

SOUP'S
ON

Pasta makes everything better, and if you choose the right shape and size, it will be more than an afterthought in your soup. The smaller pasta shapes on this list will be best in a lighter soup, while the larger shapes will hold up better in a hefty soup. In any case, add your noodles last to avoid the risk of soggy pasta.

TOP TEN NOODLES
FOR SOUPS

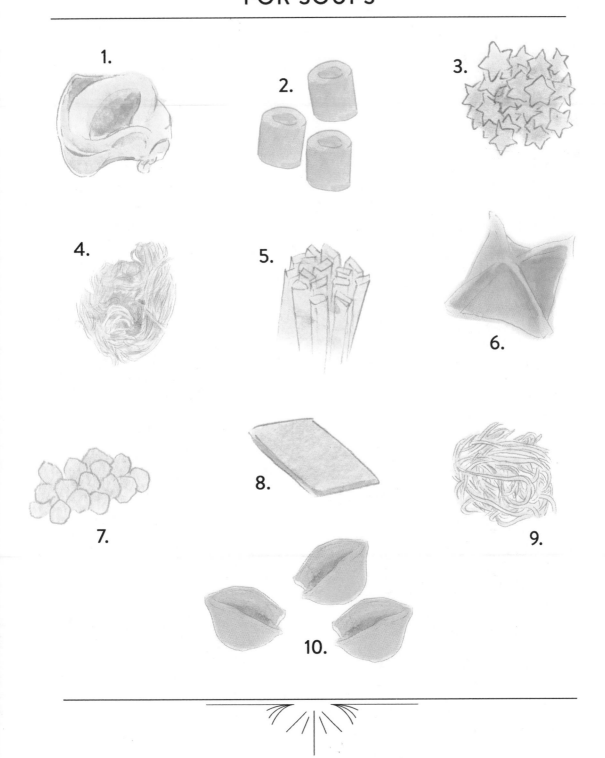

1. Tortellini   2. Ditalini   3. Pastine Minute   4. Ramen   5. Udon
6. Wonton   7. Pasta Grattata   8. Quadrucci   9. Chinese Egg Noodles   10. Assabesi

STIR
IT UP

Don't let your noodle choice hold back the delicious flavor of a stir-fry dish. While you can technically stir-fry with any type of noodle, the following 10 are our favorites, because of their tasty, chewy, texture. These noodles will support all of the beef, chicken, or vegetables that you choose to incorporate.

TOP TEN NOODLES
FOR STIR-FRIES

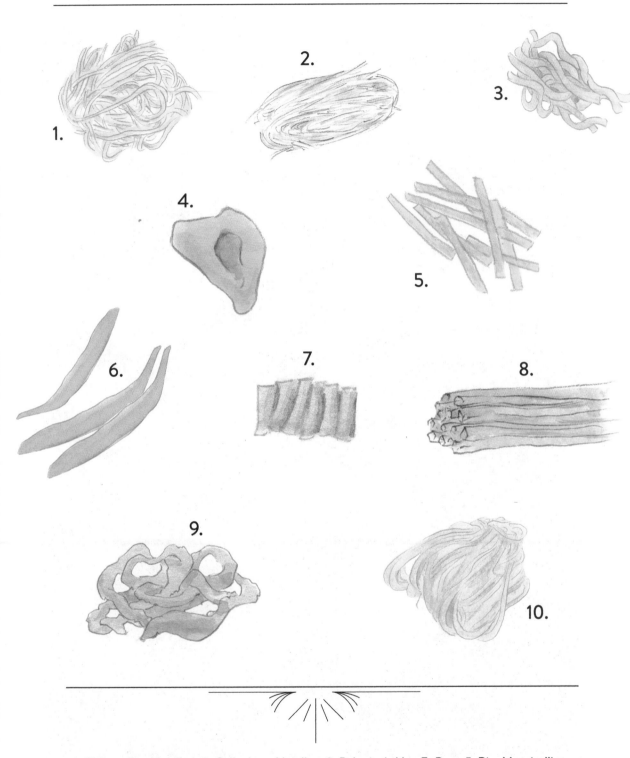

1. Chinese Egg Noodles   2. Cellophane Noodles   3. Bakmi   4. Mao Er Duo   5. Rice Vermicelli
6. Lao Shu Fěn   7. Ding Ding Chao Mian   8. Dotori Guksu   9. Dao Xiao Mian   10. Lamian

INDEX

ABOUT THE AUTHOR

Serena Cosmo is the writer behind *Rustic Plate*, a blog devoted to creating fresh, bold dishes from scratch. She also wears a number of other hats as a columnist, food educator, photographer, self-appointed spokesperson for neglected kitchens, and mother.

Originally from the Piedmont region of Italy, Serena grew up immersed in authentic Italian cuisine. A world traveller and one-time singer/songwriter, she currently resides in the university town of Auburn, Alabama, with her husband, two daughters, a cat, two kittens, two goldfish, and 27 wooden cooking spoons.

ABOUT CIDER MILL PRESS BOOK PUBLISHERS

Good ideas ripen with time. From seed to harvest, Cider Mill Press brings fine reading, information, and entertainment together between the covers of its creatively crafted books. Our Cider Mill bears fruit twice a year, publishing a new crop of titles each spring and fall.

KENNEBUNKPORT, MAINE

"Where Good Books Are Ready for Press"

Visit us on the Web at

www.cidermillpress.com

or write to us at

PO Box 454
12 Spring St.
Kennebunkport, Maine 04046